Financial Accounting Principles
An Introductory Financial Accounting Course

AME | Learning

Instructions to access the AME online course

1. Go to www.amelearning.com
2. Click on CREATE A NEW ACCOUNT
3. Follow the steps to create a new account

UNIQUE PIN NUMBER

`PQDDHGOPJL`

ONE TIME USE

4. Your enrollment key will be provided to you by your instructor
5. Click on Create My New Account

For assistance, call 1.888.401.3881 x 2 or email support@amelearning.com

Neville Joffe

AME | Learning

Textbook ISBN: 978-1-926751-44-3

Workbook ISBN: 978-1-926751-45-0

Financial Accounting Principles
Author: Neville Joffe
Publisher: AME Learning
Content Contributor: Penny Parker
Content Contributor: Graeme Gomes
Developmental Editor: Melody Yousefian
Typesetter: Paragon Prepress Inc.
Project Manager: Linda Zhang
Cover Design: Edward Phung
Online Course Design & Production: AME Multimedia Team

This book is written to provide accurate information on the covered topics. It is not meant to take the place of professional advice.

For more information contact:

AME Learning Inc.
410-1220 Sheppard Avenue East
Toronto, ON, Canada M2K 2S5
Phone: 416.848.4399
Toll-free: 1.888.401.3881
E-mail: info@amelearning.com
Visit our website at: www.amelearning.com

Content Reviewers

A special thank you to the following reviewers:

Ann Boeck, Sinclair Community College

Charles Barrett, Fashion Institute of Design and Merchandising

Cathy Duffy, Carthage College

Terry Holmes, Terra State Community College

Gerry Tryhane, Folsom Lake College

Kristina Unutoa, Los Angeles Southwest College

About the Author

Neville Joffe is the founder and CEO of AME Learning Inc. Prior to AME Learning, Neville spent over 20 years as owner, President, and manager of small and large manufacturing companies internationally. Neville is a member of the Worldwide Presidents Organization and former member of the Young Presidents Organization. He holds a patent related to the unique methodology he developed to teach accounting concepts. Neville is the author of five leading college textbooks. He has been featured in newspapers and magazines, and is a frequent speaker at national conferences where he presents as a thought leader in introductory accounting curriculum. The AME system has been used to train tens of thousands of employees at leading Fortune 1000 firms and students at premier colleges and universities across North America. Students have commented that they find the course remarkably easy to follow, using the numerous interactive tools that supplement the textbook and workbook. Students using AME materials consistently achieve higher grades compared to those who use traditional materials, and student engagement and retention rates have improved significantly. Professors have described the AME methodology as "refreshing", "intriguing", "amazing", "never thought it could be this simple", "inspiring to see that someone has changed the rules of teaching accounting" and "you have broken the mold of the way this subject has been taught".

Preface by Neville Joffe

Fifteen years ago, I founded AME Learning with a mission to change the perception of accounting from dry and boring to intuitive, engaging, and an essential life skill. Today, the AME system is used by some of the most prestigious corporations and academic institutions in the world with outstanding results, and the company has been recognized with top training and education awards including the 2009 CODiE Finalist for the Best Postsecondary Instructional Solution.

The AME System was initially conceived after I experienced the power of financial education as part of a turnaround I managed at a mid-size manufacturing company. As part of the turnaround process I adopted an assortment of initiatives including Just In Time Inventory (JIT), Lean Manufacturing, The Theory Of Constraints (TOC), and Total Quality Management (TQM). The most powerful enabler of the turnaround was the creation of an open book environment and profit-sharing program with 400 unionized workers. The initiative required non-finance employees to understand and interpret financial statements and the financial implications of their actions.

I began educating the employees about income statements and balance sheets using traditional materials, including some content from college accounting curriculum. The materials over-complicated simple concepts and ineffectively connected the lessons to the practical implications of personal and business financial management. I then tried a very non-traditional approach to teaching these concepts. I cashed $2,000 in small bills and crumpled them into a plastic garbage bag. I assembled all the staff in a room and then poured the crumpled bills onto a table. "This is called revenue" I said. I placed a handful of cash in a bucket and labelled it "wages". I continued the exercise with different buckets labelled "material", "rent", "maintenance", "insurance" and then started tearing up $20 bills and throwing them into a bucket called "waste". The employees were silently shocked when I tore up the bills. "Why are you so surprised?" I asked, "you do this every day but just don't see it".

At the end of the demonstration, some cash remained on the table and I said "what is left and lying on the table is called profit." I shifted some of the remaining cash toward the crowd and said "this is for all of you for your special hard work performed this year. The remainder is for the owners in return for all the financial risk they take to support this business." The group was stunned, and they finally understood the message I was trying to deliver. As a result of successfully implementing this initiative, key financial metrics dramatically improved; inventory levels decreased, accounts receivable were collected faster, low margin products were eliminated, unprofitable customers were turned away.

So how did the crumpled-money exercise have such a profound impact on the company? It was not the employees' fault they didn't understand the traditional materials, it was the fault of the materials that taught the concepts from the teacher's point of view.

Elizabeth Newton summed it up:

> *In 1990, Elizabeth Newton earned a Ph.D. in psychology at Stanford by studying a simple game in which she assigned people to one of two roles: "tappers" or "listeners." Tappers received a list of twenty-five well-known songs, such as "Happy Birthday to You" and "The Star Spangled Banner." Each tapper was asked to pick a song and tap out the rhythm to a listener (by knocking on a table). The listener's job was to guess the song, based on the rhythm being tapped.*
>
> *The listener's job in this game is quite difficult. Over the course of Newton's experiment, 120 songs were tapped out. Listeners guessed only 2.5 percent of the songs: 3 out of 120. But here's what made the result worthy of a dissertation in psychology. Before the listeners guessed the name of the song, Newton asked the tappers to predict the odds that the listeners would guess correctly. They predicted that the odds were 50 percent. The tappers got their message across 1 time in 40, but they thought they were getting their message across 1 time in 2. Why?*
>
> *When a tapper taps, she is hearing the song in her head and it's impossible to avoid hearing the tune in your head. Meanwhile, the listeners can't hear that tune — all they can hear is a bunch of disconnected taps, like a kind of bizarre Morse Code.*
>
> *It's hard to be a tapper. The problem is that tappers (teachers) have been given knowledge (the song title) that makes it impossible for them to imagine what it's like to lack that knowledge. When they're tapping, they can't imagine what it's like for the listeners (the student) to hear isolated taps rather than a song. This has been referred to as the Curse of Knowledge. Once we know something, we find it hard to imagine what it was like not to know it. And it becomes difficult for us to share our knowledge with others, because we can't readily re-create our listeners' state of mind.*

After successfully turning around the company and selling my ownership, I founded AME Learning and spent years refining a teaching tool that would help teach non-financial people financial accounting principles. The AME system has been used to train over 30,000 people ranging from front line employees to Directors of publicly traded companies. I am still surprised at the lack of financial literacy of managers and executives. Why is it then, that so many adults in the business world lack basic financial acumen when they have studied one or more accounting courses at college or university? It would appear that many people underestimate the importance and usefulness of basic accounting skills and learn by rote memory rather than practical lessons that have long term retention and applicability. Perhaps our economic world would be better off if more people were financially literate.

Over the years I have learned to appreciate the concept of "tappers and listeners" every time I deliver a management training program or when writing textbooks for college and university students. My years of research and experiments both on the factory floor and in the boardroom was the start of the development of AME, which has become an award winning patented system of teaching accounting as it is used today.

I strongly believe in "getting the basics right and the rest will follow". I believe that basic financial literacy is a crucial life skill that is required of everyone, not only accountants. I have written this material from the students' point of view while still meeting curriculum requirements. You will notice that I have eliminated unnecessary jargon wherever possible.

I have a wonderful dedicated team that produces world class material with one thought in mind: to educate the student so they can transfer basic accounting skills either to their professional lives or be better prepared for a higher level of accounting. Like all good science, AME is a solid base that prepares students for either an accounting or business career.

I am a true advocate of student-centric teaching and believe that I have successfully offered the opportunity to bring together the minds of both the "tappers" and the "listeners".

So my message to you the student is this: whether you choose to continue your accounting studies or not, take this subject seriously since it will stand you in good stead when you enter your professional life regardless of the career you choose.

Neville Joffe
Author

Brief Table of Contents

Introduction

Chapter 1: Financial Statements: Personal Accounting

Chapter 2: Linking Personal Accounting to Business Accounting

Chapter 3: Accounting Principles and Practices in a Business

Chapter 4: Revenue and Expense Recognition

Chapter 5: Business Accounting Cycle Part I

Chapter 6: Business Accounting Cycle Part II

Chapter 7: Merchandising Corporation

Chapter 8: Accounting Information Systems

Chapter 9: Cash Controls

Chapter 10: Accounts and Notes Receivable

Chapter 11: Inventory

Chapter 12: Long-Term Assets

Chapter 13: Current Liabilities

Chapter 14: Long-Term Liabilities

Chapter 15: Partnerships

Chapter 16: Corporations: Contributed Capital and Dividends

Chapter 17: Corporations: The Financial Statements

Chapter 18: Investments

Chapter 19: The Statement of Cash Flow

Chapter 20: Financial Statement Analysis

Detailed Table of Contents

Chapter 1: Financial Statements: Personal Accounting

Meaning of Accounting 11

Principal of Networth...12

The Balance Sheet...13

The Income Statement...15

Accounting Periods 16

The Accounting Equation...16

    Net Worth Calculation 19

    Introduction to T-Accounts...19

    The Process...20

Accrual Accounting 21

    Cash Flow vs. Accruals..22

    Cash-Based vs. Accrual-Based Accounting 22

    The Matching Principle...23

Borrowing Money and Repaying Debts...26

Buying & Selling Assets 29

Depreciation..30

Prepaid Expenses 32

Materiality...35

Capital 36

The Three Sources and Uses of Cash 36

Market Value vs. Book Value 37

Chapter Summary..38

Review Exercises 39

Chapter 2: Linking Personal Accounting to Business Accounting

Business Accounts...41

    Sequence of Assets and Liabilities...42

    Owner's Equity vs. Net Worth 42

Forms of Organizations 44

    Sole Proprietorship...44

    Partnership...45

    Corporation...46

    Not-for-Profit-Organization 47

Stakeholders 48

Financial Statements of Different Types of Business 48

    Service Business 49

    Merchandising Business 49

    Manufacturing Business 50

Business Transactions 51

    Explanation of Transactions 54

Chapter Summary 57

Review Exercises 58

Chapter 3: Accounting Principles and Practices in a Business

Fields of Accounting 61

    Financial Accounting 61

    Managerial Accounting 61

    Accounting Designations 62

Generally Accepted Accounting Principles 62

    Characteristics of GAAP 63

    Basic Concepts and Principles 65

    GAAP in Different Jurisdictions 67

International Financial Reporting Standards 68

    What is IFRS 68

Controls in Business 69

    Definition of Controls 69

    Implementing Controls 70

Ethics and Insights 72

    The 4-Way Test..74

    The Attributes of a Good Accounting System 75

Chapter Summary 76

Review Exercises 77

Chapter 4: Revenue and Expense Recognition

Revenue Recognition 81

    Customer Pays when the Service is Performed..82

    Customer Pays after the Service is Performed 83

    Customer Pays before the Service is Performed 84

Unearned Revenue 84

Expense Recognition 86

    Pay Cash when the Expense is Incurred..87

    Pay Cash after the Expense is Incurred..87

Pay Cash before the Expense is Incurred 88

Prepaid Expenses 88

Office Supplies: An Alternate Example of Prepaid Expenses 90

Relationship between Unearned Revenue and Prepaid Expenses 91

Introduction to Adjustments 91

Adjustments: Unearned Revenue 92

Adjustments: Prepaid Expenses..93

Adjustments: Accrued Interest Expense 94

Adjustments: Depreciation 95

Ethics and Controls 95

Accounts Receivable Controls 96

Chapter Summary 98

Review Exercises 99

Chapter 5: Business Accounting Cycle Part I

An Introduction to Bookkeeping...101

Transition to Debits and Credits 101

Debit and Credit Reference Guide 102

Transition to Journal Entries..103

Chart of Accounts 104

Defining Accounts 105

The Accounting Cycle 106

Step 1 – Journals 106

Step 2 – General Ledger 110

Step 3 – Trial Balance 114

Ethics and Controls 116

Chapter Summary..118

Review Exercises 119

Chapter 6: Business Accounting Cycle Part II

Adjusting Entries 125

Contra Accounts 125

Worksheet 127

Adjusted Trial Balance 130

Income Statement and Balance Sheet 131

Step 4 – Income Statement 133

Statement of Owner's Equity 134

Step 5 – Balance Sheet 135

Step 6 – Post-Closing Trial Balance 136

    Option 1: Close Directly to the Capital Account 137

    Option 2: Close Using the Income Summary 142

    Post-Closing Trial Balance 147

The Evolution from Manual to Computerized Accounting 148

    Modern Accounting Systems 149

Ethics and Controls 150

Chapter Summary 151

Review Exercises 152

Chapter 7: Merchandising Corporation

Financing a Business 161

Merchandising Sales 164

Perpetual vs. Periodic Inventory 165

    Purchase and Sale of Inventory 166

Gross Profit Margin: A Profitability Ratio 167

Classified Balance Sheet 168

    Current Assets vs. Long-Term Assets 168

    Current Liabilities vs. Long-Term Liabilities 169

Multistep Income Statement 172

Ethics and Control 174

Chapter Summary 175

Review Exercises 176

Chapter 8: Accounting Information Systems

An Integrated Approach to Learning Accounting 181

The Accounting Paper Trail 182

    Special Journals 183

    Subsidiary Ledgers 184

Using Special Journals and Subsidiary Ledgers 186

    The Sales Journal 186

    The Cash Receipts Journal 188

    The Purchases Journal 191

    The Cash Payments Journal 192

Modern Accounting Information Systems 197

Controls and Ethics 199

Chapter Summary 200

Review Exercises 201

Chapter 9: Cash Controls

Cash Controls: An Introduction 207

Bank Reconciliations 208

    Unrecorded Deposits from the Bank Statement 208

    Outstanding Deposits 213

    Outstanding Checks 215

    Bank Errors 216

    Recording Errors 217

    Bank Reconciliation Summary 219

Petty Cash 222

    Setting Up a Petty Cash Fund 223

    Posting Petty Cash to the General Ledger 224

    Petty Cash Controls 226

Ethics and Cash Control Guidelines 228

    Record Cash Immediately when it is Received 228

    Protect Cash when it is on the Premises 229

    Remove Cash from the Premises as soon as Possible 229

Chapter Summary 231

Review Exercises 232

Chapter 10: Accounts and Notes Receivable

Accounts Receivable: An Introduction 235

Accounting for Bad Debt: Direct and Allowance Methods 237

    The Direct Method 237

    The Allowance Method 239

Approached to Estimate Bad Debt 242

    The Income Statement Approach 243

    The Balance Sheet Approach 244

Managing Accounts Receivable Information Using Reports 246

The Accounts Receivable Subledger 247

    Alternation Presentation Formats 248

Measuring the Effectiveness of Collection Using Ratios 249

    Days Sales Outstanding 249

    Accounts Receivable Turnover Ratio 250

Accounts Receivable Controls 250

    Credit Controls 251

    Credit Approval 251

    Credit Information 251

Terms of Sale 251

Credit Policy 252

Converting Accounts Receivable into Cash 252

Setting Firm Credit Terms 252

The Promissory Note and Notes Receivable 253

An Ethical Approach to Managing Accounts Receivable 256

Chapter Summary 258

Review Exercises 259

Chapter 11: Inventory

Inventory: An Introduction 263

Perpetual vs. Periodic Inventory Systems 264

The Perpetual Inventory System 265

Purchases 265

Purchase Allowances 266

Freight Cost 268

FOB Shipping Point 268

FOB Destination 269

Sales 270

Sales Returns 270

Sales Allowances 271

Sales Discounts 272

Income Statement 273

Closing Entries 274

Methods of Valuing Inventory 277

Determining the Cost of Inventory 277

Applying Valuation Methods 277

Using Specific Identification 278

Using First-In-First-Out (FIFO) 279

Using Weighted Average Cost 280

Using Last-In-First-Out (LIFO) 281

The Effect of Different Valuation Methods 282

Determining the Actual Quantity of Inventory 283

The Physical Inventory Count 283

Effect of Inventory Errors 284

The Impact of Cost of Goods Sold on Gross Profit 284

The Effect of Overstating Inventory 285

The Impact of Inventory Errors 286

Valuation of Inventory at the Lower of Cost or Market...287

Estimating Inventory...288

    The Gross Profit Method...289

    The Retail Method..290

Measuring Inventory Using Financial Ratios..291

    Inventory Turnover Ratio...292

    Inventory Days on Hand..293

Controls Related to Inventory...294

    Compliance with Plans, Policies, Procedures, Regulations and Laws...................295

    Safeguarding Inventory...296

    The Economical and Efficient Use of Resources...296

    Inventory Objectives...296

An Ethical Approach to Inventory Estimation and Valuation....................................297

    Impact on Financial Statements..297

    Who Commits Fraud and Why..297

Chapter Summary...299

Review Exercises...300

Appendix 11A: The Periodic Inventory System..308

Chapter 12: Long-Term Assets

Long-Term Assets: The Big Picture...331

Defining a Long-Term Asset..333

The Acquisition of Long-Term Assets..334

    Lump Sum Purchases of Capital Assets..335

Changes in a Capital Asset..336

The Concept of Depreciation..338

    Residual Value..338

    Actual Salvage Value...339

Three Methods of Depreciation..339

    The Straight-Line Method..340

    The Declining and Double-Declining-Balance Method...343

    The Units-of-Production Method..345

    Which Depreciation Method Should be Used..346

Depreciation for Partial Years...347

Disposal and Depreciation..349

    Trading-In..353

Revising Depreciation...354

Natural Resources..355

Intangible Assets 357

    Goodwill 358

    Patents 361

    Copyright 362

    Trademark and Trade Name 363

    Leasing Long-Term Assets 363

Long-Term Assets, Total Assets and Financial Ratios 364

    Asset Turnover 364

    Return on Assets 364

    Using the Ratios 365

Controls Related To Long-Term Assets 365

An Ethical Approach to Long-Term Assets 367

Chapter Summary 369

Review Exercises 371

Chapter 13: Current Liabilities

A Company's Current Liabilities 375

Short-Term Notes Payable 376

    Accrued Interest and Notes Payable 377

    Current Portion of Long-Term Liabilities 378

Sales Tax 379

Payroll Accounting 381

    Gross Pay to Net Pay 382

    Employee Payroll Deductions 383

    Employee Payroll Contributions 385

    Paying the Deduction Liability 386

Payroll for Roofus Construction 386

    Employer Payroll Contributions 390

    Paying the Liabilities 391

Estimated and Contingent Liabilities 394

    Product Warranties 394

    Contingent Liabilities 397

Current Liabilities and Financial Ratios 398

    Current Ratio 398

    Quick Ratio 399

Controls Relating to Current Liabilities 400

An Ethical Approach to Current Liabilities 400

Chapter Summary 402

Review Exercises 404

Chapter 14: Long-Term Liabilities

Long-Term Liabilities: An Introduction 407

Characteristics and Types of Bonds 407

The Concept of Present Value 409

    Time Value of Money and Bonds Payable 411

Issuing Bonds at Par 412

Issuing Bonds at a Discount 415

Issuing Bonds at a Premium 420

Retiring Bonds 423

Financial Ratios Related to Liabilities 424

    Debt-to-Total Assets Ratio 424

    Debt-to-Equity Ratio 424

Controls Related to Long-Term Liabilities 425

An Ethical Approach to Long-Term Liabilities 425

Chapter Summary 427

Review Exercises 429

Chapter 15: Partnerships

Proprietorships, Partnerships and Corporations 431

Advantages and Disadvantages of Partnerships 432

    Advantages 432

    Disadvantages 433

Types of Partnerships 434

    General Partnership 434

    Limited Partnership 434

    Limited Liability Partnership 434

Formation of a Partnership 435

Division of Income or Loss 436

    Dividing Earnings Equally 437

    Dividing Earnings According to an Agreed-Upon Ratio 437

    Dividing Earnings According to the Capital Contribution of Each Partner 438

    Dividing Earnings According to Agreed-Upon Salary Allocations, Plus a
    Share of the Remainder 438

Partner Drawings 439

Addition and Withdrawal of a Partner 440

When Market Value Differs from Book Value 441

Liquidation of a Partnership 443

Chapter Summary 446

Review Exercises 447

Chapter 16: Corporations: Contributed Capital and Dividends

The Professionalization of the Ownership Structure..449

Public vs. Private Corporation...450

Corporate Structure: Separating Management from Ownership...451

Financial Statements and Stockholders' Equity..452

Issuing Stock...455

    Issuing stock in exchange for assets..456

    Issuing stock in exchange for services...456

Issuing Stock that is Common or Preferred..457

    Par and No Par Value Stock...458

    Stated Value..459

Accounting for Cash Dividends..460

    Dividends in Arrears..462

Stock Splits and Stock Dividends...463

Treasury Stock...464

    Resale of Treasury Stock..465

An Ethical Approach to Corporations and Inside Trading...466

Chapter Summary..468

Review Exercises..469

Chapter 17: Corporations: The Financial Statements

Earnings of a Corporation: An Introduction...473

Income Tax Expense..474

Closing Entries for Corporations..476

Measuring Income...477

Measuring Changes in Equity...479

    Prior Period Adjustments...480

    Changes in Accounting Policies..481

Measuring Financial Position..482

Calculation of Financial Ratios...483

    Book Value per Share...483

    Debt-to-Equity Ratio..485

    Dividend Payout Ratio...486

    Earnings per Share (EPS)..487

    Variations in Presentation of Earnings per Share..488

    Price-Earnings Ratio..489

Chapter Summary..490

Review Exercises..491

Chapter 18: Investments

Investments: An Introduction 495
    Types of Investments 496
    Classification of Investments 497
Trading Investments 499
Held to Maturity Investments 505
    Purchasing Bonds between Interest Dates 507
Available for Sale Investments 511
Significant Influence 514
    Controls 516
Chapter Summary 519
Review Exercises 520

Chapter 19: The Statement of Cash Flow

Beyond the Balance Sheet and Income Statement 523
Cash Flow Statements: Follow the Money 524
    Three Ways of Generating Cash Flow 524
Preparing a Cash Flow Statement 526
    Examine the Balance Sheet and the Income Statement 526
    Indirect Method 528
    Cash Flow from Operations 529
    Cash Flow from Investments 531
    Cash Flow from Financing 532
    Summary of the Indirect Method 536
Sale of Property, Plant and Equipment 537
Direct Method 541
    Summary of the Direct Method 544
Ethics and Controls 545
Chapter Summary 546
Review Exercises 547
Appendix 19A: Selling Long-Term Assets 549

Chapter 20: Financial Statement Analysis

The Importance of Financial Statement Analysis 557
Revenues are Vanity 559
Profits are Sanity 560
    EBIT 561
    EBIT Percentage of Sales 562

Interest Coverage Ratio..564

Net Profit Margin 565

Return on Equity (ROE) 566

Return on Assets (ROA) 568

Asset Turnover..569

The DuPont Framework 570

Cash Flow is Reality..573

Current Ratio..573

Quick Ratio 575

Debt-to-Equity Ratio 576

Management Ensures Stability..578

Investors Measure Performance 582

Horizontal and Vertical Financial Statement Analysis...585

Ethics and Controls...590

Chapter Summary..592

Review Exercises 593

Appendix I – Summary of Financial Ratios **597**

Appendix II – Home Depot's Financial Statements **601**

Glossary...**605**

Index...**621**

The AME Method of Learning Accounting

AME utilizes a unique and patented method that has simplified accounting principles, using step-by-step logic to ensure that the subject is extremely easy to understand. Accounting concepts are communicated using straightforward language and AME Accounting Maps™ that make potentially complex transactions simpler and easier to follow.

This textbook is part of a larger and blended program that is being used to teach the course. The steps of the program are as follows:

1. A highly interactive online section must be completed before attending each class.
2. At the start of the class, a quiz will be given to test your knowledge and comprehension of the online section that you would have completed before class.
3. Building on the online segment and the quiz, the class will then reinforce and improve your understanding of the concepts that have already been introduced and studied.
4. Once the basic learning is done, it will be time to take the next step and apply the lessons learned by completing the exercises provided in the workbook.

The *name, value,* and *timing* of each transaction

As you embark on this unique way of learning accounting you should be aware of the importance of financial statements to both internal and external stakeholders. You should also be familiar with the balance sheet, income statement and cash flow statement — and how they link together. Students familiar with our approach will know that the technical process of double entry accounting isn't really that complicated and that there are very few debit and credit combinations.

Additionally, there are three basic components to every accounting transaction that must be remembered each time entries are made or accounts are adjusted. These three components are:

1. *Name:* What are the names of the accounts involved?
2. *Value:* What value is involved?
3. *Timing:* When is it occurring?

These three components need to be considered in any adjustment made on the company's records to ensure accuracy and thoroughness.

Here is a brief example to illustrate the importance of these three components.

Assume that you are an accountant for a company whose fiscal year ends on December 31. On December 20, an upfront payment of $60,000 (related services to be rendered in the following year) is deposited in the company's bank account. The project is expected to be completed in about six months (i.e. by June of the next year).

What are the names of the accounts that should be used for the transaction? As any introductory accounting course indicates, Cash is debited for the amount deposited. However, which account receives the corresponding credit? If you guessed Revenue, your guess is incorrect. Since the money isn't earned until the service is performed, it is the Unearned Revenue account that is used. This makes a big difference when the company reports its financial position.

What is the value of the transaction? Your first thought may be that the value of this transaction is $60,000. However, the transaction may need to be sliced into smaller sections to reflect work performed in due course. This may be done on a monthly basis, using a measure such as materials delivered. Depending on the kind of transaction involved, the amount to be recorded isn't as obvious as it might appear.

What is the timing of the transaction? The first two questions have touched upon the third. Revenue should only be recognized in the period in which it is earned. In our present example, this cannot be done in the current fiscal period. It has to be done in the next fiscal period (when the work is finally started) and in a way that reflects the gradual completion of the work done. In other words, the revenue cannot be recognized as earned right away. It will take six months to complete this project, and the same amount of time to transfer the entire $60,000 into the Revenue account.

We will explore these principles throughout the remainder of the course.

The AME Approach

The AME approach has always emphasized the importance of accounting in our everyday lives and how these principles can be applied to professional accounting in general. This approach will be expanded upon in this course. We will examine various aspects of the balance sheet and income statement and how the information contained therein impacts both internal and external stakeholders.

The course begins with an application of accounting principles and transactions in our personal life before making the transition to applying accounting principles in a business environment. By the time debit and credit terminology are introduced, students will be comfortable increasing and decreasing accounts. Making the switch to debit and credit rules will be relatively straight-forward.

Once the accounting cycle is covered, the design and structure of this course is based on the format in which the accounts on the balance sheet are laid out. Each chapter will focus on one aspect of the balance sheet in order, which is why we look at Cash first (the top item on the balance sheet), then move on Accounts Receivable, Inventory and so on. The further we go down the list of accounts, the less liquid the assets are, until we finally examine Long-Term Assets such as property, equipment and goodwill. These assets are not easily converted into cash, which is why they are also known as Fixed Assets.

The other side of the balance sheet is where we find a listing of the company's liabilities. These liabilities will form the basis of the next part of this course. Just as with assets, liabilities are listed on the balance sheet with a purpose. Those that need to be paid first, such as Notes Payable and Accounts Payable, are listed near the top. The least immediate liabilities (such as bonds) are listed last.

The latter part of this course will involve an in-depth examination of equity and how it is structured in entities such as corporations and partnerships. We will also complete our look at financial statements, with an examination of the structure and logic of the income statement, also known as a profit and loss statement (P&L).

Each chapter will contain a structure. The first part of a chapter will discuss inputs, or how activities are accounted for on a company's financial statements. The second part of the chapter will discuss outputs, or how companies collect and organize information to generate reports and make managerial decisions. Where applicable, each chapter will end with a discussion of controls, ethics and financial ratios relevant to the topic at hand.

Navigating the Accounting Map™

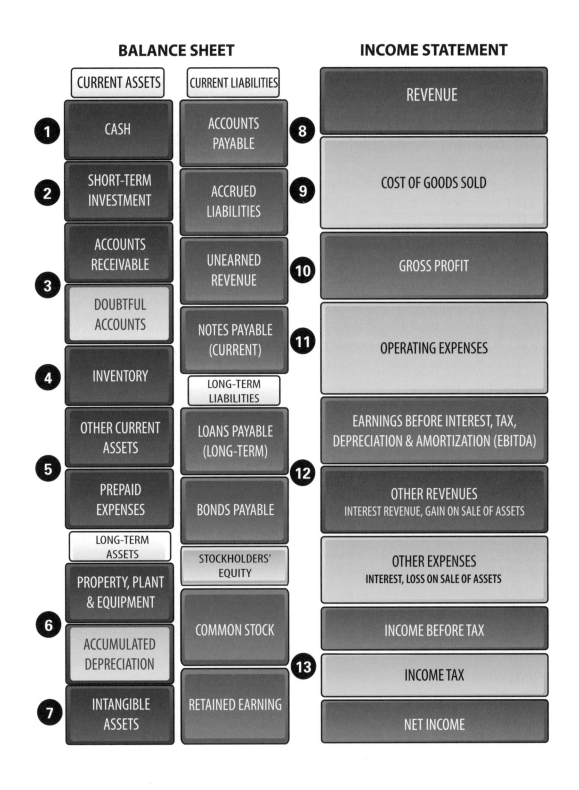

BALANCE SHEET

CURRENT ASSETS	CURRENT LIABILITIES
① CASH	⑧ ACCOUNTS PAYABLE
② SHORT-TERM INVESTMENT	⑨ ACCRUED LIABILITIES
③ ACCOUNTS RECEIVABLE	⑩ UNEARNED REVENUE
DOUBTFUL ACCOUNTS	⑪ NOTES PAYABLE (CURRENT)
④ INVENTORY	LONG-TERM LIABILITIES
OTHER CURRENT ASSETS	LOANS PAYABLE (LONG-TERM)
⑤ PREPAID EXPENSES	BONDS PAYABLE
LONG-TERM ASSETS	STOCKHOLDERS' EQUITY
PROPERTY, PLANT & EQUIPMENT	COMMON STOCK
⑥ ACCUMULATED DEPRECIATION	RETAINED EARNING
⑦ INTANGIBLE ASSETS	

INCOME STATEMENT

- REVENUE
- COST OF GOODS SOLD
- GROSS PROFIT
- OPERATING EXPENSES
- EARNINGS BEFORE INTEREST, TAX, DEPRECIATION & AMORTIZATION (EBITDA)
- ⑫ OTHER REVENUES — INTEREST REVENUE, GAIN ON SALE OF ASSETS
- OTHER EXPENSES — INTEREST, LOSS ON SALE OF ASSETS
- INCOME BEFORE TAX
- ⑬ INCOME TAX
- NET INCOME

Why learn this material?

Many of you may be taking this course as a step towards becoming an accountant. Learning this material will help you understand the importance and logic underlying most business decisions. For example, a manager of a medium-sized business needs to operate the company in a responsible fashion, while at the same time providing financial statements to the board of directors every month. This course will help a student do just that, as well as calculate net income, award bonuses based on those profits, and do a number of other things that are crucial for any size of business.

In other words, a thorough knowledge of a company's accounts, and the procedures involved in recording and analyzing related transactions, is vital for most important decision-makers within a company.

How this material is organized

The following is a description of the financial statement items that will be examined in Financial Accounting Principles.

1. **Cash** — This account includes petty cash, bank reconciliations and the controls necessary to protect cash. The Cash account is at the centre of almost every transaction. For example, businesses often find themselves with a surplus of cash that needs to be invested for short periods of time.

2. **Investments** — Organizations often invest surplus cash in investments outside the company. These investments can include short-term and long-term debt and equity.

   ### Issues to keep in mind:
   - Where is the cash to be invested?
   - What is the risk of losing the money being invested?
   - Is the return worth the investment?
   - What happens if the business needs to cash the investment urgently? Does the investment chosen allow for such cashing out (i.e. is it liquid)?
   - How is the interest or return on the investment recorded? If it is recorded as a regular form of revenue, it may give the impression that the business is operating with a larger net income than is actually the case.

3. **Accounts receivable and doubtful debts** — One of a company's most important assets is its accounts receivable, which constitutes debt owed by customers who have bought goods or services using payment terms. This course will examine how transactions involving accounts receivable are input, as well as how to deal with non-paying customers, and allowing for bad or doubtful debts. Various controls, as well as reports used to manage accounts receivable and related information will also be examined.

Issues to keep in mind:

- Are there adequate controls to ensure that customers pay on time?
- How certain is it that the company will actually get paid? Some methods to predict frequency of payment will be examined.
- How do we know that customers are being billed correctly?
- Are there adequate controls to ensure that no unauthorized refunds are being issued?
- How are potential losses being assessed? If these losses are underestimated, then it will appear as though the company is making more net income than it actually is.
- Conversely, an overestimation of losses will understate net income. Among other things, this could have an impact on taxes and payment of bonuses.
- Higher or lower earnings may also influence the manner in which pricing policies are established for the upcoming year.

4. **Inventory** — The basic concepts associated with inventory, including cost of goods sold (COGS) and the perpetual inventory system are covered in this course. In addition, we will also examine the different methods of valuing inventory, as well as issues related to inventory controls and ethics.

Issues to keep in mind:

- Is the inventory system being used appropriate for the industry?
- How is the inventory valued? Overstated values will affect figures related to gross and net income. Conversely, if the value of inventory is too low, it will appear that gross profit margins have been compromised, reflecting badly on management.
- The value of inventory impacts net income and bonuses.
- Lack of proper controls for inventory could lead to theft and lower than expected inventory levels.

5. **Prepaid expenses and other current assets** — This type of asset addresses prepayments that are not considered expenses at the time they are paid or assets that are not used on a regular basis and do not warrant a special account code. We will examine prepaid expenses in connection with other parts of a company's financial statements.

Issues to keep in mind:

- Are staff members informing the accounting department that travel expenses, for example, are related to a future event? Is the staff aware of the implications of not reporting these expenses properly?
- Not accruing prepaid expenses can skew the operating results of the company.
- Is the value of prepaid services being monitored as to when the services are actually provided? How much of the prepaid expense should be recognized? When?
- What happens to refunds? Are proper controls in place to ensure that these refunds are made to the company, and not specific to individuals?

6. **Property, Plant & Equipment and depreciation** — Property, plant and equipment are long-term assets. They usually consist of the company's most highly valued assets and often consume most of the available cash resources. We will examine different methods of depreciating long-term assets and their impact on company profits.

    ## Issues to keep in mind:

    - Who in the company is authorized to purchase long-term assets?
    - Are some expenses considered assets, which will falsely increase net income?
    - Are assets properly depreciated over their expected useful life?
    - Are the company's long-term assets financed using long-term debt or operating capital?
    - Does the business generate sufficient profits and cash flow to finance debt?
    - Does the business have an asset register to keep track of its long-term assets, such as laptops, that may disappear?

7. **Intangible assets** — The word intangible literally describes something that cannot be touched or felt. It is therefore understood that intangible assets comprise things that aren't physical in nature but that, nevertheless, the company owns — such as goodwill, copyright, trademarks and patents.

    ## Issues to keep in mind:

    - The decision to capitalize or expense an item is one of the most important on the company's balance sheet. It affects the bottom line, as well as bonuses awarded to employees.
    - What is the company's policy when capitalizing intangible assets related to the creation of material such as software?
    - If an item is to be capitalized, over what period should its total cost be amortized?
    - The method of amortization chosen could impact other aspects of the business, such as pricing policy.

8-11. **Debt** — Items 8 to 11 on our Accounting Map™ represent the company's current liabilities, or debt owing, ranging from accounts payable to loans payable. We will examine the various ways in which these items should be categorized, as well as the transactions associated with each.

    ## Issues to keep in mind:

    - Can the business actually pay its debts? Are there sufficient current assets to pay for current liabilities?
    - Are discount opportunities taken advantage of?
    - How are unearned revenues accounted for? Falsely classifying them as earned when deposited will significantly overstate net income for the period.
    - Are unearned revenues properly matched to related expenses?
    - Are unearned revenues recognized as earned by sales staff, simply to collect a commission?

12. **Long term debt and bonds** — This category of liabilities represents amounts owing after 12 months.

Issues to keep in mind:

- Can the business finance its debt?
- Are the lenders taking more risk than the owners? If so, it may be difficult to secure additional loans.
- If the business is running out of operating capital to finance inventory and accounts receivable, should some of the current debt be converted to long-term debt?
- Is the business generating sufficient profits and cash flow to support any additional debt?

13. **Equity** — Equity represents a company's net worth and is structured according to entity type. Proprietorships will be the initial focus of the course. Later, how to account for partnerships and corporations will be examined in detail.

Issues to keep in mind:

- Should profits be distributed to owners for personal use, or should some of the profits be retained in the business?
- If the business needs more cash but cannot secure more financing from the bank, should shares be issued? At what price? Will control of the business change as a result?

Beyond the company's balance sheet, other aspects of financial statements examined in this course, will include:

The income statement - Although every company has an income statement on its books, they do not all look the same. We will examine the various types of income statements that companies use, their layouts and which are most common or appropriate for certain industries.

Cash flow - Once the balance sheet and income statement are fully understood, we will address the cash flow statements that provide information related to the sources and uses of cash.

Financial analysis - Sometimes it is the simple numbers that can tell the story of a business. We will examine various financial ratios and key performance indicators that provide a telling glimpse into the health of a company.

In summary, this course should not only serve as preparation for the accounting profession, it should also serve as preparation for business decision-making in general. By knowing the name, value and timing associated with any transaction of interest, the business professional has at their disposal the tools to make informed and strategic decisions. This is the basic foundation of the course, one which you can take with you in all your future endeavors.

Some additional segments

This textbook was designed to make your learning experience productive and engaging. To that end, we have added some segments to each chapter that highlight learning objectives. They include:

A CLOSER LK

The *Closer Look* segments in each chapter are meant to more closely examine a part of the chapter that might need to be expanded in order to broaden your understanding of an underlying concept or principle. Or they might include an example that applies the concepts being learned, in a way that is easy to understand and follow.

WORTH REPEATING...

The *Worth Repeating* segments in each chapter are meant to remind students of concepts in accounting already learned, and to highlight current concepts being taught that are "worth repeating."

IN THE REAL WORLD

The *In The Real World* segments in each chapter are meant to provide applied examples of elements being learned in a particular chapter. They are meant to put some of the concepts being learned in context and to drive home the point that eventually, accounting has to be done outside the classroom. We hope that these segments give you a sense of what "the real world" can be like for the accountant or business professional.

Notes

Chapter 1
FINANCIAL STATEMENTS: PERSONAL ACCOUNTING

LEARNING OUTCOMES:

❶ Describe and calculate net worth

❷ Interpret the balance sheet and the income statement

❸ Explain how the accounting equation works

❹ Record double entries in T-Accounts

❺ Explain accrual accounting

❻ Understand and apply the matching principle and the concept of materiality

❼ Understand the concept of depreciation under the personal context

❽ Distinguish between capital and revenue

❾ Describe the three sources and uses of cash

❿ Understand the differences between market value and book value

Meaning of Accounting

Accounting accurately measures all the financial activities of an individual or a business. Personal accounting tracks how much an individual is worth. Whether you choose a simple or luxurious lifestyle, you need money to sustain your personal life. Most people want to save enough money to allow them to retire comfortably. The more you save and invest, the more you will be worth.

It is important to maintain records of the activities that increase or decrease your net worth (i.e. how much you earn, how much you invest and how much you spend). The key principles that drive your personal economic life are very similar to those used in business. In fact, learning basic accounting is a crucial life skill for everyone.

Most people associate accounting with calculators, computers and long lists of numbers. That may be true to some degree when you are a practicing bookkeeper or accountant; however, understanding accounting principles involves not only numbers but also a logical way of thinking.

Here is an example of the logic behind one of the principles that you will learn in this course: the concept of net worth. Which scenario in figure 1.1 would you prefer?

Scenario 1

Assets (what we own)

Cash	$3,000
House	80,000
Automobile	15,000
Contents of Home	6,000
Total Assets	**$104,000**

Scenario 2

Assets (what we own)

Cash	$5,000
House	100,000
Automobile	20,000
Contents of Home	8,000
Total Assets	**$133,000**

FIGURE 1.1

Scenario 2 appears to be preferable. However, some crucial information is missing.

In examining the scenarios in figure 1.2, which one would you now prefer? You must not only look at how much you **own** (assets) but also consider how much you **owe** (liabilities).

Scenario 1

Assets (what we own)

Cash	$3,000
House	80,000
Automobile	15,000
Contents of Home	6,000
Total Assets	**$104,000**

Liabilities (what we owe)

Bank Loan	$0
Credit Card Account	2,000
Mortgage	60,000
Automobile Loan	5,000
Student Loan	5,000
Total Liabilities	**$72,000**
Net Worth*	**$32,000**

Scenario 2

Assets (what we own)

Cash	$5,000
House	100,000
Automobile	20,000
Contents of Home	8,000
Total Assets	**$133,000**

Liabilities (what we owe)

Bank Loan	$8,000
Credit Card Account	4,000
Mortgage	80,000
Automobile Loan	5,000
Student Loan	10,000
Total Liabilities	**$107,000**
Net Worth*	**$26,000**

FIGURE 1.2   *Net worth = things you own - things you owe.

Even though you may own more in scenario 2, you also owe a lot more. The end result is that scenario 2 is worth less than scenario 1.

Principle of Net Worth

If you choose to *cash out* (i.e. successfully sell all your assets and get the value equivalent to the recorded amount) and pay everything that you owe, the remaining cash will represent your **net worth.** In accounting, what you own are called *assets*, and what you owe are called *liabilities*.

Tracking the amount you are worth is a fundamental component of accounting in both your personal life and your business life.

Assets = all that you OWN

Value of Assets = $75,000

Liabilities = all that you OWE

Value of Liabilities = $50,000
Net Worth = $25,000

The most common way to increase your net worth is to earn revenue. **Revenue** is an increase in net worth caused by providing goods or services. In your personal life, one way revenue is earned is by working and earning a salary. **Expenses** are a decrease in net worth from the costs of day-to-day activities. In your personal life, expenses can include items such as rent or food.

An overall increase to net worth for a period will happen when revenue exceeds expenses. If you do not maintain a record of your revenues and expenses, you will never know what activities caused your net worth to increase or decrease. This principle remains the same in business.

The Balance Sheet

The **balance sheet** is a permanent document that is used to record what you own (assets) and what you owe (liabilities) on a specific date. The balance sheet provides a snapshot of your financial position. The difference between the value of what you own and what you owe represents your net worth. The date of the balance sheet is presented as 'As at …' because it represents a snapshot of your finances at a particular point in time. For example, a balance sheet prepared on December 31, 2011 would have the date "As at December 31, 2011".

Here are some examples:

In figure 1.3, note that you have only $7,000 in cash. At this point, if you needed to pay everything that you owe ($105,500), you would need to sell some of your assets (i.e. convert the value of your assets into cash, also known as *liquidating*

Personal Balance Sheet As at December 31, 2011			
Assets		**Liabilities**	
Cash (Checking Account)	$7,000	Unpaid Accounts	$500
Cash (Savings Account)	0	Mortgage	100,000
House	120,000	Bank Loan	5,000
Automobile	10,000		
Contents of Home	5,000	**Total Liabilities**	**$105,500**
Total Assets	**$142,000**	**Net Worth**	**$36,500**

FIGURE 1.3

your assets). Although you may think that you are worth only the $7,000 you have in the bank as cash, your true value (or net worth) is $36,500.

Note that net worth is equal to assets less liabilities. We will discuss this relationship later in the chapter.

In figure 1.4, despite the fact that your cash balance is lower, your net worth is higher compared to figure 1.3.

In figure 1.5, you have a negative bank (cash) balance which means that your bank account is over-drawn which can also be called a **bank overdraft**. However, your net worth is significantly higher than in figures 1.3 and 1.4.

Note that in accounting, negative numbers are expressed in parentheses. For example, −$2,000 is shown as ($2,000).

In figure 1.6, you have a large amount of cash, a valuable home and an expensive car. However, your net worth is lower than the previous three scenarios. This is because you have borrowed a significant amount from the bank for your house and car, and you have borrowed money from your family.

Even through figure 1.5 shows a negative cash balance, it has the highest net worth compared to the other figures as a result of the greater difference between its total assets and its total liabilities.

Personal Balance Sheet
As at December 31, 2011

Assets		Liabilities	
Cash (Checking Account)	1,000	Unpaid Accounts	$5,000
Cash (Savings Account)	0	Mortgage	100,000
Pension Savings	18,000	Bank Loan	0
House	120,000		
Automobile	10,000		
Contents of Home	4,500	Total Liabilities	$105,000
Total Assets	$153,500	Net Worth	$48,500

FIGURE 1.4

Personal Balance Sheet
As at December 31, 2011

Assets		Liabilities	
Cash (Checking Account)	($2,000)	Unpaid Accounts	$10,000
Cash (Savings Account)	0	Mortgage	80,000
Pension Savings	10,000	Bank Loan	0
House	180,000	Car Loan	6,000
Automobile	10,000	Family Loan	7,000
Contents of Home	5,000		
Investments	20,000	Total Liabilities	$103,000
Total Assets	$223,000	Net Worth	$120,000

FIGURE 1.5

Personal Balance Sheet
As at December 31, 2011

Assets		Liabilities	
Cash (Checking Account)	$50,000	Unpaid Accounts	$15,000
Cash (Savings Account)	0	Mortgage	220,000
Pension Savings	3,000	Bank Loan	50,000
House	250,000	Car Loan	40,000
Automobile	50,000	Family Loan	10,000
Contents of Home	12,000		
Investments	5,000	Total Liabilities	$335,000
Total Assets	$370,000	Net Worth	$35,000

FIGURE 1.6

The Income Statement

The **income statement** is primarily used as a temporary document to record transactions relating to revenue and expenses. The purpose of this statement is to determine the change in net worth over a specific period of time. The date of the income statement is presented as 'For the Period Ended ...' since the statement covers a period of time. For example, an income statement prepared on December 31, 2011 covering a year would have the date "For the Year Ended December 31, 2011".

If you did not want to use a formal income statement, you could merely record every transaction in the net worth section on the balance sheet. Since revenue increases net worth and expenses decrease net worth, you could record every revenue and expense amount directly into net worth on the balance sheet.

Figure 1.7 illustrates this example:

1. Earned and deposited your $3,000 salary.
2. Paid cash for your $80 telephone bill for the month.
3. Received a bill for $150 for car maintenance.
4. Received a bill for $500 for insurance.
5. Paid cash of $800 for your monthly rent.
6. Spent $200 cash on groceries.

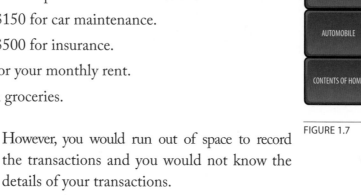

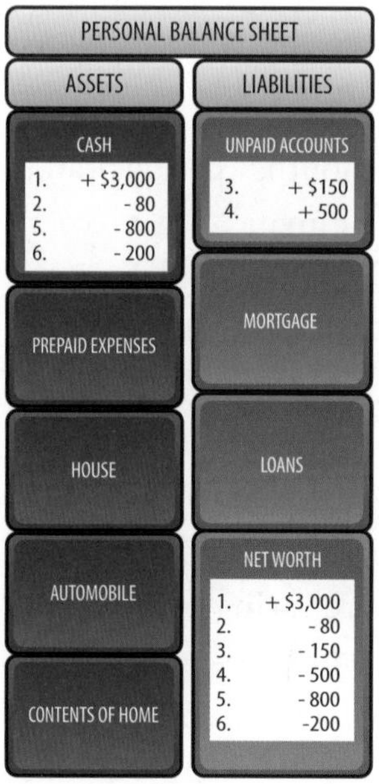

FIGURE 1.7

However, you would run out of space to record the transactions and you would not know the details of your transactions.

Instead, you could make note of revenue and expenses on a separate document (the income statement).

Using an income statement, as shown in figure 1.8, allows you to keep a clean record of changes to your net worth over a period of time. It also allows you to review your records at any time to see what caused the changes in net worth.

FIGURE 1.8

A CLOSER LOOK

Imagine playing a sports game without a scorecard. It would be very difficult to play the game effectively without knowing the score while the game is played. Your economic life is no different in principle. It is crucial to monitor how your day to day activities impact your net worth on a monthly basis to allow sufficient time to change spending behaviors to fit within your income. Remember that there is a difference between cash and your net worth.

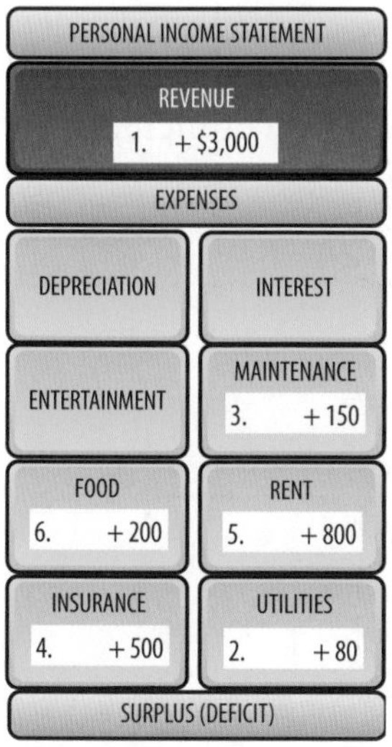

Accounting Periods

You can keep changing net worth continuously; however, for accounting purposes, it would be more convenient to record changes to net worth in separate periods. You can use any period you choose as an accounting period: one year, six months or one month, as shown in figure 1.9.

If you use a month as your accounting period, you can look back at previous months (periods) and estimate what your expenses and income will be in the coming months. You can also estimate the surplus or deficit you generate each month. If you are saving for a major purchase such as a car, a new computer or an

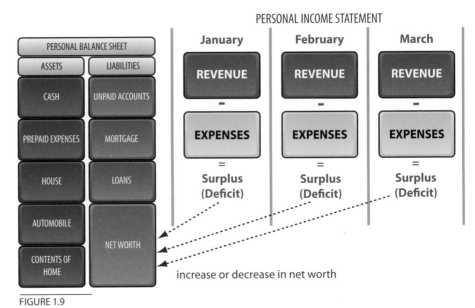

FIGURE 1.9

expensive entertainment system, you will be able to determine when you will have enough money to buy the desired item or at least to provide a down payment.

Some advantages of using monthly accounting periods in your personal balance sheet include
- tracking regular monthly living expenses (e.g. rent, cell phone)
- frequently comparing against your personal financial plan or budget
- preventing and detecting errors effectively

The Accounting Equation

The accounting equation is shown in figure 1.10.

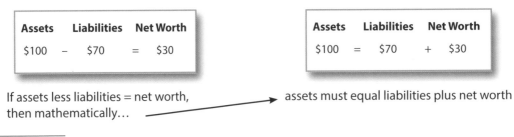

FIGURE 1.10

While Newton's Third Law applies to science, the same principle can be applied to the logic of the accounting equation: "For every action there is an equal and opposite reaction" – that is, transaction and financial consequence. In accounting terms, a double entry of the same value is always made for every transaction. This means that each transaction has at least two entries. The logic of the double entry is based on the accounting equation:

Assets = Liabilities + Net Worth

In the absence of a logical opposite entry, the balance sheet will not balance, as shown in figure 1.11.

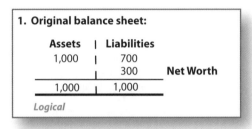

1. Original balance sheet:

Assets		Liabilities	
1,000		700	
		300	**Net Worth**
1,000		1,000	

Logical

2. Deposit $500 in wages:

Assets		Liabilities	
1,500		700	
		300	**Net Worth**
1,500		1,000	

1,500 ≠ 1,000 (not logical)

Assets		Liabilities	
1,500		700	
		800	**Net Worth**
1,500		1,500	*Net worth increase, which is revenue*

1,500 = 1,500 (logical)

3. Pay cash expenses of $100:

Assets		Liabilities	
1,400		700	
		800	**Net Worth**
1,400		1,500	

1,400 ≠ 1,500 (not logical)

Assets		Liabilities	
1,400		700	
		700	**Net Worth**
1,400		1,400	*Net worth decreases, which is an expense*

1,400 = 1,400 (logical)

FIGURE 1.11

Imagine the accounting equation as a scale with each side in balance; the left side of the scale would include assets and the right side would include liabilities and net worth.

The scale must always be in balance, as shown in figure 1.12.

Assets
122,000

Liabilities + Net Worth
80,000 + 42,000

Assets = Liabilities + Net Worth
$122,000 = $80,000 + $42,000

FIGURE 1.12

If you received $3,000 cash, it would increase your assets. Only recording the increase in cash will cause the scale to go out of balance, as shown in figure 1.13.

Increase cash
by $3,000

Liabilities + Net Worth
80,000 + 42,000

Assets
125,000

Assets = Liabilities + Net Worth
$125,000 ≠ $80,000 + $42,000

FIGURE 1.13

To get the scale back into balance, you must ask yourself why you received the cash. If you received the cash because you earned it at your job, then the $3,000 must also increase net worth. This will be recorded as revenue and bring the scale back into balance, as shown in figure 1.14.

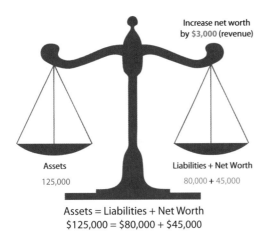

Increase net worth
by $3,000 (revenue)

Assets
125,000

Liabilities + Net Worth
80,000 + 45,000

Assets = Liabilities + Net Worth
$125,000 = $80,000 + $45,000

FIGURE 1.14

Soon after, if you made a cash payment of $1,000, your assets would decrease in value. The scale would only stay in balance if you record the $1,000 somewhere else. Ask yourself, "Why did I make a $1,000 payment?" If you made the payment for rent for the month, then the $1,000 must also decrease net worth. This will be recorded as an expense and leave the scale in balance, as shown in figure 1.15.

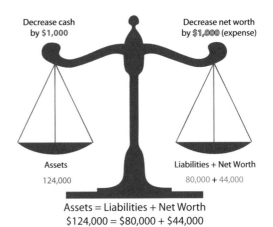

Decrease cash
by $1,000

Decrease net worth
by $1,000 (expense)

Assets
124,000

Liabilities + Net Worth
80,000 + 44,000

Assets = Liabilities + Net Worth
$124,000 = $80,000 + $44,000

FIGURE 1.15

Net Worth Calculation

As discussed, net worth can be calculated by rearranging the accounting equation (Net Worth = Assets – Liabilities). If you want to calculate your net worth using this method at a particular date, the balance of total liabilities is simply deducted from total assets. However, net worth changes over time as you earn revenue and incur expenses. The calculation below shows how to calculate the change in net worth over a period of time.

Opening Net Worth + Capital + Surplus (Deficit) = Closing Net Worth

Opening net worth is the balance of net worth at the beginning of the period that is being considered. Capital refers to increases to net worth that is not considered revenue. Capital will be discussed in detail later in the chapter. Surplus (or deficit) is the amount by which revenues exceed expenses (or expenses exceed revenues) for the period. The amount is taken from the personal income statement. A surplus increases net worth and a deficit decreases net worth. To double check if your accounting records and your calculation of net worth are accurate, you can use the accounting equation to ensure that assets are equal to liabilities plus net worth.

Introduction to T-Accounts

To demonstrate the link between the income statement and the balance sheet, consider the opening balances and transactions shown in figure 1.16. The opening balances are the values of the assets, liabilities and net worth before transactions are recorded. A transaction occurs any time you trade with someone else to receive something of value. We will use the opening balances and the transactions to determine the changes in net worth and the ending balances of the assets, liabilities and net worth. This will be shown in figure 1.17.

Every transaction in this example involves cash, so cash is on one side of the double entry each time. For the other side of the double entry transaction, ask yourself why cash is being affected (e.g. to pay for rent or to pay for food). That will help you determine what the other account will be.

Opening Balances		Transactions		
Cash	$5,000	*Receive cash for revenue:*		
House	100,000	1. Receive Salary	$3,000	
Contents of Home	5,000	*Pay cash for expenses:*		
Mortgage	80,000	2. Entertainment	200	
Net Worth	30,000	3. Food	400	
		4. Home repairs	200	
		5. Insurance	100	
		6. Gas	100	
		7. Rent	800	

FIGURE 1.16

At this stage, the entries from figure 1.16 will be marked for you on each account. A **T-Account** allows us to track detailed information about the values of individual items (i.e. Cash, Unpaid

Accounts, Food Expense, etc.). We will be using formatted T-Accounts throughout the textbook. T-Accounts, so called because they are in the shape of a T, are used to record accounting transactions. This form allows you to record the double entries for each transaction on opposite sides (increase or decrease) of each account. It is important to note that each transaction will have at least one entry on the left side of the T-Account and at least one entry on the right side of another T-Account. The total of all the numbers entered on the left side must equal the total of all the numbers entered on the right side.

The Process

① If applicable, enter the opening balances in the appropriate accounts. Then check that the accounting equation is in balance before you begin entering transactions.

② Enter both sides of the transaction under the correct account in the balance sheet and/or income statement. Be sure to record the transaction numbers so that you may check your work.

③ Calculate the surplus or deficit in the income statement and transfer the amount to net worth in the balance sheet. A surplus increases net worth, and a deficit decreases net worth.

④ Complete the accounting equation at the bottom of the balance sheet to check that it balances.

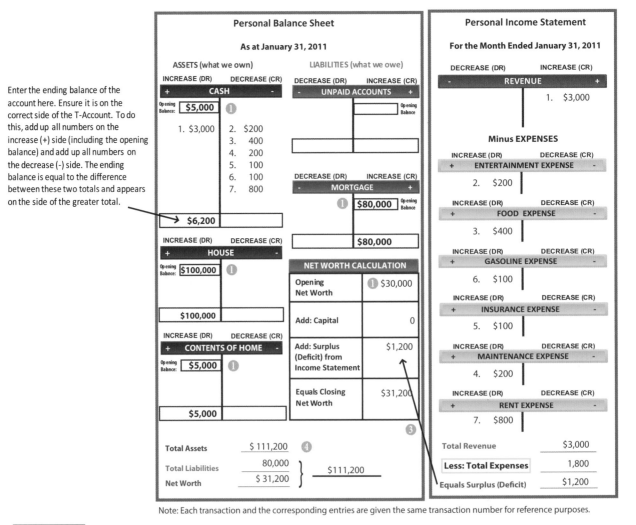

Note: Each transaction and the corresponding entries are given the same transaction number for reference purposes.

FIGURE 1.17

Accrual Accounting

A typical reason for personal financial failure (and small business failure) is a lack in understanding the principle of accruals. People tend to think intuitively that an increase in cash represents an increase in wealth, and vice versa. The notion of the accrual is recognizing how much you are worth at a point in time. The principle of **accrual accounting** states the following:

Revenue (an increase to net worth) and expenses (a decrease to net worth) should be recognized in the time period in which they occur, regardless of when the cash payment is received or made.

So far we have assumed that every expense is paid when it is incurred. In reality, many expenses are not paid until a later date. The examples in figures 1.18 and 1.19 illustrate how expenses are recorded as they occur.

Assume that you have $1,000 of cash and net worth of $1,000. If you pay for a $300 expense with cash, your cash and your net worth will decrease by $300 (see figure 1.18).

If instead you receive a phone bill for $300 to be paid next month, there would be no change in cash in the current month. However, the phone debt (or unpaid accounts) would increase by $300 and net worth would decrease by $300 (see figure 1.19). In other words, you would *recognize* the expense which decreases net worth.

FIGURE 1.18

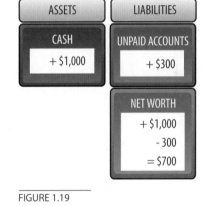

FIGURE 1.19

In general, keep in mind that the word "expense" relates to a decrease to net worth, which does not necessarily relate to cash.

Cash Flow vs. Accruals

There are two key principles to understand as shown in figure 1.20:

1. *Cash flow* relates to cash flowing into and out of the bank account, which is not necessarily directly connected to net worth.

2. *Accruals* relate to net worth, which does not necessarily connect to cash flow.

Both principles are important and distinct.

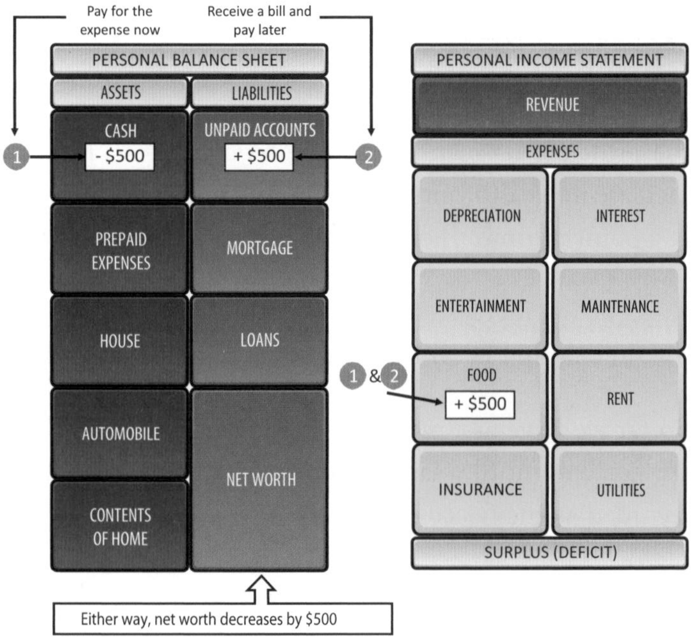

FIGURE 1.20

Cash-Based vs. Accrual-Based Accounting

If a cash-based method of accounting is used, then revenue and expenses are recorded only when the cash is received or paid.

As illustrated in figure 1.21, at the end of January, you deposit your $3,000 salary earned during the month and you pay expenses of $2,000 using cash from the bank. The difference between revenue and expenses results in an increase in net worth of $1,000, which happens to be the same as the increase in cash.

Suppose that you deposit salary of $3,000 in January, but choose to charge all $2,000 worth of expenses to your credit card, which is to be paid in February. When you use cash-based accounting, your net worth appears to be $3,000 in January since no cash is used to pay your expenses.

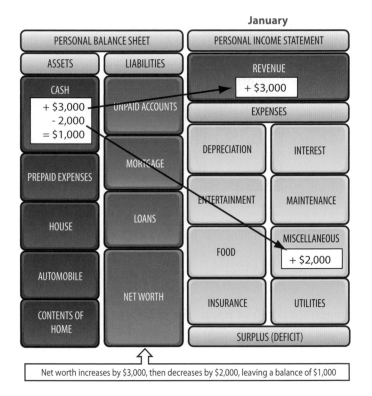

FIGURE 1.21

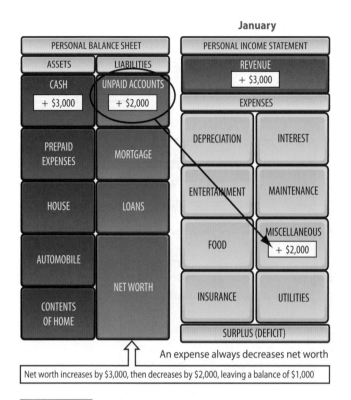

FIGURE 1.22

If you are using accrual-based accounting, you need to recognize the expense in January, the month in which it was actually incurred.

In figure 1.22, the income statement for the month of January shows that you have matched the revenue of $3,000 (an increase in net worth) to the expenses in January of $2,000 (a decrease in net worth), resulting in an overall increase in net worth of $1,000. Cash remains at $3,000 because you have not spent any of it yet.

The accrual system of accounting recognizes the change in net worth even though payment is not necessarily received or paid.

The Matching Principle

The **matching principle** requires expenses to be reported in the same period as the revenues to which they are related. This conforms to accrual accounting. Four transactions that occurred in January are presented below. Their impact on the balance sheet and income statement are shown in figure 1.23. Keep in mind that the accounting equation must always stay in balance.

1. Earn and deposit $5,000 in salary. Cash increases by $5,000 which increases the total assets in the accounting equation. Why did cash increase? Because you deposited your salary. Net worth increases, which is shown as revenue on the income statement.

2. Pay $1,000 in cash for food expenses. Cash decreases by $1,000 which decreases the total assets in the accounting equation. Why did cash decrease? Because you bought some food. Thus, net worth decreases, which is shown as food expense on the income statement.

3. Record a $500 credit card bill for gas expenses (due in one month). Cash is not affected; however, you have a debt which must be paid next month. Debt increases which increases the total liabilities in the accounting equation. Why did your debt increase? Because you will have to pay for the gas at some point in the future. Net worth decreases, which is shown as gasoline expense on the income statement.

4. Record a $1,500 credit card bill for entertainment expenses. Debt increases which increases the liabilities in the accounting equation. Why did your debt increase? Because you will have to pay for the entertainment at some point in the future. Net worth decreases, which is shown as entertainment expense on the income statement.

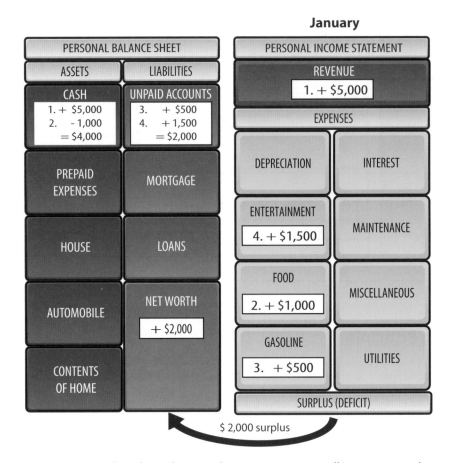

January

Remember: Everything that is shown on the income statement will impact net worth

FIGURE 1.23

The same information can be illustrated using income statement and balance sheet T-Accounts. T-Accounts are the preferred way to record these transactions, and are illustrated in figure 1.24.

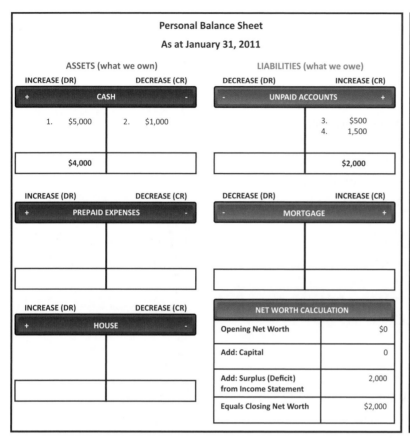

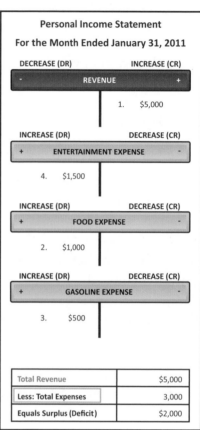

Remember that the income statement lists all individual items that cause a change to net worth.

FIGURE 1.24

The accounting equation is balanced:

$$\text{Assets} = \text{Liabilities} + \text{Net Worth}$$
$$\$4,000 = \$2,000 + \$2,000$$

As the examples in figure 1.23 and 1.24 illustrate, you need to match what you earn each month to your expenses for that month. According to the principle of accruals, the credit card expenses would be recognized in January when they were incurred, not in February when they will be paid.

You will note that cash initially increased by $5,000 and then decreased by $1,000, which may leave you with the impression that your net worth decreased by the same amount. In fact, your net worth decreased by $3,000 (instead of $1,000) because the revenue and expenses were matched in the same time period, regardless of when the expenses were actually paid.

Borrowing Money and Repaying Debt

Other than cash in your bank account, every other financial aspect of your life relates to values – not to cash. The things you own are called assets.

Examples of assets that have value would include:

- A house has *value*, but is not actually cash.
- An automobile has *value*, but is not actually cash.
- An entertainment system has *value*, but is not actually cash.

In other words, at some point you purchased these assets with cash (or you may have borrowed the money), but they now represent a value. When you eventually sell these assets, they will then be converted into cash.

The things you owe are called liabilities.

For example:

- The amount of money you owe a friend is not cash; it is an IOU (I owe you).
- The amount of money you owe against your credit card account is not cash; it is how much you owe (also an IOU or a debt).

However, when you pay your friend or the credit card company, you will be required to pay them with cash. Until that happens, the amount that you owe is simply a value. Accounting includes the process of recording these values, whether they represent real cash or simply a value. See the example in figure 1.25.

Example:

Assets (what you own)		Liabilities (what you owe)	
Cash	$2,000	Value of loan from the bank	$6,000
Value of house	100,000	Value of loan from a friend	2,000
Value of automobile	20,000	Value of credit card balance	2,000
Value of furniture	6,000	**Total value of liabilities**	$10,000
Value of computer	2,000		
Total value of assets	**$130,000**	**Assets – Liabilities = Net Worth**	**$120,000**

FIGURE 1.25

When you borrow money, you have more cash, but your net worth does not change. When you pay your debt, you are "cash flow poorer," not "net worth poorer."

For example, assume you borrow money from a friend and then repay the money:

1. Borrow $100 from a friend: you have more cash, but your net worth does not change.
2. Repay your friend: you have less cash, but your net worth still does not change.

The T-Account entries are shown in figure 1.27.

FIGURE 1.26

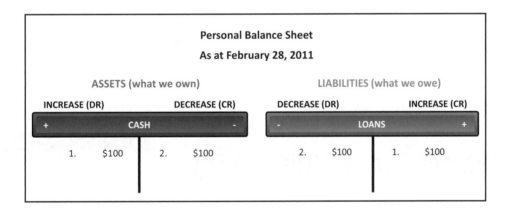

FIGURE 1.27

No entry is reflected in the income statement because there is no change in net worth.

Figure 1.28 demonstrates that not all the cash you spend would necessarily be used to pay expenses. For example, you arrange for a loan of $15,000 and your loan repayments are $500 each month. The payment involves two transactions:

Transaction 1:

Pay the interest portion of $400. (Recall Newton's Third Law: *For every action there is an equal and opposite reaction*). Net worth has decreased. Therefore, an expense should be recognized.

Transaction 2:

Pay the principal of $100, thereby reducing the amount owing to the loan company. Your net worth does not change and therefore there is no need to record this transaction in the income statement.

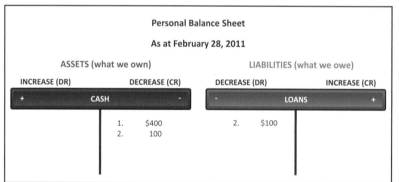

FIGURE 1.28

The transactions would appear on the T-Accounts, as in figure 1.29:

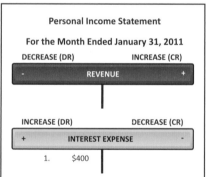

FIGURE 1.29

Even though your cash decreased by $500, your net worth decreased by $400 as a result of the expense.

Buying and Selling Assets

Buying or selling assets (according to the value stated in the balance sheet) has no impact on net worth. For example, you purchase a new car for $10,000; pay $3,000 cash and take a loan from the bank for the remaining $7,000.

FIGURE 1.30

When you pay $3,000 cash for the car, one asset is exchanged for another asset (cash for a car), with no change in net worth. This is shown in figure 1.30.

By borrowing $7,000 from the bank, you will be able to pay for the balance owing on the car (see figure 1.31). When you borrow money to buy a car, you increase the asset and increase the liability, with no change in net worth.

Although you now own a $10,000 car, there has been no change in your net worth.

FIGURE 1.31

The transactions would appear on the T-Accounts as shown in figure 1.32. The $3,000 and the $7,000 increase to the automobile account have been combined into a single increase of $10,000.

The car you purchased for $10,000 is expected to last you several years. Over these years, you will benefit from the use of the car while, simultaneously, the car will lose value. This reduction in value of your car is called depreciation and will be discussed in the next section.

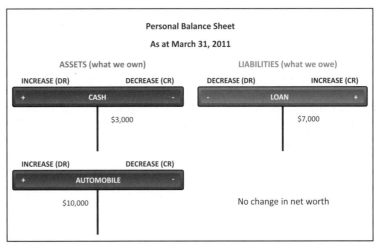

FIGURE 1.32

So, borrowing and repaying debt does not impact net worth, and neither does buying or selling assets for the value stated in the balance sheet. The primary way you can change your net worth is to have revenue exceed expenses (net worth increases) or have expenses exceed revenue (net worth decreases). Capital can also change your net worth, which will be discussed later.

Depreciation

Both assets and expenses start out the same way: you usually use cash (or your credit card) to buy an asset or pay for an expense. Assets differ from expenses in the sense that assets will provide benefits to you in the future. This means that the asset can be used for a long period of time, in some cases for one year or more. However, the assets shown on your personal balance sheet (cell phone, entertainment system, computer, vehicle, etc.) that you can use for one year or more will eventually wear out or become obsolete and outdated. Therefore, if you were to sell your assets, you would not get the same value that you paid for them.

It is not reasonable to show the asset in your balance sheet indefinitely. Since the asset deteriorates, or eventually has no value, it should be removed from the balance sheet at some point.

The solution is to **depreciate** the asset. Depreciation takes a portion of the asset's cost and records it as an expense for each period you use the asset. This is in line with the matching principle and reports the depreciation expense in the same period as the revenue to which it is related.

To illustrate this principle, assume you purchased a computer for $1,200. The computer is expected to last for three years before it is worn out or becomes worthless. At the time you bought the computer, your cash decreased and there was no change in net worth. As the computer is used, it needs to be depreciated to reflect the reduction in value. Since you predict the computer will last for three years, it will decrease by one third of its value every year: $1,200 \div 3 = $400 per year.

A CLOSER LOOK

For personal accounting, it is acceptable to decrease the asset directly with the yearly depreciation. In a business environment, the asset account will not directly be affected by depreciation. Instead, another account will be used to track the total depreciation over the useful life of the item (termed "accumulated depreciation").

Each year, the value of your asset will decrease by $400 and net worth will decrease by $400 since depreciation is treated as an expense. By the end of the third year, the computer will have no value at all.

Cash does not decrease when you record depreciation. Rather, the value of the asset is reduced and so is net worth. Cash decreases when you buy the asset, *not* when you record depreciation. Net worth decreases when you depreciate the asset, *not* at the time of the purchase.

The following table illustrates the impact of depreciation on the balance sheet and income statement.

Depreciation of Computer		
Period	**Balance Sheet**	**Income Statement**
Date of Purchase (Year 0)	On the date of purchase, 3/3 of the value is shown in the balance sheet. $1,200	On the date of purchase, no part of the value is shown in the income statement. $0
Year 1	At the end of Year 1, 2/3 of the value is shown in the balance sheet. $1,200 – $400 = $800	During Year 1, 1/3 of the value is transferred to the income statement. $400
Year 2	At the end of Year 2, 1/3 of the value is shown in the balance sheet. $800 – $400 = $400	During Year 2, 1/3 of the value is transferred to the income statement. $400
Year 3	At the end of Year 3, zero value is shown in the balance sheet. $400 – $400 = 0 At this time, we are assuming the computer will not be worth anything.	During Year 3, the remaining 1/3 of the value is transferred to the income statement. $400

FIGURE 1.33

If you assessed your net worth at the end of the three-year period, you would have adjusted it to exclude the value of the computer. You would record the depreciation in the balance sheet and income statement in each period.

There are some assets that can also increase in value (i.e. appreciate) over time. These assets are considered investments, and some examples are:

- Cash investments
- Stocks
- Home
- Antiques
- Jewelry

When these assets increase in value, so does net worth. These assets may also depreciate in value, causing a decrease in net worth. So net worth will likely fluctuate from year to year based on the change in value of these assets.

Changes in net worth due to increases in the value of these investments should have a separate record from your regular monthly income and expenses. To a large extent, you can neither control the value of these investments nor live off the profits that could be made from them on a month-to-month basis. It is therefore important to monitor revenue and expenses on a monthly basis to ensure that you are managing your personal finances in a responsible manner.

Prepaid Expenses

It is a common practice to pay for various expenses in advance – for example, insurance and rent. These prepayments are not considered an expense at the time they are paid because the services have not been provided. The following example illustrated in figure 1.34 explains the prepayment of $1,200 for insurance for one year:

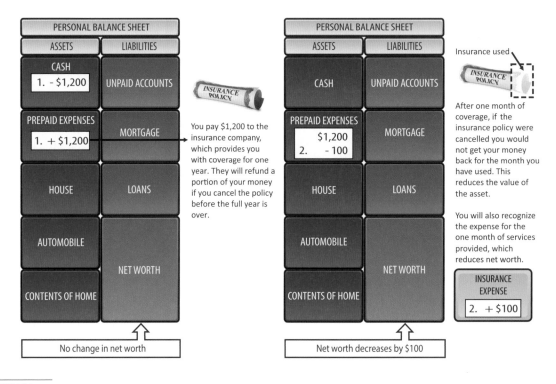

FIGURE 1.34

When you prepay your insurance, you might think intuitively that your net worth decreased because the cash is no longer in your bank account. However, what you have really done is purchased a one year insurance policy, which you now own. Anything you own is considered an asset and recorded on the balance sheet. In this case the insurance policy is considered a prepaid expense. A **prepaid expense** is an item (like insurance) that you pay for before you use it. You own the policy for one year and the insurance company must provide you with coverage for that period of time. Technically, your own cash is sitting in the insurance company's bank account. It can be considered your own cash because they have not yet provided services to you. If you cancel the insurance policy before the year is up, they will have to refund your money for the amount of the policy that you did not use.

Figure 1.35 illustrates another example of a prepaid expense. Assume that you hire a gardening service that costs $600 per year ($50 per month). The service provider requests that you prepay the full $600 in January. If you were to cancel the contract with the company the next morning, you would receive all the money back because it does not belong to the company since it has not yet provided the service. In effect, you have simply given the company an interest-free loan. Therefore, if you were to cancel the contract in three months, you would get back $450 [$600 - ($50 per month × 3 months)]; if it were cancelled in six months, you would get back $300; and so on.

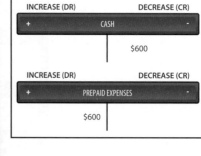

FIGURE 1.35

You have paid the $600 in advance but the service provider owes you cash if the services are not provided. As a result, this payment is considered an asset (which is a prepaid expense). There is no expense (i.e. a decrease in net worth) until the service is provided.

As each month goes by, the value of the prepaid expense will decrease together with your net worth. In other words, you are recognizing the expense in the month in which it is used – not when it is paid.

After the first month's service is provided, you will recognize $50 as an expense for that month (which decreases net worth) and the remaining prepaid portion will be $550 as shown in figure 1.36.

An increase in expenses relates to a decrease in net worth. Cash does not have to be involved to increase an expense and decrease net worth. You will recognize $50 as an expense for each of the next 11 months as the supplier provides the service.

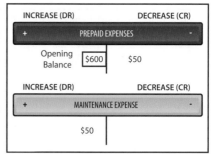

FIGURE 1.36

In summary, there are only three ways to pay for an expense. In all cases, the expense must be recognized when it is incurred. If we assume an expense is $100, the three transactions are:

1. Pay as the expense occurs (cash).

2. Pay before the event and recognize the expense when the event occurs (prepaid expense).

3. Pay after the event has occurred (unpaid account).

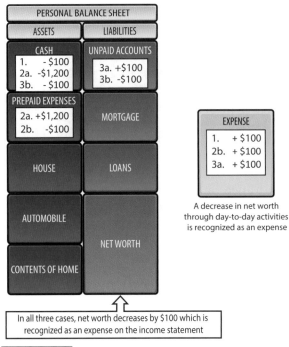

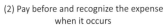

FIGURE 1.37

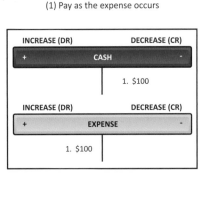

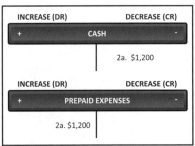

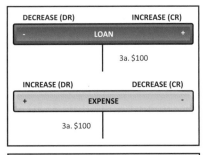

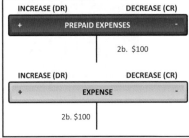

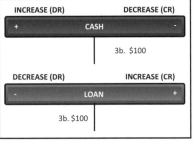

FIGURE 1.38

Materiality

As you now know, if you buy an asset your net worth will not change. Similarly, if you sell an asset for the value that is recorded in your balance sheet, your net worth will not change.

The big question is, "What is the true value of your assets and how much is your actual net worth?" We all know the value of our liabilities, but we don't know the true value of our assets until we sell them. In reality, we do not know our net worth unless we sell all our assets, pay off all our liabilities and see how much cash remains.

Accounting (in both our personal and our business lives) helps us record the value of our assets as accurately as possible. This is not always easy. Before continuing, let us provide a further definition of an asset and how an asset is different from an expense.

In simple terms, an asset is something of value that can be sold for cash – for example a TV, video camera, furniture, car or a house. An expense is something that cannot be converted to cash and reduces your "wealth" – for example gas, food, movie tickets or maintenance.

Sometimes the difference is not quite so clear. One person may consider DVDs an expense because she believes that once they are opened, they have no value. Another person could logically argue that even though you paid $30 for the DVD, someone may be willing to pay you $10 for it in six months' time. It is often a question of judgment. However, we need to use common sense in determining how much we think the item is really worth. In other words, we need to determine if the item is material relative to net worth. Applying the concept of **materiality** means that we can record an asset as an expense if it does not make a significant difference to the balance sheet and income statement.

In the case of someone who is extremely wealthy, a $200 DVD player is not material enough to be recorded as an asset. In this case, it would be expensed.

If you think that an item you purchased will have any material value at the end of the year relative to your total assets, you need to record the full value that you paid for it as an asset and then decrease its value to the amount you think you would obtain for it at the end of the year. In other words, you need to depreciate the value of your assets in the balance sheet according to their realistic value.

Materiality is one of the criteria in the decision to record an item as an asset (i.e. capitalize) or expense. However, it is not the only one. Another criteria is examining the ongoing benefits of the item purchased. For example, although a new TV may only cost a few hundred dollars, it will last and benefit the owner for several years. This should be considered an asset instead of an expense. In fact, in the business world, there are numerous accounting standards that provide guidance on this issue. The decision to capitalize an item or recognize it as an expense, in some cases, can be a very complicated issue.

Capital

So far, we have discussed that the most common way to increase net worth is to earn revenue in an amount that exceeds your expenses. There are other ways to increase your net worth, such as winning the lottery or receiving a gift. These are not considered as revenue since they were not earned; but they do increase your net worth. They are known as **capital**. Recall that capital was a component in the calculation of net worth presented earlier in the chapter.

FIGURE 1.39

Closing Net Worth = Opening Net Worth + Capital + Surplus (Deficit)

Part of the accounting function is to manage your finances by recording your monthly expenses and matching them to your monthly revenue. Capital items (such as gifts or lottery winnings) are not everyday revenues and are therefore recorded directly to net worth instead of the revenue account.

It is important to separate these records because pooling all your revenues together (including profit that is made on the sale of investments or the sale of your old car) will limit your ability to manage your finances on a month-by-month basis.

The Three Sources and Uses of Cash

It should now be apparent that an increase or decrease in cash does not necessarily mean that net worth has increased or decreased. There are essentially three ways of increasing or decreasing cash:

1. Through day-to-day activities of earning and spending money on regular expenses; ideally you want to increase your cash position by ensuring that your revenue exceeds your expenses;

2. By investing in or selling investments such as properties, stocks and mutual funds;

3. Through borrowing or paying back loans — called financing.

You should always strive to ensure that your cash increases through day-to-day activities, which will ultimately increase your wealth. If you have to rely on your investments to increase your wealth, you may be in for an unpleasant surprise. It is therefore important to maintain an income statement on a regular basis to ensure that your revenue exceeds your expenses. If you can successfully increase your wealth through investments, this should be monitored separately from your day-to-day activities. These same principles apply to businesses.

Market Value vs. Book Value

Your personal assets should be valued according to their **market value**, which is the amount for which the asset could be sold on the open market. **Book value**, on the other hand, is the difference between the purchase price and the amount of depreciation.

Example 1:

In your personal financial statements, you may choose to depreciate furniture over a five-year period. Assume that the book value of the furniture is $1,000, but the market value is $1,200. You should value the furniture in your balance sheet at the market value of $1,200.

For businesses, strict rules are in place with regard to valuing assets. A business would value the furniture at its book value of $1,000.

Example 2:

If you purchase stock in a public company such as IBM or Toyota, the value of the stock (on the asset side of your balance sheet) will change almost daily. You should increase or decrease the value of the stock every time you decide to update your net worth. An increase is called a gain on investments and a decrease is called a loss on investments. Gains are not considered regular income.

A business would initially record the value of shares at book value. Under certain circumstances it would adjust the value of the shares in the balance sheet and record a gain or loss when the investments are sold.

IN THE REAL WORLD

During 2009, the economic world changed due to the collapse of large American banks and many other banks across the world. While there was a number of complex issues that caused this catastrophe, one of the more common reasons was that many homeowners did not understand the notion of the true value of assets (their home) and their ability to service the debt (mortgage).

Essentially, revenues must exceed expenses in order to create a surplus which will be used to pay for day to day living expenses, interest and principal of the mortgage. While the market value of homes was increasing, mortgage companies often awarded loans higher than the amount paid for the homes hoping that the homes would increase in value.

Despite the fact that many home owners had less-than-perfect credit ratings and their ability to service the debt was questionable, they were still offered home loans. These types of risky loans are called subprime debt.

When the borrower is considered subprime, lenders charge a greater interest rate to make up for possible default on the loan.

What does the understanding of financial statements have to do with all this? When an individual understands the consequences of different financial decisions, the wrong decision is less likely to be made.

In Summary

↪ If you choose to sell all your assets and pay everything you owe, the remaining cash represents your net worth.

↪ The balance sheet represents what you own (assets) and what you owe (liabilities), and is a permanent record.

↪ The income statement is a temporary record and is used to determine the change in net worth (revenue minus expenses) over a period of time.

↪ The accounting equation: **Assets = Liabilities + Net Worth**

↪ An increase or decrease in cash does not necessarily mean that net worth has increased or decreased.

↪ **Accrual accounting** is recognizing revenue (increases net worth) and expenses (decreases net worth) in the time period in which they occur, regardless of when the payment is received or made.

↪ **Cash flow vs. accruals** involve two key principles: (1) cash flow relates to cash flowing into and out of the bank account, regardless of the effect on net worth; and (2) accruals relate to net worth, regardless of cash flow. Both principles are important and distinct.

↪ The matching principle requires that revenue and expenses be matched in the same time period, regardless of when the revenue is received or when the expenses are paid.

↪ Buying or selling assets for the value stated in the balance sheet has no impact on net worth. When you borrow money, you have more cash but your net worth does not change. When you pay back your debt, you are "cash flow poorer," not "net worth poorer."

↪ The reduction in the value of your assets, which decreases net worth, is called depreciation expense.

↪ There are only three ways to pay for an expense: (1) pay as the expense occurs (cash); (2) pay before the event and recognize the expense when the event occurs (prepaid expense); (3) pay after the event occurs (unpaid accounts).

↪ Determining the value of an asset relative to net worth or how important it is to record the item as part of net worth is partially based on materiality.

↪ Capital: gifts and lottery winnings are not part of everyday revenues and are therefore recorded directly to net worth instead of the revenue account.

↪ The three ways to generate and consume cash are: (a) earning and spending through day-to-day activities; (b) buying and selling investments; (c) borrowing or paying back loans.

↪ Your personal assets are essentially valued according to their market value (i.e. the value of the asset on the market if it were sold immediately).

Review Exercise

Complete the T-Account worksheet on the opposite page for the following transactions and calculate ending net worth.

Opening balances:

Cash	$3,000
House	100,000
Contents of Home	3,000
Mortgage	70,000
Net Worth	36,000

Transactions for the month of January:

Revenue

1. Earned and deposited salary	$2,000
2. Earned and deposited interest on savings	300

Expenses (all paid by cash)

3. Food	300
4. Entertainment	200
5. Clothing	100
6. Maintenance to home	500
7. Utilities (electricity, water, gas)	100

Others

8. Deposited lottery winnings	600
9. Received cash gift	150

Review Exercise – Answer

T-Account Worksheet

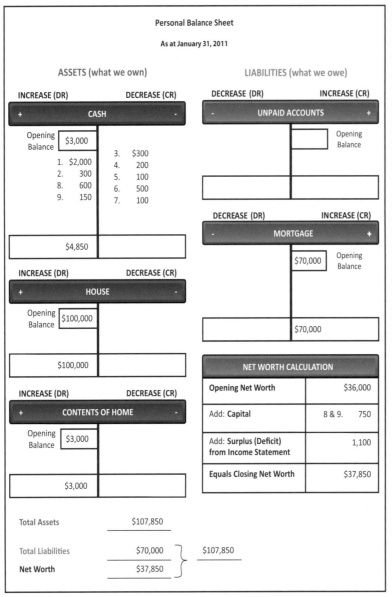

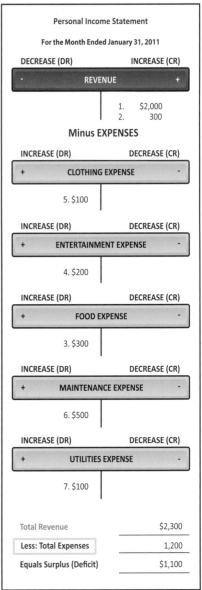

Chapter 2
LINKING PERSONAL ACCOUNTING TO BUSINESS ACCOUNTING

LEARNING OUTCOMES:

❶ Understand the differences between personal accounts and business accounts

❷ Explain the sequence of assets and liabilities as they appear on the balance sheet

❸ Define owner's equity and calculate the balance of the capital account

❹ Describe the different forms of organizations

❺ Define stakeholder

❻ Explain the three main types of businesses

❼ Record business transactions

Business Accounts

Accounting principles in a personal context are similar to the principles in a business context, with a few exceptions. The following are examples of account names and principles that will change when dealing with accounting in a business:

1. Cash in the bank is usually referred to as *cash* or *cash and cash equivalents*. These terms are used interchangeably in this textbook.

2. Computers and other assets that are expected to last for more than a year are referred to as **property, plant and equipment, long-term assets** or **fixed assets.** Property, plant and equipment will be abbreviated as PPE in account titles for the rest of this text.

3. Net worth is referred to as *owner's equity*.

4. The income statement is occasionally referred to as a *profit & loss statement* (or P&L).

5. Personal revenue (e.g. salary earned) is referred to as *business revenue* (e.g. sales revenue or service revenue).

6. Surplus (deficit) is referred to as *net income (loss)*, or *net profit (loss)*. The terms can be used interchangeably.

Figure 2.1 shows the comparison between the personal balance sheet and the business balance sheet.

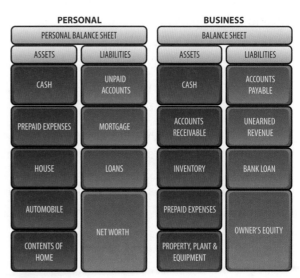

FIGURE 2.1

41

Sequence of Assets and Liabilities

The assets of a business are listed in sequence according to their level of liquidity. **Liquidity** is the ease with which the asset can be converted to cash. Cash is the most liquid asset and is therefore listed first on the balance sheet, followed by accounts receivable (the amount of money owed by customers to the business), inventory, and so on. Property, plant and equipment, such as buildings and machinery, are the least liquid and are therefore listed last.

FIGURE 2.2

Liabilities are also listed in sequence in a similar way. Those that are payable within the shortest amount of time are listed first (e.g. accounts payable, which represents the amounts a business owes to its suppliers and are payable within one year), and debts that are due more than one year in the future are to be listed last.

Owner's Equity vs. Net Worth

If the owner sells all the assets of the business for the values reflected in the balance sheet and uses the cash received to pay all the debts, the remaining cash would represent owner's equity. Different terms are used to describe owner's equity:

- In a proprietary business, it is referred to as *owner's equity*.
- In a corporation, it is referred to as *stockholders' equity* or *shareholders' equity*. If all the assets of the company were sold for cash and some of the cash was used to pay all the liabilities, the remaining cash would belong to the owners (in proportion to the amount of stock that they own).
- Some government institutions refer to it as *accumulated surplus (deficit)*.

All these terms represent owner's equity of an organization, which is similar to net worth introduced in personal accounting (chapter 1). At the end of the accounting period, the ending owner's equity balance can be calculated as follows:

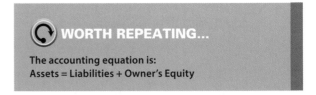

WORTH REPEATING...

The accounting equation is:
Assets = Liabilities + Owner's Equity

Ending Owner's Equity Balance = Beginning Owner's Equity Balance
+ Owner's Contributions + Net Income (Loss) – Owner's Withdrawals

Owner's contributions is the amount of cash or assets invested into the business by the owner. **Owner's withdrawals** is the amount of cash or assets taken by the owner of the business for personal use.

In business accounting, owner's equity is a category on the balance sheet but not an account. Separate accounts are required to record transactions such as owner's contribution and owner's withdrawals. In this chapter, we will examine these accounts in a proprietary business.

The **capital account** is used to record the amount of the owner's equity including owner's contributions. Owner's contributions are added directly into the capital account. Owner's withdrawals is recorded in a separate account called *owner's drawings*. Owner's withdrawals decrease the business's assets and the value of owner's equity.

In the personal T-Account worksheet from chapter 1, there exists a table for calculating net worth immediately following the section containing the T-Accounts for liabilities. In the context of a business, this table will be replaced by a separate T-Account section for owner's equity. This section will have a T-Account for the capital account and a T-Account for owner's drawings. Refer to figure 2.3 below.

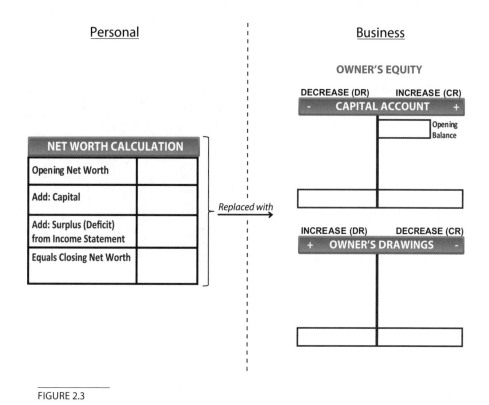

FIGURE 2.3

We will illustrate the T-Account entries related to the capital account and owner's drawings with an example. Suppose that the owner of a newly formed company invested an additional $30,000 in cash into the company (transaction #1). This will result in an increase to the capital account and an increase to cash. For simplicity, assume that all opening account balances are $0.

Also suppose that the owner withdrew $5,000 from the company for personal use (transaction #2). This transaction will cause cash to decrease and owner's drawings to increase. These transactions related to owner's equity are summarized below in figure 2.4.

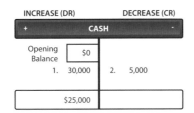

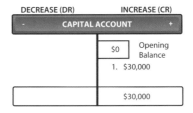

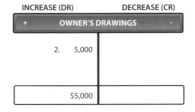

FIGURE 2.4

Forms of Organizations

Sole Proprietorship

A **sole proprietorship** is owned and generally operated by one owner. A proprietorship is usually a small business, and could provide services such as bookkeeping, gardening, painting or general contracting. Many proprietorships have only a small amount of money invested by the owner. Starting a proprietorship can be an easy process, often it is just enough to register a business name and obtain a business license. The proprietorship will last as long as the owner wishes to run the business, or as long as the owner is alive.

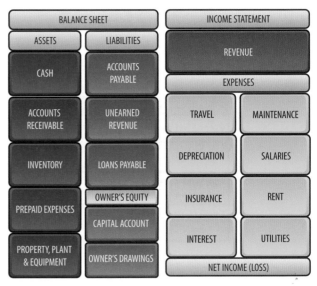

FIGURE 2.5

From an accounting perspective, the financial affairs of the business must be *separate* from the financial affairs of the owner. From a legal perspective, a sole proprietorship is *not a separate entity* from its owner. This means that the assets and liabilities of the business legally belong to the owner, even though the financial activities are recorded separately. If the business is unable to pay its debts, creditors of the business can force the owner to sell his or her personal assets to pay the business debts. This is called **unlimited liability.**

In other words, the owner will receive all the net income, suffer any net loss and be personally liable for all financial obligations of the business.

During our discussions over the next few chapters, we will be using a proprietorship to illustrate various transactions. Figure 2.5 is an example of the financial statements used in a proprietary service business.

It is common for a proprietary business owner to incorrectly record business transactions in the same set of records as his/her personal records. This practice makes it very difficult, if not impossible, to monitor the activities of the business in order to evaluate its performance.

Consider this scenario: Emilio operates a gardening service and combines all his business and personal records. He also has a job at night to help him make more money to pay for personal expenses and to finance the gardening business. The gardening business has become very busy to the extent that he needs to hire some help and arrange a bank loan to help buy more equipment and supplies. By maintaining both personal and business records together, Emilio faces the following challenges:

1. He does not know how much of the night job and the gardening business is contributing toward his income.

2. By not separating business and personal expenses, he will not know which expenses are being used to generate sales. This is important because business expenses can be tax deductible.

3. He also needs to establish how much is spent for each gardening job to help identify the profitability of the business. These expenses could include insurance, gas for the truck, etc.

Before lending money to Emilio, the bank will want to see financial statements to assess if the business is capable of servicing the loan. This can be a problem for Emilio in the current situation.

Partnership

A **partnership** is a business owned by two or more people called *partners*. As in a proprietorship, the only special legal requirements that must be met in order to start a partnership are registering the business name and obtaining a business license. To manage a business together, the partners need an oral or a written agreement that would usually set out how profits and losses are to be shared. The partnership will last as long as the partners continue to run the business, or as long as all partners are still alive.

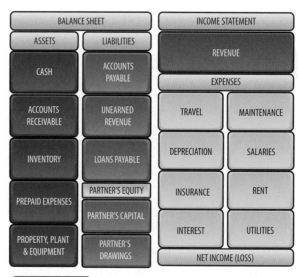

FIGURE 2.6

A partnership, like a proprietorship, is not legally separated from its owners. Depending on the type of partnership, partners may be subject to unlimited liability, which means that the partners are jointly responsible for all the debts of the partnership. In a partnership, **mutual agency** exists. Mutual agency means that each partner is able to speak for the other partners and bind them to business contracts. In other words, each partner is bound by the business actions of the other partners.

There are three types of partnerships that can be created.

1. A **general partnership** is a partnership in which all partners are subject to unlimited liability. In this situation, all partners are considered to be general partners. Unless special provisions are made (as shown in the next two items), all partnerships are general partnerships.

2. A **limited partnership** includes at least one general partner who accepts unlimited liability and one or more limited partners with liability limited to the amount they invested. All partnerships must have at least one general partner. The limited partners are sometimes referred to as silent partners, since they are not allowed to provide any management input for the business.

3. A **limited liability partnership** (LLP) allows partners to have limited liability regarding the misconduct or negligence of the other partners. For example, if a partner in a law firm that is an LLP is sued for misconduct, only the partner in question will be responsible for paying any damages. Note that an LLP does not remove the liability of the partners if the business is unable to pay its debts.

A **cooperative** is an enterprise or organization that is organized, owned and democratically controlled by the people who use its products and services, and whose earnings are distributed on the basis of use rather than investment. The people who use and own the cooperative are referred to as *members*. A cooperative operates for the benefit of its members.

Corporation

A **corporation** is a business that is registered with the State government or Securities and Exchange Commission (SEC) as a separate legal entity from its owners, the stockholders. As a separate legal entity, the corporation has all the rights of a person and is responsible for its own activities and is liable for its own debts. It can enter into contracts and buy and sell products or assets. It can also sue others and be sued.

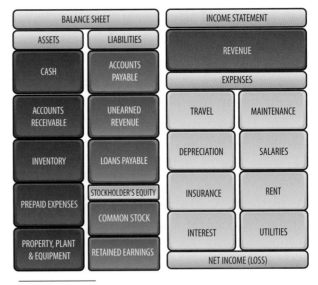

FIGURE 2.7

A **stockholder** is an owner of the business through ownership of **shares**. Each share of stock provides partial ownership of the business. For example, if a person owns one share of stock and there are 100 shares available, the person owns 1/100th of the corporation. If a stockholder owns more than 50% of all the stock of a corporation, they can control the business as they see fit. Stockholders are legally distinct from the business, and their financial risk is limited to the amount that they have invested in the form of stock. Thus, owners or stockholders have limited liability.

Moreover, the life of a corporation is indefinite and is independent of the lives of the stockholders. The corporation's operations are not directly controlled by its stockholders, but they elect a board of directors to oversee the corporation. Members of the board of directors and senior management can be financially and legally accountable for the actions of the corporation. The behavior of officers of the corporation is governed by a number of rules including those relating to responsible accounting and cash management.

As mentioned, the ownership of a corporation is divided into units called *shares*. For example, if the assets are worth $100,000 and the liabilities are worth $60,000, the stockholders' equity is equal to $40,000. If the corporation were to sell all its assets for $100,000 and use some of the cash to pay the liabilities of $60,000, the remaining $40,000 cash would represent the stockholders' equity and would belong to the stockholders. If there were two equal stockholders, each one would be paid $20,000. If there were 20 equal stockholders, each would be paid $2,000. In other words, the stockholders' equity is divided among the stockholders in proportion to the number of stock that they own.

Corporations can be set up as private or public businesses. A public corporation allows its stock to be sold to anyone who wishes to buy them. This allows the public corporation to gain access to a large amount of cash to help grow the business. Typically, a public corporation will have thousands of individual stockholders. You may have heard about stock exchanges such as the New York Stock Exchange or the NASDAQ. These stock exchanges allow buyers and sellers to trade stock of public corporations.

A private corporation does not allow their stock to be sold to just anyone, and often the stock is held by a few individuals. Private corporations allow for less stringent reporting requirements than public corporations, such as not making their financial statements public.

The **book value** of shares can be determined by the values provided on the balance sheet. The **market value** of the shares, however, depends upon what a buyer is willing to pay for it on a stock exchange.

Not-for-Profit Organizations

Unlike regular businesses, profits made by **not-for-profit organizations** may be paid out (redistributed) to the community by providing services. Not-for-profit organizations include religious organizations, community care centers, charitable organizations and hospitals. They do not have an identifiable owner but, require financial statements because they are accountable to donors, sponsors, lenders, tax authorities, etc.

Accounting records provide key information pertaining to the activities of not-for-profit organizations, enabling them to operate as permitted.

Stakeholders

Stakeholders rely on accurate information about an organization, enabling them to make appropriate decisions. Stakeholders can be divided into two categories:

1. *Internal stakeholders*, people who own the business and/or work in the business.
2. *External stakeholders*, the people or organizations that are outside the business, such as suppliers, banks and external accountants.

Internal stakeholders rely on financial statements to enable them to manage the business efficiently. In other words, they will assess the business by examining the financial results on a regular basis. To an internal stakeholder, financial statements serve the same purpose as a scoreboard does to a sports team.

Typically, external stakeholders need financial statements to ensure that their investment in the business, whether in the form of cash loans or supplying product or services on credit, is protected. If a business is poorly operated or is not operating profitably, external stakeholders have the choice of deciding whether or not to supply the business. They want to ensure that their loans can be repaid or that they receive payment for services they rendered to the business.

There are also indirect external users of the financial statements – for example, the tax authorities, who will want to look at the financial statements to ensure that the business is paying the appropriate amount of taxes. Indirect external users include customers and trade unions.

The following case illustrates how stakeholders can be affected: During 2011, a NBA lockout took place. The players (internal stakeholders) went on strike over money and other issues. However, the players were not the only stakeholders who were affected by the strike. The absence of basketball games resulted in no business for external stakeholders such as hot dog vendors (and the factories that make the hot dogs, napkins, ketchup, plastic cutlery, etc.), restaurants and other food suppliers. Breweries, advertisers and all other suppliers of materials and services relating to basketball were also adversely affected.

Financial Statements of Different Types of Businesses

Different types of businesses use different financial statement layouts – for example, a small consulting firm would use a very simple income statement and balance sheet compared to a complex manufacturing company that produces goods. The manufacturing company requires a more detailed set of financial statements, which provide the information a manager needs to know in order to operate the business effectively.

The following examples display financial statements for three main types of businesses.

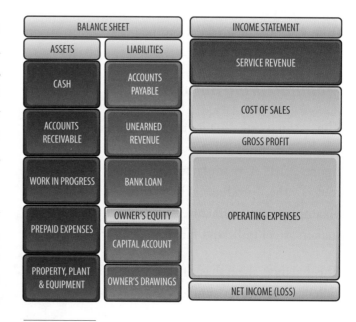

Service Business

The financial statements shown in figure 2.8 represent a simple service business. Examples of services are accounting, consulting, lawn maintenance or general contracting, to name a few. A few new items are presented on the income statement and balance sheet: cost of sales, gross profit and work in progress.

Cost of sales are the expenses directly tied to the service revenue earned. In a consulting firm, this would be the salary of the consultants. All other expenses would be part of the operating expenses (i.e. rent, insurance, depreciation, etc.). The difference between service revenue

FIGURE 2.8

and cost of sales is called gross profit. **Gross profit** is used to pay for all other expenses and will be discussed in detail later in the text. Not all service businesses will use cost of sales, in which case every expense is considered an operating expense and there is no gross profit.

On the balance sheet, there may be an asset account called work in progress. This represents jobs that are currently being worked on but are not yet complete. An example could be a training company in the middle of developing a training program. This partially completed work would be eventually recognized as cost of sales and matched to revenue when the service is delivered to the client.

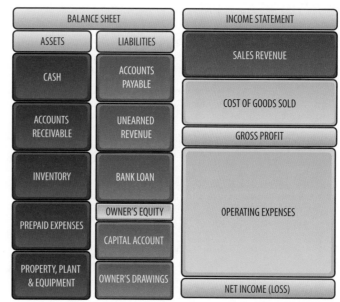

Merchandising Business

The financial statements shown in figure 2.9 represent a merchandising business. Any company that buys goods to resell to customers is considered a merchandising business. A common example of one is a retail store. Examples of retail stores would include hardware, clothing, toy and convenience stores.

On the balance sheet, there is a new asset called inventory. This account would track the value of all the goods the store has purchased and intends to sell to their

FIGURE 2.9

customers. Once these items are sold, the value of the inventory is transferred to cost of goods sold on the income statement. Cost of goods sold is the value of all the goods sold and is subtracted from sales revenue to determine gross profit. Inventory and cost of goods sold will be covered in later chapters.

Manufacturing Business

The financial statements of a manufacturing company are shown in figure 2.10. A manufacturing company makes the products that they sell. Examples of manufacturers include auto makers, steel mills and furniture makers.

The balance sheet has an asset account called inventory, similar to a retail store. However, a manufacturer will have different types of inventory at various stages of production. Raw material represents the items that will be transformed into the product that can be sold (e.g. lumber used to make furniture). Work in progress represents partially completed products and finished goods

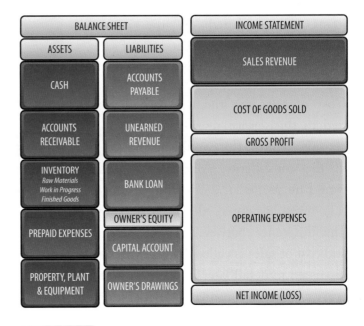

FIGURE 2.10

represent products that are complete and can be sold to customers. Once the items are sold, they are recorded in cost of goods sold.

IN THE REAL WORLD

It is simple to grasp the nature of a particular business by labeling it as either a service, merchandising or manufacturing business. However, in reality, there are some companies that operate as a combination of two or more of these types of businesses. For instance, consider Apple Inc. Apple is well known as a manufacturer of breakthrough technology such as the Macintosh operating system, iPod, iPhone and iPad.

However, the company also has a merchandising segment as it operates an online store and a retail store. These stores predominantly sell its own self-manufactured products, but also sell complementary products produced by other manufacturers such as security software and computer speakers.

Lastly, Apple is in part a service business because the company provides online support as well as warranty and repair services for its products. It also provides online services such as MobileMe which is a subscription-based service that allows user to store personal data on a server, create web pages, back up key files and so on.

Therefore, Apple is technically a hybrid of a service, merchandising and manufacturing business. However, it is reasonable to deem the company as primarily a manufacturing business since sales of its own products represent over 95% of its total sales (for fiscal year 2010).

Business Transactions

There are many similar concepts between personal accounting and business accounting. Some of the transactions a business records can be easily related to the personal transactions demonstrated in chapter 1. Let us examine some typical business transactions for a sample service business, Ace Bookkeepers. This business operates as a sole proprietorship.

Transactions for Ace Bookkeepers during March 2011

1.	The owner deposited cash into the business in the form of owner's equity	$30,000
2.	Borrowed cash from the bank	10,000
3.	Bought furniture with cash	8,000
4.	Performed services for cash	15,000
5.	Paid rent for the month with cash	1,100
6.	Paid salaries to employees	6,000
7.	Paid interest on the bank loan	200
8.	Paid for repairs and maintenance expense with cash	900
9.	Incurred telephone expenses, to be paid next month	300
10.	Incurred travel expenses, to be paid next month	2,000
11.	Prepaid insurance for one year with cash	6,000
12.	Repaid a portion of bank loan principal	3,000
13.	The owner withdrew cash for personal use	2,000
14.	Recognized prepaid insurance as an expense for this month	500

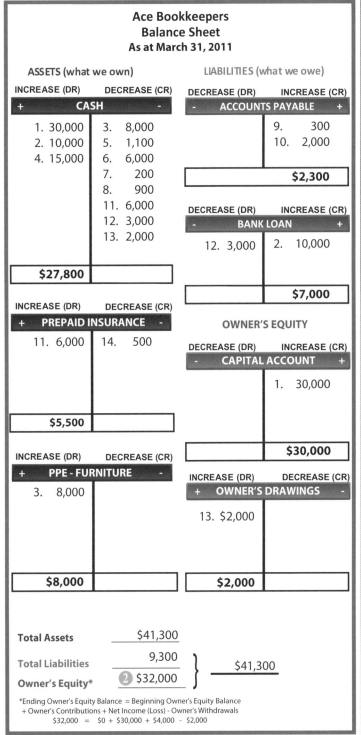

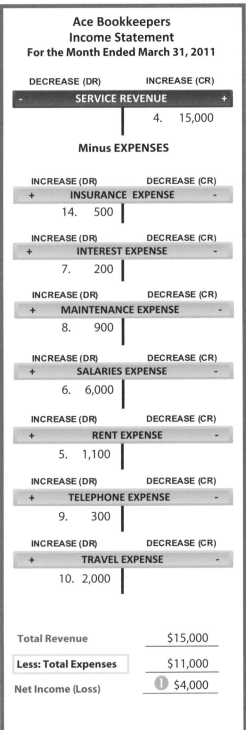

Ace Bookkeepers
Balance Sheet
As at March 31, 2011

ASSETS (what we own)

INCREASE (DR)	DECREASE (CR)
+ CASH -	
1. 30,000	3. 8,000
2. 10,000	5. 1,100
4. 15,000	6. 6,000
	7. 200
	8. 900
	11. 6,000
	12. 3,000
	13. 2,000
$27,800	

INCREASE (DR)	DECREASE (CR)
+ PREPAID INSURANCE -	
11. 6,000	14. 500
$5,500	

INCREASE (DR)	DECREASE (CR)
+ PPE - FURNITURE -	
3. 8,000	
$8,000	

LIABILITIES (what we owe)

DECREASE (DR)	INCREASE (CR)
- ACCOUNTS PAYABLE +	
	9. 300
	10. 2,000
	$2,300

DECREASE (DR)	INCREASE (CR)
- BANK LOAN +	
12. 3,000	2. 10,000
	$7,000

OWNER'S EQUITY

DECREASE (DR)	INCREASE (CR)
- CAPITAL ACCOUNT +	
	1. 30,000
	$30,000

INCREASE (DR)	DECREASE (CR)
+ OWNER'S DRAWINGS -	
13. $2,000	
$2,000	

Total Assets	$41,300
Total Liabilities	9,300
Owner's Equity*	② $32,000
	} $41,300

*Ending Owner's Equity Balance = Beginning Owner's Equity Balance
+ Owner's Contributions + Net Income (Loss) - Owner's Withdrawals
$32,000 = $0 + $30,000 + $4,000 - $2,000

Ace Bookkeepers
Income Statement
For the Month Ended March 31, 2011

DECREASE (DR)	INCREASE (CR)
- SERVICE REVENUE +	
	4. 15,000

Minus EXPENSES

INCREASE (DR)	DECREASE (CR)
+ INSURANCE EXPENSE -	
14. 500	

INCREASE (DR)	DECREASE (CR)
+ INTEREST EXPENSE -	
7. 200	

INCREASE (DR)	DECREASE (CR)
+ MAINTENANCE EXPENSE -	
8. 900	

INCREASE (DR)	DECREASE (CR)
+ SALARIES EXPENSE -	
6. 6,000	

INCREASE (DR)	DECREASE (CR)
+ RENT EXPENSE -	
5. 1,100	

INCREASE (DR)	DECREASE (CR)
+ TELEPHONE EXPENSE -	
9. 300	

INCREASE (DR)	DECREASE (CR)
+ TRAVEL EXPENSE -	
10. 2,000	

Total Revenue	$15,000
Less: Total Expenses	$11,000
Net Income (Loss)	① $4,000

FIGURE 2.11

Figures 2.12 and 2.13 show the completed income statement and balance sheet, respectively, using the information provided in the worksheets.

Ace Bookkeepers Income Statement For the Month Ended March 31, 2011	
Revenue	
Service Revenue	$15,000
Expenses	
Insurance Expense	500
Interest Expense	200
Maintenance Expense	900
Salaries Expense	6,000
Rent Expense	1,100
Telephone Expense	300
Travel Expense	2,000
Total Expenses	11,000
Net Income	$4,000

FIGURE 2.12

Ace Bookkeepers Balance Sheet As at March 31, 2011			
Assets		**Liabilities**	
Cash	$ 27,800	Accounts Payable	$ 2,300
Prepaid Insurance	5,500	Bank Loan	7,000
PPE - Furniture	8,000	**Total Liabilities**	9,300
		Owner's Equity	32,000
Total Assets	$ 41,300	**Total Liabilities & Owner's Equity**	$ 41,300

FIGURE 2.13

Notice there are three categories of accounts in the balance sheet. They are assets, liabilities and owner's equity. The ending balance of owner's equity is simply calculated in the t-account and recorded in the balance sheet at this point. The formal presentation and the details of this category will be further discussed in the upcoming chapters.

Explanation of Transactions

Transaction 1: The owner deposited cash into the business in the form of owner's equity

When an owner invests his or her own cash into a proprietary business, the cash is directly recorded in the capital account and is regarded as owner's equity. Since the owner is responsible for all the debts of the business, all amounts deposited by the owner into the business or taken out of the business for personal use represent an increase or decrease directly to owner's equity.

Transaction 2: Borrowed cash from the bank

When an owner of a proprietary business borrows money from the bank, he or she is personally responsible for the repayment of the debt. This transaction is recorded by increasing cash (an asset) and increasing the value of bank loan (a liability). The transaction has no impact on owner's equity; therefore nothing is recorded on the income statement.

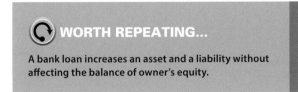

WORTH REPEATING...

A bank loan increases an asset and a liability without affecting the balance of owner's equity.

Transaction 3: Bought furniture with cash

Furniture, computers and cars are considered to be **property, plant and equipment** (also referred to as **long-term assets** or **fixed assets**). They are classified as *long-term assets* because they essentially last for a long time (more than one year) and should not be sold to raise cash to pay for day-to-day expenses. The assets are used to run the business and generate sales. In contrast, **current assets** are assets that are expected to last for less than a year and are used for day-to-day activities. When recording property, plant and equipment, each different type of assets usually has its own specific account. In this chapter, we will use "PPE - Asset's Name" to record any long-term assets. This transaction is recorded by increasing PPE - Furniture and decreasing cash.

Transaction 4: Performed services for cash

Selling services for cash in a business is similar to an individual earning and depositing their salary. Selling services is called revenue and it increases owner's equity. This transaction is recorded by increasing revenue and increasing cash.

As well as generating revenue, a business needs to pay expenses. An expense can be paid in one of three ways:

1. Pay as the expense occurs (decrease cash, increase expense) – decreases owner's equity;

2. Pay later (increase accounts payable, increase expense) – decreases owner's equity; or

3. Pay in advance (initially decrease cash, increase prepaid expense). Later on, when the expense is recognized, owner's equity decreases (increase expense, decrease prepaid expense).

Transactions 5 through 8: Paid cash for expenses

All these transactions relate to cash expenses. The transactions are recorded by increasing the value of the corresponding expense account and decreasing the value of the cash account.

Transactions 9 and 10: Incurred expenses to be paid later

The telephone expense is due to be paid next month, and travel expenses were billed to a credit card that is also to be paid next month. These expenses must be recorded this month because they were incurred and used to generate sales this month. In other words, expenses incurred are matched to revenue earned in the same month. This transaction is recorded by increasing the corresponding expense and increasing accounts payable, as illustrated in figure 2.14.

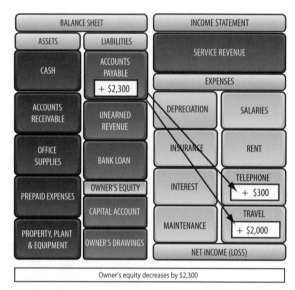

FIGURE 2.14

Transaction 11: Prepaid an annual expense

It is common for a business to prepay various expenses such as insurance, web hosting fees, consulting fees and legal fees. You will recall from the previous chapter how prepaid expenses are recorded. The same principle is practiced in business. Figure 2.15 shows how the prepayment for insurance is recorded. The actual recognition of the expense will be shown in transaction 14. Prepaid expenses will be discussed in detail in chapter 4.

Transaction 12: Repaid a portion of the bank loan principal

This transaction is recorded by decreasing cash and decreasing the bank loan with no impact on the owner's equity. It is fairly common for a business's cash to be depleted and for the business to be unable to pay its debts. Therefore, it is important to maintain a daily record of the amount of cash the business is expected to collect and to pay out. This is called **cash flow**. Throughout this textbook, we will refer regularly to cash flow issues and how to manage them.

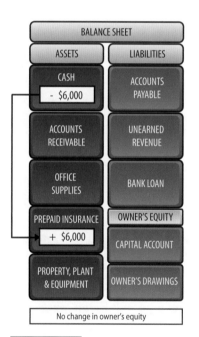

FIGURE 2.15

Transaction 13: The owner withdrew cash for personal use

In a proprietary business, since the owner withdraws cash out of net income of the business, it is not considered to be a salary, but rather a direct decrease to the owner's equity. Note that the income statement is not affected in this case, even though the equity has decreased. This transaction is recorded by decreasing cash and increasing the owner's withdrawals, and is shown in figure 2.16.

Transaction 14: Recognized prepaid insurance as an expense for this month

The insurance for the entire year was paid in advance. It was recorded as an asset because the service had not yet been provided by the insurance company at the time of purchase.

You own the insurance policy and the insurance company must provide you with the coverage for one year. If you cancel the policy before the year is up, the insurance company will have to refund the money for the portion of the policy (i.e. the amount of time) you did not use.

Each month, as the service is provided by the insurance company, the value of the prepaid insurance must be adjusted to reflect the correct balance owing. This is done by decreasing the prepaid expense and increasing the insurance expense for the month.

Figure 2.17 shows how one month's worth of insurance is recognized. The entire year of insurance was paid in transaction 11. This amounted to $6,000. One month's worth of insurance is equal to $500 ($6,000 ÷ 12 months). This monthly amount is recognized as an expense and decreases the prepaid insurance account at the end of each month.

BALANCE SHEET

ASSETS	LIABILITIES
CASH - $2,000	ACCOUNTS PAYABLE
ACCOUNTS RECEIVABLE	UNEARNED REVENUE
OFFICE SUPPLIES	BANK LOAN
PREPAID EXPENSES	OWNER'S EQUITY
	CAPITAL ACCOUNT
PROPERTY, PLANT & EQUIPMENT	OWNER'S DRAWINGS + $2,000

Owner's drawings increases, which causes owner's equity to decrease

FIGURE 2.16

WORTH REPEATING...

The matching principle requires expenses to be reported in the same period as the revenues that were earned as a result of the expenses.

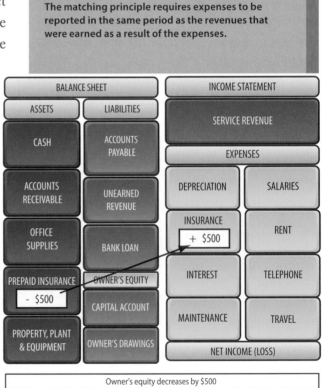

Owner's equity decreases by $500

FIGURE 2.17

In Summary

↪ There are different terms to describe the value (assets less liabilities) of a business, such as owner's equity, stockholders' equity, net assets and accumulated surplus (deficit).

↪ The assets of a business are listed in sequence according to their level of liquidity.

↪ The liabilities of a business are listed in sequence, starting with those that are payable within the shortest amount of time and ending with long-term debts.

↪ A small business that is owned by one person is generally structured in the form of a proprietorship.

↪ From an accounting perspective, the financial affairs of a proprietary business are *separate* from the financial affairs of the owner. From a legal perspective, a sole proprietorship is *not a separate entity from its owner.*

↪ A partnership is a business owned by two or more persons.

↪ A corporation is a business that is registered with the State government or Securities and Exchange Commission and is a separate legal entity from its owners, the stockholders.

↪ Unlike regular businesses, profits made by not-for-profit organizations may be paid out (redistributed) to the community by providing services.

↪ Internal stakeholders own the business and/or work in the business. External stakeholders are the people or organizations that are outside the business such as suppliers, banks and external accountants.

↪ There are three main types of business: service, merchandising and manufacturing.

Review Exercise

Miranda Jones owns a salon called Style House. Record the following transactions for Miranda's business on the T-Account worksheets provided on the opposite page, and then complete the income statement and balance sheet.

Opening balances:

Cash	$3,000
PPE - Equipment	12,000
Accounts payable	5,000
Owner's equity (Capital account)	10,000

Transactions for the month of March:

1.	Borrowed money from the bank	$12,000
2.	Used cash to purchase equipment	8,000
3.	Paid the principal portion of the bank loan	333
4.	Paid the interest portion of the bank loan	50
5.	Signed a maintenance contract with a company - the service fee is $100 per month - Miranda decided to prepay the full amount for a six-month contract	600
6.	Performed services for cash	8,000
7.	Paid salary expense to employees	4,000
8.	Received a bill for telephone expenses, which is not due until next month	250
9.	Incurred various expenses to be paid later ($500 for travel expenses, and $300 for newspaper advertising)	800
10.	Paid rent for the month with cash	2,000
11.	Paid amount owing that was outstanding to a supplier	1,000
12.	Miranda withdrew cash for personal use	3,000

Review Exercise – Answer

T-Account Worksheet

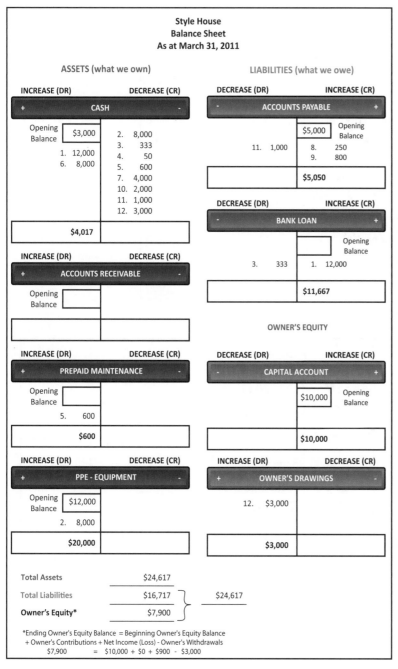

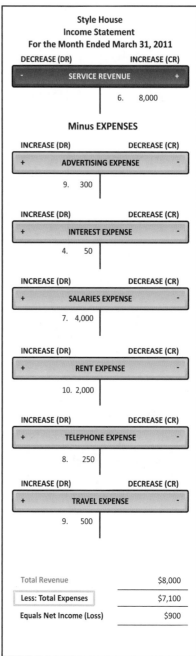

Complete the income statement and balance sheet for this exercise.

Style House Income Statement For the Month Ended March 31, 2011	
Revenue	
Service Revenue	$8,000
Expenses	
Advertising Expense	300
Interest Expense	50
Salaries Expense	4,000
Rent Expense	2,000
Telephone Expense	250
Travel Expense	500
Total Expenses	7,100
Net Income	$900

Style House Balance Sheet As at March 31, 2011			
Assets		**Liabilities**	
Cash	$4,017	Accounts Payable	$5,050
Prepaid Maintenance	600	Bank Loan	11,667
PPE - Equipment	20,000	**Total Liabilities**	16,717
		Owner's Equity	7,900
Total Assets	$24,617	**Total Liabilities and Owner's Equity**	$24,617

Chapter 3

ACCOUNTING PRINCIPLES AND PRACTICES IN A BUSINESS

LEARNING OUTCOMES:

❶ Identify the types of accountants

❷ Explain the characteristics of GAAP

❸ List and explain GAAP principles

❹ Explain the International Financial Reporting Standards (IFRS)

❺ Define and understand the importance of controls

❻ Explain the importance of ethics in accounting

Fields of Accounting

Businesses large and small need accountants to assist with recordkeeping, making business decisions or preparing tax returns. The needs of the business will determine the type of accountant required. The two broad ranges of accounting are financial accounting and managerial accounting.

Financial Accounting

Financial accounting is concerned with the recordkeeping or bookkeeping of the business and preparing the financial statements, similar to what you have learned so far. Financial accountants can assume the role of accounting clerks focusing on one area of the business (i.e. accounts receivable, accounts payable or payroll) or can be the chief financial officer (CFO) of the business. Financial accountants do not have to be employees of the business. Smaller companies may hire a financial accountant to look after their recordkeeping and financial statements on a monthly or yearly basis. Accountants that provide their services to many businesses are called **public accountants**.

Managerial Accounting

Managerial accounting serves the internal users of the business by providing special analysis of financial statements and assisting with decision making. The analysis and prepared reports will follow the internal policy of the company and do not have to follow any standards that financial accounting must follow. Managerial accountants track and classify costs, prepare and analyze budgets and assist with decision making. They are often employees of the business they work for.

In order to work in the accounting field, you need to obtain accounting-related education. While becoming a bookkeeper may require no more than a college diploma, many accounting positions (financial or managerial) require an individual to acquire further specialized education and certification. The accounting certifications are Certified Public Accountant (CPA) and Certified Management Accountant (CMA).

Accounting Designations

Certified Public Accountants

Certified Public Accountants (CPAs) are the specialists for applying accounting standards in the US. To obtain the CPA designation, you must successfully complete the required CPA program of study and pass rigorous exams offered by the American Institute of Certified Public Accountants (AICPA). CPAs must take continuing education classes annually to retain their licenses. Although the eligibility requirements to sit for the CPA exams can be different from state to state, the exams themselves are identical. CPAs are not necessarily employees of the business for which they prepare the financial statements.

Certified Management Accountant

Certified Management Accountants (CMAs) are specialists in managerial accounting topics and assist internal users in making business decisions. CMAs will work in a variety of industries and in many areas of the business (i.e. accounting, marketing, operations, etc). CMAs are usually employees of the company they work for.

To become a CMA, one must successfully complete all the requirements of the CMA program from the Institute of Management Accountants. This includes passing two four-hour exams in the areas of financial planning, performance and control, and financial decision making.

Generally Accepted Accounting Principles

Imagine a football or a hockey game with no rules or consistent method to keep score. Both the players and spectators would quickly become frustrated because of the lack of consistency. By having rules to follow and a consistent method to keep score, players know how to play the game and spectators know what to expect as they watch.

Accounting for business is similar. If there were no rules to follow, business owners and accountants could make up rules regarding what to report. External users would find the reports to be unreliable and inconsistent. Thus, accounting standards have been created that allow for reliable and consistent reporting that all users of the reports can trust.

Financial statements that are prepared using accounting standards accurately report various business events that both internal and external stakeholders find useful. Managers can make strategic decisions relating to products, sales prices, policies and a host of other issues that influence business results. Investors can decide whether to invest in the business.

Generally Accepted Accounting Principles (GAAP) is a set of standards and acceptable ways of reporting accounting activities. In the US, GAAP is developed and maintained by the Financial Accounting Standards Board (FASB). Accountants and companies are expected to follow GAAP when preparing financial statements. It is important to point out that GAAP only offers guidelines for financial reporting. It can be interpreted and applied differently under different circumstances.

Characteristics of GAAP

There are some fundamental characteristics upon which GAAP is based. These characteristics form the foundation of GAAP and define how the information is presented in financial statements. In order for financial statements to be effective, GAAP states that financial information should be **relevant, reliable, understandable, comparable and consistent**. Each of these characteristics is discussed further below.

Relevance

Relevant means that all information useful for decision making is present in the financial statements. In other words, if a piece of relevant information is omitted or misstated, the user's interpretation of the statement would change. Information that helps in predicting the outcome of past, present or future events is relevant and is said to have **predictive value**. For example, if an investor wants to assess the financial position of a company, and the company purposefully avoided reporting a bank loan, the investor would not understand the company's debt correctly. Therefore, the investor's decision to invest or not invest in the company may change. This means the balance of the bank loan would be considered to be relevant financial information.

Suppose the investor feels confident about the company and decides to invest, he would most likely review the company's financial information on a regular basis after making the investment. This is because the information has **feedback value** and tells him how well the company is doing. In other words, the information helps the investor confirm his prediction about the company's performance. If the company is not performing well, the investor may decide to withdraw his investment based on the feedback information.

Another component of relevance is **timeliness**. Information is timely if there is no delay in the reporting of crucial information. For instance, a business owner may want to have monthly statements prepared to monitor the company's performance. If they only receive yearly statements, it may be too late to correct problems with the company.

Reliability

Reliability means that information is free from material error and bias. In other words, different independent people looking at the evidence will arrive at the same conclusions. This implies that the information is **neutral**; it must not be presented in a manner that favors one set of users over the other. Business records must be based on objective evidence. A component of reliability is **verifiability**. Verifiability means that every transaction must have proof that it occurred. For example, if a company records an expense transaction in its financial records, an invoice must be present to back it up (i.e. the expense can be verified).

Another component of reliability is **representational faithfulness**. In simple words, representational faithfulness means being truthful. Lynn Turner, the SEC Chief Accountant, used the following analogy to illustrate the truthfulness of financial statements: "A map's representational faithfulness may be determined by how well the map describes the coastline."

Understandability

Understandable means that the financial information can be reasonably understood by its users if the users have a reasonable knowledge of the business and a basic knowledge of accounting. To be understandable, companies often include notes in the financial statements to explain many of the numbers, especially those that are based on company policy. For example, depreciation is usually supported by a note explaining the methods the company used to calculate the figure.

Comparability and Consistency

Comparable means the financial statements of a company must be prepared in a similar way year after year. This allows for a comparison of this year's performance to last year's performance. By comparing yearly statements, users can identify trends in the company's financial position and performance. For example, an investor may be interested in observing the change in a company's debt balance from one year to the next to see if the company incurred additional debt or was able to pay off its creditors. The financial information should also be comparable between companies in the same industry.

Consistency prevents people from changing accounting methods for the sole purpose of manipulating figures on the financial statements. Consistency requires accountants to apply the same methods and procedures from period to period. For example, the method used for depreciation should be the same from year to year. When a method changes from one period to another, the change must be clearly explained on the financial statements. The readers of financial statements have the right to assume that consistency has been applied if there is no statement to the contrary.

Trade-off of Reliability and Relevance

Under GAAP, it is required for financial information to be relevant, reliable, understandable, comparable and consistent. However, sometimes it is difficult to fully represent all characteristics. There could be a trade-off among some of the characteristics. A trade-off is an exchange of part of one characteristic for part of another.

A commonly discussed trade-off is the one between relevance and reliability. In order for information to be relevant, it needs to be timely. For example, presenting information that is a few years old on today's financial statements is likely not very relevant. However, reliable information often requires time to gather.

Suppose that a company chooses to prepare financial statements on a monthly basis instead of on a quarterly or semi-annual basis. In this case, the financial statements are very timely and relevant. However, some reliability may be given up since there is less time for the accounting staff to scrutinize and make necessary adjustments to the monthly financial figures. If the financial statements were less frequent (such as quarterly or semi-annually), the accounting staff can allocate more time to verify the accuracy and effectiveness of the statements.

Basic Concepts and Principles

The basic objective of financial accounting is to accurately present the financial information related to a company's performance and its financial position. Building on the four characteristics of relevance, reliability, understandability and comparability, GAAP is formed using basic accounting principles and concepts. Some of these basic concepts and principles are provided below.

The Economic Entity Principle states that accounting for a business must be kept separate from the personal affairs of its owner or any other business. This means that the owner of a business cannot record personal transactions on the income statement or the balance sheet of the business. The financial statements of the business must reflect the financial position of the business alone. Any personal expenses of the owner are charged to the owner and are not allowed to affect the operating results of the business.

The Going Concern Principle assumes that a business will continue to operate into the foreseeable future. Determining the value of the assets belonging to a business that is alive and well is not complicated. For example, items such as property, plant and equipment are listed on the balance sheet at their cost, or original purchase price. This would not be the case if the company was going out of business. In that case, property, plant and equipment have their value changed to what they could be sold for. When a company is going out of business, the value of the assets usually suffers because they have to be sold under unfavorable circumstances.

 *The Monetary Unit Principle* requires that the accounting records are expressed in terms of money. These accounting records should all be reported in a single currency, such as US dollars or Euros. This allows accountants to assign monetary values to business events. For instance, suppose that a company hires a salesman. The event of officially hiring the employee is not reflected in the company's accounting records since a value cannot be easily assigned to the event (i.e. expressed in terms of money). However, over time, the financial impact of the hiring will be evident (e.g. recognizing the salary expense for the salesman and realizing an increase in sales). Furthermore, it is also assumed that the unit of measure used in the accounting records remains fairly constant over time and that transactions can be measured relevantly in current monetary units. That is, inflation (a rise in prices) or deflation (a drop in prices) is ignored when comparing dollars of different years.

The Objectivity Principle states that transactions will be recorded on the basis of objective and verifiable evidence. It means that different people looking at the evidence will arrive at the same values for the transaction. Or, this means that accounting entries will be based on fact and not on personal opinion. The source document (e.g. sales receipt or purchase invoice) for a transaction is always the best objective evidence because it shows the amount agreed to between the buyer and the seller.

The Cost Principle states that the accounting for purchases must be at their cost price. It is related to the monetary unit principle and the objectivity principle discussed above. In almost all cases, the cost is the amount that appears on the source document for the transaction. If the owner purchased some office furniture on sale for $5,000, but knew the furniture was actually worth $7,000 (the price before the sale), the furniture would be recorded as $5,000, which is what is shown on the receipt. There are times when the above type of objective evidence is not available. For example, a building could be received as a gift. In such a case, the transaction would be recorded at fair market value which must be determined by some independent means.

The Conservatism Principle states that whenever an accountant needs to exercise their own interpretation or judgment in applying an accounting standard and has several options, the least optimistic or least favorable option should be selected. This means choosing the option that would result in a lower balance of assets, lower net income or a higher balance of debt. In other words, the accountant should have a *conservative* mindset when making estimates to avoid overstating assets, overstating net income or understating debt.

The Time Period Principle requires that accounting takes place over specific time periods known as fiscal periods. These fiscal periods are of equal length, and are used when measuring the financial progress of a business.

The Revenue Recognition Principle states that revenue can only be recorded (recognized) when goods are sold or when services performed. If a transaction is made with cash, the revenue is recorded when the sale is completed and the cash is received. If the transaction involves a large project such as building a dam, it may take a construction company a number of years to complete such a project. The construction company does not wait until the project is entirely completed before it recognizes the revenue. Periodically, they send a bill for the amount of work completed and recognize revenue for the work completed since the last bill was sent.

The Matching Principle states that an expense must be recorded in the same accounting period in which it was used to produce revenue. For example, a manufacturing business would recognize both sales (revenue) and the costs to produce goods when the goods are sold to the customer, not when the items are produced or when payments for the costs occur. If the matching principle is not applied, the financial statements will not fairly reflect the results of the company's operations.

The Materiality Principle requires accountants to use Generally Accepted Accounting Principles except when doing so would be more expensive or complicated relative to the value of the transaction. For example, a company purchases a new $100 keyboard for a computer. They can record the keyboard directly as an expense, or record it as an asset (capitalize) and depreciate it over a few years. Recording this small amount as an expense is the less complicated way of recording the purchase, and it will not have a material impact on the financial statements. Choosing to capitalize versus expense an item must not significantly affect the company's income, nor should the reader's ability to judge the financial statements be impaired.

The Full Disclosure Principle states that any and all information that affects the full understanding of a company's financial statements must be included with the financial statements. Some items may not affect the accounting records directly. These items would be included in the notes accompanying the statements. Examples of such items are outstanding lawsuits, tax disputes and company takeovers.

GAAP in Different Jurisdictions

The profession of accounting is currently governed by Generally Accepted Accounting Principles (GAAP) in many countries.

GAAP is often believed to entail one set of rules and principles that regulate accounting conduct worldwide. In reality, most countries have established their own versions of GAAP to be applied to their domestic accounting profession.

 A set of accounting standards are often described as a rules-based or principles-based system. In **rules-based accounting**, the accounting standards are stated as a list of specific, detailed rules that must be followed when preparing financial statements. To apply these rules, little or no interpretation is required by the accountants. In **principles-based** accounting, the standards are designed as guidelines for accountants. In other words, accountants are allowed more judgment and flexibility in applying the accounting standards when creating financial statements. US GAAP is primarily rules-based, whereas Canadian GAAP is primarily principles-based.

International Financial Reporting Standards

As the world changes, so does the accounting profession. The increase in global business activity has created a need for international standards of reporting a company's financial position and performance. These standards are referred to as **International Financial Reporting Standards (IFRS)**. Specifically, instead of following GAAP guidelines, most of the world will soon be adhering to IFRS. This is a new and uniform set of international accounting standards that many countries have already adopted.

At this time, the United States has decided not to adopt IFRS accounting standards, instead sticking with GAAP. In total, more than 100 countries have adopted IFRS guidelines. That number will grow in the coming years as IFRS becomes a global reality that all businesses and accountants will need to accept.

What is IFRS?

The accounting standards and interpretations that form the foundation of IFRS were established in 2001 by the International Accounting Standards Board (IASB). The IASB was established to create IFRS and to subsequently oversee its execution. The board is responsible for the development and issuance of what was initially called International Accounting Standards. These standards are now known as International Financial Reporting Standards (IFRS).

GAAP presents problems when attempting to compare companies from different countries because application of accounting standards (such as GAAP) varies from country to country. The purpose of IFRS is quite simple: establish a universal accounting standard that can be applied by all accountants no matter where they practice.

A CLOSER LOOK

It is common for countries that adopted IFRS to experience various advantages and disadvantages. Some examples are shown below.

Advantages: It allows for better comparability between companies, even if they are located in different countries. It also allows for more streamlined reporting of multinational corporations. Investors may also be more inclined to invest in foreign businesses.

Disadvantages: On the other hand, IFRS can be costly to implement in the short-term if a company must switch from GAAP to IFRS. Countries also lose control over domestic accounting standards.

As mentioned previously, relevance, reliability, understandability as well as comparability and consistency are characteristics required for information to be useful under GAAP. IFRS has the same characteristics as its guideline and trade-offs still occur between them. Furthermore, the basic principles of IFRS are aligned with all of the basic principles of GAAP (business entity principle, the going concern principle, conservatism, etc.). Some of the IFRS principles may have different names than their GAAP counterpart. For example, the principle of conservatism under GAAP is referred to as **prudence** under IFRS. The entire GAAP and IFRS standards are comprised of a collection of accounting characteristics and principles as shown in figure 3.1.

Diagram of Accounting Fundamentals

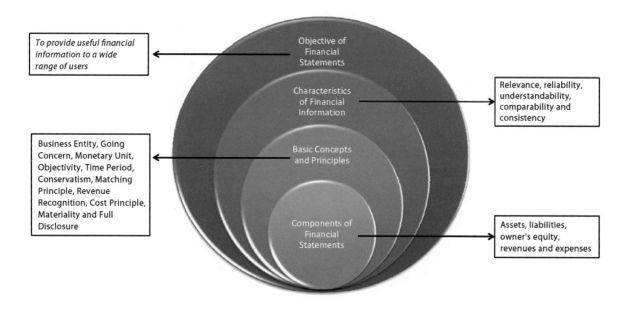

FIGURE 3.1

Controls in Business

Examine the controls in your personal life for a moment. You have a lock on the doors and windows to your house or apartment. You have a PIN on your bank card or credit card. You have access to a bank statement which allows you to monitor all the deposits and withdrawals from your bank account. The lock, PIN and bank statement are all considered controls. Why do you have controls? Although you might believe that most people are honest and trustworthy, you want to protect the things you own and make sure that all payments and transactions are authorized. Businesses also implement controls to protect what they have.

Definition of Controls

Controls are procedures and methods used to protect assets, monitor cash payments, ensure transactions are authorized and the accounting records are accurate. These procedures can include cash controls, budgetary controls, credit controls, working procedures, inventory controls, production processes, hiring policies and quality measures.

The purpose of internal controls is to provide reasonable assurance regarding the:

- effectiveness and efficiency of operations
- reliability of financial reporting
- compliance with applicable laws and regulations

Internal controls are designed to:

- align objectives of the business
- safeguard assets
- prevent and detect fraud and error
- encourage good management
- allow action to be taken against undesirable performance
- reduce exposure to risks
- ensure proper financial reporting

Implementing Controls

Under an adequate system of internal controls, each business transaction is complete, accurate, authorized, real (i.e. it exists), and valid. In addition, when internal controls are present, errors in the system are automatically identified and corrected, duties are segregated and financial reports are timely.

Generally, internal controls can be classified as preventive (i.e. to stop an incident before it happens), or detective (i.e. to discover an incident after it happens). Obviously, it is better to prevent incidents than to discover them after they occur.

Imagine why a motor vehicle may be involved in an accident:

1. The driver lost control because of speeding - the driver's fault.
2. The brakes failed - the mechanic's fault.
3. Another car drove through a red light - someone else's fault.
4. A tree fell on the car - just plain bad luck.

In all these scenarios something different caused the accident.

Operating and controlling a business is not dissimilar to this metaphor. Consider the following situation:

Michael purchased a family restaurant, which he managed himself. He bought supplies, paid bills, opened and closed the restaurant himself each day. He was doing so well that he decided to buy another location in another suburb of the city. He promoted an employee, who had worked with him for the past three years, to manage the old location while he focused on setting up the new location.

Michael disliked anything to do with accounting. He operated a simple hands-on business and his bookkeeper updated the books each month to ensure that sales taxes were paid and payroll was disbursed on time. Other than these two functions, the bookkeeper relied on the accountant to complete the financial statements at the end of each year and complete Michael's annual tax return.

Michael's business was performing well, so Michael and his wife decided to take a vacation. Not long after they returned, Michael received a call from one of his suppliers to say that a payment he had issued a few days before was returned by the bank because of insufficient funds in Michael's account. Michael was not only frustrated but also extremely embarrassed. He had to transfer money from his savings account to cover the shortfall and immediately started looking into what might have happened.

Since Michael knew very little about accounting, he contacted his accountant to investigate the matter. An entire year had passed since the accountant had worked with Michael's financial statements, so the investigation was no easy task. After some time, Michael discovered the following issues:

1. Cash was only being deposited every few days, rather than daily and the cash receipts did not match the cash register.

2. Payroll was considerably higher, relative to sales, than it had been in previous years.

3. His trusted manager was stealing food supplies and selling them for cash. This increased the food costs and decreased profits.

4. It appeared that the manager was paying ghost employees - he was making payments to contract staff that did not actually exist.

5. Some of the servers were 'sweet-hearting' customers - meaning that friends were being served with free meals or extras at no charge.

As a result of a lack of controls, poor bookkeeper oversight and fraudulent behavior, Michael nearly went bankrupt. He hired a new manager, and with the help of his accountant, he implemented the following controls to prevent this from happening again.

1. The new manager does not handle any sales and deposits the cash every day. Any discrepancies between the cash receipts and the register are investigated by the manager immediately.

2. The new manager is responsible for scheduling and keeping payroll costs to a certain percentage of sales.

3. The head chef at the restaurant counts food supplies at the beginning of each day and is responsible for ordering replacement food. The manager compares the daily inventory counts to the inventory used in the daily sales to ensure there are no anomalies.

4. A hiring package was created which collected personal information on new employees (such as name, address, Social Security and bank account number). Michael had to approve all new hires and payroll was deposited directly into employee's bank accounts.

5. A computerized system to record sales is now used. All servers have their own pass code to record sales. Discounts or free meals must be approved by the manager entering a special code to allow the discount or free meal.

6. Overall, the bookkeeper still updates the books every month, but also prepares financial statements on a monthly basis for Michael to examine.

IN THE REAL WORLD

Lack of proper controls and shady accounting led to the bankruptcy of Enron in 2001. Enron was a large energy company that earned about $100 billion in revenue in the year before they went bankrupt. As a result of the bankruptcy and discovery of misleading accounting practices, the United States introduces the Sarbanes-Oxley Act (SOX) in 2002.

SOX impacts all public US corporations by setting higher standards for reporting and ensuring that controls are in place to properly report all aspects of the financial statements. Also, any international company that wishes to trade on a stock market in the US must also comply with SOX.

Ethics and Insights

In the previous example of Michael and the family restaurant, his manager was behaving in a way that most would consider wrong. The manager was treating Michael unfairly and unethically. While the manager's behavior may be easy to label as unethical, not all behavior may be so blatantly wrong. Accountants must also behave in an ethical manner because others rely on the information the accountant provides.

Stakeholders place significant trust in the accuracy of financial records to enable them to make sensible decisions regarding the business. For that reason, it is an accountant's responsibility to ensure that the financial status of the business is accurately reported. The standards, by which these actions are judged as being honest versus dishonest, right or wrong, fair or unfair, are also known as **accounting ethics**.

The professional accounting bodies mentioned earlier (CPA and CMA) have strict rules governing the behavior of their members. There are cases on record that have resulted in jail sentences for violating these rules. Two of the most infamous examples relate to Enron and Worldcom. The senior executives of these companies were found guilty of various offences, including using company funds for their own personal use, and covering up certain negative financial information. In addition to these offences were other types of activities that were not regarded as legal or moral by the stockholders and government authorities.

These are some typical ethical standards for accountants:

- Members shall act with trustworthiness, integrity and objectivity.

- Members shall not participate in any activity or provide services to any company that the member, or a reasonably prudent person, would believe to be unlawful.

- Members shall not engage in a discriminatory practice on prohibited grounds for discrimination, as those terms are defined in the US Civil Liberties Act.

- Members shall not criticize another professional colleague without first submitting this criticism to that colleague for explanation.

- Members shall act in the interest of their clients, employers, and interested third parties, and shall be prepared to sacrifice their self-interest to do so. Members shall honor the trust bestowed upon them by others, and shall not use their privileged position without their principal's knowledge and consent. Members shall avoid conflicts of interest.

- Members shall not disclose or use any confidential information concerning the affairs of any client, former client, employer or former employer.

- Members shall, when engaged to audit or review financial statements or other information, be free of any influence, interest or relationship with respect to the client's affairs, which impairs the member's professional judgment or objectivity, or which, in the view of a reasonable observer, may have that effect.

- Members shall not, without an employer's or client's consent, use confidential information relating to the business of the member's employer or client to directly or indirectly obtain a personal advantage. Members shall not take any action, such as acquiring any interest, property or benefit, that is for unauthorized use, or is confidential relating to an employer's or client's affairs, obtained in the course of his or her duties.

- Members shall strive to continually upgrade and develop their technical knowledge and skills in the areas in which they practice as professionals. This technical expertise shall be employed with due professional care and judgment.

- Members shall adhere to acknowledged principles and standards of professional practice.

- Members shall not be associated with any information that the member knows, or ought to know, to be false or misleading, whether by statement or omission.

- Members shall always act in accordance with the duties and responsibilities associated with being members of the profession, and shall carry on work in a manner that will enhance the image of the profession and the association.

Some of the common concerns about ethics in a business are issues related to:

- cash discounts
- operation of a petty cash fund
- manipulation of expenses to manage earnings
- trading a company's stock based on insider information (insider trading)
- recognizing sales before products or services are delivered
- mixing personal and business expenses

There is often a fine line between the law and ethics. A behavior can be quite legal, but immoral. For example, a manager may employ his nephew in the company where he is working. He decides to pay his nephew a much higher salary than others in a similar position in the business. While this practice may not be illegal, it is certainly immoral and unethical. Many organizations create their own set of rules pertaining to ethics and morals. An internationally recognized code of conduct is the *4-way test*.[1]

The 4-Way Test

From the earliest days of Rotary organizations (major national and international service clubs), Rotarians were concerned with promoting high ethical standards in their professional lives. The 4-Way Test is one of the world's most widely printed and quoted statements of business ethics. It was created in 1932 by Rotarian, Herbert J. Taylor (who later served as Rotary International President), when he was asked to take charge of a company that was facing bankruptcy. This 24-word test for employees to follow in their business and professional lives became the guide for sales, production, advertising, relations with dealers and customers, and the survival of the company. Adopted by Rotary in 1943, this simple philosophy has been translated into more than one hundred languages and published in thousands of ways. It asks the following four questions:

Of the things we think, say or do:

1. Is it the **truth**?
2. Is it **fair** to all concerned?
3. Will it build **goodwill** and **better friendships**?
4. Will it be **beneficial** to all concerned?

---

[1] The Rotary Foundation (Accessed March 11, 2011)

The Attributes of a Good Accounting System

Imagine playing a sport such as hockey, baseball or golf without a scoreboard or scorecard. It would be difficult to measure your performance. In fact you would be confused as you played the game, because you would never know whether you were winning or losing.

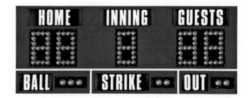

Financial records are the scoreboard of a business. A business owner or manager needs regular financial statements (records) to help him or her make appropriate management decisions in the business, based upon the information provided by accountants. A good accounting system will accurately record the business sales matched against the various expenses, to assess if the business is making a profit. A good system will also provide an accurate balance sheet to inform the reader how much the assets are worth, how much the business owes in the form of liabilities, and the equity of the business. The financial records will also inform the reader where cash came from and how the cash was used.

Different types of businesses require different types of information. For example, a simple business such as a consulting service will require less information than a complicated manufacturing business that calculates the value of inventory. Whatever the business type, a manager requires the services of an accountant to help sort the information and financial data into a format that can be used to make decisions. Depending on the size of a business, there is often a requirement for many people to gather and record different types of information.

In Summary

- Financial accountants keep track of the records of a business and prepare financial statements.

- Management accountants provide valuable information to internal users.

- Certified Public Accountants and Certified Management Accountants are accounting designations, and all of these designated practitioners assist with business recordkeeping and business decisions.

- Generally Accepted Accounting Principles (GAAP) is a set of conventions, rules and procedures that serve as guidance for the preparation of financial reports.

- The characteristics of GAAP are relevance, reliability, understandability, comparability and consistency.

- Accountants may face a trade-off between two characteristics (e.g. relevance and reliability).

- The conceptual framework for GAAP is comprised of various principles. Some of the principles are:
  - Business Entity Principle
  - Going Concern Principles
  - Monetary Unit Principle
  - Objectivity Principle
  - Cost Principle
  - Conservatism Principle
  - Time Period Principle
  - Revenue Recognition Principle
  - Matching Principle
  - Materiality Principle
  - Full Disclosure Principle

- Rules-based accounting is based on a specific list of rules that must be followed. Principles-based accounting allows accountants to use their judgment when applying accounting standards.

- IFRS is similar in many respects to GAAP.

- IFRS is considered to be principles-based standards.

- A key advantage of IFRS is the improved comparability of financial statements across jurisdictions.

- Controls are measures, procedures and performance indicators that check and regulate business operations.

- Internal controls ensure effective and efficient operations, reliable financial reporting and comply with laws and regulations.

- Accountants must adhere to a high standard of ethics.

Review Exercise

Hollinger Runners Inc. (HRI) is a publicly traded manufacturer of high quality, stylish sneakers with hundreds of stockholders. The company has been in business for over 20 years and has endured both good and bad economic times. The company's financial performance has usually been aligned with the state of the economy. As of late, the economy has been booming.

The company has a year-end of April 30. It is now May 31, 2011. HRI produces financial statements on an annual basis. The company's accountant has prepared the balance sheet as at April 30, 2011 using GAAP. A portion of this balance sheet (i.e. the assets portion) is shown below.

Hollinger Runners Inc.
Balance Sheet
As at April 30, 2011

	2011	2010
ASSETS		
	(in thousands)	
Current Assets		
Cash	10	500
Accounts receivable	10	140
Inventory	5	120
Other current assets	60	70
Total Current Assets	85	830
Long-Term Assets		
Available-for-sale investments	60	65
Property, plant and equipment	1,210	2,120
Goodwill	40	50
Total Non-Current Assets	1,310	2,235
TOTAL ASSETS	1,395	3,065

On May 1, 2010, the company changed the location of its headquarters from Europe to the US. Therefore, the '2010' column in the balance sheet is presented in the currency unit of Euros and the '2011' column is presented in US dollars. The company did not disclose this information in the notes to the financial statements. Also, the Euro was much stronger than the US dollar during 2010 and 2011.

Here is some additional information with regards to HRI's financial statements and accounting records:

- HRI has indicated in the notes to the financial statements that in 2011 they had changed the method they used for depreciating assets. However, they did not justify their reason for doing so.

- The cash account is comprised of two sub-accounts: cash related to the business and personal cash savings of a few of the stockholders.

- Purchases have all been valued at fair market value at the year-end date.

- With regards to expenses, there are numerous invoices which did not match the cost amounts reported in the accounting records. The amounts on the invoices are significantly greater than the amounts in the accounting records.

- The company's income statement has shown a significant net loss for the past three years.

Part 1

Which of the GAAP characteristics has HRI failed to apply? Explain.

Part 1 – Answer

Relevance

- A particular piece of information is relevant if its omission means that the user's decision would change. In the financial statements, the company did not disclose that two different currencies were used in the comparative balance sheet (one for 2011 and another for 2010). This omission can potentially affect users' (investors') decisions.

- A component of relevance is timeliness. HRI only prepares financial statements on an annual basis. However, the company has hundreds of stockholders that would benefit from more timely financial statements (e.g. quarterly or monthly).

Reliability

- A component of reliability is verifiability. Since several invoices did not match the cost amounts listed in HRI's accounting records, the reported costs are not verifiable. Therefore, total expenses are not a reliable number in the company's income statement.

Comparability and Consistency

- Even though the company provided balance sheet amounts from the previous year, two different currencies are used from one year to the next. One currency has consistently been stronger than the other. Therefore, it is not straightforward to compare the financial information of HRI through time.

- The method of depreciation is inconsistent from 2010 to 2011. Sometimes, an inconsistency can be fully justified. However, HRI did not explain the reason or provide backup for changing this particular accounting method.

Part 2

Which of the basic concepts and principles of accounting has HRI violated? Explain.

Part 2 – Answer

The Business Entity Principle

- The cash account of HRI includes the personal savings of some of the stockholders. This indicates that the accounting for the business was not kept separate from the personal affairs of the owners.

The Objectivity Principle

- The objectivity principle is closely linked to the reliability characteristic. Many invoices did not match the cost amounts listed in HRI's accounting records. Therefore, the accounting for expenses was not done objectively.

The Cost Principle

- The cost principle includes that the accounting for purchases must be at their cost price. However, HRI has valued their purchases at fair market value.

The Full Disclosure Principle

- HRI did not disclose the justification for changing the depreciation method.

- HRI did not disclose the change in net income due to changing the depreciation method.

- HRI did not disclose the information related to changing the location of the headquarters and the inconsistent measures of currency.

The Going Concern Principle *(requires critical thinking)*

- The following is evidence that the company may not exist and operate in the foreseeable future:

    o HRI has experienced a significant net loss for each of the past three years (even before adjusting for the unverified expense amounts).
    o The cash balance and inventory balances are extremely low in 2011.
    o The company's property, plant and equipment balance has declined significantly from 2010 and 2011 (even after adjusting for exchange rates). It may be possible that some of these assets were sold during 2011.
    o The above examples of HRI's poor financial performance occurred during a time when the economy was booming. The performance of HRI is normally aligned with the state of economy. This discrepancy should cause stockholders to question the going concern assumption with respect to HRI.

Notes

Chapter 4
REVENUE AND EXPENSE RECOGNITION

LEARNING OUTCOMES:

❶ Record revenue transactions

❷ Record expense transactions

❸ Explain the purpose of adjustments

❹ Record adjustments related to unearned revenue, prepaid expenses and accrued interest

Revenue Recognition

The earnings of a business generated by selling products or providing services over a period of time are called **revenue**. The earnings can also be called *income*, *proceeds*, or *sales*. In this book, we refer to earnings generated from providing services as ***service revenue*** and earnings generated from selling products as ***sales revenue***. To familiarize you with a commonly used term in this chapter, **recognizing** revenue or an expense simply means to record the revenue or expense in the accounting records (i.e. on the income statement).

Consider the example of Huntington Safety Consulting (Huntington), a mid-sized service company which provides advice to construction companies on how they can manage and improve their workplace health and safety. Huntington refers to its revenue as *service revenue*.

During the past week, Huntington provided its services to three large clients. The company delivered its standard one-day workshop on occupational safety to each of these three clients. One of the three clients paid Huntington for their services immediately after the workshop session. Another client has promised to pay for the workshop in one month. The third client paid two months before the workshop even took place.

In all three scenarios, Huntington earned revenue by providing the workshop. The only difference between the scenarios is when the cash payment was collected. When a business sells products or services, there are three ways to receive cash. In all cases, revenue must be recognized when the service is provided or the product is sold. The three scenarios are:

1. The customer pays cash when the service or product is delivered
2. The customer pays after the service or product is delivered
3. The customer pays before the service or product is delivered

In the above three scenarios, not only is the timing of the collection of cash different, but so is the transaction that is required. We will now examine how each scenario is accounted for in detail.

WORTH REPEATING...

The revenue recognition principle states that revenue must be recorded (or recognized) at the time duties are performed.

Customer Pays when the Service is Performed

When a company performs a service and the customer pays for it immediately, the transaction is fairly straightforward. From the service provider's perspective, cash increases and equity increases. The increase is equity is recognized as revenue.

Consider Huntington's first client who paid for the workshop immediately after the session. Suppose that the cost of the workshop was $1,100. The impact on cash and revenue from Huntington's perspective is shown below in figure 4.1.

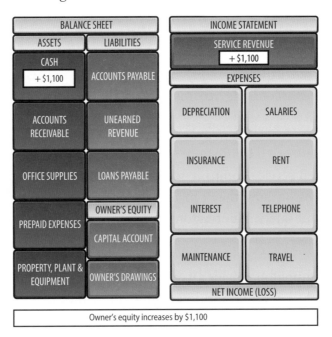

FIGURE 4.1

Customer Pays after the Service is Performed

Most businesses provide customers with payment terms, which allow customers to pay after they have received the product or service (e.g. 30 days to pay the balance owing). This form of making sales is sometimes referred to as "selling on account." You may think that the value of owner's equity would not change when selling on payment terms because no cash was received from the sale. However, the principle of revenue recognition requires revenue to be recorded at the time the product is sold or the service is delivered, regardless of when the payment is received.

When a company provides payment terms to sell its products or services, the money owed by its customers is recorded as an asset, called *accounts receivable*. After a service is provided, the seller issues an **invoice** to the buyer. The invoice includes the details of the service rendered and the agreed upon price. This indicates that the customer now owes the balance and needs to pay the seller by the date stated on the invoice. From the seller's perspective, this indicates an increase in accounts receivable (an asset) and an increase in owner's equity (recognized as revenue). This transaction is illustrated in figure 4.2. Later, when the customer actually pays the outstanding amount, the issuing company increases cash and decreases accounts receivable. The decrease in accounts receivable shows that the service provider received cash and is no longer owed any amount from the customer (i.e. nothing is "receivable"). This is shown in figure 4.3.

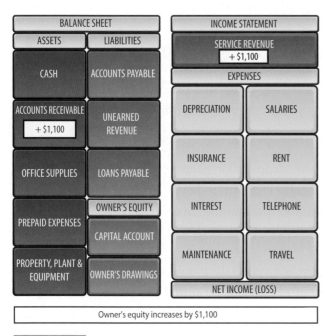

FIGURE 4.2

Let us return to the example of Huntington Safety Consulting and their client that has promised to pay in one month. Even though this client is not paying for Huntington's services immediately, Huntington will still issue an invoice as soon as the workshop has concluded. Assume that Huntington is charging $1,100 for its one-day workshop. Figure 4.2 shows the impact on the applicable accounts when the invoice is issued. Notice that equity increases and is recognized as revenue.

Now assume that one month has passed and Huntington receives payment of $1,100 from the client. Figure 4.3 illustrates the accounting impact of this transaction. This transaction is often referred to as "receipt of account". Equity does not change since one asset is exchanged for another.

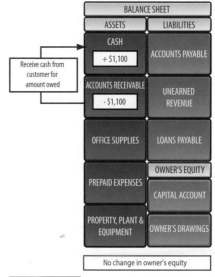

FIGURE 4.3

Customer Pays before the Service is Performed

The third scenario, in which the client paid before the workshop was delivered, can be viewed as a customer deposit. A new liability account known as unearned revenue must be used. The following section will explain how this account is used to deal with customer deposits.

Unearned Revenue

We have discussed two ways in which revenue can be recognized:

1. The customer pays cash immediately; or
2. The customer is given payment terms and pays after receiving the service.

The third way a customer can pay for services is to pay before the service is delivered. When a customer pays before receiving the product, they are making a prepayment or deposit. The amount paid is initially recorded by increasing cash and increasing **unearned revenue** (a liability account). The payment generates a liability because the company *owes* the service. They have not done anything to *earn* the revenue.

A number of different types of businesses require deposits or prepayments for their services. Examples include banquet halls (hall rental fees), health clubs (memberships), magazine publishers (subscription dues) and insurance companies (insurance premiums). In each of these scenarios, the business receives cash up front and provides their service at a later date.

Once the service is provided, the unearned revenue account is decreased and the revenue account is increased. Recall that the third client for Huntington Safety Consulting paid two months before Huntington provided its training workshop. Assume that the cost of the workshop to the customer is still $1,100.

Figure 4.4 illustrates the impact on the accounts of Huntington at the time the customer paid for the services (two months in advance). The prepayment by the customer is a liability for Huntington (unearned revenue) because Huntington now has an obligation to provide the workshop training service to the customer. The payment is essentially *held in trust* on behalf of the customer. At this point, there is no impact on equity because even though cash is received, revenue is not recognized because no work has been completed.

Figure 4.5 shows the impact on Huntington's accounts when the training workshop has been provided. The previous *unearned* revenue of $1,100 is now essentially *earned*.

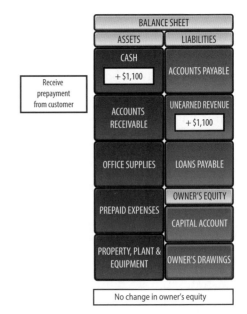

FIGURE 4.4

Therefore, the liability account, unearned revenue, decreases by $1,100 and equity increases by $1,100. This is recorded in revenue. Notice that even though there was no change in cash with this transaction, owner's equity on the balance sheet increased by $1,100.

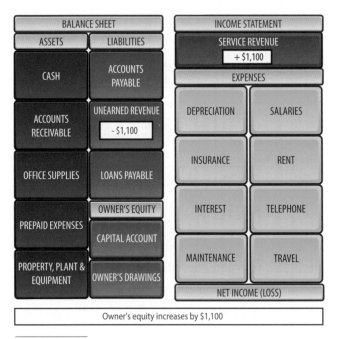

FIGURE 4.5

Unearned revenue is a commonly used transaction that can lead to business failure when not fully understood. Consider the following scenario:

Ella owns a web design and hosting company. She needs cash to operate her business and cannot raise any more money from the bank or other lenders. She decides to offer an incentive to her customers to pay in advance in exchange for a discount. Each of her 100 customers chooses to prepay $600 in January, instead of paying $60 per month (which would be $720 per year). So Ella receives $60,000 cash in January and $50 worth of services is provided to each customer every month.

Unfortunately Ella does not fully understand the revenue recognition principle and she prepared a $600 invoice for each customer in January. Once an invoice is issued, it indicates that services have actually been delivered and recorded as revenue. This results in a significant profit for the month of January. As a result of the large deposit of cash and large net income in January, Ella starts spending money without realizing that there would be no more sales for the year and no more cash coming in. Thus, she over-spent and ran out of cash part-way through the year.

Ella's Incorrect Records

Month	Revenue	Expenses	Net Income
January	$60,000	$3,000	$57,000
February	0	3,000	(3,000)
March	0	3,000	(3,000)
April	0	3,000	(3,000)
May	0	3,000	(3,000)
June	0	3,000	(3,000)
July	0	3,000	(3,000)
August	0	3,000	(3,000)
September	0	3,000	(3,000)
October	0	3,000	(3,000)
November	0	3,000	(3,000)
December	0	3,000	(3,000)
Totals	$60,000	$36,000	$24,000

FIGURE 4.6

Figure 4.6 shows how Ella recorded the revenue in January and expenses in each month they occurred.

Her records incorrectly show a very large profit for January that, in conjunction with all the cash received, made her believe that she could spend freely. For the remainder of the year there was no revenue, resulting in net losses for those months.

Ella's Correct Records

Figure 4.7 shows the way Ella's records should have been completed. Instead of recording the full $60,000 as revenue in January, the amount received is spread evenly throughout the year as Ella provides the services and they are earned. The $60,000 would have initially been recorded as unearned revenue on the liability side of the balance sheet. To avoid the temptation of spending all that cash at once, Ella may have deposited the cash into a separate business savings account.

Month	Revenue	Expenses	Net Income
January	$5,000	$3,000	$2,000
February	5,000	3,000	2,000
March	5,000	3,000	2,000
April	5,000	3,000	2,000
May	5,000	3,000	2,000
June	5,000	3,000	2,000
July	5,000	3,000	2,000
August	5,000	3,000	2,000
September	5,000	3,000	2,000
October	5,000	3,000	2,000
November	5,000	3,000	2,000
December	5,000	3,000	2,000
Totals	$60,000	$36,000	$24,000

FIGURE 4.7

Each month, Ella should have transferred $5,000 from the savings account to the daily bank account. She also would transfer $5,000 from the unearned revenue account to the revenue account on the income statement, indicating it has now been earned. This amount would be matched to the $3,000 worth of expenses each month. This even distribution of revenue and systematic transfer of cash would cause Ella to be mindful of her spending so she would not run out of cash.

Expense Recognition

You have learned about revenue recognition and how there are three transactions related to revenue recognition, which reflect the different timing of cash collection. There are also three ways to pay for an expense. In each case, the expense must be recognized when it is incurred to conform to the matching principle. All expenses incurred to operate the business, such as salaries, rent, insurance, advertising and maintenance should be considered as **operating expenses**.

There are three possible ways to pay for an expense:

1. Pay cash when the expense is incurred
2. Pay cash after the expense has been incurred
3. Pay cash before the expense has been incurred

Notice we use the term "incurred" in all three scenarios presented above. An expense is incurred by a company if the activities related to the expense have been used or consumed. For example, if a company has hired a lawn care service company to water the grass on their premises on August 16, the expense has been incurred once the grass has actually been watered on that date. As another example, if a company pays for internet services, the internet expense for a given month has been incurred once that month has ended (i.e. the internet services for one month have been used up).

Referring back to Huntington Safety Consulting, suppose that their operating expenses include travel expense, maintenance expense and insurance expense. Huntington's travel expense is paid for as soon as it is incurred. Maintenance expense is paid for after it has been incurred (i.e. paid on account). Lastly, insurance expense is usually paid for before it has been incurred (i.e. prepaid).

We will now discuss the above three scenarios regarding the expense transactions in more depth and discuss the financial impact each one will have on a typical service business.

Pay Cash when the Expense is Incurred

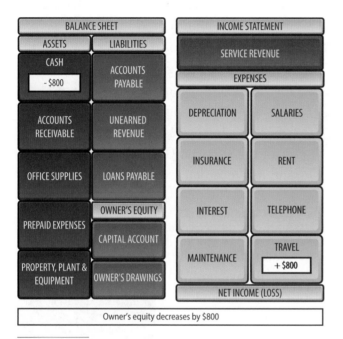

FIGURE 4.8

When a company incurs an expense and pays for it immediately, the transaction is fairly straightforward. From the company's perspective, cash decreases and owner's equity decreases. Since owner's equity decreases, it is recorded as an expense.

Huntington pays for travel expenses for as soon as they are incurred. This would seem logical since this expense account is comprised only of the costs to commute to different clients' sites (e.g. gas, parking, train tickets, etc.). Suppose that the cost to travel to a particular client's head office was $800. Figure 4.8 illustrates the accounting treatment when paying for travel expenses immediately in cash.

Pay Cash after the Expense is Incurred

Many expenses are paid after they have been incurred. This form of paying expenses is sometimes referred to as "paying on account." You may think that the value of owner's equity would not change until the expense is paid for. However, the matching principle requires expenses to be recorded at the time it is incurred, regardless of when the payment is made.

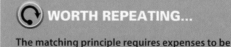

WORTH REPEATING...

The matching principle requires expenses to be reported in the same period in which it was used to operate the company and produce revenue.

A business that provides products or services to another business is known as a supplier. When a company owes a supplier for a product or service, the money owed is recorded as a liability called **accounts payable**. When an invoice is issued to the company by the supplier (after the expense has been incurred), the value of the invoice is treated as an increase to the accounts payable account and an increase to the appropriate expense account. Later, when the company actually pays off the outstanding amount, the transaction is a decrease to cash and a decrease to accounts payable. The company used cash to pay and it no longer owes any amount to the supplier (i.e. nothing is "payable").

Return to the example of Huntington Safety Consulting, suppose that Huntington pays for

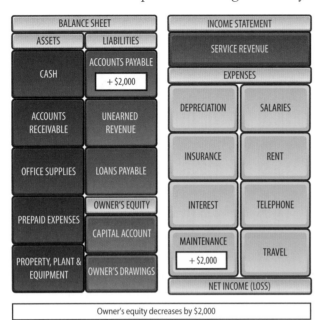

FIGURE 4.9

maintenance expense two months after it has been incurred. In other words, the payment is made to the supplier of the maintenance service after the maintenance service has been performed. Even though Huntington is not paying for the services immediately, the supplier will still issue an invoice to Huntington as soon as the maintenance work is done. Assume that the supplier is charging $2,000 to Huntington for its maintenance services. Figure 4.9 shows the impact on the applicable accounts when the invoice is issued to Huntington from the supplier. Owner's equity decreases and it is recorded as expense.

Now assume that two months have passed and Huntington pays the $2,000 owed to the maintenance supplier. Figure 4.10 illustrates the accounting impact of this transaction. This transaction is often referred to as a "payment of account." Equity does not change. Only an asset (cash) and a liability (accounts payable) are affected.

Pay Cash before the Expense is Incurred

The third scenario, in which the company pays before the expense has been incurred, can be viewed as a supplier prepayment. This scenario leads to the introduction of a new asset account known as prepaid expenses, which was discussed in the context of personal accounting in chapter 1. The following section will explain how this account is used to deal with supplier prepayments.

FIGURE 4.10

Prepaid Expenses

We have discussed two ways in which expenses can be recognized:

1. The company pays cash immediately; or

2. The company is given payment terms and pays after the expense is incurred

The third way a company can pay for expenses is to pay in advance. When a company pays before using the product or service, the amount paid is initially recorded by decreasing cash and increasing **prepaid expenses** (an asset account). These prepayments are not considered an expense at the time they are paid because the services or the product has not been used. The concept of prepaid expenses was already discussed in chapter 1 with respect to personal accounting. The same principles apply to accounting for prepaid expenses in the context of a business.

For example, if a company pays its insurance premiums one year in advance, it is paying for services not yet received. The premiums should only be expensed in the months to which they apply – hence they are called *prepaid* expenses. Common examples of prepaid expenses are rent and office supplies, although any time a company pays for products or services in advance, they can be considered prepaid expenses.

In our example, Huntington Safety Consulting paid their insurance premium before the expense was incurred, so it is considered a prepaid expense. So what does it mean to pay for insurance before the expense is incurred? It

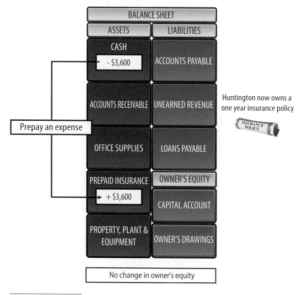

FIGURE 4.11

means that Huntington paid cash ahead of time to the insurance company for insurance coverage to be provided for the upcoming year. At the time of the payment, cash decreases and a prepaid expense called *prepaid insurance* increases. This prepaid expense is considered an asset because it could be turned back into cash if the entire year of insurance is not used up (e.g. the policy is cancelled).

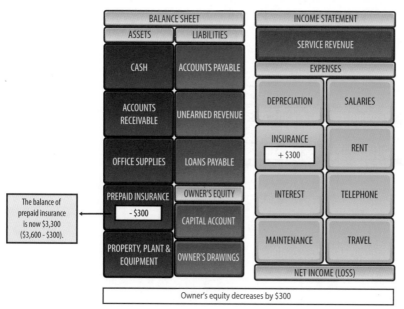

FIGURE 4.12

Let us assume Huntington paid the insurance company $3,600 on January 1, 2011 for insurance coverage throughout 2011. On January 1, 2011, when the payment is made, Huntington's cash (an asset) decreases by $3,600 and prepaid insurance (another asset) increases by $3,600. At this point, equity is not affected. One asset was exchanged for another asset. This is shown in figure 4.11.

For each month that passes in 2011, Huntington will recognize $300 of the prepaid insurance as an actual expense ($3,600 ÷ 12 months = $300/month) at the end of the month. Therefore, on January 31, 2011, Huntington's prepaid expenses account (an asset) will decrease by $300 and owner's equity will decrease by $300. The decrease to owner's equity will be recorded as an expense. The adjustment on January 31, 2011 is summarized in figure 4.12. Immediately after recognizing the month's insurance expense, the insurance company now owes the business $3,300 worth of insurance services ($3,600 - $300).

Office Supplies: An Alternate Example of Prepaid Expenses

Another accounting principle that must be taken into consideration when dealing with a company's prepaid expenses is materiality. In other words, is the prepaid amount significant enough to warrant increasing the prepaid expense account in advance and decreasing it regularly thereafter? It is a duty that comes with some administrative responsibilities. If the amount is deemed immaterial, the company can expense the entire amount in advance and not be concerned about administering the prepaid expense account.

For example, if a prepaid expense amounts to only $100 for the whole year, the entire amount would be expensed immediately. Cash would decrease, expenses would increase and prepaid expenses would not be affected at all.

In addition to prepaid expenses such as prepaid insurance, there are prepaid expenses of a tangible nature, such as office supplies. Depending on the materiality of the supplies, companies may choose to allocate office supplies as an asset and expense them as they are used. For example, a business would immediately expense a few erasers, but may record a large quantity of expensive laser printer cartridges and photocopier toner as assets. This is largely a matter of judgment.

Assume that a company had $2,000 worth of office supplies (an asset) on hand on January 1, 2011. At the end of January, the office clerk calculated that $1,200 worth of supplies remained on hand. The adjustment for the $800 supplies expense ($2,000 - $1,200) on January 31, 2011 would be recorded as follows:

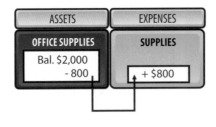

FIGURE 4.13

In summary, there are only three ways to pay for expenses, which reflect the different timing of cash payment:

1. Pay as the expense occurs (cash)
2. Pay after the event has occurred (accounts payable).
3. Pay before the event and recognize the expense when the event occurs (e.g. prepaid expense).

Relationship between Unearned Revenue and Prepaid Expenses

One company's accounts receivable is another company's accounts payable, and one company's unearned revenue is another company's prepaid expense. It is all about the point-of-view. Examine figure 4.14.

1. If the seller provides a service for $2,000 and allows their customer to pay later, the seller will increase their accounts receivable. From the buyer's perspective, they have just bought something on account and will have to pay for it later. To the buyer, this represents an increase in accounts payable.

FIGURE 4.14

2. If the seller receives $1,000 cash from a customer as a deposit for future services, the seller will increase their unearned revenue to record the liability. From the buyer's perspective, they have paid for services in advance. To the buyer, this represents an increase in prepaid expenses.

Introduction to Adjustments

Certain transactions are not recorded on a daily basis because they are not triggered by obvious business events. Rather, they are recorded at the end of each accounting period with the purpose of correctly allocating revenue and expenses. Recall that an accounting period is the period of time covered by the financial statements. Accrual accounting states that revenue and expenses should be recognized in the accounting period when they occur, regardless of when the cash payment is received or made.

Transactions made at the end of an accounting period to allocate accrued revenue and accrued expenses are called ***adjustments.*** Adjustments will not only update assets and liabilities, they will also update owner's equity to its correct balance by adjusting revenue and expense accounts. Examples of adjustments include depreciating assets, recording interest owed on bank loans or recording interest earned on investments.

For example, suppose a company prepaid a one year insurance policy on December 31, 2010 for $1,200 (or $100 per month). As we have already learned, this involves decreasing cash (an asset) and increasing prepaid expenses (an asset). The company can decide not to make any changes to the prepaid expense account until their year-end. If their year-end is May 31, 2011, they will have to prepare financial statements at that date, and adjust prepaid expenses to show that five months ($500) of insurance has been used. The timeline of this transaction is illustrated below in figure 4.15.

FIGURE 4.15

On May 31, 2011, the prepaid expense account will be reduced by $500 so that the asset is reported accurately. Also, insurance expense will increase by $500 to properly record the expense on the income statement. If the prepaid expense was not recognized as an expense on May 31, 2011, then assets would be overvalued by $500 and owner's equity would also be overvalued by $500 since an expense was not recognized. Although no obvious business event has occurred at the end of the period, it is important to recognize any prepaid expenses to correctly reflect the true value of owner's equity.

In this current section, we will describe and illustrate three particular adjustments: recognition of unearned revenue, recognition of prepaid expenses and accrued interest expense.

Adjustments: Unearned Revenue

Unearned revenue was covered in detail earlier in this chapter. When unearned revenue decreases and revenue increases (i.e. when the service is performed and revenue is earned), it is considered an adjustment.

To illustrate the concept of adjustments related to unearned revenue, we will use an example. Consider Raina Property Management (Raina). Raina just recently bought a large office building in a suburban area, which it rents out as separate offices to tenants. The company has a policy of collecting the first three months' rent in advance when a new tenant moves in. For each office, Raina charges $2,200 per month for rent. On March 1, 2011, a new tenant moved in and paid $6,600 immediately to Raina to cover rent for March, April and May. Raina makes adjustments to its accounting records at the end of each month because it produces financial statements internally on a monthly basis.

In Raina's books, on March 1 when the payment is received, Raina will increase cash (an asset) by $6,600 and increase unearned revenue (a liability) by $6,600. As of March 31, Raina has *earned* one month's worth of revenue. On this date, the company will decrease unearned revenue (a liability) by $2,200 and increase owner's equity by $2,200 with an increase to rent revenue (an income statement account). In other words, the amount owing to the customer relating to unused funds is adjusted. This particular transaction is considered an adjustment. The same adjustment will be made on April 30 (to recognize April's rent revenue) and May 31 (to recognize May's rent revenue). Figure 4.16 summarizes these transactions related to unearned revenue.

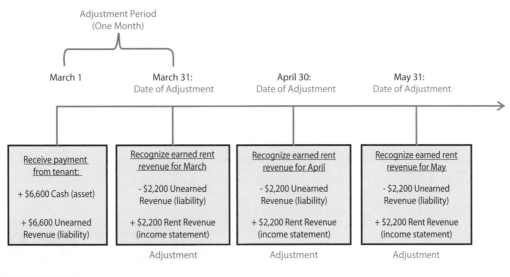

FIGURE 4.16

Adjustments: Prepaid Expenses

Similar to unearned revenue, accounting for prepaid expenses involves making adjustments. Recall that when a prepaid expense is recognized as an actual expense, prepaid expenses (an asset) decreases and the expense (an income statement account) increases. When this happens, it is referred to as an adjustment (similar to the treatment of unearned revenue above).

Before continuing, remember the following general rule: Suppose Company A pays Company B for services before the service is delivered. From the perspective of Company A, they have a prepaid expense (an asset) recorded in their accounts. From the perspective of Company B, they have an unearned revenue (a liability) recorded in their accounts. This notion was illustrated earlier in figure 4.14.

This general rule can be applied in the example with Raina Property Management, which we introduced in the previous section. Let us now examine the financial impact of the transactions from the perspective of the tenant who paid Raina three months of rent in advance. Also, assume that the tenant's accounting period is one month. The timeline of adjustments will look as follows:

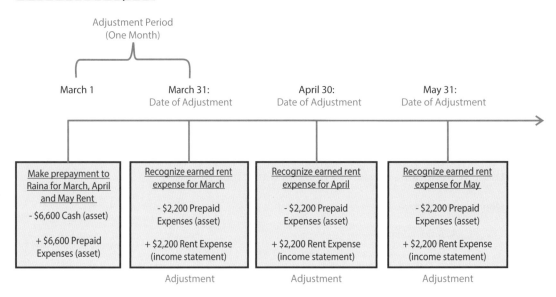

FIGURE 4.17

Adjustments: Accrued Interest Expense

Expenses incurred in one accounting period but not paid until a later accounting period are called **accrued expenses**. At the end of an accounting period, an accrued expense is recorded by an adjusting entry.

Accrued interest expense is an example of a common accrued expense. To illustrate the accounting for accrued interest expense, assume that a company with a year end of December 31 borrowed a bank loan on August 1, 2010. The loan has a repayment term of two years. The bank loan requires the company to accrue interest in the amount of $1,500 per month. For simplicity, assume that all interest is payable when the bank loan is due (in two years). Note that the period from August 1, 2010 to December

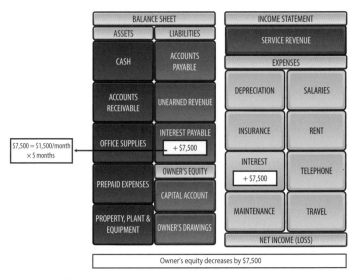

FIGURE 4.18

31, 2010 is five months in length. At the year-end date of December 31, 2010, when the financial statements are prepared, the company determines that it owes $7,500 in interest ($1,500 interest per month × 5 months). On December 31, 2010, this will cause an increase to interest expense (an income statement account) and an increase to interest payable (a liability account on the balance sheet) in the amount of $7,500. This transaction is illustrated in figure 4.18.

Adjustments: Depreciation

You have already been introduced to the concept of depreciation as it applies to your personal life. The decrease in the value of property, plant and equipment (long-term assets) is recorded as a depreciation expense in the income statement and decreases owners' equity.

For example, suppose property, plant and equipment is currently valued at $1,000. Depreciation of $100 must be recorded. Owner's equity will decrease by $100, represented by a $100 increase to depreciation expense. The $100 will also reduce the value of property, plant and equipment to $900, which is considered the book value of the asset.

However, GAAP requires the original amount (or historical amount) of the asset to be recorded in the balance sheet. Accounting for depreciation requires a special account which will be introduced in a later chapter.

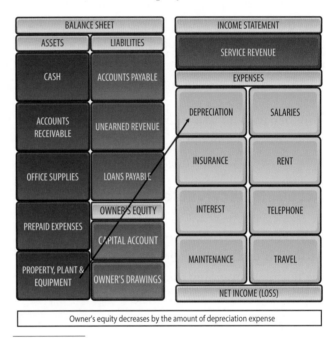

FIGURE 4.19

Ethics and Controls

Owners and managers of businesses have some control over how revenue and expenses are recorded and reported on the income statement. Perhaps the most famous example of misrepresenting revenue comes from Enron. Enron was a large energy company in the United States which, over a period of five years, reported an increase in revenue of over 750%. This massive increase in revenue was partly due to counting the full amount of trading contracts, instead of just brokerage fees, as revenue.

Another example of corporate fraud is WorldCom, a telecommunication company. In addition to misrepresenting revenue, they also took certain expenses and recorded them as assets on the balance sheet. Thus, by increasing revenue and eliminating certain expenses, they were able to show very large profits.

On a smaller business level, the owner of a banquet hall may receive deposits from customers to book the hall months in advance. As we have learned, customer deposits are to be treated as a liability (unearned revenue) until the service is actually performed. Suppose the owner requires additional financing from the bank to help pay for an expansion to the hall and feels her income may not be enough to get the loan.

In order to make her net income appear higher, the owner may decide to record the customer deposits as revenue instead of a liability. By inflating her revenue and profits, she hopes the bank will grant her the loan she needs. The misrepresentation is unethical, and if she does not earn enough to repay the loan, the bank will lose money.

Consider a sole proprietor that is attempting to minimize the amount of taxes he must pay to the government on his business income. If he has a significant amount of prepaid expenses recorded as assets, he may be tempted to report them all as expenses. He may also be tempted to overstate the expenses by including personal expenses in his business records. All these would reduce the net income and the amount of taxes that have to be paid.

This behavior is also unethical. By manipulating the accounting records, the government does not collect the amount of taxes that it should. Also, the owner could face financial penalties if the government were to find out what he did.

Accounts Receivable Controls

When customers are allowed to pay later for services provided, they are in effect being provided with an interest free loan that they must pay back within a certain timeframe. Unfortunately for the business providing the payment terms, customers sometimes default on their payments (do not pay the amount owed).

One of the primary reasons for a shortage of cash in a business is that they are unable to collect accounts receivable. Thus, it is important for a company to implement good accounts receivable controls to handle collection issues.

Ideally, a company will hire a full-time accounts receivable clerk to oversee all aspects of sending invoices to customers, collecting payments from customers and other duties related to accounts receivable. Some controls that could be implemented are:

Credit Approval

A business does not have to grant credit to every customer. There is always an element of risk when extending credit terms, so only authorized employees should be allowed to give credit to customers. Extending credit to a customer is a at the discretion of the business. The process of granting credit usually involves performing a credit check on the customer.

Customer Billing

Sending an invoice to a customer promptly is important. The sooner the customer receives the invoice, the sooner the customer can pay the amount owing.

Customer Payments

Receiving payments in a timely manner is crucial to good cash flow in a business. Another reason for quickly collecting payments is that as customers take longer to pay, odds increase that the customer will never pay. If a customer is late paying their bill, the business should remind them of the amount outstanding and request the amount be paid immediately.

Separation of Duties

The person opening the mail should not be the same person recording the customer payments. If payment comes by check, one person should record that the check was received and another should record that amount in the books against the amount the customer owed. This provides for two records of the check and ensures that the amount is properly deposited in the company's bank account.

In Summary

⇨ Earnings of a business are called revenue.

⇨ A business can be paid for services in one of three ways; 1) paid when the service is delivered, 2) paid after the service is delivered or 3) paid before the service is delivered.

⇨ **Accounts receivable** tracks the amount customers owe for services already provided. Accounts receivable is an asset.

⇨ Collecting accounts receivable does not affect service revenue.

⇨ **Unearned revenue** arises when customers pay before the service is delivered. The income statement is not initially affected. Unearned revenue is a liability.

⇨ When a business provides the service they were prepaid for, revenue increase and unearned revenue decreases. Cash is not affected.

⇨ **Operating expenses** represent the various costs of running a business.

⇨ Businesses can pay for expenses in one of three ways; 1) pay when the expense is incurred, 2) pay after the expense is incurred or 3) pay before the expense is incurred.

⇨ **Accounts payable** tracks the amount a business owes a supplier. Accounts payable is a liability.

⇨ Paying accounts payable does not affect expenses.

⇨ **Prepaid expenses** arise when a business pays for expenses before they are incurred. The income statement is not initially affected. Prepaid expenses are asset accounts.

⇨ When an expense is incurred that has already been paid for, expenses increase and prepaid expenses decrease. Cash is not affected.

⇨ **Adjustments** ensure that all account values are properly reported. Adjustments are done at the end of an accounting period.

⇨ Accounting for unearned revenue that has been earned and prepaid expenses that have been incurred are examples of adjustments.

⇨ **Accrued interest expense** is interest expense incurred in one accounting period but not paid until a later accounting period. An adjusting entry is required to account for accrued interest expense.

⇨ Implementing proper controls for accounts receivable will ensure customers pay on time and the business has good cash flow.

Review Exercise

Complete the T-Account worksheet on the next page for the following business transactions during April 2011 for JKF Company. Also, calculate owner's equity as of April 30, 2011.

Balances as at March 31, 2011:

Cash	$11,000
Accounts Receivable	5,000
Prepaid Expenses	3,200
PPE - Equipment	72,500
Accounts Payable	7,900
Unearned Revenue	11,200
Loans and Interest Payable	24,000
Owner's Equity (Capital Account)	48,600

Transactions for April:

1. Received $2,225 from a customer, immediately after a service was rendered
2. Paid $3,600 cash on April 1 for March's rent
3. Received invoice in the amount of $800 for maintenance services (to be paid by JKF in one month)
4. Issued an invoice to a customer in the amount of $7,220 for services already performed in April (to be paid by customer in six weeks)
5. Received a $1,000 deposit on April 1 from a customer for a service to be performed later in the month
6. The service referred to in Transaction #5 was fully performed at month-end by JKF.
7. Recognized one month's worth of insurance expense (note that JKF made a prepayment to the insurance company in the amount of $3,600 at the beginning of the year for a one-year coverage period)
8. Prepaid advertising expense in the amount of $1,900 with cash
9. Accrued $6,000 in interest expense for April

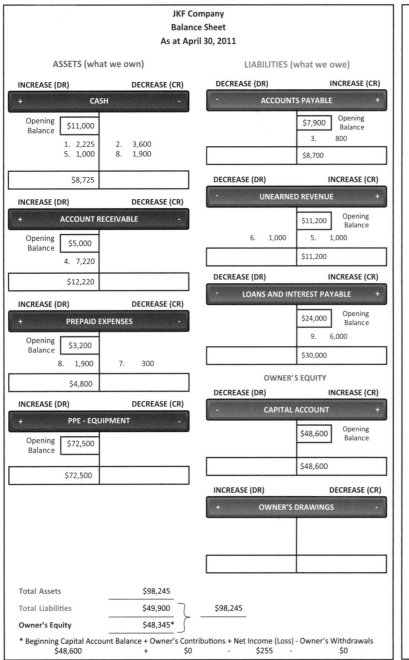

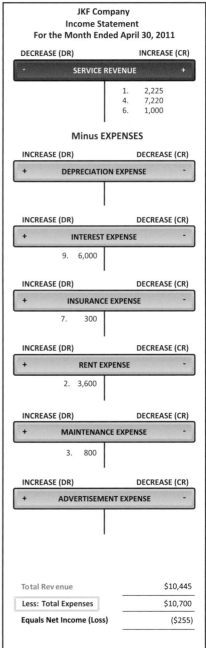

Chapter 5
BUSINESS ACCOUNTING CYCLE PART I

LEARNING OUTCOMES:

❶ Understand the use of debits and credits

❷ Record transactions in the general journal

❸ Post journal entries to the general ledger

❹ Prepare a trial balance

An Introduction to Bookkeeping

One of the challenges in teaching a modern accounting course is the need to combine traditional concepts and methods with modern technology. The reality is that today's accounting students may never see or use an actual set of accounting books.

Computerized accounting systems have all but replaced the manual way of keeping records for a company. Computers make gathering and analyzing information easier. They automate the process of recording the entry of transactions and simultaneously update the necessary accounting records. In a traditional paper-based accounting system, the updating of accounting records after making an entry is done manually, which is time consuming and leaves ample opportunity for making errors.

However, learning about paper-based accounting provides a foundation for understanding what accounting is all about. By studying manual accounting systems, it allows you to better understand the flow of financial information, understand what the computerized system does behind the scenes, and increases your chances of detecting mistakes within a computerized system.

Transition to Debits and Credits

We have been using the terms *increase* and *decrease* to record transactions up to this point, but formal accounting requires the use of **debits** and **credits**. In the debit and credit system (unlike increases and decreases), a debit is always recorded on the left-hand side of an account and a credit is always recorded on the right-hand side. You will see DR to represent debits and CR to represent credits.

An important point to remember about debits and credits is that they do not always mean increase or decrease. A credit means an entry on the right side of the account, and it may cause the account to increase or decrease, depending on the type of account it is. A similar explanation holds for debits. Remember, the accounting equation is:

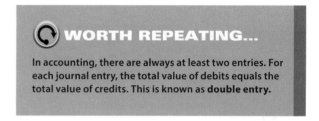

WORTH REPEATING...

In accounting, there are always at least two entries. For each journal entry, the total value of debits equals the total value of credits. This is known as **double entry**.

Assets = Liabilities + Owner's Equity

Owner's equity is a category that includes the capital account and the owner's drawings account. At this point it is important to separate the two in the owner's equity category, since each behaves differently under the debit and credit rules.

Debit and Credit Reference Guide

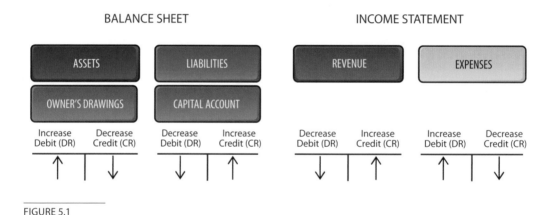

FIGURE 5.1

For the accounting equation to be correct and for the balance sheet to stay in balance, the total value of the debits must *always* equal the total value of the credits. Use the *Accounting Map™* on the right and the *Debit and Credit Reference Guide* above to follow the flow of these transactions.

1. Receive $2,000 payment from a customer:
   - increase cash (DR)
   - increase revenue (CR)

2. Reduce bank loan debt by $500:
   - decrease bank loan (DR)
   - decrease cash (CR)

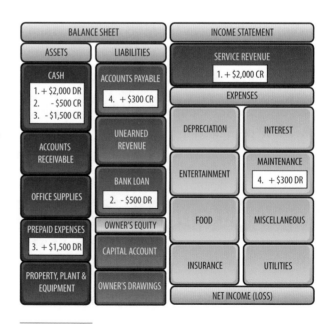

FIGURE 5.2

3.   Prepay $1,500 in cash for insurance:

 •   increase prepaid expenses (DR)
 •   decrease cash (CR)

4.   Record $300 maintenance expense on account:

 •   increase maintenance expense (DR)
 •   increase accounts payable (CR)

Every transaction will have at least one debit and one credit. The total of all debits in a transaction must equal the total of all credits. If debits do not equal credits, the accounting equation will not balance.

Each type of account also has a normal balance. A **normal balance** will correspond to the side of the T-Account that records the increase (e.g. assets have a debit normal balance and liabilities have a credit normal balance). A normal balance indicates a positive balance for the account. The normal balance for an account is simply the type of balance (debit or credit) that the account typically has. For instance, the cash account (an asset) has a debit normal balance.

Transition to Journal Entries

The format for recording **journal entries** (double entry transactions) is slightly different from what you have learned so far. The difference between T-Accounts and journals is that instead of recording the transactions directly into each account, you will now list all transactions in one place, the journal.

To help you to understand how increases and decreases translate into debits and credits, consider the following common transactions:

 1. Provided services to a customer and received $6,300 cash.
 2. Received a $600 bill for advertising, which you will pay later.
 3. Received $1,500 cash from a customer for work to be completed next month.
 4. Paid $2,400 towards the bank loan.
 5. Paid $5,200 in advance for four months' rent.
 6. Purchased office furniture with $4,100 cash.
 7. Provided services to a customer who will pay $2,300 next month.
 8. Paid off $400 of the advertising bill.
 9. A customer paid $1,800 towards the amount they owed.

Instead of recording these transactions directly into the T-Accounts, we will simulate how a journal would be prepared and illustrate how increases and decreases translate into debits and credits.

	Account Name	Increase or Decrease	Debit	Credit
1	Cash	Increase	6,300	
	Service Revenue	Increase		6,300
2	Advertising Expense	Increase	600	
	Accounts Payable	Increase		600
3	Cash	Increase	1,500	
	Unearned Revenue	Increase		1,500
4	Bank Loan	Decrease	2,400	
	Cash	Decrease		2,400
5	Prepaid Rent	Increase	5,200	
	Cash	Decrease		5,200
6	PPE - Equipment	Increase	4,100	
	Cash	Decrease		4,100
7	Accounts Receivable	Increase	2,300	
	Service Revenue	Increase		2,300
8	Accounts Payable	Decrease	400	
	Cash	Decrease		400
9	Cash	Increase	1,800	
	Accounts Receivable	Decrease		1,800

FIGURE 5.3

Chart of Accounts

Each account in an accounting system is given a unique number. The listing of all the accounts used by a business is called a **chart of accounts**.

To set up a chart of accounts, you must first define the various accounts to be used by the business and then give each account an identifying number. For small businesses, three-digit account numbers may be sufficient, although more digits are desirable to allow for new accounts to be added as the business grows. Large organizations may have thousands of accounts and require longer account numbers.

It is important to assign account numbers in a logical manner and to follow specific industry standards. An example of a numbering system is shown below:

Account Numbering
1000 - 1999: **Asset** accounts
2000 - 2999: **Liability** accounts
3000 - 3999: **Equity** accounts
4000 - 4999: **Revenue** accounts
5000 - 5999: Expense accounts

Separating each account by several numbers will allow new accounts to be added while maintaining the same logical order. Note that the account numbering follows the order of the financial statements: balance sheet (assets, liabilities and owner's equity); income statement (revenue and expenses).

Defining Accounts

Different types of businesses utilize different types of accounts. For example, a manufacturing business will require various accounts for reporting manufacturing costs. A retail business, however, will have accounts for the purchase of merchandise. Many industrial associations publish recommended charts of accounts for their respective industries in order to establish a consistent standard of comparison among organizations. Accounting software packages often provide a selection of predefined account charts for various types of businesses.

Tax reporting requirements must also be considered when creating accounts (e.g. some tax authorities require that travel, entertainment and meals be tracked using individual accounts).

Figure 5.4 shows how a service company may set up their accounts. Other accounts can be set up as needed – for example, if the business has more than one bank account, the chart of accounts would include an account for each of them.

Account Description	Account #	Account Description	Account #
ASSETS		**REVENUE**	
Cash	101	Service Revenue	400
Accounts Receivable	105	Interest Earned on Savings	410
Prepaid Insurance	110		
Office Supplies	115	**EXPENSES**	
PPE - Equipment	120	Advertising Expense	500
		Bad Debts Expense	505
LIABILITIES		Depreciation Expense	510
Accounts Payable	200	Insurance Expense	515
Interest Payable	205	Interest Expense	520
Unearned Revenue	210	Maintenance Expense	525
Bank Loan	215	Office Supplies Expense	530
		Professional Fees Expense	535
OWNER'S EQUITY		Rent Expense	540
Capital Account	300	Salaries Expense	545
Owner's Drawings	310	Telephone Expense	550
Income Summary	315	Travel Expense	555

FIGURE 5.4

The Accounting Cycle

The accounting cycle refers to the steps required to complete the financial statements. Recall that businesses prepare financial statements at the end of each accounting period, whether it is a month or a year. Every period, the cycle repeats.

The figure below shows the steps required to generate a formal set of financial statements. A computerized system will prepare most of these steps automatically, while a manual system requires each step to be complete by hand. This chapter will cover the first three steps of the cycle and the next chapter will cover the last three steps.

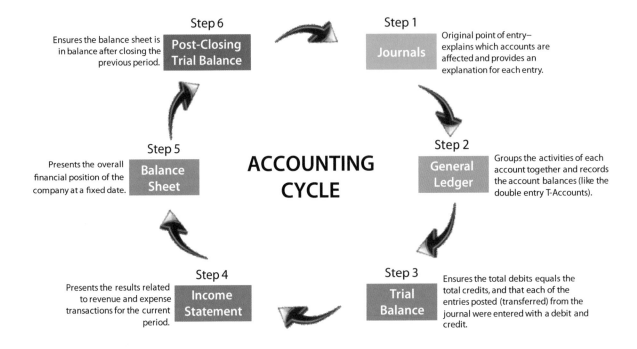

FIGURE 5.5

IN THE REAL WORLD

Accounting software such as QuickBooks and Simply Accounting automatically perform the functions of double entries. For example, assume that a cash payment is received by the company and the user defines the payment as a payment for services or goods provided. The user is usually the company's bookkeeper or accountant. The software will automatically realize that an asset account must be debited and the revenue account must be credited. After the entry is journalized by the software, the amounts are automatically posted to the general ledger and the trial balance. There is a significant level of automation provided by accounting software, which can reduce the number of accounting errors and misstatements if used correctly.

Step 1 - Journals

Journals are also known as books of original entry. All business activities are recorded initially in a journal. It contains all the initial entries used to record every transaction (each of which includes at least one debit and one credit) and the purpose of the transactions. This process is called **journalizing**.

Consider MP Consulting, a service company that provides financial advice to its clients. We will illustrate the posting of journal entries for all of MP's transactions during the month of January 2014. The opening account balances are shown below in the balance sheet in figure 5.6. You will notice that the beginning balance of owner's equity is listed in the capital account and the capital account is located under the owner's equity category heading. In practice, this is how the owner's equity section would look like on a formal balance sheet. The details of the owner's equity section will be further discussed in the next chapter.

These balances are required to complete step 2 of the accounting cycle (posting to the general ledger), to be discussed in the next section.

MP Consulting Balance Sheet As at December 31, 2013			
ASSETS		**LIABILITIES**	
Cash	$3,000	Accounts Payable	$1,000
Prepaid Insurance	1,200	Unearned Revenue	900
PPE - Equipment	6,000	Bank Loan	3,000
		Total Liabilities	4,900
		OWNER'S EQUITY	
		Capital Account	5,300
TOTAL ASSETS	$10,200	**TOTAL LIABILITIES & EQUITY**	$10,200

FIGURE 5.6

Note that the above balance sheet is dated December 31, 2013. In other words, it is comprised of the ending account balances for the month of December 2013, which are also the beginning balances for the month of January 2014. In general, an account's ending balance for a given accounting period is the beginning balance of the next period. In this book, the term "opening balance" will be used synonymously with "beginning balance" and "closing balance" is synonymous with "ending balance".

MP Consulting had the following transactions for the month of January 2014. The transactions have been entered in the journal in figure 5.7.

1. On January 2, completed some work for a client and the client paid $1,500 cash
2. On January 3, paid $800 cash for the month's rent
3. On January 5, the owner invested $5,000 cash into the business
4. On January 7, paid $2,300 cash for equipment
5. On January 10, completed some work for a client who will pay $1,800 next month
6. On January 16, paid $500 against the principal of a bank loan
7. On January 19, received $1,100 cash from a client for work to complete next month
8. On January 20, received a bill for the telephone for $250. This will be paid next month
9. On January 30, the owner withdrew $2,000 cash for personal use

JOURNAL				Page 1
❶ Date	**Account Title and Explanation ❷**	**PR ❸**	**Debit ❹**	**Credit**
2014				
Jan 2	Cash ❷ⓐ	101	1,500	
	Service Revenue ❷ⓑ	400		1,500
	Completed work for client ❷ⓒ			
	❺			
Jan 3	Rent Expense	540	800	
	Cash	101		800
	Paid rent for month of January			
Jan 5	Cash	101	5,000	
	Capital Account	300		5,000
	Owner invested cash			
Jan 7	PPE - Equipment	120	2,300	
	Cash	101		2,300
	Bought equipment			
Jan 10	Accounts Receivable	105	1,800	
	Service Revenue	400		1,800
	Completed work on account			
Jan 16	Bank Loan	215	500	
	Cash	101		500
	Paid bank loan principal			
Jan 19	Cash	101	1,100	
	Unearned Revenue	210		1,100
	Received customer deposit			
Jan 20	Telephone Expense	550	250	
	Accounts Payable	200		250
	Received telephone bill			
Jan 30	Owner's Drawings	310	2,000	
	Cash	101		2,000
	Owner took cash for personal use			

FIGURE 5.7

The journal lists all the activities of the business in chronological order and provides a set of complete, organized record of all the transactions of the business. Recording all the transactions in one place reduces the risk of potential errors and makes it easier to trace any mistakes.

Note that not all accounts have been affected by January's day-to-day transactions. Up until this point, prepaid insurance (an asset) still has the same balance as what it started with. However, an adjustment will be made to this account in a subsequent step of the accounting cycle. This will be covered in the next chapter.

The format of the journal is relatively standard and generally includes the following items, as shown in figure 5.7.

❶ Date

The date column includes the current year at the top of the first column, followed by the month and day of the transaction. The journal entries are entered in chronological order.

❷ Account Title and Explanation

This column indicates the names of the accounts being affected. It is important to note that the logic you have been using to indicate the accounts to be used has not changed. For example, if an expense is being paid with cash, cash will decrease (credit) and the expense will increase (debit). The journal merely places this information in a standard order to keep information organized.

a) Any accounts that will be debited for the transaction will be listed first.
b) Any accounts that will be credited for the transaction will be listed after the debited accounts and indented slightly. This is simply a formatting standard which makes it easier to read long lists of transactions.
c) A brief explanation will be listed immediately after the transaction.

❸ PR (Posting Reference)

The PR column indicates the number assigned to the account from the chart of accounts (e.g. cash = 101, rent expense = 540). It is simply used for identification purposes and as a means for organizing the accounts. For practical purposes, the journal entries in this text will include the PR column in chapter 5 and 6 only.

❹ Debit or Credit

These two columns are used to record the amount of the transaction in the appropriate side – debit or credit.

❺ Lastly, leave a space between journal entries to make it easier to read and separate them.

Step 2 - General Ledger

Although all the activities for the month have been recorded in the general journal, the ending balance for each account has not yet been determined. For example, there may have been several transactions relating to cash. If you are required to calculate the closing cash balance, the accounts need to be sorted into a manageable format where each account is assigned a separate page in which all transactions affecting that account will be recorded.

The **general ledger** organizes the accounts in the order shown on the chart of accounts and tracks the balance of each account. There is a separate ledger for each account. You will need to record the date of the transaction, a short description (if needed), the journal page in which the transaction originated, the amount, whether it was a debit or credit, and the new balance. Think of the ledger as an expanded T-Account. In figure 5.8, notice the red "T" under the debit and credit columns. This is shown to illustrate its similarity to the T-Accounts you have been working with up until this point.

Account: Cash						GL No. 101	
Date	Description	PR	Debit	Credit	Balance		

FIGURE 5.8

Each entry must be posted (recorded) to the relevant ledger account. These accounts are then used for preparing the trial balance and financial statements. The posting of journal entries to the ledgers should be completed on a regular consistent basis.

The posting to the general ledger is completed as shown in figure 5.9 (note that the general ledger account in the example is cash and it has an opening balance of $3,000):

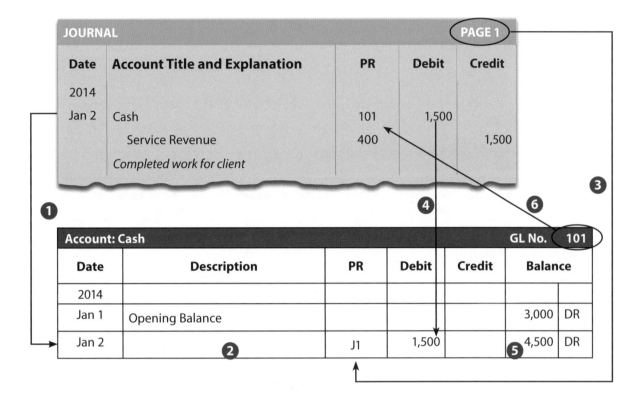

FIGURE 5.9

As seen in the figure above, there are a number of steps to complete posting items from the journal to the general ledger.

1. Transfer the date of the transaction.
2. The description in the ledger does not have to be completed for every transaction, provided you have a description already recorded in the journal.
3. Transfer the page number of the journal to the posting reference column in the ledger.
4. Enter the transaction amount into the appropriate debit or credit column.
5. Calculate the new account balance (i.e. the ending, or closing balance). Remember to increase and decrease the previous balance according to the debit and credit rules shown in figure 5.1.
6. Enter the ledger number from the ledger into the posting reference in the journal as a checking process once the amount has been posted.
7. Repeat the steps for all lines in the journal entry.

It is good practice to double check that the balance shown in the ledger for each account is a normal balance (e.g. accounts payable is a liability and liabilities have a credit normal balance). If an account does not have a normal balance, this may indicate that an error has occurred. Double check that the balance was calculated correctly, the figure in the ledger was correctly copied from the journal and the journal entry was created correctly.

In the modern accounting system, the posting process is automatically done by the computer system. Accountants no longer need to refer to a specific page in the journal book to look for transactions.

The following figure shows how the general ledger would look for all the journal entries from figure 5.7.

GENERAL LEDGER

Account: Cash   **GL. No.   101**

Date	Description	PR	Debit	Credit	Balance	
2014						
Jan 1	Opening Balance				3,000	DR
Jan 2		J1	1,500		4,500	DR
Jan 3		J1		800	3,700	DR
Jan 5		J1	5,000		8,700	DR
Jan 7		J1		2,300	6,400	DR
Jan 16		J1		500	5,900	DR
Jan 19		J1	1,100		7,000	DR
Jan 30		J1		2,000	5,000	DR

Account: Accounts Receivable   **GL. No.   105**

Date	Description	PR	Debit	Credit	Balance	
2014						
Jan 1	Opening Balance				0	DR
Jan 10		J1	1,800		1,800	DR

Account: Prepaid Insurance   **GL. No.   110**

Date	Description	PR	Debit	Credit	Balance	
2014						
Jan 1	Opening Balance				1,200	DR

Account: PPE - Equipment   **GL. No.   120**

Date	Description	PR	Debit	Credit	Balance	
2014						
Jan 1	Opening Balance				6,000	DR
Jan 7		J1	2,300		8,300	DR

Account: Accounts Payable   **GL. No.   200**

Date	Description	PR	Debit	Credit	Balance	
2014						
Jan 1	Opening Balance				1,000	CR
Jan 20		J1		250	1,250	CR

Account: Unearned Revenue					GL. No. 210	
Date	**Description**	**PR**	**Debit**	**Credit**	**Balance**	
2014						
Jan 1	Opening Balance				900	CR
Jan 19		J1		1,100	2,000	CR

Account: Bank Loan					GL. No. 215	
Date	**Description**	**PR**	**Debit**	**Credit**	**Balance**	
2014						
Jan 1	Opening Balance				3,000	CR
Jan 16		J1	500		2,500	CR

Account: Capital Account					GL. No. 300	
Date	**Description**	**PR**	**Debit**	**Credit**	**Balance**	
2014						
Jan 1	Opening Balance				5,300	CR
Jan 5		J1		5,000	10,300	CR

Account: Owner's Drawings					GL. No. 310	
Date	**Description**	**PR**	**Debit**	**Credit**	**Balance**	
2014						
Jan 30		J1	2,000		2,000	DR

Account: Service Revenue					GL. No. 400	
Date	**Description**	**PR**	**Debit**	**Credit**	**Balance**	
2014						
Jan 2		J1		1,500	1,500	CR
Jan 10		J1		1,800	3,300	CR

Account: Rent Expense					GL. No. 540	
Date	**Description**	**PR**	**Debit**	**Credit**	**Balance**	
2014						
Jan 3		J1	800		800	DR

Account: Telephone Expense					GL. No. 550	
Date	**Description**	**PR**	**Debit**	**Credit**	**Balance**	
2014						
Jan 20		J1	250		250	DR

FIGURE 5.10

Step 3 - Trial Balance

Remember that in every journal entry, the total value of the debits must equal the total value of the credits (at *all* times). To ensure that this rule has been adhered to, we need to create a trial balance. A **trial balance** lists all accounts in the general ledger and their balances. If the total debits equals total credits, then the trial balance balances. The trial balance is created at the end of the accounting cycle and is used as an internal report for the preparation of financial statements. Some accountants choose to total the debit and credit columns in journals as well, as an added control.

The trial balance has a title which indicates the company name, the name of the report (Trial Balance) and the date the trial balance was prepared. It then lists each account in the order they appear in the general ledger and their final balances in the debit or credit column. The following trial balance is based on the accounts and balances from figure 5.10.

MP Consulting Trial Balance January 31, 2014		
Account	**Debit**	**Credit**
Cash	$5,000	
Accounts Receivable	1,800	
Prepaid Insurance	1,200	
PPE - Equipment	8,300	
Accounts Payable		$1,250
Unearned Revenue		2,000
Bank Loan		2,500
Capital Account		10,300
Owner's Drawings	2,000	
Service Revenue		3,300
Rent Expense	800	
Telephone Expense	250	
Total	$19,350	$19,350

FIGURE 5.11

If the trial balance does not balance, the financial statements cannot be prepared because there is an error somewhere in the accounts. Double check the following items to track down the error:

1. Do all accounts on the trial balance show a normal balance?
2. Were the balances on the trial balance copied correctly from the ledger accounts?
3. Was the calculation of the ledger account balances done correctly?
4. Were the amounts in the ledger accounts copied correctly from the journal?
5. Were the journal entries created correctly?

The fact that a trial balance balances does not necessarily mean that all transactions were correctly recorded. And since locating errors can be a frustrating experience, it is important to ensure that entries are made correctly the first time.

A CLOSER LOOK

Some errors that can be made that will leave the trial balance in balance are:

1. Error of Principle: You credited cash and debited an asset instead of debiting an expense. The trial balance will balance, but the financial statements will be incorrect.

2. Error of Total Omission: A journal entry may have been omitted.

3. Repeated Entry Error: A journal entry may have been posted twice.

4. Original Entry Error: Incorrect amounts may have been posted for both the debit and credit entry.

5. Reversal Error: Correct amounts are entered in the credit side as opposed to the debit side or vice versa.

Transposition Errors

Transposition occurs when two adjacent numbers are switched, for example 530 may be written as 350. This type of error can be very difficult to track down, especially in a long list of numbers. If only one figure has been transposed, then there is an easy mathematical trick to find the error. Figure 5.12 recreates the trial balance shown before, except that PPE - Equipment has been written incorrectly as $3,800 instead of $8,300.

MP Consulting Trial Balance January 31, 2014		
Account	**Debit**	**Credit**
Cash	$5,000	
Accounts Receivable	1,800	
Prepaid Insurance	1,200	
PPE - Equipment	3,800	
Accounts Payable		$1,250
Unearned Revenue		2,000
Bank Loan		2,500
Capital Account		10,300
Owner's Drawings	2,000	
Service Revenue		3,300
Rent Expense	800	
Telephone Expense	250	
Total	**$14,850**	**$19,350**	× Does not balance

FIGURE 5.12

Notice the totals of the debit and credit column do not match. To determine if this is a transposition error, find the difference and divide by 9.

$$($19,350 - $14,850) \div 9 = $500$$

If the answer ($500) is a whole number, then a transposition has likely occurred. The number 5 from the answer is in the hundreds column, so the transposition must be between the hundreds column and column to the left (thousands column). The difference between the numbers in the two columns will be 5.

In the trial balance, there are two accounts where the difference between the hundreds and thousands column is 5: cash ($5,000) and PPE - Equipment ($3,800). By comparing the ledger account balances for these accounts to the trial balance, we find that it is PPE - Equipment that is written incorrectly.

This check also works if a number is missing a zero or has an extra zero. The drawback to this trick is that it is only effective if there is only one figure transposed or does not have the correct number of zeros.

Once the trial balance is completed and balanced, we are ready to begin the period end procedures to start preparing the financial statements. This will be covered in the next chapter.

Ethics and Controls

Regardless of whether the company uses accounting software or records transactions manually, there is ample opportunity to manipulate the books. Keep in mind that computerized accounting information is only as reliable and accurate as the information that goes into the system. Most of the time, the accounting system used by a company is not fully automated. This means that the user needs to input information into the system or interact directly with the software at one point or another, which provides opportunity for unethical behavior.

For instance, certain accounting software allow for automated recurring entries. In other words, they can be set up to repeat the same entry at various time intervals. As an example, consider GG Property Management, which manages and rents out high-end office buildings. Since the company receives rent from its tenants on a monthly basis (at month end), it has set up its accounting software to record rent revenue automatically at the end of each month. Suppose  that a tenant decides to move out and, thus, stops paying rent to GG. However, the rent revenue for the tenant continues to be recorded in GG's accounting system for every subsequent month after the office has been vacated. Allowing the entries to continue being recorded automatically will result in inaccuracies on the financial statements. The additional entries for rent revenue will automatically flow to the general ledger, the trial balance, the income statement and ultimately the balance sheet. Earnings for the period will be inflated. The financial statements will be misstated and this significant error may mislead the users of the financial statements if it goes undetected.

If the above behavior is done intentionally and management takes further steps to conceal the misstatement, then it is considered highly unethical and fraudulent. However, assume that the error was done unintentionally. A possible control that may detect the error is to compare the current list of tenants to the transaction details in the journal at regular intervals (such as at month end). Another method of preventing this error is to set up the software to automatically prompt the software administrator to authorize each entry or avoid using automated recurring entries entirely.

In Summary

↻ Debits are recorded on the left side of an account and credits are recorded on the right side. For the accounting equation to be correct, the total value of the debits must equal the total value of the credits. This will ensure that the balance sheet stays in balance.

↻ A journal is a record in which transactions are recorded before they are posted. Journals are known as *books of original entry*. Amounts are posted from the journals to the general ledger.

↻ Double-entry transactions are called *journal entries*.

↻ The general ledger is a book used to record all the accounts of the business. These accounts represent the complete financial position of the business. They also make up the accounting data from which all reports are generated.

↻ The listing of all the accounts being used by a business is called a *chart of accounts*.

↻ The trial balance lists all accounts in the general ledger and their balances. If the total debits equals total credits, then the trial balance is said to be "balanced."

↻ A transposition error occurs when two adjacent numbers are switched (e.g. 450 mistakenly written as 540).

↻ The order of the accounting cycle is as follows: journals → general ledger → trial balance → income statement → balance sheet → post-closing trial balance.

Review Exercise

CG Accounting provides bookkeeping services to small and mid-sized companies. The company had the following closing balances at the end of May 2014.

CG Accounting Balance Sheet As at May 31, 2014			
Assets		**Liabilities**	
Cash	$4,200	Accounts Payable	$2,300
Accounts Receivable	3,100	Unearned Revenue	600
PPE - Equipment	6,000	Bank Loan	4,000
		Total Liabilities	6,900
		Owner's Equity	
		Capital Account	6,400
Total Assets	$13,300	**Total Liabilities & Owner's Equity**	$13,300

CG Accounting uses the following accounts and account numbers in their accounting records:

Account Description	Account #
ASSETS	
Cash	101
Accounts Receivable	105
Prepaid Insurance	110
PPE - Equipment	120
LIABILITIES	
Accounts Payable	200
Interest Payable	205
Unearned Revenue	210
Bank Loan	215
OWNER'S EQUITY	
Capital Account	300
Owner's Drawings	310
Income Summary	315

Account Description	Account #
REVENUE	
Service Revenue	400
EXPENSES	
Advertising Expense	500
Bad Debts Expense	505
Depreciation Expense	510
Insurance Expense	515
Interest Expense	520
Maintenance Expense	525
Office Supplies Expense	530
Professional Fees Expense	535
Rent Expense	540
Salaries Expense	545
Telephone Expense	550
Travel Expense	555

During the month of June 2014, CG Accounting had the following transactions:

Jun 1	Paid $900 cash for rent for the month of June.
Jun 3	Prepaid $1,200 cash for a one year insurance policy.
Jun 6	Completed work for a client who immediately paid $2,100 cash.
Jun 11	Received a bill for advertising for $450 which will be paid next month.
Jun 13	The owner contributed an extra $3,000 cash to the business.
Jun 16	Received $300 from a client for work to be completed in July.
Jun 18	Completed work for a client who will pay $1,500 next month.
Jun 23	Paid $950 cash towards the principal portion of the bank loan.
Jun 30	The owner withdrew $1,000 cash for personal use.

Required:

a) Complete the journal entries.

b) Post the journal entries to the general ledger.

c) Prepare a trial balance.

a) Journal Entries

JOURNAL				Page 1
Date	**Account Title and Explanation**	**PR**	**Debit**	**Credit**
2014				
Jun 1	Rent Expense	540	900	
	Cash	101		900
	Paid cash for month's rent			
Jun 3	Prepaid Insurance	110	1,200	
	Cash	101		1,200
	Prepaid a one year insurance policy			
Jun 6	Cash	101	2,100	
	Service Revenue	400		2,100
	Received cash for services			
Jun 11	Advertising Expense	500	450	
	Accounts Payable	200		450
	Received invoice for advertising			
Jun 13	Cash	101	3,000	
	Capital Account	300		3,000
	Owner invested cash in business			
Jun 16	Cash	101	300	
	Unearned Revenue	210		300
	Received deposit from customer			
Jun 18	Accounts Receivable	105	1,500	
	Service Revenue	400		1,500
	Provided services on account			
Jun 23	Bank Loan	215	950	
	Cash	101		950
	Paid bank loan principal			
Jun 30	Owner's Drawings	310	1,000	
	Cash	101		1,000
	Owner drawing for personal use			

b) General Ledger

GENERAL LEDGER

Account: Cash   GL. No. 101

Date	Description	PR	Debit	Credit	Balance	
2014						
Jun 1	Opening Balance				4,200	DR
Jun 1		J1		900	3,300	DR
Jun 3		J1		1,200	2,100	DR
Jun 6		J1	2,100		4,200	DR
Jun 13		J1	3,000		7,200	DR
Jun 16		J1	300		7,500	DR
Jun 23		J1		950	6,550	DR
Jun 30		J1		1,000	5,550	DR

Account: Accounts Receivable   GL. No. 105

Date	Description	PR	Debit	Credit	Balance	
2014						
Jun 1	Opening Balance				3,100	DR
Jun 18		J1	1,500		4,600	DR

Account: Prepaid Insurance   GL. No. 110

Date	Description	PR	Debit	Credit	Balance	
2014						
Jun 1	Opening Balance				0	DR
Jun 3		J1	1,200		1,200	DR

Account: PPE - Equipment   GL. No. 120

Date	Description	PR	Debit	Credit	Balance	
2014						
Jun 1	Opening Balance				6,000	DR

Account: Accounts Payable   GL. No. 200

Date	Description	PR	Debit	Credit	Balance	
2014						
Jun 1	Opening Balance				2,300	CR
Jun 11		J1		450	2,750	CR

Account: Unearned Revenue   GL. No. 210

Date	Description	PR	Debit	Credit	Balance	
2014						
Jun 1	Opening Balance				600	CR
Jun 16		J1		300	900	CR

Account: Bank Loan — GL. No. 215

Date	Description	PR	Debit	Credit	Balance	
2014						
Jun 1	Opening Balance				4,000	CR
Jun 23		J1	950		3,050	CR

Account: Capital Account — GL. No. 300

Date	Description	PR	Debit	Credit	Balance	
2014						
Jun 1	Opening Balance				6,400	CR
Jun 13		J1		3,000	9,400	CR

Account: Owner's Drawings — GL. No. 310

Date	Description	PR	Debit	Credit	Balance	
2014						
Jun 30		J1	1,000		1,000	DR

Account: Service Revenue — GL. No. 400

Date	Description	PR	Debit	Credit	Balance	
2014						
Jun 6		J1		2,100	2,100	CR
Jun 18		J1		1,500	3,600	CR

Account: Advertising Expense — GL. No. 500

Date	Description	PR	Debit	Credit	Balance	
2014						
Jun 11		J1	450		450	DR

Account: Rent Expense — GL. No. 540

Date	Description	PR	Debit	Credit	Balance	
2014						
Jun 1		J1	900		900	DR

c) **Trial Balance**

CG Accounting Trial Balance June 30, 2014		
Account	**Debit**	**Credit**
Cash	$5,550	
Accounts Receivable	4,600	
Prepaid Insurance	1,200	
PPE - Equipment	6,000	
Accounts Payable		$2,750
Unearned Revenue		900
Bank Loan		3,050
Capital Account		9,400
Owner's Drawings	1,000	
Service Revenue		3,600
Advertising Expense	450	
Rent Expense	900	
Total	$19,700	$19,700

Chapter 6
BUSINESS ACCOUNTING CYCLE PART II

LEARNING OUTCOMES:

❶ Record adjustments on the worksheet and complete the worksheet

❷ Prepare an adjusted trial balance

❸ Prepare financial statements using an adjusted trial balance

❹ Journalize adjustments

❺ Close the books and prepare a post-closing trial balance

❻ Describe the difference between manual and computerized accounting systems

Adjusting Entries

The previous chapter discussed the first three steps in the accounting cycle: 1) Journals, 2) General Ledger and 3) Trial Balance. Those three steps lead to the end of an accounting period, at which point an accountant must begin to prepare the financial statements. However, before creating the financial statements, accountants must ensure that all accounts accurately reflect their proper values.

For example, prepaid expenses such as rent and insurance are recorded as assets. In chapter 4, we learned how to adjust the balances of prepaid expenses to properly update the asset account and record the expense. If this step is not done, prepaid expenses (an asset) will be too high and owner's equity will be too high because an expense is not recognized.

In addition to the adjustments shown in chapter 4, an adjustment for depreciation must also be recorded. Recall that GAAP requires the original (or historical) amount to be shown in the balance sheet. Thus, a special account called a contra account must be used to help record depreciation.

Contra Accounts

Contra means opposite. A contra account is linked to another account and records decreases in the value of that account without changing the original value shown. The value of the contra account is subtracted from the other account, thus reducing the overall value of the item. In the case of property, plant and equipment (PPE), the contra account is called *accumulated depreciation*. This contra asset account will reflect the decrease in the value of PPE without overriding the original cost of the asset.

Depreciation essentially spreads the recognition of the cost of the asset over its useful life. Items in the property, plant and equipment section of the balance sheet are considered tangible items, that is, they have physical substance and can be touched. With the exception of land, every asset that is considered part of property, plant and equipment will have its own separate accumulated depreciation account to track the decrease in value.

Land does not depreciate because it does not get used up, experience wear and tear, or have a limited useful life. The real estate value of the land may fluctuate up and down due to market conditions, but this is not depreciation.

Suppose an asset was purchased for $10,000 and since it was purchased, $2,000 worth of depreciation has been recorded.

To preserve the original amount paid of $10,000, the asset account PPE is not directly adjusted. Instead, accumulated depreciation records the total decrease in value of the asset. The result of subtracting the accumulated depreciation from the asset's original cost represents the book value of the asset (also referred to as the net value). The contra asset account is called accumulated depreciation because the depreciation accumulates each period as the asset decreases in value.

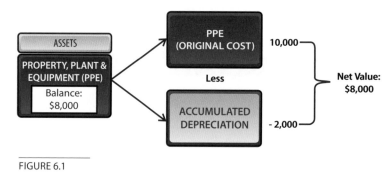

FIGURE 6.1

The contra asset account behaves in a manner opposite to the way a regular asset account behaves. Recall that an asset account will increase in value with a debit and decrease in value with a credit. The contra asset account (accumulated depreciation) will increase in value with a credit and decrease in value with a debit. Figure 6.2 illustrates the T-Accounts for property, plant and equipment and accumulated amortization.

FIGURE 6.2

The entry to record depreciation will increase depreciation expense on the income statement with a debit entry and increase the accumulated depreciation contra asset account with a credit entry. Assuming the depreciation is $2,000, figure 6.3 illustrates how the entry will affect the accounting map.

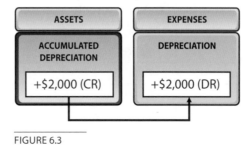

FIGURE 6.3

There are different methods to calculate depreciation. These methods and calculations will be explained in detail later in this text.

FIGURE 6.4

Worksheet

To start the period end procedures, a behind-the-scenes document called a worksheet can be used. We will continue with the example of MP Consulting discussed in the previous chapter.

The trial balance prepared from the previous chapter is the first step to creating the worksheet. The worksheet consists of five sections used by accountants to test that the accounts balance and will continue to balance during the period end procedures. The first three sections are shown in figure 6.5.

| MP Consulting Worksheet January 31, 2014 | | | | | | |
| Account | Unadjusted Trial Balance | | Adjustments | | Adjusted Trial Balance | |
	Debit	Credit	Debit	Credit	Debit	Credit
Cash	$5,000					
Accounts Receivable	1,800					
Prepaid Insurance	1,200					
PPE - Equipment	8,300					
Accounts Payable		$1,250				
Unearned Revenue		2,000				
Bank Loan		2,500				
Capital Account		10,300				
Owner's Drawings	2,000					
Service Revenue		3,300				
Rent Expense	800					
Telephone Expense	250					
Total	$19,350	$19,350				

FIGURE 6.5

Our original trial balance from chapter 5 is called an "Unadjusted Trial Balance" because these values represent account balances before adjustments are made.

Consider the following adjustments that MP Consulting will make at the end of January 2014.

1. As of January 31, 2014, MP Consulting owes $25 in interest on the bank loan. This is considered an accrued expense. This will cause an increase (debit) to interest expense, an income statement account and an increase (credit) to interest payable, a liability account on the balance sheet.
2. The balance of prepaid insurance represents a one year insurance policy that started on January 1, 2014. At the end of January, one month of insurance has been used, so prepaid insurance must be adjusted. This will increase (debit) insurance expense and decrease (credit) prepaid insurance (an asset) by $100 ($1,200 ÷ 12 months).
3. Part of the balance of unearned revenue was earned during the month of January in the amount of $200. To adjust unearned revenue for the amount earned, we must decrease (debit) unearned revenue (a liability) and increase (credit) service revenue.
4. During the month of January, PPE - Equipment depreciated $140 in value. This adjustment for depreciation will increase (debit) depreciation expense and increase (credit) accumulated depreciation (a contra asset account).

While it may be tempting to immediately create the journal entries for these adjustments, accountants will often complete the worksheet before creating the journal entries. The worksheet provides a complete view of the impact of the adjustments on the accounts and the financial statements. Also, if errors are discovered during the period end procedures, it is easier to fix them on a worksheet than in the journals, ledgers and financial statements.

Once the entire worksheet has been completed and any errors have been corrected, the adjustments will be recorded in the journal and posted to the general ledger accounts.

The adjustments are shown in figure 6.6, and each is numbered to correspond to the descriptions given above.

MP Consulting Worksheet January 31, 2014						
	Unadjusted Trial Balance		Adjustments		Adjusted Trial Balance	
Account	Debit	Credit	Debit	Credit	Debit	Credit
Cash	$5,000					
Accounts Receivable	1,800					
Prepaid Insurance	1,200		❷	$100		
PPE - Equipment	8,300					
Accumulated Depreciation - Equipment		$0	❹	140		
Accounts Payable		1,250				
Interest Payable		0	❶	25		
Unearned Revenue		2,000	$200	❸		
Bank Loan		2,500				
Capital Account		10,300				
Owner's Drawings	2,000					
Service Revenue		3,300	❸	200		
Depreciation Expense	0		140	❹		
Insurance Expense	0		100	❷		
Interest Expense	0		25	❶		
Rent Expense	800					
Telephone Expense	250					
Total	$19,350	$19,350	$465	$465		

FIGURE 6.6

The total of the debit and credit columns of the adjustments must balance in order for the accounts to remain in balance.

Notice that some accounts were added to the unadjusted trial balance with zero balances (accumulated depreciation, interest payable, depreciation expense, insurance expense and interest expense). If a company anticipates using these accounts, they can include them in the unadjusted trial balance. If they do not, the new accounts being used can be entered below the total, as shown in figure 6.7.

MP Consulting Worksheet January 31, 2014						
	Unadjusted Trial Balance		Adjustments		Adjusted Trial Balance	
Account	Debit	Credit	Debit	Credit	Debit	Credit
Cash	$5,000					
Accounts Receivable	1,800					
Prepaid Insurance	1,200			$100		
PPE - Equipment	8,300					
Accounts Payable		$1,250				
Unearned Revenue		2,000	$200			
Bank Loan		2,500				
Capital Account		10,300				
Owner's Drawings	2,000					
Service Revenue		3,300		200		
Rent Expense	800					
Telephone Expense	250					
Total	$19,350	$19,350				
Accumulated Depreciation - Equipment				140		
Interest Payable				25		
Depreciation Expense			140			
Insurance Expense			100			
Interest Expense			25			
Total			$465	$465		

FIGURE 6.7

As you may have noticed, the worksheet lists all the accounts and includes their debit or credit balances. It does not indicate whether each account is an asset, liability, owner's equity or income statement account because the worksheet has a different purpose. The purpose of the worksheet is to ensure that total debits equal total credits and to provide a template to record adjustments. Note that the accounts listed in the worksheet are still ordered in the same manner as in the chart of accounts.

Adjusted Trial Balance

After entering the adjustments in the worksheet, the adjustments are added or subtracted to the original balance in a new column called the adjusted trial balance. This provides the new totals of all accounts. Accounts that were not adjusted are just copied over to the adjusted trial balance. Once again, it is important to ensure that total debits equals total credits. Bear in mind that it is a difficult task to go back and find errors. Constant checking is necessary to ensure that all accounts remain in balance. The completed adjusted trial balance is shown in figure 6.8.

MP Consulting Worksheet January 31, 2014						
	Unadjusted Trial Balance		Adjustments		Adjusted Trial Balance	
Account	**Debit**	**Credit**	**Debit**	**Credit**	**Debit**	**Credit**
Cash	$5,000				$5,000	
Accounts Receivable	1,800				1,800	
Prepaid Insurance	1,200			$100	1,100	
PPE - Equipment	8,300				8,300	
Accumulated Depreciation - Equipment		$0		140		$140
Accounts Payable		1,250				1,250
Interest Payable		0		25		25
Unearned Revenue		2,000	$200			1,800
Bank Loan		2,500				2,500
Capital Account		10,300				10,300
Owner's Drawings	2,000				2,000	
Service Revenue		3,300		200		3,500
Depreciation Expense	0		140		140	
Insurance Expense	0		100		100	
Interest Expense	0		25		25	
Rent Expense	800				800	
Telephone Expense	250				250	
Total	$19,350	$19,350	$465	$465	$19,515	$19,515

FIGURE 6.8

This adjusted trial balance does not yet indicate whether the business is operating with an income or a loss. One further step is required to complete this process.

Income Statement and Balance Sheet

In figure 6.9, the income statement accounts are separated from the balance sheet and equity accounts. Notice that the initial debit and credit totals of the income statement accounts do not balance. This is expected because the company should report an income or loss. In this case, MP Consulting shows a greater credit balance (see numbers 1 and 2). Since the credit total is higher, they generated an income. Find the difference between the two figures and add the difference to the smaller total. In the case of MP Consulting, the difference is $2,185 (see number 3) and is added to the smaller debit total to get $3,500. This ensures the income statement columns balance

A similar process is completed for the balance sheet and equity columns. The difference is calculated and added to the smaller total (see number 4) to ensure the balance sheet and equity columns balance. Notice that the difference between the income statement columns and the difference between the balance sheet and equity columns are identical. This should always be the case. A net income will increase the capital account, therefore it will always be a credit to the balance sheet and equity accounts. Figure 6.9 shows the completed worksheet.

MP Consulting
Worksheet
January 31, 2014

Account	Unadjusted Trial Balance		Adjustments		Adjusted Trial Balance		Income Statement		Balance Sheet & Equity	
	Debit	Credit	Debit	Credit	Debit	Credit	Debit	Credit	Debit	Credit
Cash	$5,000				$5,000				$5,000	
Accounts Receivable	1,800				1,800				1,800	
Prepaid Insurance	1,200			$100	1,100				1,100	
PPE - Equipment	8,300				8,300				8,300	
Accumulated Depreciation - Equipment		$0		140		$140				$140
Accounts Payable		1,250				1,250				1,250
Interest Payable		0		25		25				25
Unearned Revenue		2,000	$200			1,800				1,800
Bank Loan		2,500				2,500				2,500
Capital Account		10,300				10,300				10,300
Owner's Drawings	2,000				2,000				2,000	
Service Revenue		3,300		200		3,500		$3,500		
Depreciation Expense	0		140		140		$140			
Insurance Expense	0		100		100		100			
Interest Expense	0		25		25		25			
Rent Expense	800				800		800			
Telephone Expense	250				250		❷ 250	❶		
Total	$19,350	$19,350	$465	$465	$19,515	$19,515	$1,315	$3,500	$18,200	$16,015
Net Income (Loss)							❸ 2,185			❹ 2,185
Total							$3,500	$3,500	$18,200	$18,200

FIGURE 6.9

Step 4 - Income Statement

Since the worksheet is a working paper for accountants, it is not meant to be read by external users of financial information. It is therefore important to create readable documents in the form of an income statement, a statement of owner's equity and a balance sheet.

The income statement takes the values from the income statement column of the worksheet and organizes them into a readable format that shows the net income or loss. To help stress the importance of preparing the adjustments in the worksheet, first look at the income statement in figure 6.10. This income statement was prepared before any adjustments were made. Net income shows $2,250.

MP Consulting Income Statement (Pre-Adjustment) For the Month Ended January 31, 2014		
Service Revenue		$3,300
Expenses		
Rent Expense	$800	
Telephone Expense	250	
Total Expenses		1,050
Net Income (Loss)		$2,250

FIGURE 6.10

After the adjustments, the income statement can be prepared properly. In figure 6.11, net income is properly reported as $2,185. If no adjustments were made, net income would have been overstated, which would have caused owner's equity to also be overstated.

MP Consulting Income Statement For the Month Ended January 31, 2014		
Service Revenue		$3,500
Expenses		
Depreciation Expense	$140	
Insurance Expense	100	
Interest Expense	25	
Rent Expense	800	
Telephone Expense	250	
Total Expenses		1,315
Net Income (Loss)		$2,185 ⓐ

FIGURE 6.11

Before moving on to the balance sheet, there is a statement to prepare that links the income statement to the balance sheet.

Statement of Owner's Equity

The statement of owner's equity reports any changes in equity over the reporting period. It is usually prepared as a separate statement but it can be included as a component of the balance sheet. The statement of owner's equity for MP Consulting is shown in figure 6.12.

MP Consulting Statement of Owner's Equity For the Month Ended January 31, 2014		
Capital Account at January 1		$5,300
Add:		
Additional Investment	$5,000	
Net Income	2,185 ⓐ	7,185
Subtotal		12,485
Less:		
Owner's Drawings		2,000
Capital Account at January 31		$10,485 ⓑ

FIGURE 6.12

The statement of owner's equity represents the change to owner's equity over the accounting period and thus is presented with a date format of an elapsed time period similar to the income statement.

The above statement is just a formal representation of the formula for ending owner's equity you learned in chapter 2.

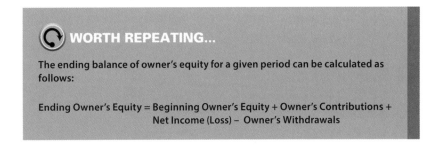

WORTH REPEATING...

The ending balance of owner's equity for a given period can be calculated as follows:

Ending Owner's Equity = Beginning Owner's Equity + Owner's Contributions + Net Income (Loss) – Owner's Withdrawals

The statement begins with the opening balance of the capital account (or owner's equity). In our example, the opening balance was $5,300 (see figure 5.6 from chapter 5) on January 1, 2014.

Owner's equity will increase if the owner invests more cash or assets into the business, or if the business earned a profit during the period. In our example, the owner invested $5,000 into the business during the month (see the transaction on January 5 from figure 5.7 in chapter 5). Notice the net income (marked 'a') from the income statement in figure 6.11 is also added.

The equity will decrease if the owner withdraws any capital (cash or assets) from the business for personal use, or if the business suffered a loss during the period. There was no loss in our example, but there was a $2,000 withdrawal, as shown in the worksheet under owner's drawings.

The final closing balance of the capital account is transferred to the owner's equity section of the balance sheet.

Step 5 - Balance Sheet

The balance sheet is prepared using the values from the balance sheet and equity column from the worksheet. Previous chapters showed the balance sheet organized horizontally, with assets beside liabilities and owner's equity. An alternate way, and the way balance sheets are most commonly presented, is vertically. Assets are listed above liabilities and owner's equity.

MP Consulting Balance Sheet As at January 31, 2014		
Assets		
Cash		$5,000
Accounts Receivable		1,800
Prepaid Insurance		1,100
PPE - Equipment	$8,300	
Accumulated Depreciation - Equipment	(140)	8,160
Total Assets		$16,060
Liabilities		
Accounts Payable	$1,250	
Interest Payable	25	
Unearned Revenue	1,800	
Bank Loan	2,500	
Total Liabilities		$5,575
Owner's Equity		
Capital Account		10,485 ⓑ
Total Liabilities and Owner's Equity		$16,060

FIGURE 6.13

Notice that the capital account (marked 'b') comes directly from the statement of owner's equity in figure 6.12 and not from the worksheet. The journal entries used to update the capital account will be demonstrated in the next section.

Examine how PPE - Equipment is presented. The accumulated depreciation is subtracted from the asset account, giving the book value of $8,160.

Now that the financial statements are prepared, the journal and the ledgers must be updated with the adjusting entries that appear in the adjustments column of the worksheet. These entries are made after the statements are completed so any errors can be detected and corrected. The entries are shown in figure 6.14. Remember that these amounts must be posted to the appropriate ledger accounts. The updated ledgers will be shown later in this chapter.

JOURNAL				Page 2
Date	**Account Title and Explanation**	**PR**	**Debit**	**Credit**
2014				
Jan 31	Interest Expense	520	25	
	Interest Payable	205		25
	Accrued interest on bank loan			
Jan 31	Insurance Expense	515	100	
	Prepaid Insurance	110		100
	Recognize one month of insurance			
Jan 31	Unearned Revenue	210	200	
	Service Revenue	400		200
	Recognize revenue previously unearned			
Jan 31	Depreciation Expense	510	140	
	Accumulated Depreciation - Equipment	125		140
	Record depreciation of PPE			

FIGURE 6.14

A CLOSER LOOK

The timing of journalizing the adjustments will differ from one company's accounting system to another. Some companies may record the adjustments in the journals immediately before the financial statements are prepared. This is done so that the journals and general ledgers reflect the information in the financial statements at the time the financial statements are prepared. Some companies even prefer journalizing the adjustments when the initial journal entries are prepared in step 1 of the accounting cycle. Ultimately, it depends on the preference of each business.

Step 6 - Post-Closing Trial Balance

The post-closing trial balance is prepared after the owner's equity account is updated to reflect the changes in the statement of owner's equity from figure 6.12. This process is called closing the books. **Closing the books** updates the capital account (owner's equity) and starts a new income statement for the next accounting period.

In a computerized accounting system, owner's equity is automatically updated with every related transaction that is entered into the system. In a manual accounting system, owner's equity is only updated at the end of the period. That means that all accounts that impact owner's equity must have their balances transferred to the capital account. Thus, revenue and expenses are considered to be temporary accounts because they are brought back to a zero balance at the end of each period. This is done so that a new income statement can be prepared for the next period with a fresh start.

Recall that an income statement reports net income (or net loss) for a specific period of time. For example, if MP Consulting had net income of $100,000 for a period ended December 31, 2014, this amount would relate exclusively to the period ended on that date and would not be carried over to the next period. Therefore, all revenue and expense accounts are classified as temporary. They must be cleared at the end of an accounting period to commence a new fiscal year.

Besides revenue and expenses, the drawings account is also a temporary account which needs to be closed at the end of the period. This is because the drawings account measures the amount the owner takes from the business during a specific accounting period and is used to calculate the value of owner's equity.

There are two methods to close the books, and we will use MP Consulting to illustrate both methods.

Option 1: Close Directly to the Capital Account

To illustrate the concept of closing entries, examine MP Consulting's balance sheet at the beginning of January 2014 (i.e. the end of December 2013). At the beginning of the period, MP Consulting's balance sheet was in balance, as shown in figure 6.15. This shows the balances before any journal entries were made for January 2014. T-Accounts are also used to illustrate the overall values of three categories: assets, liabilities and owner's equity.

MP Consulting Balance Sheet As at December 31, 2013			
ASSETS		**LIABILITIES**	
Cash	$3,000	Accounts Payable	$1,000
Prepaid Insurance	1,200	Unearned Revenue	900
PPE - Equipment	6,000	Bank Loan	3,000
		Total Liabilities	4,900
		OWNER'S EQUITY	
		Capital Account	5,300
TOTAL ASSETS	$10,200	**TOTAL LIABILITIES & EQUITY**	$10,200

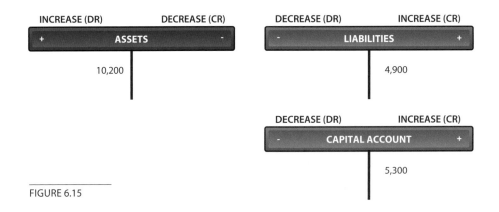

FIGURE 6.15

Notice what happens when we provide services to a customer who pays cash:

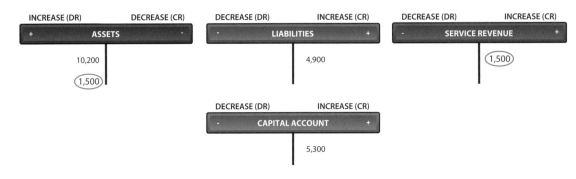

FIGURE 6.16

The balance sheet is now out of balance because assets have increased, but the capital account has not been updated. A similar discrepancy occurs if a telephone bill is received and will be paid later.

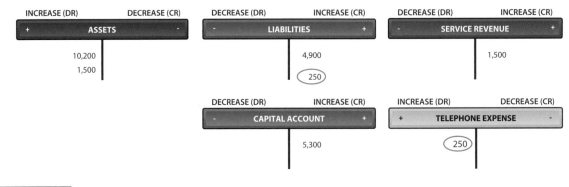

FIGURE 6.17

To get the balance sheet back into balance, the capital account must be updated with the revenue and expense transactions. To do this, the revenue account must be closed by decreasing revenue and increasing the capital account. The revenue account is now reduced to a zero balance.

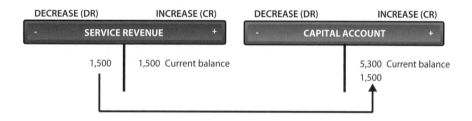

FIGURE 6.18

The expense account must also be closed by decreasing the expense and decreasing the capital account. The expense account is now reduced to zero.

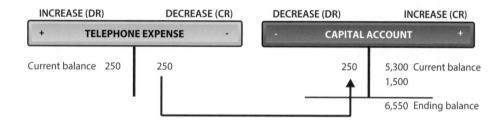

FIGURE 6.19

The end result is that the capital account will have a new balance and assets will equal liabilities plus owner's equity.

To see how to close the books for MP Consulting, we will use the adjusted trial balance on the worksheet, which shows all the balances we need. It is shown again in figure 6.20.

MP Consulting Adjusted Trial Balance January 31, 2014		
Account	**Debit**	**Credit**
Cash	$5,000	
Accounts Receivable	1,800	
Prepaid Insurance	1,100	
PPE - Equipment	8,300	
Accumulated Depreciation - Equipment		$140
Accounts Payable		1,250
Interest Payable		25
Unearned Revenue		1,800
Bank Loan		2,500
Capital Account		10,300
Owner's Drawings	2,000	❸
Service Revenue		3,500 ❶
Depreciation Expense	140	
Insurance Expense	100	
Interest Expense	25	❷
Rent Expense	800	
Telephone Expense	250	
Total	**$19,515**	**$19,515**

FIGURE 6.20

Notice that the revenue balance is a credit, the expense balances are debits and the owner's drawings balance is also a debit. To reset (close) the balances back to zero in order to prepare for the next accounting period, we must decrease the value of each of these accounts. Thus, revenue will be debited, expenses will be credited and owner's drawings will be credited. In the context of closing entries, the terms "close", "reset" and "zero out" can be used interchangeably.

Figure 6.21 illustrates the journal entries to close the accounts directly to the capital account. The steps involved are explained below.

JOURNAL				Page 3
Date 2014	**Account Title and Explanation**	**PR**	**Debit**	**Credit**
Jan 31	Service Revenue	400	3,500		❶
	Capital Account	300		3,500
	To close revenue			
Jan 31	Capital Account	300	1,315	
	Depreciation Expense	510		140
	Insurance Expense	515		100
	Interest Expense	520		25	❷
	Rent Expense	540		800
	Telephone Expense	550		250
	To close expenses			
Jan 31	Capital Account	300	2,000	
	Owner's Drawings	310		2,000	❸
	To close owner's drawings			

FIGURE 6.21

Step 1: Zero out the revenue account

The transaction is recorded by debiting (decreasing) the current revenue balance with $3,500 and crediting (increasing) the capital account with the same amount. The revenue account is now reduced to zero.

Step 2: Zero out the expense accounts

The transaction is recorded by crediting (decreasing) the current expense balances and debiting (decreasing) owner's capital account with the total of all expense amounts. The expense accounts are now reduced to zero. Notice in figure 6.21 that instead of closing each expense account individually to the capital account, all expenses were listed in one transaction. This saves time and effort (imagine if the company had 50 or more expenses). The debit to the capital account is the total of all the expenses.

Step 3: Zero out the owner's drawings account

The transaction is recorded by crediting (decreasing) the current owner's drawings balance with $2,000 and debiting (decreasing) the capital account with the same amount. The owner's drawings account is now reduced to zero.

Net Result

The capital account has been increased by the total revenue and decreased by the total expenses and the owner's drawings. The new balance is $10,485. This is the same figure shown as the ending value on the statement of owner's equity from figure 6.12.

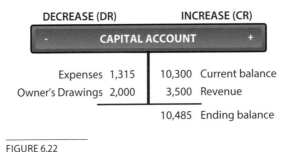

FIGURE 6.22

Option 2: Close Using the Income Summary

Instead of debiting and crediting the owner's equity account directly, some accountants use an account called income summary to calculate the change in equity with one summary entry. Using our T-Account example, the summary shown in the figure below would work as follows:

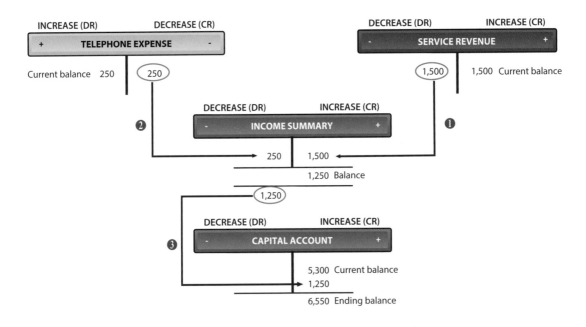

FIGURE 6.23

1. Debit revenue to clear the account and credit the income summary.
2. Credit expenses to clear the account and debit the income summary.
3. Calculate a profit or loss. Credit owner's capital and debit income summary with the net income amount, or debit owner's capital and credit income summary with the net loss amount.

The income summary is only used to close the revenue and expense accounts. The owner's drawings account is not closed through the income summary account because owner's withdrawals do not affect the amount of net income or net loss.

Using the adjusted trial balance amounts for our existing company (figure 6.20), the closing entries are presented as shown in the journal below:

JOURNAL				Page 3
Date	**Account Title and Explanation**	**PR**	**Debit**	**Credit**
2014				
Jan 31	Service Revenue	400	3,500	
	Income Summary	315		3,500
	To close revenue			
Jan 31	Income Summary	315	1,315	
	Depreciation Expense	510		140
	Insurance Expense	515		100
	Interest Expense	520		25
	Rent Expense	540		800
	Telephone Expense	550		250
	To close expenses			
Jan 31	Income Summary	315	2,185	
	Capital Account	300		2,185
	To close Income Summary			
Jan 31	Capital Account	300	2,000	
	Owner's Drawings	310		2,000
	To close owner's drawings			

FIGURE 6.24

The first two transactions are nearly the same as shown in option 1 (figure 6.21), except that the income summary account is used instead of the capital account.

The third transaction is used to close the income summary to the capital account. The value is the difference ($2,185) between the revenue and expenses accounts. Note that $2,185 is the same value shown on the worksheet in figure 6.9 when calculating the difference in the income summary column. It is also the net income reported on the income statement in figure 6.11.

The last transaction is identical to the one shown in option 1 (figure 6.21).

Remember, all journal entries must be posted to the general ledger. Assuming MP Consulting uses option 2 to close their books, the following figure shows how the ledger accounts would look at the end of the period. All journal entries from chapter 5 and the adjustments and closing entries from this chapter are reflected here. Notice that adjustments and closing entries have a description to make them stand out in the ledger.

GENERAL LEDGER

Account: Cash — GL. No. 101

Date	Description	PR	Debit	Credit	Balance	
2014						
Jan 1	Opening Balance				3,000	DR
Jan 2		J1	1,500		4,500	DR
Jan 3		J1		800	3,700	DR
Jan 5		J1	5,000		8,700	DR
Jan 7		J1		2,300	6,400	DR
Jan 16		J1		500	5,900	DR
Jan 19		J1	1,100		7,000	DR
Jan 30		J1		2,000	5,000	DR

Account: Accounts Receivable — GL. No. 105

Date	Description	PR	Debit	Credit	Balance	
2014						
Jan 1	Opening Balance				0	DR
Jan 10		J1	1,800		1,800	DR

Account: Prepaid Insurance — GL. No. 110

Date	Description	PR	Debit	Credit	Balance	
2014						
Jan 1	Opening Balance				1,200	DR
Jan 31	Adjustment	J2		100	1,100	DR

Account: PPE - Equipment — GL. No. 120

Date	Description	PR	Debit	Credit	Balance	
2014						
Jan 1	Opening Balance				6,000	DR
Jan 7		J1	2,300		8,300	DR

Account: Accumulated Depreciation - Equipment — GL. No. 125

Date	Description	PR	Debit	Credit	Balance	
2014						
Jan 31	Adjustment	J2		140	140	CR

Account: Accounts Payable — GL. No. 200

Date	Description	PR	Debit	Credit	Balance	
2014						
Jan 1	Opening Balance				1,000	CR
Jan 20		J1		250	1,250	CR

Account: Interest Payable — GL. No. 205

Date	Description	PR	Debit	Credit	Balance	
2014						
Jan 31	Adjustment	J2		25	25	CR

Account: Unearned Revenue — GL. No. 210

Date	Description	PR	Debit	Credit	Balance	
2014						
Jan 1	Opening Balance				900	CR
Jan 19		J1		1,100	2,000	CR
Jan 31	Adjustment	J2	200		1,800	CR

Account: Bank Loan — GL. No. 215

Date	Description	PR	Debit	Credit	Balance	
2014						
Jan 1	Opening Balance				3,000	CR
Jan 16		J1	500		2,500	CR

Account: Capital Account — GL. No. 300

Date	Description	PR	Debit	Credit	Balance	
2014						
Jan 1	Opening Balance				5,300	CR
Jan 5		J1		5,000	10,300	CR
Jan 31	Closing Entry	J3		2,185	12,485	CR
Jan 31	Closing Entry	J3	2,000		10,485	CR

Account: Owner's Drawings					GL. No.	310	
Date	Description	PR	Debit	Credit	Balance	
2014						
Jan 30		J1	2,000		2,000	DR
Jan 31	Closing Entry	J3		2,000	0	DR

Account: Income Summary					GL. No.	315	
Date	Description	PR	Debit	Credit	Balance	
2014						
Jan 31	Closing Entry	J3		3,500	3,500	CR
Jan 31	Closing Entry	J3	1,315		2,185	CR
Jan 31	Closing Entry	J3	2,185		0	CR

Account: Service Revenue					GL. No.	400	
Date	Description	PR	Debit	Credit	Balance	
2014						
Jan 2		J1		1,500	1,500	CR
Jan 10		J1		1,800	3,300	CR
Jan 31	Adjustment	J2		200	3,500	CR
Jan 31	Closing Entry	J3	3,500		0	CR

Account: Depreciation Expense					GL. No.	510	
Date	Description	PR	Debit	Credit	Balance	
2014						
Jan 31	Adjustment	J2	140		140	DR
Jan 31	Closing Entry	J3		140	0	DR

Account: Insurance Expense					GL. No.	515	
Date	Description	PR	Debit	Credit	Balance	
2014						
Jan 31	Adjustment	J2	100		100	DR
Jan 31	Closing Entry	J3		100	0	DR

Account: Interest Expense					GL. No.	520	
Date	Description	PR	Debit	Credit	Balance	
2014						
Jan 31	Adjustment	J2	25		25	DR
Jan 31	Closing Entry	J3		25	0	DR

Account: Rent Expense					GL. No. 540	
Date	Description	PR	Debit	Credit	Balance	
2014						
Jan 3		J1	800		800	DR
Jan 31	Closing Entry	J3		800	0	DR

Account: Telephone Expense					GL. No. 550	
Date	Description	PR	Debit	Credit	Balance	
2014						
Jan 20		J1	250		250	DR
Jan 31	Closing Entry	J3		250	0	DR

FIGURE 6.25

Post-Closing Trial Balance

Once the closing entries are completed, it is necessary to ensure that the balance sheet still balances. This is done by completing another trial balance called the post-closing trial balance. The **post-closing trial balance** only lists accounts that have a balance. Since the closing entries have been journalized and posted, only assets, liabilities and the capital account should have a balance. The post-closing trial balance is shown in figure 6.26.

MP Consulting Post-Closing Trial Balance January 31, 2014		
Account	**Debit**	**Credit**
Cash	$5,000	
Accounts Receivable	1,800	
Prepaid Insurance	1,100	
PPE - Equipment	8,300	
Accumulated Depreciation - Equipment		$140
Accounts Payable		1,250
Interest Payable		25
Unearned Revenue		1,800
Bank Loan		2,500
Capital Account		10,485
Total	$16,200	$16,200

FIGURE 6.26

Once the post-closing trial balance is complete, the entire accounting cycle for the period is done. The company is ready to begin the next accounting cycle for the upcoming accounting period.

The Evolution from Manual to Computerized Accounting

One of the challenges in teaching a modern accounting course is the need to combine traditional concepts and methods with modern technology. However, the reality is that today's accounting students may never see or use an actual accounting ledger.

Although computerized systems are becoming more common, and while they make gathering and analyzing information easier for the accountant, having a sound knowledge of traditional paper-based systems provides a foundation for understanding what accounting is all about. This book has therefore been designed to combine the new with the old — to use the foundations of accounting theory and apply them to the realities of modern accounting practice.

Before the advent of computers, bookkeepers used various types of journals to maintain company financial records. The main books required were the following:

Special journals: individual journals that were used to record similar repetitive activities on a regular basis – for example, sales and purchases journals.

General journal: used to record transactions that did not occur on a regular basis or with sufficient volume to justify maintaining a separate book. However, in modern accounting systems, all business activities are recorded in one journal, known as the general journal.

General ledger: used as the main accounting record in which information was extracted from the other journals and grouped together into various accounts.

Journals included sales, purchases, payroll, cash receipts, cash payments...

The journals are combined into one double-entry bookkeeping book called the general ledger, so that records can be easily accessed and sorted by account.

Useful information required to operate the business can be extracted from the general ledger.

FIGURE 6.27

In manual systems, recording procedures often provide the analytical structure for the accountant. If accounts receivable needs analyzing, the accountant would refer to all related journals and ledgers. If, on the other hand, inventory is being analyzed, the paper trail from receipt to shipping would be tracked accordingly.

In most modern computerized systems, however, the accounting logic is already built into the software. There is no need to keep a separate set of books and documents for specific types of transactions. Instead, every transaction is input into the system to produce one central database (general ledger). The software will then process the information, transfer it to the correct location and produce the report that the accountant wants at any given time.

Some examples of reports that can be generated with a few clicks of a mouse are:

- Financial statements
- Aged accounts receivable and payable listings
- Detailed product inventory listings
- Detailed long-term asset reports containing asset cost and depreciation schedules
- Breakdown of sales by product, department and division
- Breakdown of expense accounts
- Loan payment schedules

It is the responsibility of management and the accounting department to work with information technology personnel to buy or design a system that meets organizational objectives. Manual systems help accountants learn the basics of their profession; however, in today's business world, a properly designed computer system, tailored to the needs of a specific company, can make accounting more efficient.

Modern Accounting Systems

IN THE REAL WORLD

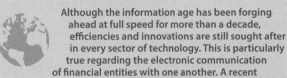

Although the information age has been forging ahead at full speed for more than a decade, efficiencies and innovations are still sought after in every sector of technology. This is particularly true regarding the electronic communication of financial entities with one another. A recent development – namely, the development of Extensible Business Reporting Language, or XBRL, may constitute a significant advance. XBRL is a new computer language that will help to facilitate the exchange of financial information in all sectors of the economy.

XBRL essentially packages bits of financial information, standardizes this information and makes it easier to use and manipulate. The ramifications of this type of development are almost unlimited. Companies can use XBRL to publish financial reports for the public. Governments and regulators can use XBRL to receive and transmit information. Stock exchanges can serve as a conduit between business and government in exchanging financial information quickly and easily. Software companies can create various IT solutions for specific sectors.

XBRL will transform the communication of financial information in the same way that highways did for the transportation of people in vehicles. This new information system is upon us already.

Both manual and computerized accounting systems require a paper trail or an electronic trail of information, starting with the **source documents**. Source documents come in many forms for various business transactions. The most common examples are associated with accounts receivable and accounts payable, such as invoices and purchase orders. The information obtained from the source documents are recorded in entries made in the general journal, followed by posting to the general ledger.

Some computerized systems require an initial manual entry of source documents into the system, whereas other systems have moved away from paper documents altogether. For example, *Electronic Data Interchange* (EDI) is a computerized system that allows companies to transfer electronic information to one another. Sending an invoice electronically to a customer is one potential use of this system.

In the early days of manual bookkeeping, it was difficult and time-consuming to extract a sales report from the sales journal or to determine how much was owing to a vendor. With modern computerized systems, the logic of accounting is already built into the software. The software processes the information almost instantaneously and transfers it when and where it is needed.

Ethics and Controls

The need for adjusting entries provides management an opportunity to unethically manage the financial performance and position of the company. For example, consider the accrual of interest on a bank loan. Management should not wait until the interest is payable to accrue interest. Interest should be accrued at the end of an accounting period and thus reflected as interest expense on the income statement. If management fails to accrue interest at the end of an accounting period, the financial statements will understate liabilities (since accrued interest is understated) and overstate net income (since interest expense is understated). This will provide investors and creditors an incorrect representation of the company's performance and debt position.

As an internal control, management should review the terms of the debt contracts for all outstanding long-term liabilities at the end of an accounting period. This will provide management with a reasonable idea of what the interest expense should be for the period after including accrued interest as well.

In Summary

⇨ In the accounting cycle, after the first trial balance is prepared, the worksheet needs to be created.

⇨ The worksheet includes the unadjusted trial balance, adjustments and the adjusted trial balance.

⇨ The purpose of the worksheet is to ensure total debits equal total credits and to provide a template to record adjustments.

⇨ Following the completion of the adjusted trial balance, the financial statements are prepared (income statement, statement of owner's equity and balance sheet).

⇨ The adjustments are journalized after the preparation of the financial statements.

⇨ Closing the books: the income statement needs to be zeroed out at the end of each fiscal year, and a new income statement commenced for the next accounting period.

⇨ There are two ways to close the income statement accounts:

  ✦ Close directly to owner's capital

  ✦ Close to an intermediary income summary account

⇨ A post-closing trial balance is created after the books are closed.

⇨ The adjustments and closing entries should all be reflected in the general ledger as well.

⇨ Both manual and computerized accounting systems require a paper (or electronic) trail of information, starting with source documents.

Review Exercise

CG Accounting provides bookkeeping services to small and mid-sized companies. The company was introduced in the review exercise from chapter 5. Before you begin this exercise, familiarize yourself with the review exercise in chapter 5 since this is a continuation.

The journal entries for the month of June have already been entered in the journal and posted to the ledger. The trial balance, before adjustments, is presented below.

CG Accounting Trial Balance June 30, 2014		
Account	**Debit**	**Credit**
Cash	$5,550	
Accounts Receivable	4,600	
Prepaid Insurance	1,200	
PPE - Equipment	6,000	
Accounts Payable		$2,750
Unearned Revenue		900
Bank Loan		3,050
Capital Account		9,400
Owner's Drawings	1,000	
Service Revenue		3,600
Advertising Expense	450	
Professional Fees Expense	900	
Total	$19,700	$19,700

The balance of owner's equity as at May 31, 2014 was $6,400. Also recall from the chapter 5 review exercise that during June the owner contributed $3,000 cash to the business and withdrew $1,000 cash for personal use.

CG Accounting uses the following accounts and accounting numbers in their accounting records:

Account Description	Account #
ASSETS	
Cash	101
Accounts Receivable	105
Prepaid Insurance	110
PPE - Equipment	120
Accumulated Depreciation - Equipment	125
LIABILITIES	
Accounts Payable	200
Interest Payable	205
Unearned Revenue	210
Bank Loan	215
OWNER'S EQUITY	
Capital Account	300
Owner's Drawings	310
Income Summary	315

Account Description	Account #
REVENUE	
Service Revenue	400
EXPENSES	
Advertising Expense	500
Bad Debts Expense	505
Depreciation Expense	510
Insurance Expense	515
Interest Expense	520
Maintenance Expense	525
Office Supplies Expense	530
Professional Fees Expense	535
Rent Expense	540
Salaries Expense	545
Telephone Expense	550
Travel Expense	555

At the end of June 2014, CG accounting had to make the following adjustments:

Jun 30   One month of the insurance policy ($100) has been used.

Jun 30   Earned $450 of the unearned revenue.

Jun 30   Accrued $20 interest on the bank loan.

Jun 30   PPE - Equipment depreciated by $125.

Required:

a) Complete the worksheet.

b) Complete the journal entries for the adjusting entries and post them to the general ledger.

c) Prepare the income statement, statement of owner's equity and balance sheet.

d) Compete the closing entries using the income summary account and post them to the general ledger.

e) Prepare the post-closing trial balance.

a) Complete the worksheet.

CG Accounting
Worksheet
June 30, 2014

Account	Unadjusted Trial Balance Debit	Unadjusted Trial Balance Credit	Adjustments Debit	Adjustments Credit	Adjusted Trial Balance Debit	Adjusted Trial Balance Credit	Income Statement Debit	Income Statement Credit	Balance Sheet & Equity Debit	Balance Sheet & Equity Credit
Cash	$5,550				$5,550				$5,550	
Accounts Receivable	4,600				4,600				4,600	
Prepaid Insurance	1,200			$100	1,100				1,100	
PPE - Equipment	6,000				6,000				6,000	
Accumulated Depreciation - Equipment		$0		125		$125				$125
Accounts Payable		2,750				2,750				2,750
Interest Payable		0		20		20				20
Unearned Revenue		900	$450			450				450
Bank Loan		3,050				3,050				3,050
Capital Account		9,400				9,400				9,400
Owner's Drawings	1,000				1,000				1,000	
Service Revenue		3,600		450		4,050		$4,050		
Advertising Expense	450				450		$450			
Depreciation Expense	0		125		125		125			
Insurance Expense	0		100		100		100			
Interest Expense	0		20		20		20			
Rent Expense	900				900		900			
Total	$19,700	$19,700	$695	$695	$19,845	$19,845	1,595	4,050	18,250	15,795
Net Income							2,455			2,455
Total							$4,050	$4,050	$18,250	$18,250

b) Prepare the adjusting journal entries. (The ledger will be shown later).

JOURNAL				Page 2
Date	**Account Title and Explanation**	**PR**	**Debit**	**Credit**
2014				
Jun 30	Insurance Expense	515	100	
	Prepaid Insurance	110		100
	Recognized one month of insurance used			
Jun 30	Unearned Revenue	210	450	
	Service Revenue	400		450
	Recognized revenue previously unearned			
Jun 30	Interest Expense	520	20	
	Interest Payable	205		20
	Accrued interest on bank loan			
Jun 30	Depreciation Expense	510	125	
	Accumulated Depreciation - Equipment	125		125
	Recorded depreciation of PPE			

c) Prepare the income statement, statement of owner's equity and balance sheet.

CG Accounting Income Statement For the Month Ended June 30, 2014		
Service Revenue		$4,050
Expenses		
Advertising Expense	$450	
Depreciation Expense	125	
Insurance Expense	100	
Interest Expense	20	
Rent Expense	900	
Total Expenses		1,595
Net Income (Loss)		$2,455

CG Accounting Statement of Owner's Equity For the Month Ended June 30, 2014		
Capital Account at June 1		$6,400
Add:		
Additional Investment	$3,000	
Net Income	2,455	5,455
Subtotal		11,855
Less:		
Owner's Drawings		1,000
Capital Account at June 30		$10,855

CG Accounting Balance Sheet As at June 30, 2014		
Assets		
Cash		$5,550
Accounts Receivable		4,600
Prepaid Insurance		1,100
PPE - Equipment	$6,000	
Accumulated Depreciation - Equipment	(125)	5,875
Total Assets		$17,125
Liabilities		
Accounts Payable	$2,750	
Interest Payable	20	
Unearned Revenue	450	
Bank Loan	3,050	
Total Liabilities		$6,270
Owner's Equity		
Capital Account		10,855
Total Liabilities and Owner's Equity		$17,125

d) Complete the closing entries using the income summary account and post them to the general ledger.

JOURNAL				Page 3
Date	**Account Title and Explanation**	**PR**	**Debit**	**Credit**
2014				
Jun 30	Service Revenue	400	4,050	
	Income Summary	315		4,050
	Close revenue to income summary			
Jun 30	Income Summary	315	1,595	
	Advertising Expense	500		450
	Depreciation Expense	510		125
	Insurance Expense	515		100
	Interest Expense	520		20
	Rent Expense	540		900
	Close expenses to income summary			
Jun 30	Income Summary	315	2,455	
	Capital Account	300		2,455
	Close income summary to capital			
Jun 30	Capital Account	300	1,000	
	Owner's Drawings	310		1,000
	Close drawings to capital			

GENERAL LEDGER						
Account: Cash					**GL. No.**	**101**
Date	**Description**	**PR**	**Debit**	**Credit**	**Balance**	
2014						
Jun 1	Opening Balance				4,200	DR
Jun 1		J1		900	3,300	DR
Jun 3		J1		1,200	2,100	DR
Jun 6		J1	2,100		4,200	DR
Jun 13		J1	3,000		7,200	DR
Jun 16		J1	300		7,500	DR
Jun 23		J1		950	6,550	DR
Jun 30		J1		1,000	5,550	DR

Account: Accounts Receivable — GL. No. 105

Date	Description	PR	Debit	Credit	Balance	
2014						
Jun 1	Opening Balance				3,100	DR
Jun 18		J1	1,500		4,600	DR

Account: Prepaid Insurance — GL. No. 110

Date	Description	PR	Debit	Credit	Balance	
2014						
Jun 1	Opening Balance				0	DR
Jun 3		J1	1,200		1,200	DR
Jun 30	Adjusting Entry	J2		100	1,100	DR

Account: PPE - Equipment — GL. No. 120

Date	Description	PR	Debit	Credit	Balance	
2014						
Jun 1	Opening Balance				6,000	DR

Account: Accumulated Depreciation - Equipment — GL. No. 125

Date	Description	PR	Debit	Credit	Balance	
2014						
Jun 30	Adjusting Entry	J2		125	125	CR

Account: Accounts Payable — GL. No. 200

Date	Description	PR	Debit	Credit	Balance	
2014						
Jun 1	Opening Balance				2,300	CR
Jun 11		J1		450	2,750	CR

Account: Interest Payable — GL. No. 205

Date	Description	PR	Debit	Credit	Balance	
2014						
Jun 30	Adjusting Entry	J2		20	20	CR

Account: Unearned Revenue — GL. No. 210

Date	Description	PR	Debit	Credit	Balance	
2014						
Jun 1	Opening Balance				600	CR
Jun 16		J1		300	900	CR
Jun 30	Adjusting Entry	J2	450		450	CR

Account: Bank Loan   GL. No.   215

Date	Description	PR	Debit	Credit	Balance	
2014						
Jun 1	Opening Balance				4,000	CR
Jun 23		J1	950		3,050	CR

Account: Capital Account   GL. No.   300

Date	Description	PR	Debit	Credit	Balance	
2014						
Jun 1	Opening Balance				6,400	CR
Jun 13		J1		3,000	9,400	CR
Jun 30	Closing Entry	J3		2,455	11,855	CR
Jun 30	Closing Entry	J3	1,000		10,855	CR

Account: Owner's Drawings   GL. No.   310

Date	Description	PR	Debit	Credit	Balance	
2014						
Jun 30		J1	1,000		1,000	DR
Jun 30	Closing Entry	J3		1,000	0	DR

Account: Income Summary   GL. No.   315

Date	Description	PR	Debit	Credit	Balance	
2014						
Jun 30	Closing Entry	J3		4,050	4,050	CR
Jun 30	Closing Entry	J3	1,595		2,455	CR
Jun 30	Closing Entry	J3	2,455		0	CR

Account: Service Revenue   GL. No.   400

Date	Description	PR	Debit	Credit	Balance	
2014						
Jun 6		J1		2,100	2,100	CR
Jun 18		J1		1,500	3,600	CR
Jun 30	Adjusting Entry	J2		450	4,050	CR
Jun 30	Closing Entry	J3	4,050		0	CR

Account: Advertising Expense   GL. No.   500

Date	Description	PR	Debit	Credit	Balance	
2014						
Jun 11		J1	450		450	DR
Jun 30	Closing Entry	J3		450	0	DR

Account: Depreciation Expense   GL. No.   510

Date	Description	PR	Debit	Credit	Balance	
2014						
Jun 30	Adjusting Entry	J2	125		125	DR
Jun 30	Closing Entry	J3		125	0	DR

Account: Insurance Expense   GL. No.   515

Date	Description	PR	Debit	Credit	Balance	
2014						
Jun 30	Adjusting Entry	J2	100		100	DR
Jun 30	Closing Entry	J3		100	0	DR

Account: Interest Expense   GL. No.   520

Date	Description	PR	Debit	Credit	Balance	
2014						
Jun 30	Adjusting Entry	J2	20		20	DR
Jun 30	Closing Entry	J3		20	0	DR

Account: Rent Expense   GL. No.   540

Date	Description	PR	Debit	Credit	Balance	
2014						
Jun 1		J1	900		900	DR
Jun 30	Closing Entry	J3		900	0	DR

e) Prepare the post-closing trial balance.

CG Accounting Post-Closing Trial Balance June 30, 2014		
Account	**Debit**	**Credit**
Cash	$5,550	
Accounts Receivable	4,600	
Prepaid Insurance	1,100	
PPE - Equipment	6,000	
Accumulated Depreciation - Equipment		$125
Accounts Payable		2,750
Interest Payable		20
Unearned Revenue		450
Bank Loan		3,050
Capital Account		10,855
Total	$17,250	$17,250

Chapter 7
MERCHANDISING CORPORATION

LEARNING OUTCOMES:

❶ Record the initial capital investment for a business

❷ Understand how net income (loss) affects retained earnings and stockholders' equity

❸ Describe the difference between the perpetual and the periodic inventory systems

❹ Explain cost of goods sold and how it is recorded

❺ Calculate gross profit and gross margin percentage

❻ Prepare a classified balance sheet and a multistep income statement

Financing a Business

So far, our discussion of accounting has focused on sole proprietorships that provided a service. To start a proprietorship, cash and assets must be invested by the owner or borrowed from a third party. Usually, the owner will have access to limited cash and credit.

A **merchandising business** can be defined as any business that buys and sells product for the purpose of making a profit. Examples of merchandising businesses include retailers and wholesalers. A **manufacturing business** turns raw materials into new products for resale. Examples of manufacturing businesses include steel manufacturers and auto makers. We will focus on merchandising in this chapter. While a service business may be able to start up with a minimal investment from the owner, merchandisers require much more capital to start their operations. Cash would be required to lease a building, purchase inventory and store inventory.

An option available to owners is to set up the business as a corporation. A corporation allows many individuals to invest cash into the business in exchange for part ownership. Ownership is indicated in the form of **stock,** also called *contributed capital*. Each unit of stock is called *a share of stock*. The more shares an individual owns, the greater the piece of the organization's profit he or she is entitled to.

To demonstrate how to set up a new merchandising company as a corporation, assume that two owners will invest cash into the business in exchange for stock.

Owner 1 will contribute $70,000, and Owner 2 will contribute $30,000. This means that Owner 1 will own 70% of the business and Owner 2 will own 30%. If the owners agree that 100 shares of stock will be issued by the corporation, Owner 1 will receive 70 shares of stock and Owner 2 will receive 30 shares of stock. Suppose that they will also borrow $50,000 from the bank to meet their initial setup requirements. This loan will be paid back over five years.

The transactions for owners' investments and bank loan arrangement are shown in figure 7.1:

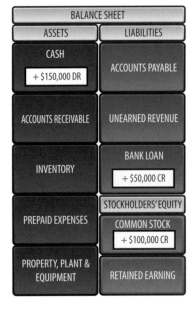

BALANCE SHEET	
ASSETS	LIABILITIES
CASH + $150,000 DR	ACCOUNTS PAYABLE
ACCOUNTS RECEIVABLE	UNEARNED REVENUE
INVENTORY	BANK LOAN + $50,000 CR
PREPAID EXPENSES	STOCKHOLDERS' EQUITY COMMON STOCK + $100,000 CR
PROPERTY, PLANT & EQUIPMENT	RETAINED EARNING

Stockholders' equity increases by $100,000

JOURNAL			Page 1
Date	Account Title and Explanation	Debit	Credit
Jan 1	Cash	100,000	
	Common Stock		100,000
	Investment made by owners		

JOURNAL			Page 1
Date	Account Title and Explanation	Debit	Credit
Jan 1	Cash	50,000	
	Bank Loan Payable		50,000
	Received loan from bank		

FIGURE 7.1

The owner's equity category in a corporation goes by a different name. It is called **stockholders' equity** and shows how much of the business is owned by the owners, or stockholders. Stockholders' equity is composed of at least two parts: contributed capital and retained earnings.

1. Contributed capital represent money invested directly in a company by its owners, who received shares of the company in return. Contributed capital will have different types of stock such as common or preferred, depending on the corporation. At this point, only common stock will be used and shown in the accounting map.

2. **Retained earnings** represent all the profits that the business has retained (i.e. not paid to the owners).

Common Stock + Retained Earnings = Stockholders' Equity

Although there are some different terms involved with a corporation, there are a number of similarities between a proprietorship and a corporation. The capital account in a proprietorship is similar to retained earnings. The owner's drawings account is similar to dividends. **Dividends** are payments made to stockholders from the profits of the company. The dividend amount is divided among the stockholders in proportion to the amount of stock they own. It is generally paid in cash, but can also be paid in the form of more stock. Dividends are usually discretionary, which means that the corporation can choose when to pay out dividends and in what amounts. In other words, paying dividends is not a contractual obligation.

Here is an example of how the stockholders' equity would change after the initial investment of $100,000 by the owners.

Year 1

The company earns net income of $10,000 in the first year of operations. The owners decide not to distribute the net income, but rather to retain it in the company (see part B in figure 7.2 below).

Year 2

The company earns net income of $20,000. This time the owners decide to distribute $5,000 of the net income to themselves. This payment is called a dividend.

In this example, Owner 1 will receive $3,500 ($5,000 total dividend x 70% share = $3,500) and Owner 2 will receive $1,500 ($5,000 total dividend x 30% share = $1,500). The remaining net income of $15,000 will be retained in the company. This amount will be added to the previous $10,000 of retained earnings to reflect the new balance of $25,000 (see part C in figure 7.2 below).

Year 3

The company suffers a net loss of $12,000. Retained earnings will decrease by the amount of the net loss reported in the income statement (see part D in figure 7.2 below).

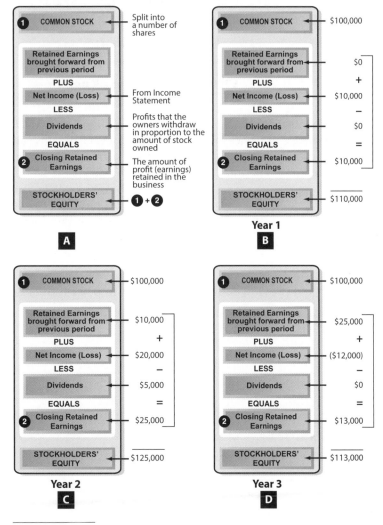

FIGURE 7.2

Merchandising Sales

A merchandising business purchases products and resells them at a higher price to make profits. Products that are purchased by the merchandising business for resale purposes are called **inventory**. Inventory is listed as an asset on the merchandiser's balance sheet. When the inventory is sold, its cost, known as **cost of goods sold (COGS)**, is matched against the value of the sale. Cost of goods sold is an expense account and is shown on the income statement below sales revenue. The difference between the selling price of the product and the cost of goods sold is called **gross profit**. Gross profit is used to cover all other expenses incurred in operating the business. **Operating expenses** are the expenses incurred in promoting and selling products or services and in running the operations that make and sell the products or services.

To see how revenue, cost of goods sold, gross profit and operating expenses interact, consider the following example. A business purchases T-shirts for $5.00 each and plans to sell them for $7.00 each. The business also incurs a variety of operating expenses, totaling $700. Figure 7.3 shows the results of selling 200 T-shirts.

Operating expenses of the business:	
1. Travel	$100
2. Business Cards	100
3. Flyers for Advertising	300
4. Temporary rental space	200
Total Operating Expenses	**$700**

Sell 200 T-shirts:	
Total sales (200 x $7.00)	**$1,400**
Less Cost of Goods Sold	1,000
= Gross Profit	**400**
Less Operating Expenses	700
= Net Income (Loss)	**($300)**

Every business has various monthly operating expenses that will occur regardless of services or products sold. The sale of merchandise, less merchandise cost, contributes toward paying these expenses.

Remember, these T-shirts may have been purchased several months earlier. You are now recognizing (matching) the cost of the shirts against the value of the sale. If you only sell 200 T-shirts (COGS = 200 x $5.00), there is not enough gross profit to pay operating expenses, resulting in a net loss of $300.

FIGURE 7.3

You need to sell more T-shirts to provide enough gross profit to pay for operating expenses. Figure 7.4 shows the results of selling 350 T-shirts and 500 T-shirts.

Sell 350 T-shirts:

Total sales (350 x $7.00)	$2,450
Less Cost of Goods Sold	1,750
= **Gross Profit**	**700**
Less Operating Expenses	700
= **Net Income (Loss)**	**$0**

By selling 350 T-shirts (COGS = 350 x $5.00), you manage to break even (which means that revenues equal expense). Therefore, you have not produced net income or suffered a net loss).

Sell 500 T-shirts:

Total sales (500 x $7.00)	$3,500
Less Cost of Goods Sold	2,500
= **Gross Profit**	**1,000**
Less Operating Expenses	700
= **Net Income (Loss)**	**$300**

By selling 500 T-shirts (COGS = 500 x $5.00), you have made sufficient gross profit to cover operating expenses and produce net income.

FIGURE 7.4

Perpetual vs. Periodic Inventory

Imagine you are shopping for a particular item at a department store. You cannot find it on the shelf, so you ask an employee if there are any left. The employee checks the computer, which says there is one left. The employee finds it in the storage room, gives it to you and you go to the cashier. The cashier scans the item, you pay the bill and you leave the store. If another customer were to ask for that same item after you bought it, the computer would show that there are none in stock.

This example illustrates the perpetual inventory system. The **perpetual inventory system** updates inventory levels after every purchase and sale. Most merchandising companies use technology such as scanners to update their records for inventory, as well as COGS. All the updates happen automatically when the item is scanned by the cashier. The purchase and sale example to be presented in figures 7.5 and 7.6 are examples of the perpetual inventory system.

On the other hand, some small merchandising companies such as a small convenience store may not have scanning technology in place. Without the scanning technology, the business can track their sales, but inventory and COGS will not be updated automatically or regularly. The **periodic inventory system** only updates the inventory and COGS values after physically counting the items on hand. These inventory counts occur periodically, usually at the end of the month or year. Since most large businesses use computers to track purchases and sales, the periodic inventory system is not commonly used today. In this text, we will primarily illustrate merchandising transactions under the perpetual inventory system. Unless otherwise stated, we will always assume the perpetual inventory system is used.

Purchase and Sale of Inventory

Assume a company purchased products costing $6,000 for resale purposes. The purchase should be recorded as a debit to inventory (an asset) and a credit to cash (an asset). This transaction has no impact on the value of stockholders' equity.

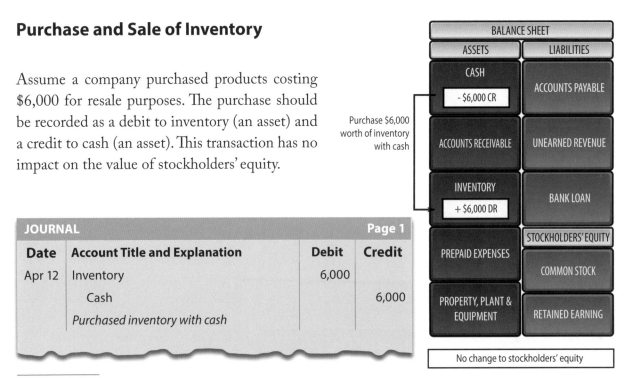

JOURNAL		Page 1	
Date	**Account Title and Explanation**	**Debit**	**Credit**
Apr 12	Inventory	6,000	
	Cash		6,000
	Purchased inventory with cash		

FIGURE 7.5

Now the company can sell the inventory they purchased in figure 7.5. We will assume the inventory is sold for $10,000 cash. The sale of inventory will be recorded by using two entries (two sets of transactions):

1. Debit (increase) cash to show the receipt of cash and credit (increase) sales revenue to show that the business earned profit. Both cash and sales revenue will be increased by the amount charged to the customer. This amount does not represent gross profit but rather the proceeds from the sale.

    Note that if the sale was made on account, then accounts receivable would increase instead of cash.

2. Credit (decrease) inventory to show that inventory has been removed from the store and debit (increase) COGS to show the expense. Both inventory and COGS are affected by the cost of the product sold.

JOURNAL			Page 1
Date	**Account Title and Explanation**	**Debit**	**Credit**
Apr 23	Cash	10,000	
	Sales Revenue		10,000
	Sold inventory for cash		
Apr 23	Cost of Goods Sold	6,000	
	Inventory		6,000
	Record cost of product sold		

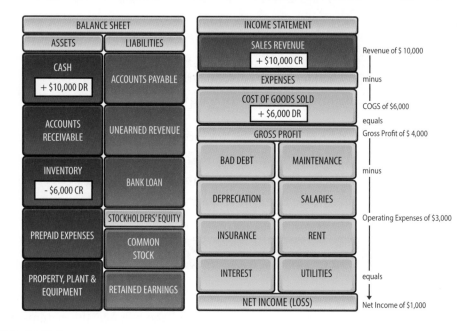

FIGURE 7.6

When the product (inventory) is sold, it can no longer be regarded as an asset by the company because it is now owned by the customer. Stockholders' equity decreases, so cost of goods sold (COGS) is recorded in the income statement.

The difference between revenue and COGS is called *gross profit*, which in this example amounts to $4,000. Net income is calculated by deducting the operating expenses (assume $3,000) from the gross profit ($4,000 − $3,000 = $1,000 net income).

Gross Profit Margin: A Profitability Ratio

Examining the ratio of gross profit to revenue: If Company A has sales of $100,000, and its COGS is $60,000, the gross profit is $40,000. When gross profit is expressed as a percentage, it is calculated as follows:

$$\text{Gross Profit Margin} = \text{Gross Profit} \div \text{Sales} \times 100$$

Gross profit expressed as a percentage of sales is called ***gross profit margin***. The gross profit margin represents the percentage of sales left over to pay for all the operating expenses.

Gross profit margin is more meaningful when comparing the results from one period to another or among different companies. If Company B has sales of $500,000, with a gross profit of $175,000, which of the two companies is performing better? You may think that Company B is performing better because a gross profit of $175,000 is greater than a gross profit of $40,000. However, to assess the results properly, it is important to compare the following two percentages:

Company A: $40,000 Gross Profit ÷ $100,000 Sales × 100 = 40%

Company B: $175,000 Gross Profit ÷ $500,000 Sales × 100 = 35%

The results show that Company A is more efficient because it used only 60% of revenue to cover the cost of the product, leaving 40% of every dollar to contribute toward its operating expenses. Company B, on the other hand, used 65% of its revenue to cover the cost of goods sold, leaving only 35% of each dollar to contribute toward its operating expenses.

Keep in mind that ratios should be compared within industry groups, taking industry norms into account. Suppose Company A and Company B are both hardware stores and other hardware stores have a gross profit margin of 38%. In this situation, Company A is doing better than the industry average and Company B is doing worse than the industry average.

Classified Balance Sheet

The balance sheet of a corporation is prepared using the same basic concepts as those of a proprietorship. To this point in the course, we have divided the balance sheet items into the three main categories: assets, liabilities and stockholders' equity. However, it is useful to group together similar assets and similar liabilities on the basis of their financial characteristics. Before we go into the details of a classified balance sheet, we will first discuss the groupings of assets and liabilities.

Current Assets vs. Long-Term Assets

Assets are divided into two categories:

1. **Current assets** are those that are likely to be converted into cash or used up within the next 12 months through the day-to-day operations of the business. Some examples of current assets are cash, inventory, accounts receivable and prepaid expenses.

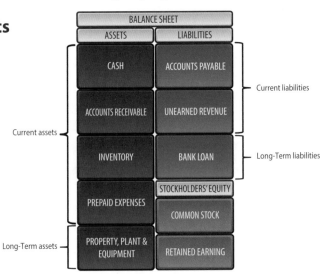

FIGURE 7.7

2. **Long-term assets** are used to operate a business and are not expected to be turned into cash or be used up within the next 12 months unless they are sold for reasons other than the day-to-day operations of the business. Property, plant and equipment (PPE) is considered a long-term asset. Assets that are PPE, and thus long-term assets, include buildings, land, machinery, vehicles, computers and furniture.

Current Liabilities vs. Long-Term Liabilities

Liabilities are divided into two categories:

1. **Current liabilities** are amounts due to be paid within the next 12 months. Examples of current liabilities would include accounts payable, interest payable and unearned revenue (assuming the related revenue will be earned within the next 12 months).

2. **Long-term liabilities** are amounts due to be paid after 12 months. Examples of long-term liabilities would include bank loans and mortgages.

Long-term liabilities usually have a portion that is considered current. That is, a portion must be repaid within the next 12 months. In order to properly plan for cash payments in the upcoming year, accountants will separate the current portion from the long-term portion on the classified balance sheet.

For example, suppose the $50,000 bank loan from figure 7.1 was to be paid off in five equal installments; in this case, $10,000 ($50,000 ÷ 5 years) would be considered current and the rest ($40,000) would be considered long-term. In other words, $10,000 is due within one year and $40,000 is due after one year. This separation of current debt from long-term debt is done on the date of the balance sheet. Each year, the amount of long-term debt would decrease, as a portion is classified as current debt.

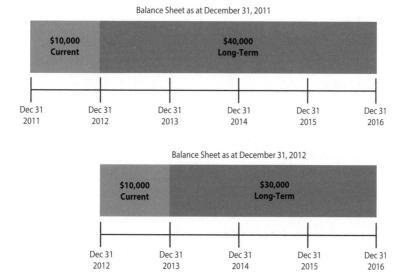

FIGURE 7.8

What is the reason for splitting the balance sheet assets and liabilities between current and long-term items? Readers of the financial statements are interested in the ability of the company to be able to pay the upcoming debt, and where they will get the money to do so. Current liabilities indicate the upcoming debt and current assets indicate where the money will come from. The classified balance sheet also indicates how much the company has invested in itself by means of long-term assets. The amount of long-term liabilities and equity also provide a snapshot of how the company finances its operations.

Now that we have defined current and long-term assets, as well as current and long-term liabilities, we can demonstrate the difference between the balance sheet that we have been using so far and a classified balance sheet.

Figure 7.9 shows a balance sheet for Star Corporation. This is not a classified balance sheet, so all assets and liabilities are each grouped under one heading. The bank loan will have $20,000 of the principal paid off by December 31, 2015.

Star Corporation Balance Sheet As at December 31, 2014		
Assets		
Cash		$12,700
Accounts Receivable		56,000
Prepaid Expenses		12,000
Inventory		45,000
PPE - Equipment	$170,000	
Accumulated Depreciation - Equipment	(24,000)	146,000
Total Assets		$271,700
Liabilities		
Accounts Payable	$30,000	
Unearned Revenue	29,000	
Bank Loan	70,000	
Total Liabilities		$129,000
Stockholders' Equity		
Common Stock		100,000
Retained Earnings		42,700
Total Stockholders' Equity		142,700
Total Liabilities and Stockholders' Equity		$271,700

FIGURE 7.9

By contrast, the classified balance sheet would define the assets and liabilities as current or long-term. The classified balance sheet is shown in figure 7.10. Notice that $20,000 of the bank loan is classified as current because it will be paid within the next one year period.

Star Corporation Balance Sheet As at December 31, 2014		
Assets		
Current Assets		
Cash	$12,700	
Accounts Receivable	56,000	
Prepaid Expenses	12,000	
Inventory	45,000	
Total Current Assets		$125,700
Long-Term Assets		
PPE - Equipment	170,000	
Accumulated Depreciation - Equipment	(24,000)	
Total Long-Term Assets		146,000
Total Assets		$271,700
Liabilities		
Current Liabilities		
Accounts Payable	$30,000	
Unearned Revenue	29,000	
Current Portion of Bank Loan	20,000	
Total Current Liabilities		$79,000
Long-Term Liabilities		
Long-term Portion of Bank Loan	50,000	
Total Long-Term Liabilities		50,000
Total Liabilities		129,000
Stockholders' Equity		
Common Stock		100,000
Retained Earnings		42,700
Total Stockholders' Equity		142,700
Total Liabilities and Stockholders' Equity		$271,700

FIGURE 7.10

This presentation, which separates current from long-term items, allows for the easy calculation of the current ratio. The **current ratio** measures a company's ability to pay off short-term debt. The higher the current ratio, the more current assets the company has to pay off debt that is due within one year. The formula is shown below:

$$\text{Current Ratio} = \frac{\text{Current Assets}}{\text{Current Liabilities}}$$

From the balance sheet in figure 7.10, the current ratio is calculated as shown below:

$$\text{Current Ratio} = \frac{\$125,700}{\$79,000}$$

$$= 1.59$$

This indicates that the company has $1.59 in current assets for every $1.00 in current liabilities. Star Corporation is doing well, since they have enough current assets to cover their upcoming debt payments.

Multistep Income Statement

The income statement of a merchandising business follows the same principles as those of a service business. Until now, we have been grouping revenue accounts together and listing all expenses together, without further categorizing. This is shown in figure 7.11.

Star Corporation Income Statement For the Year Ended December 31, 2014		
Revenue		
Sales Revenue	$230,200	
Interest Revenue	5,100	
Total Revenue		$235,300
Expenses		
Cost of Goods Sold	103,590	
Salaries Expense	72,654	
Rent Expense	24,500	
Utilities Expense	8,426	
Depreciation Expense	4,156	
Supplies Expense	5,234	
Interest Expense	2,163	
Total Expenses		220,723
Net Income		$14,577

FIGURE 7.11

A multistep income statement divides revenue and expenses further to show subtotals such as gross profit, operating expenses and operating income. This format highlights significant relationships because gross profit and operating income are two different but important measures for a merchandising business. A multistep income statement is illustrated in figure 7.12.

Star Corporation Income Statement For the Year Ended December 31, 2014		
Sales Revenue		$230,200
Cost of Goods Sold		103,590
Gross Profit		126,610
Operating Expenses		
Salaries Expense	$72,654	
Rent Expense	24,500	
Utilities Expense	8,426	
Depreciation Expense	4,156	
Supplies Expense	5,234	
Total Operating Expenses		114,970
Income From Operations		11,640
Other Revenue and Expenses		
Interest Revenue	5,100	
Interest Expense	(2,163)	2,937
Net Income		$14,577

FIGURE 7.12

The operating expenses could be further divided into selling and administrative expenses. Selling expenses are those related to actually selling inventory. Examples would include sales salaries, rent for the retail space and store supplies. Administrative expenses are those related to running the business, which are not directly tied to selling inventory. Examples would include office salaries, office supplies and depreciation of office equipment.

The multistep income statement further groups the revenues and expenses that are not part of the main operations of the business, such as interest expense, interest revenue or loss from a lawsuit, under a separate category called *Other Revenue and Expenses*.

IN THE REAL WORLD

An actual company's balance sheet and income statement will usually look similar to what we have shown you up to this point. However, most companies' financial statements will also have an additional column to show amounts from the previous fiscal year. For instance, a company reporting for fiscal year 2011 will have a column with the header '2011' in each of the balance sheet and income statement to report financial information for the most recent fiscal year. There may also be an additional column with the header '2010' to show amounts from the previous fiscal year. This form of the financial reports is referred to as comparative financial statements. This allows users to easily compare the financial performance and position of a company to that of the previous year.

Some companies go beyond the two-year comparison. For example, Telus Corporation shows comparative amounts for eight years in their most recent annual financial statements (i.e. there are eight columns in their financial statements: 2003 to 2010). This allows users, such as investors, to identify both short-term and long-term trends in the financial data. The investors can then assess whether or not the business is growing at a rate they anticipated.

Ethics and Controls

Earlier in the chapter, the notion of splitting a particular liability into its current and long-term portions was discussed. The importance of making this allocation is often underestimated. Some believe it is not significant to show whether the debt is due within a year or due after one year because, ultimately, the debt is still due at some point.

However, the allocation of the current and long-term portions of a liability is crucial. Management needs to ensure that the current portion of debt is not understated. For instance, earlier we introduced the current ratio (current assets ÷ current liabilities). Assume that a particular company is desperate for financing. Since they are having difficulty raising funds from equity investments, they apply for a bank loan. However, in order for the loan to be approved, the bank requires that the company has a current ratio of at least 1.5 for the most recent fiscal year. This shows the bank that the company is not hindered by a lack of ability to meet upcoming debt obligations and therefore will likely not default on their loan. Unfortunately, the company's management knows that they do not have the minimum current ratio requirement of 1.5. In their desperation for financing, they manipulate the reported amount of current liabilities on the balance sheet by under-allocating the current portion of an existing loan. As a result, this inflates the company's current ratio to above 1.5.

Clearly, management has demonstrated unethical and fraudulent behavior. From the bank's perspective, they can implement controls to prevent the issuance of a loan that the borrower really does not deserve. For instance, they can add the requirement that the financial statements of the company be audited (i.e. examined for accuracy by a qualified, independent party). Alternatively, the bank can send its own staff members to perform a review of the potential borrower's financial statements. This is done to ensure that the financial statements are an accurate representation of the financial performance and position of the company.

In Summary

⇨ A **merchandising business** buys and resells products for a profit.

⇨ Corporations sell **common stock** to raise cash to invest in the business. Common stock represent money invested in the company by its owners.

⇨ Owner's equity in a corporation is called **stockholders' equity**.

⇨ **Retained earnings** represent all the profits kept by the business (i.e. not distributed).

⇨ Payments made to the owners of a corporation are called **dividends.**

⇨ **Inventory** is the collection of products a merchandising business buys and sells. Inventory is an asset, but becomes an expense called **cost of goods sold** when the inventory is sold to a customer.

⇨ **Gross profit** is the amount of profit remaining after selling inventory that is used to cover operating expenses.

⇨ The **perpetual inventory system** constantly updates inventory whenever a purchase or sale is made.

⇨ The **periodic inventory system** only updates inventory when a physical count of the inventory is taken, usually at the end of a period.

⇨ **Gross profit margin** is the gross profit as a percentage of sales. The formula is: Gross Profit ÷ Sales × 100.

⇨ A classified balance sheet separates assets and liabilities into current and long-term items.

⇨ **Current assets** are items that will be converted into cash within the next 12 months. **Current liabilities** are items that are due to be paid within the next 12 months.

⇨ The **current ratio** is calculated by dividing current assets by current liabilities. It shows the company's ability to pay off its short-term debt.

Review Exercise

Derek Toward is starting up a business to sell bicycles and bicycle parts and accessories. He decides to incorporate his business and call it DT Bikes. In order to raise enough cash to start the business, Derek will sell stock in his business and get a bank loan.

The store that Derek will rent has a space that Derek will sublet (rent) to another person who does bicycle repairs. This rental income is not part of the main operations of the business.

On January 1, 2014, Derek sells stock in his business and receives $150,000 cash. He also receives a loan from the bank for $80,000. He will have to make equal payments on the principal over the next five years.

At the end of the year, December 31, 2014, Derek had the following financial statements prepared.

DT Bikes Income Statement For the Year Ended December 31, 2014		
Revenue		
Sales Revenue	$564,300	
Rent Revenue	8,400	
Total Revenue		$572,700
Expenses		
Cost of Goods Sold	338,580	
Salaries Expense	184,200	
Rent Expense	24,600	
Utilities Expense	12,400	
Depreciation Expense	2,400	
Insurance Expense	3,020	
Interest Expense	4,800	
Total Expenses		570,000
Net Income		$2,700

DT Bikes Balance Sheet As at December 31, 2014		
Assets		
Cash		$37,600
Accounts Receivable		12,600
Prepaid Insurance		4,800
Inventory		62,500
PPE - Equipment	$110,000	
Accumulated Depreciation - Equipment	(2,400)	107,600
Total Assets		$225,100
Liabilities		
Accounts Payable	$8,400	
Bank Loan	64,000	
Total Liabilities		$72,400
Stockholders' Equity		
Common Stock		150,000
Retained Earnings		2,700
Total Stockholders' Equity		152,700
Total Liabilities and Stockholders' Equity		$225,100

Required:

1. Prepare the journal entries to record the sale of stock and the bank loan on January 1, 2014.

2. Prepare a multistep income statement for 2014.

3. Prepare a classified balance sheet as at December 31, 2014.

4. Calculate the gross margin percentage.

5. Calculate the current ratio.

1. Journal entries

JOURNAL			Page 1
Date	**Account Title and Explanation**	**Debit**	**Credit**
Jan 1	Cash	150,000	
	Common Stock		150,000
	Recorded investment by owners		
Jan 1	Cash	80,000	
	Bank Loan Payable		80,000
	Received loan from bank		

2. Multistep income statement

DT Bikes Income Statement For the Year Ended December 31, 2014		
Sales Revenue		$564,300
Less: Cost of Goods Sold		338,580
Gross Profit		225,720
Operating Expenses		
Salaries Expense	$184,200	
Rent Expense	24,600	
Utilities Expense	12,400	
Depreciation Expense	2,400	
Insurance Expense	3,020	
Total Operating Expenses		226,620
Income (Loss) From Operations		(900)
Other Revenue and Expenses		
Rental Revenue	8,400	
Interest Expense	(4,800)	3,600
Net Income		$2,700

3. Classified balance sheet

DT Bikes Balance Sheet As at December 31, 2014		
Assets		
Current Assets		
Cash	$37,600	
Accounts Receivable	12,600	
Prepaid Insurance	4,800	
Inventory	62,500	
Total Current Assets		$117,500
Long-Term Assets		
PPE - Equipment	110,000	
Accumulated Depreciation - Equipment	(2,400)	
Total Long-Term Assets		107,600
Total Assets		$225,100
Liabilities		
Current Liabilities		
Accounts Payable	$8,400	
Current Portion of Bank Loan	16,000	
Total Current Liabilities		$24,400
Long-Term Liabilities		
Long-term Portion of Bank Loan	48,000	
Total Long-Term Liabilities		48,000
Total Liabilities		72,400
Stockholders' Equity		
Common Stock		150,000
Retained Earnings		2,700
Total Stockholders' Equity		152,700
Total Liabilities and Stockholders' Equity		$225,100

Note: The $80,000 bank loan is payable over five years. One year has already been paid ($80,000 ÷ 5 years = $16,000), which reduces the balance owing to $64,000. Of the amount owing, $16,000 is considered current.

4. Gross margin percentage

$$\text{Gross Margin Percentage} = \text{Gross Profit} \div \text{Sales} \times 100$$
$$= \$225,720 \div \$564,300 \times 100$$
$$= 40\%$$

5. Current ratio

$$\text{Current Ratio} = \text{Current Assets} \div \text{Current Liabilities}$$
$$= \$117,500 \div \$24,400$$

Notes

Chapter 8
ACCOUNTING INFORMATION SYSTEMS

LEARNING OUTCOMES:

❶ Understand the flow of accounting information and the use of modern accounting systems

❷ Describe and record in special journals

❸ Describe and post in subsidiary ledgers

❹ Apply controls and ethics related to the accounting information system

An Integrated Approach to Learning Accounting

The accounting information system refers to the system companies use to collect and process financial transactions as well as provide financial information. The challenge in teaching a modern course in accounting involves the need to integrate traditional concepts and methods with modern technology. This can easily become a challenging task considering that modern accounting information systems have been incorporated so quickly into business that many of the education materials available to accounting students have become outdated.

The reality is that with current "point-and-click" software, accounting students may never see or get to use a set of paper journals and ledgers. This means that the traditional methods used to develop modern accounting systems are being used less and less.

Due to their affordability and usefulness, computerized systems are now a common occurrence in the workplace. They make gathering and analyzing information easier for the accountants and are capable of providing a high level of internal control. Understanding the flow of information in a manual accounting system (journal to ledger to financial statements) will make it easier to understand the flow of information in a computerized accounting system.

The Accounting Paper Trail

Basic elements of a manual/paper-based accounting system include source documents, journals, subsidiary ledgers, ledgers, worksheets, trial balances and financial statements. Subsidiary ledgers provide more details regarding the balance of an account in the general ledger and will be expanded upon in the next section.

Source Documents, which provide evidence that a business transaction has occurred, come in many different forms. The most common examples of source documentation are usually associated with accounts payable and accounts receivable. Source documentation includes purchase orders, sales invoices, cash receipts and contracts.

Accountants use source documentation (in addition to other sources of information) to update the accounting records of an organization. For example, when the accounting department issues a sales invoice, the corresponding journal entry regarding the sale should be made. Note that the procedures surrounding this entry will differ slightly between manual and computerized accounting systems (e.g. in a computerized accounting system, the revenue and accounts receivable accounts are automatically updated while the sales invoice is generated). Our focus in this section, however, will be on manual accounting systems.

Figure 8.1 below outlines the traditional accounting paper trail. Once source documentation is received, the accountant updates the journal. At specified points, this information is transferred to the general ledger (either directly or through a subsidiary ledger). At the end of the accounting period, a trial balance is produced. A trial balance lists all the company's accounts and their corresponding balances. The main purpose of a trial balance is to ensure that all debits equal all credits. The trial balance may need to be adjusted (e.g. to take into account recognition of prepaid expenses, depreciation of assets etc.) before the financial statements are produced. The financial statements are then organized into a financial report for management to review.

The Traditional Accounting Paper Trail

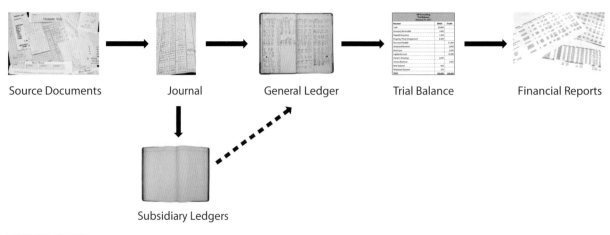

Source Documents   Journal   General Ledger   Trial Balance   Financial Reports

Subsidiary Ledgers

FIGURE 8.1

Regardless of whether one is dealing with a manual or a computerized system, an effective accounting system should ensure:

- Adequate internal controls to prevent misuse of assets
- Accurate information is provided on a timely basis
- Effective communication across the various components of the system
- Flexibility to allow for changes as the organization grows and evolves
- Maximum benefits at a reasonable cost

In this section, we will focus on two components of the traditional accounting information system. They are *special journals* and *subsidiary ledgers*.

Special Journals

Following our manual accounting paper trail, after the source documentation has been received, the next step for the accountant is to record the transaction in **journal** format.

In a traditional accounting system, recording all business transactions in one journal could be very time consuming – especially when there are lots of activities concerning specific transactions. For transactions that occur regularly, it is wise to maintain a separate book called a **special journal**. Examples of regular transactions include sales, purchases, cash payments, cash receipts and payroll. Maintaining these events in a separate set of books will allow one to easily access information pertaining to these activities. For example, if a sales manager wants to see the amount of credit sales generated in May, she could examine the sales journal and add up all the sales for that month. In other words, accounting information is organized into a specific category so that people can look back later and easily extract information. Examples of special journals are listed below.

Sales Journal: This journal is used to record all sales made on account.

Purchases Journal: This is similar to the sales journal, but is used to record all purchases (products or services) made on account.

Cash Payments Journal: This journal is used to record all cash payments made by the business (e.g. rent and wages expense) including payments made to suppliers.

Cash Receipts Journal: This journal is used to record all cash deposits (e.g. cash sales) and collections from outstanding accounts receivable.

When transactions are not recorded in sufficient volume to justify a special journal or they don't 'fit' into one of the special journals, they are recorded directly in the **general journal**. The general journal is simply another name for the journal that has been used in previous accounting courses. The term *general* simply separates it from the other special journals. Some typical entries that would be recorded in the general journal may include:

- Purchase or sales returns
- Depreciation
- Recognition of a prepaid expense as an expense
- Correction of a mistake

Subsidiary Ledgers

Subsidiary ledgers (also called *subledgers*) are used to provide details that are not kept in the general ledger because there is so much information that it will clutter up the general ledger accounts. For example, a company usually deals with many suppliers and customers at the same time and certain information about each supplier and customer is important to the accounting function. This information would include invoice numbers and amounts, dates of purchases or sales and terms of the purchase or sale. Thus, the accounts receivable account in the general ledger would have a subledger for each individual customer, and the accounts payable account in the general ledger would have a subledger of each individual supplier.

Transactions are initially recorded in the general journal or the special journals and are then posted to the general ledger or the subledgers as needed. The subledgers are usually updated after each transaction, while the general ledger is updated after a specified period, such as a month. The general ledger has one summary amount representing the total of all the activity. Since subledger accounts only contain details about general ledger accounts and are not used in preparing financial statements or for posting to the general ledger, they are not assigned account numbers.

The accounts receivable account in the general ledger is a *control* account for the individual accounts in the accounts receivable subledger. A control account keeps track of the grand total of the amounts in the subledger. For example, suppose a company had the following list of customers that each owed a certain amount:

- Customer A owes $400
- Customer B owes $500
- Customer C owes $600

The subsidiary ledger tracks each customer and the amount owing, while the accounts receivable control account would simply show the total amount, $1,500. It is important to note that we do not post amounts from the subledger to the general ledger. Subledgers simply keep a record of detailed information about specific general ledger accounts. All amounts in the general ledger are posted from either the special journal or the general journal.

At the end of a period, the total of the subledger accounts is compared with their respective control account balance. If the sum of the individual ledger accounts is not equal to the control account, an error has occurred and must be corrected. The comparison between the subsidiary and control account acts as a detective control because it is designed to find errors or irregularities after they have occurred.

Subsidiary ledgers protect assets by confirming that accounts receivable are properly accounted for and can, similarly, be used to confirm that accounts payable (liabilities) are correctly recorded. For example, a manager may want to know how much product was purchased from a particular supplier, over what time period, when it was paid for, what discounts were allowed for early payment, etc. To have easy access to this information, an individual ledger should be maintained for each supplier. The ledger, which records the activities for each individual supplier, is called the **accounts payable subsidiary ledger**. The total of all the closing balances for each account in the accounts payable subsidiary ledger would be equal to the accounts payable general ledger balance.

The relationship between the general ledger and the subledger is demonstrated in figure 8.2 and figure 8.3.

Subsidiary Ledger

Accounts Payable Subsidiary Ledger					
Sellmore Advertising Agency					
DATE	**PR**	**DR**	**CR**	**BALANCE (DR or CR)**	
O/B				4,600	CR
Apr 1		4,600		0	
Apr 12			4,600	4,600	CR

ABC Prize Supply Store					
DATE	**PR**	**DR**	**CR**	**BALANCE (DR or CR)**	
Apr 12			500	500	CR

Sparkies Computer Repairs					
DATE	**PR**	**DR**	**CR**	**BALANCE (DR or CR)**	
Apr 8			400	400	CR
Apr 12		100		300	CR

Control Account

General Ledger				
Accounts Payable				
DATE	**PR**	**DR**	**CR**	**BALANCE**
Apr 12			5,400	5,400

Sellmore	$4,600
ABC Prize	$500
Sparkies	$300
Accounts Payable	$5,400

> A **subsidiary ledger** is a group of accounts.
>
> The total of the subsidiary ledger accounts is equal to the **control account**

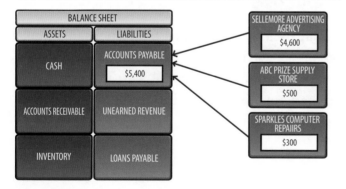

FIGURE 8.2

There are different subsidiary ledgers to control various activities (e.g. inventory, cash and sales). Figure 8.3 shows how the accounts payable, accounts receivable and inventory subsidiary ledgers are totaled and reconciled to their corresponding control account in the general ledger.

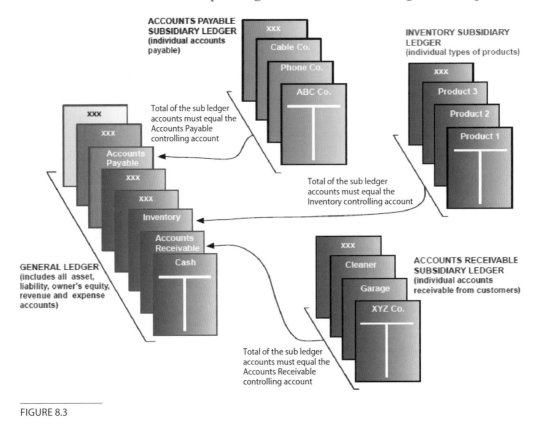

FIGURE 8.3

Once the subledgers have been reconciled to the control accounts in the general ledger, a trial balance can be created with the general ledger accounts and balances. The rest of the accounting cycle continues as you have already learned.

Using Special Journals and Subsidiary Ledgers

It is important to repeat that the special journals are used to group similar transactions that would normally appear in the general journal. Transactions are entered into the appropriate journal when they occur. For the most part, the subledgers are updated from the special journals immediately, while the general ledger is updated at the end of the accounting period. The details of posting from the special journals to the ledgers will be discussed with each journal.

The Sales Journal

The sales journal records all the details of sales on account. Cash sales are not included in this journal. They will appear in the cash receipts journal, since that is where all cash received is recorded. The sales journal includes 1) the date of the sale, 2) the name of the customer, 3) the invoice number and 4) the value of the sale and inventory. These items are shown in figure 8.4.

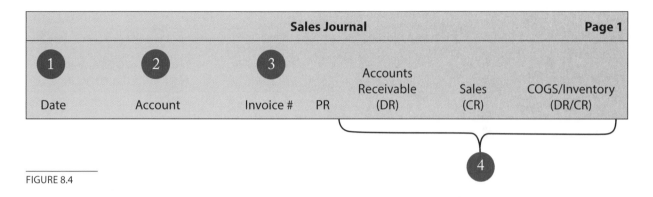

FIGURE 8.4

When a sale is made, as shown on January 5 in figure 8.5, the customer subledger account must be updated immediately. The date and the amount of accounts receivable is transferred from the journal to the subledger. The PR in the subledger is the page number of the sales journal. The subledger account does not have a number like the general ledger does, so the post reference in the sales journal will show a checkmark to indicate the amount was properly posted to the subledger account. Every sales transaction made on account will be recorded the same way.

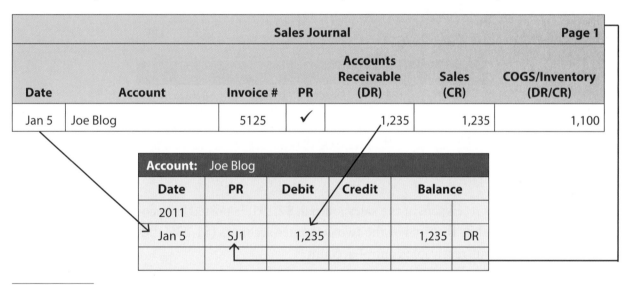

FIGURE 8.5

At the end of the month, the totals of all the columns will be posted to the appropriate ledger accounts. As shown in figure 8.6, the numbers in brackets under the totals represent the ledger numbers of the accounts being used. In this example, we are focusing on accounts receivable, which is account number 110. Assume accounts receivable totals to $2,191.

Sales Journal						Page 1
Date	Account	Invoice #	PR	Accounts Receivable (DR)	Sales (CR)	COGS/Inventory (DR/CR)
Jan 5	Joe Blog	5125	✓	1,235	1,235	1,100
Jan 16	Furniture Retailers	5126	✓	956	956	850
Jan 31	Total			$2,191	$2,191	$1,950
				(110)	(400)	(500/120)

Account:	Accounts Receivable				GL. No.	110	
Date	Description	PR	Debit	Credit	Balance		
2011							
Jan 31		SJ1	2,191		2,191	DR	

Account:	Joe Blog				
Date	PR	Debit	Credit	Balance	
2011					
Jan 5	SJ1	1,235		1,235	DR

Account:	Furniture Retailers				
Date	PR	Debit	Credit	Balance	
2011					
Jan 16	SJ1	956		956	DR

FIGURE 8.6

The total of accounts receivable in the sales journal, $2,191, is posted to accounts receivable in the general ledger as a debit. The total of the two customer accounts ($1,235 and $956) is equal to the balance of the accounts receivable control account.

The Cash Receipts Journal

The cash receipts journal will record all receipts of cash for whatever reason. A list of common reasons for the receipt of cash is listed in the columns (Accounts Receivable, Sales and Bank Loan) which will vary depending on the company. A column titled *Other* is used to record cash receipts that do not fall under one of the common reasons.

Cash (DR)	Accounts Receivable (CR)	Sales (CR)	Bank Loan (CR)	Other (CR)	COGS/Inventory (DR/CR)

FIGURE 8.7

A cash sale would be recorded in the cash receipts journal, as shown in figure 8.8. Since accounts receivable is not affected, nothing must be posted to the subledger accounts. Also, since the Other column was not used, no entry is posted to the general ledger at this time. Only at the end of the month when the columns are totaled will the general ledger be updated.

Cash Receipts Journal							Page 3
				Accounts			
Date	Account	PR	Cash (DR)	Receivable (CR)	Sales (CR)	Bank Loan (CR)	Other (CR)	COGS/Inventory (DR/CR)
Jan 2	Cash Sale		350		350			280

FIGURE 8.8

The transaction on January 4 in figure 8.9 is an investment into the company by the owner. Since there is no column with Capital Account as a heading, the amount will be recorded in the Other column. The post reference (300) indicates that the amount of the investment shown is immediately updated to the capital account in the general ledger. At the end of the month, the total of the Other column will not be posted since any amount in this column is posted immediately to the appropriate ledger account.

Cash Receipts Journal								Page 3
				Accounts				
Date	Account	PR	Cash (DR)	Receivable (CR)	Sales (CR)	Bank Loan (CR)	Other (CR)	COGS/Inventory (DR/CR)
Jan 2	Cash Sale		350		350			280
Jan 4	Capital Account	300	4,000				4,000	

FIGURE 8.9

The partial payment from a customer on January 10 will immediately update the subledger account because it impacts the accounts receivable account. Similar to the sales journal, the posting to the subledger is shown in the cash receipts journal with a checkmark.

Cash Receipts Journal								Page 3
				Accounts				
Date	Account	PR	Cash (DR)	Receivable (CR)	Sales (CR)	Bank Loan (CR)	Other (CR)	COGS/Inventory (DR/CR)
Jan 2	Cash Sale		350		350			280
Jan 4	Capital Account	300	4,000				4,000	
Jan 10	Joe Blog	✓	600	600				

Account:	Joe Blog				
Date	PR	Debit	Credit	Balance	
2011					
Jan 5	SJ1	1,235		1,235	DR
Jan 10	CR3		600	635	DR

FIGURE 8.10

At the end of the month, all columns will be totaled and the amounts posted to the appropriate general ledger accounts. In figure 8.11, this means that $600 is posted as a credit to accounts receivable. The Other column total is not posted, thus an X is used to indicate that no posting is required.

Cash Receipts Journal								Page 3
				Accounts				
Date	Account	PR	Cash (DR)	Receivable (CR)	Sales (CR)	Bank Loan (CR)	Other (CR)	COGS/Inventory (DR/CR)
Jan 2	Cash Sale		350		350			280
Jan 4	Capital Account	300	4,000				4,000	
Jan 10	Joe Blog	✓	600	600				
Jan 22	Bank Loan		2,000			2,000		
Jan 31	Total		$6,950	$600	$350	$2,000	$4,000	$280
			(101)	(110)	(400)	(220)	(X)	(500/120)

Account:	Accounts Receivable				GL. No.	110
Date	Description	PR	Debit	Credit	Balance	
2011						
Jan 31		SJ1	2,191		2,191	DR
Jan 31		CR3		600	1,591	DR

Account:	Joe Blog				
Date	PR	Debit	Credit	Balance	
2011					
Jan 5	SJ1	1,235		1,235	DR
Jan 10	CR3		600	635	DR

Account:	Furniture Retailers				
Date	PR	Debit	Credit	Balance	
2011					
Jan 16	SJ1	956		956	DR

FIGURE 8.11

The Purchases Journal

The purchases journal records all purchases on account. Several columns are provided to account for the more common items that the company purchases on account (inventory and office supplies in our example). If anything else is purchased, it would be recorded in the Other column.

Inventory (DR)	Office Supplies (DR)	Other (DR)	Account Payable (CR)

FIGURE 8.12

When a purchase is made, as shown on January 3 in figure 8.13, the supplier subledger account must be updated immediately. The date and the amount of accounts payable is transferred from the journal to the subledger. As with the other journals, a checkmark is used to indicate the amount was properly posted to the subledger account. Every purchase transaction made on account will be recorded the same way.

Purchases Journal							Page 6
Date	Account	Invoice #	PR	Inventory (DR)	Office Supplies (DR)	Other (DR)	Account Payable (CR)
Jan 3	Antonio's Electric	2089	✓	4,200			4,200

Account:	Antonio's Electric				
Date	PR	Debit	Credit	Balance	
2011					
Jan 3	PJ6		4,200	4,200	CR

FIGURE 8.13

At the end of the month, the total of the columns are posted to the general ledger accounts. Assume the company also purchased $80 worth of office supplies from Young Office Supplies this month and total amounts to $4,280. The posting of the accounts payable is shown in figure 8.14. The totals of the individual subledger accounts must equal the balance of accounts payable.

Purchases Journal							Page 6
Date	Account	Invoice #	PR	Inventory (DR)	Office Supplies (DR)	Other (DR)	Account Payable (CR)
Jan 3	Antonio's Electric	2089	✓	4,200			4,200
Jan 19	Young Office Supplies	6091	✓		80		80
Jan 31	Total			$4,200	$80		$4,280
				(120)	(115)		(200)

Account: Accounts Payable					GL. No. 200	
Date	Description	PR	Debit	Credit	Balance	
2011						
Jan 31		PJ6		4,280	4,280	CR

Account: Antonio's Electric					
Date	PR	Debit	Credit	Balance	
2011					
Jan 3	PJ6		4,200	4,200	CR

Account: Young Office Supplies					
Date	PR	Debit	Credit	Balance	
2011					
Jan 19	PJ6		80	80	CR

FIGURE 8.14

The Cash Payments Journal

The cash payments journal records all cash payments made by the company. There is a column to record the check number, since a good control is to have all payments made by a check. Various columns are provided for the most common reasons for paying with cash, and the column of Other is used to record cash payments for items that do fall under one of the given columns. Notice that Inventory appears with both a debit and credit column. The debit side will be used if inventory is purchased with cash (check) and the credit side will be used if the company pays a supplier of inventory early and receives a discount.

Check #	PR	Accounts Payable (DR)	Other (DR)	Inventory (DR)	Cash (CR)

FIGURE 8.15

A cash purchase would be recorded in the cash payments journal, as shown in figure 8.16. Since accounts payable is not affected, no entry should be posted to the subledger accounts. Also, since the Other column was not used, no entry should be posted to the general ledger at this time. Only at the end of the month when the columns are totaled will the general ledger be updated.

Cash Payments Journal							Page 4
Date	Account	Check #	PR	Accounts Payable (DR)	Other (DR)	Inventory (DR)	Cash (CR)
Jan 6	Inventory	748				1,500	1,500

FIGURE 8.16

The transaction on January 15 in figure 8.17 is a withdrawal from the company by the owner. Since there is no column with Owner's Drawings as a heading, the amount will be recorded in the Other column. The post reference (310) indicates that the amount of the withdrawal shown is immediately updated to the owner's drawings in the general ledger. At the end of the month, the total of the Other column will not posted since any amount in this column is posted immediately to the appropriate ledger account.

Cash Payments Journal							Page 4
Date	Account	Check #	PR	Accounts Payable (DR)	Other (DR)	Inventory (DR)	Cash (CR)
Jan 6	Inventory	748				1,500	1,500
Jan 15	Owner's Drawings	749	310		500		500

FIGURE 8.17

The payment to a supplier on January 18 will immediately update the subledger account since it impacts the accounts payable account. Similar to the other journals, the posting to the subledger is shown in the cash payments journal with a checkmark.

Cash Payments Journal							Page 4
				Accounts Payable	Other	Inventory	Cash
Date	Account	Check #	PR	(DR)	(DR)	(DR)	(CR)
Jan 6	Inventory	748				1,500	1,500
Jan 15	Owner's Drawings	749	310		500		500
Jan 18	Antonio's Electric	750	✓	4,200			4,200

Account:	Antonio's Electric				
Date	PR	Debit	Credit	Balance	
2011					
Jan 3	PJ6		4,200	4,200	CR
Jan 18	CP4	4,200		0	CR

FIGURE 8.18

At the end of the month, all columns will be totaled and the amounts posted to the appropriate general ledger accounts. In figure 8.19, this means that $4,200 is posted as a debit to accounts payable. The Other column total is not posted, thus an X is used to indicate that no posting is required.

Cash Payments Journal							Page 4
				Accounts Payable	Other	Inventory	Cash
Date	Account	Check #	PR	(DR)	(DR)	(DR)	(CR)
Jan 6	Inventory	748				1,500	1,500
Jan 15	Owner's Drawings	749	310		500		500
Jan 18	Antonio's Electric	750	✓	4,200			4,200
Jan 31	Total			$4,200	$500	$1,500	$6,200
				(200)	(X)	(120)	(101)

Account:	Accounts Payable				GL. No.	200	
Date	Description	PR	Debit	Credit	Balance		
2011							
Jan 31		PJ6		4,280	4,280	CR	
Jan 31		CP4	4,200		80	CR	

Account:	Antonio's Electric				
Date	PR	Debit	Credit	Balance	
2011					
Jan 3	PJ6		4,200	4,200	CR
Jan 18	CP4	4,200		0	CR

Account:	Young Office Supplies				
Date	PR	Debit	Credit	Balance	
2011					
Jan 19	PJ6		80	80	CR

FIGURE 8.19

Remember that at the end of the month, when the general ledger is updated by the journals, the total of all the subledger accounts must equal the balance of the appropriate control account (accounts receivable or accounts payable).

To prove that the total of the individual subledger accounts is equal to the respective control account balance in the general ledger, a reconciliation is prepared. From figure 8.11, the balance of accounts receivable was $1,591 in figure 8.20. By finding the total of the accounts receivable subledger account, we can prove that the control account and subledger are in balance.

Company Name Schedule of Accounts Receivable January 31, 2011 General Ledger	
Accounts Receivable	$1,591

Control account in the general ledger

Company Name Schedule of Accounts Receivable January 31, 2011	
Joe Blog	$635
Furniture Retailers	956
Total Accounts Receivable	$1,591

The total of all subledger accounts

FIGURE 8.20

A similar listing can be done for the accounts payable subledger. From figure 8.19, the balance of accounts payable was $80. The total of the accounts payable subledger is shown below.

Company Name Schedule of Accounts Payable January 31, 2011 General Ledger	
Accounts Payable	$80

Control account in the general ledger

Company Name Schedule of Accounts Payable January 31, 2011	
Antonio's Electric	$0
Young Office Supplies	80
Total Accounts Payable	$80

The total of all subledger accounts

FIGURE 8.21

If the comparison of the general ledger control account and the total of the subledger accounts shows that they do not balance, the difference must be investigated. The difference must be resolved before the trial balance can be completed.

Shown below is an example of how reports generated from the accounts receivable subledger and sales journal can be used to examine amounts owing from individual customers. Figure 8.22 shows amounts owing from four different customers and is otherwise known as an aging analysis of accounts receivable. It shows how long it has been since customers have been invoiced (e.g. Better Late Ltd. was invoiced 60-90 days ago and have still not paid their bill(s) which amounts to $1,720). In this particular figure we are also drawn to Slo-Pay Joe because the amount owing ($5,950) makes up over 70% of the total accounts receivable balance of $8,290.

ANALYZE RECEIVABLES					
Customer Report - all customers					
Customer	**Total**	**0-30**	**31-60**	**60-90**	**90+**
Slo-Pay Joe	5,950.00	580.00	900.00	3,900.00	570.00
On The Ball Inc.	50.00		50.00		
Better Late Ltd.	1,720.00			1,720.00	
Way Past Due Corp.	5,70.00				570.00
Total	8,290.00	580.00	950.00	5,620.00	1,140.00
Percent of total	100%	7%	11%	68%	14%

This drills down to detailed analysis per customer below.

FIGURE 8.22

The accounts receivable subsidiary ledger and the sales journal are used to generate a detailed customer report for Slo-Pay Joe (see figure 8.23). This report gives us the breakdown of each invoice billed to Slo-Pay Joe and how long it has been since the outstanding invoice was billed. When we contact Slo-Pay Joe regarding the billable amounts, we can use this report to focus on Invoice #122222 which has an amount of $3,900 that has not been paid in at least two months, to determine the cause of the late payment. This is one way in which special journals and subledgers can be used in the course of regular business operations.

Detailed Customer Report - by customer:		Slo-Pay Joe			
Invoice #	**Amount**	**0-30**	**31-60**	**60-90**	**90+**
122222	4,470.00			3,900.00	570.00
122255	900.00		900.00		
122280	300.00	300.00			
122262	280.00	280.00			
Total	5,950.00	580.00	900.00	3,900.00	570.00
Percent of total	100%	10%	15%	65%	10%

This drills down to each invoice

FIGURE 8.23

Modern Accounting Information Systems

In the traditional systems, all financial records need to be examined manually. For example, if the accountant needs to analyze accounts receivable, then all related journals and ledgers are pulled and looked at for reference. If inventory needs to be examined, then the paper trail from receipt to shipping must be tracked accordingly.

With most modern computerized systems, however, the logic of accounting is already built into the software. There is no need to keep a separate set of books and documents for specific types of transactions. Instead, just about every transaction is entered as an input to the system to produce one central database (general ledger). The software will then process and store the information for future use. At any time, the accountant can create and print reports for any aspect of the business.

The data in a modern, computerized accounting system flows through three stages:

1. The first stage is user *input*. These can come from source documents such as sales receipts and purchase orders. A user with access to the accounting system would enter the necessary information on the source document into the computer.

2. The second stage is *data processing*. In this stage, after user input is complete, the computer automatically creates a journal entry in the system and posts the data to the ledger, which eventually flows through to the financial statements. In other words, the computer is processing the information inputted by the user.

3. The third stage is *output*. Output is the set of reports and financial statements that are created after all necessary information has been processed. They are used internally for decision making purposes and may also be provided to external users such as creditors and investors.

Depending on how comprehensive the data is regarding recorded transactions, the accounting software will be able to produce a variety of useful reports to aid in the management of the business. Note that with computerized accounting systems, information in the special journal and subledger can be accessed as an output report with relative ease.

As an example, the recording of a payment from a customer can contain ten fields of information as follows:

Transaction Type	Date	Debit Account	Debit Amount	Credit Account	Credit Amount	Payee Name	Payee a/c #	Invoice Date	Due Date

FIGURE 8.24

These fields are not only used for accounts receivable, but for any purpose at any point in the traditional document trail — from initial sale to financial reporting. Countless transactions can be entered as an input into a system, which can then be sorted to produce the following reports:

- Financial statements
- Accounts receivable and accounts payable aging reports
- Detailed product inventory listings
- Detailed fixed asset reports containing asset costs and depreciation schedules
- Breakdown of sales per product, department, division etc...
- Breakdown of expense accounts
- Loan amortization schedules
- Income tax preparation reports

Although some computerized systems require an initial manual entry of source documentation into the system, other systems do not require any paper documentation. For example, electronic data interchange, or EDI, is a computerized system that allows companies to transfer electronic information to one another. Sending a bill electronically to a customer is one potential use of such a system.

With the heavy reliance on electronic data in modern accounting systems, you may be concerned about how this information is stored. Many companies store financial data in-house (on the premises) and/or at off-site locations for disaster recovery or backup purposes. Storing the information in-house under the eye of internal employees can increase privacy controls and allow for quicker service when required. On the other hand, many smaller companies may not have the resources to hire an IT expert and have to outsource the data storage function. Note that even though an accountant does not have to be an expert in these systems, he or she should have a clear idea of what IT services are available and what issues can come up so that he or she can protect the integrity of the company's accounting information.

Ultimately, it is up to the management and the accounting department to work with information technology personnel to buy and design a system that meets organizational objectives. Manual systems help accountants learn the ABC's of their profession. However, in today's business world, a properly designed computer system, tailored to the needs of a specific company, can make accounting more efficient.

IN THE REAL WORLD

Although the information age has been forging full speed ahead for more than a decade, efficiencies and innovations are still sought after in almost every sector of technology. This is particularly true regarding how financial entities communicate electronically with one another. A recent development in the field might constitute a great leap forward.

Extensible Business Reporting Language, or XBRL, is a new computer language that will facilitate the exchange of financial information in all sectors of the economy – and it is coming very soon.

What XBRL does is essentially package bits of financial information, standardize this information and make it easier to use and manipulate. The ramifications for this kind of development are almost limitless.

XBRL can be used by companies to publish financial reports for the public. Governments and regulators can use XBRL to receive this information and transmit their own. Stock exchanges can serve as a conduit between business and government in exchanging financial information quickly and easily. Even software companies can get in on the action to create various IT solutions for specific sectors.

In a sense, what XBRL will do for the communicating of financial information is similar to what highways did for the transport of people in vehicles. One system can be used more quickly and efficiently by everyone.

Controls and Ethics

By having a detailed subledger for both accounts receivable and accounts payable, a business is able to properly monitor and control these accounts.

The accounts receivable subledger will provide information on amounts due, and when they are due. Customers who are struggling to make payments can be identified in order to properly collect funds from them. It is also easy to view the history of sales and payments related to a particular customer.

Accounts payable controls will ensure that suppliers are paid on time. If discounts are available for early payment, the subledger will identify when payments should be made to take advantage of these discounts.

Both the customer list and the list of suppliers can be valuable information. For example, the list of clients of an insurance company should be considered private information since it can be valuable to competing insurance companies. Thus, access to the client list should be limited only to those that need client information. Publishing or making the client list widely available may be breaking confidentiality agreements.

From another perspective, employees that do have access to client lists while employed at one company may be tempted to take that client list with them if they decide to change jobs and work for a competing company. This type of behavior is actually considered theft. The client list is private information belonging to the first employer. Depending on the type of employment contract that the employee signed, the employee could be sued for theft of information and confidentiality breaches.

In Summary

The challenge for today's accountant is to use principles established with traditional methods and apply them using today's technology. This involves knowledge and familiarity with the traditional paper trail. It also involves an understanding of how these traditional methods are handled today using computer software. This chapter essentially provides a basic framework, which is to use traditional techniques to understand how modern accounting is done.

Here is a summary of some of the specific concepts and principles you have learned in this chapter:

- ⇨ Modern accounting involves a need to understand traditional accounting procedures and apply them to current technological realities.

- ⇨ The basic elements of the traditional accounting paper trail include: *source documents, journals, subsidiary ledgers, general ledgers, worksheets, trial balances* and *financial statements*.

- ⇨ Special journals are special books used to record events of a regular nature such as sales, purchases, cash receipts/payments, payroll, etc.

- ⇨ Subsidiary ledgers provide supporting details on individual balances.

- ⇨ Accountants used to categorize transactions and track them accordingly. Today, computer software simply gathers all the information in one database and distributes it as instructed.

Review Exercise

Lin-Z Inc. is an owner-operated office furniture retailer. The following is a list of transactions for the month of June.

Jun 4	Received $4,000 from a cash sale to Gus Van Sand (sold office furniture costing $2,015)
Jun 5	Lin-Z received a bill (Invoice #4053) for $100 worth of supplies from Stapl-EZ Inc.
Jun 6	Received $480 from Bo Didley regarding outstanding accounts receivable
Jun 9	Received $2,160 for the cash sale of a lounge suite (costing $1,050) to ReetaPetita
Jun 9	Lin-Z received a bill from Building Services Inc. (Invoice #124) for $350 for repairs and maintenance of office building
Jun 10	Received $25 in interest from loan to Kurt Domino
Jun 12	Paid amount owing (Invoice #4053) to Stapl-EZ Inc. (Check #465)
Jun 15	Jo Jo Inc. paid back loan of $2,400
Jun 18	Made a sale on account (Invoice #10022) to Richard Starkey Jr., for office furniture for $3,000 (and costing $2,000).
Jun 21	Handed over check #466 to Noel's Inc for $4,000 worth of inventory
Jun 22	Paid amount owing (Invoice #124) to Building Services Inc. for repairs (Check #467)
Jun 25	Paid $175 to SKG Inc., for general expenses (Check #468)
Jun 26	Received bill from The Brick & Mortar Inc. (Invoice #404241) for $3,500 worth of inventory
Jun 28	Made a sale, on account (Invoice #10023), to Pete Best for $5,000 worth of desks and tables (costing $3,700)

Required

Record these transactions in the Cash Receipts, Sales, Purchases and Cash Payments Journal.

Use the following headings:

Cash Receipts Journal									Page 1
Date	Account	PR	Cash (DR)	Sales (CR)	Accounts Receivable (CR)	Interest Revenue (CR)	Loans Payable (CR)	Other (CR)	COGS/ Inventory (DR/CR)

Sales Journal						Page 1
Date	Account	Invoice #	PR	Sales (CR)	Accounts Receivable (DR)	COGS/Inventory (DR/CR)

Purchases Journal							Page 1
Date	Account	Invoice #	PR	Repairs Expense (DR)	Office Supplies (DR)	Inventory (DR)	Accounts Payable (CR)

Note: *the column titled "Terms" in the purchase journal is not included for the purpose of this exercise. This "Terms" column will be presented in the workbook questions wherever necessary.*

Cash Payments Journal							Page 1
Date	Account	Check #	PR	Other (DR)	Inventory (DR)	Accounts Payable (DR)	Cash (CR)

Post from the special journals to the accounts receivable subledger. At the end of the month, post from the special journals to the general ledger control account. Assume opening subledger balances of:

- Bo Didley : $2,000 (DR)
- Richard Starkey Jr. : $1,000 (DR)
- Pete Best : $1,500 (DR)

Note that Lin-Z's accounts receivable records consist of only these three subledgers. Assume no entries were made directly to accounts receivable through the general journal. Reconcile the subledger to the control account at the end of the month.

Use the following ledgers:

Accounts Receivable Subsidiary Ledger Bo Didley				
Date	PR	Debit	Credit	Balance

Accounts Receivable Subsidiary Ledger Richard Starkey Jr.				
Date	PR	Debit	Credit	Balance

Accounts Receivable Subsidiary Ledger Pete Best				
Date	PR	Debit	Credit	Balance

General Ledger Accounts Receivable				
Date	PR	Debit	Credit	Balance

Post from the special journals to the accounts payable subledger and then to the general ledger control account at the end of the month. Assume opening subledger balances of:

- Staple-EZ : $500 (CR)
- Building Services Inc.: $750 (CR)
- Brick & Mortar Inc: $2500 (CR)

Note that Lin-Z's accounts payable records consist of only these three subledgers. Assume no entries were made directly to accounts payable through the general journal. Reconcile the subledger to the control account at the end of the month.

Use the following ledgers:

Accounts Payable Subsidiary Ledger Stapl-EZ Inc.				
Date	PR	Debit	Credit	Balance

Accounts Payable Subsidiary Ledger Building Services Inc.				
Date	PR	Debit	Credit	Balance

Accounts Payable Subsidiary Ledger Brick & Mortar Inc.				
Date	PR	Debit	Credit	Balance

General Ledger Accounts Payable				
Date	PR	Debit	Credit	Balance

Review Exercise - Answer

Cash Receipts Journal								Page 1
Date	Account	PR	Cash (DR)	Sales (CR)	Accounts Receivable (CR)	Interest Revenue (CR)	Loans Payable (CR)	Other (CR)	COGS/ Inventory (DR/CR)
Jun 4	G.V.Sand sale		4,000	4,000					2,015
Jun 6	B. Didley paid account	✓	480		480				
Jun 9	R.Petita sale		2,160	2,160					1,050
Jun 10	Interest from K. Domino		25			25			
Jun 15	Jo Jo Inc. returned principal		2,400				2,400		
	TOTAL		9,065	6,160	480	25	2,400		3,065

Sales Journal						Page 1
Date	Account	Invoice #	PR	Sales (CR)	Accounts Receivable (DR)	COGS/ Inventory (DR/CR)
Jun 18	Richard Starkey Jr.	10022	✓	3,000	3,000	2,000
Jun 28	Pete Best	10023	✓	5,000	5,000	3,700
	TOTAL			8,000	8,000	5,700

Purchases Journal						Page 1
Date	Account	Invoice #	PR	Repairs Expense (DR)	Office Supplies (DR)	Inventory (DR)	Accounts Payable (CR)
Jun 5	Stapl-EZ	4053	✓		100		100
Jun 9	Building Services Inc.	124	✓	350			350
Jun 26	Brick & Mortar	404241	✓			3,500	3,500
	TOTAL			350	100	3,500	3,950

Cash Payments Journal							Page 1
Date	Account	Check #	PR	Other (DR)	Inventory (DR)	Accounts Payable (DR)	Cash (CR)
Jun 12	Stapl-EZ Inc.	465	✓			100	100
Jun 21	Noel's Inc	466			4,000		4,000
Jun 22	Building Services Inc.	467	✓			350	350
Jun 25	SKG Inc.	468		175			175
	TOTAL			175	4,000	450	4,625

Accounts Receivable Subsidiary Ledger Bo Didley				
Date	PR	Debit	Credit	Balance
Opening Bal				2,000 DR
Jun 6	CR1		480	1,520 DR

Accounts Receivable Subsidiary Ledger Richard Starkey Jr.				
Date	PR	Debit	Credit	Balance
Opening Bal				1,000 DR
Jun 18	SJ1	3,000		4,000 DR

Accounts Receivable Subsidiary Ledger Pete Best				
Date	PR	Debit	Credit	Balance
Opening Bal				1,500 DR
Jun 28	SJ1	5,000		6,500 DR

Post to general ledger.

General Ledger Accounts Receivable				
Date	PR	Debit	Credit	Balance
Opening Bal.				4,500 DR
Jun 30	CRI		480	4,020 DR
Jun 30	SJ1	8,000		12,020 DR

Lin-Z Inc. Schedule of Accounts Receivable June 30, 2011 General Ledger	
Accounts Receivable	$12,020

Lin-Z Inc. Schedule of Accounts Receivable June 30, 2011	
Bo Didley	$1,520
Richard Starkey Jr.	4,000
Pete Best	6,500
Total Accounts Receivable	$12,020

Accounts Payable Subsidiary Ledger Stapl-EZ Inc.				
Date	PR	Debit	Credit	Balance
Opening Bal.				500 CR
Jun 5	PJ1		100	600 CR
Jun 12	CP1	100		500 CR

Accounts Payable Subsidiary Ledger Building Services Inc.				
Date	PR	Debit	Credit	Balance
Opening Bal.				750 CR
Jun 9	PJ1		350	1,100 CR
Jun 22	CP1	350		750 CR

Accounts Payable Subsidiary Ledger Brick & Mortar Inc.				
Date	PR	Debit	Credit	Balance
Opening Bal.				2,500 CR
Jun 26	PJ1		3,500	6,000 CR

Post to general ledger.

General Ledger Accounts Payable				
Date	PR	Debit	Credit	Balance
Opening Bal.				3,750 CR
Jun 30	PJ1		3,950	7,700 CR
Jun 30	CP1	450		7,250 CR

Lin-Z Inc. Schedule of Accounts Payable June 30, 2011 General Ledger	
Accounts Receivable	$7,250

Lin-Z Inc. Schedule of Accounts Payable June 30, 2011	
Staple-EZ Inc.	$500
Building Services Inc.	750
Brick & Mortar Inc.	6,000
Total Accounts Payable	$7,250

Chapter 9
CASH CONTROLS

LEARNING OUTCOMES:

❶ Prepare a bank reconciliation and the related journal entries

❷ Establish a petty cash fund and record related transactions

❸ Apply cash controls

Cash Controls: An Introduction

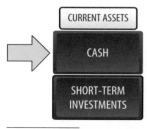

FIGURE 9.1

Our Accounting Map™ in figure 9.1 starts with cash because it is the most liquid asset and the first asset to appear on a balance sheet. A business receives cash from providing services or selling products to customers and uses that cash to purchase assets and pay for expenses. Without cash, a business will likely fail. Thus, it is important for a business to ensure that controls are in place to protect this valuable asset.

While it is important to have sufficient cash on hand, if a business earns more cash than it currently needs, leaving it in a checking account will earn little return. Instead of having the cash sitting idle, some companies choose to invest their excess cash into *short-term investments,* expecting to generate a higher return. Short-term investments are generally kept for less than one year and they are recorded in the current assets section of the balance sheet. Since they can be quickly converted to cash when needed, these types of investments are also called *cash equivalents.* The details of short-term investments will be discussed later in the text.

This chapter will focus on monitoring the movement of cash in and out of the business bank account and how to use a petty cash fund for small and incidental purchases.

Bank Reconciliations

Although banking institutions have high standards, it is still possible for them to make errors. At the end of each month, a bank provides its clients with records (bank statements) prepared by its computer system and employees. A company requires its bookkeeper to update the general ledger on a regular basis. Errors that may occur include recording incorrect amounts and charging amounts to the wrong account.

Moreover, even if both the bank and the company record their transactions correctly, differences between the bank statement and the company's general ledger cash account may still occur as a result of the time lag in recording transactions. A simple internal control involves comparing and reconciling the items in the company's cash records with the items shown on the bank statement. This is achieved by preparing a schedule called a *bank reconciliation*.

In the process of comparing the items in your records with the items shown on the bank statement, you may notice that some items shown correctly on the bank statement may not appear in your records. Similarly, some items shown correctly in your records may not appear on the bank statement.

The following are some typical reasons for the bank making additional deductions from the company's cash account:

- loan interest charges
- repayment of a bank loan
- bank charges
- electronic fund transfers (EFTs): automatic cash payments to other accounts

The following are some typical reasons for the bank making additional deposits to the company's cash account:

- interest deposited directly into the account
- payment from a customer deposited directly into the account
- EFTs: automatic cash receipts from other accounts

Unrecorded Deposits from the Bank Statement

From time to time, the bank may automatically record a deposit, such as interest earned on the bank balance, in the company's bank account. The company would be unaware of the amount until it receives the bank statement. For example, let us compare the bank statement for HR Clothing Company to the company's cash ledger entries.

Company's Records:

GENERAL LEDGER

Account: Cash				GL. No.	101	
Date	**Description**	**Debit**	**Credit**	**Balance**	
Jun 1	Opening Balance			5,000	DR
Jun 2	Check #1		300	4,700	DR
Jun 3	Check #2		500	4,200	DR
Jun 10	Check #3		700	3,500	DR

Bank's Records:

Bank Statement			June 1 - June 30, 2011	
Date	**Description**	**Withdrawal**	**Deposit**	**Balance**
Jun 1	Opening Balance			5,000
Jun 2	Check #1	300		4,700
Jun 3	Check #2	500		4,200
Jun 10	Check #3	700		3,500
Jun 30	Interest		5	3,505

FIGURE 9.2

If the deposit is correct, you will have to record it in the ledger account. For example, in figure 9.2, the bank has recorded interest of $5 in the account of HR Clothing on June 30. All the other checks have been recorded by the bank as well as by the company. Since the interest earned is correctly shown on the bank statement, it should also be recorded in the general ledger by debiting (increasing) cash and crediting (increasing) interest revenue.

Assume that HR Clothing's ledger balance is $3,500, and the bank statement for the month shows a balance of $3,505. The bank reconciliation for this item would look like this:

HR Clothing Bank Reconciliation June 30, 2011		
	Ledger	**Bank**
Balance as per records	$3,500	$3,505
Add: Unrecorded deposits		
Interest June 30	5	
Reconciled balance	$3,505	$3,505

FIGURE 9.3

Notice that the adjusting amount is in the ledger column. This means that you must correct the general ledger balance with an adjusting journal entry. The entry is shown in figure 9.4.

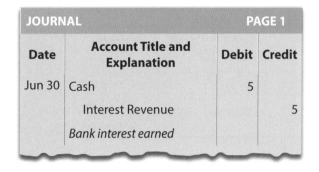

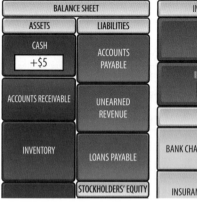

FIGURE 9.4

Unrecorded Charges from the Bank Statement

As with unrecorded deposits, there may be charges shown on the bank statement that are not yet recorded in the general ledger. Typical examples are the monthly bank charges or an annual fee for a safe deposit box. Such charges are legitimate and should be adjusted in the ledger.

Consider the following:

As reflected in figure 9.5, HR Clothing has a cash ledger balance of $3,500. The bank statement reflects a balance of $3,450. All checks are recorded in both the bank statement and the general ledger. Upon comparison, the bookkeeper of the company notices that the bank recorded bank charges of $50 on the last day of the month. This change must be updated in the general ledger.

GENERAL LEDGER					
Account: Cash				**GL. No.**	**101**
Date	**Description**	**Debit**	**Credit**	**Balance**	
Jun 1	Opening Balance			5,000	DR
Jun 2	Check #1		300	4,700	DR
Jun 3	Check #2		500	4,200	DR
Jun 10	Check #3		700	3,500	DR

Bank Statement			June 1 - June 30, 2011	
Date	Description	Withdrawal	Deposit	Balance
Jun 1	Opening Balance			5,000
Jun 2	Check #1	300		4,700
Jun 3	Check #2	500		4,200
Jun 10	Check #3	700		3,500
Jun 30	Bank Charges	50		3,450

FIGURE 9.5

The bank reconciliation for this item would look like this:

HR Clothing Bank Reconciliation June 30, 2011		
	Ledger	**Bank**
Balance as per records	$3,500	$3,450
Less: Unrecorded charges		
Bank Charges June 30	(50)	
Reconciled balance	$3,450	$3,450

FIGURE 9.6

As with the unrecorded deposit shown previously, the adjustment is shown in the ledger column, so it must be updated with a journal entry as shown in figure 9.7.

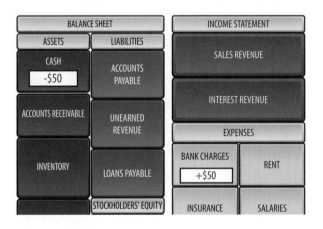

FIGURE 9.7

The journal entry is recorded by debiting (increasing) bank charge expense and crediting (decreasing) cash (an asset).

Another type of bank charge can occur as a result of **non-sufficient funds (NSF)** checks. These are usually payments made to the company by a customer who does not have sufficient funds in their bank account to cover the amount of the check. For example, HR Clothing receives a $500 check from a customer and deposits the check into the company bank account on June 17. However, the bank cannot successfully collect the $500 from the customer's account because the customer does not have enough money in his account to support this withdrawal. The bank would return the check to the company and charge an additional service fee.

GENERAL LEDGER					
Account: Cash				**GL. No.**	**101**
Date	**Description**	**Debit**	**Credit**	**Balance**	
Jun 1	Opening Balance			5,000	DR
Jun 2	Check #1		300	4,700	DR
Jun 3	Check #2		500	4,200	DR
Jun 10	Check #3		700	3,500	DR
Jun 17	Deposit	500		4,000	DR

Bank Statement				June 1 - June 30, 2011
Date	**Description**	**Withdrawal**	**Deposit**	**Balance**
Jun 1	Opening Balance			5,000
Jun 2	Check #1	300		4,700
Jun 3	Check #2	500		4,200
Jun 10	Check #3	700		3,500
Jun 17	Deposit		500	4,000
Jun 19	NSF Check	500		3,500
Jun 19	NSF Charge	10		3,490

FIGURE 9.8

The bank reconciliation would look like this:

HR Clothing Bank Reconciliation June 30, 2011		
	Ledger	**Bank**
Balance as per records	$4,000	$3,490
Less: **NSF check**	(500)	
Charges for NSF check	(10)	
Reconciled balance	$3,490	$3,490

FIGURE 9.9

This adjustment should also be recorded in the journal and updated in the ledger. Since an NSF check represents the amount of cash receipts unsuccessfully collected, this amount should be added back to the company's accounts receivable account. In addition, the bank charge associated with the NSF check should also be recorded. The journal entries are shown in figure 9.10:

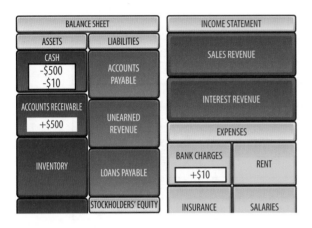

JOURNAL			PAGE 1
Date	**Account Title and Explanation**	**Debit**	**Credit**
Jun 30	Accounts Receivable	500	
	Cash		500
	NSF check returned by bank		
Jun 30	Bank Charge Expense	10	
	Cash		10
	Bank charge for NSF check		

FIGURE 9.10

Notice that HR Clothing received a charge because the customer was unable to honor the check. The company will not want to have to pay the extra fee for the customer's error. What HR Clothing will do is create a new invoice to the customer, charging them an extra amount to cover the NSF fee.

IN THE REAL WORLD

Non-sufficient funds (NSF) checks are commonly known as bad checks or bounced checks in the real world. In our example, it is assumed that non-sufficient funds (NSF) checks occur because the issuer of the check does not have enough money in their own bank account to support the check. However, NSF checks can result from a variety of reasons, including the following:

1. The issuer purposely cancels the check
2. The account is frozen
3. The account does not exist (i.e. the issuing party engaged in a fraudulent act)
4. The account is under investigation

Outstanding Deposits

An outstanding deposit is one that has been recorded in the company's general ledger but not shown on the bank statement. These are also referred to as ***deposits in transit***. This can occur when the company makes a deposit in the bank (perhaps using the night deposit box) on the last day of the month, but the bank does not record the deposit until the following business day in the next month. The bank statement and the company's ledger account may appear as shown in figure 9.11.

GENERAL LEDGER

Account: Cash — GL. No. 101

Date	Description	Debit	Credit	Balance	
Jun 1	Opening Balance			5,000	DR
Jun 2	Check #1		300	4,700	DR
Jun 3	Check #2		500	4,200	DR
Jun 10	Check #3		700	3,500	DR
Jun 30	Deposit	1,000		4,500	DR

Bank Statement — June 1 - June 30, 2011

Date	Description	Withdrawal	Deposit	Balance
Jun 1	Opening Balance			5,000
Jun 2	Check #1	300		4,700
Jun 3	Check #2	500		4,200
Jun 10	Check #3	700		3,500

FIGURE 9.11

The balance on the bank statement is $3,500. The balance in the general ledger is $4,500. There was a deposit of $1,000 on June 30 that was not recorded by the bank. Since the balance is missing from the bank statement, it should be added to the bank balance as shown in figure 9.12.

HR Clothing
Bank Reconciliation
June 30, 2011

	Ledger	Bank
Balance as per records	$4,500	$3,500
Add: **Outstanding deposit June 30**		1,000
Reconciled balance	$4,500	$4,500

FIGURE 9.12

Notice that the reconciled balances are the same for the bank and the ledger columns. As the entry is only in the bank account column of the bank reconciliation worksheet, there is no adjustment required in the ledger. The outstanding deposit is a timing difference; it should appear on the bank statement which includes the following business day (in July). If the deposit does not show up within one or two business days, further investigation should be made to rule out theft or fraud.

Outstanding Checks

The next reconciling item to consider is *outstanding checks*. An outstanding check (issued by the company) is one that has been recorded in the general ledger, but has not been recorded on the bank statement. This can happen because after the company records the check, it is mailed to the supplier. The supplier then records it in their books, prepares the deposit and takes it to the bank. The process can take several days, so the check mailed on June 29 may not appear on the bank statement until July 2 or 3.

Consider the following:

Three checks have been recorded in the ledger between June 28 and 30, as reflected in figure 9.13. None of these checks have been processed by the bank by June 30. The checks are therefore outstanding.

To reconcile the ledger account with the bank statement, we must treat the checks as if the transaction had been completed by the bank (i.e. deduct the amounts from the bank record).

GENERAL LEDGER

Account: Cash — GL. No. 101

Date	Description	Debit	Credit	Balance	
Jun 1	Opening Balance			5,000	DR
Jun 2	Check #1		300	4,700	DR
Jun 3	Check #2		500	4,200	DR
Jun 10	Check #3		700	3,500	DR
Jun 15	Deposit	1,000		4,500	DR
Jun 28	Check #4		400	4,100	DR
Jun 29	Check #5		800	3,300	DR
Jun 30	Check #6		700	2,600	DR

Bank Statement — June 1 - June 30, 2011

Date	Description	Withdrawal	Deposit	Balance
Jun 1	Opening Balance			5,000
Jun 2	Check #1	300		4,700
Jun 3	Check #2	500		4,200
Jun 10	Check #3	700		3,500
Jun 15	Deposit		1,000	4,500

FIGURE 9.13

The bank reconciliation for outstanding checks would look as follows:

HR Clothing Bank Reconciliation June 30, 2011		
	Ledger	**Bank**
Balance as per records	$2,600	$4,500
Less: **Outstanding checks**		
Check #4 June 28		**(400)**
Check #5 June 29		**(800)**
Check #6 June 30		**(700)**
Reconciled balance	$2,600	$2,600

FIGURE 9.14

No adjustment is required in the ledger account because the checks are correctly recorded in the general ledger but have not been cashed by the bank. The bank will eventually include them on the bank statement.

Bank Errors

Although rare, it is possible that banks will make errors, such as charging the company incorrectly with a check belonging to another company. In that case, the company's ledger balance is correct and the bank must correct the error.

Consider the following as shown in figure 9.15.

When the bookkeeper receives the bank statement and compares it with the company records, she notices that the bank processed a check for $800 on June 8, but the company has no knowledge of the check.

At that point, the bookkeeper calls the bank and discovers that the check belongs to another bank client.

GENERAL LEDGER					
Account: Cash				GL. No.	**101**
Date	**Description**	**Debit**	**Credit**	**Balance**	
Jun 1	Opening Balance			5,000	DR
Jun 2	Check #1		300	4,700	DR
Jun 3	Check #2		500	4,200	DR
Jun 10	Check #3		700	3,500	DR

Bank Statement				June 1 - June 30, 2011
Date	Description	Withdrawal	Deposit	Balance
Jun 1	Opening Balance			5,000
Jun 2	Check #1	300		4,700
Jun 3	Check #2	500		4,200
Jun 8	Check #108	800		3,400
Jun 10	Check #3	700		2,700

FIGURE 9.15

The bank reconciliation for this item looks like this:

HR Clothing Bank Reconciliation June 30, 2011		
	Ledger	Bank
Balance as per records	$3,500	$2,700
Add: **Bank Error**, check incorrectly charged to account June 8		800
Reconciled balance	$3,500	$3,500

FIGURE 9.16

Since the adjustment is in the bank column, it does not need to be adjusted in the company's books. The amount is an error, not a timing difference, and the bank must correct the error by depositing funds back into the company's account. The company needs to follow up to ensure that the bank corrects the error.

An incorrect deposit may also appear on the bank statement. In that case, the bank reconciliation would reflect a deduction from the bank balance because it is overstated as a result of the deposit. The company would follow up to ensure that the amount was deducted from its bank account.

Recording Errors

It is possible for bookkeepers to make errors. These errors would appear in the company's records.

Consider this situation as shown in figure 9.17:

Upon investigating the difference between the bank statement and the ledger, the bookkeeper discovers that a check recorded as $950 in the ledger should have been recorded as $590.

The bank cashed the correct amount of the check ($590). The bank reconciliation for this item looks like this:

GENERAL LEDGER					
Account: Cash				**GL. No.**	**101**
Date	**Description**	**Debit**	**Credit**	**Balance**	
Jun 1	Opening Balance			5,000	DR
Jun 2	Check #1		300	4,700	DR
Jun 3	Check #2		950	3,750	DR
Jun 10	Check #3		700	3,050	DR

Bank Statement				June 1 - June 30, 2011
Date	**Description**	**Withdrawal**	**Deposit**	**Balance**
Jun 1	Opening Balance			5,000
Jun 2	Check #1	300		4,700
Jun 3	Check #2	590		4,110
Jun 10	Check #3	700		3,410

FIGURE 9.17

In this situation, more was deducted from the general ledger than was on the check. To correct this error, the bookkeeper will have to add back to the general ledger the difference between what was recorded and the actual amount deducted by the bank. This amounts to $360 ($950 - $590). The bank reconciliation would appear as shown in figure 9.18.

HR Clothing Bank Reconciliation June 30, 2011		
	Ledger	**Bank**
Balance as per records	$3,050	$3,410
Recording error		
Add: **Error on check #2**	360	
Reconciled balance	$3,410	$3,410

FIGURE 9.18

Because the correcting entry is in the ledger column, an adjusting entry must be recorded in the journal. Assuming the original check was written to purchase inventory, the journal entry to correct the ledger is shown in figure 9.19.

JOURNAL			PAGE 1
Date	**Account Title and Explanation**	**Debit**	**Credit**
Jun 30	Cash	360	
	Inventory		360
	Correct error in ledger		

FIGURE 9.19

For an error that is made by the bookkeeper, the bookkeeper must go back into the records to determine what the original entry was for. This will determine which account will be used to offset the cash account. In our example, the payment was for inventory. If the payment was to pay off an account, use accounts payable; to pay this month's rent, use rent expense; to pay a telephone bill, use telephone expense, etc.

As with the previous examples, any discrepancy between the bank statement and the ledger record should be examined and then corrected with the appropriate entries.

Incorrect amounts in the ledger can be more or less than the amounts shown on the bank statement. Each error must be analyzed carefully for appropriate adjustments.

A CLOSER LOOK

In a computerized accounting system, errors in the ledger, such as the one described in figure 9.19, are corrected using two entries instead of one. The first entry would be a $950 debit to cash and a $950 credit to inventory. This entry reverses the original incorrect entry. The second entry would be a $590 debit to inventory and a $590 credit to cash to record the correct amount of the June 3rd check. The net result is the same as the single entry in the amount of $360 shown above. Manual accounting systems will not use this method because it requires more entries and provides more room for error.

Bank Reconciliation Summary

Once all the items on a bank statement and the ledger have been matched up, only a few items should remain that need to be reconciled. The table below summarizes how items will be treated on a bank reconciliation.

Add to Bank Balance	Subtract from Bank Balance
• Outstanding deposits • Bank error	• Outstanding checks • Bank error
Add to Ledger Balance*	Subtract from Ledger Balance*
• Interest earned • Direct deposit from customer • Receipts through EFT • Bookkeeper error	• Loan interest charges • Repayment of bank loan • Bank service charges • Payments through EFT • NSF checks • Bookkeeper error

*Must also create a journal entry to update the ledger balance.

FIGURE 9.20

To illustrate a complete bank reconciliation with journal entries, examine the following bank statement, ledger and journal entries for HR Clothing for the month of October 2011.

Before comparing the new items, it is always important to consider the outstanding items from the last period. We need to ensure these items have been cleared.

From the September bank reconciliation, HR Clothing had the following outstanding items:

Outstanding Deposit   ✓ $2,200

Outstanding Check #57   ✓ $350

Outstanding Check #59   ✓ $480

GENERAL LEDGER						
Account: Cash					**GL. No.**	**101**
Date	Description	Debit	Credit	Balance		
Oct 1	Opening Balance			6,300	DR	
Oct 2	Check #62		✓ 140	6,160	DR	
Oct 4	Deposit M. Smith	✓ 200		6,360	DR	
Oct 7	Check #63		570	5,790	DR	
Oct 15	Check #64		820	4,970	DR	
Oct 17	Deposit	✓ 1,200		6,170	DR	
Oct 21	Check #65		✓ 540	5,630	DR	
Oct 25	Check #66		320	5,310	DR	
Oct 29	Check #67		410	4,900	DR	
Oct 31	Deposit	900		5,800	DR	

Bank Statement			October 1 - October 31, 2011	
Date	Description	Withdrawal	Deposit	Balance
Oct 1	Opening Balance			4,930
Oct 1	EFT Rent	1,300		3,630
Oct 2	Deposit		✓ 2,200	5,830
Oct 4	Check #57	✓ 350		5,480
Oct 5	Deposit		✓ 200	5,680
Oct 6	NSF Check	200		5,480
Oct 6	NFS Fee	15		5,465
Oct 8	Check #62	✓ 140		5,325
Oct 10	Check #59	✓ 480		4,845
Oct 15	EFT Deposit		300	5,145
Oct 18	Deposit		✓ 1,200	6,345
Oct 23	Check #63	750		5,595
Oct 25	Check #65	✓ 540		5,055
Oct 31	Service Charge	10		5,045

Check #63 was for advertising and was cashed for the correct amount by the bank
The NSF check was from a customer as payment of their account
The EFT deposit was a customer paying their account

FIGURE 9.21

The green check marks indicate that the item on the bank statement matches an item from the ledger or September's bank reconciliation. Only the items without a check mark will need to be included on the bank reconciliation for October.

HR Clothing Bank Reconciliation October 31, 2011		
	Ledger	Bank
Balance as per records	$5,800	$5,045
Add: Outstanding Deposit		900
Less: Outstanding Checks		
Check #64		(820)
Check #66		(320)
Check #67		(410)
Add: EFT Deposit	300	
Less: EFT Rent	(1,300)	
NSF Check	(200)	
NSF Fee	(15)	
Service Charge	(10)	
Error on Check #63	(180)	
Reconciled balance	$4,395	$4,395

FIGURE 9.22

Once the bank is reconciled to the ledger, all items that increase or decrease the ledger balance must be recorded in the journal.

JOURNAL			PAGE 1
Date	**Account Title and Explanation**	**Debit**	**Credit**
Oct 31	Cash	300	
	Accounts Receivable		300
	Collection from customer		
Oct 31	Rent Expense	1,300	
	Cash		1,300
	Payment for rent		
Oct 31	Accounts Receivable	200	
	Cash		200
	NSF check from customer		
Oct 31	Bank Charge Expense	25	
	Cash		25
	NFS fee and service charge		
Oct 31	Advertising Expense	180	
	Cash		180
	Correct error on check		

FIGURE 9.23

Petty Cash

At times, a business may require small amounts of cash to pay for petty (small) expenses such as parking, postage stamps and courier fees. Instead of issuing a check each time, the business will set up a petty cash fund to pay for these small amounts in cash.

Petty cash is usually operated on what is known as an *imprest system*. An imprest system for petty cash ensures that spending is limited to the amount available in petty cash fund. For example, if a petty cash fund starts with $100, that is the maximum amount that can be spent. When the amount spent approaches the $100 limit, the petty cash fund will be replenished up to $100.

Setting Up a Petty Cash Fund

1.   **Designate one individual as the petty cash custodian.** There are many ways in which petty cash can be mishandled. Having one person responsible for the fund increases transparency and accountability. The petty cash custodian ensures that petty cash is properly safeguarded and disbursed for legitimate reasons and that an accurate record is maintained for all activities related to the fund.

2.   **Establish the amount of the fund.** The petty cash custodian needs to determine the amount of the fund as well as the frequency with which it is replenished.

3.   **Record the initial petty cash transaction.** The establishment of a petty cash fund requires one initial transaction. Here is the journal entry:

JOURNAL			PAGE 1
Date	**Account Title and Explanation**	**Debit**	**Credit**
Dec 10	Petty Cash	100	
	Cash		100
	To set up the petty cash fund		

FIGURE 9.24

4.   **Require users of petty cash to provide receipts.** Any employee who requires petty cash should provide a receipt from the supplier indicating the amount of money spent. The petty cash custodian will require the person to sign the receipt, indicating that the person has been reimbursed. Figure 9.25 shows a petty cash receipt.

RECEIVED IN PETTY CASH		
Date: *December 13, 2011*		
Description	**Amount**	
Office supplies	7	00
TOTAL	7	00
Received By	*Rebecca McGillivray* Approved By	

FIGURE 9.25

5. **Provide a summary of petty cash.** At the end of the period, which in this example is one week, the petty cash custodian prepares a summary that lists the details of the fund before it is reimbursed. The summary sheet is shown in figure 9.26.

The petty cash summary should include a list of all the items, in groups, paid with the petty cash fund.

Petty Cash Summary Sheet

Period: Dec. 10 - Dec. 17

Opening Balance		$100.00
Parking		
Dec. 10	$10.00	
Dec. 12	6.00	
Dec. 14	5.00	$21.00
Freight in		
Dec. 10	$18.00	
Dec. 11	6.00	$24.00
Office Supplies		
Dec. 13	$ 7.00	
Dec. 16	13.00	$20.00
Gasoline		
Dec. 14	$18.00	$18.00
Total Disbursements		$83.00
Cash over and short	$2.00	
Total to be reimbursed to Petty Cash		$85.00

Opening balance less disbursements

FIGURE 9.26

Both subtotals and a grand total should be calculated. In this example the grand total comes to $83. Subtracting $83 from the original balance of $100 gives us an amount of $17. This should be the remaining balance in the petty cash box.

6. **Reconcile any overage or shortage.** The petty cash custodian must take care of any amounts short or over in the petty cash box. This is done by making additions or subtractions to the account called *cash over and short*. In our current example, there was only $15 in the petty cash box, meaning there was a $2 shortage. Such discrepancies can result from a miscount of coins or an overpayment during the period. The total disbursements recorded, along with any cash short or over, constitute the total amount to be reimbursed to petty cash to restore it to its original value of $100. In this case, the amount is $85.

7. **Summary slip is presented to a supervisor.** The petty cash custodian presents her supervisor with a summary slip, together with all supporting vouchers. After reviewing these documents, the supervisor provides the petty cash custodian with a check to reimburse the petty cash fund. The vouchers are stamped "paid" so that they cannot be reused.

8. **Reimburse the petty cash fund.** The petty cash custodian cashes the check (in this example the check is for $85) and replenishes the fund to its original amount ($100).

Posting Petty Cash to the General Ledger

We have examined the steps that an organization must take when establishing a petty cash fund. Now let us take a closer look at how this process affects the organization's general ledger.

We have already described the transaction that occurs when the petty cash fund is initially established. Cash is credited and petty cash is debited — both for the same amounts, which in our example was $100 as shown in figure 9.24. Until now, all the activity has been in the physical

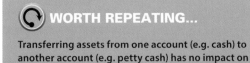
WORTH REPEATING...

Transferring assets from one account (e.g. cash) to another account (e.g. petty cash) has no impact on owner's equity.

petty cash box itself, with no transactions affecting the ledger. When it is time to replenish the fund, we need to increase the amount of petty cash to $100 and allocate the amounts used to the appropriate expense accounts.

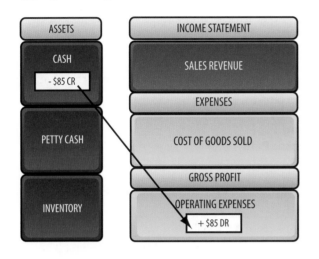

No change is made in the amount of the petty cash ledger account when the reimbursement check is issued, and the reimbursed cash is placed in the petty cash box. You may think that the transaction should be recorded by debiting expenses and crediting petty cash, followed by a debit to petty cash and a credit to cash. However, in practice, when the bookkeeper records the check, there is *no change to the petty cash account.* The check is recorded with a debit to various expenses (parking, delivery, office supplies, gasoline, cash over and short), and a credit to cash in the amount of $85.

JOURNAL			PAGE 1
Date	Account Title and Explanation	Debit	Credit
Dec 17	Parking Expense	21	
	Delivery Expense	24	
	Office Supplies Expense	20	
	Gasoline Expense	18	
	Cash Over and Short	2	
	Cash		85
	Replenish the petty cash fund		

FIGURE 9.27

The cash over and short account behaves like an expense account when there is a shortage. It will be debited in the journal entry. If there is an overage, the cash over and short account behaves like a revenue account. It will be credited in the journal entry.

It is important to note that the *only* time the petty cash account in the ledger is debited or credited is when the account is established or when the amount in the petty cash fund is increased or decreased.

Assume that on December 31, the manager decided to increase the petty cash fund to $150. The journal entry to record the $50 increase would be as follows:

JOURNAL			PAGE 1
Date	Account Title and Explanation	Debit	Credit
Dec 31	Petty Cash	50	
	Cash		50
	Increase the petty cash fund		

FIGURE 9.28

When the petty cash fund is increased, the petty cash account should be debited (increased) and the cash account should be credited (decreased).

Petty cash can also increase at the same time it is replenished. If we combine the transactions from figure 9.27 and 9.28, petty cash would be debited $50 along with the expenses. Cash would then be credited by $135 to replenish and increase the petty cash fund.

A spreadsheet may be maintained listing the various expenses so that each month the general ledger can be updated with the correct allocation of expenses. Here is an example:

HR Clothing
Petty Cash Expenses Paid
July 2011

Description	Receipt #	Amount	Office	Travel	Meals	Marketing
Photo Developing	1	8.07				8.07
Taxis	2	65.00		65.00		
Meals	3	33.00			33.00	
Batteries	4	11.00				11.00
Photocopying - brochures	5	23.32				23.32
Photocopying - general	6	3.05	3.05			
Parking	7	1.87		1.87		
Parking	8	10.26		10.26		
Parking	9	3.00		3.00		
Parking	10	4.00		4.00		
Parking	11	6.50		6.50		
Parking	12	7.00		7.00		
Parking	13	6.00		6.00		
Parking	14	3.94		3.94		
Parking	15	1.00		1.00		
Gas	16	10.00		10.00		
Meals	17	8.10			8.10	
Travel	18	49.01		49.01		
TOTALS		**$254.12**	**$3.05**	**$167.58**	**$41.10**	**$42.39**

Cash will be credited with this amount.

= $254.12
Each of these amounts will be debited to the respective GL expense accounts.

FIGURE 9.29

Petty Cash Controls

Using petty cash funds can be a convenient way to purchase small items. However, the funds also provide opportunities for abuse. It is therefore important to regulate the use of the petty cash fund to ensure that it is not mishandled. Here are four tips to ensure that petty cash is used appropriately:

1. Establish guidelines regarding when and how petty cash may be available.
2. Consistently maintain documentation regarding the use of petty cash.

3. Review the rules regularly with employees.

4. Ensure that petty cash is controlled by one person – the petty cash custodian.

5. Periodically count the petty cash fund.

1. **Establish guidelines.** The first step in ensuring that your petty cash is used properly is to draw up a list of items that can be purchased with petty cash. Determine what purchases may be made with purchase orders, and then make a list of other types of regular purchases. The fund should be reserved strictly for small ("petty") expenses and not for items such as long-term assets or inventory, or for paying accounts payable and independent contractors.

2. **Maintain documentation.** It is difficult to keep accurate records unless you have a uniform documentation system. Establish an easy-to-use system and follow it consistently. The easiest way to do this is by keeping track of all receipts, whether they are register receipts or written invoices. Each receipt should have the date of purchase, the name of the vendor, a list of the items or services purchased, the price of each item and the total cost. Accurate recordkeeping also ensures that

   • the person who made the purchase signs the receipt.

   • all receipts are filed correctly so that they can be checked to determine if there are any discrepancies.

3. **Review the rules with employees.** If the regulations are not well-known, abuse of the petty cash fund becomes easier. Keep everyone up-to-date and do not allow exceptions to the rules.

4. **Ensure that petty cash is controlled by one person – the petty cash custodian.** The appointment of one person to administer and be exclusively responsible for the fund limits the opportunities for mismanagement.

5. **Periodically count the petty cash fund.** Have a person independent from the petty cash custodian, such as a manager, count the fund with the custodian present. This discourages misuse of the funds and can detect shortages early.

SUMMARY OF PETTY CASH CONTROLS	
Control	**Explanation**
Specific guidelines	Determine what purchases can be made with purchase orders. High value items and regular types of purchases should **never** be made through the petty cash fund. The fund should be strictly reserved for small ("petty") expenses.
Documentation	Track all receipts. Ensure each receipt has the date of purchase, name of company or vendor, list of items or services purchased and total cost. The receipts should be signed by the purchaser and filed correctly.
Rules	Establish a clear and precise method for recording petty cash. Designate a petty cash clerk who prepares petty cash reports each month.
Accountability	Appoint one person as the petty cash administrator.
Counting	Independent count of the fund to discourage misuse and find shortages early.

FIGURE 9.30

Ethics and Cash Control Guidelines

Cash is very important to a business and it can be tempting for employees to try and misuse cash. Therefore, it is important to have rules for dealing with cash. Three rules are shown below and will be discussed in detail.

- Record cash immediately when it is received
- Protect cash when it is on the premises
- Remove cash from the premises as soon as possible

Record Cash Immediately when it is Received

After the receipt of cash is recorded, its movement through an organization should be tracked and its removal detected and noted.

The method of recording cash depends on the size of the business and the systems used. For a small business, a simple book of pre-numbered receipts will suffice. When the customer offers cash for merchandise, a paper receipt is prepared in duplicate (one copy for the customer, and the other copy retained as a permanent record of the receipt of cash). Proper controls include the recording of the receipts. Receipts are issued in numerical order and are accounted for on a regular basis by a responsible staff member. The amounts shown on the receipts are totaled and compared with the cash on hand on a daily basis.

An improvement to preparing receipts by hand is to use a cash register. The cash register prepares two copies of the receipt, similar to handwritten receipts – one copy being maintained in the cash register itself and the second copy provided to the customer. As with handwritten receipts, individual sales amounts are added and compared to the amount of cash on hand.

For larger companies, the cash register is replaced with a point-of-sale (POS) computer terminal. The terminal connects directly with the company's accounting system, but performs the same functions as a handwritten receipt. Specifically, a receipt is given to the customer and a record is maintained in the system. The sales are totaled and compared with the cash on hand on a regular basis.

All of the above systems require the participation of the customer. When the customer is handed the receipt, he or she is expected to examine the receipt to ensure that it reflects the exact amount of cash paid. For instance, if the amount on the receipt is less than the actual amount on paid, the customer will complain and a correction will be made, ensuring that the receipt for the correct amount is recorded.

The second feature of these systems is a regular summing-up of the sales amounts and comparison of the total with the cash on hand. Cash shortages and overages are dealt with by management. Cash should be deposited intact into a bank account. The total amount of sales should be the amount deposited into the bank, without any deductions being made.

Protect Cash when it is on the Premises

Having cash present on the premises of a business may be a temptation to a dishonest employee. It therefore becomes necessary to protect surplus amounts of cash. When the money reaches a predetermined amount, the overage is placed in a safe area (i.e. a locked office or backroom). In addition, the business may make use of a safe to store the cash until it is deposited in a bank. The combination or key to the safe should only be made available to a limited number of people.

As described previously, cash receipts should be deposited intact. Deposits may be made more than once a day to minimize the amount of cash on the premises. If deposits are to be made after hours, the company can make use of the bank's night deposit box.

For larger companies that have substantial amounts of cash on hand, security guards may be employed to physically protect the premises. Similarly, security firms may be employed when moving large amounts of cash from the company's premises to the bank.

Checks received, which may be treated like cash, should be stamped "for deposit only" on the back to discourage fraudulent cashing of the check.

Remove Cash from the Premises as soon as Possible

Since cash is portable and highly vulnerable to theft, a company should retain minimal cash on site by making regular bank deposits.

In addition, the establishment of a properly controlled bank account is required to keep cash on the premises to a minimum. As all cash receipts are deposited in the bank, all payments are made with checks, thus removing the need to keep a large amount of cash on the premises. For the few expenses that must be paid in cash, a small amount can be kept as petty cash.

The above information covers only the minimal controls required for internal control over cash. Figure 9.31 provides a sample of detailed controls over cash, some of which were discussed in this chapter.

Control	Explanation
Petty cash custodian	Custodian is responsible for controlling cash.
Use pre-numbered receipts	Review numbers used, accounting for the numerical sequence on a regular basis by a responsible official. Missing receipts can be easily detected.
Stamp "for deposit only"	If checks and money orders are stamped "for deposit only" (preferably with the bank account number), they cannot be cashed or deposited to another company's bank account.
Count cash	Count cash received and balance with total receipts; deposit daily. Ensures the correct amount is deposited.
Use safe or vault	Keep undeposited cash receipts in a safe place to protect cash.
Bank reconciliation	Locates fraudulent checks and missing deposits.
Issue receipts	Issuing receipts for *all* sales and other cash received is the key to controlling cash.
Pay by check	Pay all disbursements by check to avoid keeping cash on hand.
No "cash"	Payee's name on check is required, as opposed to checks written to "cash", for adequate documentation of payments.
Check writing	Making two people responsible for signing checks discourages the writing of fraudulent checks.
Pay on original documents	Prepare checks only on presentation of original, approved documents - photocopies not allowed.
Compare invoices	Compare invoices with quotes and contracts before payment - avoids paying inflated/incorrect invoices.
No pre-signed checks	A supply of pre-signed checks can be misused.
Stamp invoices "paid"	Invoices cannot be presented a second time for payment.
Bank statement security	Send bank statements directly to the person who prepares bank reconciliations so that statements cannot be tampered with before reconciliation is prepared.

FIGURE 9.31

In Summary

This chapter has examined how accountants should deal with back reconciliation and petty cash in the balance sheet. We have also examined the various controls necessary to ensure that cash is properly safeguarded.

Here is a summary of some of the specific concepts and principles you have learned in this chapter.

- ⇨ The bank reconciliation is an internal control that involves comparing and reconciling the items in the company's cash records with the items shown on the bank statement.

- ⇨ The petty cash account is established with one accounting transaction. The petty cash custodian deals with specific transactions involving the petty cash fund.

- ⇨ While it is easy to think that petty cash is unimportant, small abuses can lead to larger abuses down the line. That is why organizations should establish a formal process to implement a petty cash fund and follow up with controls to ensure that the fund is safeguarded and that employees are informed about its use.

Review Exercise 1

The following is the general ledger and bank statement for Martin Furniture Inc.

General Ledger Report May 31, 2010 to June 30, 2010						
Account 1020	Cash					
Date	Comment	Source #	JE#	DR	CR	Balance
Jun 1	*Opening Balance*					3,100.50
Jun 6	Chicago Hardware Traders Inc.	541	J1		900.50	2,200.00
Jun 9	Reo's Interiors Inc.	700	J3	1,925.00		4,125.00
Jun 10	Air-conditioning Repair & Co.	543	J7		1,600.00	2,525.00
Jun 16	Alex Santiago Payroll	542	J10		400.00	2,125.00
Jun 16	Martin Furnishings Inc.	256	J11	2,000.00		4,125.00
Jun 19	Line-wire Electric	544	J20		110.00	4,015.00
Jun 19	Rice Inc.	545	J21		500.00	3,515.00
Jun 30	*Closing Balance*					3,515.00

Reserve Bank
146 Lineage Avenue, Chicago

Martin Furniture Inc.
234 Lakeview Drive
Chicago 19112

Date	Information	Withdrawal	Deposits	Balance
Jun 1	Balance Forward			3,100.50
Jun 8	Check #541	900.50		2,200.00
Jun 9	Deposit		1,925.00	4,125.00
Jun 10	Check #543	1,600.00		2,525.00
Jun 16	Deposit		2,000.00	4,525.00
Jun 16	Check #542	400.00		4,125.00
Jun 18	NSF Check #256	2,000.00		2,125.00
Jun 21	Check #544	110.00		2,015.00
Jun 27	Deposit Interest		5.00	2,020.00
Jun 29	Service Charge	20.00		2,000.00
Jun 29	Loan Interest	100.00		1,900.00
Jun 30	Ending Balance			1,900.00

You are required to reconcile the ledger and bank statement and record the relevant transactions on the general journal.

Review Exercise 1 – Answer

BANK RECONCILIATION WORKSHEET		
Explanation	**Ledger**	**Bank**
Balance as per records	3,515	1,900
Add: deposit interest	5	
Less: service charge	20	
Less: loan interest	100	
Less: NSF check	2,000	
Less: outstanding check		500
Reconciled balance	1,400	1,400

Date	Account Title and Explanation	Debit	Credit
Jun 18	Accounts Receivable	2,000	
	Cash		2,000
	Reinstate accounts receivable for NSF check		
Jun 27	Cash	5	
	Interest Revenue		5
	To record deposit of interest earned		
Jun 29	Bank Service Charges	20	
	Cash		20
	To record payment of bank service charges		
Jun 29	Interest Expense	100	
	Cash		100
	To record payment of bank service charges		

—————————— **Review Exercise 2** ——————————

On April 1st, Clayton Company established a petty cash fund of $200.

During the month the custodian paid out the following amounts:

Apr 6	– Postage	$40
Apr 8	– Fedex for delivery of package	20
Apr 10	– Public Transit fares for employees on company business	25
Apr 14	– Coffee and donuts for client during a meeting	8
Apr 15	– Purchased a package of paper for the copy machine	7

The custodian counted the fund on April 16 and found $95 in the petty cash box.

a) Prepare the journal entry to record the establishment of the fund.

b) Prepare the journal entry to record the reimbursement of the fund on April 16.

Review Exercise 2 – Answer

a)

Date	Account Title and Explanation	Debit	Credit
Apr 1	Petty Cash	200	
	Cash		200
	To establish petty cash fund		

b)

Date	Account Title and Explanation	Debit	Credit
Apr 16	Postage Expense	40	
	Delivery Expense	20	
	Travel Expense	25	
	Entertainment Expense	8	
	Office Expenses	7	
	Cash Over and Short	5	
	Cash		105
	To reimburse petty cash fund		

Chapter 10

ACCOUNTS AND NOTES RECEIVABLE

LEARNING OUTCOMES:

❶ Understand the importance of accounts receivable

❷ Account for bad debt using the direct method

❸ Account for bad debt using the allowance method

❹ Estimate bad debt using the income statement approach

❺ Estimate bad debt using the balance sheet approach

❻ Calculate financial ratios pertaining to accounts receivable

❼ Record promissory notes and notes receivable

❽ Apply controls and ethics relating to accounts receivable and notes receivable

Accounts Receivable: An Introduction

The next stop on our tour of the balance sheet is accounts receivable, since it ranks immediately after cash and short-term investments in terms of liquidity.

When customers purchase a product or service from a company, they often do so using payment terms. In other words, they receive the product or service, but pay for it later – usually on credit terms established by the company. Accounts receivable represents the amounts customers owe as a result of the company exchanging goods or services in return for the promise to pay.

FIGURE 10.1

Moving down the current assets section of the balance sheet generally involves not only a decrease in liquidity but also an increase in risk. When compared with cash, accounts receivable is less liquid since it takes some time for them to be converted into cash through collection from customers. There is also some risk that a customer will not pay the amount they owe.

Nevertheless, accounts receivable are an integral part of doing business in a modern economy. Sales may be increased by allowing customers to pay at a later date since some customers may be unable to pay for their purchases immediately.

Since many businesses have accounts receivable on their books, it is important to know how to record and manage them. Throughout this chapter, we will take a closer look at how this is achieved.

Accounts receivable is a different type of asset from those higher up on the balance sheet. One difference involves the way in which information about the asset is collected and managed.

Cash is held in a bank account and the bank provides the account holder with a statement outlining the movement of the cash and the status of the account. Indeed, it is the bank that is essentially responsible for handling the day-to-day administration of the cash being held in the account.

On the other hand, employees need to spend a significant amount of time on the administration of accounts receivable. In fact, perhaps nothing differentiates accounts receivable from other current assets more than their day-to-day administration.

Even a business with a relatively small number of customers has many transactions to record and manage on a daily basis.

In the days before computers, transactions were entered into a journal. While a general journal may be used for transactions that are infrequent, accountants have often used specialized journals for transactions of a specific nature. For example, a purchase journal can be kept to record transactions involving the purchases of the business, and a cash receipts journal can be used to record transactions involving the receipt of money from outside sources.

IN THE REAL WORLD

 One of the most prominent business trends of the past decade has been outsourcing, whereby one company hires another company to take over a certain business function — whether it is call center duties or specialized manufacturing capabilities.

The accounts receivable department has not escaped this outsourcing trend. Accounts receivable may represent only a small percentage of a company's total assets; yet the administrative burdens associated with this asset can be overwhelming, and a company's resources in dealing with it are often inadequate.

To handle this challenge, companies have the option of hiring firms that specialize in taking over the accounts receivable function. Such specialists possess the technical hardware, expertise and experience to maximize this important asset.

Outsourcing accounts receivable offers certain advantages, especially for those companies that don't have a good track record in managing this asset. Outsourcing can

- improve a company's profitability by having the asset managed and controlled more efficiently;

- make a company's accounts receivable function more consistently, thereby making customers more satisfied;

- ensure financial reporting is more accurate; and

- allow a company to focus on its core business, while leaving some of the administrative duties to specialists.

Accounts receivable is an important asset for most companies. Leaving it in good hands is necessary for business success, and that may involve outsourcing the accounts.

Before the advent of computers, every sales transaction was entered in the sales journal. Today, sales transactions can be tracked using computer scanning and software, which can generate reports with the click of a mouse. A sample sales report is shown in figure 10.2.

Sales Report		
Archer Limited	Purchased 6 boxes of tiles	$1,000
Beta Company	Purchased 8 boxes of tiles	1,250
Cooper Inc.	Purchased a cord of timber	1,800
Dunwoody Company	Purchased spare parts	200
Archer Limited	Purchased truck of concrete	2,000
Beta Company	Purchased tools	900
	Total Sales	**$7,150**

FIGURE 10.2

If only one account in the general ledger were dedicated to accounts receivable, the general ledger would be overwhelmed with many accounts receivable transactions. This is the reason why accountants use an *accounts receivable subsidiary ledger*, or *subledger*, which is kept separately in order to track each customer's activity. The total of the subsidiary ledger is matched to the accounts receivable balance in the general ledger (called the *control account*).

Accounting for Bad Debt: Direct and Allowance Methods

There is an upside and a downside to selling goods and services to customers on credit. The upside is that selling on credit encourages people to buy. For the most part, people pay their bills when they are due. The downside is that there will inevitably be customers who will either delay paying their bills or will never pay. The latter is referred to as **bad debt**.

All businesses must investigate outstanding accounts receivable in order to identify and account for bad debt. This can be challenging because it is sometimes difficult to know whether the customer is late with the payment or is unable to pay. Assumptions must be made in this regard, because the records need to reflect the company's current financial position as accurately as possible. Generally Accepted Accounting Principles (GAAP) provides two accounting methods for doubtful accounts and bad debt: the direct (write-off) method and the allowance method. The direct method can only be allowed in very specific circumstances, which will be discussed below.

The Direct Method

When a sale is made on account, it is recorded as a debit to accounts receivable and a credit to sales. The debit to accounts receivable increases the asset of the company while the credit to sales increases equity and is recorded as sales revenue.

However, consider this example:

A customer informs you that his company has filed for bankruptcy and is therefore unable to pay its outstanding account balance of $5,000.

When it is determined that the bill will not be paid, the direct method requires a journal entry to increase (debit) *bad debt expense* and decrease (credit) *accounts receivable*. Figure 10.3 shows the required journal entry for this transaction.

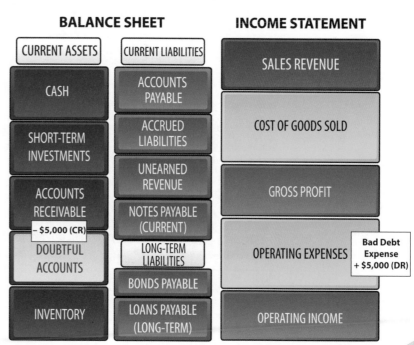

Equity Decreases

One drawback of using the direct method to write off bad debt is that it does not always satisfy the matching principle. Recall that the matching principle states that expenses must be recorded during the same period in which the related revenue is generated.

JOURNAL

Date	Account Title and Explanation	Debit	Credit
	Bad Debt Expense	5,000	
	Accounts Receivable - Customer Name		5,000
	Direct write-off of bad debt from accounts receivable		

FIGURE 10.3

The write-off should be made in the same accounting period in which the sale was recorded in order to conform to the matching principle; however, it is more likely to be made in a later period, which violates the matching principle. The write-off is usually made in later periods because it takes time to determine whether a customer will pay or not. For businesses that experience very few bad debts or the dollar amount involved is considered immaterial to the business, the direct method may be used. In the above example, assume that the year-end balance of accounts receivable was $50 million and that credit sales for the year were $650 million, the company experiences very few write–offs and $5,000 is considered by management to be immaterial. In this case, using the direct method may be considered acceptable.

The second drawback to using this method arises if the customer is able to repay the account *after* the account has been written off. Figure 10.4 shows the journal entries that would need to be recorded if this occurs.

JOURNAL

Date	Account Title and Explanation	Debit	Credit
	Accounts Receivable - Customer Name	5,000	
	Bad Debt Expense		5,000
	To reinstate the customer's account		

JOURNAL

Date	Account Title and Explanation	Debit	Credit
	Cash	5,000	
	Accounts Receivable - Customer Name		5,000
	To record receipt of payment on account		

FIGURE 10.4

You will need to reinstate the amount into the customer's account. This requires a journal entry to increase (debit) accounts receivable and decrease (credit) bad debt expense, which will cause a reduction in expenses and an overstatement of net income for the current period. Unless the write-off and the subsequent reinstatement occur in the same period, the matching principle is being violated.

After you have reinstated the amount, you would need to make a second journal entry to record the receipt of the payment from the customer.

The Allowance Method

Since the direct method will violate the matching principle if the bad debt is not recorded in the same period as the sale, accountants have devised what is called an ***allowance for doubtful accounts*** (AFDA). It is located directly beneath Accounts Receivable on our Accounting Map™, and is also known as a ***contra account.*** A contra account is linked directly to another account and is used to decrease the account balance. In this case, the AFDA contra account is linked directly to accounts receivable.

Under the direct method, a bad debt is recorded by debiting the bad debt expense and crediting accounts receivable when the actual bed debt occurs. The allowance method, on the other hand, estimates an amount that will be bad debt and records it in the books. This method uses the bad debt expense account and the AFDA to record bad debt on a consistent basis. Bad debt is recorded in the same period in which revenue is generated in order to adhere to the matching principle.

For example, let us assume that at the end of year 1, your customers owe a total of $100,000. After analyzing the existing data and the current economy, it has been determined that $5,000 of the accounts receivable may not be collectable. However, since there is still a chance that you will collect, you will not remove them from the accounts receivable list. Note that the amount estimated to be uncollectable is not based on one specific customer who will not pay. Rather this is an overall estimate for the entire accounts receivable.

The accounts receivable account of $100,000 does not change. It remains as a debit on the balance sheet. Instead, the AFDA contra account is credited with $5,000, which decreases the combined amount of the accounts receivable and the AFDA by $5,000, resulting in net accounts receivable of $95,000. Bad debt expense is in turn increased, or debited, by $5,000 and this amount is reported as an expense for the period in the income statement. The journal entry at the end of year 1 for this transaction is recorded as follows:

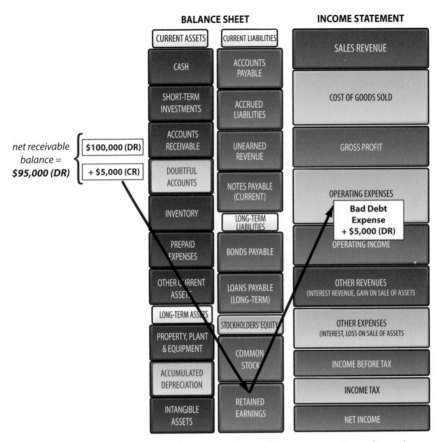

BALANCE SHEET

INCOME STATEMENT

The Accounts Receivable account remains unchanged.
The effect of this transaction decreases equity.

JOURNAL			
Date	**Account Title and Explanation**	**Debit**	**Credit**
	Bad Debt Expense	5,000	
	Allowance for Doubtful Accounts		5,000
	Record an allowance for doubtful accounts		

FIGURE 10.5

The AFDA contra account allows a company to account for the possibility that some of the accounts receivable generated in the current period will not be collected. The debit to bad debt expense supports the matching principle, since this amount will be deducted as an expense in the period during which the sale was recorded. Note that the company's equity decreases as a result of recognizing the bad debt expense.

It should also be noted that according to GAAP, any amount of money originally credited to the AFDA contra account, and thus deemed uncollectible, must be justified with backup documentation. In other words, a company must have good reason to believe that some amounts will not be paid in order to justify the adjustments made to the assets and expenses. Such measures are warranted since estimates such as AFDA are easy targets for manipulation.

After companies anticipate bad debt by setting up the AFDA contra account, several scenarios can exist:

1. A customer is unable or unwilling to pay the debt and the amount is considered uncollectible.
2. After an account is written off as uncollectible, the customer informs you that he or she will pay the amount.
3. The customer is unable to pay the debt immediately, but will be able to pay it in the future.

We will now examine each scenario.

Scenario 1: During year 2, a customer who owes you $250, informs you that he is unable to pay his account.

FIGURE 10.6

JOURNAL			
Date	**Account Title and Explanation**	**Debit**	**Credit**
	Allowance for Doubtful Accounts	250	
	Accounts Receivable - Customer Name		250
	To write-off account as uncollectible		

The amount is now considered uncollectible and needs to be written off.

Since the allowance method was used, a debit to the bad debt expense was recorded in the previous period when the sale occurred; therefore, the AFDA account will now be debited and the accounts receivable account credited to remove the amount from the company's records. The above entry will have no impact on the company's equity, since this was already accounted for by the original debit to bad debt expense in year 1.

The same transaction would be made if a customer simply refuses to pay. Usually a company will attempt to contact and collect from a customer for many months. After a period of time, the company may realize the customer just will not pay or can not be contacted. Figure 10.6 is the journal entry to write off that account.

Scenario 2: The customer in scenario 1 has experienced a windfall and is now eager to pay his account (which you previously wrote off as uncollectible).

This will result in your having to record two journal entries: (1) to reinstate the customer's account balance, and (2) to show the amount being paid.

1. Reverse the previous entry.

JOURNAL			
Date	Account Title and Explanation	Debit	Credit
	Accounts Receivable - Customer Name	250	
	Allowance for Doubtful Accounts		250
	To reinstate amount previously written off		

FIGURE 10.7

2. Record receipt of payment on account.

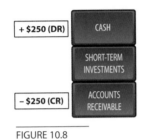

JOURNAL			
Date	Account Title and Explanation	Debit	Credit
	Cash	250	
	Accounts Receivable - Customer Name		250
	To record receipt of payment from customer		

FIGURE 10.8

Scenario 3: The customer is unable to pay the debt at present, but will be able to do so in the future.

Even customers with a good credit record sometimes take time to settle their bills. After many months of attempting to collect from a customer, a company would face the decision of writing off the account as uncollectable. If they do write it off, the transaction in scenario 1 would be made. When the customer finally does pay, the two transactions in scenario 2 would be made.

However, if it is relatively certain that the customer will pay eventually, the company can decide to take no action, except to periodically issue a reminder to the customer. The original amount in accounts receivable will remain on the books and will be credited when the account is finally paid. Another alternative would be to convert the accounts receivable into a notes receivable, which will be covered later in this chapter.

Approaches to Estimate Bad Debt

Managing accounts receivable includes assessing how much of it will end up as bad debt. This not only has an impact on how a company reflects its financial position on a timely basis, but also has implications for meeting GAAP requirements. In other words, businesses should always have good reasons for their treatment of bad debt and should maintain the necessary documentation to justify it.

We will examine two approaches for estimating bad debt: the income statement approach and the balance sheet approach.

The Income Statement Approach

The income statement approach or the percentage of sales method, is so called because credit sales from the income statement are used as a basis to predict future bad debt. More specifically, the current year's bad debt expense is calculated by multiplying a certain percentage by the credit sales. Different companies use different percentages based on their own collection history and credit policy.

For example, if the collection history of a company suggests that 1% of credit sales will result in bad debt, that rate is used to estimate the portion of each period's sales that will not be collectible.

Total credit sales for ABC Company amounted to $1,000,000, of which $200,000 is currently owing by customers. On the basis of historical sales, 1% of $1,000,000 will be uncollectible. Therefore, the bad debt expense for the period will be:

$$\$1,000,000 \times 1\% = \$10,000$$

JOURNAL			
Date	Account Title and Explanation	Debit	Credit
	Bad Debt Expense	10,000	
	Allowance for Doubtful Accounts		10,000
	To record bad debt expense based on percentage of credit sale		

FIIGURE 10.9

As previously discussed, the accounts receivable account, or control account, maintains the same debit amount, which in this case is $200,000. The amount calculated above will be added to the current balance in the AFDA account. Assuming that the AFDA starts with a zero balance, it will now have a $10,000 credit balance. This leaves a net accounts receivable balance of $190,000, which represents a decrease in the company's assets. The income statement includes a debit balance of $10,000 for bad debt expense.

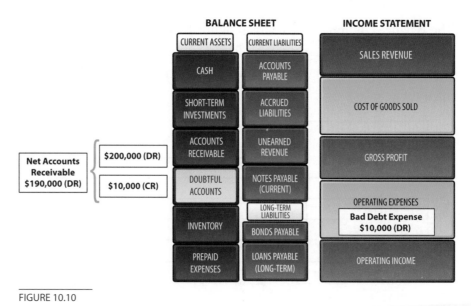

FIGURE 10.10

This approach is called the income statement approach since the name is taken from the way the bad debt expense is calculated. Nevertheless, adjustments must be made to both the income statement and the balance sheet accounts when accounting for the bad debt expense.

The Balance Sheet Approach

The balance sheet approach or aging method, uses percentage of receivables to calculate bad debt expense. The percentage is applied to the accounts receivable account. Specifically, percentages are often applied to accounts receivable according to groupings based on the age of uncollectible amounts. We will use an example to illustrate this procedure.

The chart in figure 10.11 contains three groups of customers:

1.   those who have not paid within 30 days;

2.   those who have not paid for 31 to 60 days; and

3.   those who have not paid for over 60 days.

Aging Category	Bad Debt % (probability of being uncollectible)	Balance of Accounts Receivable
30 days	2%	80,000
31–60 days	3%	90,000
over 60 days	5%	30,000
Total		200,000

The above percentages are based on historical performance

FIGURE 10.11

A percentage is applied to each aging category. A 2% rate is applied to the first group, 3% to the second group and 5% to the third group. The longer that a customer takes to pay, the less likely he or she will pay; that is the reason why the highest rate is used for the third group.

The Balance column of the chart in figure 10.12 shows the amounts that each group still owes the company. The percentages are applied to these amounts to calculate the expected total bad debt per customer group. These are then added to give us the total amount of bad debt expected in the upcoming period.

Aging Category	Bad Debt % (probability of being uncollectible)	Balance of Accounts Receivable	Estimated Bad Debt*
30 days	2%	80,000	1,600
31–60 days	3%	90,000	2,700
over 60 days	5%	30,000	1,500
Total		200,000	5,800
* Balance x Bad Debt %			

FIGURE 10.12

Uncollectible accounts receivable in the upcoming period is estimated at $5,800. Notice that the $5,800 of estimated bad debt will be the ending balance of AFDA for the period regardless of AFDA's existing balance. Under the balance sheet approach, the adjustments required could be grouped into three different scenarios based on AFDA having a credit, zero or debit balance. These scenarios are presented through the following examples.

Scenario 1: AFDA has a credit balance of $3,000.

If there is already an amount credited in the AFDA account, it needs to be subtracted from the $5,800 total to give us the bad debt expense for the period. A credit balance indicates the company has overestimated bad debt expense in the past. In this example, the AFDA account had a credit balance of $3,000. Subtracting that from the calculated amount of $5,800 leaves us with an adjustment in the AFDA account of $2,800. In effect, this "tops up" the AFDA account, since we are adjusting it to reflect the total amount of bad debt expected. Figure 10.13 shows the journal entry for this transaction and the accounting map shows the impact of scenario 1 on the balance sheet and income statement.

Scenario 2: AFDA has a balance of zero.

If AFDA has a zero balance, then the amount calculated as uncollectible becomes the amount of the adjustments. The amount of the credit to the AFDA account would be $5,800. In effect, this "tops up" the AFDA account, since we are adjusting it to reflect the total amount of bad debt expected. Figure 10.13 shows the journal entry for this transaction.

Scenario 3: AFDA has a debit balance of $1,000.

If there is already an amount debited in the AFDA account, it needs to be added to the $5,800 total to give us the bad debt expense for the period. A debit balance indicates the company has underestimated bad debt expense in the past. In this example, the AFDA account had a debit balance of $1,000. Adding that to the calculated amount of $5,800 leaves us with an adjustment in the AFDA account of $6,800. In effect, this "tops up" the AFDA account, since we are adjusting it to reflect the total amount of bad debt expected. Figure 10.13 shows the journal entry for this transaction.

Scenario 1

ALLOWANCE FOR DOUBTFUL ACCOUNTS	
	$3,000 Opening balance
$2,800	
	$5,800 Desired ending balance

JOURNAL			
Date	**Account Title and Explanation**	**Debit**	**Credit**
	Bad Debt Expense	2,800	
	Allowance for Doubtful Accounts		2,800
	To adjust the AFDA account to the correct balance		

Scenario 2

ALLOWANCE FOR DOUBTFUL ACCOUNTS

	$0	Opening balance
	$5,800	
	$5,800	Desired ending balance

JOURNAL			
Date	Account Title and Explanation	Debit	Credit
	Bad Debt Expense	5,800	
	Allowance for Doubtful Accounts		5,800
	To adjust the AFDA account to the correct balance		

Scenario 3

ALLOWANCE FOR DOUBTFUL ACCOUNTS

Opening balance	$1,000	
	$6,800	
	$5,800	Desired ending balance

JOURNAL			
Date	Account Title and Explanation	Debit	Credit
	Bad Debt Expense	6,800	
	Allowance for Doubtful Accounts		6,800
	To adjust the AFDA account to the correct balance		

FIGURE 10.13

Note that the net adjustment of accounts receivable adheres to the principle of conservatism under GAAP, which requires assets to be valued at the lower amount of possible alternatives and, as a result, reflects a reduced income for the period. This approach allows the business to make decisions based on figures that don't overstate assets, net income or the financial position of the company.

Managing Accounts Receivable Information Using Reports

Much of our analysis of accounts receivable has involved the method of accounting for accounts receivable in the company's books. This is important because these records give management accurate information on which to make good business decisions. This also allows companies to adhere to external reporting standards and principles.

However, another important aspect of accounts receivable is managing or controlling them. It is important for a business to know not only the amount of its accounts receivable but also which policies and procedures will lead to the collection of the maximum possible amount.

Having too many customers owing the company too much money on overdue bills restricts cash flow and working capital. Among other things, it limits the ability of the company to meet its commitments, such as accounts payable and loans.

Since the accounts receivable section of the balance sheet plays such a prominent role in the financial well-being of a company, it is important that information about this asset is efficiently organized.

Fortunately, computer software is available to collect, organize and process information in different ways. Many reports can be produced to give management insight into financial affairs in ways that raw data cannot.

A CLOSER LOOK

A number of strategies will ensure that a company manages and controls its accounts receivable. These include the following:

- Commitment to efficiency. Management commits to ensuring that accounts receivable are handled efficiently.

- Measuring results. After using ratios and reports to manage information, it is essential to determine whether these measures are working.

- Cutting-edge technology. Having the company's technology up-to-date to provide accurate and useful information about accounts receivable will assist in informed decision-making.

The Accounts Receivable Subledger

The list in figure 10.14 is a customer-by-customer list of outstanding amounts owing to a company; these amounts represent the total in the accounts receivable control account.

Accounts Receivable listing as at July 31					
	Current	31-60 days	61-90 days	91 days +	Total
Archer Limited	1,300	900	1,500		3,700
Beta Company	1,200	1,800	1,300	150	4,450
Cooper Limited	1,800	150			1,950
Dunwoody Company	200	500	200		900
Harry's Supplies	4,000	3,000	1,600	1,200	9,800
Lino Inc.	400	600	100		1,100
Total	**8,900**	**6,950**	**4,700**	**1,350**	**21,900**
	40.64%	31.74%	21.46%	6.16%	

FIGURE 10.14

Presenting the data in this form facilitates the analysis of accounts receivable by customer. It also highlights the figures that stand out from the others. In this case, the areas of note have been marked in yellow, red and green in the revised chart that follows.

Accounts Receivable listing as at July 31					
	Current	31-60 days	61-90 days	91 days +	Total
Archer Limited	1,300	900	1,500		3,700
Beta Company	1,200	1,800	1,300	150	4,450
Cooper Limited	1,800	150			1,950
Dunwoody Company	200	500	200		900
Harry's Supplies	4,000	3,000	1,600	1,200	9,800
Lino Inc.	400	600	100		1,100
Total	8,900	6,950	4,700	1,350	21,900
	40.64%	31.74%	21.46%	6.16%	

FIGURE 10.15

As the yellow and red areas show, two customers have bills outstanding over 90 days.

The yellow area shows us an amount of $150 from Beta Company that has not been paid for over 90 days. However, this is a relatively small amount, especially in comparison with Beta's total amount owing. It could be the result of an invoice discrepancy or some other minor issue. Although Beta is one of only two customers with balances owing for over 90 days, management should not be too concerned about this balance. There should still be controls in place to follow up with the customer either to correct or adjust the amount.

The other customer with a balance exceeding 90 days, Harry's Supplies, should certainly be a cause for concern. The amount marked in red, $1,200, represents a significant portion of its outstanding balance. Furthermore, the amount might be even more problematical, given that the same customer has been given $4,000 credit in the current month. This account is not being well-managed, and management should follow up with the company while also reconsidering the credit policies that have allowed such a situation to develop.

The green area of this chart is notable because, unlike all the other customers on the list, Cooper Limited does not have an outstanding balance for the 61–90 day period. Furthermore, it has only $150 outstanding for the 31–60 day period. Therefore the $1,800 credit given to Cooper in the current period appears to be justified: this customer has paid his bills promptly and providing more credit for that customer would make good business sense.

Alternative Presentation Formats

The preceding examples represent just a few ways in which accounts receivable information can be organized and presented. Computer software provides unlimited possibilities. Management should tailor computer programs to meet the specific needs and objectives of the company with regard to information about accounts receivable, bad debts, internal controls and all other related issues.

The reports that can be generated involving accounts receivable include the following:

- Current active customers
- Past customers not active for the last 12 months
- Customer activities listing value of sales per month
- Customer activities listing value of sales per product
- Categorization of customers according to sales representative or geographic location
- Overdue accounts

Measuring the Effectiveness of Collections Using Ratios

Another approach to measuring the effectiveness of the company's collection efforts is through the use of financial ratios. We examine two types of ratios: **days sales outstanding** and **accounts receivable turnover**.

Days Sales Outstanding

One way of organizing accounts receivable information is to use days sales outstanding (DSO). DSO tracks how long customers take to pay their bills. This is done by using two basic figures from the financial records: net accounts receivable (accounts receivable less allowance for doubtful accounts) and net credit sales for the past 12 months.

The average net accounts receivable figure is divided by the net credit sales of the past 12 months. The result is then multiplied by 365 (days in the year). The result provides the company with the average number of days that customers take to pay their bills. The following two examples illustrate the use and function of this particular ratio.

Company 1

Let us assume that the total average net accounts receivable amount for Company 1 is $200,000, and the total net credit sales amount for the past year was $1,200,000. Our DSO ratio is calculated as follows:

Days Sales Outstanding = (*Average Net Accounts Receivable ÷ Net Credit Sales) x 365
$$= (\$200{,}000 \div \$1{,}200{,}000) \times 365$$
$$= 61 \text{ days}$$

*Average net accounts receivable is calculated by adding the opening net accounts receivable balance to the closing net accounts receivable balance and dividing the result by 2

* Net credit sales = Total Credit Sales – Sales discount – Sales Returns and Allowances

In other words, it takes an average of 61 days to collect amounts outstanding.

Company 2

Let us assume that the total average net accounts receivable amount for Company 2 is $135,000, and the total net credit sales for the past year were $1,650,000. Our DSO ratio is calculated as follows:

$$(\$135{,}000 \div \$1{,}650{,}000) \times 365 = 30 \text{ days}$$

On the basis of these calculations, Company 2 is collecting its accounts receivable from customers twice as fast as Company 1. Because of the importance of cash in operating a business, it is in a company's best interest to collect outstanding accounts receivable as quickly as possible. By quickly turning sales into cash, a company has the opportunity to effectively use the cash for reinvestment and to produce more revenue. One of the most important factors that affect DSO is the company's credit terms.

If both companies allow customers 30 days to pay for their purchase on account, Company 2 is doing well in terms of collection whereas Company 1 is doing poorly.

Accounts Receivable Turnover Ratio

The accounts receivable turnover (ART) ratio is similar to DSO. It involves dividing a company's net credit sales by the average amount of net accounts receivable.

$$ART = Net\ Credit\ Sales \div Average\ Net\ Accounts\ Receivable$$

Company 3

Company 3 has net credit sales of $1,000,000 and the average amount of its net accounts receivable is $100,000.

$$ART = \$1,000,000 \div \$100,000 = 10\ times$$

Company 4

Company 4 has net credit sales of $3,000,000 and the average amount of its net accounts receivable is $400,000.

$$ART = \$3,000,000 \div \$400,000 = 7.5\ times$$

A higher ratio indicates a greater ability to convert accounts receivable into cash. In this case, Company 3 is collecting its receivables faster than Company 4.

If a business turns its receivables over 12 times per year, it would mean that it is collecting the average balance of receivables every month.

Accounts Receivable Controls

Now that we have examined various ways of organizing, presenting and managing accounts receivable information, some of the information can be used to implement sound control policies. In other words, there is no value in collecting all that data unless it is used to better manage a company's accounts receivable.

Indeed, this is the purpose of accounts receivable internal controls – to help a company get the most out of one of its largest and most crucial assets. We will look specifically at how a credit policy can serve as a control mechanism to ensure that the accounts receivable asset is managed, protected and maximized in value.

Credit Controls

One of the first issues a company should consider when establishing a credit policy is whether to adopt a lenient or restrictive approach to providing credit. Two broad factors can influence such a decision: the company's own financial position and its market position relative to the competition.

For example, if a company is already financially constrained, it probably cannot afford to extend credit to customers at risk. Similarly, low sales volumes for custom-made products leave a company with less room to extend generous credit terms. A company with little or no competition does not need to increase market share, and therefore has no incentive to adopt lenient credit policies.

Decisions involving credit terms can have a significant impact on sales volume. The more lenient a company's credit policy, the more likely it is to generate additional sales. It provides potential customers with the incentive to buy goods without having to pay for them immediately. Therefore, a more competitive market environment, homogeneous products and high sales volumes provide a company with greater incentive to extend more lenient credit terms to customers.

Credit Approval

Providing payment terms to customers involves making unsecured loans to the customers so that they can buy the company's product or service. Instead of automatically offering these terms, a company can implement various measures to better understand their customers and follow up when necessary. This is the essence of credit approval. It can involve having the customer complete a credit application and update the information regularly. The company can also request a customer's financial statements to ensure that it is in a position to pay its bills.

Credit Information

Of course, customers may not always be completely open about their financial health or ability to pay their bills. Companies therefore get independent credit information about customers from credit reporting agencies, financial institutions and even from other vendors.

Credit agency reports can be very useful in getting up-to-date information on current and potential customers. They can provide payment history, claims against the customer, banking information, existing credit granted, a record of recent inquiries as well as any credit ratings.

Terms of Sale

Another credit control at a company's disposal is setting the terms of sale. A certain period, such as 30 days, can be used and enforced against all customers.

Credit Policy

Finally, deciding on the methods of collecting from customers is yet another control in credit policy. The invoice is always the first tool of collection. If a customer is overdue with his payment, the company can send a second. If that does not prove successful, other measures such as letters, phone calls and even personal visits can be used to put pressure on the customer. If all else fails, a collection agency can be hired to enforce payment, especially when the account is long overdue.

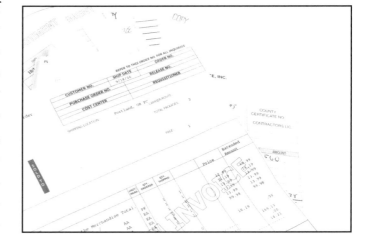

Other controls for accounts receivable that may be implemented are the following:

- Keeping individual records for each customer.
- Following up on large accounts that are overdue.
- Writing off a bad debt when it has been determined that all reasonable measures have been exhausted in collecting the debt.
- Ensuring that the original write-off is reversed when payments are received for a previously written-off account.

A CLOSER LOOK

An important objective for any successful business is to maximize its control and management of accounts receivable. To that end, a company can establish a checklist of items to monitor how well it is doing in meeting this objective. Such a checklist may include the following items:

- Is the staff fully trained to handle accounts receivable issues?
- Is all sensitive accounts receivable information adequately secured?
- Are invoices being processed accurately?
- Are customers informed quickly enough of credit decisions made by the company?
- Are third party collection agencies being properly monitored?

Converting Accounts Receivable into Cash

Having too many customers that are not paying on time, or not at all, can create serious problems for a company's cash flow and working capital. Certain measures can be taken to convert a company's accounts receivable into cash in the most efficient manner possible (see "In the Real World" on the next page for a description of one of these measures).

Setting Firm Credit Terms

Perhaps most important, a company should try to assess whether its collection period is stringent enough. Accounts receivable should not be extended more than 10 or 15 days beyond the credit terms. Industry standards differ, so assessing what the competition is doing, then setting a benchmark to meet or surpass those expectations, may be a wise business strategy. Setting a high standard and routinely enforcing it might improve the collection of accounts.

The Promissory Note and Notes Receivable

There is another way to look at accounts receivable. In a sense, the transaction is much like a loan. Since the customers do not initially pay for the goods or services they receive from the company, the selling company is in effect lending customers the money to pay for them until the loan is due. However, this loan usually does not come with interest within the credit period.

A **promissory note**, or **note receivable** makes an account receivable resemble a formal loan by adding precise terms of repayment to which the customer adds his signature.

For example, if a customer is overdue on her account, the company may request that the customer sign a promissory note, which would formalize the arrangements involved in the repayment of the debt – much like a formal loan specifies its terms of repayment. Both a loan and a promissory note can set terms that include naming the parties to the document, the amount to be paid, when the amounts are due, as well as the interest charges related to the payments.

A promissory note, or note receivable, is used not only to formalize an accounts

WORTH REPEATING...

Two factors are taken into consideration when deciding on how stringent or lenient the company's credit policy should be:

- The company's own financial situation. The stronger it is, the better it can afford to make sales on credit.

- The company's competitive situation. The more competition a company has, the greater the pressure to extend credit in order to increase sales.

IN THE REAL WORLD

Companies have various means at their disposal to convert their accounts receivable into cash. One that has become more frequent in recent years is known as *factoring*, which can help a company's cash flow and working capital in the short term.

Factoring involves selling accounts receivable assets at a discount price to a third party, the factor. The factor is then responsible for collecting payment from the debtor.

At one time a factor was brought in as a last resort — only after all previous attempts at collecting failed, including the use of a collection agency.

However, factoring has become quite common place, with tens of billions of dollars being factored each year.

Today, as it becomes increasingly difficult for businesses to secure loans, factoring is turning into a viable option for raising funds. The cost to the seller involves receiving a discounted price for the total value of accounts receivable. In essence, this amounts to decreasing the value of the company assets. However, it receives cash for its accounts receivable, and the discount price may be worth more than the amount the company could hope to collect from its customers on its own.

receivable item but also to extend unusual credit terms to a specific customer, such as an agreement that may involve lengthening the terms of repayment to more than one year. In addition, the note can be used to extend credit to a customer with no formal credit history. The stronger legal claim associated with a note provides greater protection for the selling company when dealing with uncertain or riskier customer accounts. Provided that the seller is confident the customer will eventually pay the note, there should be no objection to issuing the note.

PROMISSORY NOTE

_____, 201__

At any time after the above date, the undersigned promises to pay the lender the sum of $_____ with _____ % interest until _____ 201__. The makers, endorsers, and guarantors hereof waive presentment, demand of payment, notice of nonpayment, protest, notice of protest, and all exemptions.

_____   _____
NAME OF LENDER   NAME OF BORROWER

_____   _____
LENDER'S SIGNATURE   BORROWER'S SIGNATURE

For example, on April 1, 2010, Kay Fernandez Alonso has $1,000 of outstanding accounts receivable with Bennet Company. Bennet's year-end is October 31. Kay cannot pay the amount immediately, but is willing to sign a note. The interest is 6% per annum, to be collected when the note is due. Kay promises to pay on April 1, 2011. The entry to record the conversion of the accounts receivable to a note receivable is as follows:

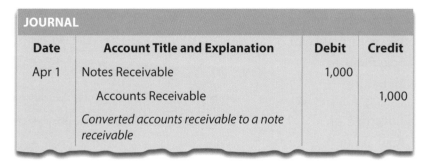

JOURNAL			
Date	**Account Title and Explanation**	**Debit**	**Credit**
Apr 1	Notes Receivable	1,000	
	Accounts Receivable		1,000
	Converted accounts receivable to a note receivable		

ACCOUNTS RECEIVABLE
− $1,000 (CR)

ACCOUNTS

NOTES RECEIVABLE
+ $1,000 (DR)

FIGURE 10.16

On October 31, when Bennet Company prepares its financial statements, it will need to accrue the interest earned from Alonso. Notice that the interest earned is classified as "Other Revenue" rather than regular earned revenue.

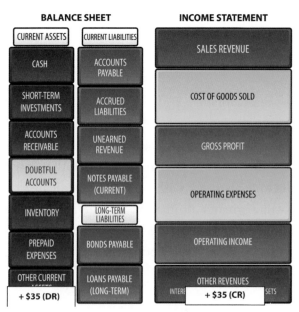

JOURNAL			
Date	**Account Title and Explanation**	**Debit**	**Credit**
Oct 31	Interest Receivable	35	
	Interest Revenue		35
	To record accrued interest revenue *$1,000 x 6% x 7/12*		

FIGURE 10.17

When Kay pays the amount due on April 1, 2011, the following entry is recorded on the statements of Bennet Company.

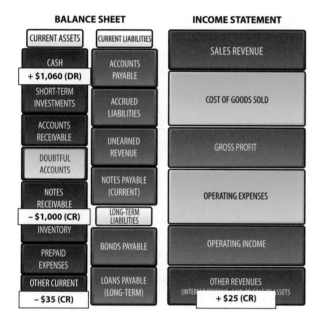

BALANCE SHEET

INCOME STATEMENT

Explanation of this transaction:

- Kay paid $1,060 (debit to cash).
- An amount of $25 was recorded as interest revenue by crediting interest revenue.
- The interest receivable of $35 was eliminated by crediting the account.
- The note receivable of $1,000 was eliminated by crediting the note receivable account.

JOURNAL			
Date	**Account Title and Explanation**	**Debit**	**Credit**
Apr 1	Cash	1,060	
	Interest Receivable		35
	Interest Revenue		25
	Notes Receivable		1,000
	Record the receipt of note principal & interest ($1,000 x 6% x 5/12)		

FIGURE 10.18

An Ethical Approach to Managing Accounts Receivable

As some of the discussion in this chapter has already illustrated, a company's accounts receivable asset can be both simple and complex. Its simplicity can be found in the fact that it is represented on the balance sheet as one debit figure in one control account, with a corresponding contra account representing the bad debt allowance. The asset will therefore have one net value, reflecting the balance expected to be collected from customers.

However, the complexity of accounts receivable is revealed by looking at the subledger. This consists of many transactions, which must be regularly updated to reflect ongoing payments or non-payments. Managing these accounts involves different procedures and requires various tools at the accountant's disposal. We looked at some of these tools earlier in the chapter.

The company and its accounting department are responsible for managing these tasks accurately and ethically.

There is little dispute regarding the impact of the value of accounts receivable on the company's financial statements and that the management and accounting of the asset is open to manipulation.

Various ethical principles and standards have been established to prevent or detect manipulation of accounts receivable. Here is a case study that illustrates unethical behavior, which violates the full disclosure principle outlined in GAAP.

Charles owns a manufacturing business, which has been growing steadily. His bank wants to examine his financial statements before approving his loan to finance his increasing need for additional capital. His records show a total of $450,000 in accounts receivable, and he has earned net income of $80,000 for the current year. Charles is also aware that there is an amount of $50,000 that is likely to be uncollectible; however, he knows that if he allows for the bad debt in his statements, he may not be successful in securing the loan. Charles justifies his non-disclosure by committing himself to allowing for the bad debt the following year because there is a slight chance that he may still get paid.

What Charles did was unethical. He deliberately overstated the value of his assets to try to secure the loan. He believed that the debt was not going to be paid, but he represented it otherwise to distort the current value of the accounts receivable.

Charles consciously violated the full disclosure principle by withholding information relevant to the valuing of these assets.

Let us look at another example of unethical behavior. This time we will examine the importance of maintaining the integrity of the accounts receivable information that a company collects and manages. A failure to do so can put into doubt the accuracy of the company's books, as well as the ethics of the people in charge.

Sophie has been hired by the controller, Rick, to manage the company's accounts receivable. Upon assuming the job, Sophie soon notices that the company's accounts receivable have been poorly managed. The computer system was old and the invoices were not detailed enough, thus leading to customers questioning their invoices. Furthermore, the company would increase prices on the date of shipment instead of on the date the order was placed. Customers would complain and did not want to pay invoices showing prices they had not agreed to.

Sophie brought her concerns to Rick, who told her to keep quiet about her concerns and to do the best she could. Rick was afraid that he would be held accountable if the extent of the problems was made known to upper management, so he tried to hide the problems as much as he could. Sophie did not know what to do about the unethical accounting practices. If she remained silent, the integrity of the company's accounts receivable would be in serious jeopardy.

An accountant is responsible for maintaining the integrity of the information in the books. Rick should have dealt with these problems as soon as he became aware of them. Instead, when these problems were pointed out to him, he tried to hide them and absolve himself of any responsibility. The company's customers were being treated unfairly, the integrity of the financial information of the company was compromised and the tactics used in response to the problems were ethically unacceptable. Furthermore, he imposed an unacceptable dilemma on his employee, Sophie, requiring her to choose between her job and the proper management of the company's assets.

Unless Rick accepts responsibility for the problems and corrects them, he puts both himself and his company in a vulnerable position both financially and ethically.

A CLOSER LOOK

An important feature of the income statement approach is that the calculation produces an amount by which the bad debt expense needs to be adjusted regardless of what the existing balance of AFDA is. On the other hand, the balance sheet approach's calculation produces an amount which would be the ending balance of AFDA and not necessarily the amount of adjustment required.

Under the income statement approach, after the amount based on a percentage of credit sales is calculated, bad debt expense is debited and AFDA is credited. The idea behind basing the expense on sales is to appropriately match the bad debt expense with the credit sales of the period.

The total amount of the allowance is essentially ignored. Each period bad debt expense is debited, and AFDA is credited. If the percentage of credit sales used realistically reflects the actual amount of bad debt experienced, the allowance account will reflect a reasonable balance.

On the other hand, if the actual bad debt experienced are materially lower than the estimate (based on a percentage of sales), the allowance for doubtful accounts may build to an unrealistically large amount. This would occur because the increase in AFDA based on the estimate of bad debt is not consistent with a corresponding reduction resulting from actual bad debt write-offs.

If you observe that the allowance account is becoming unusually large, you could forego recording additional bad debt expenses (and the corresponding credit to the allowance account), until debits (i.e. actual bad debt write-offs) reduce the allowance account to a reasonable balance once again. What is a reasonable balance? As with many items in accounting, the answer is based on professional judgment.

In Summary

↪ Accounts receivable often represents a significant percentage of a company's assets.

↪ Since accounts receivable losses usually occur after the end of the fiscal year in which the sale was made, an allowance for doubtful accounts (AFDA) needs to be used. This procedure allows a company to conform to GAAP rules.

↪ AFDA is a contra account attached to the accounts receivable account. AFDA entries are recorded in reverse of the entries recorded in accounts receivable.

↪ There are two approaches to evaluate AFDA: The income statement approach and the balance sheet approach.

↪ The effectiveness of accounts receivable collections can be gauged with the use of two ratios: days sales outstanding (DSO) and accounts receivable turnover (ART).

↪ Accounts receivable can be converted into promissory notes, or notes receivable, which are legally binding documents.

↪ Credit controls and policies are necessary to manage and protect the accounts receivable asset.

↪ Reports are used to monitor paying trends by customers and ensure that credit terms are not abused.

↪ Since accounts receivable often represents a significant percentage of a company's assets, there can be a temptation to manipulate its value. Ethical behavior is therefore crucial in maintaining the integrity of a company's financial statements.

Review Exercise 1

Part 1

You are the accountant for Booe Company. Your company uses the direct write-off method to account for bad debt. Record the following transactions:

1. Sale to Guy Tygart on account – 1,000 gadgets @ $5 on June 30
2. Collect $4,900 from Guy Tygart on July 10
3. Write off the remaining balance owing from Guy Tygart on July 31
4. Collect 50% of the amount written off on December 15.

Assume the cost of inventory is only updated at the end of the year (i.e. do not consider cost of goods sold for the transactions above).

Part 1 – Answer

Date	Account Title and Explanation	Debit	Credit
Jun 30	Accounts Receivable – Tygart	5,000	
	Sales Revenue		5,000
	To record sale on credit		
Jul 10	Cash	4,900	
	Accounts Receivable – Tygart		4,900
	To record receipt of payment in part		
Jul 31	Bad Debt Expense	100	
	Accounts Receivable – Tygart		100
	To record bad debt using the direct write-off		
	method		
Dec 15	Accounts Receivable – Tygart	50	
	Bad Debt Expense		50
	To reinstate customer's account		
Dec 15	Cash	50	
	Accounts Receivable – Tygart		50
	To record receipt of payment		

Part 2

Using the same scenario as above, recalculate all the transactions and record the entries assuming that your company uses the allowance for doubtful accounts method.

Assume that $5,000 had been credited to the allowance account for the year.

Part 2 – Answer

Date	Account Title and Explanation	Debit	Credit
Jun 30	Accounts Receivable – Tygart	5,000	
	Sales Revenue		5,000
	To record sale on credit		
Jul 10	Cash	4,900	
	Accounts Receivable – Tygart		4,900
	To record receipt of payment in part		
Jul 31	Allowance for Doubtful Accounts	100	
	Accounts Receivable – Tygart		100
	To write-off accounts as uncollectible		
Dec 15	Accounts Receivable – Tygart	50	
	Allowance for Doubtful Accounts		50
	To reinstate amount previously written-off		
Dec 15	Cash	50	
	Accounts Receivable – Tygart		50
	To record receipt of payment		

Review Exercise 2

ABC Company uses the allowance method to account for bad debt. During the current year, 2010, the company had $350,000 in sales of which 80% were on account and the remaining 20% were cash sales.

During the year the company received $250,000 from customers as payment on their accounts. In June, it also wrote-off $1,500 for a customer who notified them they were filing for bankruptcy and would not be able to pay. However, the same customer notified them that they had received money from a wealthy relative and would be able to pay their account early in the new year after the account was written off. The company expects that $5,000 of the accounts receivable balance at the end of the year may be uncollectible.

Required:

a) Using the general journal and Dec 31 as the date for all transactions, record the sales, collections for customers on account, write-off of accounts and bad debt expense for 2010. You may omit explanations for each entry.

Assume accounts receivable had a debit balance of $35,000 and that the AFDA had a credit balance of $2,500 at the beginning of the year (Jan.1, 2010).

b) Show how the above transactions would be posted in the related T-Accounts

c) Show how accounts receivable would be reported on the Dec 31, 2010 balance sheet after the above entries had been posted.

Note: do not consider cost of goods sold in the above transactions.

Review Exercise – Answer

a) Show how the above transactions would be recorded in the journal

Date	Account Title and Explanation	Debit	Credit
Dec 31	Cash	70,000	
	Accounts Receivable	280,000	
	Sales Revenue		350,000
	To record sales for the year		
Dec 31	Cash	250,000	
	Accounts Receivable		250,000
	To record collection of accounts for the year		
Dec 31	Allowance for Doubtful Accounts	1,500	
	Accounts Receivable		1,500
	To write-off uncollectible account		
Dec 31	Accounts Receivable	1,500	
	Allowance for Doubtful Accounts		1,500
	To reverse write-off of account		
Dec 31	Bad Debt Expense	2,500	
	Allowance for Doubtful Accounts		2,500
	To reinstate bad debt for the year		

b) Show how the above transactions would be posted in the related T-Accounts

Cash	
$70,000	
250,000	
$320,000	

Sales Revenue	
	$350,000

Accounts Receivable	
Beg. Bal.: $35,000	$250,000
280,000	1,500
1,500	
$65,000	

Allowance for Doubtful Accounts	
$1,500	Beg. Bal.: $2,500
	1,500
	2,500
	$5,000

Bad Debt Expense	
$2,500	

c) Show how accounts receivable would be reported on the Dec 31, 2010 balance sheet after the above entries had been posted

Current Assets:	Dec 31, 2010	Jan 01, 2010
Accounts Receivable	$65,000	$35,000
Less: Allowance for Doubtful Accounts	5,000	2,500
Net Accounts Receivable	$60,000	$32,500

Chapter 11
INVENTORY

LEARNING OUTCOMES:

❶ Understand the difference between the perpetual and the periodic inventory systems

❷ Record journal entries under the perpetual inventory system

❸ Determine inventory values under the perpetual system

❹ Determine the impact of inventory errors

❺ Use the lower of cost or market to value inventory

❻ Estimate inventory using the gross profit method and the retail method

❼ Calculate ratios to determine inventory efficiency

❽ Apply controls and understand ethics related to inventory

Appendix

❾ Record journal entries under the periodic inventory system

❿ Determine inventory values under the periodic system

Inventory: An Introduction

As our examination of the balance sheet continues, it will become increasingly clear that each type of current asset has its own defining characteristics. For example, cash is the most liquid type of asset and is used to buy other assets, while other assets are sold for cash.

Much like accounts receivable, inventory involves the day-to-day operations of the business; and can also comprise a large portion of the company's current assets. However, unlike accounts receivable and any of the other assets we have studied so far, inventory isn't just a number or monetary concept.

Inventory represents physical goods that a company has bought or manufactured in order to sell to its customers. The inventory has a value that can change unpredictably and even decrease over time. Accountants can make errors in tracking the value of inventory as it moves from receiving to shipping. They can also have a hard time figuring out what inventory to count and how to count it. These are some of the challenges confronting a company in handling its inventory assets.

CURRENT ASSETS

CASH

SHORT-TERM INVESTMENT

ACCOUNTS RECEIVABLE

INVENTORY

FIGURE 11.1

Perpetual vs. Periodic Inventory Systems

Under a **perpetual inventory system**, a continuous record of the changes to inventory is maintained. This means all purchases and sales of goods are recorded directly in the inventory account as they occur. With the advent of scanning technology, most retail businesses can now use a perpetual inventory system. With one swipe of the scanner at the point of sale, the value of the specific item can be accounted for and adjusted directly in the company's inventory account. The cost of goods sold is readily available at the end of the period, as the inventory account has been constantly updated.

However, not all companies choose to track their inventory this way. A small grocery store might not have access to scanning technology. In this case, a company can use what is known as the **periodic inventory system**, which determines the quantity of inventory on hand only periodically. Under a periodic inventory system, a physical count is taken at the end of the period to determine the value of the cost of goods sold.

Figure 11.2 highlights the difference between the perpetual and periodic inventory system. It shows sample revenue amounts for a company under both systems over a period of three months. Notice that the perpetual system updates cost of goods sold continuously while the periodic system updates cost of goods sold only when a physical inventory count is performed (at the end of March).

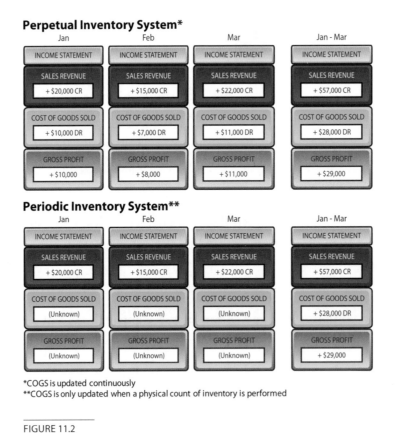

FIGURE 11.2

Since the periodic inventory system is not widely used in today's computerized environment, our discussion will focus on the perpetual inventory system.

The Perpetual Inventory System

As mentioned above, a perpetual inventory system involves recording all transactions affecting the balance of inventory on hand as they occur. In reality, most businesses have separate, detailed records for each type of product they sell. For simplicity, our examples will focus on one type of product, where all transactions affect a single inventory account directly.

We will demonstrate various inventory-related transactions using an example of a retail store called Tools 4U Inc., which buys and sells various tools. Assume the inventory account has a beginning balance of $20,000 and the following transactions occurred during the accounting period.

Purchases

When inventory is purchased for resale using a perpetual inventory system, the inventory account is debited and the cash or the accounts payable account is credited. Tools 4U Inc. purchased inventory at a cost of $4,800 on January 1, 2011. Assume all purchases and sales are made on account.

JOURNAL			Page 1
Date	Account Title and Explanation	Debit	Credit
Jan 1	Inventory	4,800	
	Accounts Payable		4,800
	Purchased inventory on account		

FIGURE 11.3

Purchase Returns

Goods often need to be returned for reasons such as incorrect product, over-shipments, or inferior product quality.

When the manager of Tools 4U examined the new shipment of inventory from the company's supplier, Roof Tiles Inc., he noticed that there were some damaged goods in the shipment. The damaged goods cost $500. The goods were returned and the journal entry would be the exact reverse of the original purchase transaction.

BALANCE SHEET

CURRENT ASSETS	CURRENT LIABILITIES
CASH	ACCOUNTS PAYABLE - $500 DR
SHORT-TERM INVESTMENTS	ACCRUED LIABILITIES
ACCOUNTS RECEIVABLE	UNEARNED REVENUE
DOUBTFUL ACCOUNTS	NOTES PAYABLE (CURRENT)
INVENTORY - $500 CR	LONG-TERM LIABILITIES

JOURNAL			Page 1
Date	Account Title and Explanation	Debit	Credit
Jan 2	Accounts Payable	500	
	Inventory		500
	Goods returned to Roof Tiles		

FIGURE 11.4

Purchase Allowances

Purchase allowances occur when the buyer agrees to keep the undesirable goods at a reduced cost. Continuing with the above example, assume Tools 4U found another $500 worth of unsatisfactory goods and the supplier had offered a 20% allowance for the company to keep the goods, rather than returning them. The journal entry would be recorded by debiting accounts payable and crediting inventory. The transaction amount would be $100 ($500 × 20%).

After recording purchase returns and purchase allowance, a balance of $4,200 ($4,800 - $500 - $100) is still owing to Roof Tiles Inc.

JOURNAL			Page 1
Date	Account Title and Explanation	Debit	Credit
Jan 4	Accounts Payable	100	
	Inventory		100
	Allowance from Roof Tiles		

BALANCE SHEET

CURRENT ASSETS	CURRENT LIABILITIES
CASH	ACCOUNTS PAYABLE - $100 DR
SHORT-TERM INVESTMENTS	ACCRUED LIABILITIES
ACCOUNTS RECEIVABLE	UNEARNED REVENUE
DOUBTFUL ACCOUNTS	NOTES PAYABLE (CURRENT)
INVENTORY - $100 CR	LONG-TERM LIABILITIES

FIGURE 11.5

Purchase Discounts

Various types of discounts exist when purchasing products or services. Some common reasons for a seller to give discounts are to:

- avoid changes in a price catalogue
- apply price discrimination (i.e. quote different prices for different customers)
- hide the true invoice price from competitors
- encourage customers to purchase more
- encourage early payments

Two types of common discounts given are **trade discounts** and **cash discounts**. Only cash discounts will be discussed in detail for the purpose of this chapter.

Cash discounts are usually given to encourage prompt payment from customers. For example, a seller may offer a 2% cash discount if the payment is made within 10 days of the date of invoice, otherwise the full amount is payable within 30 days. The term for this arrangement is commonly shown as: 2/10, n/30 (read as: a 2 percent discount is applied if paid within 10 days, the net amount owing is due in 30 days). Another example could be: 3/15, n/30, which means a 3 percent discount is applied if paid within 15 days, otherwise the full amount (net amount owing) is payable within 30 days. The following example illustrates how to record a purchase discount.

Tools 4U made the original purchase from Roof Tiles Inc. on January 1, 2011 for $4,800. The amount Tools 4U owes has been reduced by $600 due to returns and allowances, so that only $4,200 must be paid. The supplier (Roof Tiles Inc.) allows 2/10, n/30 on all invoices. Since Tools 4U has excess cash at this time, the manager decides to take advantage of the cash discount by paying the invoice within 10 days.

Assume Tools 4U Inc. made the payment on January 10, the amount for the bill will be $4,200 less the $84 discount ($4,200 × 2%). Since the business is paying less for the inventory, the value of the inventory needs to decrease by the value of the discount. The entry to record the payment is shown in figure 11.6.

BALANCE SHEET

CURRENT ASSETS	CURRENT LIABILITIES
CASH - $4,116 CR	ACCOUNTS PAYABLE - $4,200 DR
SHORT-TERM INVESTMENTS	ACCRUED LIABILITIES
ACCOUNTS RECEIVABLE	UNEARNED REVENUE
DOUBTFUL ACCOUNTS	NOTES PAYABLE (CURRENT)
INVENTORY - $84 CR	LONG-TERM LIABILITIES

JOURNAL			Page 1
Date	**Account Title and Explanation**	**Debit**	**Credit**
Jan 10	Accounts Payable	4,200	
	Cash		4,116
	Inventory		84
	Paid invoice and took discount for early payment		

FIGURE 11.6

The discount of $84 is credited to inventory because the downward adjustment is made to reflect the true cost of the goods.

If Tools 4U decides not to pay the amount owing within 10 days, then they are not entitled to take the discount. They must pay the full amount of $4,200 within 30 days of the invoice date. This payment is just like paying any other amount that is owed to a supplier. Cash will decrease (credit) and accounts payable will decrease (debit) by the amount owed. The entry is shown in figure 11.7. Notice the date is more than 10 days past the invoice date.

BALANCE SHEET

CURRENT ASSETS	CURRENT LIABILITIES
CASH - $4,200 CR	ACCOUNTS PAYABLE - $4,200 DR
SHORT-TERM INVESTMENTS	ACCRUED LIABILITIES
ACCOUNTS RECEIVABLE	UNEARNED REVENUE
DOUBTFUL ACCOUNTS	NOTES PAYABLE (CURRENT)
INVENTORY	LONG-TERM LIABILITIES

JOURNAL			Page 1
Date	**Account Title and Explanation**	**Debit**	**Credit**
Jan 24	Accounts Payable	4,200	
	Cash		4,200
	Paid amount owing to Roof Tiles		

FIGURE 11.7

Freight Cost

When one company purchases goods from another, the items purchased must somehow be transported from the seller's place of business to the buyer's place of business. There are a number of ways to transport goods (sea, rail, truck, etc.). The selling company may have their own fleet of vehicles to deliver goods to customers, or they may use a common carrier. A common carrier in this context is a company that provides shipping service to the general public. Examples would be railroad or trucking companies.

In addition to arranging transport of the goods, at some point ownership of the goods must be legally transferred from the seller to the buyer. The term used to determine when ownership of the goods changes hands is called the FOB point. FOB stands for Freight On Board. There are two possible FOB points: FOB shipping point and FOB destination. Each of these points have implications regarding who pays for shipping, when ownership passes from the buyer to the seller and who bears the risk for the goods during transport.

FOB Shipping Point

FOB shipping point indicates that ownership of the items being purchased changes when the goods leave the seller's place of business. In other words, ownership changes at the point when shipping begins. In this case, a common carrier is often used to deliver the items to the buyer. The buyer will pay for shipping and is responsible to insure the items while they are in transport. If anything were to happen to the items while they are being transported, the buyer bears the risk of loss.

The seller will record revenue earned and the buyer will record an increase to inventory as soon as the goods are loaded on the truck (or other transport). The buyer will also have to record the shipping cost into inventory. The reason the buyer includes shipping costs as inventory is that the value of the goods must include all costs (such as transportation) that were incurred to get the goods ready to sell. Figure 11.8 illustrates who pays the shipping costs.

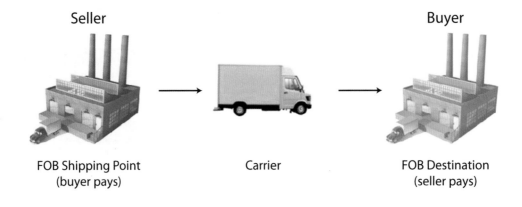

FIGURE 11.8

FOB Destination

FOB destination indicates that ownership of the items being purchased changes when the goods arrive at the buyer's place of business. In other words, ownership changes at the point of destination. In this case, the seller may pay an independent carrier or have a fleet of vehicles and use them to deliver goods to their customers. Thus, the seller pays for the shipping and is responsible for the items while they are in transport. If anything were to happen to the items while they are being transported, the seller bears the risk of loss.

The seller will record revenue earned and the buyer will record an increase to inventory once the goods reach their destination (the buyer's place of business). The seller will also record the cost of shipping the goods as an expense. This expense is part of the seller's cost of doing business.

A summary of FOB shipping point and FOB destination are presented in figure 11.9. Basically, whoever pays for shipping owns the goods while they are being transported and bears the risk of loss.

	FOB Shipping Point	FOB Destination
Ownership Change	When goods leave the seller on a common carrier	When goods arrive at the buyer's place of business
Transportation Costs	Paid by the buyer and recorded in inventory	Paid by the seller and recorded as an expense
Risk of Loss	Buyer bears risk of loss during transport	Seller bears risk of loss during transport

FIGURE 11.9

Assume that Tools 4U had inventory shipped to them FOB shipping point. This means that Tools 4U will have to pay the cost of shipping. If they paid $100 on January 2, that amount would have to be added to the inventory account. The journal entry is shown in figure 11.10.

BALANCE SHEET

CURRENT ASSETS — CASH: - $100 CR; SHORT-TERM INVESTMENTS; ACCOUNTS RECEIVABLE; DOUBTFUL ACCOUNTS; INVENTORY: + $100 DR

CURRENT LIABILITIES — ACCOUNTS PAYABLE; ACCRUED LIABILITIES; UNEARNED REVENUE; NOTES PAYABLE (CURRENT); LONG-TERM LIABILITIES

JOURNAL			Page 1
Date	Account Title and Explanation	Debit	Credit
Jan 2	Inventory	100	
	Cash		100
	Paid for freight costs		

FIGURE 11.10

Sales

Under a perpetual inventory system, two entries are needed to record the sale of inventory. One entry is needed to record the sale, which involves debiting accounts receivable (or cash) and crediting sales revenue; and another entry is needed to record the cost of goods sold, which involves debiting cost of goods sold and crediting inventory.

Both the COGS and the amount of inventory will be updated immediately in the accounting records when using a perpetual inventory system.

Assume Tools 4U Inc. sold $9,000 worth of inventory for $15,000 on January 15. The journal entry is presented as shown in figure 11.11.

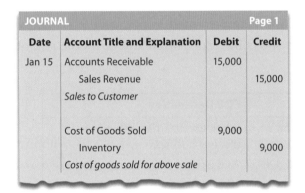
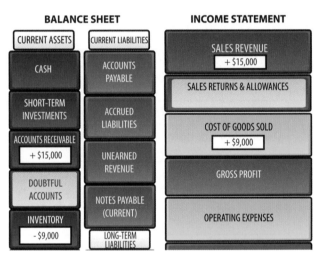

FIGURE 11.11

Sales Returns

A business may have to deal with numerous returns from customers, and these returns must be tracked over a period of time. High return levels may indicate serious problems with the products being sold. Therefore, instead of reversing the revenue account with a debit when recording returns, a contra-revenue account called **sales returns and allowances** is used to track the amount of returns.

Sales returns and allowances is a **contra-revenue account** with a normal debit balance. It behaves like an expense account, since it reduces the equity of the business. It is generally used to record both sales returns and sales allowances. **Sales returns** occur when undesirable products are returned to the seller. **Sales allowances** occur when the customer decides to keep such undesirable products at a reduced price.

Continuing with our example, if a customer returned Tools 4U Inc. $4,000 of undesirable goods (the cost of the goods is $3,000), the journal entry using the contra-revenue account would be:

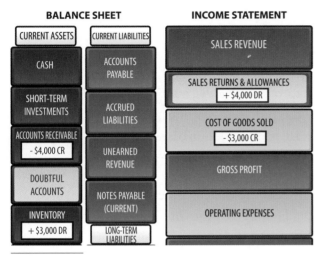

FIGURE 11.12

There will be a $4,000 increase in the sales returns and allowances account. This amount decreases revenue since the contra revenue account has the opposite normal balance of the revenue account.

In the example in figure 11.12, the inventory that was returned was not what the customer wanted. There was nothing wrong with the product in terms of quality, so it was placed back on the shelf to be sold again. If the items returned by the customer were damaged, then the inventory can not be sold again. Tool 4U would either have to absorb the cost of the damaged items (with an adjusting entry shown later), or return the damaged inventory to their supplier to get their money back (a purchase return).

Sales Allowances

There are circumstances where a reduction to the original selling price is given to a customer.

Assume the customer from January 15 discovered that some goods were damaged during shipping. Instead of returning the items, the customer agreed to accept an allowance of 5% on the price of the goods they kept. The customer kept $11,000 ($15,000 original sale - $4,000 return) of goods, so they will get a $550 ($11,000 × 5%) reduction on what they owe Tools 4U. The journal entry is shown in figure 11.13. The amount is recorded as a debit to sales returns and allowances and a credit to accounts receivable. Since the allowance decreases equity, it must be recorded on the income statement by debiting sales returns and allowances.

JOURNAL		Page 1	
Date	Account Title and Explanation	Debit	Credit
Jan 18	Sales Returns & Allowances	550	
	Accounts Receivable		550
	Sale allowance for damaged goods		

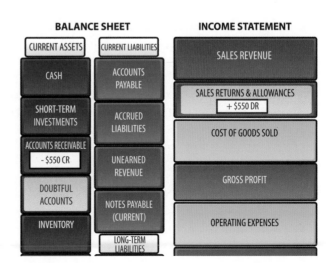

FIGURE 11.13

A balance of $10,450 ($15,000 - $4,000 - $550) is still owed by Tools 4U's customer.

Sales Discounts

When selling products or services, it is common to offer sales discounts to customers for early payment. The concept works in the same way as the purchase discount. Assume that Tools 4U offered their customer from January 15 terms of 2/10, n/30 in the invoice. If the customer pays by January 25, they can take a 2% discount on the $10,450 they still owe.

Assume the customer made the payment on January 20; the amount will be for $10,241 ($10,450 less the 2% discount). The journal entry to record this transaction is shown in figure 11.14.

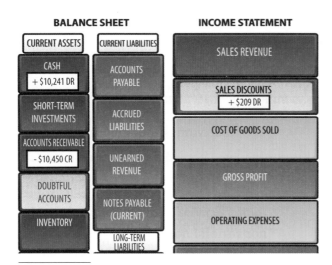

JOURNAL			Page 1
Date	Account Title and Explanation	Debit	Credit
Jan 20	Cash	10,241	
	Sales Discount	209	
	Accounts Receivable		10,450
	Payments received from customer less discount		

FIGURE 11.14

The $209 is recorded as a debit in the **sales discount**. Sales discount is a contra-revenue account which can be increased with a debit and decreased with a credit.

If the customer decides not to pay the amount owing within the discount period, then they are not entitled to take the discount that Tools 4U offers. Instead, the customer will have to pay the full amount of $10,450 within 30 days of the sale. The receipt of cash from the customer is just like receiving cash from any customer that owes the company money. Cash will increase (debit) and accounts receivable will decrease (credit). The entry is shown in figure 11.15. Notice that the date is more than 10 days past the date of the sale.

BALANCE SHEET

CURRENT ASSETS — CURRENT LIABILITIES

CASH
+ $10,450 DR

ACCOUNTS PAYABLE

SHORT-TERM INVESTMENTS

ACCRUED LIABILITIES

ACCOUNTS RECEIVABLE
- $10,450 CR

UNEARNED REVENUE

DOUBTFUL ACCOUNTS

NOTES PAYABLE (CURRENT)

INVENTORY

LONG-TERM LIABILITIES

JOURNAL			Page 1
Date	Account Title and Explanation	Debit	Credit
Feb 2	Cash	10,450	
	Accounts Receivable		10,450
	Payment received from customer		

FIGURE 11.15

Income Statement

A multistep income statement is prepared (shown in figure 11.16) based on the sales transactions that have occurred.

Tools 4U Inc. Income Statement For the Month Ended January 31, 2011		
Sales Revenue		$15,000
Less:		
Sales Returns & Allowances	($4,550)	
Sales Discounts	(209)	(4,759)
Net Sales		10,241
Cost of Goods Sold		6,000
Gross Profit		4,241

FIGURE 11.16

The sales revenue amount comes from figure 11.11. However, this is not the true value of what was sold. The customer returned some items, was given an allowance for a slightly damaged product, and paid early to receive the discount. Each of these items will reduce the value of sales revenue to provide net sales. **Net sales** is the value of sales after taking into account sales returns and allowances and sales discounts. The gross profit amount represents how much profit is left to pay for operating expenses.

In a situation where a company tracks sales returns and discounts separately, the gross profit margin is calculated using the value of net sales, not sales revenue:

$$\text{Gross Profit Margin} = \text{Gross Profit} \div \text{Net Sales} \times 100$$

$$= \$4,241 \div \$10,241 \times 100$$

$$= 41.4\%$$

The perpetual inventory system is typically used in the retail sector where the cost of products can easily be identified through technology such as bar coding. In its simplest form, when a product is purchased for resale, the value of goods available for sale is automatically updated. When a product is sold, the inventory is deducted from stock and the value of cost of goods sold is updated immediately. Gross profit can be determined right away since the cost of goods sold is known at any given time. If any adjustment to the value of the inventory is required, it can be determined when a physical inventory count is performed at the end of the year (or from time to time).

Closing Entries

When using a perpetual inventory system, inventory is immediately updated after each purchase and sale transaction. However, the value of inventory on the balance sheet may not accurately represent the value of inventory actually on hand. To verify the accuracy of the accounting records, a physical inventory count should be performed at the end of the reporting period. If the count does not match the records, an adjustment must be made to bring the inventory to its correct balance. This difference is often referred to as "inventory shrinkage", resulting either from an error in recording transactions, theft or breakage. If the amount is considered immaterial, the following entry would be made where the balance in the inventory account was more than the physical count. Assuming that the amount of shrinkage is $200, the journal entry for this transaction is shown in figure 11.17.

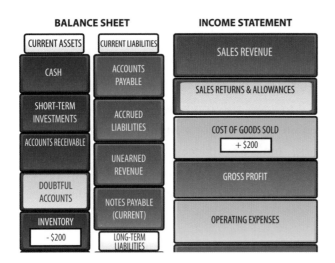

FIGURE 11.17

After this adjustment and all other adjustments have been made, assume Tools 4U has the adjusted trial balance shown in figure 11.18.

Tools 4U Inc. Adjusted Trial Balance January 31, 2011		
Account	**Debit**	**Credit**
Cash	$5,200	
Accounts Receivable	3,750	
Inventory	12,470	
Prepaid Expenses	3,200	
Property, Plant & Equipment	6,840	
Accumulated Depreciation		$340
Accounts Payable		5,260
Unearned Revenue		2,450
Bank Loan		6,500
Common Shares		10,000
Retained Earnings		4,010
Sales Revenue		18,700
Sales Returns & Allowances	2,300	
Sales Discounts	420	
Cost of Goods Sold	7,480	
Salary Expense	3,460	
Rent Expense	2,140	
Total	$47,260	$47,260

FIGURE 11.18

The steps to close the books of a merchandising company are similar to closing a service company. The first step is to close the revenue account and is shown in figure 11.19.

JOURNAL			Page 1	
Date	**Account Title and Explanation**		**Debit**	**Credit**
Jan 31	Sales Revenue		18,700	
	Income Summary			18,700
	Close revenue accounts			

FIGURE 11.19

The second step is to close expenses. In this step, we will also close the two contra-revenue accounts (sales returns and allowances and sales discounts) because they have debit balances like the rest of the expense accounts.

JOURNAL			Page 1
Date	**Account Title and Explanation**	**Debit**	**Credit**
Jan 31	Income Summary	15,800	
	Sales Returns & Allowances		2,300
	Sales Discounts		420
	Cost of Goods Sold		7,480
	Salary Expense		3,460
	Rent Expense		2,140
	Close expense and debit balance accounts		

FIGURE 11.20

Step 3 closes the income summary account. If this were a proprietorship, the income summary would be closed to the capital account. Since Tools 4U is a corporation, the income summary will be closed to retained earnings.

JOURNAL			Page 1
Date	**Account Title and Explanation**	**Debit**	**Credit**
Jan 31	Income Summary	2,900	
	Retained Earnings		2,900
	Close income summary		

FIGURE 11.21

The end result, just as in a service company, is that the equity in the business is updated with the net income.

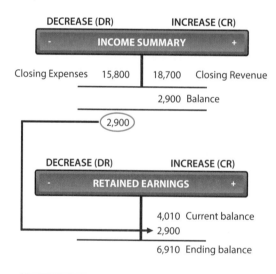

FIGURE 11.22

Methods for Valuing Inventory

Determining the Cost of Inventory

Once an inventory system has been chosen, there are four methods that companies can use, based on the type of business and choice of management, to value the inventory.

Here is a brief description of what they are and under what circumstances they are used:

- **Specific identification** is used when a business wants to value specific items individually. High value items such as cars, houses and diamonds are often valued in this way.
- **The first-in-first-out (FIFO)** method is used when a business assumes that the first items received in inventory are also the first items moved out of inventory. Perishable items that expire within a certain amount of time, such as fruit and vegetables, are often valued in this way.
- **The weighted average cost method** is used when a business simply applies an average cost to its entire inventory. Homogeneous (standardized) materials, such as plastic used in the making of garbage bags, or oil used in making gasoline, are often valued in this way.
- **The last-in-first-out (LIFO)** method is used when a business assumes that the last items received in inventory are also the first items moved out. Think of a product that is kept in a pile, with newer purchases being added to the top of the pile. A non-perishable product such as interlocking paving stones would be a good example. Suppose the paving stones are stacked on top of each other in layers. Newer purchases are simply added to the stack resulting in the oldest purchases being left at the bottom of the stack and sold last.

There are two principles that apply when a company chooses an inventory valuation method:

1. The method chosen can be somewhat arbitrary, since it does not have to actually reflect the physical movement of goods. For example, if a business chooses the first-in-first-out (FIFO) method, a newly received product can still end up being sold before an older product.
2. Once a valuation method is chosen, the company has to stay with it. The reason for this is that a company may be tempted to change the method used in order to impact cost of goods sold and closing inventory values, which can both change depending on the valuation method. (This adheres to the GAAP principle of consistency).

Applying Valuation Methods

Cool Ink Company sells a number of different high quality pens, pencils, markers and highlighters. Let us examine one item from their inventory to illustrate specific identification, FIFO, weighted average and LIFO inventory valuation methods. Assume that Cool Ink uses a perpetual inventory system to account for purchases and sales.

Cool Ink Company currently has ten collector pens in inventory with a cost of $10 each. During the month of March, the following transactions took place:

Date	Transaction	Quantity	Unit Cost
March 5	Purchase from Pen Distributers	50	$12
March 7	Sale	15	
March 15	Purchase from Promotional Pens	40	$14
March 19	Purchase from Promotional Pens	20	$16
March 27	Sale	50	

FIGURE 11.23

During the month, the cost of the pen changed. This implies that the cost of goods sold applied to each sale will likely be different, based on which pens are actually sold. We can apply the four methods of valuing inventory to the transactions to arrive at different values for inventory and cost of goods sold. This will demonstrate that the choice of inventory valuation method can make a difference on the financial statements of a company.

Using Specific Identification

When using specific identification, it is helpful to list the purchases separately from each other to easily identify the costs associated with each batch of inventory. The opening balance and the transactions from figure 11.23 are listed in figure 11.24. At the bottom of the figure is the value of ending inventory.

Date	Purchases			Sales			Balance		
	Quantity	Unit Cost	Value	Quantity	Unit Cost	Value	Quantity	Unit Cost	Value
March 1							10	$10	$100
March 5	50	$12	$600				10	$10	$100
							50	$12	$600
March 7				8	$10	$80	2	$10	$20
				7	$12	$84	43	$12	$516
March 15	40	$14	$560				2	$10	$20
							43	$12	$516
							40	$14	$560
March 19	20	$16	$320				2	$10	$20
							43	$12	$516
							40	$14	$560
							20	$16	$320
March 27				2	$10	$20	10	$12	$120
				33	$12	$396	25	$14	$350
				15	$14	$210	20	$16	$320
Ending Inventory									$790

FIGURE 11.24

Step 1:   The purchase of 50 pens on March 5 is added to the value of inventory.

Step 2:   The sale of 15 pens on March 7 can be specifically identified. Eight of the pens came from opening inventory and seven of the pens came from the purchase on March 5. As a result, the opening balance of 10 pens is reduced to two and the batch of 50 pens is reduced to 43. The value of cost of goods sold for this sale is $164 ($80 + $84).

Step 3:   The purchase of 40 pens on March 15 is added to the value of inventory.

Step 4:   The purchase of 20 pens on March 19 is added to the value of inventory.

Step 5:   The sale of 50 pens on March 27 can be specifically identified. Two came from opening inventory, 33 from the purchase on March 5 and 15 from the purchase on March 15. The value of the cost of goods sold for this sale is $626 ($20 + $396 + $210).

Step 6:   The value of ending inventory is made up of 10 pens remaining from the March 5 purchase, 25 pens remaining from the March 15 purchase and 20 pens remaining from the March 19 purchase. Total value of ending inventory is $790 ($120 + $350 + $320).

Using First-In-First-Out (FIFO)

When using the FIFO method, it is helpful to list the purchases in the order they were received. This will allow you to easily see which items were the first ones purchased, which will also be considered the first ones sold. The opening balance and the transactions from figure 11.23 are listed in figure 11.25. At the bottom of the figure is the value of ending inventory.

Date	Purchases			Sales			Balance		
	Quantity	Unit Cost	Value	Quantity	Unit Cost	Value	Quantity	Unit Cost	Value
March 1							10	$10	$100
March 5	50	$12	$600				10	$10	$100
							50		$12	$600
March 7				10	$10	$100	45	$12	$540
				5	$12	$60			
March 15	40	$14	$560				45	$12	$540
							40	$14	$560
March 19	20	$16	$320				45	$12	$540
							40	$14	$560
							20	$16	$320
March 27				45	$12	$540	35	$14	$490
				5	$14	$70	20	$16	$320
Ending Inventory									$810

FIGURE 11.25

Step 1:   The purchase of 50 pens on March 5 is added to the value of inventory.

Step 2:   The sale of 15 pens on March 7 must first use the costs from the opening balance. Since there were only 10 pens in the opening balance, another five will have to be taken from the purchase on March 5. This means that the entire opening balance inventory has been sold and only 45 units remain from the purchase on March 5. The value of cost of goods sold for this sale is $160 ($100 + $60).

Step 3:   The purchase of 40 pens on March 15 is added to the value of inventory.

Step 4:   The purchase of 20 pens on March 19 is added to the value of inventory.

Step 5:   The sale of the 50 pens on March 27 must first use the costs from the purchase on March 5. Since there are only 45 pens left from that purchase, another five will have to be taken from the purchase on March 15. The value of cost of goods sold for this sale is $610 ($540 + $70).

Step 6:   The value of ending inventory is made up of 35 pens remaining from the March 15 purchase and 20 pens from the March 19 purchase. Total value of inventory is $810 ($490 + $320).

Using Weighted Average Cost

When using the weighted average cost method, the total inventory value will be divided by the total quantity on hand to arrive at an average cost for each unit. The opening balance and the transactions from figure 11.23 are listed in figure 11.26. At the bottom of the figure is the value of ending inventory.

Date	Purchases			Sales			Balance		
	Quantity	Unit Cost	Value	Quantity	Unit Cost	Value	Quantity	Unit Cost	Value
March 1							10	$10.00	$100
March 5	50	$12	$600				60	$11.67	$700
March 7				15	$11.67	$175	45	$11.67	$525
March 15	40	$14	$560				85	$12.76	$1,085
March 19	20	$16	$320				105	$13.38	$1,405
March 27				50	$13.38	$669	55	$13.38	$736
Ending Inventory									$736

FIGURE 11.26

Step 1:   The purchase of 50 pens on March 5 is added to the quantity on hand. The value of the 50 pens is added to the value of the opening inventory. The unit cost is approximately $11.67 ($700 ÷ 60 units).

Step 2:   The sale of 15 pens on March 7 is taken from inventory. The most recent unit cost of approximately $11.67 per unit is used to calculate the cost of goods sold ($175). Both the quantity and value of inventory decrease, and the unit cost is still approximately

$11.67 ($525 ÷ 45 units). The unit cost of inventory will never change after a sale; it can only change after a purchase.

Step 3: The purchase of 40 pens on March 15 is added to the quantity on hand. The value of the 40 pens is added to current value of inventory. The unit cost is now approximately $12.76 ($1,085 ÷ 85 units).

Step 4: The purchase of 20 pens on March 19 is added to the quantity on hand. The value of the 20 pens is added to current value of inventory. The unit cost is now approximately $13.38 ($1,405 ÷ 105 units).

Step 5: The sale of the 50 pens on March 27 is taken from inventory. The most recent cost of approximately $13.38 per unit is used to calculate the cost of goods sold ($669).

Step 6: The value of ending inventory is 55 pens at the unit cost of approximately $13.38. Total value of inventory is $736.

Using Last-In-First-Out (LIFO)

When using the LIFO method, it is helpful to list the purchases in the order they were received. This will allow you to easily see which items were the last ones purchased and will be the first ones to be sold. The opening balance and the transactions from figure 11.23 are listed in figure 11.27. At the bottom of the figure is the value of ending inventory.

Date	Purchases			Sales			Balance		
	Quantity	Unit Cost	Value	Quantity	Unit Cost	Value	Quantity	Unit Cost	Value
March 1							10	$10	$100
March 5	50	$12	$600				10	$10	$100
							50	$12	$600
March 7				15	$12	$180	10	$10	$100
							35	$12	$420
March 15	40	$14	$560				10	$10	$100
							35	$12	$420
							40	$14	$560
March 19	20	$16	$320				10	$10	$100
							35	$12	$420
							40	$14	$560
							20	$16	$320
March 27				20	$16	$320	10	$10	$100
				30	$14	$420	35	$12	$420
							10	$14	$140
Ending Inventory									$660

FIGURE 11.27

Step 1. The purchase of 50 pens on March 5 is added to the value of inventory.

Step 2. The sale of 15 pens on March 7 must first use the costs from the purchase on March 5. Since the purchase from March 5 had 50 pens, the entire 15 units will come from that purchase. This means that only 35 units from the purchase on March 5 and the entire opening balance remain. The value of cost of goods sold for this sale is $180.

Step 3.   The purchase of 40 pens on March 15 is added to the value of inventory.

Step 4.   The purchase of 20 pens on March 19 is added to the value of inventory.

Step 5.   The sale of the 50 pens on March 27 must first use the costs from the purchase on March 19. Since there are only 20 pens from that purchase, another 30 will have to be taken from the purchase on March 15. The value of cost of goods sold for this sale is $740 ($320 + $420).

Step 6.   The value of ending inventory is made up of 10 pens from the opening balance inventory, 35 pens remaining from the March 5 purchase and 10 pens remaining from the March 15 purchase. Total value of inventory is $660 ($100 + $420 + $140).

The Effect of Different Valuation Methods

As the inventory valuation methods demonstrate, different ending inventory figures are produced using different valuation methods. The following chart summarizes these differences when applied to the Cool Ink example:

	Specific Identification	FIFO	Weighted Average	LIFO
Inventory Available for Sale (beginning inventory + purchases)	$1,580	$1,580	$1,580	$1,580
Ending Inventory	790	810	736	660
Value of COGS	790	770	844	920

FIGURE 11.28

From the above, we can make the following assumptions:

1. In times where product cost increases over the period, FIFO will result in the highest value of ending inventory and LIFO will result in the highest value of cost of goods sold.
2. While specific identification provides the true value of ending inventory and cost of goods sold, it is costly to implement and therefore not practical for items of small value.
3. FIFO reports a more accurate value of ending inventory than weighted average, as it is based on the most recent purchases.
4. LIFO matches current revenues with the closest current cost to replace the goods sold (cost of most recent purchase) resulting in a lower profit.

Conclusion: When ending inventory amounts change, so does the cost of goods sold, gross profit and net income. Therefore, companies can dramatically change their financial results by manipulating the inventory valuation method.

Determining the Actual Quantity of Inventory

Goods are moved in and out of inventory all the time, which is why recording the amount and quantities bought and sold is so important. This is done when the goods enter the premises at purchase and when they leave the premises at sale. The reliability of the information recorded at these points must be assured.

For example, the items must be counted when they are received, and these amounts should be compared to the amounts listed on the original purchase order. Any discrepancies must be noted and followed up. Once the inventory count is complete, the company's records should be updated immediately.

Before goods can leave the premises, a release order, such as a packing slip, must be written up and authorized. Just as goods coming in have to be recorded, goods moving out must also be recorded. The shipper should note which goods are leaving and forward the documents to the accounting department to ensure the information is entered into the system.

Some of this paperwork can take time using a manual system. Computer scanning software can eliminate much of the paperwork and time involved in recording the movement of goods in inventory. Whether items are coming in or moving out, a swipe of the scanner can immediately track their location and status while in inventory.

The Physical Inventory Count

As required by GAAP, a business must take a physical count of its inventory accounts at least once a year. While a business may have its own policies and procedures for the process of taking a physical inventory count, the following steps are generally included:

1. Designate an area to a specific person.
2. Count and record each item on pre-numbered sheets that are distributed and controlled by the accounting department.
3. The counts must include all inventory owned by the company, even it if is not physically in the warehouse. This means that inventory shipped FOB shipping point must be counted.
4. Once completed, the sheets are returned to the accounting department where items are valued and summarized.
5. Where a perpetual system is used, the inventory record (ledger account) is compared to the physical count. Differences are noted and adjustments are recorded accordingly.
6. Where major differences occur between the inventory record and the physical count, further investigation is required.

Effect of Inventory Errors

Inventory is a type of asset that differs somewhat from other assets we have discussed in previous chapters. Unlike cash, the value of which is quite definitive (except when it comes to exchange rates between currencies), or accounts receivable which is also quite definitive, the value of inventory is largely a matter of judgment.

Attaching a value to inventory involves a different kind of challenge. A warehouse can be full of various products which were bought at a certain price and will sold at another price, with no clarity as to which items moved when. As we have already demonstrated, the choice of valuation system often settles the matter. However, even a valuation system only serves to create a snapshot in time, one which management can influence by choosing one valuation system over another.

In other words, matching physical items in inventory to specific dollar values using any valuation method can be complicated. This is why the process is prone to errors, and errors can have an impact on the way that a company presents its financial figures — both internally and externally. Let's examine the impact that an inventory error can have on gross margin percentage and other aspects of financial reporting.

The Impact of Cost of Goods Sold On Gross Profit

Before we continue, we must first clarify the use of the terms gross profit and gross margin. These terms are used in various ways by different businesses, and there is no right or wrong version. For the purpose of this course, we will refer to **gross profit** *as the* **dollar amount** *calculated by subtracting the COGS from revenues, and* **gross margin** *as the* **percentage** *of gross profit divided by sales.*

Although inventory is a balance sheet account, it can have an immediate impact on the income statement, since the cost of goods sold is used to calculate gross profit. Gross profit in turn, is used to calculate the gross margin percentage. The gross margin percentage represents the percentage of sales left to pay the remaining operating expenses of the company.

This relationship between inventory and gross profit is demonstrated in this diagram:

It should become clear that the cost of goods sold serves as a focal point when dealing with inventory on a company's financial statements.

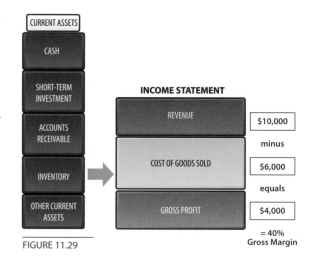

FIGURE 11.29

In a periodic inventory system, COGS is calculated by adding total inventory purchases to the value of inventory on hand at the beginning of the period, then deducting the closing value of inventory at the end of the period. The closing value of inventory is determined by a physical count. An example of the calculation is shown in figure 11.30.

In other words, a company's COGS represents the amount of inventory that is used/sold in a period.

Errors in valuing closing inventory can impact COGS and, as a result, gross profit. Just one broken link in the chain — that of an error in closing inventory — can render many of the other links broken. Beyond affecting COGS and gross profit, an incorrect inventory value impacts opening inventory for the next period. We will examine the impact on gross profit while ignoring the effects on net income for the year.

Inventory Calculation	
Opening Inventory	10,000
Plus: Purchases	60,000
Cost of Goods Available for Sale	70,000
Less: Closing Inventory	20,000
Cost of Goods Sold	50,000

FIGURE 11.30

The Effect of Overstating Inventory

We will use two examples: one set of charts will include the correct amount for closing inventory. The other set of charts will include an incorrect amount for closing inventory.

We will then look at how this error impacts the other important figures on the company's financial statements. Here are the correct numbers:

Inventory Calculation	
Opening Inventory	5,000
Plus: Purchases	75,000
Cost of Goods Available for Sale	80,000
Less: Closing Inventory	9,000
Cost of Goods Sold	71,000

Income Statement Year 1	
Sales	$100,000
Less: Cost of Goods Sold	71,000
Gross Profit	$29,000

FIGURE 11.31

When closing inventory is correctly valued at $9,000, a COGS value of $71,000 is produced. As a result, the gross profit for the year is $29,000. The gross margin for the reporting period would then be: 29,000 ÷ 100,000 = 29%

What happens if we over-value closing inventory by $1,000?

Gross profit for the year is $30,000. Gross margin is then: 30,000 ÷ 100,000 = 30%

Inventory Calculation	
Opening Inventory	5,000
Plus: Purchases	75,000
Cost of Goods Available for Sale	80,000
Less: Closing Inventory	10,000
Cost of Goods Sold	70,000

Income Statement Year 1	
Sales	$100,000
Less: Cost of Goods Sold	70,000
Gross Profit	$30,000

FIGURE 11.32

As a result, COGS is understated by $1,000, gross profit is overstated by $1,000, and gross margin is overstated by 1%. Note that the same error while performing a physical account for a company that uses the perpetual inventory system will lead to the same problem.

If this error is found and corrected before the end of the period, then the following journal entry is made:

JOURNAL			
Date	Account Title and Explanation	Debit	Credit
	Cost of Goods Sold	1,000	
	Inventory		1,000
	Corrected overstated inventory		

FIGURE 11.33

If the error is made after the financial reporting period is over, then an assessment of the materiality of the error must be made.

If the error is considered material, then the company's financial statements would have to be reissued with the amended figures. It is obviously a scenario that companies want to avoid. Such a high profile mistake can only cast doubt on how the company is being run. Nevertheless, if such material errors are found, they must be reported — regardless of any embarrassment they may cause the company.

This is just a snapshot of what errors in valuing inventory can do to a company's financial statements. Both internal and external stakeholders are impacted by inventory errors. Such errors can affect things like business decision-making, tax reporting and adherence to GAAP procedures.

The Impact of Inventory Errors

Overstated gross profits resulting from inflated inventory can give management a false sense of confidence in the company. This could lead to bad decisions when it comes to pricing, discounts, target market share, or other aspects of business performance. The reverse would be true for understated numbers, which could create unnecessary panic and desperation on the part of ownership.

An inaccurate gross profit figure can also have consequences when it comes to paying taxes. A higher gross profit leads to higher net income, which means that a company is paying more tax than it should. Perhaps even more importantly, an understated gross profit figure leads to an understated net income amount, which means that the government is getting less in taxes from the company than it should.

Finally, a company could use its inflated financial figures to create a false impression of its performance on external stakeholders, or even on banks when trying to secure loans. This can represent an ethical breach in violation of GAAP rules of disclosure.

Valuation of Inventory at the Lower of Cost or Market

Market conditions can fluctuate. With regard to inventory, this means that sometimes a company sells its inventory for a lower price than what it was purchased for in the first place (i.e. the selling price is lower than cost).

The GAAP principle of conservatism asserts that, given a choice, the accounting alternative that produces a lower value for assets must always be used. This prevents companies from providing an overly optimistic state of their finances.

As a result, the **lower of cost or market (LCM)** principle must be used when valuing inventory.

So when inventory is sold below cost, it is the selling price that is used to value the inventory — not the purchase price. In other words, an inventory item can never be valued at more than the purchase price.

The LCM principle can be applied on three different levels: individual item; category; and total inventory. We will demonstrate how this is done by using Elan's Camera Shop as an example. The following is a chart detailing the cost and selling price of their inventory.

1	2	3	4	5	6	7
				Lower of Cost and Market applied to …		
Description	**Category**	**Cost**	**Selling Price (market)**	**Individual**	**Category**	**Total**
Film type 1	Supplies	$100	$90	$90		
Film type 2	Supplies	500	520	500		
Total Supplies		600	610		$600	
Camera A	Cameras	1,000	1,000	1,000		
Camera B	Cameras	2,000	2,200	2,000		
Total Cameras		3,000	3,200		3,000	
Accessory 1	Accessories	3,000	2,900	2,900		
Accessory 2	Accessories	4,000	3,500	3,500		
Total Accessories		7,000	6,400		6,400	
Total		$10,600	$10,210	$9,990	$10,000	$10,210

FIGURE 11.34

- Column 1 is a description of a particular inventory item.
- Column 2 categorizes the item into supplies, cameras and accessories.
- Column 3 provides the cost of the item.
- Column 4 indicates the market selling price of the item.
- Columns 5, 6 and 7 cover inventory values based on LCM: Column 5 lists the LCM for individual inventory items, Column 6 lists the LCM for each category, and Column 7 simply picks the lower of cost or market after all the inventory items are added together.
- The items marked in grey represent a total cost or selling price per category. For example, the total cost for all supplies is $600, and the total selling price for all supplies is $610.

- The last row of totals, including the items marked in orange, are the final inventory values using the three different methods.

If the LCM is applied to individual items, the total inventory value is $9,990. If applied to the three categories, we get an inventory value of $10,000, and if applied to the total amount of inventory, we get a value of $10,210. You will note that this last number (bottom right-hand corner) is the total selling price of all the inventory. This amount is lower than the total purchase price of $10,600. In other words, it is the most obvious demonstration of the LCM principle at work.

The last step in applying the lower of cost or market principle is to properly reflect the results of figure 11.34 in the accounting records of the company. This is done by recording a journal entry to reduce the value of inventory. For example, suppose Elan's Camera Shop applies LCM to individual items and uses the perpetual inventory system. The entry is a debit to cost of goods sold and a credit to inventory. The amount of the adjustment is equal to the original cost of the inventory less the LCM value applied to individual items. In this case, the adjustment is equal to $610 ($10,600 - $9,990). The journal entry is shown in figure 11.35.

In the above journal entry, cost of goods sold is debited. If the amount of the adjustment is deemed material, the company can instead debit another income statement account called "Loss on Write-down of Inventory."

JOURNAL			
Date	**Account Title and Explanation**	**Debit**	**Credit**
	Cost of Goods Sold	610	
	Inventory		610
	To adjust inventory to LCM (on an individual item basis)		

FIGURE 11.35

Estimating Inventory

In a perpetual inventory system, a company maintains a continuous record of the changes to inventory. This means that, at any given point in time, a company can take an instant snapshot of its inventory value, including the amounts for cost of goods sold and ending inventory. That is why modern scanning and computer technology can help a company update its financial situation with the click of the mouse.

Alternatively, a periodic inventory system poses greater challenges in obtaining up-to-date inventory information, since the value of the inventory cannot be tracked from start to finish. Taking a physical count of inventory can be very costly, so companies will often just perform a count at the end of the year. If a company wishes to create financial statements throughout the year for their own purposes, they will want to avoid the timely and costly inventory count. Therefore, they will estimate the value of inventory for these financial statements. When it is time to report the company's financial numbers, some value for inventory must be stated. That is where inventory estimation methods come in handy.

We will examine two methods of estimating inventory under a periodic inventory system: the **gross profit method** and the **retail method**.

The Gross Profit Method

As the name suggests, the gross profit method uses a company's gross profit figure in calculating an estimation of inventory value. More specifically, a company analyzes the gross profit numbers of prior years in order to come up with a current gross profit number to apply to estimation figures.

IN THE REAL WORLD

Every now and then, you might come across the term: pro forma financial statements. Simply stated, these are statements prepared by a company that do not adhere to GAAP rules.

There are various reasons why companies might want to prepare such reports. They can be used in an informal way to temporarily guide managerial decision-making. They can also be used to present financial figures in a way that at times might be distorted by GAAP rules. For example, costs associated with a previous accounting scandal have to be included in GAAP reports, yet such numbers may inaccurately reflect how the company is currently performing.

Pro forma statements can provide the public with a clearer snapshot of current organizational performance. In fact, pro forma financial figures were reported publicly and often during the dot.com boom of the late 1990's. However, regulators began to crack down on such practices, since even pro forma statements have their limitations and should not act as a substitute for documents that adhere to GAAP. For example, critics of pro forma statements argue that financial stresses from previous periods happen often and are part of the capitalist economic system. Leaving them out can itself be a distortion of a company's status and not fully reflect its performance.

Nevertheless, pro forma financial statements serve as a tool for company management when they want a financial snapshot of their company that isn't as formal, or potentially cumbersome, as GAAP disclosure principles require.

Other figures that a company needs to complete the gross profit method that can be taken from the general ledger are: sales, opening inventory and purchases. Once an accountant has these numbers, then the rest of the numbers needed to estimate inventory can be filled in one at a time.

Here is an example: Van Der Linden Inc. has to prepare financial statements for the quarter and needs to value its inventory in order to do this. It will use the gross profit method.

Sales	$100,000	
Cost of Goods Sold		
Opening Inventory	3,000	
Purchases	70,000	
Cost of Goods Available for Sale	73,000	
Closing Inventory		
Cost of Goods Sold	?	
Gross Profit	?	50%

FIGURE 11.36

- Based on an analysis of gross margin in previous years, a figure of 50% will be used for current calculations.

- Additionally, the following financial numbers were taken from the accountant's general ledger:

Sales	100,000	
Cost of Goods Sold		
Opening Inventory	3,000	
Purchases	70,000	
Cost of Goods Available for Sale	73,000	
Closing Inventory	?	
Cost of Goods Sold	?	
Gross Profit	$50,000	50%

FIGURE 11.37

Sales: $100,000
Opening Inventory: $3,000
Purchases: $70,000

Van Der Linden Inc.'s accountant will use a pro forma income statement (prepared in addition to those used for reporting purposes) to plug-in these numbers and calculate the others needed in estimating the value of the inventory.

The cells with a question mark are those that need to be calculated step-by-step to complete the estimation process.

If our gross margin is 50% (marked in red) then it is applied to the sales figure (marked in blue). $100,000 \times 50\% = \$50,000$

We now have all the information we need to fill in one of the two remaining question marks: *Cost of Goods Sold*.

Remember:

Sales – Gross Profit = COGS
$100,000 – \$50,000 = \$50,000$

The $50,000 COGS is plugged into the chart and marked in grey.

Sale	100,000	
Cost of Goods Sold		
Opening Inventory	3,000	
Purchases	70,000	
Cost of Goods Available for Sale	73,000	
Closing Inventory		
Cost of Goods Sold	50,000	
Gross Profit	50,000	50%

FIGURE 11.38

There is one question mark left in Van Der Linden Inc.'s pro forma income statement, which is the figure we need to complete the balance sheet for the quarter: *Closing Inventory*.

Closing inventory is calculated by subtracting the Cost of Goods Sold from the Cost of Goods Available for Sale:

Cost of Goods Available for Sale – Cost of Goods Sold = Closing Inventory

$73,000 – \$50,000 = \$23,000$

Therefore, the gross profit method yields a closing inventory estimation value of $23,000, which is marked in grey. This figure will now be used on the quarterly balance sheet for Van Der Linden Inc.

To summarize: The gross profit method starts with historical analysis that yields a gross profit margin. This is applied to sales, which yields a gross profit figure. Each subsequent step fills out another part of the pro forma income statement, until a final figure for closing inventory is obtained. This is the estimation that will be used for the quarterly financial statements in this example.

Sales	100,000	
Cost of Goods Sold		
Opening Inventory	3,000	
Purchases	70,000	
Cost of Goods Sold Available for Sale	73,000	
Closing Inventory	23,000	
Cost of Goods Sold	50,000	
Gross Profit	50,000	50%

FIGURE 11.39

The Retail Method

The retail method of estimating inventory requires less information and fewer steps than the gross profit method. Specifically, it requires two things: (1) the value of sales at retail (which is why it is called the retail method); and (2) the company's cost of goods sold section on the income statement.

Here is an example using Leung Retail Company.

As you can see in figure 11.40, the cost of goods sold section is marked in brown, and the sales figure at retail is marked in red.

The section marked in green, which is the *Cost of Goods Available for Sale*, is calculated by adding *Opening Inventory* and *Purchases*. This section is important because the cost and retail figures for *Cost of Goods Available for Sale* will be used in ratio format as follows:

$$\frac{\text{Cost of Goods Available for Sale at Cost}}{\text{Cost of Goods Available for Sale at Retail}}$$

The ratio for the Leung Retail Company is:

$$\frac{\$73,000}{\$140,000} = 52.1\%$$

This ratio needs to be applied to the *Closing Inventory at Retail* figure, which is marked in blue:

$$\$70,000 \times 52.1\% = \$36,500$$

This is the *Closing Inventory at Cost* figure, using the retail method of inventory estimation, which is added to the bottom of the Leung Retail Company chart.

	At Cost	At Retail
Cost of Goods Sold		
Opening Inventory	3,000	6,000
Purchases	70,000	134,000
Cost of Goods Sold Available for Sale	73,000	140,000
Less: Sales at Retail		70,000
Closing Inventory at Retail		70,000

FIGURE 11.40

	At Cost	At Retail
Cost of Goods Sold		
Opening Inventory	3,000	6,000
Purchase	70,000	134,000
Cost of Goods Sold Available for Sale	73,000	140,000
Less Sales at Retail		70,000
Closing Inventory at Retail		70,000
Closing Inventory at Cost	$36,500	

FIGURE 11.41

Measuring Inventory Using Financial Ratios

Generally speaking, a business wants to be as precise as possible in buying inventory for resale. Ideally, inventory should be sold as soon as it is bought. In other words, the less time that an item spends in inventory, while still meeting customer demand, the better.

A company can measure the extent to which it is moving inventory in this way through the use of two ratios: **inventory turnover ratio** and **days inventory on hand**.

Inventory Turnover Ratio

The extent to which an organization can quickly sell inventory on hand is known as **inventory turnover**. Specifically, the inventory turnover ratio estimates how many times a year a company is buying inventory. The more often a company buys inventory, the less likely it is that the inventory sits for extended periods of time, and the more likely it is that the turnover is high.

The inventory turnover ratio is calculated by taking the cost of goods sold for a year and dividing it by average inventory:

$$\text{Inventory Turnover Ratio} = \frac{\text{Cost of Goods Sold}}{\text{Average Inventory}}$$

We'll use a few real life examples to demonstrate how the inventory turnover ratio is applied to a company's inventory numbers.

Blackberry is the maker of the Blackberry mobile device that people all over the world use for e-mail, the Internet, and even taking pictures. The following is a listing of their relevant inventory numbers for the 2012 fiscal year:

	$ Millions
Inventory – February 26, 2011	$618
Inventory – March 5, 2012	$1,027
Cost of Goods Sold	$11,217

FIGURE 11.42

Average inventory is calculated by adding the opening and closing inventory numbers and dividing the total by 2.

This number is entered into the inventory turnover ratio as follows:

Average Inventory	(618 + 1,027) ÷ 2 = 822.5

FIGURE 11.43

Turnover	11,217 ÷ 822.5 = 13.6

FIGURE 11.44

Blackberry's inventory turnover ratio for fiscal year 2012 is 13.6. This means that the company bought its inventory over 13 times during the year.

As a comparison, we'll calculate the 2012 inventory turnover ratio for NewTech Mobile Corporation, a fictional company in the same industry:

Inventory – December 31, 2011	$501.3
Inventory – December 31, 2012	$428.1
Cost of Goods Sold	$2,882.8
Average Inventory (501.3 + 428.1) ÷ 2 = 464.7	
Turnover 2,882.8 ÷ 464. 7 = 6.2	

FIGURE 11.45

The inventory turnover ratio is 6.2, which means that for the 2012 fiscal year, NewTech Mobile Corporation bought inventory approximately 6.2 times.

Comparing these two examples, Blackberry has a higher inventory turnover ratio, which is desirable. These ratios are comparable since both companies are in the same industry.

Inventory Days on Hand

There is another way of looking at inventory turnover. Instead of estimating how often a company sells and replaces inventory over a period of time (which is indicated by the inventory turnover ratio), turnover can be calculated by estimating how many days it takes to move items out of inventory. Expressed in another way: how many days will the inventory last given the current rate of sales?

The number of days in a year (365) is divided by the inventory turnover ratio, resulting in the inventory days on hand.

$$\text{Inventory Days on Hand} = \frac{365}{\text{Inventory Turnover Ratio}}$$

The inventory days on hand carves up the calendar year into equal sized chunks. The number of chunks equals the inventory turnover ratio. The size of the chunks translates into the inventory days on hand.

For example, if a company's inventory turnover ratio is 10, then the inventory days on hand will have 10 chunks in the year. Since there are 365 days in the year, each chunk will be 36.5 days long.

$$\frac{365}{10} = 36.5$$

Therefore, 36.5 days would be the inventory days on hand ratio.

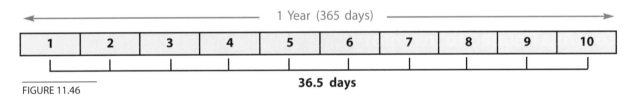

FIGURE 11.46   **36.5 days**

Here is an example using the inventory turnover ratios we calculated for Blackberry and the NewTech Mobile Corporation.

If you recall, Blackberry had the more desirable inventory turnover ratio. The inventory days on hand simply reorganizes the same information as follows:

Blackberry inventory days on hand: 365 ÷ 13.6 = 26.8 days

NewTech Mobile Corporation inventory days on hand: 365 ÷ 6.2 = 58.9 days

Another way of calculating inventory days on hand is as follows:

$$\frac{\text{Average Inventory}}{\text{Cost of Goods Sold}} \times 365$$

Here is the logic of this calculation. The relationship (ratio) is between: (1) how much inventory is in stock; and (2) the amount of inventory used for the year (which is the Cost of Goods Sold). Dividing the average inventory by how much was used and multiplying this number by 365 (number of days in the year) will convert the ratio to the number of days on hand based on how much was used.

Using the Blackberry inventory and cost of goods sold from figure 11.42 let us test this formula:

$$\frac{\$822.5 \text{ (Average)}}{\$11,217} \times 365 = 26.8 \text{ Inventory Days on Hand}$$

The results show that Blackberry has the more desirable inventory days on hand ratio. A lower number for this ratio means that it takes less time for a company to move its inventory. This is another way of saying that its inventory turnover is better.

Management should not be making decisions regarding inventory based on ratios alone. There could be many factors that impact such numbers. For example, some industries might require companies to wait longer periods of time to have goods shipped to them. High turnover in these instances may lead to empty warehouses and customer demands not being met.

As an example, a grocery store will have higher inventory turnover than an appliance store. Alternatively, car engines will move out of an auto plant warehouse much slower than light bulbs in a hardware store.

It is the responsibility of accountants and management to know what inventory levels are best for business. Ratios can help in this regard, but they are only one of many tools that can be used.

Controls Related to Inventory

The way a company handles its inventory can have a major impact on the state of the business. After all, basic economic theory is about supply and demand. If customers demand goods or services, the goal of a business is to meet that demand. In essence, this is what inventory management is about: to manage supply in order to meet demand.

A company with too much inventory on hand risks tying up capital that could be used productively in other areas. A company with too little inventory on hand risks not having enough supply to meet customer demand. Thus there is a delicate balance that needs to be maintained by a company. Perpetual inventory systems help companies to maintain such a balance.

Keeping track of inventory is one of the primary challenges of doing business. This is why transactions need to be recorded properly and relevant information presented in a way that helps company decision-makers.

Keeping track of a company's inventory can be a challenge, but computer software can help mitigate this challenge. However, every accountant should have an understanding of how inventory is tracked and recorded manually.

First, it should be noted that even with the use of technology, errors can be made. It is the responsibility of the accounting department and management to ensure that inventory information is accurate and reliable. The responsibility stops with them.

Second, a thorough knowledge of manual accounting procedures helps the accountant to develop the kinds of controls necessary to ensure that this type of asset is managed responsibly and with integrity.

We will provide examples to show how an accountant can develop a personal method of controlling inventory manually. We will then take a closer look at the kinds of controls needed when dealing with the inventory section of the balance sheet.

Compliance with Plans, Policies, Procedures, Regulations and Laws

All aspects of doing business should be governed by the appropriate plans, policies, procedures, laws and regulations. This is certainly true regarding a company's handling and control of inventory.

All businesses should have plans that are formalized through general policies that lead to specific procedures. These should all comply with the regulations and laws in place within the jurisdiction of the business.

Maintaining the integrity of information is an obligation that companies have when implementing inventory controls.

For example, a company can have a plan to train all inventory personnel. This plan can include detection controls that single out instances of procedures not being followed. An example of such a procedure could be to have all items tagged and scanned at checkout. If this procedure is not followed, then a backup measure could be implemented, with alarms going off upon exit.

All these plans, policies and procedures must adhere to relevant laws and regulations. For example, customers cannot be strip-searched because the alarm goes off as they are leaving the store as this would be a violation of their rights.

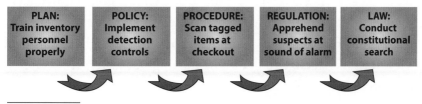

FIGURE 11.47

All employees should be trained in the inventory procedures in place. For example, the receiver should count all goods that enter the premises and match the count with the one written on the invoice or packing slip. It should be the job of the supervisor to ensure that this procedure is followed. Internal auditors can engage in field visits to ensure that both the supervisor and the receiver are implementing procedures according to plans and policies in place.

Safeguarding Inventory

All company assets must be physically protected. Cash is generally deposited in a bank; securities can be kept with the brokerage house. Inventory, on the other hand, is often located on company premises in a warehouse or onsite storage facility. The location needs to be easily accessible for receiving or shipping, but it also needs to be protected from the possibility of theft. That is why inventory facilities are usually locked up after closing. The more valuable the inventory, the more elaborate the security measures needed to protect it. These measures can include anything from fences and guard dogs to alarm systems, security guards or even the hiring of an inventory custodian who is charged specifically with protecting the inventory.

The Economical and Efficient Use of Resources

The concept that resources should be used economically and efficiently is especially applicable to inventory. First, financial ratios can be used to determine if there is too much or too little inventory on hand. If there is too much inventory, then capital is tied up that could be used more efficiently elsewhere. If there is too little, then customer demand will not be met.

Second, the physical condition of the inventory should be checked regularly. This can be done visually or through inventory reports. Any inventory items that are old or in disrepair, and therefore difficult to sell at market value, can be sold at reduced prices or disposed of so that valuable storage space can be maximized.

Inventory Objectives

All aspects of a business should be guided by the objectives set by management. This not only allows for the accomplishment of specific objectives, but allows all organizational objectives to be properly coordinated. For example, sales objectives can be tied to inventory objectives; and profit objectives can be tied to those set by the marketing department.

All employees should be aware of the company's objectives. For example, if a company wishes to keep items in inventory for only a short period of time before being shipped out, then both the receiver and shipper should be aware of this. This objective would guide much of their short-term and long-term activities.

Meeting inventory objectives needs to be a total team effort. If inventory levels are not close to management's objective, then initiatives should be implemented to ensure that objectives are reassessed or changed. For example, if inventory levels are higher than expected, the sales department can view it as a challenge to get items moving out faster. The more sales increase, the less inventory builds up in the warehouse.

An Ethical Approach to Inventory Estimation and Valuation

As mentioned earlier, management is able to choose how they wish to value inventory. Thus, inventory may be open to manipulation. A company can purchase, store and sell many items throughout the course of a business year, and how all these items are valued can have a significant impact on a company's bottom line.

For example, inventory can sometimes be used as collateral when taking out a bank loan; or employees may steal from the company's inventory. That is why the inventory asset on a company's balance sheet should be subject to ethical guidelines. We will examine some of these guidelines and suggest how organizations should approach estimating and valuing inventory in an ethical manner.

Impact on Financial Statements

The impact of inflating closing inventory is significant. It reduces the cost of goods sold and increases net income for the year. It will also inflate cost of goods sold and reduce net income for the following year. Therefore, any manipulation of inventory value has negative consequences that extend beyond the current fiscal year. The ethical responsibility of management is to ensure this does not happen by detecting errors and the causes behind them.

Who Commits Fraud and Why?

Companies need to know the kinds of inventory fraud that can be perpetrated and understand who would be most likely to commit fraud.

Inventory fraud from the top down

Various methods are used to pad a company's inventory value. One such method is to overstate the value of items deemed obsolete, shop-worn or generally unsalable. This would overstate the overall value of inventory. Similarly, various overhead costs can be attributed to inventory. These figures can also be manipulated in a way that affects the company's bottom line. In addition, a manufacturer might be tempted to overstate the completion of work-in-process inventories and, again, pad the value of its inventory.

Generally speaking, these kinds of attempts to pad inventory numbers tend to come from the top. Unlike determining fixed costs such as rent, determining inventory costs is a more subjective exercise. Accountants and executives can abuse the subjectivity involved in some of these decisions and errors can be rationalized as a matter of opinion.

Such abuses can be avoided by laying out specific policies and guidelines in handling and valuing inventory. Controls should be in place to ensure that these policies are being followed. Companies can also have both internal and external auditors review the design and effectiveness of inventory controls and detect any possible ethical breaches.

In the end, management is responsible for any errors arising from the way its financial situation is being reported. There is no excuse for manipulating the value of inventory. Any wrongful reporting should be dealt with at the earliest opportunity.

Inventory fraud from the bottom up

Lower level employees and thieves can also create havoc with inventory. Their motivation is often associated with greed.

Inventory items are goods that have value and that people want to buy. That is why companies purchase these items and eventually sell them. People who have routine access to such items, such as employees, might be tempted to simply take them without paying for them. Alternatively, an employee might even take funds from the company, buy the inventory, then resell it and pocket the profits. Even borrowing an item without permission, such as a car on a sales lot, is theft, and needs to be prevented.

Some forms of inventory fraud originate from the executive level. Ethical guidelines are needed that detect wrongdoing at any level of the company.

There are various red flags that help a company monitor and prevent inventory shrinkage. One such red flag occurs when sales lag inventory levels. In other words, the company is buying more than it is selling. Some of that inventory is obviously not going to the customer. Another potential inventory red flag should pop up when shipping costs lag inventory. Again, this indicates that the company is not shipping out as many items as it is receiving in inventory. The missing items might well have been taken by thieves.

All companies should be in the practice of noting these red flags and ensuring measures are in place to prevent or detect theft. Furthermore, all businesses should implement security measures that properly safeguard inventory on their premises. Some of these measures were discussed earlier in this chapter.

IN THE REAL WORLD

Perhaps no business philosophy captures the spirit of high inventory turnover more than Just In Time, also known as JIT.

The Japanese first started developing JIT in their manufacturing industries after Word War II. The goal was to gain a competitive advantage by reducing the amount of inventory a company had in storage at any given time, since inventory is often a larger but less liquid asset than others on the balance sheet. JIT eventually made its way to North America and has been used to improve manufacturing efficiency in many different industries.

At the heart of JIT is a comprehensive approach not just to reducing inventory, but to managing a business. Under JIT, it is the customer that drives the manufacturing process. That is why JIT systems are often implemented in conjunction with what is known as Total Quality Management, or TQM. Under such philosophies, everything is done to ensure that the customer gets quality goods and services on time and every time.

To that end, JIT systems mobilize all efforts to coordinate manufacturing processes and reduce waste. This involves the goal of having virtually no excess inventory on hand at any time. This can only be achieved if a company thoroughly understands what the customer wants and when they want it. Receiving and shipping schedules, assembly parts, and labor flexibility are all adapted to ensure that customer demand is met while enhancing organizational efficiency and profitability.

JIT stresses the importance of reducing a company's inventory while enhancing customer service. It is a comprehensive approach that has achieved success on a global scale.

In Summary

⇨   Organizations can use a **perpetual system** for valuing inventory, which tracks the value of specific items from purchase to sale, or a **periodic system**, which values inventory items at specific points in time (periodically).

⇨   The major differences between the perpetual and periodic inventory systems are in the accounts used to record purchases, sales and returns of merchandise, reporting the **cost of goods sold** on the income statement and the **closing entries**.

⇨   Depending on the type of business and the direction taken by management, organizations can also use four specific methods of valuing inventory: **specific identification, FIFO, average cost and LIFO**. Applying different inventory systems can produce different inventory values for the same set of goods.

⇨   Various **controls** can be implemented by accountants to preserve the integrity of inventory numbers. Some of these can be personalized and are used on an industry wide basis.

⇨   Like most assets on the balance sheet, inventory must be managed and handled in an ethical way. **Fraud** can sometimes occur from the top down so that net income can be unduly inflated. Fraud can also occur from the bottom up when employees or thieves steal items from inventory.

Review Exercise

1. Record the following transactions for Mike's Tikes Toys for the month of March 2011. The company uses a perpetual inventory system and values inventory using the FIFO method. There are 100 items in opening inventory that cost $12 each.

Mar 1	Purchased1,000 items at a cost of $15 each on credit (on account)
Mar 10	Sold 100 items at $45 each on credit
Mar 12	Sold 800 items at $50 each for cash
Mar 20	Purchased 500 items at $20 each on credit

2. Prepare the inventory record to demonstrate the closing inventory after each transaction listed in part 1 above, using the weighted average cost method.

3. Prepare the top portion of the income statement showing Sales, Cost of Goods Sold and Gross Profit for the month ended March 31, 2011. Use the values from the inventory record in part 2.

4. The company physically counted their inventory on March 31st, and found that there was an inventory shortage of $945. Record the adjusting entry required.

5. Prepare the revised income statement reflecting the correct inventory amount from part 2. Calculate the gross profit margin.

Review Exercise 1 - Answers

1.

JOURNAL				Page 1
Date	**Account Title and Explanation**		**Debit**	**Credit**
Mar 1	Inventory		15,000	
	Accounts Payable			15,000
	Purchased inventory on account			
	1,000 units × $15			
Mar 10	Accounts Receivable		4,500	
	Sales Revenue			4,500
	Sale to customer on account			
	100 units × $45			
	Cost of Goods Sold		1,200	
	Inventory			1,200
	Cost of goods sold for above sale			
	100 units × $12			
Mar 12	Cash		40,000	
	Sales Revenue			40,000
	Sale to customer for cash			
	800 units × $50			
	Cost of Goods Sold		12,000	
	Inventory			12,000
	Cost of goods sold for above sale			
	800 units × $15			
Mar 20	Inventory		10,000	
	Accounts Payable			10,000
	Purchased inventory on account			
	500 units × $20			

2.

Date	Purchases			Sales			Balance		
	Quantity	Unit Cost	Value	Quantity	Unit Cost	Value	Quantity	Unit Cost	Value
Mar 1							100	$12.00	$1,200
Mar 1	1,000	$15	$15,000				1100	$14.73	$16,200
Mar 10				100	$14.73	$1,473	1000	$14.73	$14,727
Mar 12				800	$14.73	$11,782	200	$14.73	$2,945
Mar 20	500	$20	$10,000				700	$18.49	$12,945
Ending Inventory									$12,945

3.

Mike's Tikes Toys Income Statement For the Month Ended March 31, 2011		
Sales Revenue		$44,500
Cost of Goods Sold*		13,255
Gross Profit		31,245

*$1,473 + 11,782

4.

JOURNAL				Page 1
Date	Account Title and Explanation		Debit	Credit
Mar 31	Cost of Goods Sold		945	
	Inventory			945
	Adjust inventory to match count			

5.

Mike's Tikes Toys Income Statement For the Month Ended March 31, 2011		
Sales Revenue		$44,500
Cost of Goods Sold		14,200
Gross Profit		30,300

Gross Profit Margin		68.1%

Review Exercise 2

The following information was presented by the bookkeeper for George's Gardening Supplies for the month of December 2011.

DATE	BUSINESS EVENT
Dec 1	Owner George G. deposited $120,000 of his own money into the business account.
Dec 3	The company purchased $50,000 of inventory on account, terms 2/10, net 30.
Dec 6	The company sold $80,000 of inventory to Greenland Care on account, terms 2/10, net 30; cost of goods sold $32,000.
Dec 7	The company purchased $20,000 of inventory on account, terms 2/15, net 30.
Dec 8	The company returned $2,000 of defective merchandise from the purchase on December 7.
Dec 11	The company paid for inventory bought on December 7, less the return and discount.
Dec 12	The customer from December 6 returned $1,000 of goods purchased on account. The cost of goods sold for returned inventory is $600.
Dec 14	The company purchased $10,000 of inventory on account, terms 2/10, net 30.
Dec 15	The company paid $500 freight bill for transportation of inventory purchased in transaction above.
Dec 16	The company collected the amount owing from the customer from December 6.
Dec 19	The company sold $33,500 of goods to Green House Inc. on account, terms 2/10, net 30. The value of cost of goods sold is $13,300.
Dec 22	The company paid for the purchase from December 3.
Dec 28	The following cash transactions were made: prepaid insurance of $3,600; maintenance expense of $600; salary expense of $11,000; rent expense of $6,000; owner's withdrawals of $5,000; property, plant and equipment of $45,000; utility expense of $750; and advertising expense of $2,500.

Assuming that George's Gardening Supplies uses the perpetual inventory system, complete the following exercise.

Part 1

Journalize all the transactions for December.

Part 1 - Answer

JOURNAL			Page 1
Date	**Account Title and Explanation**	**Debit**	**Credit**
Dec 1	Cash	120,000	
	Capital Account		120,000
	Owner invested cash in business		
Dec 3	Inventory	50,000	
	Accounts Payable		50,000
	Purchased inventory on account		
Dec 6	Accounts Receivable	80,000	
	Sales Revenue		80,000
	Sold to customer on account		
	Cost of Goods Sold	32,000	
	Inventory		32,000
	Cost of goods sold for above sale		
Dec 7	Inventory	20,000	
	Accounts Payable		20,000
	Purchased inventory on account		
Dec 8	Accounts Payable	2,000	
	Inventory		2,000
	Purchase return		
Dec 11	Accounts Payable	18,000	
	Inventory		360
	Cash		17,640
	Paid supplier and took discount		
Dec 12	Sales Returns & Allowances	1,000	
	Accounts Receivable		1,000
	Customer returned items		
	Inventory	600	
	Cost of Goods Sold		600
	Return items to inventory		

JOURNAL			Page 1
Date	**Account Title and Explanation**	**Debit**	**Credit**
Dec 14	Inventory	10,000	
	Accounts Payable		10,000
	Purchased inventory on account		
Dec 15	Inventory	500	
	Cash		500
	Paid for freight		
Dec 16	Cash	77,420	
	Sales Discount	1,580	
	Accounts Receivable		79,000
	Customer paid account		
Dec 19	Accounts Receivable	33,500	
	Sales Revenue		33,500
	Sold to customer on account		
	Cost of Goods Sold	13,300	
	Inventory		13,300
	Cost of goods sold for above sale		
Dec 22	Accounts Payable	50,000	
	Cash		50,000
	Paid supplier		
Dec 28	Prepaid Insurance	3,600	
	Maintenance Expense	600	
	Salary Expense	11,000	
	Rent Expense	6,000	
	Owner's Drawings	5,000	
	Property, Plant & Equipment	45,000	
	Utility Expense	750	
	Advertising Expense	2,500	
	Cash		74,450
	Paid cash for various items		

Part 2

Given the trial balance at the end of December, prepare the closing entries.

George's Gardening Supplies Trial Balance December 31, 2011		
Account	**Debit**	**Credit**
Cash	$54,830	
Accounts Receivable	33,500	
Inventory	33,440	
Prepaid Insurance	3,600	
Property, Plant and Equipment	45,000	
Accounts Payable		$10,000
Capital Account		120,000
Owner's Drawings	5,000	
Sales Revenue		113,500
Sales Returns & Allowances	1,000	
Sales Discount	1,580	
Cost of Goods Sold	44,700	
Advertising Expense	2,500	
Maintenance Expense	600	
Rent Expense	6,000	
Salary Expense	11,000	
Utility Expense	750	
Total	**$243,500**	**$243,500**

Part 2 - Answer

JOURNAL				Page 1
Date	**Account Title and Explanation**		**Debit**	**Credit**
Dec 31	Sales Revenue		113,500	
	Income Summary			113,500
	Close revenue account			
Dec 31	Income Summary		68,130	
	Sales Returns & Allowances			1,000
	Sales Discount			1,580
	Cost of Goods Sold			44,700
	Advertising Expense			2,500
	Maintenance Expense			600
	Rent Expense			6,000
	Salary Expense			11,000
	Utility Expense			750
	Close expense and debit accounts			
Dec 31	Income Summary		45,370	
	Capital Account			45,370
	Close income summary			
Dec 31	Capital Account		5,000	
	Owner's Drawings			5,000
	Close drawings account			

Appendix 11A: The Periodic Inventory System

As mentioned in chapter 11, the periodic inventory system determines the quantity of inventory on hand only periodically. A physical count is taken at the end of the period to determine the value of the ending inventory and cost of goods sold.

Thus, a periodic inventory system actually does not update the inventory account on a regular basis, only when a physical count is taken. On a regular basis, the periodic inventory system updates a new list of income statement accounts which are used to calculate cost of goods sold.

Consider the differences between the perpetual and the periodic inventory system. Figure 11A.1 illustrates the perpetual inventory system. A business that has the technology to properly implement the perpetual inventory system will record purchases, discounts, allowances and other adjustments into the inventory asset account. Inventory is then transferred to cost of goods sold when a sale is made. Cost of goods sold is immediately matched to sales and gross profit is reported every month, although gross profit may be slightly incorrect if an inventory count is not performed.

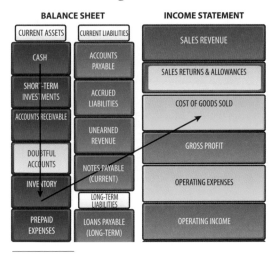

FIGURE 11A.1

A business that does not have the technology to constantly update inventory like in the perpetual inventory system described earlier must instead use the periodic inventory system. Figure 11A.2 illustrates the periodic inventory system. Inventory shows an opening value at the beginning of the period, but will only be adjusted up or down at the end of the period when an inventory count is performed. All purchases, discounts, allowances and other adjustments will be recorded directly into the income statement.

If purchases were recorded in the inventory account on the balance sheet, they would always remain in inventory since inventory is not transferred to cost of goods sold when a sale is made. This would leave a large amount of inventory remaining on the balance sheet and no cost of goods sold on the income statement. It is more practical to record purchases directly on the income statement, and adjust the inventory account only at year end.

Keep the concept of the periodic inventory system in mind as the journal entries are presented. The transactions are very similar to the perpetual inventory system, except that income statement accounts are affected instead of inventory.

FIGURE 11A.2

Purchases

When inventory is purchased for resale using a periodic inventory system the inventory account is not debited. Instead, we debit an account called *purchases* on the income statement, which is part of cost of goods sold. If the inventory was paid for on credit, then accounts payable is credited. If the inventory was paid for with cash, then the cash account is credited. In this example, Tools 4U Inc. purchased inventory of $10,000 on January 1, 2011. Assume all purchases and sales are made on account.

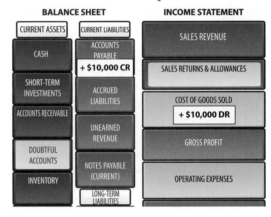

JOURNAL			
Date	Account Title and Explanation	Debit	Credit
Jan 1	Purchases	10,000	
	Accounts Payable		10,000
	Record purchase of inventory		

FIGURE 11A.3

The purchases account is a temporary account located on the income statement. It records all the inventory purchased by a company during a specific period of time under the periodic inventory system.

The value of inventory and cost of goods sold are not adjusted until the end of the period when the physical inventory count is taken. As a result, we need to track the costs related to inventory in separate accounts.

Purchase Returns

Continuing with the example of Tools 4U Inc., assume the company returned $300 worth of inventory to its supplier. Instead of just crediting the purchases account, businesses that use a periodic inventory system track these returns by using a temporary contra-expense account called **purchase returns and allowances**. This new account is also part of cost of goods sold. The following journal entry is recorded to reflect the above return:

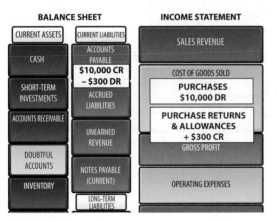

JOURNAL			
Date	Account Title and Explanation	Debit	Credit
Jan 2	Accounts Payable	300	
	Purchase Returns and Allowances		300
	Record purchase returns		

FIGURE 11A.4

Purchase Allowances

Continuing with the above example, assume Tools 4U found another $300 worth of unsatisfactory inventory. The supplier had offered a 20% **allowance** to Tools 4U to keep the goods, rather than returning them. The transaction resulted in an allowance of $60 ($300 x 20%). When a periodic inventory system is used, the credit will also be recorded in the purchase returns and allowances account as shown in figure 11A.5:

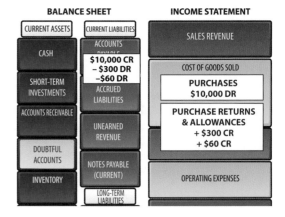

JOURNAL			
Date	**Account Title and Explanation**	**Debit**	**Credit**
Jan 5	Accounts Payable	60	
	Purchase Returns and Allowances		60
	Record purchase allowance for a supplier		

FIGURE 11A.5

Purchase Discounts

The supplier may offer credit terms and a discount period to encourage early payments. In a periodic inventory system, the amount of the discount is credited to a contra-expense account called **purchase discounts**. This is another account that is part of cost of goods sold. By crediting this account, instead of simply crediting the inventory account like we did in the perpetual inventory system, management is able to track the amount they are saving in paying their suppliers within the discount period. We will now show the journal entries for both the purchase and payment from Tools 4U Inc. who bought goods from Roof Tiles Inc. in the amount of $4,200 on January 10. The supplier allows 2/10, n/30 on all invoices. Since Tools 4U had excess cash at this time, the manager chose to take advantage of the cash discount by paying the invoice within 10 days.

The original entry for the purchase is:

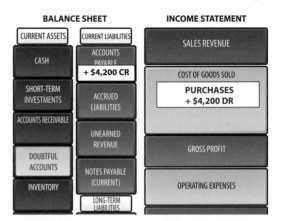

JOURNAL			
Date	**Account Title and Explanation**	**Debit**	**Credit**
Jan 10	Purchases	4,200	
	Account Payable		4,200
	Purchase of goods from Roof Tiles		

FIGURE 11A.6

The payment amount for the bill would be $4,200 less the $84 discount ($4,200 × 2%). Since the business was paying less for the purchases of inventory, the value of the purchase needed to decrease by the discount amount. The entry to record the discount when the payment was made to Roof Tiles Inc. on January 12 is:

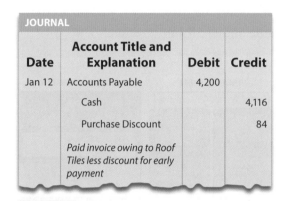
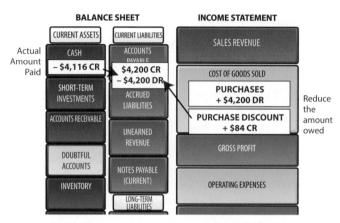

FIGURE 11A.7

Both purchase returns and allowances and purchase discounts are known as contra accounts as they have the opposite balance to the account to which they are related to. They reduce the balance of purchases when reported on the financial statements.

Calculation of Net Purchases

From the above journal entries, the amount of net purchases is determined in figure 11A.8.

Purchases		$14,200
Less: Purchase Returns and Allowances	$360	
Purchase Discounts	84	444
Net Purchases		$13,756

FIGURE 11A.8

Freight-In

In a periodic inventory system, shipping charges on incoming inventory is recorded by debiting the **freight-in** account which is an income statement account that is part of cost of goods sold. Assume Tools 4U Inc. paid $100 freight cost for the inventory on January 10, the journal entry is shown in figure 11A.9.

JOURNAL			
Date	**Account Title and Explanation**	**Debit**	**Credit**
Jan 10	Freight-In	100	
	Cash		100
	Record the payment of freight cost		

FIGURE 11A.9

Sales

The major difference between the periodic and perpetual system occurs at the point of sale. Unlike the perpetual system which immediately records cost of goods sold when revenue from the sale of inventory is recognized, the periodic system calculates cost of goods sold at the end of the period when ending inventory is determined with a physical count. Assuming inventory is sold on account, the entry should be recorded by debiting accounts receivable and crediting revenue.

Assume Tools 4U Inc. sold $13,000 worth of goods for $20,000 on January 15. In a periodic system, this transaction would be recorded as shown in figure 11A.10:

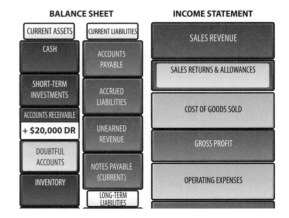

JOURNAL			
Date	Account Title and Explanation	Debit	Credit
Jan 15	Accounts Receivable	20,000	
	Sales		20,000
	Record sales on account		

FIGURE 11A.10

The entry is recorded by debiting accounts receivable and crediting sales. The cost of goods sold and inventory accounts are not updated immediately. Instead, they will be updated at the end of the period when the physical count is taken.

Sales Returns

If a customer returns goods, in a periodic inventory system, only one journal entry is required to record the sales return and credit the amount owing from the customer (assuming the goods were sold on account). The journal entry for a return of $4,000 worth of goods by a customer is shown in figure 11A.11.

The entry is recorded by debiting sales returns and allowances and crediting accounts receivable. Unlike the perpetual inventory system, the cost of goods sold and inventory are not updated immediately.

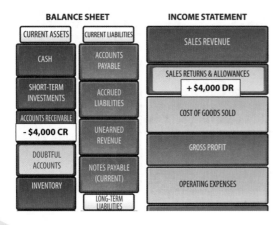

JOURNAL			
Date	Account Title and Explanation	Debit	Credit
	Sales Returns and Allowances	4,000	
	Accounts Receivable		4,000
	Record return of items by customer for credit		

FIGURE 11A.11

Sales Allowances

Sales allowances are recorded in the same way as when a perpetual inventory system is used. Referring to the sales allowances example from the previous section, we recall that Tools 4U granted a $300 sales allowance. The journal entry is recorded as shown in figure 11A.12 in a periodic inventory system.

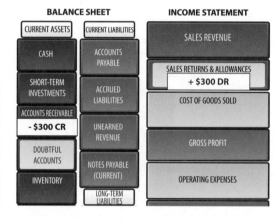

JOURNAL			
Date	Account Title and Explanation	Debit	Credit
	Sales Returns & Allowances	300	
	Accounts Receivable		300
	Record sales allowances provided for customer		

FIGURE 11A.12

Sales Discounts

Sales discounts are recorded in the same way as when a perpetual inventory system is used. In our example, the customer paid within the discount period and received a $250 discount as shown in the following journal entry:

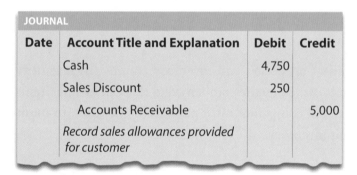

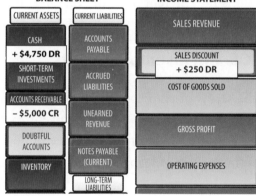

JOURNAL			
Date	Account Title and Explanation	Debit	Credit
	Cash	4,750	
	Sales Discount	250	
	Accounts Receivable		5,000
	Record sales allowances provided for customer		

FIGURE 11A.13

Net sales is determined by deducting sales returns and allowances and sales discounts from sales revenue as follows:

$$\$20,000 - \$4,000 - \$300 - \$250 = \$15,450$$

Reporting the Cost of Goods Sold

In a periodic system, the cost of goods sold is not known until the end of the period, when the ending inventory is known. This is because, unlike the perpetual system where all costs flowed through the inventory account, the costs that make up the cost of goods available for sale are kept in separate accounts (beginning inventory, purchases, and freight-in). Once ending inventory is determined, it is subtracted from the cost of goods available for sale to determine the cost of goods sold. Assuming the beginning inventory in our example is $20,000 and the ending inventory is $22,856, the cost of goods sold is determined on the income statement as shown in figure 11A.14.

Cost of Goods Sold = Beginning Inventory + Net Purchases + Freight-In − Ending Inventory		
Beginning Inventory		$20,000
Net Purchases	$13,756	
Freight-In	100	13,856
Cost of Goods Available for Sale		$33,856
Less: Ending Inventory		22,856
Cost of Goods Sold		$11,000

FIGURE 11A.14

The freight-in is added to net purchases to determine cost of goods available for sale. The value of ending inventory is determined by a physical count and subtracted from cost of goods available for sale to determine cost of goods sold. The amounts included in the inventory and cost of goods sold is no different from the example under the perpetual inventory system. It is mainly a timing difference regarding when these amounts are updated.

FOB and Inventory Counts

The terms of shipping items will have an impact on period end inventory counts. An inventory count is supposed to include all inventory that is owned by the company, and this can include items that are not physically at the place of business. All companies must pay careful attention to items in the process of being shipped when counting inventory.

For example, suppose Company A purchases items with a cost of $10,000 with terms of FOB shipping point. This means that Company A takes ownership of the goods as soon as they are loaded onto the carrier, and should include these as part of their inventory. While these goods are in transit, Company A performs an inventory count and does not include the inventory that they just purchased. This means that the value of their ending inventory on their balance sheet will be too low, or understated by $10,000. If Company A uses the periodic inventory system, an understated ending inventory will cause COGS to be overstated and net income to be understated. This is shown in figure 11A.15.

	Correct	Incorrect
Sales	$160,000	$160,000
Cost of Goods Sold		
Beginning Inventory	50,000	50,000
Net Purchases	65,000	65,000
Cost of Goods Available for Sale	115,000	115,000
Less: Ending Inventory	45,000	35,000
Cost of Goods Sold	70,000	80,000
Gross Profit	90,000	80,000
Operating Expense	50,000	50,000
Net Income	$40,000	$30,000

FIGURE 11A.15

Similar problems would occur if a company sells inventory with terms of FOB destination. Although the items are not in the seller's warehouse, the seller still owns the items while they are in transit and must include them as part of their inventory.

To summarize the differences between the perpetual and periodic journal entries, the following table indicates which accounts are affected by the types of transactions we have learned.

Transaction	Perpetual*		Periodic*	
	Debit	Credit	Debit	Credit
Purchase	Inventory (B/S)	Cash or Accounts Payable	Purchases (I/S)	Cash or Accounts Payable
Purchase Return	Cash or Accounts Payable	Inventory (B/S)	Cash or Accounts Payable	Purchase Returns & Allowances (I/S)
Purchase Allowance	Cash or Accounts Payable	Inventory (B/S)	Cash or Accounts Payable	Purchase Returns & Allowances (I/S)
Payment with Discount	Accounts Payable	Cash Inventory (B/S)	Accounts Payable	Cash Purchase Discounts (I/S)
Freight	Inventory (B/S)	Cash or Accounts Payable	Freight-In (I/S)	Cash or Accounts Payable
Sales	Cash or Accounts Receivable Cost of Goods Sold (I/S)	Sales Revenue (I/S) Inventory (B/S)	Cash or Accounts Receivable	Sales Revenue (I/S)

Transaction	Perpetual*		Periodic*	
	Debit	**Credit**	**Debit**	**Credit**
Sales Returns	Sales Returns & Allowances (I/S)	Cash or Accounts Receivable	Sales Returns & Allowances (I/S)	Cash or Accounts Receivable
	Inventory (B/S)	Cost of Goods Sold (I/S)		
Sales Allowance	Sales Returns & Allowances (I/S)	Cash or Accounts Receivable	Sales Returns & Allowances (I/S)	Cash or Accounts Receivable
Receipt with Discount	Cash Sales Discounts (I/S)	Accounts Receivable	Cash Sales Discounts (I/S)	Accounts Receivable

*B/S = Balance Sheet and I/S = Income Statement

FIGURE 11A.16

In essence, the mechanisms behind recording these transactions under both inventory tracking methods are the same. They only differ in the way that no "inventory" and "cost of goods sold" accounts are present under the periodic inventory transactions.

A CLOSER LOOK

The accurate financial performance of a company that uses the periodic system can only be calculated when an inventory count is performed and the cost of goods is calculated. If a business wanted to see how they were performing between inventory counts, they may have to make some adjustments to the reports before the numbers can be useful for decision making.

For example, a nursery selling flowers and other plants may operate from May to October. After closing in October, they perform a physical count of inventory and prepare formal financial statements.

Before they open in May, they have to purchase soil and seeds and start growing plants in their greenhouses in preparation for spring. These purchases are made before any sales are made. Recall that under a periodic inventory system, cost of goods sold = beginning inventory + purchases - ending inventory. If the company uses the periodic inventory system and wanted to see their performance after one month of operations (May), without counting inventory, only the beginning inventory and purchases amount would be available for the purposes of calculating cost of goods sold. That is, ending inventory would be missing. By not deducting ending inventory, the information presented would be distorted and it would appear that they are operating at a loss.

To prevent the distortion of the financial statements, management can instead estimate what cost of goods sold was using the gross profit method discussed earlier in chapter 11.

For example, if the nursery typically operates at 40% gross profit during their sales season, the following figure illustrates how the income statement could be estimated without doing a physical inventory count.

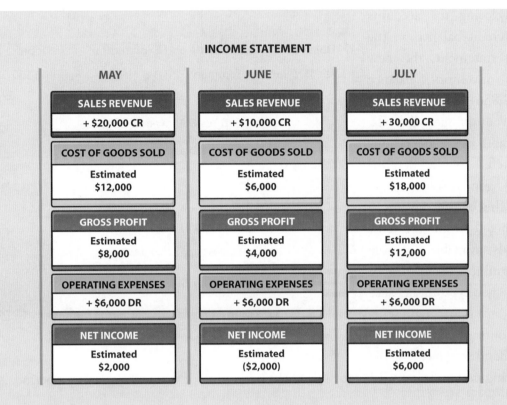

This estimation can only be used for management purposes and interim statements. Formal financial statements can only be prepared after a physical count has been performed.

Closing Entries

Closing Entries and Inventory in a Periodic System

Although there are a few variations of how inventory is adjusted through the closing entries when a periodic system is used, the main objective is the same – to remove the beginning inventory balance and add the new ending inventory balance.

Here is one approach that is frequently used as shown in figure 11A.17.

JOURNAL			
Date	Account Title and Explanation	Debit	Credit
Mar 31	Revenue	20,000	
	Inventory	22,856	
	Purchase Returns & Allowances	360	
	Purchase Discounts	84	
	Income Summary		43,300
	To close revenue and other income statement credit balance accounts and to set up ending inventory balance for the period		

FIGURE 11A.17

When closing the accounts with a credit balance on the income statement, the new ending inventory balance of $22,856 is debited to the inventory account. To understand the logic of this entry, refer to the detailed cost of goods sold section above. The ending inventory is deducted from the cost of goods available for sale to determine the amount of cost of goods sold because ending inventory represents the amount a company still has on hand at the end of the

JOURNAL

Date	Account Title and Explanation	Debit	Credit
Mar 31	Income Summary	40,360	
	Inventory		20,000
	Sales Returns & Allowances		4,300
	Sales Discounts		250
	Purchases		14,200
	Freight-in		100
	Operating Expenses		1,510
	To close expense and other debit balance income statement accounts and to remove beginning inventory for the period		

FIGURE 11A.18

accounting period. It is available for sale at the beginning of the next accounting period.

In closing the expense accounts, notice that the beginning inventory balance of $20,000 is credited. Refer to figure 11A.14, the detailed cost of goods sold section is shown. What effect does the beginning inventory have on the cost of goods available for sale? It is added together with purchases and therefore represents an expense of the period. The logic is: expenses are credited through the closing entries; therefore, the beginning inventory balance of $20,000 must be credited.

After the closing entries are posted to the accounts, the inventory account will be updated to reflect the actual amount of inventory on hand, $22,856.

The final step of the closing entry process is to close the income summary account to the owners' capital (proprietorship) or retained earnings (corporations). Assuming the company operates as a proprietorship, the journal entry on January 31 is shown in figure 11A.19.

JOURNAL

Date	Account Title and Explanation	Debit	Credit
Jan 31	Income Summary	2,940	
	Capital Account		2,940
	To close income summary and transfer net income to owner's capital account		

FIGURE 11A.19

The T-Accounts below summarize the closing entries under the periodic inventory system. Note how the inventory account is updated following the physical inventory count. Each item that is closed to the income summary account is shown separately so the opening and ending inventory amounts can be highlighted.

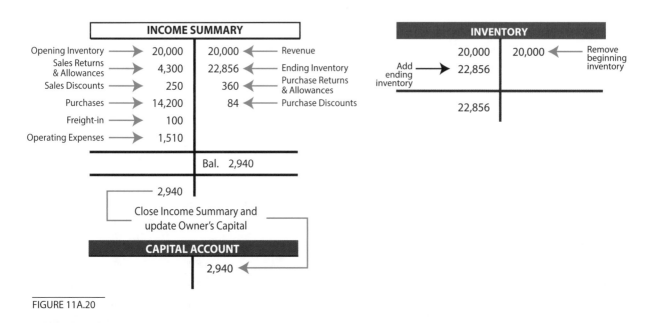

FIGURE 11A.20

Methods for Valuing Inventory: Periodic

Cool Ink Company sells a number of different pens, pencils, markers and highlighters. Let us examine one item from their inventory to illustrate specific identification, FIFO, weighted average and LIFO inventory valuation methods. Assume that Cool Ink uses a periodic inventory system to account for purchases and sales.

Cool Ink Company currently has 10 pens in inventory with a cost of $10 each. During the month of March, the following transactions take place:

Date	Transaction	Quantity	Unit Cost
March 5	Purchase from Pen Distributers	50	$12
March 7	Sale	15	
March 15	Purchase from Promotional Pens	40	$14
March 19	Purchase from Promotional Pens	20	$16
March 27	Sale	50	

FIGURE 11A.21

During the month, the cost of the pen changed. This implies that the cost of goods sold applied to the sales will likely be different, based on which pens are actually sold. We can apply the four methods of valuing inventory to the transactions to arrive at different values for inventory and cost of goods sold. This will demonstrate that the choice of inventory valuation method can make a difference on the financial statements of a company.

The main difference between the perpetual and the periodic inventory system is when costs are assigned to the sales. The perpetual system, as illustrated in chapter 11, assigns costs to the sales as the sales are made. The periodic system only assigns costs at the end of the period, when a physical count of the inventory is made.

Using Specific Identification

When using specific identification, list the purchases separately from each other to easily identify the costs associated with each batch of inventory. The opening balance and the transactions from figure 11A.21 are listed in figure 11A.22. At the bottom of the figure is the value of ending inventory.

Date	Purchases			Sales			Balance		
	Quantity	Unit Cost	Value	Quantity	Unit Cost	Value	Quantity	Unit Cost	Value
March 1							10	$10	$100
March 5	50	$12	$600				10	$10	$100
							50	$12	$600
March 15	40	$14	$560				10	$10	$100
							50	$12	$600
							40	$14	$560
March 19	20	$16	$320				10	$10	$100
							50	$12	$600
							40	$14	$560
							20	$16	$320
Sales for the Month				10	$10	$100	10	$12	$120
				40	$12	$480	25	$14	$350
				15	$14	$210	20	$16	$320
Ending Inventory									$790

FIGURE 11A.22

Step 1: The purchase of 50 pens on March 5 is added to the value of inventory.

Step 2: The purchase of 40 pens on March 15 is added to the value of inventory.

Step 3: The purchase of 20 pens on March 19 is added to the value of inventory.

Step 4: The sales are tallied at the end of the month and are identified based on which batch of inventory they came from. In this example, the entire amount of opening inventory was sold, 40 items from the March 5 purchase were sold and 15 items from the March 15 purchase were sold. Total cost of goods sold is $790 ($100 + $480 + $210).

Step 5: The value of ending inventory is made up of 10 pens remaining from the March 5 purchase, the 25 pens remaining from the March 15 purchase and the 20 pens remaining from the March 19 purchase. Total value of inventory is $790 ($120 + $350 + $320).

Using First-In-First-Out

When using the FIFO method, list the purchases in the order they were received. This will allow you to easily see which items were the first ones purchased and will be the first ones to be sold. The opening balance and the transactions from figure 11A.21 are listed in figure 11A.23. At the bottom of the figure is the value of ending inventory.

Date	Purchases			Sales			Balance		
	Quantity	Unit Cost	Value	Quantity	Unit Cost	Value	Quantity	Unit Cost	Value
March 1							10	$10	$100
March 5	50	$12	$600				10	$10	$100
							50	$12	$600
March 15	40	$14	$560				10	$10	$100
							50	$12	$600
							40	$14	$560
March 19	20	$16	$320				10	$10	$100
							50	$12	$600
							40	$14	$560
							20	$16	$320
Sales for the Month				10	$10	$100	35	$14	$490
				50	$12	$600	20	$16	$320
				5	$14	$70			
Ending Inventory									$810

FIGURE 11A.23

Step 1:   The purchase of 50 pens on March 5 is added to the value of inventory.

Step 2:   The purchase of 40 pens on March 15 is added to the value of inventory.

Step 3:   The purchase of 20 pens on March 19 is added to the value of inventory.

Step 4:   There was a total of 65 items sold (15 units + 50 units). Costs will be taken from the list of inventory, starting with the first item at the top of the list. The entire amount of opening inventory, the entire amount of the March 5 purchase, and five items from the March 15 purchase are considered sold. Total cost of goods sold is $770 ($100 + $600 + $70).

Step 5:   The value of ending inventory is made up of 35 pens remaining from the March 15 purchase and the 20 pens remaining from the March 19 purchase. Total value of inventory is $810 ($490 + $320).

Using Weighted Average Cost

When using the weighted average cost method, the average cost per unit only has to be calculated at the end of the period. The opening balance and the transactions from figure 11A.21 are listed in figure 11A.24. At the bottom of the figure is the value of ending inventory.

Date	Purchases			Sales			Balance		
	Quantity	Unit Cost	Value	Quantity	Unit Cost	Value	Quantity	Unit Cost	Value
March 1							10		$100
March 5	50	$12	$600				60		$700
March 15	40	$14	$560				100		$1,260
March 19	20	$16	$320				120	$13.17	$1,580
Sales for the Month				65	$13.17	$856	55	$13.17	$724
Ending Inventory									$724

FIGURE 11A.24

Step 1: The purchase of 50 pens on March 5 is added to the quantity on hand. The value of the 50 pens is added to the value of the opening inventory.

Step 2: The purchase of 40 pens on March 15 is added to the quantity on hand. The value of the 40 pens is added to current value of inventory.

Step 3: The purchase of 20 pens on March 19 is added to the quantity on hand. The value of the 20 pens is added to current value of inventory.

Step 4: At the end of the month, there are 120 pens available for sale with a total cost of $1,580. The average cost per pen is approximately $13.17 ($1,580 ÷ 120 units). This average cost will be applied to the total sales of 65 pens for the month. Total cost of goods sold is $856 (65 units x $13.17).

Step 5: The value of ending inventory is 55 pens at the unit cost of approximately $13.17. Total value of inventory is $724.

Using Last-In-First-Out (LIFO)

When using the LIFO method, it is helpful to list the purchases in the order they were received. This will allow you to easily see which items were the last ones purchased and will be the first ones to be sold. The opening balance and the transactions from figure 11A.21 are listed in figure 11A.25. At the bottom of the figure is the value of ending inventory.

Date	Purchases			Sales			Balance		
	Quantity	Unit Cost	Value	Quantity	Unit Cost	Value	Quantity	Unit Cost	Value
March 1							10	$10	$100
March 5	50	$12	$600				10	$10	$100
							50	$12	$600
March 15	40	$14	$560				10	$10	$100
							50	$12	$600
							40	$14	$560
March 19	20	$16	$320				10	$10	$100
							50	$12	$600
							40	$14	$560
							20	$16	$320
Sales for the Month				20	$16	$320	10	$10	$100
				40	$14	$560	45	$12	$540
				5	$12	$60			
Ending Inventory									$640

FIGURE 11A.25

Step 1.   The purchase of 50 pens on March 5 is added to the value of inventory.

Step 2.   The purchase of 40 pens on March 15 is added to the value of inventory.

Step 3.   The purchase of 20 pens on March 19 is added to the value of inventory.

Step 4.   There was a total of 65 items sold (15 units + 50 units). Costs will be taken from the list of inventory, starting with the item at the bottom of the list. The entire amount of the March 19 purchase, the entire amount of the March 15 purchase, and five items from the March 5 purchase are considered sold. Total cost of goods sold is $940 ($320 + $560 + $60).

Step 5.   The value of ending inventory is made up of 10 pens from the opening balance inventory, 45 pens remaining from the March 5 purchase. Total value of inventory is $640 ($100+ $540).

The Effect of Different Valuation Methods: Periodic

As the previous example with Cool Ink Company demonstrates, different ending inventory figures are produced using different valuation methods. The following chart summarizes these differences when applied to the Cool Ink examples:

Periodic Inventory System	Specific Identification	FIFO	Weighted Average	LIFO
Inventory Available for Sale (beginning inventory + purchases)	$1,580	$1,580	$1,580	$1,580
Ending Inventory	790	810	724	640
Value of COGS	790	770	856	940

FIGURE 11A.26

From the above, we can make the following assumptions:

1. In times where product cost increases over the period, FIFO will result in the highest value of ending inventory and LIFO will result in the highest value of cost of goods sold.

2. While specific identification provides the true value of ending inventory and the cost of goods sold, it is costly to implement and therefore not practical for items of small value.

When ending inventory amounts change, so does the cost of goods sold, gross profit and net income. Therefore companies can dramatically change their financial results by manipulating the inventory valuation method.

When comparing inventory valuation methods between the perpetual and periodic systems in figures 11A.26 and 11A.27, notice the following figure of ending inventory and cost of goods sold. Specific identification will always provide the same values since the company is able to specifically identify which items are being sold, regardless of the inventory system being used. FIFO will also provide the same values because the most recent purchases are always in ending inventory.

Perpetual Inventory System	Specific Identification	FIFO	Weighted Average	LIFO
Inventory Available for Sale (beginning inventory + purchases)	$1,580	$1,580	$1,580	$1,580
Ending Inventory	790	810	736	660
Value of COGS	790	770	844	920

FIGURE 11A.27

The weighted average method and LIFO show different values for ending inventory and COGS. This is because the perpetual inventory system assigns costs as the items are sold, whereas the periodic inventory system only assigns costs at the end of the period.

Review Exercise

The following information was presented by the bookkeeper for George's Gardening Supplies for the month of December 2010.

DATE	BUSINESS EVENT
Dec 1	Owner George G. deposited $100,000 of his own money into the business account
Dec 2	The company purchased $50,000 of inventory on account, terms 2/10, net 30.
Dec 3	The company sold $80,000 of inventory to Greenland Care on account, terms 2/10, net 30; cost of goods sold $32,000.
Dec 4	The company purchased $20,000 of inventory on account, terms 2/15, net 30.
Dec 5	The company returned $2,000 of defective merchandise to the suppliers.
Dec 6	The company paid for inventory bought on Dec 4, less $400 discount.
Dec 7	A customer returned $1,000 of goods purchased on account. The cost of goods sold for returned inventory is $600.
Dec 8	The company purchased $10,000 of inventory on account, terms 2/10, net 30.
Dec 9	The company paid $500 freight bill for transportation of supplies purchased in transaction above.
Dec 9	The company collected $39,000 outstanding accounts receivable less approved sales discount of $780.
Dec 10	The company sold $33,500 of goods to Green House Inc. on account, terms 2/10, net 30. The value of cost of goods sold is $13,300.
Dec 11	The company paid $48,000 for inventory bought previously less a $960 discount.
Dec 12	The following cash transactions were made: Prepaid insurance of $3,600; Repairs and maintenance of $600; Salary expense of $11,000; Rent expense of $6,000; Withdrawals of $5,000, Equipment of $45,000, Utility expense of $750, and Advertising Expense of $2,500.

Assume that George's Gardening Supplies uses the periodic inventory system. Complete the following exercises.

Part 1

Journalize all transactions.

Part 1 - Answer

Journal			
Date	**Account Title and Explanation**	**Debit**	**Credit**
Dec 1	Cash	100,000	
	G. George, Capital		100,000
	Owner's initial investment in business		
Dec 2	Purchases	50,000	
	Accounts Payable		50,000
	Purchase of inventory on account, terms 2/10,		
	net 30		
Dec 3	Accounts Receivable	80,000	
	Sales Revenue		80,000
	Record sales on account, terms 2/10, net 30		
Dec 4	Purchases	20,000	
	Accounts Payable		20,000
	Record purchase of inventory on account,		
	2/15, net 30		
Dec 5	Accounts Payable	2,000	
	Purchase Returns & Allowance		2,000
	Returned defective merchandise for credit		
Dec 6	Accounts Payable	20,000	
	Purchase Discounts		400
	Cash		19,600
	Paid for merchandise less return and discount		
Dec 7	Sales Returns & Allowances	1,000	
	Accounts Receivable		1,000
	Customer returned goods bought on account		
Dec 8	Purchases	10,000	
	Accounts Payable		10,000
	Purchase of inventory on account, terms		
	2/10,net 30		
Dec 9	Freight-in	500	
	Cash		500
	Paid freight bill on above purchase		

Date	Account Title and Explanation	Debit	Credit
Dec 9	Cash	38,220	
	Sales Discounts	780	
	Accounts Receivable		39,000
	Received payment on account, less return and		
	discount		
Dec 10	Accounts Receivable	33,500	
	Sales Revenue		33,500
	Sales on account, terms 2/10, net 30		
Dec 11	Accounts Payable	48,000	
	Purchase Discounts		960
	Cash		47,040
	Paid for merchandise, less return and discount		
Dec 12	Prepaid Insurance	3,600	
	Repairs and Maintenance	600	
	Salary Expense	11,000	
	Rent Expense	6,000	
	Withdrawals	5,000	
	Equipment	45,000	
	Utilities Expense	750	
	Advertising Expense	2,500	
	Cash		74,450
	Record payment of various items		

Part 2

Given the following year-end trial balance (prior to closing entries), prepare the schedule of cost of goods sold and close the accounts at the period end. Assume the physical count determined the value of ending inventory to be $39,940.

George's Garden Centre Trial Balance December 31, 2010		
Account Title	**DR**	**CR**
Cash	$16,630	
Accounts Receivable	73,500	
Inventory	7,500	
Prepaid Insurance	1,800	
Equipment	45,000	
Accumulated Depreciation-Equipment		$9,000
Accounts Payable		17,500
Salary Payable		1,000
G. George, Capital		120,000
G. George, Withdrawals	5,000	
Sales Revenue		113,500
Sales Discounts	780	
Sales Returns and Allowances	1,000	
Purchases	80,000	
Purchase Discounts		1,360
Purchase Returns and Allowances		2,000
Freight-in	500	
Salary Expense	12,000	
Rent Expense	6,000	
Advertising Expense	2,500	
Utilities Expense	750	
Repairs & Maintenance	600	
Depreciation Expense-Equipment	9,000	
Insurance Expense	1,800	
Totals	$264,360	$264,360

Part 2 – Answer

Schedule of COGS:

Beginning inventory		$7,500
Purchases	$80,000	
Less:		
Purchase returns & allowances	2,000	
Purchase discounts	1,360	
Add:		
Freight-in	$500	
Net purchases		77,140
Cost of goods available for sale		86,640
Less:		
Ending inventory		39,940
Cost of goods sold		$44,700

Part 3

Prepare the closing entries for the company at the end of December.

Part 3 – Answer

Date	Account Title and Explanation	Debit	Credit
Dec 31	Inventory (Ending)	39,940	
	Sales Revenue	113,500	
	Purchase Discounts	1,360	
	Purchase Returns & Allowances	2,000	
	Income Summary		156,800
	To close revenue and other income statement		
	credit balance accounts and to set up ending		
	inventory balance for the period		

Date	Account Title and Explanation	Debit	Credit
Dec 31	Income Summary	122,430	
	Inventory (Beginning)		7,500
	Sales Discounts		780
	Sales Returns & Allowances		1,000
	Purchases		80,000
	Freight-in		500
	Salary Expense		12,000
	Rent Expense		6,000
	Advertising Expense		2,500
	Utilities Expense		750
	Repairs & Maintenance Expense		600
	Depreciation Expense-Equipment		9,000
	Insurance Expense		1,800
	To close expense and other debit balance		
	income statement accounts and to remove		
	beginning inventory for the period		
Dec 31	Income Summary	34,370	
	G. George, Capital		34,370
	To close income summary and transfer net		
	income to owner's capital account		
Dec 31	G. George, Capital	5,000	
	G. George, Withdrawals		5,000
	To close the withdrawal account		

Chapter 12
LONG-TERM ASSETS

LEARNING OUTCOMES:

❶ Define long-term assets

❷ Record the acquisition and changes in value of long-term assets

❸ Apply the three methods of depreciation of long-term assets

❹ Account for the gain or loss on the sale of long-term assets

❺ Account for natural resources

❻ Define intangible assets and describe the different types of intangible assets

❼ Account for intangible assets

❽ Calculate asset turnover and return on asset ratios

❾ Understand controls and ethical approach related to long-term assets

Long-Term Assets: The Big Picture

You will recall from our examination of the *current assets* section of the balance sheet that current assets are defined as those owned for less than a year. On the other hand, *long-term assets* are those that will be owned and will be used by the company as part of normal operations for longer than a year. Long-term assets comprise tangible assets, which have physical substance – that is, they can be perceived with our senses, especially by touch; and intangible assets, which have no physical substance and can only be perceived by the mind or imagination; intangible assets represent amounts paid for "rights" of ownership. We will cover each group of assets in this chapter.

Long-term assets tend to be worth large amounts of money and constitute major items on a company's balance sheet. Accountants often face the challenge of classifying, recording and monitoring the value of long-term assets. In this chapter, we will have a detailed discussion on how accountants perform these tasks.

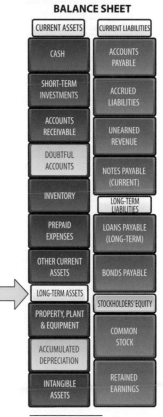

FIGURE 12.1

The *Long-Term Assets* section of the Accounting Map™ is divided into two parts. The first part, labeled *Property, Plant & Equipment*, pertains to a company's long-term assets that are of a tangible nature. The second part is labeled *Intangible Assets* and we will discuss these later in the chapter.

A company has to have long-term tangible assets in order to get physical tasks accomplished – for example, machines that package bottles, trucks that deliver catalogues and computers that scan and compute inventory data. Indeed, long-term tangible assets often form the physical backbone of a company. Without them, a business will not have the property, buildings and machinery it needs to deliver goods and services to its customers. This is particularly true for manufacturers or companies involved in the transportation industry whose capital assets are often the largest on the balance sheet.

FIGURE 12.2

For example, look at figure 12.3, which shows an excerpt of the balance sheet for Amtrak for the years ended September 30, 2012 and September 30, 2011.

National Railroad Passenger Corporation and Subsidiaries (Amtrak) Consolidated Balance Sheet For the Year Ended September 30 (In Thousands of Dollars, Except Share Data)		
ASSETS	**2012**	**2011**
Current Assets:		
Cash and cash equivalents	210,820	126,779
Restricted Cash	8,130	57,247
Accounts receivable, net of allowances of $7,236 and $8,556 at September 30, 2012 and 2011, respectively	209,760	172,450
Materials and supplies – net	234,896	213,575
Prepaid Expenses	13,712	13,746
Other current assets	25,091	32,832
Total current assets	702,409	616,629
Property and Equipment:		
Locomotives	1,485,812	1,447,556
Passenger cars and other rolling stock	2,699,572	2,572,583
Right-of-way and other properties	10,689,217	9,971,446
Construction in progress	1,020,317	1,367,223
Leasehold improvements	496,353	374,740
Property and equipment, gross	16,391,271	15,733,548
Less - Accumulated depreciation and amortization	(6,024,334)	(5,633,117)
Total property and equipment, net	**10,366,937**	**10,100,431**
Other Assets, Deposits, and Deferred Charges:		
Notes receivable on sale-leasebacks	51,850	50,012
Deferred charges, deposits, and other	253,295	304,304
Total other assets, deposits, and deferred charges	**305,145**	**354,316**
Total Assets	**11,374,491**	**11,071,376**

FIGURE 12.3

You can see that for both fiscal years 2012 and 2011, the company's largest assets were its property, plant and equipment. These are obviously important investments for the business and need to be properly managed to achieve long-term success.

Defining a Long-Term Asset

Various components distinguish a long-term asset from a current asset. An asset can be considered to be long-term if it contains certain characteristics related to time, money and purpose. In fact, these characteristics can be determined by the accountant who asks three questions when presented with the purchase of an item:

1. How long will the company use the item?
2. How much does the item cost?
3. What will the item be used for?

1. How long will the company use the item?

As already mentioned, a period of one year is the dividing line between current and long-term assets. If a business intends to use an item for more than a year, it meets one of the most important criteria for defining a long-term asset.

Different types of capital assets tend to have different life spans – all exceeding one year. Office equipment, such as computers and printers, tend to have life spans averaging five years. The life span of buildings can often be measured in decades. Land can be considered to have an infinite life span; it can be used for as long as the company is in business.

2. How much does the item cost?

When one hears the term *capital* being used, it usually refers to items worth large sums of money that are integral to the finances of an organization, industry or even the country. This certainly holds true for long-term tangible (capital) assets, which normally make up a large portion of the value of the assets on a company's balance sheet. Yet, how much does something have to cost for it to be classified as a capital asset in the financial statements? The short answer is this: it depends. It depends on the size of the organization and the guidelines used to classify capital assets. The accounting principle of *materiality* should be applied – that is, companies need to decide the dollar amount they will use as the basis on which amounts will either be set up as long-term assets or expensed during the current accounting period.

What a large multinational corporation considers to be a significant amount of money will almost invariably differ from the amount a small business would consider significant. A large organization could, for example, establish the guideline that something needs to cost at least $2,000 to be considered a tangible long-term asset. A small business might set $500 as a threshold. For businesses large and small, if an item is less than the threshold, it is recorded as an expense on the income statement.

It is important to keep in mind that once a rule is chosen, a company should adhere to it. This is what the GAAP rule of consistency is about, and it seeks to prevent accountants from manipulating the numbers after the fact.

3. What will the item be used for?

For something to be considered a capital asset, an organization should acquire it for the purpose of generating income (i.e. it must be used for business purposes). Businesses buy land in order to build factories; they buy buildings in order to set up stores; they buy trucks in order to deliver goods; and they buy machines in order to make products. All these items should be considered capital assets as long as they meet the first two criteria discussed.

The Acquisition of Long-Term Assets

When companies purchase physical items such as land, buildings and equipment, the accountant must consider the cost, purpose and expected useful life of the item. According to the materiality principle, an item can be considered a capital asset on the balance sheet instead of an expense in the income statement if it satisfies the following: it has material value relative to the size of the business and it is expected to last for longer than one year.

Once the decision has been made to record the item as a capital asset, focus shifts to the cost principle to ensure that all the costs associated with acquiring the asset are properly recorded. A company pays not only for the asset in question

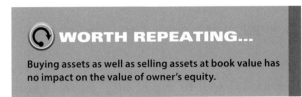

WORTH REPEATING...

Buying assets as well as selling assets at book value has no impact on the value of owner's equity.

but also for all the costs associated with acquiring the asset – for example, the freight that was paid to bring a machine to the factory; the infrastructure upgrades involved in connecting electricity and water lines; and the installation fees paid to set up the machines and have them ready for operation.

Note that since these costs are directly related to the asset itself, they are not treated as expenses but as part of the cost of the asset. This cost is then recorded on the company's balance sheet.

For example, the Sunshine Juice Company has purchased a new bottling machine for its orange juice line. It was purchased at a price of $120,000 and shipped at a cost of $5,000, with installation costs amounting to $2,000. Assuming one invoice for all these costs, here is the journal entry for the acquisition of this capital asset:

JOURNAL			
Date	**Account Title and Explanation**	**Debit**	**Credit**
	Machine	127,000	
	Accounts Payable		127,000
	Record the purchase of a machine for $120,000 + $2,000 for installation, and $5,000 for shipping		

BALANCE SHEET

FIGURE 12.4

When totaled, the costs amount to $127,000. This amount is debited to an account that is part of property, plant and equipment and credited to accounts payable, since the company was invoiced and owes this amount to the bottling machine manufacturer. Of course, once the bill is paid, accounts payable will be debited and cash will be credited.

Although financial statements may just show a single property, plant and equipment line item, there are actually separate accounts for each capital asset within that category. In this text, we will journalize each capital asset by using the asset's specific name.

Lump Sum Purchases of Capital Assets

Unique circumstances can throw a wrench in the way transactions are recorded. This also holds true for capital assets. Companies sometimes purchase capital assets in bundles, or what is known as a "basket of assets." Instead of buying capital assets individually from different vendors, a company may get a good price for a basket of assets by buying them from the same vendor.

The challenge with this type of transaction is that by paying a lower price for the assets, the buyer acquires them for less than their appraised value. Accountants find creative ways to resolve conflicting principles like this. In this case, the lump sum paid for all the assets will be divided and allocated to each item according to percentages based on the appraised values. For example, the Huge Bargain Store has purchased land, a building and a parking lot for the purpose of opening a new store. It bought all these assets in a bundle for the lump sum payment of $800,000. However, each asset has its own appraised value, as listed in the following chart:

Item	Appraised Value
Property	600,000
Building	300,000
Parking Lot	100,000
Total	1,000,000

FIGURE 12.5

As you can see, the total of all the appraised values is $1,000,000, which is $200,000 more than the purchase price. The first step is to take each appraised value and divide it by the total appraised values. This produces a percentage that should be allocated to each asset.

Property	600,000 ÷ 1,000,000	60%
Building	300,000 ÷ 1,000,000	30%
Parking Lot	100,000 ÷ 1,000,000	10%

FIGURE 12.6

We have based the amounts to be recorded for each asset on the appraised values, and these will be recorded as follows:

The specific capital asset accounts are debited and cash is credited.

These percentages are now allocated to the amount actually paid, which was $800,000.

Property	800,000 × 60%	480,000
Building	800,000 × 30%	240,000
Parking Lot	800,000 × 10%	80,000
		800,000

FIGURE 12.7

JOURNAL			
Date	Account Title and Explanation	Debit	Credit
	Land	480,000	
	Building	240,000	
	Parking Lot	80,000	
	Cash		800,000
	Record the purchase of land, building and parking lot		

FIGURE 12.8

Changes in a Capital Asset

Capital assets can change in value as a result of two factors: depreciation, which we will examine shortly, and changes made to the capital asset itself. As already mentioned, a challenge with capital assets is determining whether an item should be classified as a long-term asset or whether it should simply be recorded as an expense in the current year. This challenge is made even more difficult when a change to the asset takes place. Is the change an example of maintenance, which can be recorded as a routine expense? Or does the change alter the nature of the asset itself so that it is worth more, lasts longer or undergoes a change in function?

These determinations are important every time money is spent on a capital asset. Is the expenditure considered to be an asset or an expense? To make the assessment, ask four questions:

1. Does the expenditure extend the life of the asset?
2. Does the expenditure improve the productivity of the asset?
3. Does the expenditure reduce the company's operating costs?
4. Is the expenditure a material amount?

We will examine each question separately through examples.

1. Does the expenditure extend the life of the asset?

A company has a large stamping press that runs on an electric motor. The maintenance department has been adding replacement parts to keep the motor in operation. The head of the maintenance department tells the owner that these replacement parts are becoming harder to find and that the motor has only one year of operation left. The maintenance manager recommends that the company buy a new motor for the stamping press, which would extend the life of the machine by about 10 years.

If the maintenance department continues buying new parts for the motor, no material changes or upgrades are made to the stamping press; the motor's life span is not extended. These expenditures are therefore classified as expenses in the income statement. However, if the company buys a new motor, a material improvement will be made to the stamping press. Its life span will significantly increase, as will its total cost as a long-term asset on the balance sheet.

2. Does the expenditure improve the productivity of the asset?

Assume that a company originally bought a machine without a lighting system (which could be purchased as an option). The lighting system would have enabled the machine to be operated at night. Management later decided to have a night production shift, and therefore needed to install the lighting system at a substantial cost. This installation significantly increased the machine's productivity, since it could produce more products within the work week. The lighting system, along with all additional costs associated with its delivery and installation, should be considered an improvement, and added to the original cost of the machine.

3. Does the expenditure reduce the company's operating costs?

Many pieces of equipment require routine maintenance by paid staff or by outsourced help – for example, a company's Internet server, which stores web page information. Technicians periodically check the server to ensure that everything is running smoothly. However, technology is available to enable the server itself to perform many routine checks. If the company were to purchase such technology, it would reduce some of the expenses involved in having personnel perform the maintenance, thereby reducing operating costs of the company. The new technology would be classified as a capital expenditure and added to the cost of the server on the company's balance sheet.

4. Is the expenditure a material amount?

As mentioned earlier, the amount of expenditure should be capitalized (added to the cost of the asset) if the money was spent for one of the purposes described in items 1 to 3 above. However, accountants need to consider whether the expenditure is a material amount. Companies often have accounting policies that determine what dollar amount is considered to be material. If the amount is material, the cost is capitalized. If the amount is immaterial, the cost is expensed.

For example, a company that owns a $50 million capital asset may decide that any asset-related cost below $600 is automatically expensed. Therefore, when a $100 addition is made to the capital asset providing a $12,000 benefit, the cost will be considered immaterial and expensed. It is management's responsibility to decide what amount is considered material for their company.

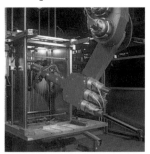

Changes to a capital asset that increases its productivity, such as the addition of an overhead light, which extends the production time of the machine, is considered a material improvement and needs to be added to its total cost.

The Concept of Depreciation

In any discussion of expenses arising from assets, the matching principle needs to be considered. Expenses associated with assets need to be matched with associated revenues. As a company generates annual revenue from using a capital asset, it also generates annual expenses. Capital assets are typically used for long periods of time and their value tends to decrease with use; in other words, as with a car, the more a capital asset is used the less value it will have on the market when it is eventually sold. This decrease in value is considered an expense of "using" the asset and is referred to as *depreciation*. We will examine various aspects of depreciation and how capital assets on the balance sheet are affected.

Residual Value

Before discussing specific methods of depreciation, we should first examine what a capital asset's **residual value** is and how it affects depreciation calculations. As already mentioned, depreciation is the process by which accountants reduce the value of a capital asset over time. At the end of its useful life, the asset might still be worth something. This is called its *salvage value*, since it is possible that the asset can be salvaged for a certain amount of money. It is also called *residual value*, since the asset is considered to have some value, despite no longer being useful to the company.

New capital assets like company trucks can gradually turn into old capital assets. Depreciation is the process by which gradual decreases in value are estimated and recorded over time.

For example, a company may no longer be able to use a delivery truck that has been on the road for six years. A buyer might see some residual value in the truck, salvage it for a price and sell its spare parts or the scrap metal it contains, or even donate it to a museum. In fact, people might want an item for a number of purposes, which is the reason why a capital asset might carry a residual or salvage value even after it is unable to do what it was designed for.

The total amount to be depreciated for a capital asset is affected by the residual value that is expected to remain at the end of the asset's useful life. In other words, if a company purchases a capital asset for $5,000, and determines that its residual value will eventually be $1,000, the amount to be depreciated over the useful life of the asset is $4,000. Even though the capital asset can no longer be used for business after its useful life expires, somebody may salvage it for a price; this price should be subtracted from the depreciation calculations made by the company.

Actual Salvage Value

One of the realities confronting accountants is that depreciation is a theoretical concept. The value of a capital asset does not decrease according to a depreciation schedule. It will decrease on the basis of the price it actually fetches on the market. In other words, depreciation involves an accountant's best estimate, which requires justified calculations of a capital asset's value over its useful life with the company.

For example, a capital asset might be purchased at an initial cost of $100,000. The accountant will examine the asset, study its potential worth over time, and make an educated guess at what someone might eventually be willing to pay to salvage it. This is not an easy task.

Let us assume that the accountant estimates a residual value of $10,000. Ten years later, the item is salvaged for $5,000. It would appear that the accountant overestimated the residual value. This is in order as long as the accountant was justified in making the initial estimate and adjusts for a loss once the asset is salvaged. The residual value was initially estimated as $10,000, though the selling price ended up being $5,000. As a result, the accountant will have to record a loss of $5,000. Similarly, if a capital asset is eventually sold for more than its estimated residual value, the difference would be recorded as a gain.

Three Methods of Depreciation

As time goes by and an asset is used, its value on the market will decline. The capital asset's book value should reflect this decline. Since no one knows what an asset will be worth until it is actually sold, an accountant must estimate how much a capital asset is depreciated while being used by the company.

This process is similar to the one used when estimating a capital asset's residual value. In other words, it is somewhat of a guessing game. The difference with depreciation, however, is that some method should be used to calculate a relatively gradual decline in the asset's worth, period after period. Additionally, once this method is chosen, adherence to the consistency principle requires that the same method be used for the entire time the company uses the asset (unless special conditions are met).

The simplest method of depreciating a capital asset is to take its total cost, deduct any residual value it is expected to have, and divide the balance by the amount of years the asset is expected to be useful. This would produce the same depreciation amount year after year.

This is called the ***straight-line depreciation*** method, which we will examine in further detail shortly. Its attraction is that it is simple. Its fault is that it may not reflect a realistic decline in the value of the asset. That is why other methods of depreciation have been developed, which we will also discuss.

We will now examine three methods of depreciation related to capital assets:

The Straight-Line Method

The Straight-Line Method	Uses simple average
The Declining-Balance Method	Try to reflect a more realistic decline in asset value
The Units-of-Production Method	

FIGURE 12.9

Let us recap what the straight-line method of depreciation does. It takes the entire cost of the capital asset, less any estimated residual value, and divides it by the number of years of its estimated useful life. This produces an average depreciation expense, which is applied each year until the asset is sold or reaches the end of its useful life.

Any method of depreciation involves changing the book value of an asset as realistically as possible

In our first example, we will apply the straight-line method to an asset that is expected to have a residual value once its useful life is over. Remember, only the value related to an asset's useful life is depreciated. This means that the residual value is subtracted from the initial cost before the depreciation method is applied.

Total Cost of Asset - Residual Value = Amount Depreciated

Smith Tools buys a machine for $5,000. The machine is expected to have a useful life of five years and its residual value is estimated to be $1,000. The amount to be depreciated is:

$5,000 - $1,000 = $4,000

Under the straight-line method, the average is calculated by dividing the amount to be depreciated (cost – residual value) by the number of years of the asset's useful life:

$$\text{Yearly Depreciation} = \frac{\text{Amount Depreciated}}{\text{Years of Useful Life}} = \frac{\$4,000}{5}$$

$$= \ \$800 \text{ depreciation per year}$$

This annual depreciation would be applied to the capital asset as follows:

Year	Cost of Capital Asset	Depreciation Expense	Accumulated Depreciation	Net Book Value
0	5,000	-0-	-0-	5,000
1	5,000	800	800	4,200
2	5,000	800	1,600	3,400
3	5,000	800	2,400	2,600
4	5,000	800	3,200	1,800
5	5,000	800	4,000	1,000

FIGURE 12.10

Depreciation of $800 is accumulated each year until the end of the asset's useful life. At that time, all that is left of the asset's book value is its residual value. In this case, the amount is $1,000, being the final net book value at the bottom right hand corner of the table.

Continuing with the Smith Tools example, we will assume this time that the asset will have no residual value at the end of its presumed useful life. This means that the total amount to be depreciated will be $5,000 (the original cost of the asset) instead of $4,000, which included a $1,000 residual value deduction from the original cost. The annual depreciation amounts would be recorded as shown in figure 12.11:

As is common in accounting, the calculations are only part of the process. The subsequent challenge is to record the results of those calculations in the financial statements.

You will recall from our examination of accounts receivable that a contra account was established that allowed bad debt to be written off for the period before the debt was proved to be uncollectible. In other words, the company expected some loss of assets during the course of the year, and a contra account was established to mark a negative change in the value of the asset without distorting the company's net worth.

Year	Depreciation Expense
1	1,000
2	1,000
3	1,000
4	1,000
5	1,000

FIGURE 12.11

A similar process is implemented with a company's capital assets. On the one hand, accountants like to see the original value of the asset remain on the balance sheet. On the other hand, the value of the asset does change over time, as does the company's equity. Contra accounts allow both the asset's original value and the book value to be reflected on the balance sheet. Remember, a contra-asset account is linked to another asset account, but works in reverse. Any addition to the contra account serves to decrease the value of the asset. The contra account for a capital asset is called *accumulated depreciation*. It reflects the decrease in value of the capital asset over time. The original cost in the capital asset account remains constant. The net value of the original cost and the accumulated depreciation equals the book value of the asset.

Figure 12.12 shows the corresponding journal entry for recording $1,000 of depreciation expense of a capital asset:

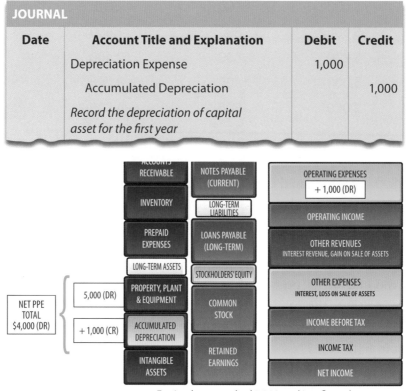

FIGURE 12.12

We now continue with our Smith Tools example to demonstrate how the contra account is used to depreciate capital assets on the balance sheet. The initial purchase of the capital asset is recorded as a debit of $5,000 to property, plant and equipment, with no change to equity. Using the straight-line method, we calculate each year's depreciation as $1,000. This amount is credited in the accumulated depreciation contra account. As you can see, this reduces the net value of the capital asset to $4,000 in the first year, but does not change the original $5,000 value recorded in the property, plant and equipment account. In the income statement, the depreciation expense of $1,000 is recorded as a debit because equity decreased by $1,000.

Each year depreciation is recorded, the amount of accumulated depreciation increases and the net book value of the capital asset decreases. This is illustrated in the following table, which can also be referred to as an *asset register*.

Year 0 marks the beginning of the year in which the capital asset is purchased. Although the $5,000 cost remains the same from year to year, as does the $1,000 amount of depreciation expense, notice that the accumulated depreciation increases annually by $1,000, while the net book value decreases annually by the same amount.

Year	Cost of Capital Asset	Depreciation Expense	Accumulated Depreciation	Net Book Value
0	5,000	-0-	-0-	5,000
1	5,000	1,000	1,000	4,000
2	5,000	1,000	2,000	3,000
3	5,000	1,000	3,000	2,000
4	5,000	1,000	4,000	1,000
5	5,000	1,000	5,000	-0-

FIGURE 12.13

The Declining and Double-Declining-Balance Method

The commonly discussed drawback to the straight-line method is that it may not reflect how asset values actually decrease over time because capital assets do not normally decrease in value by the same amount each year. Alternative depreciation methods have been developed by the accounting profession. One of them is known as the *declining–balance method*.

The most common real life example of asset depreciation is the car. Think about how that asset depreciates over time. It is common knowledge that the largest decrease in a car's value occurs the moment the car is driven off the dealership's lot. In other words, the value of the car depreciates the most during the early years of its useful life and depreciates the least during its later years. This principle is applicable for most capital assets and that is why the declining-balance method is used (and is so called): the amount depreciated on an annual basis declines over time.

The procedure used for the declining-balance method differs from the straight-line method in two ways:

It is often said that the value of a new car tumbles the second it is driven off the dealership lot. The declining method of depreciation tries to capture this more dramatic decline in the early years of the useful capital assets.

First, the straight-line method simply calculates an average annual depreciation rate. It achieves this by dividing the amount to be depreciated by the number of years of the asset's useful life.

As an example, let us consider the purchase of a capital asset worth $10,000 that has a useful life of 5 years with no residual value.

Straight–Line Method

$$\text{Annual Depreciation} = \frac{\text{Cost - Residual Value}}{\text{Years of Useful Life}} = \frac{\$10,000}{5} = \$2,000$$

Declining-Balance Method

For the declining-balance method, instead of using an equal annual depreciation amount, an annual percentage is used, which is calculated as follows:

$$\text{Annual Depreciation} = \frac{100\%}{\text{Years of Useful Life (5)}} = 20\%$$

If the useful life of an asset is 10 years, then the base depreciation rate to be applied would be 10% (100% divided by 10). If the useful life is 20 years, the depreciation rate applied each year would be 5% (100% divided by 20).

There is one more step: the **double-declining-balance method**, by which twice the depreciation rate is used each year. With the same percentages already calculated, a double-declining depreciation rate of 40% (20% × 2) would be used when the useful life of an asset is 5 years. When the useful life is 10 years, a double-declining depreciation rate of 20% would be used (10% × 2). For a useful life of 20 years, an annual rate of 10% would be used (5% × 2).

The formula for calculating the double-declining balance rate:

Double-Declining Rate = Yearly Depreciation Rate Using Declining Balance Method × 2

In essence, using a double-declining rate amounts to exaggerating the declining effect by the order of two. This ensures that much of the depreciation occurs during the early years of an asset's life span. This effect will be demonstrated in figure 12.14.

Second, the reason that the double-declining method amplifies the depreciation effect in the early years of an asset's useful life is that, unlike the straight-line method, the declining method applies the depreciation rate to the remaining balance of the book value of the asset. In other words, it does not apply the same amount of depreciation every year. Instead, it applies the same depreciation percentage rate to the remaining balance at the beginning of every year.

Continuing with our example of a capital asset purchased for $10,000, that has an estimated useful life of 5 years, the depreciation for the first year would be

$10,000 x 40% = $4,000

The remaining book value for the beginning of the second year would be

$10,000 - $4,000 = $6,000

The double-declining depreciation rate of 40% is now applied to this new balance to determine the depreciation amount for the second year:

$6,000 x 40% = $2,400

The same double-declining rate is applied to a decreasing book value on an annual basis. This means that over the years, the depreciation amounts are reduced substantially, which generally reflects the way capital assets decline in value.

The rest of the depreciation amounts in our example are shown in the following chart:

Year	Beginning of Year Book Value		@ 40% Double Declining Depreciation Rate		Remaining Book Value
1	$10,000	minus	$4,000	equals	$6,000
2	$6,000		$2,400		$3,600
3	$3,600		$1,440		$2,160
4	$2,160		$864		$1,296
5	$1,296		$518.40		$777.60

FIGURE 12.14

Applying a percentage rate to a balance every year means that there will always be a remaining balance when the double-declining method is used. In this example, the remaining book value at the end of five years is $777.60 because there was no residual value. However, if the asset has a residual value when the declining-balance (or double-declining-balance) method is used, the asset should not be depreciated below the residual value. For example, if the residual value is $1,000 for the example shown above, the last year's depreciation should amount to $296 ($1,296 - $1,000 = $296).

The Units-of-Production Method

The **units-of-production method** involves a different procedure for depreciating a capital asset – asset usage as the basis for calculating depreciation. The methods we have studied so far use a predetermined formula that is not based on usage. The first step in the units-of-production method is to choose a unit for measuring the usage of the capital asset. If the asset is a vehicle, the unit can be the number of miles driven. If the asset is a machine, the unit can be the number of hours operated. These measures are known as *units of production* – hence the name of this method.

Once the type of unit is chosen, the next step is to estimate the number of units to be used for the entire life of the asset. The total cost of the asset is then divided by this number to arrive at a cost per unit. This cost per unit is then applied to the number of units produced in a year to determine that year's depreciation amount. The same procedure is followed each year until the end of the asset's estimated useful life.

Here is an example to illustrate how the units-of-production method can be applied in depreciation of a capital asset.

Deliveries Are Us bought a truck for $110,000 to be used for deliveries. The truck has an estimated residual value of $10,000. The company wants all its trucks to be in top condition, so it retires them after 200,000 miles of usage.

1.   The unit of production to be used will be miles.

2.   The number of units to be used for the life of the truck is 200,000 miles.

3.   The cost per unit to be used in calculating annual depreciation is:

$$\frac{\text{Cost} - \text{Residual Value}}{\text{Total Units of Production}} = \frac{\$110,000 - \$10,000}{200,000} = 50\text{¢ per unit}$$

4.   If the truck is driven 30,000 miles for the first year, the depreciation for that year would be:

Units of Production Used for Year x $0.50 = 30,000 x $0.50 = $15,000

The amount of depreciation for a year is entirely dependent on its usage. For example, if in the second year, the truck was driven for 25,000 miles, the depreciation for that year would be:

25,000 x $0.50 = $12,500

If in the third year, the truck was driven for 35,000 miles, the year's depreciation would be:

35,000 x $0.50 = $17,500

This depreciation procedure would be applied annually until the truck had been driven for 200,000 miles, the initial estimation for the life of the truck. However, when the usage exceeds the estimated units of production, no additional depreciation expense should be allocated to the units produced.

Which Depreciation Method Should be Used?

As is common in accounting, no single method of calculating a balance sheet item is necessarily better or preferable than another. The challenge for the accountant is to choose a method that best reflects the nature of the asset involved. Perhaps most important, the accountant must continue to use the initial method chosen. This is what the consistency principle dictates, so that manipulation of financial figures is prevented.

However, the consistency principle does not prevent an accountant from using different methods of depreciation for different types of company assets — so long as the same method is used for the life of the particular asset. For example, a company might use the straight-line method to depreciate an advertising sign, but use the declining-balance method to depreciate a company-owned vehicle, since the value of cars and trucks decreases most during their early years.

Depreciation for Partial Years

Our examination of depreciation has been based on the assumption that capital assets are purchased at the beginning of a year, used for full year periods and sold at the end of a year. Of course, business executives do not allow depreciation methods to dictate when capital assets are bought and sold. Various tactics can be employed to accommodate the realities of the calendar year when depreciating a company's capital assets. Once a capital asset has been purchased, the accountant must choose a depreciation schedule that accommodates the timing of asset ownership. She may decide to depreciate the asset for the full month of purchase, depreciate monthly thereafter until the asset is sold, and not depreciate for the month of sale.

A number of possible combinations are available to the accountant to depreciate during the year of purchase or sale, or month of purchase or sale. These combinations provide the accountant with the flexibility to develop a depreciation schedule that best reflects the business reality of the company.

Let us examine the situation that arises from the purchase of a $120,000 packaging machine by the Jones Cookie Factory on March 27, 2001. The company determines that the packager will have a useful life of 10 years, after which it will not be salvageable; thus no residual value needs to be estimated. The machine will be depreciated by $12,000 annually and $1,000 monthly. The machine is eventually sold on October 1, 2008 at a price of $32,000. The fiscal year-end for the Jones Cookie Factory is November 30.

The company decides to use the following depreciation rules: no depreciation in the month of purchase and monthly depreciation thereafter, including the month of sale.

Figure 12.15 displays the annual depreciation calculated after the application of the chosen schedule. For fiscal years 2002–2007, each year includes 12 full months and will have $12,000 of annual depreciation at $1,000 per month. That is the easy part. The challenge is dealing with the partial years of 2001 (year of purchase) and 2008 (year of sale).

	Months	Depreciation
2001	8	8,000
2002	12	12,000
2003	12	12,000
2004	12	12,000
2005	12	12,000
2006	12	12,000
2007	12	12,000
2008	11	11,000
	Total	91,000

FIGURE 12.15

In fiscal year 2001, the month of purchase was March. The chosen schedule dictates that there is no depreciation in that month. That leaves eight months of depreciation in the fiscal year, or $8,000.

Fiscal Year 2001

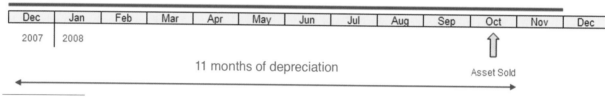

FIGURE 12.16

In fiscal year 2008, the month of sale was October. The chosen schedule dictates that even though the sale occurred on the first day of the month, depreciation for the entire month is calculated. This means that there will be 11 months of depreciation for the fiscal year amounting to a total of $11,000.

Fiscal Year 2008

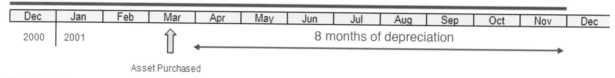

FIGURE 12.17

As figure 12.18 shows, the total amount depreciated for the packaging machine is $91,000. Subtracting this amount from the original purchase price of $120,000 produces a net book value of $29,000. The machine was sold for $32,000, generating a gain of $3,000 on the sale, or disposal. As is often true in accounting, the method chosen will affect net income. It is therefore incumbent on the accountant to choose the most appropriate method.

Packaging Machine

$91,000 Depreciated

$32,000 Sale Price - $29,000 Book Value = $3,000 Gain

FIGURE 12.18

Disposal and Depreciation

When a capital asset is disposed of, a gain or loss is usually generated from disposal of the asset. The accountant must remove from the books all the accumulated depreciation for the asset in question, since the company no longer owns the item. For example, a company has equipment (capital asset) that cost $5,000, with a useful life of 5 years and a residual value of $1,000. The asset is eventually sold for precisely that value: $1,000. The journal entry needed to record the transaction at sale would be:

JOURNAL			
Date	**Account Title and Explanation**	**Debit**	**Credit**
	Cash	1,000	
	Accumulated Depreciation - Equipment	4,000	
	Equipment		5,000
	To record the sale of used asset for $1,000		

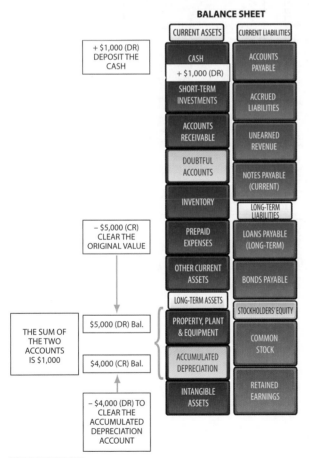

FIGURE 12.19

The amount of $1,000 is received for the asset and debited to cash; $4,000 is debited to the accumulated depreciation account, which was initially set up to record the systematic write-off of the asset each year through the adjusting entry (debit depreciation expense, credit accumulated depreciation). The amount of $5,000 is now credited to the property, plant and equipment account, since the company no longer owns the capital asset.

Now let us assume that the equipment was sold for $500, half the estimated residual value. Since only $500 was received for the asset, this amount is debited to cash and the $500 loss is debited as an *other expenses* in the income statement. The $4,000 in accumulated depreciation is still debited as an that account, and the initial cost of $5,000 is still credited to the property, plant and equipment asset account.

JOURNAL

Date	Account Title and Explanation	Debit	Credit
	Cash	500	
	Accumulated Depreciation - Equipment	4,000	
	Loss on Disposal of Asset	500	
	Equipment		5,000
	To record the sale of used asset		

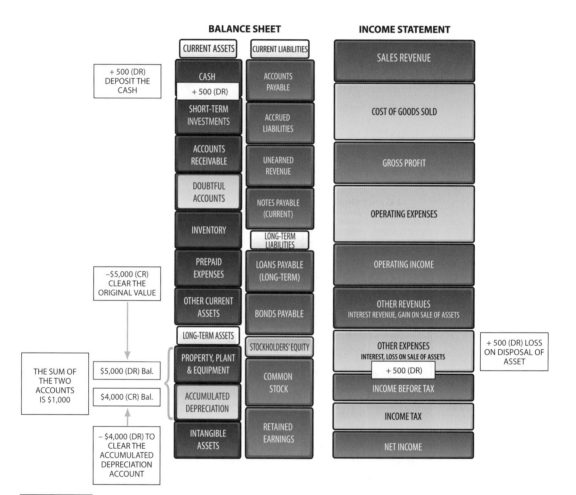

FIGURE 12.20

If the equipment was sold for $1,500, the $500 gain would change the journal entry:

JOURNAL			
Date	**Account Title and Explanation**	**Debit**	**Credit**
	Cash	1,500	
	Accumulated Depreciation - Equipment	4,000	
	Gain on Disposal of Asset		500
	Equipment		5,000
	To record the sale of used asset for $1,500		

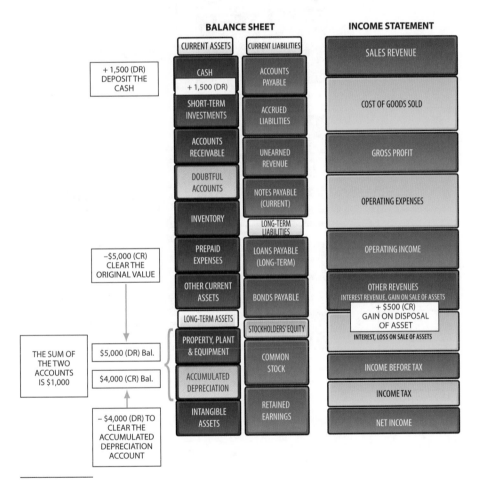

FIGURE 12.21

Debit $1,500 to cash and credit $500 as an *other revenue* in the income statement.

Instead of trying to sell the capital asset, a company may decide to donate it to charity. The transaction would involve a loss for the company and would be recorded as a donation expense. Assume the company donated the equipment from the previous example to a local charity.

JOURNAL

Date	Account Title and Explanation	Debit	Credit
	Accumulated Depreciation - Equipment	4,000	
	Donation Expense	1,000	
	Equipment		5,000
	To record the donation of used asset		

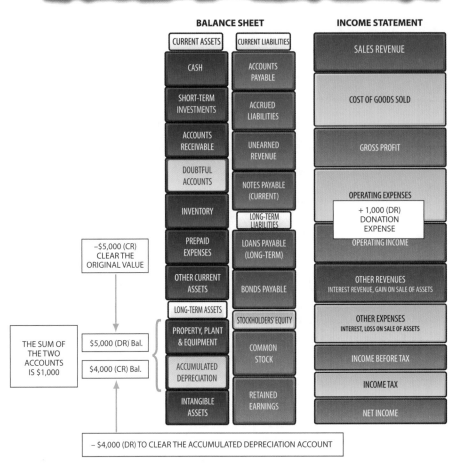

FIGURE 12.22

A capital asset can be disposed of in many ways that do not involve selling the item. For the purpose of this book, we have discussed only the routine methods of disposal and provided a solid foundation for understanding the accounting concept in general. Here is one final change to our initial example in this section. Instead of 5 years, the life of the equipment ends up being 4 years, and the asset is sold for $500.

JOURNAL

Date	Account Title and Explanation	Debit	Credit
	Cash	500	
	Accumulated Depreciation - Equipment	3,200	
	Loss on Disposal of Asset	1,300	
	Equipment		5,000
	To record the sale of used asset for $500		

FIGURE 12.23

When the useful life was 5 years, $4,000 of total depreciation had to be spread out over those 5 years, using the straight-line method. This amounted to $800 of depreciation per year. If the actual life of the asset ends up being four years, then only 4 years' worth of depreciation was accumulated, for a total of $3,200 ($800 × 4). The remaining book value, or amount yet to be depreciated, increases to $1,800. Since the asset was sold for $500, this results in a loss of $1,300.

In summary, $500 is debited to cash; $3,200 in accumulated depreciation is taken off the books by debiting that amount; $1,300 is debited as a loss in the income statement; and the original cost of the asset ($5,000) is removed from the books by crediting that amount to the account.

One final note: going back to our original example, if the company uses the capital asset for longer than the estimated useful life of 5 years, the remaining book value would be $1,000, which is the estimated residual value. In this case, no adjustments would be made and the company would continue to use the asset without further depreciation.

Trading-In

An alternative way to dispose of an asset is to trade it in for another asset. We see this type of transaction often occur when an old car is traded in for a new car. Similar to what has already been discussed, the old asset and the accumulated depreciation of the old asset must be removed from the books. Suppose an old automobile has the following values in the accounting records:

Old Automobile Purchase Price	$15,000
Accumulated Depreciation	$12,000
Old Automobile Book Value	$3,000

FIGURE 12.24

The company wishes to purchase a new car worth $20,000. The dealership will accept the old automobile as a trade-in and give the company $2,000 for it. The remaining amount owing will be paid with cash. The journal entry for this transaction is shown in figure 12.25.

JOURNAL			
Date	Account Title and Explanation	Debit	Credit
	Automobile – New	20,000	
	Accumulated Depreciation – Old	12,000	
	Loss on Disposal of Asset	1,000	
	Automobile – Old		15,000
	Cash		18,000
	To record the trade-in of an old automobile for a new one		

FIGURE 12.25

The old automobile amount is removed from the books, along with its accumulated depreciation. Since the trade-in value on the old automobile is less than the book value, a loss of $1,000 is recorded. The new automobile is added to the books with a debit entry of $20,000. The difference between the price of the new automobile and the trade-in of the old one ($20,000 - $2,000) is the amount of cash the company must spend. This is shown by the credit to the cash account for $18,000.

Revising Depreciation

Our examination of depreciation in this chapter has included numerous references to estimates. We have also looked at examples in which the residual value or the asset's useful life, or both, were incorrectly estimated. Let us take a closer look at these scenarios with a more comprehensive example.

Brian's Bricks bought a new oven for its factory at a cost of $300,000. It was expected to have a useful life of 10 years and a salvage value of $20,000.

FIGURE 12.26

After five years of use, the oven shows that it is not deteriorating as quickly as expected. After consulting with the oven manufacturer, management determines that the useful life of this capital asset could be extended to 15 years, and the salvage value increased to $40,000.

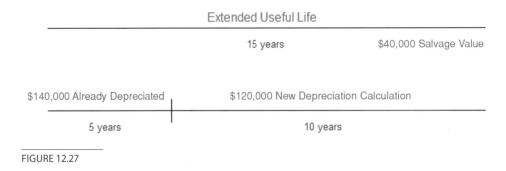

FIGURE 12.27

Using the straight-line method, the company's accountants had recorded depreciation of [($300,000 − 20,000) ÷ 10] × 5 = $140,000, which produced a net book value of $300,000 − 140,000 = $160,000.

Brian's Bricks then started a new depreciation schedule, assuming the straight-line method again, in which the amount to be depreciated for the rest of the asset's new useful life would be $160,000 - $40,000 (new salvage value) = $120,000. This amount is divided by the number of years left in the new useful life (15 years - 5 years already recorded = 10 years), to produce an annual depreciation amount of $12,000.

Note that the company should not change the depreciation already accumulated during the first five years of using the oven. An accountant should only make or change depreciation estimates for the future. Any changes that are made need to be justified with the appropriate documentation. In this case, that documentation would include consultation with the asset's manufacturer.

Natural Resources

Natural resources have a physical nature, but one that is different from the nature of other capital assets. In fact, some companies place natural resources in a separate asset category on the balance sheet. For our present purpose, we will examine these types of assets in our broader discussion of long-term assets and how we account for natural resources in the company's books.

First, as with most other assets we study in this book, natural resources come at a cost. This cost includes any expenditure made in acquiring the asset. In the case of natural resources, this cost includes expenditures involved in preparing resources for extraction. It also includes any expenditure for restoring the land upon completion of use. The total cost is to be recorded in the appropriate asset account on the balance sheet.

Second, like other capital assets we have studied, natural resources represent items that will decrease in value as a result of use. In this case, natural resources are *depleted* over time, and this depletion needs to be accounted for in the books. This is done through the process of depreciation, just as with other long-term assets. However, the term depreciation is replaced with *depletion*.

Special note:

- Some companies still use the term *amortization* or *depreciation*.
- Not all companies use the accumulated depreciation or depletion account. Instead, they credit the natural resource account directly and debit the expense.

Our examination of depreciation introduced us to the *units-of-production method* of depreciation: the method that involves actual usage of an asset. It is therefore most appropriate for use in depleting natural resources; the actual units depleted – such as cubic meters, barrels, and tons – can be used in the calculation.

We will use the example of the Standing Tall Timber Company to illustrate how the units-of-production method is applied to a natural resource asset. The company has bought land to be harvested for timber, at a total cost of $10 million. It estimates that once all the land is harvested, it will be worth $2 million. This is the asset's residual or salvage value. Furthermore, the company estimates that the total timber to be harvested will amount to 80 million MFBM (thousand board feet).

$$\frac{\text{Total Cost - Residual Value}}{\text{Total Units}} = \frac{\$10,000,000 - \$2,000,000}{80,000,000 \text{ MFBM}} = \$0.10 \text{ per MFBM}$$

If 2 million MFBM were harvested in the first year, the depletion for the year would be:
$$2,000,000 \times \$0.10 = \$200,000$$

JOURNAL

Date	Account Title and Explanation	Debit	Credit
	Depletion Expense	200,000	
	Accumulated Depletion - Standing Tall Timber		200,000
	To record depletion expense for the year for Standing Tall Timber		

The three figures above (total cost, residual value and total units) will be used to calculate a per unit depletion cost that is to be applied for every unit of timber depleted within a year.

The rate per year is $200,000 and the whole asset will be depleted over 40 years at that rate. To record this amount, $200,000 is credited to the accumulated depreciation account, and $200,000 is expensed as depletion on the income statement. The timber that is yet to be harvested remains a separate asset on the balance sheet and is valued at cost less any depletion. Any harvested timber that a company still has on hand is now considered inventory and is valued at the per unit rate that was used for depletion. In this case, it was $0.10 per MFBM.

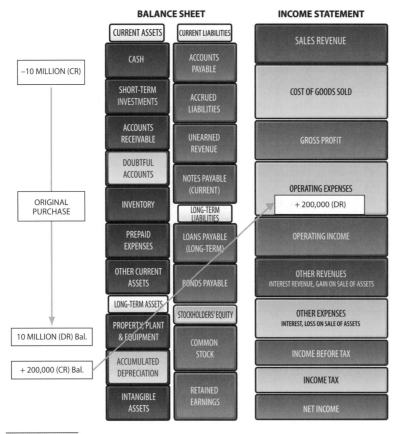

FIGURE 12.28

The following table represents the components of property, plant and equipment for Wausau Paper.

2008 Annual Report of WAUSAU PAPER Note 3: Supplement Balance Sheet Information		
Property, plant, and equipment	**2008**	**2007**
Buildings	$122,224	$124,465
Machinery and equipment	985,452	983,937
	$1,107,676	$1,108,402
Less: accumulated depreciation	(748,916)	(713,820)
Net depreciated value	$358,760	$394,582
Land	6,868	7,386
Timber and timberlands, net of depletion	5,675	5,064
Construction in progress	34,105	6,264
Total property, plant and equipment	$405,408	$413,296

FIGURE 12.29

Wasau Paper is a US paper manufacturer headquartered in Wisconsin. Figure 12.29 shows the balances included in Note 3 in the Notes to the Financial Statements section of their 2008 annual report. Given that Wausau owns and manages thousands of acres of timberland, it follows that a large portion of the company's assets are tied up in land used to harvest timber. Note that the timber and timberlands are reported "net of depletion".

Intangible Assets

Our previous discussion of capital assets covered *tangible assets*, which are physical in nature and can be touched or sensed. The value of these types of assets often constitute a large proportion of the total value of a company's assets.

In contrast, intangible assets do not have a physical form, are conceptual in nature and do not usually constitute a large component of the company's total net assets. Nevertheless, *intangible assets* (like tangible long-term assets) occupy the *long-term assets* section of the balance sheet and should remain with a company for more than a year.

A company's intangible assets largely constitute intellectual property. A large portion of the costs involved with such assets include research and development costs and legal fees to protect the intellectual property from imitation and theft, fees to obtain the necessary documentation or the purchase price to obtain certain rights from someone else. Most intangible assets have their values amortized over time.

FIGURE 12.30

All the components of a company's intangible assets will be examined more thoroughly as we progress through this chapter. The topic is the final one dealing with the assets side of a company's balance sheet.

Goodwill

Since goodwill is perhaps the most misunderstood business asset, it may be the perfect place to begin when examining the intangible assets section of the balance sheet. The value of goodwill is often not fully appreciated even by experienced business people.

Goodwill arises when a company purchases another company at a cost that is greater than the market value of that company's net assets. The excess of the cost of the company over the total of the market value of its assets, less its total liabilities, must be recorded as goodwill.

Goodwill can be attributed to factors such as a recognizable brand name, experienced management, a skilled workforce or a unique product. Unlike other company assets, items representing goodwill do not come with an easily determinable market price to be amortized over time. Nevertheless, businesses are willing to pay for goodwill, and it increases equity on the balance sheet. We will use an example to explain how goodwill works and how accountants should record such items in the company's books.

Vicky's Entrepreneurial Enterprises decides to buy Jack's Sweets, a relatively new, but established, candy maker. The purchase price amounts to $1 million. At the time of purchase, Jack's Sweets had assets with a market value of $1.5 million and liabilities totaling $700,000, giving the purchased company a net value of $800,000.

The remaining $200,000 in the company's purchase price constitutes goodwill. Vicky was willing to pay for the brand name, because Jack's Sweets had become known for great tasting candies. Jack's Sweets' low budget, but memorable, commercials featured a fictional "Uncle Jack" handing out treats to beloved customers. Indeed, Vicky considers $200,000 for this brand to be a bargain and is more than willing to pay this amount for goodwill. However, she also expects a good return on her investment for the premium paid for the business. The accountant for Vicky's Entrepreneurial Enterprises records the purchase of Jack's Sweets in two steps:

First, the values of the assets and liabilities from Jack's Sweets is recorded as follows:

Vicky pays $800,000 (a credit to cash) for $1,500,000 in assets from Jack's Sweets. This is a debit in assets and assumes $700,000 of Jack's Sweets' liabilities, which is recorded as a credit in Vicky's balance sheet.

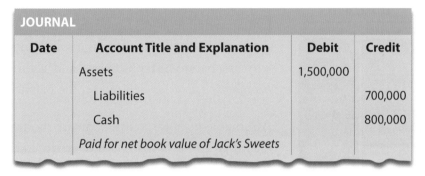

JOURNAL			
Date	**Account Title and Explanation**	**Debit**	**Credit**
	Assets	1,500,000	
	Liabilities		700,000
	Cash		800,000
	Paid for net book value of Jack's Sweets		

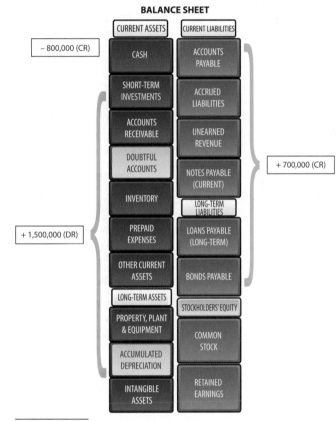

FIGURE 12.31

Second, Vicky's accountant records the portion of the purchase price involving goodwill, with the following entry:

JOURNAL			
Date	**Account Title and Explanation**	**Debit**	**Credit**
	Goodwill	200,000	
	Cash		200,000
	Paid for goodwill		

FIGURE 12.32

Unlike tangible assets, goodwill does not have a value in the books of the company being sold, and that is the reason why a separate entry is made and a different account – *intangible assets* – is debited on the balance sheet.

Alternatively, both components of the transaction can be recorded using a compound entry like the following:

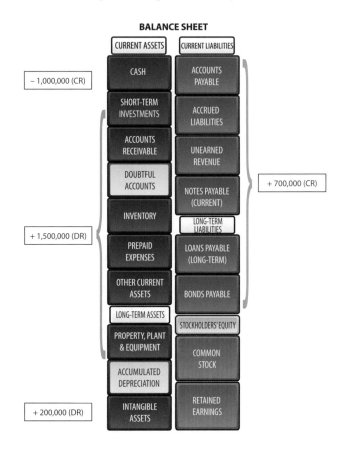

JOURNAL			
Date	**Account Title and Explanation**	**Debit**	**Credit**
	Assets	1,500,000	
	Goodwill	200,000	
	Liabilities		700,000
	Cash		1,000,000
	Paid cash for net assets and goodwill		

FIGURE 12.33

Note: we use the title "Assets" and "Liabilities" in this journal for demonstration purpose. In reality, each asset and liability would be recorded in its specific account.

Unlike other company assets, items categorized as goodwill do not have their value amortized over time. In essence, there is no book value to amortize. However, this does not mean that the value of goodwill cannot decrease. In other words, events may occur that would impair the value of goodwill.

For example, let us assume that Company A bought Company B because the latter was producing a unique product that the rest of the market could not match. The uniqueness of the product is considered to be goodwill and is worth $150,000. However, since the purchase, advances in technology led to the creation of a new product to compete with the one produced by Company B. The new product is still undergoing development and testing, but will almost certainly enter the market within a decade.

In other words, the value of goodwill associated with the innovative quality of Company B's product will be seriously reduced. But it will not be negated altogether, since it is estimated that the product will still be competitive, even after the introduction of an alternative product.

A decrease in the value of goodwill for the current year is estimated at $50,000. The journal entry to record this would be as follows:

JOURNAL			
Date	Account Title and Explanation	Debit	Credit
	Loss on Impairment of Goodwill	50,000	
	Goodwill		50,000
	Loss on impairment of goodwill		

The value of goodwill should *never* be adjusted upward, above cost. This would violate the GAAP principle of conservatism, which we previously covered. You

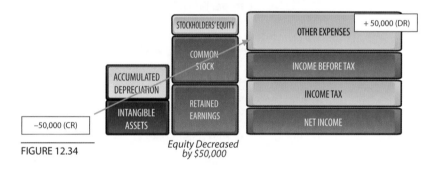

FIGURE 12.34

should now be more familiar with GAAP principles and how they apply to examples and situations highlighted in this book.

Patents

Individuals and companies invent and develop innovative products, usually at enormous cost in terms of both money and time. Inventors need to protect their intellectual property and this is achieved through patenting.

A **patent** grants the patentee the exclusive right, for a set period of time, to prevent others from making, using, selling or distributing the patented invention without permission. In most international jurisdictions, a patent term lasts for about 20 years, but the duration can differ according to the type of patent. This gives the inventor or inventing company the right to enjoy the rewards of creating a new and successful product.

The costs associated with many intangible assets involve legal fees paid in acquiring them. With regard to patents, the application process typically requires the use of patent lawyers (as does the defense and management of a patent). Depending on the product, development costs that are incurred in developing the product may be capitalized (considered as part of the cost of patent) or expensed. All legal and associated costs in acquiring a patent are recorded in the long-term assets section of the balance sheet. The value of the assets is then amortized for the remaining term of the patent.

Another aspect of a patent is that it can be bought and sold. A purchaser can buy the rights to the patent, thereby giving the new owner of the patent the same exclusive rights that originally belonged to the inventor. The price of the patent would then be amortized for the amount of time left in the patent's term.

Here is an example to illustrate this point. Henry's Lights purchases a patent from Crazy Larry Light Bulb for $28,000. The patent has seven years remaining in its term. The entries to record the purchase, as well as one year's amortization would be recorded as follows:

JOURNAL

Date	Account Title and Explanation	Debit	Credit
	Patents	28,000	
	Cash		28,000
	To record purchase of patent from Crazy Larry Light Bulbs. Remaining life is seven years.		

JOURNAL

Date	Account Title and Explanation	Debit	Credit
	Amortization Expense - Patents	4,000	
	Accumulated Amortization - Patents		4,000
	To record amortization expense for one year		

FIGURE 12.35

The $4,000 annual amortization amount is calculated using the straight-line method. The straight-line method involves taking the entire amount to be amortized or depreciated and dividing it by the number of years remaining; this calculation produces the annual amortization expense accurately reflecting amortization over time.

Copyright

Copyright is similar to a patent in that it gives exclusive rights of ownership to a person or group that has created something. The difference with copyright, however, is that it applies to artistic works such as music and literature. In addition, copyright can exist even if the work has not been registered. For example, it is automatically assumed that an article or photo posted on the Internet is protected by copyright. A person cannot simply assume that he has unlimited rights to use or copy a work from the Internet. Registration with the Copyright Office, however, puts a copyright holder in a better position if litigation arises over the copyright. In the United States, the laws regarding copyrights are governed by the Copyright Act which states that, generally, the life of a copyright lasts the life of the author plus 70 years from the end of the calendar year of his death. This means that estimates of a copyright's useful life depend on when the work was first created and how long the author of the work lived.

Overall, copyright is treated in much the same way as a patent. The costs may include legal fees paid to register the copyright, the purchase price in obtaining the copyright from someone else or any other fees involved in its acquisition. When a copyright is purchased, the remaining value of the copyright is amortized over the number of years of its term.

Trademark and Trade Name

A **trademark** is similar to a patent and copyright except that it grants ownership rights for a recognizable symbol or logo. A **trade name** grants exclusive rights to a name under which a company or product trades for commercial purposes, even though its legal or technical name might differ. Some corporations have numerous trademarks and trade names that they protect on a continuing basis. For example, *McDonald's* is not only a trade name that the company protects at all costs, but it serves as an umbrella brand for numerous other trademarks, such as the *Golden Arches*, the *Extra Value Meal* and *Hamburger University*. McDonald's finds itself in countless legal battles in fending off pretenders and imitators.

Any costs in developing and maintaining a trademark or trade name, such as those involved with advertising, are expensed during the year they are incurred. However, just as with patents and copyrights, legal fees for registering the name or logo are capitalized. Alternatively, trademarks and trade names can be purchased from someone else. The purchase cost is capitalized, which means it will be amortized for the remainder of its term.

Leasing Long-Term Assets

Instead of owning long-term tangible assets, a company can choose to lease them.

The contract that specifies the terms of the lease is known as a **lease agreement**. The owner of the asset to be leased is known as the *lessor*. The user of the leased asset is known as the *lessee*. In essence, the lessee buys the right to use the asset from the lessor. Such assets usually constitute some form of land or property.

Sometimes the lease agreement requires the lessee to pay an amount of cash in advance. In some jurisdictions, the government can even grant a 99-year lease to a lessee for a stipulated amount. Whatever amount is paid upfront for lease should be debited to the appropriate account under long-term assets on the balance sheet, and the value amortized for the remaining term of the lease.

Long-Term Assets, Total Assets and Financial Ratios

Since we are nearing the end of our examination of company assets, and long-term assets often form a large proportion of the value of these assets, we will end this chapter by examining financial ratios dealing with company assets. This should provide an understanding of the way large sections of the company's balance sheet can provide useful financial information and the significance that long-term assets play in analyzing such important data. We will specifically examine two financial ratios that measure company performance relative to total assets: **asset turnover** and **return on assets**.

Asset Turnover

As discussed in previous chapters, a turnover ratio measures how rapidly an asset's status changes and becomes productive. For example, inventory turnover measures how quickly an asset converts from inventory to becoming a sale. Asset turnover, on the other hand, measures how quickly a company converts its total assets, including long-term assets, into revenue.

To calculate asset turnover, the first figure needed is *Revenue*. The second figure needed is *Average Total Assets*, which is produced by taking the average of beginning and ending total assets:

$$\text{Average Total Assets} = (\text{Beginning of Year Total Assets} + \text{End of Year Total Assets}) \div 2$$

$$\text{Asset Turnover} = \frac{\text{Revenue}}{\text{Average Total Assets}}$$

Return on Assets

A company's return on assets is similar to asset turnover except that its focus is on net income, instead of revenue. This ratio seeks to measure the relationship between net income and assets. In other words, is the company making enough money from investment in its assets? Since the two ratios involve similar analyses, they also involve similar calculations.

$$\text{Return on Assets} = \frac{\text{Net Income}}{\text{Average Total Assets}}$$

As you can see, the ratios have the same denominator: Average Total Assets. It is their numerators that differ. One uses revenue, the other uses net income. Another difference between the two ratios, which will be illustrated in the example to follow, is that turnover is expressed as a decimal number, while return is expressed as a percentage.

Using the Ratios

Let us apply these two ratios by using the financial information made available by Amtrak and Union Pacific, two U.S. companies in the same industry; railway transportation. Using the formulas we have already outlined, the ratios have been calculated for us in the accompanying chart.

Selected Financial Information			
Year 2012	(in millions)	Amtrak	Union Pacific
A	Revenue	$ 2,453	$17,970
B	Total assets-beginning of year	$10,166	$39,722
C	Total assets-end of year	$10,300	$38,033
D=(B+C) ÷ 2	Average total assets	$10,233	$38,878
E=A ÷ D	Asset Turnover	0.24	0.46
F	Net income	-1,133	2,338
G=F ÷ D	Return on Assets	-11.07%	6.01%

FIGURE 12.36

For Amtrak and Union Pacific, both revenue and net income were divided by average total assets to produce the two financial ratios we have been examining.

With regard to asset turnover, Amtrak has a figure of 0.24 and Union Pacific has a figure of 0.46. What this means is that Union Pacific was able to generate more revenue dollars per investment in assets than Amtrak.

With regard to return on assets, Amtrak has a rate of -11.07% and Union Pacific's rate is 6.01%. This essentially means that Union Pacific was able to generate significantly more net income per investment in assets than Amtrak.

All financial ratios represent a simple snapshot of company performance. They tend to focus on one aspect of a business and give us different kinds of information about how well a company is doing. In this case, Union Pacific appears to be using its investment in assets to generate revenue and net income more effectively than Amtrak.

Controls Related To Long-Term Assets

Tangible assets, which by definition are physical in nature, are purchased by the company, used to earn an income and eventually disposed of. In the meantime, the value of a capital asset is depreciated over the period of its estimated useful life. Accounting procedures are used to control and safeguard all tangible assets while the company possesses them. Different companies and industries depend on capital assets to varying degrees. For instance, auto manufacturers General Motors and Ford rely heavily on capital assets such as machines, robots and factories. It is sometimes possible for criminals to steal large assets of a company. Security measures such as physical barriers and security personnel can be used to protect large items from theft.

Insurance is an even more useful measure to protect large capital assets. Insurance can protect a company's capital assets not only in the event of theft, for example, but also in the event of catastrophic situations such as extreme weather or unforeseen breakdowns. It is therefore incumbent upon management to make sure that the best possible insurance policies are in place and are updated or adjusted when needed. Some companies may even want to consider some self-insurance options to help protect their capital assets from catastrophic risk.

A company's largest and most protected capital assets can be lost as a result of catastrophe. Even though physical barriers can help, insurance should also be used to safeguard a business from undue risk and loss.

Big or small, pricey or inexpensive, all types of tangible assets should be tracked properly and relevant transactions recorded accurately in the company's books. Experienced accountants should be on hand to perform these control procedures. Capital assets should be tagged in some way, perhaps by bar code and scanner. The tags should be read, compared with accounting records and vice versa. Physical audits should be performed on a regular basis to ensure that all assets on the books are on the premises, still in use and accounted for.

For all company assets, paperwork and records should be completed correctly and handled securely. The first priority is to record the correct amount of cost for the capital asset. As always, any costs related to the acquisition of the asset must be included in the total cost. These can include freight, installation and even invoicing costs related to the asset.

As has been emphasized throughout our discussion of asset controls, policies, plans and procedures need to be in place, and regulations and laws followed. For example, a large company may have a policy of classifying items as capital assets only if they cost more than $1,000. A smaller company may institute a lower threshold for its policy. These policies need to be clearly communicated to the staff responsible for seeing their implementation. Adherence to all related policies, plans, procedures and regulations should be monitored, with audits when necessary.

Economic and efficient use of tangible assets involves purchasing assets at the best possible price. It also means that internal controls should include a bidding process for suppliers, which helps to ensure the best possible price is obtained. Financial ratios, which we discussed earlier in this chapter, can be used on a regular basis to monitor the efficient use of a company's capital assets. If the ratios indicate an inefficient use of these assets, measures can be taken to either dispose of or make better use of them. If sales are sluggish, this may mean that capital assets are not being used to their full capacity. A business may also find that too much money has been invested in its capital assets. Leasing them could free up some capital. As always, company goals and objectives related to capital assets should be stated, implemented, reviewed and changed when necessary.

Controls related to intangible assets are not very different from those relating to tangible assets. As always, qualified staff should be available to ensure that transactions are recorded and classified properly in the company's books and all payments are properly documented. Costs should be objectively verified and any supporting documentation should be properly maintained. The procedures involved are similar for both tangible and intangible assets.

However, with intangible assets, the only physical evidence of their existence often comes in the form of contracts, accompanying invoices and supporting cost documentation. That is why it is so important to physically protect such documents. They can be placed in a vault

IN THE REAL WORLD

Although businesses should make certain that all their assets are insured and that potential liabilities are also covered, this does not always mean that an insurance company need be involved. Businesses can self-insure to cover various risks. Companies that self-insure are sometimes regarded as being uninsured. In other words, "self-insurance" can be seen as an attempt to avoid paying for insurance. Indeed, this can be true, since some companies fail to adequately self-insure.

Proper self-insurance involves a company setting aside enough capital reserves to cover itself in case of a catastrophic event. If something happens to a company's capital assets, these capital reserves can be used to cover the loss. The advantage of self-insurance is that a company will avoid paying premiums that are often very high as a result of insurance company administrative costs or poor underwriting.

The disadvantage of self-insurance is that a company needs to tie up a certain amount of its capital to cover a disaster, and even that is sometimes insufficient. To minimize this disadvantage, alternative self-insurance strategies can be undertaken. For example, a business can still buy some insurance, but add self-insurance. Alternatively, businesses can form collaborative self-insurance groups, whereby a group of companies contributes to a pool of funds that can be used if one or more of them suffer a catastrophic event.

As with most aspects of today's business environment, various innovative solutions can be found to resolve inadequacies in the market. Self-insurance is an example of one of those innovations.

on the premises or a safe deposit box in a bank. These documents can be referenced when changes are made or when the company's books need updating.

Beyond initial registration or purchase, ongoing valuation of intangible assets needs to take place. For example, market conditions may affect the value of goodwill, or competing trademarks may diminish the value of a brand name. Furthermore, companies that own patents, copyright and trademarks should be on the lookout for entities that are using such intellectual property without permission. Any such use will diminish the value of the protected asset. All proper legal avenues should be pursued, including legal action or the threat of legal action, when improper use of protected intellectual assets has taken place.

An Ethical Approach to Long-Term Assets

Accounting for a firm's capital assets is vulnerable to manipulation to produce fraudulent figures, as has been mentioned in earlier chapters dealing with abuses of other assets. Decisions regarding classifying capital assets, depreciating them and calculating residual values can have a significant impact on a company's financial statements. It is therefore important for accountants to understand the ethical principles that exist to help prevent abuse.

Almost any accounting decision is open to abuse. Beyond GAAP principles and other accounting industry standards, the question that any accountant should ask when facing a decision is this: Should this be done because it is an accurate reflection of the business or for some other reason?

These other reasons could be to protect one's own incompetence, to seek financial gain, to succumb to pressure from management or to meet public expectation of company performance.

In other words, a good accountant should always raise a red flag when the answer to the question is anything other than, "This is being done because it is an accurate reflection of the financial condition of the business."

With regard to capital assets, figures can be manipulated to present a financial picture that does not accurately reflect the financial state of the company. For example, one of the first decisions that an accountant must make regarding capital assets is whether it is in fact a capital asset. An attempt to falsely classify the item as an expense would lead to reducing company net income. Conversely, an attempt to classify an expense as a capital asset will not reduce the company's equity. Either way, any result that does not reflect the true nature of the asset is an ethical breach and should always be avoided.

Estimating the useful life of a capital asset is another accounting decision that is open to manipulation. For example, intentionally shortening an asset's life span can unduly increase the annual depreciation charges recorded in the company's books. Similarly, intentionally increasing a capital asset's residual value will decrease the amount to be depreciated, thus decreasing those depreciation charges. An accountant has an ethical obligation to detect and avoid these abuses at all times.

Accountants are presented with a different kind of challenge when dealing with intangible assets. These assets, such as trademarks and goodwill, will only be amortized if it can be demonstrated that the value of the assets has been impaired.

Ethical considerations with respect to intangible assets relate mostly to their correct reporting in financial statements. This includes ensuring that the appropriate cost is determined, that the correct amount of amortization is calculated and that all amounts are reported accurately in the statements of operation and financial position.

Companies should always set up internal controls to ensure that ongoing transactions involving intangible assets are expensed or capitalized properly. Review procedures should be in place to ensure that annual amortization is verified and properly reported. Any review procedure should be the joint responsibility of both management and company auditors. As corporate scandals have shown, executives and accountants must take responsibility for the company's books; not doing so could lead to serious consequences.

IN THE REAL WORLD

The year 2001 saw the beginning of numerous corporate and accounting scandals, amounting to breaching ethical standards. Authorities began investigating some of America's largest corporations regarding, among other things, accounting fraud. The corporations investigated included three telecommunications companies: Global Crossing, Qwest and WorldCom.

Some of these investigations found a distortion of gains and expenses as a result of misclassifying capital assets. These errors may have been a result of incompetence. Alternatively, they may have been a deliberate attempt to mislead the public. Either way, GAAP violations were found in numerous instances. For example, both Global Crossing and Qwest engaged in billions of dollars of what are known as swaps. These companies purchased telecom capacity from customers who then bought it back from the companies. These were falsely treated as capital expenses rather than as current operating expenses. The result was that both companies recorded the revenue upfront, then expensed the amount over a period of time. This violates, among other things, the matching principle.

In addition, WorldCom classified billions of dollars of current operating expenses as capital assets. This was done over a period of 15 months. The auditing firm Arthur Andersen failed to raise any red flags over the practice.

In Summary

↪ A company's tangible long-term assets, also called *long-term assets* or *capital assets*, often constitute a significant proportion of the value of its assets.

↪ To determine whether an item is a capital asset, the accountant must ask three questions: How long will the company have the item? How much does the item cost? What will the item be used for? If an item does not qualify as a capital asset, it is recorded as an expense on the income statement.

↪ Three more questions can be asked to determine if any actions performed on a capital asset constitute routine maintenance or a material improvement: Does the expenditure extend the life of the asset? Does the expenditure improve the productivity of the asset? Does the expenditure reduce company operating costs?

↪ Depreciation is the process by which accountants reflect changes in the book value of a capital asset. It also allows expenses related to capital assets to be matched with the periods in which related revenue is generated. One of the first tasks in depreciating an item is determining its residual value or salvage value, which is deducted from the total amount to be depreciated over the useful life of the asset.

↪ Accountants can use three different methods of depreciation. The straight-line method calculates an annual average to be depreciated over the course of an asset's useful life. Two other methods have been developed to ascertain a more realistic depreciation schedule: declining-balance method (and the double-declining-balance method) and units-of-production method.

↪ A capital item can be disposed of in various ways, including selling it, donating it to charity or trading it in. The transaction will involve either a gain or loss relative to the item's book value. Revisions can also be made to a depreciation schedule. However, proper justification should always be used and prior depreciation deductions should never be changed. This would violate the *consistency principle*.

↪ Various controls can be implemented to protect a company's capital assets, ranging from accurate recording and tracking procedures to proper insurance in case of catastrophic events. Although different industries require different controls, qualified accounting personnel should always supervise the policies and measures that a company implements.

↪ An ethical approach to long-term assets involves decisions that accurately reflect the nature of the asset. Net income figures and net asset values can be distorted by manipulating decisions regarding the classification of long-term assets, the estimation of residual value and useful life, and other aspects of depreciation.

↪ A company's long-term assets usually constitute a large proportion of the total value of its assets. That is why financial ratios involving total company assets are useful when discussing performance related to long-term assets. Asset turnover measures the revenue a company generates relative to its investment in total assets. Return on assets measures the net income a company generates relative to total assets.

↪ The natural resources that a company owns – such as minerals, oil or timber – are physical in nature, but are not classified as tangible assets on the balance sheet. Some companies categorize them separately from other long-term assets. The value of natural resources gets amortized over time, using the units-of-production method.

↪ Goodwill represents the portion of a company's purchase price, above and beyond its net asset value, that is considered valuable in its own right – for example, the company's good name or its experienced and dedicated workforce.

↪ A patent gives an inventor exclusive rights to use a product. The costs related to most intangible assets are generally for legal fees or the purchase of rights from someone else. This cost is amortized over the remaining term of the patent, defined by the applicable jurisdiction. Expenditures other than legal or purchases are expensed in the period incurred.

↪ Copyright gives exclusive rights of a creation to its creator. Copyright is granted automatically to works produced and published. However, copyright is time limited and does not cover fair use privileges to others.

↪ A trademark gives exclusive rights to logos and other company symbols. A trade name provides exclusive rights to names of companies and products. Large corporations often engage in extensive efforts to legally protect the various trademarks and trade names that they own.

↪ Leasehold involves a lessor lending an asset (usually land or property) to a lessee. Any upfront fees are capitalized in the appropriate long-term asset account on the balance sheet.

Review Exercise 1

Nelson Rugasa is an entrepreneur who has just started a consulting business. During the first month of business, Nelson purchased a laptop computer for $3,000 and office equipment for $10,000.

Required:

a) Record the purchase of long-term assets, assuming Nelson paid with cash.

> **Research Component**
> to be done outside of class time
>
> Research the useful life of capital assets, and suggest the useful life for the computer and office equipment.
>
> Research the way in which the value of capital assets decline, and suggest the depreciation method(s) that should be used for the computer and office equipment.
>
> Based on your research on useful life, and the ways in which the value of capital assets decline, prepare a table showing the cost, depreciation, accumulated depreciation, and net book value of the computer, and office equipment for the first three years.

b) Explain how you calculate the profit or loss on disposal of a long-term asset.

Review Exercise 1 – Answer

a)

Date	Account Title and Explanation	Debit	Credit
	Computer	3,000	
	Office Equipment	10,000	
	Cash		13,000
	Purchase of computer and office		
	equipment for cash		

A reasonable life for a computer would be 3 years, for equipment 5-10 years. Students will arrive at various numbers based on their research.

Because computers are upgraded quickly, a declining balance method would be appropriate with large amounts of depreciation early on. For office equipment, straight-line depreciation would be reasonable.

Year	Cost	Depreciation	Accumulated Depreciation	Net Book Value
0	$3,000.00	$0.00	$0.00	$3,000.00
1	3,000.00	1,000.00	1,000.00	2,000.00
2	2,000.00	666.67	1,666.67	1,333.33
3	1,333.33	444.44	2,111.11	888.89

Year	Cost	Depreciation	Accumulated Depreciation	Net Book Value
0	$10,000.00	$0.00	$0.00	$10,000.00
1	10,000.00	2,000.00	2,000.00	8,000.00
2	8,000.00	2,000.00	4,000.00	6,000.00
3	6,000.00	2,000.00	6,000.00	4,000.00
4	4,000.00	2,000.00	8,000.00	2,000.00
5	2,000.00	2,000.00	10,000.00	0.00

b) The profit or loss on disposal of a long-term asset is the difference between the amount received, and the net book value of the asset at the time of disposal.

Review Exercise 2

Rulison Company had the following transactions during the year:

DATE	DESCRIPTION
Jan 1	Paid $250,000 to purchase Regnier Limited. Regnier Limited had $500,000 in assets and $300,000 in liabilities.
Jan 1	Purchased patents from Saundra Arneson for $50,000. The remaining life of the patents is 4 years.
Jan 1	Purchased a trademark, which will be applied to the patented product for $20,000. Management believes that the trademark will be useful for double the life of the patent, at which time it will have a value of $100.
Jan 30	Purchased mineral rights for $100,000. The company needs to extract a mineral that goes into the patented product. Rulison Company expects to extract 500,000 kg of mineral before the rights expire.
Jun 30	Rulison Company's senior executives resigned en-masse. The directors felt that the loss of the senior executives seriously affected the company's goodwill. In fact, they felt that the decrease in the value of goodwill was estimated to be $25,000.

Rulison Company prepares its financial statements with a year end of December 31. Amortization policy states that one half year's amortization is taken in both the year of purchase and year of sale. Depletion is based on units extracted. The company extracted 10,000 kg of mineral from the beginning of February to the end of December. Assume all purchases are made with cash and that the straight-line method of depreciation is used for the patent and trademark.

Required: Prepare the journal entries to record the above transactions. Also prepare the year-end adjusting entries associated with the long-term assets.

Review Exercise 2 – Answer

Date	Account Title and Explanation	Debit	Credit
Jan 1	Assets	500,000	
	Goodwill	50,000	
	Liabilities		300,000
	Cash		250,000
	Purchase of assets and liabilities of		
	Reigner company		
Jan 1	Patents	50,000	
	Cash		50,000
	Purchase of patents for cash		
Jan 1	Trademarks	20,000	
	Cash		20,000
	Purchase of trademarks for cash		
Jan 30	Mineral Rights	100,000	
	Cash		100,000
	Purchase of mineral rights for cash		
Jun 30	Loss Due to Impairment of Goodwill	25,000	
	Goodwill		25,000
	To record impairment of goodwill		
Dec 31	Amortization Expense – Patents	6,250	
	Accumulated Amortization – Patents		6,250
	Amortization for the period (50,000 ÷ 4) ×		
	½ year		
Dec 31	Amortization Expense – Trademarks	1,244	
	Accumulated Amortization – Trademarks		1,244
	Amortization for the period ((20,000 – 100) ÷		
	8) × ½ year		
Dec 31	Depletion – Mineral Rights	2,000	
	Accumulated Depletion – Mineral Rights		2,000
	Depletion for the period 10,000 × (100,000 ÷		
	500,000)		

Chapter 13
CURRENT LIABILITIES

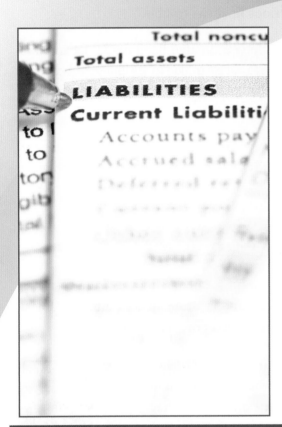

LEARNING OUTCOMES:

❶ Understand different types of current liabilities

❷ Record short–term notes payable

❸ Understand the current portion of long-term liabilities

❹ Record transactions with sales tax

❺ Record payroll transactions

❻ Record estimated liabilities

❼ Calculate financial ratios relating to current liabilities

❽ Apply controls and ethics relating to current liabilities

A Company's Current Liabilities

FIGURE 13.1

The earlier chapters of this book dealt with the assets side of the balance sheet and we examined each type of asset, both current and long-term.

This chapter deals with current liabilities. The main difference in the way that assets and liabilities are listed on the balance sheet is that the order of liabilities is dictated by the timing of the amount owed, whereas assets are placed in the order of their liquidity. Figure 13.1 illustrates this difference. Accounts payable and accrued liabilities are listed first among the current liabilities. Also, unearned revenue and the current portion of loans are listed as current liabilities. Accounts payable and unearned revenue have already been discussed in previous chapters, so we will not cover them in detail in this chapter. Recall from a previous chapter that current liabilities will be paid in the next 12 months, while long-term liabilities will be paid after 12 months.

A company's liabilities can be divided into two categories: known liabilities and unknown liabilities. These categories are sometimes referred to as *determinable liabilities* and *non-determinable liabilities*.

Determinable liabilities have a precise value. Most businesses know exactly how much they owe and when they are supposed to pay. Amounts owed to suppliers (trade payables), employees (payroll liabilities) and the government (e.g. sales taxes) constitute a debt that a company has agreed to pay. The failure to pay off debts is one of the first signs of serious financial trouble.

A company's unknown or non-determinable liabilities include estimated liabilities. They are non-determinable because the exact amount owing is unknown. This is similar to a topic we studied on the assets side of the balance sheet, where the amount of bad debt for the year was also unknown in advance.

All known company liabilities should leave an easily recognizable and traceable paper trail, and may include documents such as invoices and contracts. The exact amounts due, and when they are due, should be clearly identified.

Short-Term Notes Payable

With regard to accounts receivable, companies sometimes want greater assurance that a customer will pay its bill. To achieve this, instead of issuing an invoice and creating an account receivable, a company might make a more formal arrangement in the form of a note receivable.

In the same way that a company can have a customer agree to the terms of a note receivable, a supplier can have a company agree to the terms of a note payable. These notes are in essence the flip side of the same document. They are legally binding documents that obligate the borrower to certain terms, much like a loan.

FIGURE 13.2

Such documents outline the amount owed, when it is due and the interest payable. They are signed by the parties involved and constitute a more formalized arrangement than a basic account payable. A separate account on the balance sheet is established with short-term notes payable placed in the current liabilities section of the balance sheet. This is an example of a note payable.

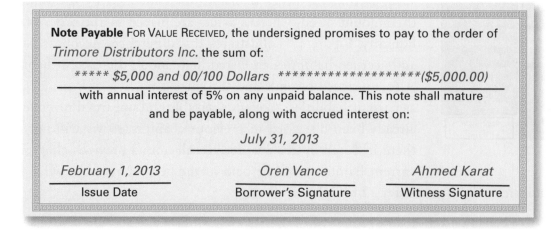

FIGURE 13.3

In the note payable presented above, Oren Vance borrowed $5,000 from Trimore Distributors Inc. on February 1, 2013. The interest rate is 5% and both principal and interest are payable in six months. The journal entry used to record the note payable is shown below:

JOURNAL			
Date	**Account Title and Explanation**	**Debit**	**Credit**
Feb 1	Cash	5,000	
	Notes Payable		5,000
	Record a 6-month, 5% note payable		

FIGURE 13.4

Notes payable also could occur as a result of transferring an accounts payable to a notes payable. This situation mainly happens when the company is unable to pay off its debt (accounts payable) on time. One way of dealing with this situation could be that the lender would extend the credit term and in exchange charge interest. This converts the original accounts payable into a notes payable.

In this case, the journal entry would be the same as figure 13.4 except that cash would be replaced with accounts payable. Therefore, the conversion is recorded by debiting the accounts payable account and crediting the notes payable account.

Accrued Interest and Notes Payable

Using Trimore Distributors' notes payable, let us assume the borrower has a June 30 year-end date. As we have seen in previous chapters, the matching principle dictates that we must report expenses in the period in which they helped to earn revenue; since no payment has been made or interest expense recognized, we must accrue the interest owing on the note to June 30. The following journal entry would be required:

In addition to the note payable for $5,000, the company would report interest payable of $104.17 on its June 30 year-end balance sheet.

JOURNAL			
Date	**Account Title and Explanation**	**Debit**	**Credit**
Jun 30	Interest Expense	104.17	
	Interest Payable		104.17
	Record interest on a 6-month, 5% note payable ($5,000 x 5% x 5/12 = $104.17)		

FIGURE 13.5

On July 31, both principal and interest will be paid to Trimore Distributors Inc. The entry to record repayment of the note, plus interest, would be as follows:

Note that the interest payable account is debited to remove the accrual recorded in the previous period and interest expense is debited with $20.83, which represents the interest expense for the month of July. In total, six months worth of interest has been recorded: five months in the previous period and one month in the current period.

JOURNAL			
Date	Account Title and Explanation	Debit	Credit
Jul 31	Interest Payable	104.17	
	Interest Expense	20.83	
	Notes Payable	5,000.00	
	Cash		5,125.00
	Record interest and payment for a 6-month, 5% note payable ($5,000 x 5% x 1/12 = $21, $5,000 + $5,000 x 5% x 6/12 = $5,125)		

FIGURE 13.6

Current Portion of Long-Term Liabilities

When the term of a note payable (loan payable) is longer than one year, the liability should be classified as a long-term liability called *loans payable*. If a portion of the loan will be paid within the next 12 months, that portion would be considered current. Although the entire portion will be contained within the long-term loans payable account, the current portion must be reported separately when the balance sheet is prepared.

For example, a company manufactures a wide range of products for consumers. It wants to purchase a new processing machine to keep up with growing demand for its product. The company has insufficient cash reserves on hand to finance the purchase. Management decides to engage in a common business practice, which is to obtain a loan from a bank to finance an important capital investment.

FIGURE 13.7

To that end, on January 2 of the current year, the company negotiates a loan from the bank of $50,000 with a term of five years, bearing an annual interest rate of 5%. Of that debt, $10,000 plus interest is payable every December 31.

Here is how the loan from the bank is recorded in the company's books:

JOURNAL			
Date	Account Title and Explanation	Debit	Credit
Jan 2	Cash	50,000	
	Loans Payable		50,000
	Borrowed $50,000 term debt payable over 5 years		

On December 31, the first installment plus interest was paid. The transaction would be recorded as follows:

JOURNAL			
Date	**Account Title and Explanation**	**Debit**	**Credit**
Dec 31	Loans Payable	10,000	
	Interest Expense	2,500	
	Cash		12,500
	Record payment for first loan installment plus interest		

FIGURE 13.8

After the first payment, the balance of the loan decreases to $40,000, $10,000 of which is still considered current. When the balance sheet is prepared at the year end, $10,000 will show as part of current liabilities and $30,000 will show as part of long-term liabilities.

Sales Tax

Sales tax is a tax that is applied by the state government to goods or services that are sold. They are calculated as a percentage of a sale, and the percentages can vary from state to state. The figure below shows some examples of states and the amount of sales taxes they charge.

California
7.5%

Utah
4.7%

Pennsylvania
6%

Note: Local sales tax may be added to state sales tax, causing actual sales tax in certain jurisdictions to be higher.

FIGURE 13.9

Although sales tax must be paid to the government, it would be impractical, if not impossible, for individual customers to send the sales tax money to the government every time they bought something. Imagine buying a coffee and having to send the government a few cents in sales tax.

Instead, businesses act as tax collectors for the government by collecting the sales tax from their customers and sending it to the government. Businesses must be careful and accurate in collecting sales taxes from customers. These taxes collected are not money that the business can spend; the money does not belong to them, it belongs to the government.

For example, if a business receives $1,500 from a customer, which includes $150 in sales tax, the business must make sure it does not spend the $150. This money must eventually be sent to the government.

FIGURE 13.10

The due date for a business to send the collected sales tax to the government can vary from business to business. Companies that have a very small amount of sales may be required to send in the sales tax once a year. As the amount of sales increase and the amount of sales tax collected increase, the business may be required to send in the money on a quarterly or monthly basis. Failure to send this money, or sending the money late, will result in interest and penalties being charged to the business by the government.

The retailer is responsible for collecting sales tax from the customer and eventually sending (remitting) the amount collected to the state government. The amount collected will be recorded in a current liability account until it is remitted. The range of sales tax varies by each state, from less than 1% to 10%. The Federal Tax Administration publishes sales tax rates for all states and cities. It is important to note that in case of certain items that are resold more than once, for example used cars, sales tax can be applied indefinitely. Each state has a list of tax exempt goods and services or items that are taxed at a reduced rate.

As an example, assume Hardware Store Inc. sells inventory to a customer for $1,000 cash on June 15, 2012. The state sales tax rate is 6%. The transaction is shown in figure 13.11. For this example, we will ignore the cost of goods sold. Notice that while cash increased by $1,060 equity only increased by $1,000.

Each sale would gradually increase the amount in the sales tax payable account until it is

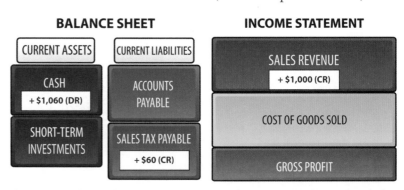

FIGURE 13.11

time for the company to send it to the state government. Assume the payment is made on August 31, 2012 and the account only has a $60 credit balance. Figure 13.12 shows the transaction.

The sales tax payable account essentially acts as a clearing account. It accumulates the sales tax collected over a period of time, and then is cleared to $0 when a payment is made to send the sales tax to the state government.

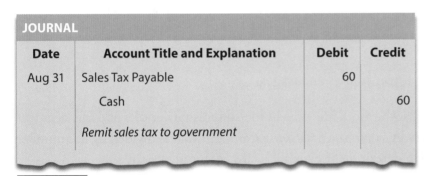 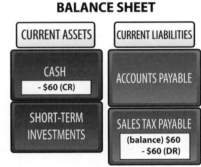

FIGURE 13.12

Payroll Accounting

Payroll is one of the most important business obligations of any organization. Employees are entitled to receive payment for services they have provided to the company.

Payroll accounting involves three types of payroll liabilities: (1) the **net pay** owed to an employee, (2) employee payroll deductions, and (3) employer payroll contributions. Any business that hires people to work on its behalf will incur these liabilities and related expenses.

The net pay owed to an employee amounts to their gross pay minus deductions made. These deductions can include:

- Social Security and Medicare
- Unemployment taxes
- Income taxes
- Other voluntary deductions

In other words, **gross pay** represents the total amount actually earned by the employee, and net pay represents the amount after the various deductions have been made.

It is important to pay attention to the pay frequency when dealing with payroll. The amount of gross pay and deductions on each paycheck is affected by the pay period (pay frequency). Pay period refers to the number of times an employee is paid during one year. The table below shows how many pay periods there are in a year for the common pay frequencies.

Pay Frequency	Number of Pay Periods in a Year
Weekly	52
Bi-weekly	26
Semi-monthly	24
Monthly	12

FIGURE 13.13

Gross Pay to Net Pay

There are two ways to pay an employee: salaries and wages.

Generally speaking, those employees who work full-time in the administrative, sales and management areas of a business are paid a salary. A salary is a *fixed annual* amount that is divided by the number of pay periods in a calendar year to determine the gross pay for each pay period.

For example, a sales manager who is paid $52,000 per year would earn $1,000 per week. If he was paid on a bi-weekly basis, his gross pay would be $2,000 for each pay period.

Individuals employed on a part-time basis (e.g. in the retail sector, in factories, or as manual labourers), are more likely to be paid a wage (hourly rate), where the pay for any given pay period is determined by the number of hours they worked in that period.

As an example, if a factory worker is paid $17.00 per hour and he works for 65 hours in a two week period, his gross pay would be $1,105.00 (65 hours x $17.00 per hour = $1,105.00).

Some of the key differences between salaries and wages are payments for overtime, sick pay and vacation pay. In most cases, employees who are paid by salary *do not* receive overtime pay, nor do they receive separate vacation pay. Instead, they continue to receive their regular pay for every pay period, including when they take vacation time. This is also true of absences for illness. Salaried employees continue to receive their pay if they are absent for a few days with legitimate reasons.

An employee that is paid an hourly wage has an opportunity to earn additional pay. Any work over and above the regular hours per pay period entitles an employee to overtime pay. The rates and circumstances for overtime pay are determined by the state, the employer, and perhaps by a union contract. In many cases, the rate paid for overtime hours is one and one-half times the regular hourly rate. An employee earning $10 an hour at a regular rate would earn $15 ($10 x 1.5) an hour for overtime hours. Hourly employees are entitled to extra pay when they work on statutory holidays such as New Year's Day. Hourly employees are also entitled to separate vacation pay. Generally, employees do not receive any pay if they are absent for personal reasons.

The gross pay shown on a pay stub is not the amount that is deposited into an employee's bank account. Gross pay is reduced by statutory and voluntary deductions, leaving a net pay amount. The amounts that are subtracted from a paycheck are referred to as payroll deductions. Net pay is your "take home pay".

Employee Payroll Deductions

Statutory Deductions

Every business is required to subtract (withhold) amounts from an employee's gross pay. Statutory deductions are paid to the appropriate tax authority in the country. In the Unites States the tax authorities are the Internal Revenue Service (IRS) for federal income tax purposes and various state authorities for state income tax purposes, such as the California Employment Development Department or in New York, the Department of Taxation and Finance. Statutory deductions in the United States are as follows:

- Federal and State income taxes
- Federal insurance contribution
- Federal unemployment taxes
- State unemployment taxes

Each of the above statutory deductions is calculated using annual tax tables. The calculated amounts are then subtracted from an employee's pay. The business is responsible for keeping track of payroll and the associated deductions to prepare tax forms for the employee (e.g. W2) at the end of each calendar year. The tax forms are then used by the employee when preparing their personal tax return for the government.

It is important to note that these deductions are made on the employee's behalf. When the employee files his annual income tax return, the amounts deducted show as payments already made and reduce the final tax amount owed. The system is designed this way to reduce the financial burden on individuals who would otherwise have to pay huge amounts when they file their tax returns every year. As well, businesses withhold and remit these amounts to the tax authorities on behalf of employees to assist in paying for the government services provided all year. Examples of these services may include education, public safety, roads and bridges. Regardless of the level of government that provides these services, the majority of the funding comes throughout the year from tax installments.

The amounts withheld are required under law, and failure to withhold the amounts from the employee's pay and remit them to the tax authorities can result in severe penalties. Therefore, payroll liabilities are kept separate from accounts payable.

Voluntary Deductions

An employer may also deduct other amounts from an employee's pay. These amounts are referred to as voluntary deductions and they cannot be withheld without the employee's permission. Examples include union dues, charitable donations, professional fees, safety or uniform allowances, pensions, medical and dental coverage, purchase of company stock, loan payments and health saving accounts. In each case, the employee would be advised of the potential deductions and would sign a contract indicating their agreement.

While these deductions are generally considered voluntary, they may be required by an employer as part of the employment agreement (typical examples would be union dues, medical and dental coverage).

An example of how to calculate an employee's net pay is:

Gross Pay	$1,700
Payroll Deductions	-650
Net Pay	$1,050

FIGURE 13.14

The journal entry to record payroll expense (wages and/or salaries) with deductions, using the example above, would be as follows:

- Record gross pay to the salaries (expense) account by debiting (increasing) salaries expense.
- Record the amounts withheld to a payable (liability) account by crediting (increasing) other payroll liabilities - this amount will be paid to the IRS. In reality, there are separate liability accounts for each type of deduction withheld. The payroll deductions liability account will be used for now to keep things simple.
- Record the net amount actually paid to the employee by crediting (decreasing) cash.

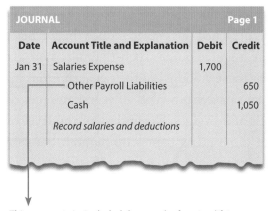

This account is included here only for simplifying your understanding of payroll accounting. In reality, this account will not exist in a company's chart of accounts. Instead, there are separate *liability accounts* for each type of deduction withheld. For instance, federal income tax payable is an example of such an account. See figure 13.18 for other examples of these accounts.

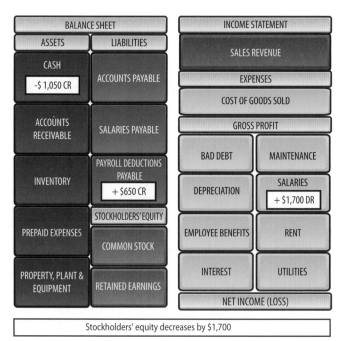

FIGURE 13.15

In a perfect world with no liabilities, all the amounts withheld from the employee's paycheck would immediately be paid to the IRS and others with cash. In reality, there is usually a difference in timing from withholding the deductions to actually sending them to the IRS and others. Businesses act as a middle-man, taking the money from the employee and sending it to the institutions at a later date. The business effectively has a debt (liability) for a short period of time until it sends the money where it is supposed to go.

Employer Payroll Contributions

Often, the government requires employers to match or contribute to the deductions made from their employee's pay. This amount is an additional expense to the business and would be recorded by debiting (increasing) employee benefits expense and crediting (increasing) other payroll liabilities (liability).

Continuing with our example, the amount deducted from the gross pay was $650. Assume that the government requires additional Social Security and Medicare contributions of $150 by the employer. This means that expenses and the amount payable to the government *both* increase by $150. The journal entry to record this additional expense would be:

- Record the additional expense by debiting (increasing) employee benefits expense.
- Record the additional amount payable to the IRS by crediting (increasing) payroll deductions payable (liability). In reality, there are separate liability accounts for each type of employer payroll contributions. The payroll deductions liability account will be used for now to keep things simple.

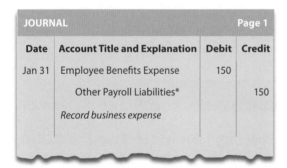

*In reality, separate liability accounts would be used. See figure 13.19 for an example of these liability accounts.

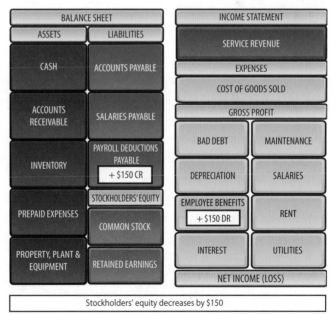

FIGURE 13.16

Paying the Deduction Liability

Amounts deducted from payroll are owed to the government and others. The amounts are required by law and usually have to be paid in the month following the deduction. To record the payment of the liability:

- Record the reduction of the liability by debiting (decreasing) other payroll liabilities.
- Record the payment to the IRS by crediting (decreasing) cash.

The journal entry to record this transaction is as follows:

JOURNAL			Page 1
Date	**Account Title and Explanation**	**Debit**	**Credit**
Feb 15	Other Payroll Liabilities*	800	
	Cash		800
	Pay payroll liability		

*In reality, separate liability accounts would be used. See figure 13.21 for an example of these liability accounts.

FIGURE 13.17

At this point, the employee has been paid, deductions have been made from their paycheck, further contributions were made by the business, and the IRS has been paid for all statutory deductions. Notice that there is no change to the income statement or equity when the deduction liability is paid.

Payroll for Roofus Construction

The above example provides an introduction to payroll accounting. Here is a more detailed example for payroll accounting using Roofus Construction as an example.

Assume that Roofus Construction's gross payroll for the period ending January 31, 2011 is $15,000. Employees are paid every two weeks and have statutory deductions withheld from their pays. In addition, there are voluntary deductions like union dues, charitable contributions, health insurance plan and retirement savings deducted from their gross earnings. As part of their benefits package, Roofus Construction matches employee contributions to health insurance and retirement plans.

The journal entry Roofus Construction must create to record payroll (wages and/or salaries) with deductions would be as follows:

- Record gross pay to the salaries (expense) account by debiting (increasing) salaries expense.

- Record the amounts withheld to various payable (liability) accounts by crediting (increasing) each of the payable accounts – these amounts will be paid to the IRS and others at a later date
- Record the net amount actually paid to the employees as a credit (decrease) to cash if the employee will be paid immediately. If there will be a delay of a few days before the employee will be paid, post the net amount as a credit (increase) to the salaries payable (liability) account for later payment.

Each numbered item in the journal entry will be discussed in detail.

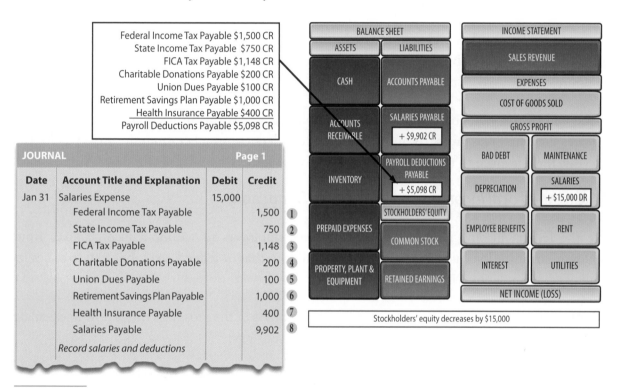

FIGURE 13.18

① Federal Income Taxes (Employee Deduction)

Every business is required to deduct (withhold) income tax from an employee's gross pay. There is no age limit for paying taxes and no maximum on the total earnings for which taxes must be paid. The more an employee earns, the more tax will be deducted from their pay.

Income tax is a major source of revenue for the federal government. The personal income tax rates depends on three factors:

- Gross pay
- Marital Status
- Withholding Allowances

The federal government allows employees to claim allowances or exemptions. These exemption allow employees to earn a certain amount of money without having to pay any tax on it. Every employee must complete and submit to their employer an Employee's Withholding Allowance Certificate (W4), which is then used to determine the amount of tax to deduct.

There are various methods for calculating federal income taxes. A common method would be to use "wage bracket method", in which government issued tables (called Employer's Tax Guide or Circular E) are used to calculate federal taxes.

If Roofus Construction applies a federal income tax rate of 10% of the gross pay, this is how to calculate how much federal income tax to deduct from the employee's pay:

Gross Pay x Income Tax Rate = Federal Income Tax Deduction
$15,000 x 10% = $1,500 Federal Income Tax Deduction

The amount of the federal income tax deduction will increase a liability account with a credit, which will show that the business will have to send the government that amount at some point in the future.

At the end of the year, the employer must complete a W2 form for each employee. This form indicates the employees gross pay and all the statutory deductions taken from the gross pay for the year. This form is given to the employee and sent to the IRS.

② State and Local Income Taxes (Employee Deduction)

Like the federal income taxes, most states require employers to withhold income taxes from employee earnings. The calculation criterion is similar to that of federal taxes. Each state issues its own tax table similar to Circular E.

If Roofus Construction applies a state income tax rate of 5% of the gross pay, this is how to calculate how much state income tax to deduct from the employee's pay:

Gross Pay x Income Tax Rate = State Income Tax Deduction
$15,000 x 5% = $750 State Income Tax Deduction

The amount of the state income tax deduction will increase a liability account with a credit, which will show that the business will have to send the government that amount at some point in the future.

③ Federal Insurance Contributions Act (Employee Deduction)

Every business is required to deduct (withhold) the Federal Insurance Contributions Act (FICA) from an employee's gross pay. The statutory deduction is to pay for federal Social Security and Medicare benefits programs. The business is also required to match the amount withheld from the employee. For example, if an employee were to have $50 deducted from her gross pay for FICA, the business would have to pay an additional $50 towards FICA.

Both Social Security and the Medicare portion have their own rates that are applied to the gross pay of an employee. The typical rate for Social Security if 6.2% and the typical rate for Medicare is 1.45% for a total FICA deduction of 7.65%. Since the employer must match this amount, the employer will pay an additional 7.65% of the employees gross pay to the federal government for FICA.

If Roofus Construction has gross payroll of $15,000, this is how to calculate how much FICA to deduct from the employee's pay:

Gross Pay x FICA rate = FICA Deduction
$15,000 x 7.65% = $1,148 FICA Deduction

The amount of the FICA deduction will increase a liability account with a credit, which will show that the business will have to send the government that amount at some point in the future.

The federal government has reduced FICA Social Security rates to 4.2% for the years 2011 to 2012 as part of the Tax Relief Act of 2010. For those two years then, FICA will be 5.65% instead of 7.65%. The Social Security rate will increase back to the normal rate in 2013.

4 5 Charitable Donations and Union Dues (Employee Deductions)

These are examples of voluntary deductions that may be required as part of employment agreement or if the employee agreed to the deduction. Unions are organizations that employees can belong to which create better working conditions for the employees. Sometimes belonging to a union is the only way an employee can get a job. Charitable donations can include local and international charities like United Way, Save Our Children or a registered local charity to whom employees would like to contribute. The donations may be tax deductible.

There are many different types of voluntary deductions, all of which depend upon what the business is willing to offer their employees. The business will deduct these amounts and eventually send them to the appropriate institution. Examples of other voluntary deductions include:

- Accidental death and dismemberment coverage (AD&D)
- Employee Stock Purchase Plan (ESOP and ESPP)
- Charitable donations
- Roth IRA
- Long-term disability (LTD)
- Medical or dental coverage
- Retirement Plan Contributions (401K)
- Short-term disability (STD)

6 7 Health and Retirement Plans (Employee Deductions)

This is an example of the employee and the business sharing the cost of a voluntary deduction. The amount shown here represents what the employee is supposed to pay for the health insurance coverage and retirement savings plan. The business will deduct these amounts and eventually send them to the appropriate institution.

8 Salaries Payable (Net Pay)

Net pay is calculated by subtracting all the deductions from the gross pay. The employee's net pay is recorded in salaries payable. This indicates that the business is recording the payroll journal entry but will not be paying the employee until a later date. If the employee was being paid immediately, then the employee's net pay would be recorded to cash.

Employer Payroll Contributions

The business now has to record its own payroll expenses. In addition to having to pay for FICA, remember that this business is paying for half of the health insurance coverage for Glen.

The journal entry to record the business expenses would be as follows:

- Record total expenses to the business by debiting (increasing) employee benefits expense.
- Record individual amounts by crediting (increasing) the various payable (liability) accounts.

Each numbered item in the journal entry will be discussed in detail.

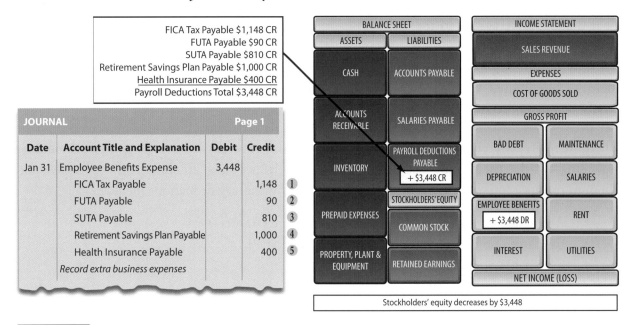

FIGURE 13.19

1 Federal Insurance Contributions Act (Employer Contribution)

As mentioned, FICA taxes are mandatory deductions from employees' pay for federal Social Security and Medicare benefits programs. The employer must also match the employee's deduction. In this case, the business will have to put aside an additional $1,148 for its portion of the taxes due.

2 3 Federal Unemployment and State Unemployment Taxes (Employer Contribution)

The business will have to contribute towards federal and state unemployment taxes on behalf of employees. The Federal Unemployment Tax Act (FUTA) rate is 6.0% of gross pay, but only applies to the first $7,000 of gross pay an employee earns in the year.

The State Unemployment Tax (SUTA) rate can change from state to state. The rate will fluctuate based on factors such as the number of unemployment claims in the state and the overall "good standing" of the state with the federal government. For this textbook, assume the SUTA rate is 5.4%. The employer is allowed to reduce the federal unemployment tax rate by the state unemployment tax rate. In this example, the FUTA rate of 6.0% will be reduced to 0.6% (6.0% - 5.4%).

If Roofus Construction has gross payroll of $15,000, this is how to calculate how much FUTA and SUTA will be payable to the government:

$$\text{Gross Pay x FUTA rate} = \text{FUTA Payable}$$
$$\$15,000 \text{ x } 0.6\% = \$90 \text{ FUTA Payable}$$

$$\text{Gross Pay x SUTA rate} = \text{SUTA Payable}$$
$$\$15,000 \text{ x } 5.4\% = \$810 \text{ SUTA Payable}$$

Both of these amounts will be recorded in liabilities and recorded as an expense to the business.

④ ⑤ *Health and Retirement Plans (Employer Contribution)*

Roofus Construction is paying for half the cost of the health insurance and retirement plans. This is an extra cost to the business. Some businesses may decide to pay for the entire benefit. If this business were to pay for the entire health insurance and retirement savings plans, then the amount shown in figure 13.19 for health insurance payable would be $800 and retirement savings plan payable would be $2,000 and there would be no deduction from the employee for these items in figure 13.18.

Paying the Liabilities

The journal entries to record paying the liabilities would be as follows:

- Record the reduction of the liabilities by debiting (decreasing) each of the payable accounts.
- Record the payment to the appropriate individual or institution by crediting (decreasing) cash.

Once the journal entries are made and the decreases to the liability accounts are complete, the liability accounts will have a balance of zero. All the amounts that were payroll debts to the company will be completely paid off. Notice that there will be no change to the income statement or equity when the liabilities are paid.

Salaries Payable

Employees do not always receive their paycheck on the same day that the payroll entry is recorded. For our example, the journal entry to record salaries and deductions in figure 13.18 was made on January 31, 2011 and the date to record paying the employee in figure 13.20 was made on February 1, 2011. When the employee receives their paycheck, we can decrease the liability and reduce cash.

JOURNAL			Page 1
Date	**Account Title and Explanation**	**Debit**	**Credit**
Feb 1	Salaries Payable	9,902	
	Cash		9,902
	Pay the employee		

FIGURE 13.20

Statutory Deductions Payable

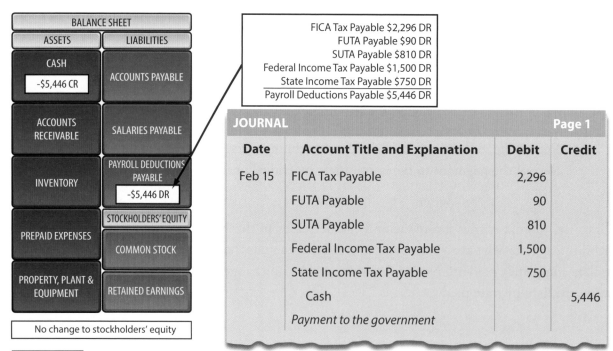

JOURNAL			Page 1
Date	**Account Title and Explanation**	**Debit**	**Credit**
Feb 15	FICA Tax Payable	2,296	
	FUTA Payable	90	
	SUTA Payable	810	
	Federal Income Tax Payable	1,500	
	State Income Tax Payable	750	
	Cash		5,446
	Payment to the government		

FIGURE 13.21

The government has strict guidelines for when the payroll liabilities are due. Businesses must pay close attention to these dates. If payments are late, the business will be required to pay penalties and interest on top of the amount owed. It is usually best to send payment through the bank. The bank teller's stamp will indicate the date payment was made if there is a question whether payment was made on time. Most moderate size businesses will have to pay their statutory deduction liabilities by the 15th of the following month.

In the example, payroll was recorded on January 31, 2011; therefore payment must be received by the government by February 15, 2011. Notice that FICA taxes include both the amounts deducted from the employee's pay and the amounts the business had to contribute.

Charitable Donations and Union Dues Payable

JOURNAL			Page 1
Date	Account Title and Explanation	Debit	Credit
Feb 28	Union Dues Payable	100	
	Cash		100
	Payment to union hall		

FIGURE 13.22

Any voluntary amounts deducted from an employee's pay must eventually be sent to the institution to which they are owed. Businesses merely act as a middle-man, taking the money from the employee and sending it to the institution. In this example, union dues are to be sent to the union hall by the end of the following month. Charitable donations would be paid in a similar manner to the appropriate charity.

Health and Retirement Plan Payable

JOURNAL			Page 1
Date	Account Title and Explanation	Debit	Credit
Feb 28	Health Insurance Payable	800	
	Cash		800
	Payment for health insurance		

FIGURE 13.23

Some voluntary amounts are split between the employee and the business. In this example, the business must combine the amount deducted from the employee in figure 13.18 and the amount the business had to contribute in figure 13.19. In this example, the payment is being made to the health insurance company. The payment for the retirement plan will be similar.

The total cash flow impact of paying all the payroll journal entries would be $18,448.

An important point to note is that the $15,000 of gross payroll actually cost the business $18,448. This means that in our example, for every $1 of gross payroll, the actual cost to the business is approximately $1.23. This actual cost can be higher. In our example we have used lower rates for federal and state income taxes. This shows that payroll can be much more expensive to a business than just the amount received by employees, depending upon the types and amounts of benefits that the business pays.

Estimated and Contingent Liabilities

We have already discussed various forms of known liabilities, also referred to as *determinable liabilities*, which are debts taken on by the company for which the terms are readily known. In other words, known liabilities leave a paper trail of invoices, contracts and purchase orders that tell the company exactly how much is due, to whom and when.

However, some company liabilities exist for which the exact terms are not precisely known and cannot be determined until future events occur. These unknown liabilities are also referred to as *non-determinable liabilities*, and can be divided further into two more categories: **estimated liabilities** and **contingent liabilities**.

Estimated liabilities are financial obligations that a company cannot exactly quantify. Examples of estimated liabilities include income and property taxes and warranties. A company needs to adhere to the matching principle when it makes an estimate of the amount of the upcoming liability.

In our discussion of accounts receivable, we described a company faced with the same challenge of matching expenses with the period in which linked revenues were generated. To meet that challenge, the company set up an allowance account based on the estimated bad debts for the period. A similar process can be established for a company's estimated liabilities.

Product Warranties

Just as a company needs to estimate how much bad debt it will have in the upcoming period, when a company sells products with warranties it needs to estimate how much warranty liability it will have. By doing this, the company can expense this liability in the period in which linked revenues are generated. Any errors in estimation can then be adjusted once the actual figures are known.

For example, Star Inc. is a manufacturer of industrial labeling machines. It offers customers a warranty of three years on the purchase of each machine. If a machine breaks down during this warranty period, it is Star Inc.'s obligation to repair it, provide necessary parts and, if necessary, replace the machine.

On the basis of an analysis of historical company trends, the company's accountant determines that an average of $100 per machine is paid out in warranty obligations. The company has sold 50 of these labeling machines during their 2009 fiscal year; therefore, the following journal entry is made to recognize the warranty expense for 2009:

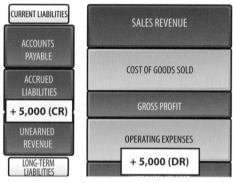

Equity decreases by $5,000.

JOURNAL			
Date	Account Title and Explanation	Debit	Credit
	Warranty Expense	5,000	
	Estimated Warranty Liability		5,000
	To record estimated warranty expense		

FIGURE 13.24

The $5,000 is expensed for this period in the income statement (since these estimates cover expected warranties for the year) and the estimated warranty liability of $5,000 is credited in the corresponding liability account.

During the next year, Star Inc. will receive some warranty claims and make some actual expenditure in meeting those claims. Let us assume that Star Inc. uses $500 in parts from its own inventory, and maintenance staff report $1,500 worth of billable hours related to warranty claims. Here is how their accountant would record these transactions:

JOURNAL			
Date	Account Title and Explanation	Debit	Credit
	Estimated Warranty Liability	2,000	
	Inventory (Parts)		500
	Cash		1,500
	To record inventory and wages for warranty work		

FIGURE 13.25

The account of estimated warranty liability is debited with $2,000, leaving a balance of $3,000 to satisfy warranty claims over the remaining two-year period. On the credit side, $500 worth of inventory is taken off the books, and $1,500 is recorded as a decrease in the bank account.

There is no change to the income statement, since the estimated warranty has already been expensed in the year the machine was sold. The company will calculate and record a debit to warranty expense and credit to estimated warranty liability accounts on the basis of the number of machines sold that year.

Assuming that this amount does not change for the remainder of the warranty period (i.e. no one else makes any warranty claims), Star Inc. would have to reconcile the original estimate with the actual claims made. This is how that process would be transacted.

The remaining $3,000 in the estimated warranty liability account is removed with a debit. In the income statement, $3,000 in expenses is removed from the books with a credit (decrease) of that amount. The company is reversing the original expense for the amount that remains in the estimated warranty liability account.

Of course, no company wants to find itself in a position of significantly erring in estimating certain liabilities as this would result in large adjustment entries after the fact.

Accountants should provide an accurate snapshot of company finances. Large errors in estimating liabilities will distort that snapshot.

INCOME STATEMENT

JOURNAL			
Date	Account Title and Explanation	Debit	Credit
	Estimated Warranty Liability	3,000	
	Warranty Expense		3,000
	To decrease the balance of estimated liability owing		

CURRENT LIABILITIES
ACCOUNTS PAYABLE
ACCRUED LIABILITIES
−3,000 (DR)
UNEARNED REVENUE
LONG-TERM LIABILITIES
LOANS PAYABLE (LONG-TERM)

SALES REVENUE
COST OF GOODS SOLD
GROSS PROFIT
OPERATING EXPENSES
−3,000 (CR)
OPERATING INCOME
OTHER REVENUES
INTEREST REVENUE, GAIN ON SALE OF ASSETS

FIGURE 13.26

To avoid such difficulties, a company should always closely monitor its estimated liability accounts. If estimates are continually and significantly wrong, then reviews should be conducted and changes made to historical and other analyses that are producing these errors. For example, if liabilities keep increasing, it would indicate that a manufacturing problem exists.

The example above demonstrated a situation of embedded warranty. Embedded warranty is provided with a product or service with no additional fee required from the customer. However, sometimes companies sell warranties separately to customers. In those cases, revenue generated on the sale of these warranties is initially recorded as unearned warranty revenue. The unearned warranty revenue is recognized throughout the life of the warranty contract.

BALANCE SHEET

CURRENT ASSETS
CASH
+$60,000
SHORT-TERM INVESTMENTS
ACCOUNTS RECEIVABLE
INVENTORY
PREPAID EXPENSES

CURRENT LIABILITIES
ACCOUNTS PAYABLE
ACCRUED LIABILITIES
UNEARNED REVENUE
+$60,000
LONG-TERM LIABILITIES
LOANS PAYABLE (LONG-TERM)

JOURNAL			
Date	Account Title and Explanation	Debit	Credit
Jun 1	Cash	60,000	
	Unearned Warranty Revenue		60,000
	Record the sale of the 3-year warranties		

FIGURE 13.27

Let us assume that Star Inc. sold $60,000 worth of three-year warranties as a separate product to its customers on June 1, 2010. This is how the transaction would be recorded in the company's books:

The receipt of $60,000 is recorded as a debit to cash and as a credit to unearned warranty revenue. Since this is a three-year warranty, $20,000 will be recognized at the end of each year. In this case, as unearned revenue decreases revenue will increase, which causes equity to increase. At the end of the first year, the company recorded the appropriate adjustment (see figure 13.28).

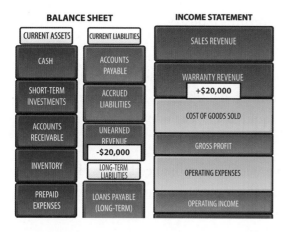

JOURNAL			
Date	Account Title and Explanation	Debit	Credit
May 31	Unearned Warranty Revenue	20,000	
	Warranty Revenue		20,000
	Recognize one year unearned warranty revenue as earned		

FIGURE 13.28

The $20,000 is recorded as a debit to the unearned warranty revenue and as a credit to the warranty revenue account. The rest of the revenue will become earned as the warranty periods elapse. At present, the unearned warranty revenue account has a $40,000 balance because there are two more years left in the warranty period. Note that only the unearned revenue in the next twelve months is counted as current liabilities.

Contingent Liabilities

Unlike estimated liabilities, a company's contingent liabilities involve a financial obligation that will occur only if a certain event takes place. As a result, not only are contingent liabilities estimated, but they are also dependent upon another event taking place.

According to the accounting rules, a company will only establish a contingent liability if payment is likely and the amount of liability can be reasonably estimated. Since it is difficult to determine what is and what is not possible, and how much of a contingency should be estimated, these items usually involve discretion and judgment by the accountants on behalf of the company.

Perhaps the most common reason to establish a contingent liability is to anticipate a costly lawsuit. If such a lawsuit does happen, it could seriously affect a company's bottom line. It would be prudent to include a note in the company's financial statements outlining any contingencies that may lead to a liability.

Current Liabilities and Financial Ratios

It is important for a company's assets to cover its liabilities. A company's current assets should always be used to cover its current liabilities. The ratio of current assets to current liabilities may be considered acceptable if it is at least 2:1. In other words, for every dollar of current liabilities, a business should have two dollars of current assets. Recall that current assets are assets will be turned into cash or used up within 12 months. However, this is just a rough guideline and should not be relied upon as a strict rule. The acceptable current ratio often depends on the company's industry. This helps to ensure that a company has enough liquidity to cover its short-term financial obligations.

Another business practice often used to ensure that a company can pay its short-term liabilities is for it to have enough assets that can be liquidated within three months. For every dollar of current liabilities, a company should have about one dollar of liquid assets, excluding current assets such as inventory.

These basic business guidelines are encapsulated in some widely used financial ratios. The current ratio (also known as the working capital ratio) and the quick ratio are used to measure and assess a company's ability to maintain a proper balance between current assets and current liabilities.

Current Ratio

The current ratio simply tracks current assets against current liabilities.

$$\text{Current Ratio} = \frac{\text{Current Assets}}{\text{Current Liabilities}}$$

In this example, the current ratio is $50,000 ÷ $50,000 or 1:1. Since a company usually needs its non-current assets to run the business over the long term, they are not included in the current ratio.

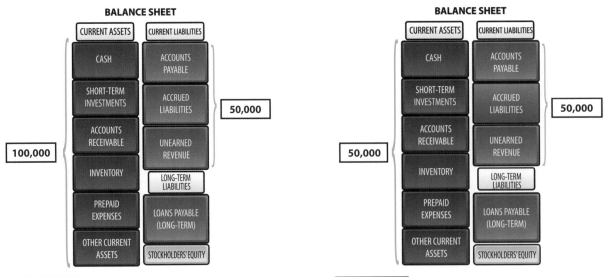

FIGURE 13.29   FIGURE 13.30

While a current ratio of 1:1 means the company can cover their current liabilities, it does not allow for unforeseen circumstances. It means that all of a company's current assets would need to be liquidated (converted to cash) to pay all its current liabilities (see figure 13.30 above).

As figure 13.29 illustrates, a ratio of 2:1 is far more desirable. It means that a company will likely have enough liquid assets on hand to cover its short-term financial obligations with some reserve in case not all accounts receivable are collected or not all inventories are sold.

Quick Ratio

One of the drawbacks of the current ratio is that it does not tell us how liquid the assets are that are being used to cover current liabilities. That is where the quick ratio is more helpful. It is also known as the **acid test**.

The quick ratio is based on current *liquid* assets: current liabilities. The equation is:

$$\text{Quick Ratio} = \frac{\text{Cash} + \text{Short-Term Investments} + \text{Net Accounts Receivable}}{\text{Current Liabilities}}$$

Figure 13.31 shows a further breakdown of the current assets section of the Accounting Map™. As illustrated, the entire current assets section totals $100,000, indicating a current ratio of 2:1. This should be an ideal situation. However, let us assume that the breakdown reveals only $40,000 of the current assets can be considered liquid. This gives us a quick ratio of less than 1:1 ($40,000 ÷ $50,000). An amount of $60,000 of the company's current assets is tied up in inventory and prepaid expenses, which are unlikely to be converted to cash in the immediate future. The company would have to sell some of its assets to get closer to the desirable quick ratio of 1:1. It would then be in a better position to cover its current liabilities with its liquid current assets.

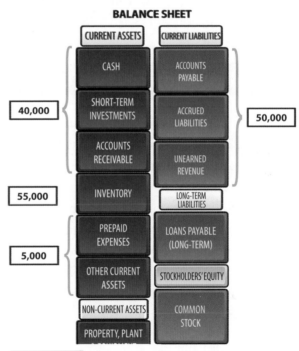

FIGURE 13.31

Controls Relating to Current Liabilities

One of the first and basic controls over a company's liabilities involves a simple principle: keep track of company bills and budget well enough to pay them on time. The inability to pay suppliers could cause serious inventory shortages. Even more important, not paying suppliers risks a company's reputation and ability to do business with others.

Ensuring that bills are paid involves implementing controls to ensure that the right bills are paid. To that end, all relevant documents should be gathered, such as purchase orders, receipts and original invoices, to ensure the legitimacy of the invoices.

After an invoice is paid, it should be marked as such and kept on file for verification purposes. The last thing that a company wants to do is pay the wrong bills or pay the same bills more than once in error. Controls related to invoices should prevent this from happening.

Accounting controls also involve ensuring that a company's resources are used efficiently and economically. This includes paying bills on time and making use of any payment discounts that may be available. Automated systems can alert the appropriate personnel when payments should be made. Manual systems can make use of "tickler files," which allow for the placement of time-sensitive documents in labeled folders that are to be reviewed on important dates.

An Ethical Approach to Current Liabilities

Much of our discussion of accounting ethics has focused on how the books can be manipulated to alter some aspect of a company's financial results. A company's current liabilities are no different in this regard. For example, management might want to understate current liabilities by classifying them as long-term liabilities because this might be helpful in securing a bank loan.

The nature of liabilities can make them a source of fraud that is difficult to detect by both internal and external auditors. In essence, a liability involves a financial obligation to another party, usually as a result of being loaned money. Yet if you're a third party looking for evidence that the transaction took place in the manner alleged, sometimes all that exists is a copy

IN THE REAL WORLD

Many people, even those experienced in the business world, usually do not give invoices a second thought. They receive a bill, take a look at how much they owe, and send the money before the due date. This is how honest people, both in business and private life, deal with their financial obligations. However, there is one potential problem with paying invoices this way: they may in fact be phony!

One of the oldest scams in business, yet one that continues to deliver success for fraudsters, is sending a phony invoice to a company. In other words, a company is sent a bill for goods or services they never asked for nor received. Nevertheless — and as strange as it may seem — honest businesses often get fooled by this practice and end up wasting their money in the process.

In a sense, it is an honest mistake. Many of these invoices look real. They often use names similar to businesses dealt with on a regular basis, such as an Internet service provider or a club offering membership. Furthermore, the people who pay these bills are often not the people responsible for making the purchases.

There are various ways in which such fraud can be detected. Collecting all necessary internal documentation is one approach. Relying on a copy of an invoice without a purchase order is a mistake. Another approach is to simply call the number provided on the invoice to see if it is a legitimate business.

Businesses have enough of a challenge to meet financial obligations they actually owe. So ensuring that phony invoices are detected and dealt with appropriately not only makes good business sense but also helps prevent one of the oldest and most embarrassing scams around.

of an invoice or an entry in the books. Experienced auditing teams will know how to follow the money.

Liability fraud often involves a company being on the receiving end of a phony invoice. That is, companies receive invoices from various suppliers and vendors, and an accounting department that doesn't implement some of the controls already discussed might be in the practice of paying any invoice that looks legitimate. It is an old scam, and one that can only be prevented through proper accounting controls.

The payroll system must also be carefully monitored to prevent abuse. There should be regulations set up by the business to ensure that an employee actually exists and is getting paid properly.

- Ensure the person hiring employees is not the same person paying employees. An employee start package should be created to collect important information about the employee, including the employee's social security number. This package should be passed to the person who prepares payroll checks. If the person hiring employees also pays them, it is possible to create a phantom employee and collect the phantom's paycheck.
- Monitor the hours worked by employees. Management should be responsible for ensuring employees work the hours they claim they work. A time clock with punch cards or electronic swipe cards can track exactly how much time employees work. It would be a good idea for managers to physically see the individuals checking in and out to ensure that they are actually starting work after checking in and that one person is not checking in many people.
- There should be proper authorization for pay increases or employee termination.
- If manual checks are being created, the person creating the checks should not be the same person who signs the checks.
- An imprest bank account could be setup for payroll. This is a separate bank account from the main bank account of the business. All payroll checks are cashed against the imprest account, and only enough cash is available in the imprest account to cover the payroll checks. This will make reconciliation easier and help prevent theft through payroll.

In Summary

⇨ A company's balance sheet should be structured in a way that its assets are used to cover its liabilities. This means that current assets should cover current liabilities, and long term assets should cover long term liabilities.

⇨ A company's known liabilities, or determinable liabilities, are financial obligations with fixed terms that can be traced using documentation (e.g. accounts payable).

⇨ Sales taxes are charged on sales. The amount collected by the business must be sent to the government. They are classified as current liabilities as they are due within the company's operating cycle.

⇨ Payroll is a crucial component of a business, for both an employee and employer. Meeting payroll means ensuring that employees are paid accurately and on time every pay period.

⇨ There are three components to accounting for payroll: (1) the net pay owed to an employee, (2) employee payroll deductions, and (3) employer payroll contributions.

⇨ Gross pay represents the total amount actually earned by the employee. Net pay represents the amount received by the employee after the various deductions have been made. Net Pay = Gross Pay - Payroll Deductions.

⇨ Accounting transactions related to payroll involve expensing gross pay, posting deductions owed to liability accounts, and then decreasing the liability accounts and crediting cash once the payments are finally made.

⇨ Statutory deductions are those required by law and are paid to the Internal Revenue Services (IRS) and other state and local governments. Voluntary deductions are those that cannot be withheld without the employee's permission.

⇨ Examples of statutory payroll deductions include FICA, SUTA, FUTA, and Federal and State Income taxes. Examples of voluntary payroll deductions include union dues, health insurance, retirement saving plans, charitable donations and professional fees.

⇨ Notes payable represent a more formalized contract between a company and a supplier for an amount owed, as opposed to a standard bill or invoice.

⇨ Estimated liabilities, such as product warranties, represent financial obligations whose specific amount will not be known until some future time. Contingent liabilities represent a financial obligation that will need to be met only if a certain event occurs. The possibility of a lawsuit might require the creation of a contingent liability.

⇨ The current ratio (also known as the working capital ratio) compares a company's current assets with its current liabilities.

⇨ The quick ratio (also known as the acid test) compares a company's current liquid assets with its current liabilities.

↳ Controls related to current liabilities should include proper tracking and monitoring of invoices and all related documentation. This ensures that the correct bills are paid on time, which is a crucial part of maintaining the company's finances.

↳ Ethics related to current liabilities should ensure that liabilities are not understated for the purpose of overstating net assets.

Review Exercise

Michelle's Crafts has three employees. They get paid bi-weekly (every two weeks). The following table lists the employees, the hours they worked over the last two weeks ending January 20, 2012 and their pay rate.

Name	Hourly Wage	Hours
Flower, Blossom	14	80
Painter, Rob	13.5	76
Scrap, Book	14.5	82

Each employee contributes $10 to charity. The appropriate deduction rates are provided below:

- Federal income tax rate is 9%
- State income tax rate is 6%
- FICA is 7.65%
- FUTA is 0.6%
- SUTA is 5.4%.

Required:

1. Prepare a journal entry for the employees.
2. Prepare a journal entry to record the additional employer expense.
3. Prepare a journal entry to make a government remittance on February 15, 2012 using just the numbers from this pay period.

Answers:

1. Pay employees

JOURNAL

Date	Account Title and Explanation	Debit	Credit
Jun 20	Salaries Expense	3,335.00	
	Federal Income Tax Payable		300.15
	State Income Tax Payable		200.10
	FICA Tax Payable		255.13
	Charitable Donations Payable		30.00
	Cash		2,549.62
	Record salaries and deductions		

2. Employer expenses

JOURNAL			
Date	**Account Title and Explanation**	**Debit**	**Credit**
Jun 20	Employee Benefits Expense	455.23	
	FICA Tax Payable		255.13
	FUTA Payable		20.01
	SUTA Payable		180.09
	Record employer payroll expenses		

3. Government remittance

JOURNAL			
Date	**Account Title and Explanation**	**Debit**	**Credit**
Jun 20	Federal Income Tax Payable	300.15	
	State Income Tax Payable	200.10	
	FICA Tax Payable	510.26	
	FUTA Payable	20.01	
	SUTA Payable	180.09	
	Cash		1,210.61
	Payment to the government		

Notes

Chapter 14

LONG-TERM LIABILITIES

❶ State the characteristics and different types of bonds

❷ Apply the concept of present value

❸ Record bonds issued at par

❹ Record bonds issued at a discount or a premium

❺ Record the retirement of bonds

❻ Calculate debt-to-total assets and debt-to-equity ratios

❼ Apply controls and ethics related to long-term liabilities

Long-Term Liabilities: An Introduction

The liabilities side of the balance sheet contains two main sections: current liabilities and long-term liabilities. Current liabilities were the focus of our discussion in chapter 13. This chapter focuses on long-term liabilities (liabilities paid after a period of more than 12 months). Two common types of long-term liabilities of business organizations are term loans and bonds payable.

The most common form of long-term financing used by a company is a loan. Term loans were partly covered in the current liabilities section because the portion of the loan due within one fiscal period is presented as a current liability on the balance sheet.

An alternative to borrowing money from a bank is to borrow money from private investors. This is done by issuing bonds, which can be sold to raise cash for the business. Bonds will be discussed in detail in this chapter.

FIGURE 14.1

Characteristics and Types of Bonds

Companies cannot always secure sufficient long-term financing from a bank or from private investors. Instead, large companies may borrow money by issuing bonds to interested investors.

The company is called the bond issuer since it issues the bond. The bondholder is the investor who purchases the bond. There a number of complexities involved with bonds but essentially, it is a contract, whereby a bondholder loans money (the principal) to a bond issuer. In return, the bond issuer promises to provide regular interest payments to a bondholder and after a set time (when the bonds mature), the principal is returned to the bondholder. Bond investors are often large organizations such as pension funds but can also include smaller institutions or individuals. The primary difference between a bond and a loan is that there is a market in which bonds are actively traded. On the other hand, a loan is usually a private agreement between two parties that is non-tradeable.

There are several types of bonds:

- Term bonds mature on a specific date, whereas serial bonds are a set of bonds that mature at different intervals.
- Companies may issue secured or mortgage bonds whereby they put up specific assets as collateral (like loans) in the event that it defaults on interest or principal repayments.
- Unsecured or **debenture bonds** are backed only by the bondholder's faith in the company's good reputation.
- Bonds may have a callable feature whereby the company has the right to buy back the bonds before maturity at a set or "call" price.
- If the bonds are convertible, bondholders have the option of converting or exchanging the bonds for a specific number of the company's stock.
- Registered bonds list the bondholders as registered owners who receive regular interest payments on the interest payment dates.
- Coupon bonds contain detachable coupons that state the amount and due date of the interest payment. These coupons can be removed and cashed by the holder.

An organization that issues bonds faces the challenge of competing with other investments in the market. A bond is an interest-bearing investment vehicle whereby money is received from investors in exchange for interest payments. For example, a 5% interest rate (coupon rate) on a bond means that 5% annual interest on the principal balance outstanding will be paid back to the investor. A company that has issued a five-year bond, with annual interest of 10% (payable twice per year) and having a $100,000 principal value, is obligated to make semi-annual (twice per year) interest payments to bondholders totaling $5,000 ($100,000 × 10% × ½). The interest rate on a bond must compete with market interest rates in general – that is, investors can earn interest through a number of other investments on the market, including bonds issued by other organizations.

That is why companies generally issue bonds at the going market interest rate. For example, if the market rate is 10%, the company is likely to issue the bond with a 10% interest rate; this is known as issuing a bond at par. Since it takes time to arrange the printing and distribution of bonds, however, rates of existing bonds can differ significantly from current market rates. We will examine what issuing companies do under these circumstances; but first, a discussion on the time value of money is necessary.

The Concept of Present Value

In our discussion of accounting methods, we have been using round figures to demonstrate various procedures. We have also assumed that the value of money remains constant. One dollar in a person's hand at one moment has been assumed to be equal in value to a dollar in that person's hand at a later time.

This, however, is not so. In fact, the value of money changes over time. This is what interest rates are all about.

In other words, money itself has a price. If it is lent, it gets repaid with interest. A deposit in a bank account is essentially a loan to a bank — with interest. Of course, a loan from a bank also comes with a price tag (in the form of interest).

The world of finance often refers to this phenomenon as the **time value of money**. It is important for accountants to be familiar with the time value of money because it is a basic principle of economics and finance. Furthermore, it almost certainly affects the amounts in transactions that an accountant records over time. If a company keeps money in a bank, its value will change even if nothing is done to it.

In the context of our current discussion of **bonds payable**, the time value of money matters because it will help determine the price the bonds will sell for when the market rate of interest differs from the stated rate. We begin with a simple example to show how a company can pay both the principal and interest over time. This involves making calculations concerning the value of money at some future point in time. We will look closely at this issue.

We will start with the basics. If you have one dollar and you invest it for one year at an interest rate of 10%, you will have made 10 cents in interest and have a total in the account of $1.10 at the end of the year.

At the start of the second year, you start with $1.10. The interest for the year will amount to 11 cents ($1.10 × 10%) and produce a year-end balance of $1.21.

You should see a pattern developing. The more money that is left in an interest-bearing account, the more the interest grows each year. In the first year, interest was 10 cents. In the second year, it was 11 cents. The following chart represents the interest that would accumulate in the account over a period of 10 years.

Year	Opening Balance	Interest at 10%	Closing Balance
1	1.000	0.100	1.100
2	1.100	0.110	1.210
3	1.210	0.121	1.331
4	1.331	0.133	1.464
5	1.464	0.146	1.611
6	1.611	0.161	1.772
7	1.772	0.177	1.949
8	1.949	0.195	2.144
9	2.144	0.214	2.358
10	2.358	0.236	2.594

FIGURE 14.2

As you can see, the amount of interest earned in year 10 is over 23 cents, more than double the amount of interest earned in Year 1.

This phenomenon is commonly referred to as *compound interest*, which refers to the piling on effect that applying the same interest rate has on an account over a period of time. Essentially, with each passing period, the interest rate is applied to interest on top of the principal.

The amount in the bottom right-hand corner of our chart ($2.59) will be the value of the money in the account after Year 10. It can also be referred to as the *future value*.

Following this basic logic, the future value of the money after Year 2 is $1.21. After year 5, it is $1.61, and so on.

Of course, calculating the value of money can work in reverse, too. In other words, an accountant can try to calculate what amount needs to be invested today to produce a certain amount in the future. This is known as the *present value*.

The following chart indicates calculations showing present values of $1.00 over 10 years, given an interest rate of 10%. The factors shown in the table are calculated using a formula that is beyond the scope of this book. However, these factors can be found in many mathematical textbooks, and are commonly included as tables in professional accounting exams. Most business calculators include functions which use the factors, as do common spreadsheet programs.

The chart provides answers for the following question: What amount needs to be invested now to create $1 in x number of years, with x representing Years 1 to 10 in this particular chart and assuming an interest rate of 10%?

10%	
Year	**Factor**
1	0.9091
2	0.8264
3	0.7513
4	0.6830
5	0.6209
6	0.5645
7	0.5132
8	0.4665
9	0.4241
10	0.3855

Excerpt from Present Value table.

FIGURE 14.3

For example, an investor requiring $1.00 after one year would have to invest about 91 cents (as indicated on the first line of the chart). If the investor wanted $1 after 10 years, it would necessitate investing about 39 cents now (as shown on the last line of the chart). Indeed, the difference between the amounts is a testament to the power of compound interest. That is, waiting 9 years to get the same payoff means initially investing less than half the money. The greater the interest rate, and the longer this interest rate is applied, the more compound interest is earned.

It should be noted that the chart provided applies only to an interest rate calculation of 10%. Separate charts need to be used when other interest rates are involved in calculating present and future values.

Time Value of Money and Bonds Payable

Now that we have some understanding of how the time value of money works, we can start applying its principles to bonds payable.

When bonds are sold at their par or face value, both the present value of the principal, and future interest payments, can be calculated. One point regarding the interest payments needs to be mentioned before we proceed. In the above calculations, interest was stated at an annual rate and paid once per year. Interest on bonds is normally paid semi-annually. Therefore, when applying present value concepts, we need to double the number of periods and divide the interest rate by two.

Using our $100,000 bond issue with 10% interest payable semi-annually over the next 5 years, we provide the following:

$$\text{Interest payments} = \$100,000 \times 5\% \ (10\% \times \tfrac{1}{2}) = \$5,000$$
$$\text{Number of Periods} = 5 \times 2 = 10$$

The present value of the $100,000 principal repayment is:

$$\$100,000 \times 0.6139 = \$61,390$$

5%	
Periods	**Factor**
1	0.9524
2	0.9070
3	0.8638
4	0.8227
5	0.7835
6	0.7462
7	0.7107
8	0.6768
9	0.6446
10	0.6139

Excerpt from Present Value of Annuity table.

FIGURE 14.4

The interest payments are different from the principal repayment in that they represent an **annuity** because they are periodic and recurring fixed payments. To calculate the present value of the interest payment annuity, we can use one of two methods:

1. We can calculate, individually, the present value of each interest payment. For example, we take the first interest payment of $5,000 in 6 months and multiply it by the 6-month factor to determine the present value of that particular payment. To this amount, we then add the second $5,000 payment in 12 months and multiply it by the 12-month factor. After this, we then add the third $5,000 payment in 18 months and multiply it by the 18-month factor. This goes on for all ten interest payments. As you can see, this can get tedious and is prone to error. For a 5-year bond, we would have to repeat this calculation 10 times (once for each interest payment) to determine the present value of all the interest payments.

2. Fortunately, annuities are a common occurrence in the financial industry and, so, tables containing factors for annuities, in particular, have been developed (see figure 14.5). Using this table, we can calculate the present value of ALL interest payments in just one calculation.

Calculate the present value of the future interest payments:

Present value of $5,000 payments (annuity) made over 10 periods
= $5,000 x 7.7217 = $38,608.50 (round to $38,610)

5%

Periods	Factor
1	0.9524
2	1.8594
3	2.7232
4	3.5460
5	4.3295
6	5.0757
7	5.7864
8	6.4632
9	7.1078
10	7.7217

FIGURE 14.5

Summary

Present value of principal	= $61,390
Present value of interest payments	= $38,610
Total proceeds	$100,000

Note: the present value of the interest payments is rounded to $38,610 for illustrative purposes.

You will notice that the interest payment value was rounded so the total would equal $100,000. This is because the tables show rounded factors. A spreadsheet or financial calculator with the present value function would not require rounding. This text will use the tables provided at the end of the chapter for illustration and exercise purposes. If you use a spreadsheet or financial calculator, your figure may be slightly different.

It is important to note that the present value of the principal and the interest payments equal the face value of the bond ($100,000). This occurred because we have discounted the 5% bond using the 5% interest rate. This shows that the face value of the bond is equal to the present value of the payments when the market rate is equal to the interest rate of the bond.

Issuing Bonds at Par

Business Time Inc., a publisher of investment-related books, magazines and newspapers, wants to raise money for long-term financing by issuing bonds. On December 31, 2009, the company issues 1,000, 10-year bonds at par at a price of $100 each with 5% annual interest. Here is how the transaction is recorded by the company's accountant:

JOURNAL			
Date	Account Title and Explanation	Debit	Credit
Dec 31	Cash	100,000	
	Bonds Payable		100,000
	Issue of $100,000 worth of bonds at par (due in 2019)		

FIGURE 14.6

The total amount of $100,000 is debited in the cash account. A corresponding liability on the other side of the balance sheet involves a credit increase of $100,000 in the bonds payable account. Since the principal for the bonds is due in 10 years, the liability is classified as long term and placed in that section of the balance sheet.

Issuing the bond for a 10-year term means that a company will have to make interest payments to its bondholders every year for 10 years. Most bonds call for semi-annual (twice per year) interest payments. For the sake of simplicity, we will assume interest is paid annually in this illustration.

A $5,000 credit represents a decrease in cash, while a $5,000 debit represents an increase in interest expense.

During the 10-year term that Business Time Inc. is making interest payments to its bondholders, the year-end may occur before the payment is made. A portion of the payment may be due, but the interest is actually paid in the following period.

JOURNAL			
Date	**Account Title and Explanation**	**Debit**	**Credit**
Dec 31	Interest Expense	5,000	
	Cash		5,000
	Record interest on bonds ($100,000 × 5%)		

The company is, therefore, required to expense the interest during the period in which it was incurred; this is regarded as an accrual and represents a decrease in the company's equity for the period. According to the matching principle, this keeps the company's books in good standing until the payment is made in the following period.

FIGURE 14.7

The previous journal entry was made on the anniversary date of the bond. Assume for a moment that the company's year end is October 31, but the bond anniversary date is December 31. On October 31, when the company prepares its financial statements, it will accrue only 10/12 of the annual interest:

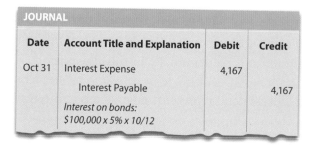

JOURNAL			
Date	Account Title and Explanation	Debit	Credit
Oct 31	Interest Expense	4,167	
	Interest Payable		4,167
	Interest on bonds: $100,000 x 5% x 10/12		

FIGURE 14.8

As with the other interest payments on the bond, $4,167 is expensed as a debit (increase) to bond interest on October 31. However, unlike the previous transaction, interest payable (accrued liabilities) is credited instead of cash.

Continuing the above example, when interest is paid on December 31, the payment should be recorded with the following entry:

JOURNAL			
Date	Account Title and Explanation	Debit	Credit
Dec 31	Interest Expense	833	
	Interest Payable	4,167	
	Cash		5,000
	Interest on bonds: $100,000 x 5%		

The logic of the transaction:

1. Cash was paid to the bondholder for $5,000.

2. The $833 applied against this period means that it is considered to be an expense in this period.

3. However, the $4,167 amount belongs to the previous period, so it cannot be regarded as an expense at this time, even though it is being paid now. It therefore needs to be recorded as a debit to accrued liabilities.

FIGURE 14.9

There is another principle involved in making annual interest payments on bonds: on the first day of every year, the company knows that interest payments will be due before the end of the year. Therefore, that year's interest payable gets classified as a current liability.

On the other hand the original principal (which will be paid back at the end of the 10-year term of the bond), is classified as a long-term liability by the company. This is like a 10-year term loan where you only pay the interest.

We have demonstrated how a bond issue is treated *at par*. However, the period from the time that a business decides to issue the bonds to the time they are printed for distribution can be several months. In the meantime, the market rate is likely to have changed. This means that the interest rate on the bond may end up being higher – or lower – than that of the market. This will affect the demand for the company's bonds. The price of the bond must, therefore, be adjusted accordingly.

A bond's **face value** is the price at which it was originally sold and is printed on the face of the bond. Another way of putting it is that the face value is the same as the principal. The principal amount gets paid back to the bondholder, regardless of any changes in market price. In other words, *regardless of the price paid for the bond*, the business needs to pay the full face value of the bond to the bondholder when payment is due.

However, the market value and the face value of a bond are not always the same. There are two scenarios to consider when such situations occur.

Scenario 1: Market value is less than face value. The bond will be sold at a discount.

Scenario 2: Market value is more than face value. The bond will be sold at a premium.

Issuing Bonds at a Discount

Continuing with our Business Time Inc. bond issue when the bonds were sold at par (or face value), the resulting transaction was relatively simple. The company received a lump sum of $100,000 and established a bonds payable for that same amount.

Things change somewhat when market interest rates rise above the interest rate attached to the bond. When that happens, investors can receive higher interest payments from other bonds and market investments.

To deter investors from those other investments and to attract them to Business Time's bonds, the company should offer the bonds at a more attractive price – at a **discount**.

But what should that discount price be? The answer is logical. The company sets a discount price which compensates the investor for the money lost with the bond's lower interest rate. Here is a demonstration of how this is done.

We know that the interest rate on the Business Time bonds is 5%. The principal is $100,000, which means that the annual interest payment is $5,000. Payment of the full amount of principal, or face value of the bond, returns a yield of 5%.

However, when the market rate is 6%, receiving a yield of 5% is not high enough to attract investors. In that case, the company must essentially lower the price of the bond to below face value so that the buyer can get an effective interest rate of 6%. It is important to understand that the buyer still expects to get $100,000 for the bond when it matures plus the $5,000 interest in the last year regardless of what was paid. Using the same present value concepts as shown above, here is how the price of the bond is determined:

> Note: Use table 14-1 and table 14-2 at the end of the chapter for factors used in the following calculations.

Present value of the principal = $100,000 x 0.5584 = $55,840
(Market interest rate of 6%, 10 periods)

Present value of future interest payments =$5,000 x 7.3601 = $36,800
(6% interest, 10 periods)

Total price bondholders are willing to pay for their investment = $55,840 + $36,800 = $92,640

The price investors are willing to pay is lower than the par value because the market rate is 6%, meaning the investors can easily get return higher than 5% elsewhere in the market. Therefore, the price they are willing to pay will be lower.

The difference between the price paid and the par value is known as the *discount*.

Here is how the receipt of $92,640 for the issue of Business Time Inc. bonds (at discount), is entered into the company's books using a contra account:

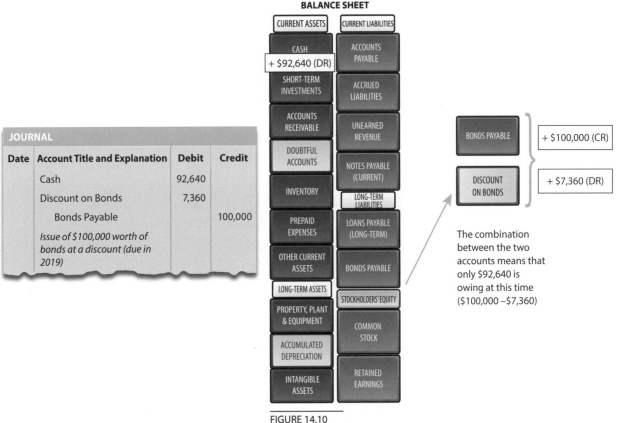

FIGURE 14.10

Here is the logic behind the entry:

1. The business deposits $92,640 instead of $100,000, due to the discount. This is recorded by debiting cash.

2. Though only $92,640 was paid by the bondholder, the full amount of $100,000 must be paid when the bond matures in 10 years. Therefore, $100,000 must be regarded as a long-term liability. This is recorded by crediting bonds payable (a long-term liability).

Consider the following possibilities of recording the discount:

a. Debit an asset: This is not possible since there is no future benefit associated with the discount.

b. Debit an expense: This is incorrect because the discount pertains to the 10 year term of the bond so expensing immediately would violate the time period concept. The discount, in fact, should be amortized over the term of the bond.

c. Solution: Debit a contra liability account called discount on bonds, and amortize the discount as an expense over the life of the bond (refer to the Accounting Map™ above).

The discount is amortized (using the straight-line method) and added to interest expense each year. At the end of 10 years, the discount on the bond will be cleared to a zero balance. The principle involved is very similar to amortizing the purchase price of property, plant and equipment, a concept we discussed in a previous chapter, which is why a discount on a bond is also amortized over the life of the bond. In this example, the discount will be amortized at $7,360 ÷ 10 = $736 per year.

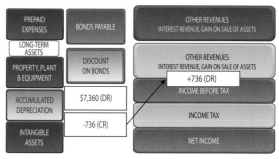

Journal entry each year when amortizing the discount

FIGURE 14.11

Each year, the company that issues the bond will pay $5,000 interest on the bond (in cash to the bondholder). The amortization of the discount of $736 is just a book entry; the total expense related to the bond for the period is $5,736.

JOURNAL			
Date	Account Title and Explanation	Debit	Credit
	Interest Expense	5,736	
	Discount on Bonds		736
	Cash		5,000
	Record interest and the depreciation of the discount for the current year.		

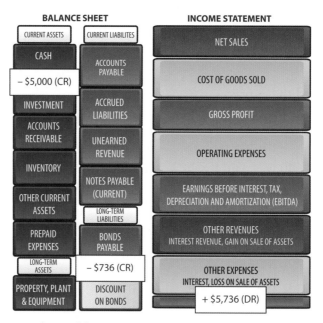

$5,000 of the expense is cash and the balance relates to the depreciation of the discount (not cash)

FIGURE 14.12

Over the period of 10 years, the journal entry shown in figure 14.12 will be repeated. As this happens, the value of the discount on the bonds will decrease and the book value (or carrying value) of the bond will increase. By the end of the 10 years, the discount will be reduced to zero and the book value of the bond will be the face value, $100,000. Figure 14.13 shows an amortization table of the bond for 10 years. Notice how the discount balance decreases while the bond book value increases.

Year	A Interest Payment ($100,000 × 5%)	B Discount Amortization (D / 10 years)	C Interest Expense (A + B)	D Discount Balance (D [Previous Year] – B)	E Bond Book Value ($100,000 – D)
0				7,360	92,640
1	5,000	736	5,736	6,624	93,376
2	5,000	736	5,736	5,888	94,112
3	5,000	736	5,736	5,152	94,848
4	5,000	736	5,736	4,416	95,584
5	5,000	736	5,736	3,680	96,320
6	5,000	736	5,736	2,944	97,056
7	5,000	736	5,736	2,208	97,792
8	5,000	736	5,736	1,472	98,528
9	5,000	736	5,736	736	99,264
10	5,000	736	5,736	0	100,000

FIGURE 14.13

FIGURE 14.14

At the end of the 10-year term, cash is credited in the amount of $100,000, and the same amount is debited to long-term debt, thereby clearing the liability. Any outstanding interest payments will be included with this final payment. The journal entry is presented as shown below:

JOURNAL			
Date	Account Title and Explanation	Debit	Credit
	Bonds Payable	100,000	
	Cash		100,000
	Repay $100,000 to bondholder		

Issuing Bonds at a Premium

We have already discussed why companies issue bonds at a discount. The higher market interest rate makes the bond's interest rate less competitive, so the selling price is reduced to make up the difference with potential investors.

Of course, there is a flip side to that scenario. By the time a company's bond issue reaches the market, the market interest rate may decline. This means that the bond's interest rate would be higher than that of the market, and produce a higher rate of return for an investor than what the market is currently offering. This creates a greater demand for the company's bond, which means the company can now sell the bond at a premium (at a price that is higher than its face value).

IN THE REAL WORLD

When using the straight-line method of amortization, the calculation doesn't necessarily produce a result that accurately reflects the changes over time in the value of an item. This is true with regard to the value of assets, and is also true with regard to the value of bonds issued at a discount or premium.

In the real world, accountants often use a method which applies a fixed interest rate to the changing value of a bond, which more accurately reflects the way that bond issues work. This is often called the Effective Interest Method of Amortization. The interest rate used is seen as a reflection of market rates in general. The changing value of the bond reflects the fact that the carrying value (or value incorporating amortization on the books) changes, even though the bond's face value remains the same.

At this level of accounting, it is not necessary to know all the details. What students should know, however, is that amortization schedules for bond discounts and premiums can get complicated. For now, the straight-line method introduces us to bond amortization. Future courses will expand on how other methods are used to more accurately reflect the value of a bond issue.

A company that issues bonds at a premium takes the same steps in recording the transaction as it would with a discount, except in reverse. Let us review those steps with an example using the Business Time Inc. publishing company again.

The interest rate for Business Time Inc. bonds is 5%. A market rate of 5% meant that the bonds could be issued at par. A market rate of 6% meant that the bonds were issued at discount. What happens when the market rate is 4%?

> Note: Use table 14-1 and table 14-2 at the end of the chapter for factors used in the following calculations.

Present value of the principal = $100,000 x 0.6756 = $67,560
(Market interest rate of 4%, 10 periods)

Present value of future interest payments =$5,000 x 8.1109 = $40,555
(4% interest, 10 periods)

Total price bondholders are willing to pay for their investment =
$67,560 + $40,555 = $108,115

The price investors are willing to pay is higher than the par value because the market rate is 4%, meaning it is difficult for investors to get return higher than 5% elsewhere in the market. Therefore, the price they are willing to pay will be higher.

This is how this bond issue is recorded on the company's books:

JOURNAL

Date	Account Title and Explanation	Debit	Credit
	Cash	108,115	
	Premium on Bonds		8,115
	Bonds Payable		100,000
	Issue of $100,000 worth of bonds at a premium (due in 2019)		

FIGURE 14.15

BALANCE SHEET

CURRENT ASSETS	CURRENT LIABILITIES
CASH **+ $108,115 (DR)**	ACCOUNTS PAYABLE
SHORT-TERM INVESTMENTS	ACCRUED LIABILITIES
ACCOUNTS RECEIVABLE	UNEARNED REVENUE
DOUBTFUL ACCOUNTS	NOTES PAYABLE (CURRENT)
INVENTORY	LONG-TERM LIABILITIES
PREPAID EXPENSES	LOANS PAYABLE (LONG-TERM)
OTHER CURRENT ASSETS	BONDS PAYABLE **+ $100,000 (CR)**
LONG-TERM ASSETS	PREMIUM ON **+ $8,115 (CR)**
PROPERTY, PLANT & EQUIPMENT	

As always, proceeds from the sale are deposited and recorded as a debit to the cash account. On the other side of the balance sheet, the principal amount of the bond ($100,000) is credited to bonds payable (a long-term liability) account. Finally, the premium on the bond of $8,115 is recorded as a credit in an account called premium on bonds. Premium on bonds appears directly below the bonds payable account on the balance sheet. So far, there is no change to equity; therefore the income statement is not impacted.

Unlike the discount on a bond, which is recorded in a contra liability account, the premium is recorded in a separate liability account. Since it is credited, it represents an amount owing. Intuitively you may think that because a discount is considered as an expense, why should a premium not be regarded as revenue? A discount is an increase to an expense (DR) and the premium simply offsets the same account and decreases the expense (CR).

Similar to a discount on a bond issue, a premium must be amortized as periodic interest payments are made. In other words, the premium liability of $8,115 should be amortized over the term of the bond. Using the straight-line method again, this amount comes to $8,115 ÷ 10 = $812 (rounded). Therefore, $812 is debited to premium on bonds every year until the amount is zero upon maturity of the bond.

Here is how that transaction would be recorded each year if the straight-line method is used:

The $5,000 interest payment is recorded each year, and is represented by a credit to cash. The expense to the company is now only $4,188 and the rest of the debit is taken care of by the $812 annual amortization of the premium calculated using the straight-line method.

JOURNAL			
Date	Account Title and Explanation	Debit	Credit
	Interest Expense	4,188	
	Premium on Bonds	812	
	Cash		5,000
	Payment of interest and depreciation of premium 1/10 x 8,155		

FIGURE 14.16

When financial statements are prepared, the premium on bonds is added to the face value of the bonds. The balance sheet would look like this at the end of the first year, after 1/10 of the premium had been applied:

Bonds payable	$100,000
Added: unamortized premium	7,303
Book value	$107,303

FIGURE 14.17

At the end of 10 years, the company will only pay the bondholder $100,000 instead of the $108,115 that was originally received.

Over the period of 10 years, the journal entry shown in figure 14.16 will be repeated. As this happens, the value of the premium on the bonds will decrease and the book value (or carrying value) of the bond will decrease. By the end of the 10 years, the premium will be reduced to zero and the book value of the bond will be the face value, $100,000. Figure 14.18 shows an amortization table of the bond for 10 years. Notice how the premium balance and the bond book value decrease.

Year	A Interest Payment ($100,000 x 5%)	B Premium Amortization (D / 10 years)	C Interest Expense (A - B)	D Premium Balance (D [Previous Year] - B)	E Bond Book Value ($100,000 + D)
0				8,115	108,115
1	5,000	812	4,188	7,303	107,303
2	5,000	812	4,188	6,491	106,491
3	5,000	812	4,188	5,679	105,679
4	5,000	812	4,188	4,867	104,867
5	5,000	812	4,188	4,055	104,055
6	5,000	812	4,188	3,243	103,243
7	5,000	812	4,188	2,431	102,431
8	5,000	812	4,188	1,619	101,619
9	5,000	812	4,188	807	100,807
10	5,000	807*	4,193	0	100,000

*$807 is due to rounding

FIGURE 14.18

Retiring Bonds

Regardless of the price at which a bond was issued, whether at par, discount or premium, the underlying terms of the bond remain the same. That means that an interest payment is made every year according to the rate on the bond. It also means that the principal amount is paid back in full. In other words, the original investor essentially loans the issuing company the principal amount.

When the bond matures, that principal amount is paid back to the current owner of the bond. This transaction is also referred to as *redeeming* the bond, or buying it back. At a basic level, it is nothing more than paying back the original amount loaned to the company.

Using our example of Business Time Inc. bonds at par, discount, or premium, this is how the final bond redemption is recorded:

| JOURNAL | | | |
Date	Account Title and Explanation	Debit	Credit
	Bonds Payable	100,000	
	Cash		100,000
	Redemption of $100,000 worth of bonds at par due in 2019		

FIGURE 14.19

Cash is credited in the amount of $100,000. The original bonds payable, created 10 years earlier at the time of bond issue, is finally taken off the books with a $100,000 debit to that account.

This transaction takes care of the redemption of the bond. However, a company sometimes issues what are known as **callable bonds**. These give the issuing company the option to buy back the bonds before the stated maturity date. The issuer might want to do this to take advantage of lower market interest rates, which would allow for the issuance of new bonds to match those lower rates. In other words, the company could now make lower annual payments on its bonds.

We have just demonstrated how bond redemption is recorded. You may realize that there is another issue that needs to be resolved when a bond is redeemed before maturity. The issue is that any remaining discount or premium must also be removed from the books. We will stay with our Business Time Inc. bonds example to see how this is achieved.

Consider our earlier example of Business Time Inc. bonds which were issued at a discount. If the company was to exercise a call option on the bonds at the end of 2017 (which includes 8 years of paid interest), the unamortized discount would amount to:

$$\$7,360 - [8 \times (\$736)] = \$1,472$$

This is how the transaction would be recorded:

JOURNAL			
Date	**Account Title and Explanation**	**Debit**	**Credit**
	Bonds payable	100,000	
	Discount on Bonds		1,472
	Cash		98,528
	Redemption of $100,000 worth of bonds at par due in 2019		

FIGURE 14.20

The cash payment of $98,528 represents the fair value paid to the present bondholders. This involves removing both the bonds payable and the discount on bonds accounts off the books. The transaction is recorded by debiting bonds payable of $100,000, crediting discount on bonds with $1,472 and crediting cash by $98,528. The $1,472 amount is what was left in the discount account after annual credits of $736 have been applied to amortize the initial amount.

If we use the bonds which were issued at a premium, then the same type of transaction would take place, except that a debit would be recorded to the premium on bonds to close the account.

Financial Ratios Related to Liabilities

Debt-to-Total Assets Ratio

Debt-to-total-assets ratio measures how much of a company's assets are financed through total liabilities. The higher the ratio, the greater the difficulty a company will have in repaying its creditors. A high debt-to-total assets ratio indicates that the company is at a greater risk of being unable to meet debt obligations. On the other hand, a low debt-to-total assets ratio is desirable to creditors.

Debt-to-Equity Ratio

Debt-to-equity ratio is used to assess how much of a company is being financed by lenders, and how much is being financed by the owners or stockholders. In other words, it measures the extent to which a business is indebted to lenders. Generally, owners or stockholders are expected to take a higher risk than lenders.

Ideally, a business should have a debt-to-equity ratio of 1:2. In other words, the company has $1 of debt for every $2 of equity. Like other ratios, though, make note that the debt-to-equity ratio must be compared to industry benchmarks to draw sound conclusions.

Controls Related to Long-Term Liabilities

Controls related to balance sheet items should include:

- Hiring qualified staff to handle transactions accurately
- Compliance with all relevant policies, plans, procedures, laws and regulations
- Setting appropriate goals and objectives that are reviewed regularly for proper implementation

Although liabilities are different from assets, the controls for both tend to mirror each other since both involve an exchange of money. With regard to loans, this means that all documents pertaining to the loan should be reviewed by legal counsel. Strong controls surrounding the negotiation of long-term liabilities should result in obtaining the best possible interest rates. The lower interest rates will increase cash flow which can be used in the operating activities of the business.

In addition, robust cash controls ensure that interest and principal payments are made on time. Other controls include verifying that interest and principal payments have been received by lenders.

An Ethical Approach to Long-Term Liabilities

We will now examine ethical violations related to long-term liabilities.

Companies assume long-term liabilities to finance large items and projects that often take years to complete. This type of financing usually takes the form of term loans and bond issues. The sheer magnitude of these transactions makes them vulnerable to abuse.

First, where large sums are concerned, management is usually closely involved. This level of company operations often has fewer internal controls, so those in place must be thorough and complete. They should include reviews by top-level executives and audits performed both internally and externally.

One cannot assume that individuals will not be tempted when dealing with large amounts of money that could possibly be siphoned off or redirected by clever

IN THE REAL WORLD

 In the fall of 2008, the world was hit by the worst financial crisis since the Depression. In a nutshell, global financial institutions had too much money invested in bad credit, especially sub-prime mortgages. The economy started to slow down when these bad debts went unpaid and the credit market crashed as a result.

In the aftermath of the crash, leading financial minds started looking for solutions to problems that had gone unsolved for years. Although many experts looked for ways to better regulate the markets, some analysts started pointing fingers at the accounting profession.

Specifically, a long-running criticism of accounting standards is that they do not require an appropriate level of disclosure. A perfect example of this is off-balance-sheet financing - the practice of keeping some forms of long-term financing off the company books.

Another example of poor disclosure practices comes in the form of reporting pension fund assets and liabilities only in footnote form. Recent standards are now forcing companies to disclose a net amount on the balance sheet itself.

Critics of the accounting profession believe that it is only through fair and open reporting that companies can gain the trust of investment markets in general. How can companies expect people to trust them with money if they are not fully open about what is reported in the financial statements?

Open and fair accounting practices can help bring back some stability and trust in world markets at a time when it is most needed.

fraudsters. Staying alert and attentive to these risks is one of the primary responsibilities of those who own and run the company.

Second, it is always necessary to be vigilant with transactions conducted with financial institutions, where the possibility of unauthorized commissions may exist. That is, some part of the loan money might end up in the hands of individuals who work out a side deal for themselves. That is why it is always important for companies to keep track of all the money.

Finally, another type of fraud related to a company's long-term liabilities involves something called off-balance sheet financing. Some businesses engage in accounting practices that keep some large financing schemes off the books. Examples include joint ventures, research and development partnerships and operating leases.

The practice of off-balance sheet financing allows a business to keep its debt to equity and leverage ratios low, which might artificially inflate share prices by overstating a company's equity position.

Operating leases were once a common example of off-balance sheet financing. Instead of owning the asset in question, a company could lease it and simply expense any rental fees involved. Accounting rules have been changed so that the leases, depending on their terms, are actually treated as a form of financing. This forces the company to record an asset and the accompanying liability to their balance sheet. This in turn increases their debt-to-equity ratio and gives users of their financial statements a more accurate picture of the company's financial position.

In Summary

- A company usually has two basic options when it comes to long-term financing: bank loans and bond issues.
- A current year's payable amount for a term loan is listed in the current liabilities section of the balance sheet, while the balance of the amount payable is listed under long-term liabilities.
- When a company needs a source of long-term financing other than a bank loan, one option would be a bond issue. A bond is a contract that a company establishes with an investor. The investor provides principal loan to the issuing company. In return, the company makes interest payments to the investor, in addition to eventually repaying the principal.
- When the bond rate equals the market rate, the company can sell the bond at par.
- When the bond rate is lower than the market rate, the company sells the bond at a discount.
- When the bond rate is higher than the market rate, the company can sell the bond at a premium.
- Both the discount and premium attached to the bond price should be amortized over the term of the bond until maturity.
- When the bond reaches maturity, it is time for the issuing company to repay the principal to whoever holds the bond at the time. This is also called redemption. The issuing company may have the option to redeem a bond early. Such securities are referred to as callable bonds.
- The time value of money involves the principle that interest attached to an investment compounds the rate of increase in the value of the investment. That is why it is called compound interest. This principle is important for accountants when breaking down amounts to be paid on loans and other long-term liabilities.
- Future value determines the value of an investment in the future if an amount is invested today. Present value determines the amount invested today to produce a certain amount in the future.
- Debt-to-total-assets ratio measures how much of a company's assets are financed through debt. Debt-to-equity ratio is used to assess how much of a company is being financed by lenders, and how much is being financed by the owners or stockholders.
- Controls related to long-term liabilities should ensure that all documents are in order and that cash flow planning accommodates future payments for loans and bonds.
- Ethics related to long-term liabilities should ensure the integrity of large amounts of cash that upper management has the responsibility of handling. Unauthorized commissions are always a risk when dealing with financial institutions. Off-balance-sheet financing is also a practice that can skew the way in which company finances are reported to the public.

Table 14-1

Present Value of $1

Periods	1%	2%	3%	4%	5%	6%
1	0.9901	0.9804	0.9709	0.9615	0.9524	0.9434
2	0.9803	0.9612	0.9426	0.9246	0.9070	0.8900
3	0.9706	0.9423	0.9151	0.8890	0.8638	0.8396
4	0.9610	0.9238	0.8885	0.8548	0.8227	0.7921
5	0.9515	0.9057	0.8626	0.8219	0.7835	0.7473
6	0.9420	0.8880	0.8375	0.7903	0.7462	0.7050
7	0.9327	0.8706	0.8131	0.7599	0.7107	0.6651
8	0.9235	0.8535	0.7894	0.7307	0.6768	0.6274
9	0.9143	0.8368	0.7664	0.7026	0.6446	0.5919
10	0.9053	0.8203	0.7441	0.6756	0.6139	0.5584
11	0.8963	0.8043	0.7224	0.6496	0.5847	0.5268
12	0.8874	0.7885	0.7014	0.6246	0.5568	0.4970
13	0.8787	0.7730	0.6810	0.6006	0.5303	0.4688
14	0.8700	0.7579	0.6611	0.5775	0.5051	0.4423
15	0.8613	0.7430	0.6419	0.5553	0.4810	0.4173

Table 14-2

Present Value of Annuity $1

Periods	1%	2%	3%	4%	5%	6%
1	0.9901	0.9804	0.9709	0.9615	0.9524	0.9434
2	1.9704	1.9416	1.9135	1.8861	1.8594	1.8334
3	2.9410	2.8839	2.8286	2.7751	2.7232	2.6730
4	3.9020	3.8077	3.7171	3.6299	3.5460	3.4651
5	4.8534	4.7135	4.5797	4.4518	4.3295	4.2124
6	5.7955	5.6014	5.4172	5.2421	5.0757	4.9173
7	6.7282	6.4720	6.2303	6.0021	5.7864	5.5824
8	7.6517	7.3255	7.0197	6.7327	6.4632	6.2098
9	8.5660	8.1622	7.7861	7.4353	7.1078	6.8017
10	9.4713	8.9826	8.5302	8.1109	7.7217	7.3601
11	10.3676	9.7868	9.2526	8.7605	8.3064	7.8869
12	11.2551	10.5753	9.9540	9.3851	8.8633	8.3838
13	12.1337	11.3484	10.6350	9.9856	9.3936	8.8527
14	13.0037	12.1062	11.2961	10.5631	9.8986	9.2950
15	13.8651	12.8493	11.9379	11.1184	10.3797	9.7122

Review Exercise

Hohl Company is planning to expand its facilities by constructing a new building, and installing new machines. In order to complete this project, the company has decided to issue $2,000,000 worth of 20-year 4% callable bonds, with interest paid every six months.

On April 1, the company completed all the necessary paperwork, and is now ready to issue the bonds. Fortunately, just as Hohl Company was issuing its bonds, the current market rate dropped to 3.5%. Their financial advisor recommended issuing the bonds at a premium of $142,124.

On March 31 of year 10, interest rates dropped to 2%. At this point, the company issues $2,200,000 of 10-year 2% bonds at par to redeem all outstanding 3.5% bonds.

Required

a) Record the journal entry for the issuance of bonds on April 1, year 1.

b) Record the payment of interest on September 30.

c) Record any required journal entries as of the company year-end, February 28, year 2. Note that the company pays interest semi-annually.

d) Record journal entries for retirement of the 3.5% bonds and issue of new 2% bonds.

e) Record the first interest payment on the 2% bonds.

Review Exercise – Answer

Premium bond price = 2,000,000 + 142,124 = 2,142,124

Date	Account Title and Explanation	Debit	Credit
Apr 1 yr. 1	Cash	2,142,124	
	Premium on Bonds		142,124
	Bonds Payable		2,000,000
	Issue of $2 million worth of bonds at a		
	premium, due in 20 years		
Sep 30 yr. 1	Interest Expense	36,447	
	Premium on Bonds	3,553	
	Cash		40,000
	Payment of interest and amortization of		
	premium $142,124 ÷ 20 × ½ = $3,553		
	$2,000,000 × 4% × 6/12 = $40,000		
Feb 28 yr. 2	Interest Expense	30,372	
	Premium on Bonds	2,961	
	Accrued Interest		33,333
	To recognize accrued interest at year-end		
	$2,000,000 × 4% × 5/12 = $33,333		
	$142,124 ÷ 20 × 5/12 = $2,961		
Mar 31 yr. 10	Cash	2,200,000	
	Bonds Payable		2,200,000
	Issuance of new bonds		
Mar 31 yr. 10	Bonds Payable	2,000,000	
	Premium on Bonds	71,062	
	Cash		2,071,062
	Redemption of bonds		
Sep 30 yr. 10	Interest Expense	22,000	
	Cash		22,000
	To record interest		
	$2,200,000 × 2% × 6/12 = $22,000		

Chapter 15
PARTNERSHIPS

LEARNING OUTCOMES:

❶ Describe the advantages and disadvantages of a partnership

❷ Understand different types of partnerships

❸ Record the formation of a partnership

❹ Record the division of income or loss and partners' drawings

❺ Account for the addition or withdrawal of a partner

❻ Record the liquidation of a partnership

Proprietorships, Partnerships and Corporations

There are three primary options for structuring the ownership of a business:

1. In a proprietorship, only one person owns the business and keeps all the earnings, which are taxed at the personal level. The owner is personally responsible for all the liabilities of the business. This means that if creditors are looking for payment, they will pursue the owner's personal assets.

2. A **partnership** is an association of two or more people who jointly own a business, its assets and liabilities, and share in its gains or losses; earnings are taxed personally. Some partners may be brought in for their technical expertise and others for their ability to raise capital.

3. In a corporation, there can be a large number of owners known as *stockholders*, many of whom may not participate in the running of the business. A corporation has many rights and duties, because it is a legal entity distinct from its owners. All earnings are taxed at the corporate level when they are earned and at the personal level when dividends are distributed to stockholders. Corporations can raise funds from the general public by issuing stock. The *stockholders* (owners) of a corporation are not personally responsible for the company's debt, and are only responsible for paying any unpaid amount owing on their stock.

In most of the examples in this book, we have focused primarily on proprietorships and corporations. In this chapter we will examine the characteristics of partnerships in detail.

We now turn our attention to the partnership form of business as we demonstrate the effect of transactions and financial reporting on the asset, liability and owners' equity accounts and how various accounting principles are applied.

If a corporation were to sell all its assets and pay its debt, the remaining cash would be divided amongst all the stockholders, according to how many shares of stock they own.

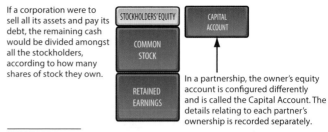

In a partnership, the owner's equity account is configured differently and is called the Capital Account. The details relating to each partner's ownership is recorded separately.

FIGURE 15.1

Advantages and Disadvantages of Partnerships

Many professional businesses are structured as partnerships, such as consulting firms, law firms and accounting firms. In addition to the characteristics listed above, certain advantages and disadvantages are associated with conducting a business as a partnership.

Advantages

Instead of one person owning and operating a business as is the case with a proprietorship, a partnership involves two or more people combining resources, both human and financial. This provides two advantages. First, the combination of human resources means that the business should benefit from the skills and experience of each partner. To illustrate, assume two lawyers, Helen White and Greg Harris decide to form the partnership White & Harris, Attorneys at Law. Helen specializes in family law and Greg specializes in criminal law. Together they are able to service twice as many clients in two different areas of law. Second, due to their combined financial resources, they are more likely than a proprietorship to be able to provide sufficient cash flow to the business without having to rely on external financing.

Another advantage of the partnership form of business is the relative ease of formation. A partnership can be formed with a simple handshake; however, most partnerships employ the services of a lawyer to have a partnership agreement drawn up to formalize the arrangement for sharing profits and losses and for other eventualities such as the addition or withdrawal of a partner or terminating the partnership.

Some contend that there is also an income tax advantage to the partnership form of business in that the partnership itself does not pay income tax. Any income or loss is taxed in the hands of the partners personally. This means that while a partnership does need to file a separate tax return, it does not pay tax as an organization. The partners are responsible for paying the tax individually.

Disadvantages

Perhaps the most serious disadvantage of the partnership form of business is the fact that each partner is responsible for the liabilities of the business; this is referred to as having *unlimited liability.* Let us assume that Partner A has no personal assets other than what she invested in the partnership. Partner B, on the other hand, owns his own home, a rental property, a cottage, a sailboat and several valuable paintings. The business suffered losses for several years and was then sued by a dissatisfied client for $1.5 million. As the partnership has very little remaining cash or assets, the partners were personally liable for the $1.5 million liability. Since Partner A had no assets, Partner B, because of unlimited liability, was required to pay the debt on behalf of the partnership.

Other disadvantages include the limited life of a partnership, which means that changes would have to be made for accounting and income tax purposes if any of the following events were to occur: death of one of the partners, bankruptcy or the addition or withdrawal of a partner. Another disadvantage is mutual agency – that is, each partner can authorize contracts and transactions on behalf of the partnership provided the activity is within the scope of the partnership's business. This is viewed as a disadvantage because it places the other partners at risk if the authorizing partner does not act in the best interests of the partnership.

Characteristics	Proprietorship	Partnership
# of owners	One	Two or more
Control	Owner has complete control	Decisions are shared among partners, with possibility of disagreement and conflict
Raising capital	Small - since only one person raising money	Larger - since more than one person is responsible for raising money
Earnings	Proprietor receives 100% of earnings	Partners share earnings in proportion to terms of the partnership agreement
Formation	Relatively simple to set up	Simple to set up, but details require close attention
Liability	Proprietor is responsible for all debts and/or legal obligations	Partners are responsible jointly and individually for actions of other partners
Skills	Reliance on the skills of the proprietor alone	Partners offer different skills in various areas of the business
Dissolution	Relatively simple to dissolve	May be dissolved upon death or withdrawal of a partner - partnership has limited life
Taxation	Earnings are taxed whether or not cash is withdrawn from the business	Partners share earnings and are taxed whether or not cash is withdrawn

FIGURE 15.2

Types of Partnerships

General Partnership

A general partnership means that all partners share the responsibility for the liabilities of the business – that is, they have unlimited liability.

Limited Partnership

Businesses sometimes find themselves in the position of being legally obligated to pay other parties a considerable amount of money. These obligations can take the form of debt owed to creditors or financial sums awarded to other parties in a lawsuit. In other words, a business is liable to others for its actions. Proprietorships and partnerships generally extend unlimited liability to all the owners of the business. Unlimited liability in a partnership can be particularly damaging because if one partner is unable to meet liability obligations that are related to the partnership, the other partners are obliged to pay. This could mean having to sell off personal assets such as houses, cars and cottages. Limited partnerships resolve the potential problem of unlimited liability by creating two categories of partners within the business: the **general partner** and the **limited partner**.

Unlimited liability is assigned to a general partner, who is responsible for the day-to-day operations of the business and is legally responsible for decisions made on behalf of the business.

Limited liability is assigned to a limited partner, who is responsible only for providing the capital to finance the business. This partner should not be involved in day-to-day operations and is therefore not considered liable for decisions made by the business that can lead to a liability. As a result, limited partners are liable only for the amount they have invested in the business.

Limited Liability Partnership

Another business legal entity – the **limited liability partnership** or **LLP** – has been developed in some jurisdictions to deal with liability. Unlike in a limited partnership, the limited partners usually participate in managing the business. LLPs are primarily used in professional partnerships to protect one partner from another partner's negligence. For example, if a lawyer is sued for negligence, other lawyers in the firm are not automatically considered liable; however, as was indicated in limited partnerships, partners usually cannot escape liability entirely. In the case of LLPs, this means that all partners are still liable for any unpaid debts to creditors. Although the details of an LLP will vary from state to state, generally an LLP can protect partners from some forms of liability, but not all.

Formation of a Partnership

Once a decision has been made to form a partnership, the next step is to record the initial journal entries to set up the asset, liability and equity accounts. The partners may have assets (other than cash) and liabilities that they would like to bring into the business. An independent market evaluation, or appraisal, of the items is required. Assume Lee Wang and Kim Chow decide to form the partnership Wang & Chow. The following is a summary of the amounts contributed by each partner:

Lee Wang			Kim Chow	
Cash	$2,500		Cash	$20,000
Accounts receivable	5,340		Building	175,000
Allowance for doubtful accounts	890		Bank loan	80,000
Equipment	10,500			
Accumulated depreciation	2,000			
Accounts payable	1,240			
Notes payable	5,000			

FIGURE 15.3

An independent appraiser determined that the allowance for doubtful accounts should be $1,200 and the market value of the equipment is $5,000. All other assets are recorded at their fair market values.

The journal entry in the books of the partnership would include the following amounts:

	DR	CR
Cash (2,500 + 20,000)	$22,500	
Accounts receivable	5,340	
Allowance for doubtful accounts		$1,200
Equipment	5,000	
Accumulated depreciation – equipment		0
Building	175,000	
Accumulated depreciation – building		0
Accounts payable		1,240
Notes payable		5,000
Bank loan		80,000
Lee Wang, capital		5,400
Kim Chow, capital		115,000

FIGURE 15.4

The amount of accumulated depreciation is not set up in the books of the partnership because the market value of the equipment, $5,000, represents the cost of the asset in the new business. A method of depreciation, useful life and residual value will all need to be determined in order to calculate depreciation for current and future years. Each owner's opening capital is calculated by deducting the total amount of liabilities from the total amount of assets.

Lee Wang, Capital = $2,500 + $5,340 - $1,200 + $5,000 - $1,240 - $5,000 = $5,400

Kim Chow, Capital = $20,000 + $175,000 - $80,000 = $115,000

Division of Income or Loss

A key difference between a partnership, a proprietorship and a corporation is the way in which earnings are distributed. In a proprietorship, the proprietor simply receives all the earnings. In a corporation, earnings are distributed in the form of dividend payments (earnings paid out to stockholders). If all the assets are sold and all debts paid, the remaining cash would be distributed among the stockholders in proportion to the amount of stock owned. For example, a stockholder with 10 times more shares than another stockholder would receive 10 times more of the remaining cash.

In a partnership, earnings are distributed differently than they are in a proprietorship or a corporation. Since partners are involved, earnings must be shared, not always on an equal basis. A partnership agreement sets out the terms of ownership, including how earnings are to be divided. A partnership's equity account on the balance sheet is referred to as the *capital account*. Here is an example of such an account:

	J. Witner	R. Pierce	Total
Capital balance (beginning)	25,000	50,000	75,000
Add: Additional contribution	0	0	0
Share of partnership net income for the period	50,000	100,000	150,000
Subtotal	75,000	150,000	225,000
Less: Drawings	40,000	80,000	120,000
Capital balance (ending)	35,000	70,000	105,000

FIGURE 15.5

The partnership's capital account is broken down by partner. In this case, J. Witner had a beginning capital balance of $25,000 and R. Pierce had a beginning capital balance of $50,000. During the year, they did not contribute additional capital to the business. At the end of the year, J. Witner's share of net income is $50,000 and $40,000 was withdrawn. R. Pierce's share of net income is $100,000 and $80,000 was withdrawn. The closing capital account balance is the net worth of the partnership.

One of the primary purposes of a partnership agreement is to stipulate how earnings are to be divided. In fact, the partners can choose any method they wish, as long as they are willing to abide by the terms of the partnership agreement.

The typical methods of dividing earnings in a partnership include the following:

*   equally
*   according to an agreed-upon ratio
*   according to the capital contribution of each partner
*   according to agreed-upon salary allocations, plus a share of the remainder

We will examine each of these methods separately.

Dividing Earnings Equally

The simplest method of dividing earnings is on an equal basis. For example, Partners A and B own a consulting practice that earned $100,000 net income for the year. The net income is credited in the income summary account after the revenue and expense accounts have been closed. For the partners to share the earnings equally, a debit is then made to the income summary account for the entire amount, while credits of $50,000 each are made to the capital accounts of the two partners, as shown in the journal entry.

WORTH REPEATING...

Closing the books for a company transfers the values in the revenue and expense accounts to the income summary account, leaving the revenue and expense accounts with a zero balance. The income summary account is then closed to the capital account. If the company had a net income for the year, the income summary account will be debited and the capital account will be credited, leaving the income summary account with a zero balance.

JOURNAL			
Date	**Account Title and Explanation**	**Debit**	**Credit**
	Income Summary	100,000	
	Capital - Partner A		50,000
	Capital - Partner B		50,000
	To close income summary account		

FIGURE 15.6

Dividing Earnings According to an Agreed-Upon Ratio

The allocation of business earnings can be done according to an agreed upon ratio. For example, if Partner A is to get 60% of the earnings and Partner B is to get 40%, the split would be recorded in the books as follows:

JOURNAL			
Date	**Account Title and Explanation**	**Debit**	**Credit**
	Income Summary	100,000	
	Capital - Partner A		60,000
	Capital - Partner B		40,000
	To close income summary account		

FIGURE 15.7

Dividing Earnings According to the Capital Contribution of Each Partner

Another method of allocating the earnings among partners is to base it on the amount that each partner invested in the business. For example, if Partner A contributed $10,000 (one-quarter) of the capital and Partner B contributed $30,000 (three-quarters), they would be entitled to their proportion of the earnings.

JOURNAL			
Date	**Account Title and Explanation**	**Debit**	**Credit**
	Income Summary	100,000	
	Capital - Partner A		25,000
	Capital - Partner B		75,000
	To close income summary account		

FIGURE 15.8

Dividing Earnings According to Agreed-Upon Salary Allocations, Plus a Share of the Remainder

Earnings can also be divided by using a fixed salary allocation, interest allocation, or both for each partner, and then dividing the remaining earnings equally. For example, if the partnership agreement stipulates that Partner A's salary is $25,000, and Partner B's salary is $40,000, then those are the first amounts to be deducted from the net income of the business and distributed to the partners. These amounts are shown in orange in figure 15.9.

	Total	A	B
Net Income	$100,000		
Salary to A	-25,000	25,000	
Salary to B	-40,000		40,000
Remainder	35,000		
Remainder - to A	-17,500	17,500	
Remainder - to B	-17,500		17,500
Capital balance (ending)		42,500	57,500

FIGURE 15.9

The $35,000 remaining after the salaries are distributed is divided equally among the partners. These amounts are shown in green on the chart.

If the distributed amounts are added up for each partner, the totals come to $42,500 ($25,000 + $17,500) for Partner A, and $57,500 ($40,000 + $17,500) for Partner B, as marked in red on the chart. These payments are the earnings to be recorded in the capital account of the business.

JOURNAL

Date	Account Title and Explanation	Debit	Credit
	Income Summary	100,000	
	Capital - Partner A		42,500
	Capital - Partner B		57,500
	To close income summary account		

FIGURE 15.10

It is important to note that the method of distributing the earnings is just allocation, not actual payments and not actual expenses. Even the salary and interest amounts are allocations. The allocation is to assign to each partner's capital account their share of the earnings. If they wish to take money from the business, it is considered a drawing, which will be discussed in the next section.

The number of ways that earnings can be divided between partners is unlimited. For example, interest can firstly be allocated (out of net income) at a fixed rate on each partner's capital account. The remaining amount of net income could then be divided according to a predetermined ratio or salary. The method chosen should meet the needs and interests of the partners involved and be clearly stated in the partnership agreement. These amounts are not to be deducted from the partnership's revenues in determining net income for the period.

Partner Drawings

The amount reported as owner's drawings does not represent the amount that has been earned by the partner during the period, but the amount that has been withdrawn from the partner's equity. During the year, partners may withdraw cash or other assets from the business for personal use. The journal entries to record the withdrawals and related year-end closing entries for the Witner and Pierce Partnership are as follows:

JOURNAL

Date	Account Title and Explanation	Debit	Credit
	Drawings - Witner	40,000	
	Drawings - Pierce	80,000	
	Cash		120,000
	To record owner drawings during the year		

JOURNAL

Date	Account Title and Explanation	Debit	Credit
	Capital - Witner	40,000	
	Capital - Pierce	80,000	
	Drawings - Witner		40,000
	Drawings - Pierce		80,000
	To close the owner drawings account		

FIGURE 15.11

Addition and Withdrawal of a Partner

The legal basis for any partnership is the partnership agreement. Once a partner leaves, or another is added, a new partnership agreement should be prepared and signed by all parties. However, this does not mean that the business needs to open a new set of books. Instead, adjustments can be made to the current set of books to reflect any change in partner status.

In figure 15.12, the first row of opening balances reflects the capital introduced by each partner plus the net income that the owners have earned to date.

	Partner A	Partner B	Partner C	Partner D	Total
Balance before admitting new partner (includes all earnings to date)	120,000	150,000	50,000		320,000
Admission of new partner				100,000	100,000
Balance after admitting new partner	120,000	150,000	50,000	100,000	420,000

FIGURE 15.12

Partner D is the new addition, therefore his opening balance is zero. The total of all the opening balances is $320,000. Partner D contributes $100,000 to the partnership, which creates a new balance of $420,000.

Here is how the admission of the new partner is recorded in journal format:

JOURNAL			
Date	Account Title and Explanation	Debit	Credit
	Cash	100,000	
	Capital - Partner D		100,000
	To record admission of new partner		

FIGURE 15.13

The receipt of $100,000 represents a debit in the company's cash account, and a corresponding credit of $100,000 is made in Partner D's section of the capital account.

This illustrates what occurs when a new partner invests cash into the business. However, the new partner could also purchase all or part of the investment (equity) held by another partner in the partnership. For example, Partner D may have bought a $100,000 share of the business from Partner A. In that case, the new partnership account would look as follows:

	Partner A	Partner B	Partner C	Partner D	Total
Balance before admitting new partner (includes all earnings to date)	120,000	150,000	50,000		320,000
Admission of new partner	- 100,000			100,000	0
Balance after admitting new partner	20,000	150,000	50,000	100,000	320,000

FIGURE 15.14

As you can see in the second row, $100,000 is deducted from Partner A's balance, and added to Partner D's balance. The journal entry would be as follows:

JOURNAL			
Date	Account Title and Explanation	Debit	Credit
	Capital - Partner A	100,000	
	Capital - Partner D		100,000
	To record admission of new partner		

FIGURE 15.15

Instead of being debited to cash, Partner A's section of the capital account is debited with the amount of $100,000, leaving Partner A with a balance of $20,000, since Partner D bought a $100,000 share of the business from Partner A.

The partnership's total net assets therefore remain at $320,000, instead of the $420,000 shown in figure 15.12. The reason should be clear. Instead of adding new cash to the partnership, Partner D purchased most of Partner A's capital (equity). Partner A would receive the cash personally from Partner D.

When Market Value Differs from Book Value

As much of our discussion has indicated, the value of items on the books for a business may not necessarily reflect their current market values. This principle can also apply to partnerships. When new partnership agreements are negotiated, the partners usually come to an understanding of what the business is really worth, relative to its stated book value. This understanding can then form the foundation of how much new partners must pay to receive a percentage or share of ownership in the business.

Here are two examples to build upon those we have already looked at in this chapter. Our opening balance originally looked like this:

	Partner A	Partner B	Partner C	Partner D	Total
Balance before admitting new partner (includes all earnings to date)	120,000	150,000	50,000		320,000

FIGURE 15.16

In our first example, we are going to assume that Partner D (the new partner) is willing to pay a premium for a share of the business. He would be willing to do this because the business could have a value that is not reflected in the capital account, such as an increase in the value of the good name of the business (goodwill), or a higher market value for assets such as land or copyright.

After negotiating the new partnership agreement, Partner D agrees to contribute $200,000 to receive a $130,000 share of the business's book value, which amounts to a quarter of the business. Here is how that transaction could be recorded:

	Partner A	Partner B	Partner C	Partner D	Total
Balance before admitting new partner (includes all earnings to date)	120,000	150,000	50,000		320,000
Admission of new partner	23,334	23,333	23,333	130,000	200,000
Balance after admitting new partner	143,334	173,333	73,333	130,000	520,000

FIGURE 15.17

The addition of Partner D's $200,000 contribution raises the total level of net assets from $320,000 to $520,000. One-quarter of this total amounts to $130,000, which is Partner D's new share. The remaining balance of Partner D's $200,000 investment, amounting to $70,000, is divided equally among the other partners.

JOURNAL			
Date	Account Title and Explanation	Debit	Credit
	Cash	200,000	
	Capital - Partner A		23,334
	Capital - Partner B		23,333
	Capital - Partner C		23,333
	Capital - Partner D		130,000
	To record admission of new partner		

FIGURE 15.18

In our second example, we are going to assume that Partner D is a partner who adds value to the business. Perhaps Partner D has a client list that would increase the value of the business once the new partnership is formed. This time we will see what happens when Partner D pays $100,000 to receive a quarter share of the business, for a value of $105,000.

	Partner A	Partner B	Partner C	Partner D	Total
Balance before admitting new partner (includes all earnings to date)	120,000	150,000	50,000		320,000
Admission of new partner	- 1,666	- 1,667	- 1,667	105,000	100,000
Balance after admitting new partner	118,334	148,333	48,333	105,000	420,000

FIGURE 15.19

The contribution made by Partner D of $100,000 creates total net assets of $420,000. One-quarter of this amount is $105,000, which is Partner D's share. Since Partner D only paid $100,000 for this share, the $5,000 difference is essentially paid for by the other partners – split three ways. This means that approximately $1,667 is deducted from the account balances of partners A, B and C.

JOURNAL			
Date	Account Title and Explanation	Debit	Credit
	Cash	100,000	
	Capital - Partner A	1,666	
	Capital - Partner B	1,667	
	Capital - Partner C	1,667	
	Capital - Partner D		105,000
	To record admission of new partner		

FIGURE 15.20

Liquidation of a Partnership

Partnerships may end for a variety of reasons, including the death of one partner or by agreement between the partners. When a partnership is liquidated, the main challenge is to establish who receives whatever remains of the business after the assets are sold and liabilities have been paid. In figure 15.21, the balance sheet of ABC Partnership is shown after liquidation. Since the only remaining asset consists of $100,000 in cash, this is distributed to the partners in proportion to their equity in the business.

The transaction would appear as follows:

JOURNAL			
Date	**Account Title and Explanation**	**Debit**	**Credit**
	Capital - Partner A	35,000	
	Capital - Partner B	40,000	
	Capital - Partner C	25,000	
	Cash		100,000
	To record cash distribution among partners		

ABC Partnership Balance Sheet As at mm/dd/yy	
Cash	**$ 100,000**
Partners' Equity	
Partner A	35,000
Partner B	40,000
Partner C	25,000
Total	**$ 100,000**

FIGURE 15.21

This was a relatively simple example. The amounts of cash received by the partners were equal to their share of equity. This example also assumes that assets were sold at their book value. As we already know, this rarely happens. Suppose before liquidation, ABC Partnership had assets valued at $700,000 and liabilities valued at $600,000. Thus, net assets are equal to $100,000. If the business's net assets are sold for $70,000, representing a loss of $30,000, the following entry would appear:

JOURNAL			
Date	**Account Title and Explanation**	**Debit**	**Credit**
	Cash	70,000	
	Liabilities	600,000	
	Loss on sale of net assets	30,000	
	Assets		700,000
	To record the sales of assets		

FIGURE 15.22

Since the assets were sold for only $70,000, a loss on sale of net assets of $30,000 must be recorded as an additional expense.

This loss is then allocated to the partners according to the same formula that would be used when distributing earnings, or whatever terms were agreed upon in the partnership agreement. For the purpose of this example, we assume that the earnings (or losses) are distributed equally.

JOURNAL			
Date	**Account Title and Explanation**	**Debit**	**Credit**
	Capital - Partner A	10,000	
	Capital - Partner B	10,000	
	Capital - Partner C	10,000	
	Loss on sale of net assets		30,000
	To allocate loss on sale of net assets		

FIGURE 15.23

The cash is then distributed to the partners based on the closing balance of their equity.

This example involved allocating a loss on sale of assets. Any gain would be allocated in the same manner – equally, unless otherwise provided for – and the cash would be divided according to each partner's final balance of equity in the business.

JOURNAL			
Date	Account Title and Explanation	Debit	Credit
	Capital - Partner A	25,000	
	Capital - Partner B	30,000	
	Capital - Partner C	15,000	
	Cash		70,000
	To record cash distrubuion among partners		

FIGURE 15.24

IN THE REAL WORLD

One of the lesser known facts of the business world is that some of the world's most famous ventures and corporations started out as partnerships.

Wilbur and Orville Wright were brothers who received a toy helicopter from their father in 1878. They went into business with one another, which led to ventures in building a printing press and publishing a newspaper. In 1886 the brothers made their own brand of bicycles. However, the toy helicopter from their father always inspired visions of machines and flight for the young men, which is why they ended up building gliders and a wind tunnel. In 1903 they built and flew the first airplane in history. Six years later they incorporated the Wright Co. and continued their pioneering work in the field of aeronautics.

Richard and Maurice McDonald were brothers from New Hampshire who decided to move to California in the late 1920s to seek their fortune. They eventually fine-tuned their hot dog stand and barbecue restaurant to limit the number of items on the menu, eliminated utensils and plates, and made the kitchen more efficient. After having sold 21 franchises by the mid-1950s, Ray Kroc came along and purchased all the rights to the business for $2.7 million. There are now approximately 31,000 McDonald's restaurants around the globe with sales of over $22 billion a year.

Bill Hewlett and David Packard graduated with engineering degrees from California's Stanford University in 1934, forging a friendship that would last a lifetime. A few years later, they started working together on a technical sound device; Disney Studios bought eight of these devices. Their partnership was formalized in 1939 and they went on to innovate in the fields of technology and management style. Today, Hewlett-Packard generates over $100 billion in sales from computer-related equipment. The name of the company was decided on a coin toss. You can guess who won.

In Summary

- A partnership differs from a proprietorship in the number of owners, the way in which earnings are divided, and the manner in which disagreement and conflict are settled.

- The characteristics of a partnership reveal several advantages and disadvantages, all of which must be carefully considered before choosing this form of business.

- A general partnership means that all partners have unlimited liability.

- A limited partnership divides a company's partners into two categories: general partners and limited partners. Unlimited liability extends to general partners because they are involved in the day-to-day decision making of the business. Limited partners, on the other hand, are only liable for the amount of capital they invest in the business. This is known as limited liability.

- A limited liability partnership or LLP is a legal ownership structure, used in some jurisdictions, that usually protects professionals from a partner's negligence. If one of the partners gets sued, the others are not necessarily liable. However, all the partners are liable for any debts owed to regular "day-to-day" creditors.

- A partnership's earnings can be divided in a number of different ways; these are usually outlined in the partnership agreement. Four common methods of dividing earnings are the following: equally; based on a ratio; based on the capital contribution of each partner; and drawing salaries before dividing the rest.

- Various stipulations can be made in a partnership agreement to accommodate the addition or withdrawal of partners. For example, a new partner can simply add in a new portion of partner's equity, or purchase some or all of another partner's share.

- The negotiated value of a partner's worth to a business might differ from what eventually appears in the books. On one hand, a new partner may pay more than book value because goodwill or other factors make it worth more. On the other hand, other partners may require a new partner to pay less, as the new partner may bring added value to the business, such as a distinguished client list.

- Partnerships may eventually be liquidated. The partnership agreement should stipulate how this should be done. If assets are sold above or below book value, the corresponding gains or losses are shared among the partners. The remaining cash can be distributed according to each partner's proportion of equity in the business.

Review Exercise

Zelma Rapoza, Serena Dennen and Sharron Throop have decided to set up a spa and operate it as a partnership. They will each contribute $10,000 to buy equipment and help pay for lease expenses. Zelma is also contributing $25,000 of her own equipment.

They agreed to pay themselves a yearly salary of $5,000 each. Since Zelma contributed the equipment, she expects $3,000 "rent" per year on the equipment for ten years. Each partner is to earn 5% on their investment (cash contribution). The net income for the year was $25,000. The profit remaining after salaries, rent, and interest is to be distributed at ratio of their cash contribution.

Required:

a) Prepare a schedule showing the changes in capital during the year.

b) Provide the journal entries that:

   i) Record the initial cash contribution

   ii) Record the equipment contribution

   iii) Record the division of partnership income. Assume that revenues and expenses have already been closed to the income summary account."

Review Exercise - Answer

Part a)

	Total	Zelma	Serena	Sharron
Cash Contribution	$30,000	$10,000	$10,000	$10,000
Contribution of Equipment	25,000	25,000		
Partner Contributions	$55,000	$35,000	$10,000	$10,000
Net Income	$25,000			
Salaries	-15,000	5,000	5,000	5,000
Equipment Rental	-3,000	3,000		
Interest	-1,500	500	500	500
Division of Income	5,500	1,834	1,833	1,833
Addition to Partners' Capital		$10,334	$7,333	$7,333
Closing Capital Balance	$80,000	$45,334	$17,333	$17,333

Part b)

Date	Account Title and Explanation	Debit	Credit
i	Cash	30,000	
	Capital - Rapoza		10,000
	Capital - Dennen		10,000
	Capital - Throop		10,000
	To record set up of partnership		
ii	Equipment	25,000	
	Capital - Rapoza		25,000
	To record contribution of equipment		
iii	Income Summary	25,000	
	Capital - Rapoza		10,334
	Capital - Dennen		7,333
	Capital - Throop		7,333
	To adjust partners' capital accounts for		
	their share of net income		

Chapter 16
CORPORATIONS: CONTRIBUTED CAPITAL AND DIVIDENDS

LEARNING OUTCOMES:

❶ Describe the characteristics of corporate organizations

❷ Outline the advantages and disadvantages of corporations

❸ Understand financial statements and stockholders' equity

❹ Record the issuance of stock

❺ Describe the differences between common stock and preferred stock

❻ Record the payment of dividends

❼ Record stock dividends and stock splits

The Professionalization of the Ownership Structure

Almost everyone has heard of **corporations**, stock markets and the investment class, but few may know what it all means and how various components interact with one another. This chapter will bring clarity and understanding to the various issues involved with corporations — especially where ownership issues are concerned.

In essence, the corporation brings business ownership to the next level. We have already discussed how partnerships involve adding more owners to a business. In this chapter, we will demonstrate the various ways in which corporations are different from both proprietorships and partnerships. Corporations come with many advantages, but they also come with some additional responsibilities.

Proprietorships and partnerships have a common characteristic of not separating the owner from the business in a legal sense. Owners are ultimately responsible for the debts of the business, and can be held accountable. On the other hand, any corporation, large or small, is legally separate from the owners. This means the owners are not responsible for the debts of the business. In some cases, owners of a corporation may have very little to do in managing the business.

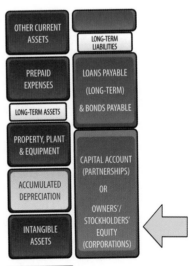

FIGURE 16.1

At the heart of a corporation is the separation of ownership and management. In a large publicly traded company, the company's stockholders do not necessarily run the business. Generally speaking, the business is run by executives hired by representatives of the stockholders: the board of directors. Accountants need to be intimately familiar with how corporations work and how their finances are managed.

Public vs. Private Corporation

A corporation can be classified as either a public or private corporation. A **public corporation** has stock listed on a stock exchange. That is, its stock is available to be traded "publicly" from one member of the general public (the current stockholder) to another (the purchaser). "Trading" simply means buying or selling. Microsoft, Apple, and Toyota are only a few of many well-known public corporations. The stock of Microsoft and Apple are traded on the NASDAQ stock exchange and Toyota stock is traded on the New York Stock Exchange (NYSE).

WORTH REPEATING...

Recall that the three main forms are organizations are sole proprietorships, partnerships and corporations. A sole proprietorship is a small business owned and generally operated by one owner. A partnership is a non-corporation owned by two or more partners. Lastly, a corporation is a business that is registered with the government as a separate legal entity from its owners.

On the other hand, a **private corporation** does not offer its stock to the general public in a stock market exchange. The company's stock is, instead, owned and exchanged privately. For example, a private company may have a single owner who never wants to sell his stock publicly. Another common example of a private corporation is a company with several owners that belong to the same family, who have no intentions of selling stock on a stock exchange. A private corporation is also commonly known as a closed corporation or a privately held corporation.

The following table shows the classification of various entities.

Entity or Individual	Classification
Toyota	Public Corporation
IKEA[1]	Private Corporation
PricewaterhouseCoopers	Partnership[2]
Bill Gates	Stockholder
Jim's Corner Bread Bakery[3]	Sole Proprietorship

(1) IKEA's few shares of stock are held privately
(2) All partnerships are essentially "privately-owned"
(3) Assume that Jim is the single owner of the company

FIGURE 16.2

Corporate Structure: Separating Management from Ownership

Corporations are legal entities whose primary characteristic is the legal separation of those who run the business from those who own the business. Specifically, owners of a corporation consist of the people who own stock in the company. Alternatively, management consists of people hired to protect the interests of stockholders, while delivering the goods or services provided by the company. The board of directors is established to ensure that management is accountable to ownership.

 WORTH REPEATING...

There are three primary options for structuring the ownership of a business:

1. In a proprietorship, only one person owns the business and keeps all the earnings which are taxed on the personal level.
2. A partnership is an association of two or more people who jointly own a business, its assets and liabilities, and share in its gains or losses; earnings are taxed personally.
3. In a corporation, there can be a large number of owners known as stockholders, many of whom may not participate in the day-to-day activities of the business. Earnings are taxed twice. Once at the corporate level and then, again, at the personal level (e.g. dividends).

When examining proprietorships, partnerships, and corporations, it becomes clear that the ownership structure is taken to the next level in the way that money is raised and the company is managed.

With respect to how money is raised, corporations do not rely solely on the finances of the proprietor, or on the financing capability of its partners. Instead, corporations can potentially raise large sums of money by issuing shares of stock to the public. Indeed, large corporations can issue many shares in order to raise large sums of money. This basic principle of corporate finance is what drives the stock market. The people who buy and sell stock on *Wall Street* are essentially exchanging a share of ownership in some of America's largest companies — and they are doing it on a daily basis.

To manage and run the business, corporations are not necessarily dependent on the brilliance of one proprietor, or on the specialties exhibited by various partners. In fact, large corporations don't rely on the business expertise of those who actually own the business: the stockholders.

Instead, large corporations rely on the expertise of hired management to run the business for them. This is why corporations have a board of directors to monitor the management team. The management team is headed by the company's chief executive officer (CEO) who presides over a team of executives responsible for various aspects of running the business.

Generally, executives are specialized and often well-trained professionals who graduated from business school and made their way up the corporate ladder. At medical school, people can learn to become doctors; at business school, they can start learning to become corporate executives.

Chapter 15 included a chart which summarized the advantages and disadvantages associated with a partnership. The following chart provides something similar with respect to corporations:

Advantages of Corporations

- *Fixed organizational structure.* The board of directors represents the interests of stockholders and is responsible for hiring executives and setting the broad direction of the organization.
- *The power to raise money.* Stock can be issued to raise amounts of money that would be much more difficult to obtain solely using the resources of proprietors or partners.
- *Limited liability.* Stockholders are only held liable for the value of the stock they hold.
- *Liquidity of stock.* The ability to sell stock quickly on the market makes them attractive investment vehicles, without affecting the stability of the business. In other words, management continues to function even while stock continue to be traded.
- *Tax treatment.* Although the business itself pays taxes, stockholders do not, until dividends are paid out.
- *Unlimited life.* The corporation remains an entity regardless of the comings and goings of stockholders. This is unlike proprietorships and partnerships which end when an owner leaves the company (with the exception of Limited Partnerships).
- *Professional management.* With proprietorships and partnerships, the owners may or may not possess specific or specialized expertise. With corporations, the board of directors ensures the hiring of experts exhibiting specialties in countless fields.

Disadvantages of Corporations

- *Red tape.* Although the corporate structure brings with it many advantages, the structure also comes with legalities that can require lawyers to be hired, forms to be completed and documents to be prepared and filed.
- *Annual requirements.* Many obligations need to be met on an annual basis, including: corporate fees, audits, financial reports, stockholder meetings, board meetings, etc.
- *Double Taxation.* Governments tax corporate earnings; stockholders who receive some of those earnings in the form of dividends are also taxed.

In summary, the corporate form of ownership allows businesses to do things on a bigger scale and in a professional manner. Yet these advantages come with regulatory and bureaucratic responsibilities that can be costly and time consuming.

Financial Statements and Stockholders' Equity

As the ownership structure gets more complicated, so does the way owners' equity is divided and reported on the balance sheet. With a proprietorship, owner's equity is literally a simple figure that represents net worth. With partnerships, owner's equity gets divided into capital accounts that outline each partner's stake in the business. With corporations, things are more complicated.

When referring to corporations, the term **stockholders' equity** is used in place of owners' equity since the stockholders actually own the company. Stockholders' equity is further divided into **contributed capital (or paid-in capital)** and **retained earnings**. Both get reported separately in the stockholders' equity section of the company's financial statements.

Contributed capital includes all the information related to a company's stock, including the types or *"class"* of stock issued, the number of shares authorized, and the number of shares that are issued or *"outstanding"*.

Retained earnings is relatively simple to define. It represents the part of a company's earnings that have not been distributed to stockholders in the form of dividends. In other words, the earnings *not* paid out to stockholders are *retained* in the business. Retained earnings can then be used for business purposes in the future.

As an example, let us take a look at the stockholders' equity section of a sample company for the fiscal year 2011 as shown in figure 16.3.

Stockholders' Equity	(in thousands of $)
Contributed Capital	
Preferred stock, $2, 10,000 shares authorized, 3,000 shares issued and outstanding	$12,000
Common stock, unlimited shares authorized, 50,000 shares issued and outstanding	5,000,000
Total Contributed Capital	5,012,000
Retained Earnings	240,000
Total Stockholders' Equity	$5,252,000

FIGURE 16.3

To properly create the stockholders' equity portion of a corporation, several values must be calculated. The quantity of shares that have been sold (issued) through the stock market must be shown for all classes of stock (common and preferred). The characteristics of common and preferred stock will be discussed later in this chapter. Also, the total value that the shares were sold for must be shown. This is considered the book value of the shares, and the value does not change as market prices for the stock increase or decrease.

Retained earnings must be calculated at the end of each period. The calculation for retained earnings is:

Ending Retained Earnings = Beginning Retained Earnings + Net Income – Dividends

A dividend is a distribution of the profits to stockholders, and will be covered in more detail later in this chapter. As an example to calculate retained earnings, suppose a company started 2011 with $100,000 in retained earnings. During the year, they earned a net income of $40,000 and paid dividends to stockholders in the amount of $15,000. Figure 16.4 shows how to calculate the value of retained earnings at the end of 2011.

Sample Company Statement of Retained Earnings For the Year Ended December 31, 2011	
Retained Earnings – January 1, 2011	$100,000
Add: Net Income	40,000
Less: Dividends	15,000
Retained Earnings – December 31, 2011	$125,000

FIGURE 16.4

You may notice that calculating the ending value of retained earnings is quite similar to calculating the ending value of owner's equity in a proprietorship.

The figure below presents the equity portion of Bombardier's consolidated balance sheet for their year-end 2011 and how they calculated the change in retained earnings for 2011. Bombardier's equity section is composed of common stock, preferred stock, retained earnings and other equity items that are beyond the scope of this course.

Bombardier Consolidated Balance Sheet (an excerpt) As at January 31, 2011 (in millions of U.S. dollars)	
Equity	
Preferred stock	$347
Common stockholders' equity	3,927
Equity attributable to stockholders of Bombardier Inc.	4,274
Equity attributable to non-controlling interests	$78

Bombardier Consolidated Statement of Stockholders' Equity (an excerpt) For the Fiscal Year Ended January 31, 2011 (in millions of U.S. dollars)	
Retained earnings	
Balance at beginning of year	$2,087
Net income attributable to stockholders of Bombardier Inc.	755
Excess of price paid over carrying value of repurchased Class B Stock	(13)

Dividends:
    Common stock
    Preferred stock, net of tax
	(173)
	(24)

Balance at end of year	$2,632

Taken from Bombardier Annual Report, Year Ended January 31, 2011, pages 162 and 167.

Accessed from the website ir.bombardier.com, October, 2012.

FIGURE 16.5

Issuing Stock

One of the strengths of adopting a corporate form of ownership involves the amount of money that can be raised by issuing and selling stock to the public. However, stock can also be issued in exchange for something other than money.

We will outline three ways in which stock can be issued and examine how they are accounted for on the company's books.

Issuing stock in exchange for cash

The most common reason for issuing stock is for the purpose of raising capital. Suppose a company issues 1,000 common shares, at $10 each, to raise a total of $10,000.

Here is how the transaction would be recorded:

JOURNAL			
Date	Account Title and Explanation	Debit	Credit
	Cash	10,000	
	Common Stock		10,000
	Issue of 1,000 common shares for cash		

FIGURE 16.6

In fact, the transaction is relatively straightforward. The receipt of $10,000 is recorded as a debit to cash, and the corresponding credit is made in the common stock account within the Contributed Capital section of the balance sheet.

However, not every type of stock issuance is as straightforward as this exchange for cash.

Issuing stock in exchange for assets

Stock represents ownership in a company that has some value. Although that value can be determined by issuing and selling stock on the market, it can also be determined by an exchange of some other kind. An example of such an exchange might involve assets instead of cash.

In other words, a company might issue stock for the purpose of receiving assets in return. For example, here's the transaction to be recorded if a company issues 1,000 shares in exchange for land that is valued at $1,000,000.

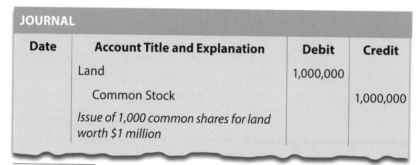

FIGURE 16.7

The receipt of the land is *capitalized* and recorded as a debit in the appropriate fixed asset account, which in this case falls under *property, plant & equipment*. The corresponding $1,000,000 credit is recorded in the common stock account.

Note that the $1,000,000 amount for the land should represent its fair value, and be determined by some objective appraisement.

Issuing stock in exchange for services

In the past, it was commonplace for stock to be issued in exchange for services rather than assets. Nowadays, however, the opposite is true. Nevertheless, it may be beneficial to show an example that involves stock issuance in exchange for services rendered.

Example: A new corporation obtained the services of an accountant for consulting. The services amounted to a cost of $10,000. Given that this is a new corporation, $10,000 expenditure might be considered quite costly. As an alternative, the company offers the accountant stock worth $10,000. The accountant accepts because he is an experienced investor and is confident that the stock will be worth much more in the not-too-distant future. Here is how that transaction is recorded on the company's books:

JOURNAL			
Date	**Account Title and Explanation**	**Debit**	**Credit**
	Accounting Fees Expense	10,000	
	Common Stock		10,000
	Issue 100 common shares in exchange for accounting services		

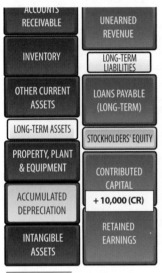

FIGURE 16.8

In this example, $10,000 is expensed in the form of a debit to the appropriate income statement account. As in the other examples, the contributed capital account receives the corresponding credit. Given the nature of such a transaction, the cash account remains untouched.

Issuing Stock that is Common or Preferred

As we have already mentioned, one of the justifications for establishing a corporate form of ownership is to raise more money. By giving the public the opportunity to buy a stake in the company, the company has access to potentially large amounts of financing.

However, as with most aspects of modern business and finance, methods have been developed to provide further incentives for potential investors, while at the same time giving corporations some flexibility in the way they finance their business. With regard to company stock, this involves offering different classes of stock: **common** versus **preferred**.

Typically, when people discuss company stock, they are referring to a company's **common stock**. Common stock represents ownership in the company, which means that they come with voting rights that involve selection of a board of directors and establishment of corporate policies.

Investors purchase common stock with the expectation that the corporation will remain or become profitable and, thus, pay out dividends. These dividends, however, are paid out at the discretion of the board of directors. So it is possible for an investor in a profitable company to not receive dividends.

In order to provide incentives for some investors, some corporations will issue what are called **preferred stock**. In essence, preferred stock addresses the primary disadvantage that comes with common stock (that dividend payments are not guaranteed). Preferred stock generally comes with regular and fixed dividend payments. As with common stock, dividends are paid out at the discretion of the board of directors, but preferred stock will have first claim on the dividends. It is this characteristic of preferred stock that makes them similar to bonds (making regular payments in the form of interest).

Preferred stock has other attributes that are similar to bonds. Specifically, they both rank ahead of common stock with regard to a claim on assets. In the event of liquidation, bondholders have a claim on assets before preferred stockholders, who, in turn, have a claim before common stockholders. However, as with bondholders, preferred stockholders have no voting rights regarding the direction of the company. In this sense, it is only common stockholders that maintain this specific right of company ownership, and it is an important one.

Features of common stock

- Represent ownership in the corporation
- Owners elect the board of directors
- Owners vote on corporate policy
- Owners rank after bondholders and preferred stockholders in the event of a liquidation
- Owners have a right to receive dividends only if declared by the directors

---

Features of preferred stock

- Owners have a higher claim on assets and earnings than do common stockholders
- Owners generally get paid a regular dividend, especially before any dividends are paid to common stockholders
- Preferred stock often has the right to accumulate dividends from previous years. If a dividend on cumulative preferred stock is missed, it will accumulate and will have to be paid off before any dividend payments are made to the common stockholders
- **Dividends in arrears** are the amount of dividends on cumulative preferred stock from past periods that have not been paid. It is not a liability, and should be disclosed in the notes to the financial statements.

Par and No Par Value Stock

Both common and preferred stock can be sold with the feature of **"par value"** or **"no-par value"**.

Par value stock is stock that is issued with a stated value on each share. Issuing par value stock would be recorded at the value as stated on the stock certificate. For example ACB Inc. is authorized to issue an unlimited number of $10 par value common shares. Suppose 1,000 of these shares are sold for $15 each. The entry to record the issuance of the stock would be as follows:

JOURNAL

Date	Account Title and Explanation	Debit	Credit
	Cash	15,000	
	Common Stock		10,000
	Additional Paid-in Capital		5,000
	Issued 1,000 shares of $10 par value common stock for $15 per share		

FIGURE 16.9

The **additional paid-in capital** account is included in the stockholders' equity section of the balance sheet right after the stock issue to which it relates. This increases the amount of equity in the business. Although not common, stock may be issued at less than the par value and are known as watered shares. When this occurs, an account called **discount on capital stock** is debited for the difference between the amounts and decreases the equity in the business.

No-par value means that the stock has no "stated value" so that when they are sold, the stock account is credited for the entire proceeds. Using the amounts from the above example, if the stock had no-par value, the following journal entry would be recorded:

JOURNAL

Date	Account Title and Explanation	Debit	Credit
	Cash	15,000	
	Common Stock		15,000
	Issued 1,000 shares of no-par common shares for $15 per share		

FIGURE 16.10

Stated Value

Some states require corporations to determine a **"stated value"** for each share of stock they are authorized to issue. The purpose of assigning a stated or "legal" value is to protect stockholders from the board of directors declaring and paying out dividends to the point where insufficient equity remains to cover the value of their stock. Having a "stated value" ensures the corporation must maintain this minimum amount of stockholders' equity so that in the event of liquidation, the stockholder's investment is somewhat protected.

Where stock is issued in excess of the stated value, the excess is credited to the additional paid-in capital account similar to the issuance of par-value stock shown above.

Accounting for Cash Dividends

From an investor's standpoint, there are two monetary reasons to buy stock in a company. One reason is the anticipation of a capital gain if the stock price rises. The other reason is the anticipation of annual **dividend payments**.

A corporation's stock price may not be entirely within management's control as it fluctuates depending on macroeconomic factors, investor confidence and analysts' recommendations. The frequency and level of dividend payments, however, are within management's control (management can set the terms of dividend payments).

Given the amount of control and responsibility that a company has over the payment of dividends, and the predictability usually associated with this responsibility, accountants need to be familiar with the transactions involved.

First, there are three dates to be kept in mind relative to dividends:

- *The date of declaration:* when the directors make the decision (or declaration) that a dividend payment is to be made to stockholders.
- *The date of record:* all those holding stock on this date are eligible to receive the dividend payment that has been declared.
- *The date of payment:* when the company eventually makes the dividend payment to eligible stockholders.

We will examine what the company's accounting responsibilities are, relative to each of these dates.

On the date of declaration

If a company decides that a dividend payment of $10,000 is in order on December 1st, and sets the terms of the payment, a journal entry like this would be recorded:

JOURNAL			
Date	**Account Title and Explanation**	**Debit**	**Credit**
Dec 1	Retained Earnings	10,000	
	Dividends Payable		10,000
	Dividend payable of $1 per share on 10,000 shares		

Dividends cannot be paid if the resulting balance in retained earnings is negative. This rule can be different in some jurisdictions.

FIGURE 16.11

Although the payment is not made right away, the company must subtract the amount of the payment from retained earnings (debit), while establishing and crediting the dividends payable account under current liabilities. In other words, the dividend payment is accrued until payment is finally made.

A CLOSER LOOK

Instead of debiting retained earnings directly when dividends are declared, some companies may instead debit a temporary equity account called Dividends. This account decreases the amount of equity in the business and is closed to retained earnings as the end of the year. The closing process for this account is similar to the way drawings are closed in a proprietorship.

You will notice that the item is not expensed, since dividend payments do not constitute a normal operating expense, so the transaction does not involve the income statement portion of the financial statements.

Although the amount of $10,000 was used in this specific example, the amount of a dividend is ultimately approved by a company's board of directors. Of course, the company must have the cash to make the dividend payment. This means that there should be enough cash to pay the dividends which the company owes.

On the date of record

The challenge for a corporation regarding the date of record is not so much one of accounting as it is one of recordkeeping. In other words, the company must determine who its stockholders are on the date of record so that it knows who is eligible for the declared dividend payment.

The person responsible for this is the corporate secretary. This person is in charge of all official company documentation. Among other things, this responsibility involves maintaining and examining the company's stock register, which serves much like a subledger, by listing information on a per individual basis. Additionally, some large corporations obtain the services of a transfer agent to record changes in ownership of stock as a result of trading on the stock market.

On the date of payment

Finally, the company's accountant must record the transaction to be made on the date of payment, which is essentially a closing out of the dividend payable liability created on the date of declaration. Assuming the date of payment is December 12, here is how this is done:

JOURNAL			
Date	Account Title and Explanation	Debit	Credit
Dec 12	Dividends Payable	10,000	
	Cash		10,000
	Payment of dividend declared (date)		

FIGURE 16.12

Since the payment is finally made, it is the cash account that receives the credit, while the original dividends payable account that was established gets closed out with the debit decrease of $10,000.

Dividends in Arrears

Dividends in arrears occurs when preferred stock is present with a cumulative feature. This means when dividends are declared, the corporation must include the amount owing to the preferred stockholders from previous years where no dividend was paid.

For example: on December 31, 2010, Corporation ABC declared $100,000 dividends, payable on January 10, 2011 to the stockholders. There are 100,000 common shares and 20,000, $2, cumulative preferred shares issued. No dividends have been declared since the end of 2008. This means the corporation owes the preferred stockholders a total of $80,000 ($2 × 20,000 from year 2009 and $2 × 20,000 from year 2010). The journal entry to record the declaration and subsequent payment of the above dividends is shown in figure 16.13 and 16.14:

JOURNAL

Date	Account Title and Explanation	Debit	Credit
Dec 31	Retained Earnings	100,000	
	Dividends Payable – Preferred		80,000
	Dividends Payable – Common		20,000
	Dividend payable on 20,000 preferred shares and 100,000 common shares		

FIGURE 16.13

JOURNAL

Date	Account Title and Explanation	Debit	Credit
Jan 10	Dividends Payable – Preferred	80,000	
	Dividends Payable – Common	20,000	
	Cash		100,000
	Payment of dividend declared		

FIGURE 16.14

Stock Splits and Stock Dividends

A **stock split** is a corporate action that increases the number of a corporation's outstanding shares which in turn diminishes the individual price of each share of stock. For example, with a 2-for-1 stock split, each stockholder now owns two shares for every one share they held in the company; however, the value of each share is reduced by half on the stock market. Because the total value of the shares outstanding is not affected, no journal entry is needed to account for a stock split. A memorandum (note) is usually recorded indicating the decreased per share value and increased number of shares outstanding.

One of the main reasons for a stock split is to increase their liquidity. If the stock price is too high, some investors may feel the stock is too expensive or unaffordable. An example demonstrating how expensive stock can be is the case of Berkshire Hathaway, a conglomerate holding company headquartered in Omaha, which has never had a stock split. During 2012, Berkshire's Class A shares traded anywhere from $115,000 to $135,000 per share. The refusal to split the stock reflects the management's desire to attract long-term as opposed to short-term investors.

Stock dividends may be issued in lieu of cash dividends when the company chooses to retain cash in the company. If a corporation declares a stock dividend of its own stock of the same class, each stockholder will own more stock, but the same percentage of the business as before.

For example, on December 31, 2010, Corporation ABC has 100,000 common shares issued. Current market price is $10 per share. The company decided to declare a 20% stock dividend. The journal entry to record the declaration and distribution of the dividend is shown in figure 16.15.

JOURNAL			
Date	**Account Title and Explanation**	**Debit**	**Credit**
Dec 31	Retained Earnings	200,000	
	Common Stock Dividends Distributable		200,000
	Stock dividend of 20,000 shares		

JOURNAL			
Date	**Account Title and Explanation**	**Debit**	**Credit**
Jan 10	Common Stock Dividends Distributable	200,000	
	Common Stock		200,000
	To record distribution of 20,000 shares		

FIGURE 16.15

The account *Common Stock Dividend Distributable* is an equity account, not a liability (like the Dividends Payable account used for cash dividends). The end result of a stock dividend is a rearrangement of the makeup of stockholders' equity. Some of the value of retained earnings is moved to the common stock account. Since only equity will be impacted by this series of transactions, only equity accounts will be used. Also, since there will be no transfer of assets, there will be no promise to pay any assets (i.e. no liability).

All of the above transactions illustrate how public corporations account for issuing stock and recording dividends. For private corporations, issuing stock would be recorded in the same manner as illustrated. However, the recording and paying of dividends is usually less formal for private corporations because the stock is not publicly traded and the list of stockholders is usually short. The table below shows the impact of cash dividends, stock dividends and stock splits.

	Common Stock		Retained Earnings	Stockholders' Equity	Assets
	Value	Quantity			
Cash Dividend	No Change	No Change	Decrease	Decrease	Decrease
Stock Dividend	Increase	Increase	Decrease	No Change	No Change
Stock Split	No Change	Increase	No Change	No Change	No Change

FIGURE 16.16

Treasury Stock

One way a corporation can reduce the number of shares it has outstanding is to buy them back on the stock market. The transaction involves a debit to treasury stock and a credit to cash for the market value of the shares. Shares held as **treasury stock** have no rights until they are reissued. They can be held by the corporation for an indefinite period of time, reissued or retired. Assume a corporation bought back 1,000 of its own stock at a price of $25 per share. The journal entry to record the purchase would be as shown in figure 16.17.

JOURNAL			
Date	Account Title and Explanation	Debit	Credit
	Treasury Stock	25,000	
	Cash		25,000
	Purchased 1,000 shares of the corporation's own common stock at $25 per share		

FIGURE 16.17

Treasury stock is not reported as an asset on the balance sheet but instead is deducted from the stockholders' equity section as shown in figure 16.18.

Contributed Capital	
Common stock, $30 par value 1,000,000 shares authorized, 40,000 shares issued, 39,000 shares outstanding	$1,200,000
Additional Paid-in Capital	15,000
Total Contributed Capital	$1,215,000
Retained Earnings	875,000
Total Contributed Capital and Retained Earning	**2,090,000**
Less: Treasury Stock, Common (1,000 shares at cost)	25,000
Total Stockholders' Equity	**$2,065,000**

FIGURE 16.18

Resale of Treasury Stock

As mentioned, shares held as treasury stock can be reissued at a later date. Assume 500 shares of the above stock were reissued for $27 per share, total proceeds of $13,500. Even though the shares were reissued for $2 ($27-$25) more per share than they were originally purchased, no gain will be recorded since a corporation cannot earn revenue by selling its own stock. Instead, the stockholders' equity account, *paid-in capital, treasury stock*, is credited for the excess. The entry to record the reissuance would be as follows in figure 16.19:

JOURNAL			
Date	**Account Title and Explanation**	**Debit**	**Credit**
	Cash	13,500	
	Treasury Stock (500 x $25)		12,500
	Paid-in Capital, Treasury Stock (500 x $2)		1,000
	Sold 500 shares of treasury stock for		
	$27 per share		

FIGURE 16.19

Now let us assume the remaining treasury stock is reissued for $21 per share for total proceeds of $10,500. As with gains, the corporation is not allowed to record a loss on the sale of treasury stock; therefore, the difference will be first debited to clear out any balance in the paid-in capital, treasury stock account and then, if needed, retained earnings is debited for any amount in excess of the balance in the paid-in capital, treasury stock account. The entry to record this sale would be as follows in figure 16.20:

JOURNAL			
Date	**Account Title and Explanation**	**Debit**	**Credit**
	Cash	10,500	
	Paid-in Capital, Treasury Stock (500 x $2)	1,000	
	Retained Earnings	1,000	
	Treasury Stock (500 x $25)		12,500
	Sold 500 shares of treasury stock for		
	$21 per share		

FIGURE 16.20

An Ethical Approach to Corporations and Insider Trading

One of the most important ethical principles for all businesses, large or small, is the need to maintain the integrity of information released publicly, which is why **insider trading** is considered one of the worst violations at the corporate level.

As some of the discussion in this chapter has already revealed, the stock market can be unpredictable at the best of times. Market trends can fluctuate, speculation can run rampant, and even the most informed investors can have a difficult time making the right decisions.

Nevertheless, one of the basic foundations of the stock market is fair and public access to all company-related information. In other words, if current or potential stockholders have a right to information about a company, then it should be disclosed to the public in a timely fashion.

Insider trading occurs when anyone involved with a company discloses stockholder-relevant information privately, before it is released publicly. For example, a secretary in a company might overhear information on an upcoming announcement of better-than expected company earnings for the year. This secretary may have a close friend who invests in the stock market, and she passes on this information to him.

Knowing that the announcement will increase the price, the friend buys a large quantity of stock and might even tell a few of his friends.

By the time the announcement is finally made, the price of the stock may increase dramatically, and the friend and his friends may have made a substantial amount of money. This, of course, is highly illegal. Everyone involved should be charged with insider trading. The crime is very serious and comes with some harsh penalties.

The purpose of insider trading laws is to give everyone a fair chance to make profits on the stock market — given the same amount of information. That is why securities regulators go to great lengths to detect the spread of information by way of insider activity. As tempting as it might be to tell a friend what's going on inside the company before anyone else knows, doing so violates the principle of fairness and openness that exists in world markets. Anything less threatens the way that capitalism and free markets should work.

IN THE REAL WORLD

Celebrity homemaking and insider trading are two concepts that do not often come to mind at the same time. However, anything is bound to happen when the stock market, money and celebrity ambition clash with one another. That is precisely what happened to Martha Stewart, and her activities in the world of finance.

What most people do not know is that Martha Stewart rose to fame and fortune by way of the stock market. In the late 1990s, she took Martha Stewart Living Omnimedia Inc. public and made a fortune on the subsequent rise of the company's stock. This is not the road to the top that most people associate with celebrity, but it is one that worked miracles for the rising homemaking star.

Stewart's familiarity and success with the stock market, however, was ultimately responsible for her downfall. It all started to unravel in late 2001 with events surrounding the stock of a company called ImClone, which is a biopharmaceutical corporation.

During that period, ImClone stock took a tumble as a result of regulatory procedures that were detrimental to the company. Records show that Stewart sold almost 4,000 shares in the company, making her a gain of $229,000, shortly before public disclosure about the regulations.

It appears that Stewart was good friends with Samuel Waksel, the CEO of ImClone. Investigations revealed that Stewart was advised by her stockbroker, Peter Bacanovic, to sell her stock, based on information he was privy to regarding Waksel. The situation was a clear case of insider trading.

As is often the case with insider trading, however, it is very hard to prove who knew what and when. The investigators therefore focused on the cover-up, and discovered that Stewart had deceived investigators numerous times as they tried to gather information on insider activity in this case. In July of 2004, she was found guilty of obstructing justice and served a five-month sentence.

In Summary

↪ The stock of public corporations is traded on a stock market exchange whereas the stock of private corporations is not.

↪ Corporations take business ownership to the next level by separating ownership, in the form of stock, from management, in the form of executives. The board of directors serves the interests of ownership by hiring senior executives who together establish the broad objectives of the corporation.

↪ Corporations essentially divide the stockholders' equity section of the balance sheet into contributed capital and retained earnings. Contributed capital is represented by the different classes of stock, common and preferred, and their respective values (dollar amount and number of shares issued and outstanding).

↪ Retained earnings represent the amount of equity that the company has kept in the business and not distributed to stockholders.

↪ While dividing corporations into shares allows companies to raise much larger sums of money, it can also create difficulties in terms of control of ownership and uncontrolled changes in the company's stock price.

↪ Although issuing stock in exchange for money is most common, and constitutes the essence of the stock market, a company can also issue stock in exchange for other things of value, such as assets or services rendered.

↪ A company has a choice of issuing common or preferred stock. Common stock constitutes ownership in the company, but doesn't come with guaranteed dividend payments. Preferred stock, on the other hand, doesn't come with voting rights, but does come with regular dividend payments and a higher claim to company assets than with common stock.

↪ There are three important dates that an accountant must keep track of with respect to the payment of dividends: the date of declaration, the date of record, and the date of payment.

↪ Insider trading involves one of the greatest violations of information integrity at the corporate level by revealing facts to private individuals that should be disclosed openly and fairly to the public at large.

Review Exercise

Marcel Campos and Fidel Feisthamel have operated their company as a partnership for several years. Over the years, the company has grown, and the partners believe that it is appropriate to incorporate their company (as Camphamel Limited) and raise more capital to expand to further geographic areas.

Accordingly, Marcel and Fidel engaged a qualified bookkeeper to provide accounting services for their new corporation. The corporate charter authorized the company to issue an unlimited number of common shares and 100,000, $3 non-cumulative preferred shares worth $100 each. On March 3, 2010, the partners transferred assets worth $2,000,000 and liabilities worth $1,250,000 to the company in exchange for 20,000 shares.

Then, Marcel and Fidel proceeded to seek investment capital from private investors. On April 15, 2010, a group of investors agreed to buy a further 20,000 shares for $1,000,000 cash.

Instead of paying the accountant $100,000 of fees in cash, Marcel and Fidel gave the accountant 1,000, $3 preferred shares on April 30, 2010. (These shares have a total value of $100,000.)

For the year ended December 31, 2010, the newly incorporated company made a net income of $200,000. At the directors' meeting held on January 15, 2011, Marcel, Fidel, and a director appointed by the private investors decided to pay out a total of 5% of the net income from 2010 to preferred and common stockholders of record on January 30, 2011. The dividend is to be paid on February 28, 2011. During the period January 1 – February 28, 2011, the company produced net income of $30,000.

Required:

a) Record the required journal entries.

b) Prepare the statement of retained earnings for the year 2010, and for the period January 1 to February 28, 2011.

c) Prepare the stockholders' equity section of the balance sheet as at December 31, 2010.

Review Exercise – Answer

Part a

Date	Account Title and Explanation	Debit	Credit
Mar 3, 2010	Assets	2,000,000	
	Liabilities		1,250,000
	Common Stock		750,000
	Issue of 20,000 common shares for net assets of partnership		
Apr 15, 2010	Cash	1,000,000	
	Common Stock		1,000,000
	Issue of 20,000 common shares for cash		
Apr 30, 2010	Accounting Fee Expense	100,000	
	Preferred Stock		100,000
	Issue of preferred stock in exchange for accounting services		
Dec 31, 2010	Income Summary	200,000	
	Retained Earnings		200,000
	To close income summary account for the year		
Jan 15, 2011	Retained Earnings	10,000	
	Dividends Payable – Common		$7,000
	Dividends Payable – Preferred		$3,000
	Total Dividends (5% × $200,000 = $10,000). Preferred ($3 × 1,000 = $3,000) Common ($10,000 – $3,000 = $7,000)		
Jan 30, 2011	No journal entry required on date of record		
Feb 28, 2011	Dividends Payable - Common	7,000	
	Dividends Payable - Preferred	3,000	
	Cash		10,000
	Recording dividends paid		

Part b

Camphamel Limited Statement of Retained Earnings For the Year Ended December 31, 2010	
Opening balance	$0
Net income for the year	200,000
Balance – December 31, 2010	$200,000

Camphamel Limited Statement of Retained Earnings For the Two Months Ended February 28, 2011	
Balance - January 1, 2011	$200,000
Add: net income for the period	30,000
	230,000
Less: dividends paid	10,000
Balance - February 28, 2011	$220,000

Part c

Camphamel Limited Stockholders' Equity As at December 31, 2010	
Contributed Capital	
Common stock, unlimited shares authorized, 40,000 shares issued and outstanding	$1,750,000
Preferred stock, $3, 100,000 shares authorized, 1,000 shares issued and outstanding	100,000
Total Contributed Capital	1,850,000
Retained Earnings	200,000
Total Stockholders' Equity	$2,050,000

Notes

Chapter 17

CORPORATIONS: THE FINANCIAL STATEMENTS

LEARNING OUTCOMES:

❶ Record income tax expense

❷ Record the closing entries for corporations

❸ Prepare an income statement

❹ Prepare a statement of retained earnings

❺ Record prior period adjustments

❻ Prepare a balance sheet

❼ Calculate financial ratios:

   ✓ Book Value per Common Share

   ✓ Debt-to-Equity Ratio

   ✓ Dividend Payout Ratio

   ✓ Earnings per Share (EPS)

   ✓ Price to Earnings Ratio

Earnings of A Corporation: An Introduction

For investors to make informed decisions about their investments, they need to obtain detailed information about the corporation's assets, liabilities, stockholders' equity and earnings. GAAP provides the rules for reporting these items. The law requires that public corporations provide financial statements that are in accordance with GAAP.

The previous chapter provided the details of the stockholders' equity accounts and, in particular, the contributed capital portion. Now that we have learned how to record the investments by stockholders, and how the accounts are reported in the stockholders' equity section of the balance sheet, we need to take a look at the earnings of the corporation and how these earnings are reported on the income statement. We will also take a closer look at how net income, dividends and other items affect the balance of the retained earnings account.

Thus far, we have learned how the income statement reports revenues and expenses. As we move from a proprietorship to a partnership and now a corporation, we see how the number of accounts and complexities of operating a business increase. Before discussing these complexities any further, we will demonstrate how to account for income taxes on corporate earnings.

Income Tax Expense

Unlike a proprietorship or partnership, a corporation must file and pay taxes on the income it has earned because it is considered a separate legal entity from its owners. Corporate income is taxed at the Federal level, and in some jurisdictions, the state and local level as well. The rules and regulations are set out in the Internal Revenue Code (IRC). Since this is not an income tax course, we will not be going into the details and intricacies of the IRC. However, we will explain how income tax is accrued and reported on the books and financial statements of a corporation.

Income tax expense is recorded in the accounting records on the accrual basis. We apply a given percentage (based on average corporate income tax rates) to the accounting income.

For example, Star Company reported a net income before tax of $266,000. Assuming the corporation pays tax at a rate (average) of 30%, the entry to record income tax expense for the year on December 31 would be:

JOURNAL			
Date	**Account Title and Explanation**	**Debit**	**Credit**
Dec 31	Income Tax Expense	79,800	
	Income Tax Payable		79,800
	To record income tax expense at the year end		

The transaction is recorded with a debit (increase) to income tax expense and a credit (increase) to income tax payable(liability).

As mentioned, the income tax owing to the government is based on laws and rates as set out in the IRC (Internal Revenue Code) and not on GAAP or our accrual basis of accounting; therefore, the actual income tax owing to the government may be quite different from that calculated above.

On occasion, the amount of tax a business should pay is different from the amount due in the current fiscal year. Using the above example, let us now assume that Star Company incurred $20,000 of warranty expenses in year 2011. However, the amount would not be paid in the same year. Based on the income tax law, the warranty expense is only allowed as a deduction on the corporation's tax return in the period it is paid. Therefore, the warranty expense decreases the accounting income with no

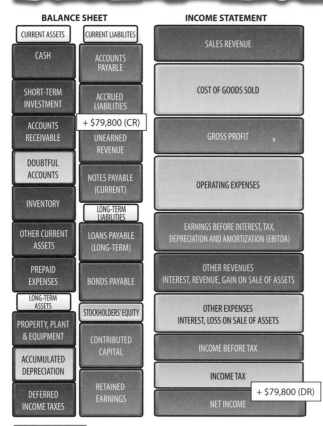

FIGURE 17.1

impact on the taxable income in fiscal 2011. **Accounting income** represents the amount of profit a company makes during a specific period of time (as reported on the income statement). **Taxable income** is the portion of income subject to taxation by law. Income tax payable is calculated from taxable income. The difference between income tax expense and income tax payable is known as *deferred income taxes*. Deferred income taxes can be an asset or liability, depending on the situation. As a result, Star Company's taxable income would be $286,000 ($266,000 + $20,000). The journal entry for this transaction is shown in figure 17.2.

In this example, the deferred income tax is an asset. This means that the company has paid more taxes than what was calculated from their accounting income. In a sense, they have prepaid a portion of their taxes. At some point in the future, the company will get a deduction based on this "prepaid" amount. This is known as a temporary or "timing" difference.

In the following year, however, the opposite could be true. There may be an expense that can be deducted for tax purposes but not for accounting purposes. This would result in taxable income being lower than accounting income. In this case, the deferred income tax would be recorded as a liability by crediting the deferred income taxes account. For example, a company may be depreciating an asset quicker for tax purposes (as per IRC rules) than through their accounting policies. This will give rise to lower taxable income than accounting income resulting in a future income tax liability.

JOURNAL			
Date	**Account Title and Explanation**	**Debit**	**Credit**
Dec 31	Income Tax Expense	79,800	
	Deferred Income Taxes	6,000	
	Income Tax Payable		85,800
	Record income tax expense ($266,000 × *30% = $79,800; $286,000 × 30% = $85,800)*		

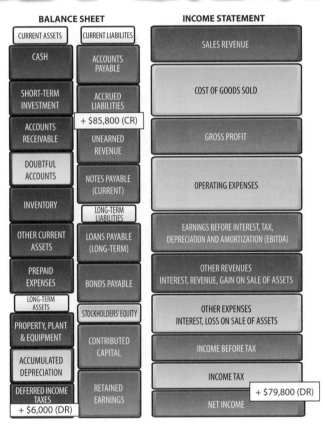

FIGURE 17.2

If the deferred income taxes has a debit balance at year end, it is reported as an asset. If it has a credit balance, it is reported as a liability. The deferred income taxes may be treated as current or long-term depending on the source of the deferred item. For example, if the deferred tax was the result of differences in depreciation amounts for accounting and tax purposes, then the balance in the deferred income taxes account would be reported as a long-term item because it was related to capital assets as shown in figure 17.2.

This topic will be covered in greater detail in more advanced accounting and taxation courses.

Closing Entries for Corporations

If you recall from our examination of partnerships, company earnings are divided at the end of the fiscal year when the income summary account is closed. The balances are transferred to the capital accounts of each individual partner.

> ### WORTH REPEATING...
>
> Recall that the term "closing the books" means updating equity and starting with a new income statement for the next period. There are two methods to accomplish this:
>
> 1. Directly, through owners' capital/retained earnings, or
>
> 2. Through the income summary account

With corporations, revenue and expenses (including income tax expense) are also closed in the income summary. However, unlike partnerships, a corporation closes out the income summary account by transferring the balance to the retained earnings account.

Thus, corporations would transfer the credit balance of revenue accounts to the income summary and transfer the debit balance of expense accounts to the income summary.

JOURNAL			
Date	Account Title and Explanation	Debit	Credit
	Sales Revenue	200,000	
	Income Summary		200,000
	Close revenue accounts		
	Income Summary	150,000	
	Cost of Goods Sold		80,000
	Salary Expense		35,000
	Rent Expense		25,000
	Income Tax Expense		10,000
	Close expense accounts		

FIGURE 17.3

In the example shown in figure 17.3, the income summary account is left with a $50,000 credit balance, which indicates that a net income was generated. To close the income summary account, the journal entry in figure 17.4 must be made.

JOURNAL			
Date	Account Title and Explanation	Debit	Credit
	Income Summary	50,000	
	Retained Earnings		50,000
	To close net income for the year to retained earnings		

FIGURE 17.4

Measuring Income

From previous studies, we have learned that revenue less cost of goods sold tells us the gross profit of the company. From gross profit, operating expenses are subtracted to provide operating income. Operating expenses are incurred to run the day-to-day operations of the company. Other revenue and expenses are then added or subtracted to provide income before tax. Other revenue and expenses are not part of the company's regular day-to-day operations. For example, selling property, plant and equipment is not part of the day-to-day operations of a business. Any gain or loss on the sale will therefore be listed as other revenue or expenses. We will use Darma Corporation as an example to illustrate different presentations of measuring income. Figure 17.5 shows a multi-step income statement which you have studied in previous chapters.

Darma Corporation Income Statement For the Year Ended December 31, 2011		
Sales Revenue		$2,505,750
Less: Sales Discounts	$1,200	
Sales Returns and Allowances	3,800	5,000
Net Sales		2,500,750
Cost of Goods Sold		1,100,000
Gross Profit		1,400,750
Operating Expenses		
Salary Expense	275,000	
Depreciation Expense	44,000	
Administrative Expenses	300,000	619,000
Results from Operating Activities		781,750
Other Revenue and Expenses		
Gain on Sale of Assets	4,500	
Interest Expense	(21,000)	(16,500)
Income before Tax		765,250
Income Tax Expense		229,575
Net Income		$535,675

FIGURE 17.5

A large corporation can have many business activities that can be very complex. Two items that are shown as separate segments on the income statement are called ***Discontinued Operations*** and ***Extraordinary Item***. The new multiple-step income statement of Darma is shown in figure 17.6. The new items on the income statement will be discussed in the paragraphs following the figure.

Darma Corporation Income Statement For the Year Ended December 31, 2011		
Sales Revenue		$2,505,750
Less: Sales Discounts	$1,200	
Sales Returns and Allowances	3,800	5,000
Net Sales		2,500,750
Cost of Goods Sold		1,100,000
Gross Profit		1,400,750
Operating Expenses		
Salary Expense	275,000	
Depreciation Expense	44,000	
Administrative Expenses	300,000	619,000
Results from Operating Activities		781,750
Other Revenue and Expenses		
Gain on Sale of Assets	4,500	
Interest Expense	(21,000)	(16,500)
Income before Tax		765,250
Income Tax Expense		229,575
Income from Continuing Operations		535,675
Discontinued Operations		
Operating Income from Discontinued Operations	125,000	
Gain on Sale of Assets from Discontinued Operations	45,000	
Less: Income Tax Expense (30%)	(51,000)	119,000
Income before Extraordinary Item		654,675
Extraordinary Item		
Loss due to Earthquake	(500,000)	
Less: Income Tax Savings (30%)	150,000	(350,000)
Net Income		$304,675

FIGURE 17.6

In figure 17.6, the term "Income from Continuing Operations" appears where you would normally expect to see "Net Income." The section below "Income from Continuing Operations" includes information for discontinued operations and extraordinary item.

A *discontinued operation* is a segment of a business that is no longer part of regular operating activities. The Accounting Principle Board defines *extraordinary item* as "events or transactions that are distinguished by their unusual nature and by the infrequency of their occurrence." This means an event can be classified as an extraordinary item if it meets the following criteria:

1. The event is unusual in nature and not typical to ordinary activities of the business.

2. Infrequency of occurrence. It is not likely the event will occur again in the foreseeable future.

For example, in addition to manufacturing computer parts, Darma Corporation also operates several divisions specializing in the creation of computer software. During the current year, Darma discontinued one of their software divisions in an attempt to become more competitive in the market. This discontinued division reported an operating income of $125,000 before it was shut down and realized a $45,000 gain from selling the capital assets. The income from the division is classified as operating income from discontinued operations.

Also, during the current year, an earthquake, which was a very unusual and infrequent event in the area, damaged the company's factory, resulting in a $500,000 loss. The loss from this event is recognized as an extraordinary loss. Losses can generate an income tax savings for a corporation. So even though the damage from the earthquake was $500,000, Darma Corporation was able to save a portion of that amount as a reduction of their income tax expense.

Even though companies prepare financial statements, GAAP requires separate disclosure of discontinued operations and extraordinary item. This is done so that stockholders will have a better understanding of the composition of net income when comparing investment opportunities.

Comprehensive Income

Some income statements may have a section called *other comprehensive income* below net income. This section would include items that are not part of continuing operations and do not belong with discontinued or extraordinary items. Other comprehensive income can occur from adjustments for items such as gains or losses caused by fair value reporting related to investments, pension and foreign currency translation transactions. The details of these topics are beyond the scope of this text.

Measuring Changes in Equity

As part of the year-end financial statements, a corporation that follows GAAP must report on how their equity changed over the year. This must include changes in retained earnings, the changes in contributed capital, and any other changes to items that must be reported in equity. These changes can be reported only in the notes of the financial statements, or within an actual statement.

An example of a statement of retained earnings will be used to illustrate how the changes to the retained earnings account will be reported. Retained earnings will increase if the company reported a net income and decrease if the company reported a net loss or paid out dividends.

Figure 17.7 shows the statement of retained earnings for Darma Corporation. The opening value of retained earnings and the dividend amount paid are assumed for this example.

Darma Corporation	
Statement of Retained Earnings	
For the Year Ended December 31, 2011	
Retained Earnings, January 1, 2011	$1,340,000
Add: Net Income	304,675
Less: Dividends	(400,000)
Retained Earnings, December 31, 2011	$1,244,675

FIGURE 17.7

The statement of retained earnings is very straight forward. The first value shown is the opening value at the beginning of the period, followed by items that will increase or decrease the value of retained earnings. After the additions and subtractions, the last value is the balance at the end of the period. This value will then appear on the balance sheet.

There are two basic calculations when it comes to calculating stockholders' equity.

$$\text{Stockholders' Equity} = \text{Contributed Capital} + \text{Retained Earnings}$$

Retained earnings can be calculated by using the figures provided in the statement of retained earnings. The formula is very similar to how owner's equity is calculated.

$$\text{Ending Retained Earnings} = \text{Beginning Retained Earnings} + \text{Net Income} - \text{Dividends}$$

Prior Period Adjustments

The statement of changes in equity is also the place where adjustments for accounting errors and changes to accounting policies having an effect on prior periods are made.

A CLOSER LOOK

The stockholders' equity section of a corporation's balance sheet is an important one for accountants and analysts to become familiar with. It is a section that in many ways separates corporations from other types of business ownership.

That is, unlike proprietorships and partnerships, corporations divide their stockholders' equity section into two: contributed capital, which represents the value of all company stock, and retained earnings, representing company earnings to date not paid out in the form of dividends.

Retained earnings is essentially calculated by adding net income to retained earnings at the start of the year and then deducting any dividends that are paid. That is precisely what is done in this sample calculation of retained earnings.

	(in thousands)
Net Income	$1,103.6
Retained Earnings, Beginning of Year	1,286.4
Change in Accounting Policy (Note 3)	0.2
Repurchase of Common Stock (Note 17)	–
Dividends	(110.6)
Retained Earnings, End of Year	$2,279.6

Assume in 2011 an auditor discovered that the 2010 records included a $25,000 debit entry in the repairs and maintenance (expense) account that should have been posted as a debit in the equipment (capital asset) account. The effect of this error is that income for 2010 was understated by $25,000. Should we simply correct the error by debiting the equipment account and crediting the expense account? The answer is no. While this entry would correct the equipment account, the reversing of the expense would understate the repairs and maintenance account for the current year. Instead, the following entry is required:

JOURNAL			
Date	Account Title and Explanation	Debit	Credit
	Equipment	25,000	
	Retained Earnings		17,500
	Income tax payable (25,000 × 30%)		7,500
	To correct accounts in 2011 for error recorded in 2010		

FIGURE 17.8

The error caused net income for 2010 to be understated by a net amount of $17,500 ($25,000 less the tax on this amount at a rate of 30%). By crediting retained earnings for the net effect of the error, we have restated (corrected) this account to reflect the income that would have been recorded had the error not occurred. Income taxes payable are also corrected to reflect the actual amount owing on the income earned.

Darma Corporation would prepare their statement of retained earnings to look like the figure shown below.

Darma Corporation Statement of Retained Earnings For the Year Ended December 31, 2011	
Retained Earnings, January 1, 2011	$1,340,000
Add: Prior Year Adjustment	17,500
Add: Net Income	304,675
Less: Dividends	(400,000)
Retained Earnings, December 31, 2011	$1,262,175

FIGURE 17.9

The adjustment to retained earnings is listed before any other items are added or subtracted from retained earnings.

Changes in Accounting Policies

A prior period adjustment may also be needed when the corporation is reporting comparative numbers (statements for two or more years) and a change in accounting policy has occurred. For example, assume Darma Corporation decided to change its inventory valuation method from LIFO to FIFO and reported 2011 and 2010 financial statements. The opening balance of retained earnings for 2010 would have to be adjusted for the cumulative effect of using one method over the other. In this case there would have been a larger depreciation expense (lower net income) for 2010.

Measuring Financial Position

The balance sheet indicates the financial standing of a business. It reports on the value of assets, liabilities and equity. Assets and liabilities are split into current and long-term items, with the current items listed first. Equity for a corporation is split between contributed capital and retained earnings as was discussed in the previous chapter. Figure 17.10 shows the balance sheet for Darma Corporation.

Darma Corporation Balance Sheet As at December 31, 2011	
Assets	
Current Assets	
Cash	$87,650
Short-Term Investments	287,580
Accounts Receivable	685,725
Inventory	1,652,840
Prepaid Expenses	16,840
Total Current Assets	2,730,635
Long-Term Assets	
Property, Plant & Equipment (net)	2,847,010
Goodwill	777,185
Total Assets	$6,354,830
Liabilities	
Current Liabilities	
Accrued Liabilities	$145,845
Accounts Payable	426,890
Current Portion of Long-Term Debt	43,870
Total Current Liabilities	616,605
Long-Term Liabilities	
Long-Term Debt	568,750
Deferred Tax Liability	24,800
Total Liabilities	1,210,155
Stockholders' Equity	
Common Stock unlimited shares authorized, 200,000 shares issued and outstanding	3,900,000
Retained Earnings	1,244,675
Total Stockholders' Equity	5,144,675
Total Liabilities and Equity	$6,354,830

FIGURE 17.10

Financial statements prepared by corporations will show the current year's performance and the previous year's performance. This allows a potential investor to see how the company has performed compared to their last year. For a real world example, the appendix shows an excerpt from Home Depot's annual report from 2012.

Calculation of Financial Ratios

Book Value per Share

When referring to the value of company stock, there are two terms that are generally used; one is market value, which represents the price at which stock is traded on the stock market. The other is book value, which represents the theoretical value of a share based on a stockholders' claim to the company's assets.

Theoretically, a share's market value should mirror its book value. In other words, what the company is worth on the financial statements should be reflected in the price at which its shares are trading. However, in the real world shares are often bought and sold for a very different price than reflected on the financial statements. In other words, the book value does not match the market value.

For various reasons, a share's market value can deviate significantly from its book value. Again, theoretically speaking, this should not happen. A share of ownership in a company should represent the stake that the stockholder has in the actual value of the company. Nevertheless, once a company issues shares and sells them on the market, the price at which they trade often takes on a life of its own.

Remember that shares in a company represent a claim on assets if they are liquidated. People buy shares for all sorts of reasons, such as an expectation of a dividend, the existence of a bull market, or the prediction of an increase in price due to speculation. All these factors and more affect the value at which shares trade on the market; therefore it does not always equate to a company's worth on its books.

The calculation of book value per share is relatively simple. Here is the formula that is often used:

$$\text{Book Value per Share} = \frac{\text{Stockholders' Equity} - \text{Preferred Equity}}{\text{Number of Common Shares Outstanding}}$$

Note that preferred equity should include preferred dividends if there are any outstanding. This is because preferred stockholders are not considered owners of the corporation, since they do not have voting rights.

In other words, the formula calculates the amount of money that each common stockholder would receive if all the company's assets were immediately liquidated.

WORTH REPEATING...

Common stockholders have voting rights and are awarded dividends at the discretion of management. Preferred stockholders usually do not have voting rights but are privy to regular and fixed dividend payments.

Let us use some actual figures to demonstrate how this formula really works. To do this, we will use the information from figure 17.11 which is part of a balance sheet.

(figures in millions)

Sample Company Balance Sheet (an excerpt) As at December 31, 2011		
Liabilities	**2011**	**2010**
Current Liabilities		
Short-term debt	$90.0	$157.9
Accounts Payable	911.7	545.2
Current Portion of Long-Term Debt	0.2	400.4
Total Current Liabilities	1,001.9	1,103.5
Long-Term Liabilities		
Long-Term Debt	1,339.4	1,357.1
Deferred Tax Liability	988.1	632.1
Accrued Pension Benefits	244.8	219.6
Accrued Environmental Costs	121.0	110.3
Other Long-Term Liabilities	2.7	14.1
Total Long-Term Liabilities	2,696.0	2,333.2
Total Liabilities	3,697.9	3,436.7
Stockholders' Equity		
Contributed Capital		
Preferred stock, $2, 10,000 shares authorized none issued and outstanding		
Common stock, unlimited shares authorized 316,411,209 and 314,403,147 shares issued and outstanding at December 31, 2011 and 2010 respectively	1,461.3	1,431.6
Total Contributed Capital	1,461.3	1,431.6
Retained Earnings	4,557.4	1,348.7
Total Stockholders' Equity	6,018.7	2,780.3
Total Liabilities and Stockholders' Equity	$9,716.6	$6,217.0

FIGURE 17.11

All the numbers we need for our formula are located in the stockholders' equity section of this company's financial statements.

Since the entire section summarizes stockholders' equity, that figure is tallied for us at the bottom of the column for 2011: $6,018,700,000.

The company has no preferred stock outstanding. Therefore, the number we plug into our formula for preferred stock is zero.

The complete calculation for book value per share is presented as shown below:

$$\text{Book Value per Share} = \frac{\text{Total Stockholders' Equity} - \text{Preferred Equity}}{\text{Number of Common Shares Outstanding}}$$

$$= \frac{\$6,018,700,000}{316,411,209} = \$19.02$$

The book value per share for this corporation at the 2011 year end is $19.02.

However, anyone looking up the actual stock price in the financial statements during 2011 might find a number ranging anywhere from $80 to $100 a share.

So, what accounts for this difference between book value and market value? Again, a number of factors can account for this discrepancy. The market price of a share is ultimately determined by speculation — speculation about how the company will do in the upcoming year, speculation about how the industry will do, as well as market trends in general.

This doesn't mean that a share price reflects a random calculation made by investors. Instead, some consensus is developed about how well the company is performing, which drives demand for the stock and ultimately determines the price.

Debt-to-Equity Ratio

The **debt-to-equity ratio** is another tool that investors and analysts have at their disposal to assess a corporation's financial statements. In fact, the name of the ratio speaks for itself, since it simply divides the company's total debt by total equity to produce a figure that the public uses to assess performance.

In other words, to calculate the debt-to-equity ratio, one goes to the balance sheet to find the figure for total liabilities, and the figure for total stockholders' equity.

If we refer back to figure 17.11 and look at the totals (at the bottom of the page), under 'liabilities', we see total amount of debt for 2011 is $3,697,900,000, and under 'stockholders' equity' the total amount of equity for 2011 is $6,018,700,000. These numbers are all we need to produce our debt-to-equity ratio as follows:

$$\text{Debt-to-Equity Ratio} = \frac{\text{Total Liabilities}}{\text{Stockholders' Equity}}$$

$$= \frac{\$3,697,900,000}{\$6,018,700,000} = 0.61$$

What does this number mean? A debt-to-equity ratio of 1:1 would mean that, for every dollar of equity a company has, it has one dollar of debt. If the debt-to-equity ratio is higher than one, it means that the company's lenders have more dollars tied up in the company than the owners — or stockholders. Consequently, if the debt-to-equity ratio is lower than one, then ownership is essentially more responsible for financing the company.

Which situation do you think is preferable for a company: to have the company financed by lenders — or have it financed by ownership? It is usually preferable that owners finance the company, more so than creditors. When that happens, more of the company's assets belong to stockholders.

This is indicative of how families approach home ownership, how small proprietorships and partnerships approach business ownership, and how small corporations ideally approach financing.

The sample corporation's debt-to-equity ratio of 0.61 calculated for the year 2011 represents a preferable way of financing the business. The alternative, which is a ratio greater than 1, would mean that the company is likely vulnerable to lenders and the interest rates they charge over the long term.

Dividend Payout Ratio

Since dividends, or at least the potential for dividends, must form part of an analysis of company stock, the investing community has produced a ratio to assess just how much in dividends a corporation is paying out to stockholders. This is called the *dividend payout ratio*. In fact, the dividend payout ratio is relatively easy to put together and analyze, because all it does is calculate dividends paid as a percentage of net income. In other words, the ratio answers the following question: How much of the company's earnings does the company pay out in dividends? Here is the basic formula that is used:

$$\text{Dividend Payout Ratio} = \frac{\text{Dividends Paid in a Year}}{\text{Net Income}}$$

For example, if a company made $1 million, and paid out $100,000 in dividends to its stockholders, the resulting dividend payout ratio would be:

$$\frac{\$100,000}{\$1,000,000} = 10\%$$

In other words, the company is paying out 10% of its earnings in the form of dividends, and the rest of net income, which is 90%, is being kept in the business in the form of retained earnings.

Earnings per Share (EPS)

Another stock market term that one might see frequently used in the financial press is **earnings per share**; this is calculated using a similar method as book value per share. Here is a basic formula for earnings per share that is used to calculate earnings per share:

$$\frac{\text{Net Income} - \text{Preferred Dividends}}{\text{Average \# Common Shares Outstanding}}$$

This ratio attempts to assess how profitable the company is for the owners. The formula is similar to the book value per share in that preferred dividends are subtracted. Preferred dividends are not included, since they are not paid out to the owners.

The paragraph under contributed capital in the balance sheet in figure 17.11 gives us the information we need here. There were 314,403,147 shares of common stock outstanding at the 2010 year end and 316,411,209 shares outstanding at the 2011 year end. The average of these two numbers produces the following to be included in the formula:

$$\frac{314,403,147 + 316,411,209}{2} = 315,407,178$$

It should also be noted that companies may use various methods to calculate the average number of shares outstanding, which is why reproducing the exact number provided in published financial statements might be difficult. For example, companies might use a monthly or daily average number instead of a yearly number.

The earnings per share ratio is:

$$\frac{\$1,103,600,000}{315,407,178} = \$3.50$$

In other words, the company is making $3.50 for every outstanding share. The general interpretation is the larger the number, the more profitable the company.

IN THE REAL WORLD

A share's book value essentially represents the value associated with a company's net assets. In an ideal world, this book value would be reflected in the stock price. In other words, a share would represent a portion of value in company assets. In fact, there was a time when stock values did in fact match book values. Although that hasn't happened in a while, the financial crisis of 2008 might mean that what was old is now new again. That is, book value might be coming back in style.

After World War II, and before the high-flying days of the 1980s on Wall Street, it was generally expected that a share would trade at a price equal to its book value. Indeed, this reflects a common sense approach to ownership. If you own part of a company, which stockholders do, then you own its assets and are entitled to the value of these assets.

However, this era of prudent investment and modest expectation of stock performance started to change. By 2004, stock prices were trading at an average of 280% of their book value. That means that stock was being bought and sold at almost three times the worth of the stock's underlying assets, so to speak. People were willing to buy stock at high prices, and even more people seemed willing to snatch them up. This was the state of affairs until recently. Then in the fall of 2008, the financial crisis hit world markets. Prices had skyrocketed, but the underlying fundamentals of investments were not solid enough. So, prices started to tumble at record rates. Pensions were plummeting in value, speculators were selling like mad, and investor confidence hit lows not seen in decades. The good times in the stock market were over as financial players worldwide started reevaluating their options.

One of those options was to start searching for stock of companies whose fundamentals were sound and whose book value actually reflected market prices. In other words, the financial crisis might lead to a new trend: the expectation that stock is sold at something closer to the value of assets owned by the company.

When strong performing companies have stock prices that mirror book prices it means, among other things, that the stock price won't suffer the stresses of a market downturn, nor is market speculation artificially propping up insane prices.

Instead, it might mean that companies and the economy might be getting back to fundamentals which bodes well for financial markets trying to see the light at the end of the tunnel during otherwise difficult times.

In addition, if our sample company had preferred dividends of $50,000,000 for 2011, this amount should be subtracted from the net income when calculating earnings per share:

$$\frac{(\$1,103,600,000 - \$50,000,000)}{315,407,178} = \$3.34$$

This results in lower earnings per share calculation.

Variations in Presentation of Earnings per Share

Sometimes companies will report EPS calculations for each area reported on the income statement. Using the information provided on the income statement of Darma Corporation, we will calculate the EPS assuming there was no preferred stock and the average number of common shares during the year was 100,000.

Earnings per Share:

Income from continuing operations: $535,675 ÷ 100,000	$5.36
Income from discontinued operations: $119,000 ÷ 100,000	1.19
Income before extraordinary item: $654,675 ÷ 100,000	6.55
Loss from extraordinary item: $350,000 ÷ 100,000	(3.50)
Net income: $304,675 ÷ 100,000	$3.05

FIGURE 17.12

Price-Earnings Ratio

Another ratio commonly used by stockholders to evaluate their investment in a corporation is that of the **price-earnings ratio** (P/E ratio), which divides the market price per share by earnings per share. This provides the investor with a measurement of share price to actual earnings of the corporation. It is sometimes used as an indicator to buy/sell or hold shares.

Assume the following details for Darma Corporation:

	2011	2010
EPS	$3.05	$4.56
Market price per share	43.50	35.80
Calculate the P/E for each year:		
P/E	43.50/3.05	35.80/4.56
	= 14.26	= 7.85

FIGURE 17.13

The ratios indicate the shares are selling for 14.26 and 7.85 times the earnings in 2011 and 2010 respectively.

It should be mentioned that an increasing P/E ratio may not necessarily mean the corporation has improved its attractiveness as an investment because stockholders may suddenly react negatively to the higher share price and sell their shares which will then cause share prices to fall.

In Summary

↪ The focus of this chapter has been on reporting and analyzing the earnings of corporations.

↪ Corporations are liable for income taxes based on profits earned by the business. While we base income tax expense on accounting income, we also recognize that actual taxes (income taxes payable) are based on government laws and rates. We account for the temporary difference between the two amounts using a deferred income taxes account.

↪ Stockholders demand timely and accurate financial information to make good investment decisions. A complex income statement reports income from continuing operations, discontinued operations and extraordinary items.

↪ Corporations sometimes have certain types of income and expenses that meet the definition of "other comprehensive items". These are presented separately on the income statement.

↪ The statement of retained earnings provides stockholders with a summary of the changes in retained earnings from the beginning to the end of the current accounting period. It takes into consideration: prior period adjustments, earnings in the current year and dividend payments.

↪ Earnings per share and price to earnings ratios are two measures stockholders use to evaluate their investment in a corporation.

Review Exercise

The following information was taken from the accounting records of Shah Inc. at December 31, 2010. Assume the tax rate is 35%.

FINANCIAL STATEMENT ITEMS	AMOUNT
Prior-year error – debit to Retained Earnings	7,500
Income tax expense on operating income from discontinued operations	12,250
Total dividends	25,000
Common stock, 40,000 shares issued	155,000
Sales revenue	710,000
Interest expense	30,000
Operating income, discontinued operations	35,000
Loss due to lawsuit	11,000
Sales Discounts	15,000
Income tax savings on sale of discontinued operations (sold at a loss)	14,000
General expenses	62,000
Income tax expense on continuing operations	74,200
Preferred stock, non-cumulative, $5.00, 1,000 shares issued	50,000
Retained Earnings, January 1, 2010 (prior to adjustment)	110,000
Loss on sale of discontinued operations	40,000
Cost of goods sold	380,000

Required:

1. Prepare an income statement for the year ended December 31, 2010.
2. Prepare a statement of retained earnings for Shah Inc. for the year ended December 31, 2010.
3. Calculate the EPS ratio.

Review Exercise – Answer

Part 1

Shah Inc.
Income Statement
For the Year Ended December 31, 2010

Sales Revenue		$710,000
Less: Sales Discounts		(15,000)
Net Sales		695,000
Cost of Goods Sold		(380,000)
Gross Profit		315,000
Less: Operating Expenses		
General Expenses	$62,000	
Operating Income		253,000
Less: Other Expenses		
Interest Expense	30,000	
Loss Due to Lawsuit	11,000	
Income Tax Expense	74,200	115,200
Income from Continuing Operations		137,800
Discontinued Operations		
Operating Income	35,000	
Less: Income Tax	(12,250)	22,750
Loss on Sale of Discontinued Operations	(40,000)	
Less: Income Tax Saving	14,000	(26,000)
Net Income		$134,550

Part 2

Shah Inc.
Statement of Retained Earnings
For the Year Ended December 31, 2010

Retained earnings, January 1, 2010 (as originally reported)	$110,000
Correction to prior-year error - debit	(7,500)
Retained earnings, January 1, 2010, as adjusted	102,500
Net Income for current year	134,550
	237,050
Dividends for 2010	(25,000)
Retained earnings, December 31, 2010	$212,050

Part 3

$$EPS = \frac{\text{Net Income} - \text{Preferred Dividends}}{\text{Average \# Common Shares Outstanding}}$$

Since Preferred Dividends = $5.00 x 1000 = $5,000 and assuming the same number of shares has been outstanding throughout the year:

EPS = ($134,550 – $5,000) ÷ 40,000 shares = $3.24

Notes

Chapter 18
INVESTMENTS

LEARNING OUTCOMES:

❶ Understand different types of short-term investments

❷ Prepare journal entries for debt (loan) investments

❸ Prepare journal entries for equity investments

❹ Understand different types of long-term investments

❺ Apply controls for investments

Investments: An Introduction

Cash is the lifeblood of a business. A business must make sure that it has enough cash to cover general operations and to pay for debt. If a business is doing well managing their cash, they may sometimes find themselves in the position of having more cash on hand than they really need. In cases like this, leaving it in a checking account generates little return. Instead, forward-looking business managers would choose investment options that would provide a good return in their desired time frame.

There are many different ways to invest, but all investments fall into three major categories: capital assets, debt or equity as shown in figure 18.1. Capital assets (property, plant and equipment) have already been discussed in previous chapters. In this chapter, we focus on investments made through purchasing debt and equity. Purchasing debt means lending money, usually by purchasing the bonds of another company. The bonds will generate interest revenue over time. Purchasing equity means buying an ownership stake (stock) in another company. The stock is expected to generate dividend revenue.

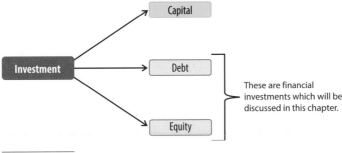

FIGURE 18.1

Types of Investments

We will now provide a more detailed overview of debt and equity investments.

Debt Investments

When a company invests its money in the form of debt, it lends money to a person or business in exchange for interest payments in addition to the return of principal at a later date. The terms of the transaction are established in advance, so that both parties to the loan agree upon the amount of the initial loan, the schedule of payments to be made, the interest rate to be charged and the length or term of the loan.

Generally two types of debt investment options are available to a business or organization: traditional loans and bonds.

Equity Investments

Investing in equities is different from investing in debt. Unlike debt, which involves lending money in return for interest, equity investment involves buying ownership, usually in the form of stock, in a company.

A vintage stock certificate issued in 1913.

Stock represents part ownership of a company. For public companies, stock is bought and sold at the price listed on a stock exchange. There are various reasons to invest in stock. One is to sell the stock for a price greater than what it was purchased. Another could be to receive dividend revenue. The stock price and the size and frequency of dividend payments often reflect the issuing company's profitability.

There are advantages and disadvantages that come with investing in debt or equity. Debt is very stable and offers guaranteed returns, however the rate of return is usually low. Equity, on the other hand, usually has a higher expected rate of return than debt. However, there is more risk involved, since the return is not guaranteed due to fluctuations of the market and the discretionary nature of dividends.

To minimize the risks associated with equities, especially in the short term, investors often choose to buy stock in profitable companies that have a history of making regular dividend payments and maintaining their stock prices. These types of stocks are often described as *blue chip stocks*.

Terms of Investments

All investments can also be grouped based on the length of time managers intend to keep them. Why do we say intend? Because although a company may plan on keeping an investment for a certain duration, circumstances can arise that will cause management to change their mind.

Let us explain the concept of intention in more detail. A company will have a plan when it comes to investing. They may be looking for a place to invest their money for a few months, or may be planning on long term returns. The plan of the company highlights their intention, and it is important because each type of investment is classified based on intent. It is important to note that the intention at the time the investment is purchased may not always be the actual outcome. For example, a company may plan to invest for the long term, but an unexpected event happens which causes them to sell their investment early to get the cash.

In accounting, the intention at the purchase date will determine how the investment is initially classified. A **short-term investment** matures or will be sold within one year. A **long-term investment** matures or will be sold within more than one year.

The short-term investment is usually very liquid and is listed immediately after cash on the balance sheet. The long-term investment account is listed before property, plant and equipment. The distinction between short-term and long-term investments is important, since it will impact certain ratios, such as the current ratio.

Classifications of Investments

GAAP segregates all debt and equity investments into three different classifications as outlined below.

1. **Trading:**
   A trading investment is one that you intend to sell within a short period of time (typically a year). The company does not plan to hold the investment beyond the short term and intends the investment to be sold for the purpose of making a profit during this period. Trading investments can be in the form of debt or equity. You may receive interest or dividends while holding the investment. Because of the short-term nature of this investment, any gains or losses on the sale of the investment will be recorded on the income statement.

2. **Held to maturity:**
   These investments have a maturity date and management intends to hold the investments to their maturity date. They could be either short-term or long-term depending on the date of maturity. These investments are usually in the form of debt (i.e. bonds) and would pay interest on a regular basis. These debt investments may be purchased at a premium or discount (like what we learned about bonds in a previous chapter). If the company later decides to sell the investment before the maturity date, any gain or loss on the sales of investments will be recorded on the income statement.

3. **Available for sale:**
   This is a category created to include any investments that are not trading or held to maturity. They could be short-term or long-term, depending on management's intention when the investment was purchased. Available for sale investments can be either debt or equity, and would therefore pay either interest or dividends. Throughout the time of holding the

investment, its value may fluctuate; therefore, at the end of each period, the investment value must be adjusted to the market value of the investment. This revaluation results in unrealized gains or losses. The term *unrealized* is used because the investment has not been sold yet. The gain or loss is only shown on paper and will not be realized until the investment is sold. Unrealized gains or losses from available for sale investments do not impact net income. The discussion of unrealized gains or losses is beyond the scope of this textbook.

The comparison of the three classifications of investments is summarized in figure 18.2.

Investment Classification

1 Trading

2 Held to maturity

3 Available for sale

Investment	Intention	Term of Investment	Type of Investment
Trading	Intend to sell in the near future	short-term	Debt or Equity
Held to maturity	Intend to keep until maturity	short-term or long-term	Debt
Available for sale	Uncertain intention	short-term or long-term	Debt or Equity

FIGURE 18.2

IN THE REAL WORLD

Assets on the balance sheet are organized according to their liquidity. That is why making the distinction between short-term and long-term assets is so important. This fact was demonstrated vividly through events that occurred on Wall Street during February, 2008.

Until that time, big investors were treating auction-rate securities as short-term assets on the balance sheet. Auction-rate securities are essentially long-term bonds. However, large financial institutions such as Goldman Sachs, Lehman Brothers and Merrill Lynch were holding monthly auctions that gave investors the opportunity to sell these bonds on an open market — an auction market.

The frequency of these auctions allowed financial institutions to sell these securities as highly liquid short-term assets that were almost as safe as cash. This all fell apart, however, when auctions started to fail and banks stopped supporting them. Investors were stuck with the bonds and unable to sell them in the short term as advertised. In other words they could no longer be classified as short term and had to be moved to the long-term assets section of the balance sheet.

In essence, auction-rate securities were an attempt to change long-term assets into short-term assets. It didn't work, and thousands of big investors were left having to adjust their balance sheets in the process.

In the following sections, we will examine how to record the different transactions for each of the three classifications along with their corresponding impacts on the accounting maps.

Trading Investments

Trading investments are very liquid financial investments. They can include debt or equity of a specific company, or investments in **Money Market Securities**. The money market is a pool of short-term debt such as commercial paper, Treasury bills (also known as T-bills) and other items that will mature in less than one year. An investment in the money market is usually considered a very low risk investment because the amount invested is not going to be lost and will generate a small profit.

An investment in debt or equity of a specific company can generate a greater profit than the money market, however there is a risk that an equity investment will actually lose money.

Traditional loans and stock purchases are illustrated for the trading investment in this section.

How Traditional Loans are Recorded

Our first example will illustrate how to record a short-term traditional loan investment for accounting purposes.

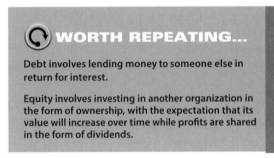

Assume on January 1, 2012, a business lends $10,000 (the principal) to another business, charging an interest rate of 5% per annum with a repayment term of one year. Interest is due on December 31, 2012. We first record the initial loan of $10,000 by crediting (decreasing) the cash account and debiting (increasing) the short-term investment account.

The journal entry and the accounting map are shown in figure 18.3.

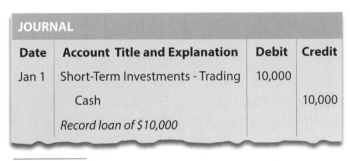

FIGURE 18.3

Interest Earned

Since the traditional loan is a debt investment, which receives interest on a fixed date, the interest earned by the lender is generally known even before the first payment is received. As long as the business that is borrowing the money (the borrower) can meet its required payments, the lender will earn $500, which is 5% interest on the loan. If the loan payments proceed as planned, the $500 in interest revenue needs to be recorded in the lender's financial statements on December 31, 2012.

The journal entry is: debit cash for $500 and credit interest revenue for $500.

JOURNAL			
Date	Account Title and Explanation	Debit	Credit
Dec 31	Cash	500	
	Interest Revenue		500
	Record interest earned on short-term loan		

FIGURE 18.4

It is important to note that the interest earned from the loan is treated as interest revenue in the other revenue section of the income statement.

In our current example, recording the interest earned as general revenue would be misleading. The revenue was not earned as a result of business operations, such as selling goods or services, but by investing surplus cash on hand. Investment decisions are independent of the day-to-day operations of the company and need to be treated as such in the financial statements.

Repayment at Maturity

To complete the process, the repayment of the principal must be recorded. This is done by debiting cash and crediting the investment on the maturity date which is December 31, 2012 in this example.

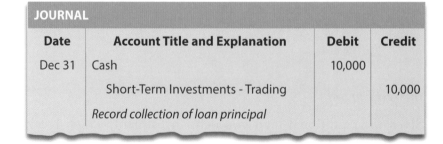

JOURNAL			
Date	Account Title and Explanation	Debit	Credit
Dec 31	Cash	10,000	
	Short-Term Investments - Trading		10,000
	Record collection of loan principal		

FIGURE 18.5

We have now completed the steps necessary to record the transactions involved in a traditional loan, including the payment of interest and repayment of the principal.

Note that beside the traditional loans, short-term investments can also be in other common forms of debt such as bonds.

The primary difference between bonds and traditional loans is that there is a market for bonds, whereas traditional loans are negotiated on an individual basis between specific parties.

A CLOSER LOOK

Let us examine the impact of erroneously recording the interest made from the loan as general revenue. What would this do to the state of the company's finances? In short, it would indicate an increase in revenues without any corresponding increase in the cost of goods sold. This would inflate gross profit and provide management with a distorted picture of the state of the business.

This could have an effect on decisions made throughout the business, such as marketing, pricing and market share. An inaccurate assessment of business finances resulting from overstated general revenues can therefore lead to bad business decisions. This is why it is so important to first record financial transactions accurately. In this case, that means treating income from short-term debt investments as interest revenue, but not general revenue (sales revenue).

How Stock Purchases are Recorded

Some conditions that must be met when buying stock that is a trading investment are shown below.

- The company must intend to sell the stock within one year for it to qualify as a trading investment.
- The company must hold less than 20% of the stock in the invested company.
- The company cannot play an important role in the operations of the business that issued the stock.

When a company purchases stock, they usually require the services of a third party called a broker. A broker will buy or sell stocks or bonds for the investor and will charge a fee. These brokerage fees are added to the cost of the investment.

IN THE REAL WORLD

Have you heard of Fannie Mae and Freddie Mac? No, they aren't someone's aunt and uncle. They were once large financial giants, and they serve as a perfect example of the risks involved in the equity market.

Putting aside the unusual names, Fannie Mae and Freddie Mac were large government-subsidized private corporations partly responsible for providing low cost mortgages to millions of Americans.

Both of these corporations were hit extremely hard by the mortgage crisis that started in 2007. By September 2008, the government had seized ownership of these two companies. One of the results was the freezing-out of countless stockholders, which involved lost ownership stake, stock value and dividend payments. Holders of the company's debt, however, were left protected.

As the saga of Fannie Mae and Freddie Mac shows, the risks associated with equity are very real. Even stockholders in seemingly can't-lose companies can end up with nothing: no value, no dividends, and no protection. It's something to keep in mind when purchasing even the surest looking forms of equity investments.

As an example, we will use the purchase of 100 shares in DEF Company Inc. on January 1 at $400 a share, with a brokerage fee of $300. The total price of the stock is $40,000 and the total cost is $40,300. The journal entry in figure 18.6 shows that this purchase is recorded by crediting (decreasing) the cash account and debiting (increasing) the short-term investment account which also includes the brokerage fees.

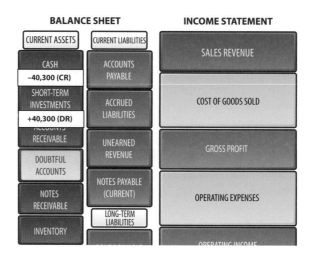

JOURNAL			
Date	**Account Title and Explanation**	**Debit**	**Credit**
Jan 1	Short-Term Investments – Trading	40,300	
	Cash		40,300
	Purchase of 100 shares of DEF Company Inc. at $400 per share plus $300 broker-age fee		

FIGURE 18.6

Note that recording the purchase of bonds maturing in less than one year is identical to recording the purchase of stock as shown in the journal entry of figure 18.6.

How Dividend Payments Are Recorded

Let us take the purchase of our stock in DEF Company Inc. to the next level by going through the appropriate steps involved in recording the receipt of a dividend payment (share of the net income).

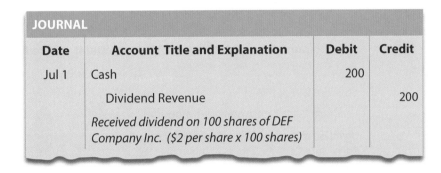

JOURNAL			
Date	Account Title and Explanation	Debit	Credit
Jul 1	Cash	200	
	Dividend Revenue		200
	Received dividend on 100 shares of DEF Company Inc. ($2 per share x 100 shares)		

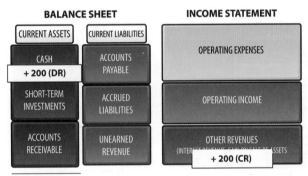

FIGURE 18.7

In our current example, a $2 per share dividend payment was paid to stockholders on July 1. This transaction involves a debit (increase) to cash, and a corresponding credit (increase) to dividend revenue.

Selling Stock and Recording the Sale

There are two ways in which an investor can receive income through owning stock: by receiving dividends (however, not all companies pay dividends) and by selling the stock. When stock is sold for a price higher than its original cost, a gain will be realized and recorded. If the stock is sold for less than its cost, a loss will be realized and recorded.

To go back to our example, our purchase of stock in DEF Company Inc. had an original cost of $40,300. We sell the stock less than a year later on November 1 for a total price of $39,900. The brokerage fee attached to this current transaction is $300 which should be deducted from the total cash received.

JOURNAL

Date	Account Title and Explanation	Debit	Credit
Nov 1	Cash	39,600	
	Loss on Sale of Investments	700	
	Short-Term Investments – Trading		40,300
	Sold DEF shares for $39,900 less a brokerage fee of $300		

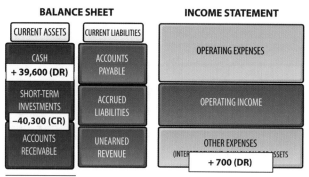

FIGURE 18.8

The net proceeds going to the company's cash account amount to $39,600 ($39,900 - $300). The cost of purchasing the stock was $40,300, but the selling price was $39,900 less the brokerage fee of $300. This represents a loss on the sale of $700 ($40,300 - $39,600). A gain or loss on the sale is the difference between the proceeds on the sale and the current carrying value of the investment (i.e. the book value).

To record this in the books, we debit cash with $39,600, and loss on sale of investments with $700. We credit the entire original amount of $40,300 to the short-term investment account.

Buying Stock for the Short Term

When a business buys stock in another company, the intention may be to make a profit when selling the shares at a later date. The shares are likely to change in value while being held. This section addresses the sale of stock within a fiscal period. However, as discussed in the next sections of this chapter, if the stock is held for more than one accounting period, the change in the stock's value may require it to be recorded as an unrealized gain or loss.

The accounting treatment would depend on the company's intention when it purchased the stock. If the stock was expected to be held for the long term, the gain in market price would not be recorded as income. If, on the other hand, the stock was held for trading in the short term, increases in market price over the accounting period are recorded as income. The details of these transactions are outside the scope of this course.

Held to Maturity Investments

Recall that held to maturity investments are usually debt investments that have a maturity date. If the maturity date is more than one year away, then the investment is considered a long-term investment. The long-term investment is considered a long-term asset and will show up on the balance sheet just before property, plant and equipment as shown earlier in figure 18.2.

The most common form of held to maturity investments are bonds. Bonds are a form of debt that can be readily bought and sold on a bond market. A bond is purchased at its fair value plus any transaction costs. Regular payments are received in the form of interest and the bond is held until its term expires or until it is resold on the market.

When buying and selling bonds, brokerage fees usually have to be paid by parties involved. The accounting treatment for a brokerage fee is the same as discussed in the trading investment section. Therefore, for simplicity, we will ignore the brokerage fees in this section.

BALANCE SHEET

Acquisition: For example, Maynard Company purchased bonds and paid $45,000 on October 1, 2011. The bonds have a par value of $45,000, pay 8% semi-annually on March 31 and September 30 and will mature on September 30, 2014. Maynard Company plans to keep these bonds until they mature, so they will be classified as a held-to maturity investment. Since the maturity date of the bond is more than one year away, the investment is considered a long term asset. The journal entry related to this acquisition is shown in figure 18.9.

JOURNAL			
Date	Account Title and Explanation	Debit	Credit
Oct 1	Long-Term Investments – Held to Maturity	45,000	
	Cash		45,000
	Purchased bonds to be held-to-maturity		

FIGURE 18.9

As shown in figure 18.9, equity would not be impacted since an increase to long-term investment is equally offset by a decrease in cash.

Interest Earned: Maynard has a December 31 year end, so they will have to record accrued interest on the bond at that date. Since the purchase price of the bond is the same as the par value, there will be no changes to the long-term investment account. The journal entry related to this acquisition is shown in figure 18.10.

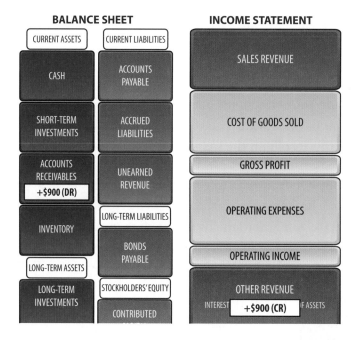

JOURNAL			
Date	**Account Title and Explanation**	**Debit**	**Credit**
Dec 31	Interest Receivable	900	
	Interest Revenue		900
	Accrued interest earned on bonds *$45,000 x 8% x 3/12*		

FIGURE 18.10

As shown in figure 18.10, interest is accrued by increasing (debiting) interest receivable and by increasing (crediting) interest revenue. Equity has increased by $900 in this example.

On March 31 of the next year, Maynard Company will receive the cash payment of interest that is owed to them from the bond as shown in figure 18.11.

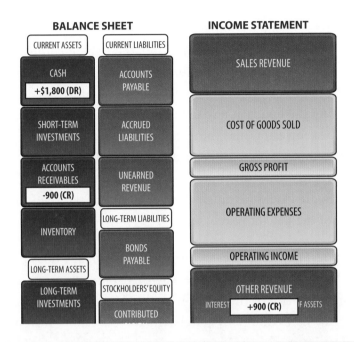

JOURNAL			
Date	**Account Title and Explanation**	**Debit**	**Credit**
Mar 31	Cash	1,800	
	Interest Receivable		900
	Interest Revenue		900
	Received six months of interest on bonds		
	$45,000 x 8% x 6/12		

FIGURE 18.11

The interest receivable that was created at the year end in figure 18.10 is cleared. The amount of interest earned in the first three months of this year is credited to interest revenue and cash increases by the total amount received.

As Maynard Company continues to receive interest payments from the bonds, interest revenue will continue to increase, causing the equity to increase.

Purchasing Bonds between Interest Dates

Note that the bond was purchased on October 1, 2011, which also happens to be the date after the last interest payment. This means that Maynard Company will earn the full amount of interest that will be paid in six months on March 31, 2012. If Maynard Company instead purchases the bonds between interest dates on November 1, 2011, then they will only earn five months on interest on March 31, 2012.

The natural response for the issuing company would be to only pay five months of interest to Maynard Company on March 31. Under this situation, the issuing company has to track the date of each bond purchased and only pay the investors the amount of interest that is earned. This can become a logistical nightmare for the company issuing the bonds, since they could have a large number of investors buying the bonds at any time between the interest dates. The company would have to make a note of these investors and the dates. In fact, each investor would receive a different amount of interest. For example, if Investor A purchased bonds on November 1, they are entitled to five months of interest, where if Investor B purchased bonds on December 1, they are only entitled to four months of interest. It would be much simpler to just make the same interest payment to each investor regardless of the date of purchase.

By making the same interest payment to each investor, the company does not have to track exactly how much interest each one should receive. The way this approach works is that the investor will pay the issuing company the price of the bond, plus the amount of interest accrued since the last interest date. Suppose Maynard Company purchased the bonds on November 1, 2011, which is one month's past the last interest date. Maynard Company would pay the purchase price of the bond plus one month's worth of interest to the issuing company on the purchase date, but will receive a full six months' worth of interest on the next interest payment date.

To illustrate this, let us re-examine the example given and show the journal entries if Maynard Company purchased the bonds on November 1, 2011. On November 1, Maynard will pay $45,000 plus $300 for one months' interest ($45,000 × 8% ×1/ 12) in exchange for the bonds. The extra $300 will be recorded in the interest receivable account, since Maynard will receive this cash back on the next interest payment date. The transaction is shown below:

JOURNAL			
Date	Account Title and Explanation	Debit	Credit
Nov 1	Long-Term Investments – Held to Maturity	45,000	
	Interest Receivable	300	
	Cash		45,300
	Purchase bonds plus one month accrued interest		

FIGURE 18.12

When Maynard Company reaches their year end on December 31, they must accrue the interest earned on the bond. They have had the bond for two months, so two months of interest must be accrued. The journal entry is similar to the one shown in figure 18.10, and is shown below.

JOURNAL			
Date	Account Title and Explanation	Debit	Credit
Dec 31	Interest Receivable	600	
	Interest Revenue		600
	Accrued interest earned on bonds		
	$45,000 × 8% × 2/12		

FIGURE 18.13

The last journal entry we have to examine is the interest payment on March 31, 2012. Maynard Company will receive the full amount of interest for six months, even though they only had the bonds for five months. They will also receive the $300 they paid for the accrued interest on November 1, 2011. This $300 is included as part of the interest receivable account. The journal entry is shown below:

JOURNAL			
Date	Account Title and Explanation	Debit	Credit
Mar 31	Cash	*1,800	
	Interest Receivable		900
	Interest Revenue		900
	Receive six months of interest on bonds		
	*$45,000 × 8% × 6/12		

FIGURE 18.14

Maturity: On September 30, 2014, Maynard Company will record two transactions for the bonds. The first will be the receipt of the last interest payment of $1,800. The second will be the receipt of the par value of the bond. The journal entries are shown in figure 18.15.

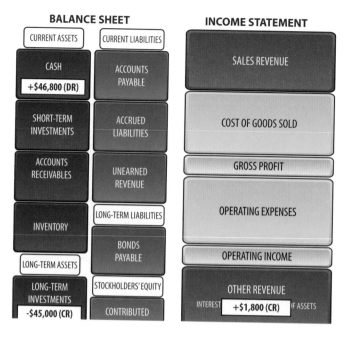

BALANCE SHEET

CURRENT ASSETS | CURRENT LIABILITIES

CASH
+$46,800 (DR)

ACCOUNTS PAYABLE

SHORT-TERM INVESTMENTS

ACCRUED LIABILITIES

ACCOUNTS RECEIVABLES

UNEARNED REVENUE

INVENTORY

LONG-TERM LIABILITIES

BONDS PAYABLE

LONG-TERM ASSETS

LONG-TERM INVESTMENTS
-$45,000 (CR)

STOCKHOLDERS' EQUITY

CONTRIBUTED

INCOME STATEMENT

SALES REVENUE

COST OF GOODS SOLD

GROSS PROFIT

OPERATING EXPENSES

OPERATING INCOME

OTHER REVENUE

INTEREST +$1,800 (CR) F ASSETS

JOURNAL

Date	Account Title and Explanation	Debit	Credit
Sep 30	Cash	1,800	
	Interest Revenue		1,800
	Received six months of interest on bonds $45,000 x 8% x 6/12		

JOURNAL

Date	Account Title and Explanation	Debit	Credit
Sep 30	Cash	45,000	
	Long-Term Investments – Held to Maturity		45,000
	Received bond's principal amount at maturity		

FIGURE 18.15

Note that the value of the long-term investment account did not fluctuate during the three years the bond was held. This is because the purchase price was identical to the maturity value. In reality, the purchase price will most likely be different than the maturity value. The difference would have to be amortized over the life of the bond whenever interest revenue is recorded.

It is worth noting that if the bonds were to mature in less than one year, similar journal entries as the ones shown in figures 18.9 to 18.11 and 18.15 would be recorded except for the fact that the account Long-Term Investments - Held to Maturity would be replaced with Short-Term Investments - Held to Maturity.

Available for Sale Investments

An equity investment, such as stock purchased in another company, is treated a little differently than a bond investment. Stock typically does not have a maturity date, therefore it cannot be classified as held-to-maturity. If the company that purchased the stock plans to keep them for longer than one year, they must be classified as available-for-sale. For this section, it is assumed that the quantity of stock purchased in another company is a very small percentage of the total number of shares that are available. In the next section, a scenario will be examined where a larger percentage of the total number of shares is purchased.

Acquisition: For example, Maynard Company purchased 1,000 shares of Company B on May 25, 2011, when the current market price was $6.60 per share. Since Maynard Company plans to keep these shares for a long period of time, they must be classified as available-for sale. Figure 18.16 shows the journal entry for this acquisition.

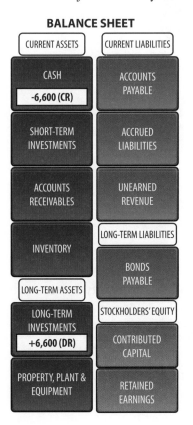

JOURNAL			
Date	Account Title and Explanation	Debit	Credit
May 25	Long-Term Investments – Available for sale	6,600	
	Cash		6,600
	Purchased 1,000 shares at $6.60 each		

FIGURE 18.16

As shown in figure 18.16, long-term investment is increased (debited) by $6,600 and cash is decreased (credited) for the same amount equal to the purchase price of the investment.

Dividend Earned: Maynard will receive cash dividends when the board of directors of Company B decides to pay them. On October 31, 2011, Maynard receives cash dividends of $0.20 per share from their investment as shown in figure 18.17.

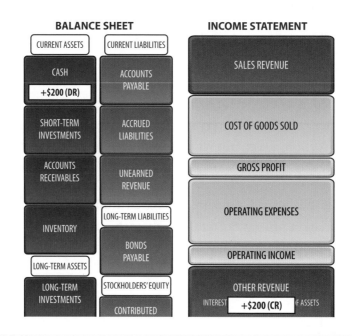

JOURNAL			
Date	**Account Title and Explanation**	**Debit**	**Credit**
Oct 31	Cash	200	
	Dividend Revenue		200
	Received a $0.20 cash dividend		
	1,000 x $0.20		

FIGURE 18.17

Disposition with a gain: Although initially a company may intend to keep an equity investment for longer than one year, under certain circumstances, they may want to sell the stock sooner. Maynard decides to sell the stock of Company B on November 22, 2011 when the market price is $7.20. Since the value of the stock has increased from the acquisition date, Maynard Company must record a gain on the investment. The gain will be recorded as other revenue on the income statement. Figure 18.18 shows the journal entry related to this disposition.

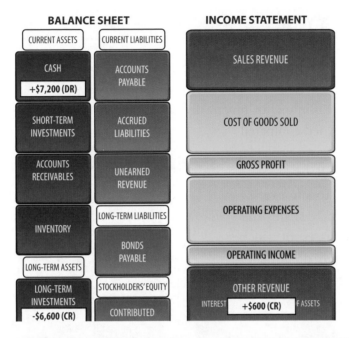

JOURNAL			
Date	Account Title and Explanation	Debit	Credit
Nov 22	Cash	7,200*	
	Long-Term Investments – Available for sale		6,600
	Gain on Sale of Investments		600
	Sold shares for $7.20 per share		
	*1,000 × $7.20		

FIGURE 18.18

As shown in figure 18.18, equity would increase by $600 as a result of recognizing a gain. If the market value of the stock had decreased instead, the journal entry to record the sale would be similar to the transaction shown in figure 18.8 of the short-term investment section.

Year-end valuation: If Maynard Company had decided to keep the Company B stock for more than one year, Maynard would have to revise the value of their available-for-sale investment. At Maynard's fiscal year end, they would revise the value of their investment based on the market value of Company B stock on that date. If the market value is higher than Maynard's current value of the investment, Maynard must record an unrealized gain on the investment. If the market value is lower than Maynard's current value of the investment, Maynard must record an unrealized loss on the investment. The term unrealized is used because Maynard Company has not sold the stock and collected any cash proceeds. Therefore, the gain or loss is not real, or realized. The details surrounding this procedure are beyond the scope of this introduction.

Significant Influence

When anyone purchases common stock in a company, the purchaser becomes a part-owner of the company and may have some influence in how the company will run. For many stockholders, though, this influence is minimal or practically non-existent. One reason for this has to do with the quantity of stock owned compared to the total number of shares available. Usually, one share will allow one vote to elect a board of directors to oversee the company. If you own 10 shares and there are 1,000,000 shares of stock available, your votes will do little to elect a board of directors or influence the company.

Significant influence is assumed to exist if one stockholder owns between 20% and 50% of the stock of a business. Although the stockholder does not own the majority of stock, they may be able to influence the company based on the quantity of stock owned. If the stockholder happens to be another company, this company must account for the investment in stock using the equity method, which will now be illustrated.

A CLOSER LOOK

In addition to the percentage of stock owned, there are other factors to consider when deciding if an investor has significant influence over their investment (or investee).

According to GAAP, there are a number of items which could indicate significant influence even though the percentage of stock owned is less than 20%. These factors include:

- substantial inter company transactions
- exchanges of executives between investor and investee
- investor's significant input in the decision making process
- investor's representation on the investee's Board of directors
- investee's dependence on investor

Acquisition: On January 1, 2011, Maynard Company purchases 40% of the stock of Company B and pays $120,000. This initial investment will be considered an available-for-sale investment, since Maynard wishes to keep the stock for a long period of time. This long-term investment will appear on the balance sheet before property, plant and equipment. The transaction to record this investment, shown in figure 18.19, is similar to the transaction to record the acquisition of the equity investment previously shown in figure 18.16.

JOURNAL			
Date	**Account Title and Explanation**	**Debit**	**Credit**
Jan 1	Long-Term Investments – Available for sale	120,000	
	Cash		120,000
	Purchased 40% of Company B shares		

FIGURE 18.19

Dividends: This is one area that differs from an equity investment shown earlier. When a company has significant influence, cash dividends are not considered revenue and will not appear on the income statement. Any cash dividends received will decrease the value of the long-term investment account because cash received comes out of the company's investment. If Company B pays out $12,000 in cash dividends on December 13, 2011, Maynard will receive 40% of the dividends and will record the receipt of cash.

JOURNAL			
Date	**Account Title and Explanation**	**Debit**	**Credit**
Dec 13	Cash	4,800	
	Long-Term Investments – Available for sale		4,800
	Record 40% of Company B cash dividends *$12,000 x 40%*		

FIGURE 18.20

As shown in figure 18.20, cash is increased (debited) and long-term investment is decreased (credited) by $4,800 as a result of receiving cash dividends from Company B.

Year-end: When Company B reports its net income for 2011, Maynard Company will record 40% of the net income as an increase in the long-term investment. When there is significant influence, the company holding the stock (Maynard Company) must record the proportionate amount of net income as an increase to the investment. This is different from an equity investment where there is no significant influence and no entry would be made. If Company B had a net income of $88,000 for 2011, Maynard would record the transaction shown in figure 18.21.

JOURNAL			
Date	**Account Title and Explanation**	**Debit**	**Credit**
Dec 31	Long-Term Investments – Available for sale	35,200	
	Income from Long-Term Investments		35,200
	Record 40% of Company B net income *$88,000 x 40%*		

FIGURE 18.21

As shown in figure 18.21, long-term investment is increased (debited) by $35,200 and the revenue of Maynard is also increased (credited) by $35,200. The income from long-term investment is considered other revenue or expenses and will show up on the income statement of Maynard Company, increasing its equity. The following T-Account shows the changes in value to the invesment in Company B.

Essentially, Maynard Company's investment in Company B will consist of the initial investment, plus the proportionate amount of Company B's net income less the proportionate amount of cash

LONG-TERM INVESTMENTS AVAILABLE FOR SALE		
Initial Investment	$120,000	$4,800	Dividends
Net Income	35,200		
	$150,400		

FIGURE 18.22

dividends that Company B pays out. This is how the equity method gets its name. The value of the long-term investment changes in proportion to the change in equity of Company B.

By December 31, 2011, the value of Maynard Company's investment in Company B has a value of $150,400. This value is considered the book value of the investment, and if Maynard Company decides to sell all the stock of Company B, the sale price is compared to the book value to determine if there is a gain or loss. As shown with the previous equity investment section, the gain or loss will appear on the income statement as other revenue or expense.

If Maynard decides to sell the stock of Company B on January 1, 2012 for $145,000, the sale would result in a loss.

JOURNAL			
Date	Account Title and Explanation	Debit	Credit
Jan 1	Cash	145,000	
	Loss on Sale of Investments	5,400	
	Long-Term Investments – Available for sale		150,400
	Sold Company B shares for a loss		

FIGURE 18.23

As shown in figure 18.23, a loss of $5,400 is recognized, resulting into a decrease of equity. Cash is increased (debited) by the sales price while long-term investment is decreased (debited) by its book value.

Controls

Unlike other assets such as cash, accounts receivable, inventory, and property, plant & equipment few are familiar with different types of investments. Nevertheless, it is important that this type of asset be managed properly and that the right controls are in place to ensure its integrity and to safeguard the interests of the business.

Adequate Funds

- Ensure that the appropriate paperwork has been completed.
- Ask the following question: Can the business afford a significant loss in the value of the investment if, for example, the share price falls below the initial purchase price?
- Perform a cash flow analysis to assess whether the business can manage without the cash that would be used to invest.

- When buying or selling shares and bonds, record brokerage fees in the company's books. This means that when shares are purchased, the brokerage fee must be added to the purchase price. When shares are sold, the brokerage fee must be subtracted from the selling price.

Integrity of Information and Bookkeeping

Regular monitoring and controls will help to maintain the integrity of investments.

To adequately safeguard information related to investments, a ledger account should be opened for each investment. If there are numerous investments, a subsidiary ledger should be established and a subsidiary ledger trial balance maintained on a regular basis and reviewed by authorized personnel to ensure that it reconciles with the control account in the general ledger. Each account should adequately describe the nature of the investment. Journal entries for the purchase and sale of investments should be properly authorized. Entries should always be recorded and posted by qualified staff and should be subject to regular review.

The receipt of income from investments should be monitored closely. This is relatively easy with investments that would involve regular receipt of interests at fixed rates and on fixed dates.

Personnel

An important control to be used in managing investments is to have the right people assigned to authorize the purchase and sale of investments and to properly record these transactions. Ensure that trustworthy people work for the company and that it employs only reputable brokerage houses and financial institutions when buying and safeguarding investments. It can be tempting for a broker and the company official in charge of investments to share unauthorized commissions, thus reducing the company's income.

Employees involved in investment transactions should always follow established company principles and procedures.

Physical Safekeeping

A business can ensure the physical safety of its investments in various ways. For example, management can choose to leave the share certificates with the brokerage firm used to purchase the investments. Alternatively, the certificates can be kept in a vault on company premises or in a safe deposit box at a bank. Maintain a list of employees who have physical access to certificates. If the certificates are held by the company, they must be registered in the name of the company to avoid potential fraudulent activities.

Safe deposit boxes, like those shown above, can be used to store valuable items like an investment certificate purchased by a company.

Managerial Oversight

Investments are a good way to make use of surplus cash. Investments of a short-term nature are often in the form of interest-bearing notes, money market funds or other near-cash assets. Regardless of the choice of investments, management must make decisions that are in the best interests of the company.

Companies should always be in the practice of doing business with people they can trust.

Setting Company Objectives

Companies should have policies that outline the types of investment to be made on a short-term or a long-term basis. Although a maximum return is always sought in any form of investment, company assets also need to be safeguarded by the assumption of an appropriate amount of risk. The investments should always be authorized in advance and any investments made should also be reviewed regularly by authorized officers of the company.

On a broader scale, well-managed organizations set strategic goals and objectives, and implement policies to pursue them. This is no different with regard to short-term or long-term investments, which can involve large amounts of funds. Goals and objectives should be communicated to the relevant employees, performance reviewed regularly and changes made when corrective action is needed.

In Summary

⮩ When a business has surplus cash, it may choose to invest it for the short term, which, for accounting purposes means less than one year.

⮩ A short-term investment is a liquid company asset and is located immediately below the cash account on the balance sheet.

⮩ If the company intends to keep the investment for longer than one year, the investment should be classified as a long-term investment under the long-term asset.

⮩ There are generally two forms of investments: debt, which involves a loan to an individual or business, and equity, which involves buying stock (ownership) in a company.

⮩ All debt and equity investments are classified into trading, held to maturity, and available for sale.

⮩ Debt can take the form of a traditional loan to an individual or business or it can take the form of a bond, which is a type of loan that can be bought and sold on the market. Both a loan and a bond earn interest, but a bond can itself change in value and be bought and sold at a lower or higher price.

⮩ Equity takes the form of stock in a company. Income is earned from the shares, either through an increase in its value or through dividend payments.

⮩ When shares are purchased, the brokerage fee must be added to the purchase price. When shares are sold, the brokerage fee must be subtracted from the selling price.

⮩ Ensure that income from investments, such as interest, dividends, gains on the sale of investments, is recorded in a special non-operating revenue account, since it is not generated from the day-to-day activities of doing business. Similarly, any losses from investments are recorded in a special non-operating expense account.

⮩ A stockholder having between 20% and 50% of the stock of a company is considered to have significant influence and must account for the investment using the equity method.

⮩ The equity method causes the investment account to increase in proportion to the net income and decrease in proportion to the dividends paid by the company invested in.

Review Exercise

Benita Sikorsky is the controller for a medium-sized enterprise that has a July 31 year-end. From time to time, her company has "surplus" cash on hand that it uses to make short-term investments. All of the investments are intended to be sold in less than one year. The types of investments vary from period to period, depending on which investments produce the highest return for the company.

During the past year, the company completed the following transactions:

Jan 1 – Lent $50,000 to another company at an annual rate of 4% and due in 6 months.

Apr 1 – Purchased 1,000 DEF Company bonds priced at $100 each with interest payable semi-annually on July 1 and December 31 at an annual rate of 6%. Also paid for any accrued interest owing.

May 10 – Purchased 1,000 shares of XYZ Company at $50 per share.

Jul 1 – Received interest payment for six months on the DEF Company bonds.

Jul 1 – Received full proceeds from the loan of Jan 1, including interest.

Jul 10 – Received the quarterly dividend of $100 on the XYZ Company shares.

Jul 31 – Year end adjustment: Record the interest accrued on the DEF bonds.

Oct 1 – Sold 100 XYZ shares for proceeds of $47 per share.

Dec 15 – Sold 900 XYZ shares for proceeds of $52 per shares.

Dec 31 – Received the second interest payment on the DEF Company bonds then immediately sold the bonds for $102,500.

Required:

Record journal entries for each of the above transactions.

Review Exercise 1 - Answer

Date	Account Title and Explanation	Debit	Credit
Jan 1	Short-Term Investments-Trading	50,000	
	Cash		50,000
	6 month, 4% loan to another company		
Apr 1	Short-Term Investments-Trading	100,000	
	Interest Receivable (100,000 × .06 × 3/12)	1,500	
	Cash		101,500
	Purchased 1,000 bonds at $100 each plus accrued interest		
May 10	Short-Term Investments-Trading	50,000	
	Cash		50,000
	Purchased 1,000 shares of XYZ Co. at $50 per		
	share		
Jul 1	Cash (100,000 × .06 × 6/12)	3,000	
	Interest Receivable		1,500
	Interest Revenue (100,000 × .06 × 3/12)		1,500
	Received 6 months interest on bonds		
Jul 1	Cash (50,000 + 50,000 × 6/12 × 4%)	51,000	
	Short-Term Investments-Trading		50,000
	Interest Revenue		1,000
	Received proceeds from loan plus interest		
Jul 10	Cash	100	
	Dividend Revenue		100
	Received quarterly dividend on XYZ shares		
Jul 31	Interest Receivable (100,000 × .06 × 1/12)	500	
	Interest Revenue		500
	Accrued interest on bonds at year end		
Oct 1	Cash	4,700	
	Loss on Sale of Investment	300	
	Short-Term Investments-Trading		5,000
	Sale of XYZ shares at a loss		
	$ (47 - 50) × 100 shares = –$300		

Date	Account Title and Explanation	Debit	Credit
Dec 15	Cash	46,800	
	Gain on Sale of Investment		1,800
	Short-Term Investments-Trading		45,000
	Sale of XYZ shares at a gain		
	$ (52 - 50) × 900 shares = $1,800		
Dec 31	Cash (100,000 × .06 × $^{6}/_{12}$)	3,000	
	Interest Revenue (100,000 × .06 × $^{5}/_{12}$)		2,500
	Interest Receivable		500
	Received 6 months interest on bonds		
Dec 31	Cash	102,500	
	Short-Term Investments-Trading		100,000
	Gain on Sale of Investment		2,500
	Sale of DEF bonds at a gain		

Chapter 19

THE STATEMENT OF CASH FLOW

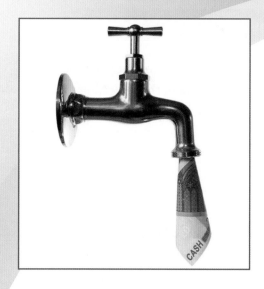

Beyond the Balance Sheet and Income Statement

Most of our discussion of accounting procedures and principles so far has focused on two types of financial statements: the balance sheet and the income statement. Indeed, these financial statements have become synonymous with the accounting profession. When people think about business finance, they usually think about balance sheets and income statements.

However, there are two reasons why analyzing the state of a business requires more than just the balance sheet and income statement.

First, balance sheets and income statements are prepared on an accrual basis. In other words, the matching principle dictates that revenues and expenses be recorded for the period in which they are earned or incurred. However, these types of transactions do not always involve an actual exchange of cash. Conversely, other transactions such as borrowing or repaying loans affect cash but do not affect net income.

Second, well-publicized accounting scandals have exposed some of the flaws of balance sheets and income statements. In other words, some businesses have become adept at manipulating them for their advantage. The financial statements are not necessarily flawed, but analysts have, to a certain extent, less confidence in them.

Cash flow statements (or statement of cash flows) essentially follow the cash within a business. They ignore accruals and other book transactions, while revealing and analyzing actual changes to a company's cash account. Cash flow statements involve a different way of looking at financial numbers. For this reason, preparing a cash flow statement can take some time to get used to. In other words, it takes practice. This chapter provides the basis for enhancing your understanding of, and proficiency with, cash flow statements.

Cash Flow Statements: Follow the Money

Accountants are required to prepare balance sheets and income statements for the business. These important documents represent the state of company finances and adhere to the matching principle, accruals and so on. Balance sheets and income statements are filled with promises of an exchange of money that must be recorded in one period, but may take place in another period. Company bills may not get paid for several months. Prepaid expenses can be left unadjusted for a number of periods. A borrower may default on a loan. Depreciation is recorded in the books, but there is no exchange of cash.

Because of the way these transactions are accounted for in balance sheets and income statements, it can be difficult to know where the cash is actually going within the business. As a result, the accounting profession has devised another financial statement whose purpose is to specifically indicate both the *sources* of cash and the *uses* of cash within an organization. This document is known as the **cash flow statement** or the **statement of cash flow**. Both terms will be used throughout this chapter.

The cash flow statement shows how net income is converted to cash. Remember, net income does not necessarily translate into cash in the bank. The way a business is structured – in terms of financing, dividend schedules, debt collection, etc. – can have a significant impact on the way net income is turned into cash. It is this aspect of a business that the cash flow statement reveals to readers, who may include management, accountants, potential lenders and investment analysts.

Though cash flow statements can be of significant help to these financial players, they also constitute a requirement under GAAP. In other words, cash flow statements are not only useful but necessary. Knowing what they are, understanding what they can do and becoming familiar with preparing them are essential tasks for an accountant. In this chapter, we explain how to perform these tasks.

Three Ways of Generating Cash Flow

A business generates and consumes cash in one of the following three ways:

- Operations
- Investments
- Financing

In fact, all cash flow statements are structured in this manner.

Cash flow from operations

This component of the cash flow statement tracks the movement of cash within a business on the basis of day-to-day activities. All items in this section would relate to transactions involving suppliers, customers or general expenses within the company, such as paying employee salaries. It is the most important section of the cash flow statement because the future of a business largely depends on the activities reported in this section.

Cash flow from investments

This component of the cash flow statement tracks the movement of cash in a business on the basis of the purchases and sales of long-term assets. For example, if a truck was sold during the year, cash flow would have increased. Alternatively, if the business purchased land, cash flow would have decreased, since the business had to use cash to buy the land.

Cash flow from financing

This component of the cash flow statement tracks the movement of cash within a business on the basis of the way a company receives money from those providing financing and pays it back. These sources of financing could be banks or bondholders. These financiers could also be stockholders, who are paid with dividend payments. All these exchanges of cash, whether considered current or long-term, need to be accounted for in this section of the cash flow statement.

The following table will help summarize the events that are recorded in each of the three sections of the cash flow statement.

Operations	Cash sales and collecting cash from customers Cash received from investments Payments made to suppliers for assets or expenses Paying employee salaries Paying interest
Investments	Buying or selling long-term assets
Financing	Issuing stock Borrowing money Paying dividends Payments made to reduce financing loans

FIGURE 19.1

Preparing a Cash Flow Statement

Two methods are used to prepare a cash flow statement: the **indirect method**, which is the most commonly used method, and the **direct method**.

The term indirect refers to tracking the changes to cash without direct reference to cash receipts or payments. In other words, the **indirect method** analyzes cash flow from operations indirectly by starting with accrual-based net income and adding or subtracting certain items from the income statement and changes on the balance sheet.

The direct method is another way of tracing the changes to cash from one period to the next. Like the indirect method, the **direct method** breaks down the three ways of generating and using cash into operating, investing and financing activities. However, unlike the indirect method, the direct method calculates cash flow from operations directly (from scratch). The direct method is often deemed as too burdensome to execute. Therefore, in this chapter we will focus primarily on the indirect method.

IN THE REAL WORLD

Academic studies have shown that if two versions of the cash flow statement are shown (i.e. direct and indirect method), investors can make better decisions. By disclosing both the direct and indirect method, a company would be improving its accounting transparency. Furthermore, through statistical studies, it has been shown that the indirect method is more useful than the direct method. However, a reason for this discrepancy was not revealed by the studies. Furthermore, the direct method is, on average, more easily understood by users than the indirect method.

Prior to executing the indirect method of preparing the cash flow statement, the balance sheet and income statement should be examined. The cash flow statement presents the change in cash over a period of time and is presented with a date format covering a specified time period similar to the income statement and statement of stockholders' equity.

Examine the Balance Sheet and the Income Statement

The first document we need is the balance sheet – or a comparative balance sheet for two periods – that tells us how much is in the cash account. Consider Soho Supplies, a manufacturer of office supplies with a year-end of December 31. Soho's financial statements will be used for cash flow analysis in this chapter. We will use this specific balance sheet for Soho Supplies for the remainder of the chapter, and keep referring to it as we move along.

When you examine the balance sheet, you will see that the last column calculates the difference between 2011 and 2012 amounts. This difference will be used when preparing the cash flow statement. As you can see from the first line of the balance sheet, the cash account decreased from $72,642 in 2011 to $13,265 in 2012. This represents a decrease of $59,377.

	2012	2011	Changes
Soho Supplies			
Balance Sheet			
As at December 31			
ASSETS			
Current Assets			
Cash	$13,265	$72,642	($59,377)
Accounts receivable	1,286,138	1,065,812	220,326
Inventory	1,683,560	840,091	843,469
Prepaid expenses	48,612	42,625	5,987
Total Current Assets	3,031,575	2,021,170	1,010,405
Property, plant & equipment[1]	322,518	170,000	152,518
Less: Accumulated depreciation	(79,262)	(36,000)	(43,262)
TOTAL ASSETS	$3,274,831	$2,155,170	$1,119,661
LIABILITIES AND EQUITY			
Liabilities			
Current Liabilities			
Accounts payable	$783,602	$475,645	$307,957
Current portion of bank loan	380,000	240,000	140,000
Notes payable	170,000	200,000	(30,000)
Total Current Liabilities	1,333,602	915,645	417,957
Long-Term portion of bank loan	420,000	356,000	64,000
TOTAL LIABILITIES	1,753,602	1,271,645	481,957
Stockholders' Equity			
Common stock	15,000	5,000	10,000
Retained earnings[2]	1,506,229	878,525	627,704
TOTAL STOCKHOLDERS' EQUITY	1,521,229	883,525	637,704
TOTAL LIABILITIES AND EQUITY	$3,274,831	$2,155,170	$1,119,661

(1) Property, Plant & Equipment:
    a) During 2012, land was sold for $50,000, which was also the cost of the land.
    b) During 2012, Soho made purchases of property, plant & equipment for $202,518.

(2) Retained Earnings:
    Soho declared and paid $10,000 in dividends in 2012.

FIGURE 19.2

We now need to examine Soho's income statement.

Soho Supplies Income Statement For the Year Ended December 31, 2012	
Sales	$8,685,025
COGS	5,998,612
Gross Profit	2,686,413
Operating Expenses	
Administration charges	8,652
Advertising & marketing	42,645
Depreciation	43,262
Bonuses	65,000
Commission	420,250
Interest	51,875
Insurance	16,000
Sales and administration salaries	610,325
Management salaries	320,560
Occupancy	52,000
Consulting	22,500
Repairs and maintenance	36,860
Professional fees	11,560
Other operating expenses	61,200
Total Operating Expenses	1,762,689
Operating Income Before Tax	923,724
Income Tax	286,020
Net Income	$637,704

FIGURE 19.3

The company's net income is $637,704 for 2012. We will be using this income statement for the remainder of the chapter, so keep it handy as we assemble our cash flow statement for 2012.

You may have asked yourself an obvious question after noticing a change in balance of the cash account (which reflects a decrease of $59,377) and a net income of $637,704. What happened to all the cash? This type of question can be answered by the cash flow statement, which ignores accruals and reflects only transactions involving cash. Let us start getting some answers.

Indirect Method

The figure we start with is the balance of cash at the end of 2011 (i.e. the beginning of 2012), which is $72,642.

Cash Flow from Operations

The following illustrations will help you understand the change in cash through day-to-day operations.

As the value of various current assets and liabilities change from one period to another, cash flow is affected. Figures 19.4 to 19.7 illustrate this principle.

If accounts receivable decreases, it means that the cash has been collected, resulting in an increase to cash (as shown in figure 19.4).

If inventory increases, it means that the cash has been used (or will be used) to pay for it, resulting in a decrease in cash (as shown in figure 19.5).

If accounts payable decreases, it means that cash has been used to pay it off, resulting in a decrease in cash (as shown in figure 19.6).

If prepaid expenses increases, this means that cash has been used to pay for it, resulting in a decrease in cash (as shown in figure 19.7).

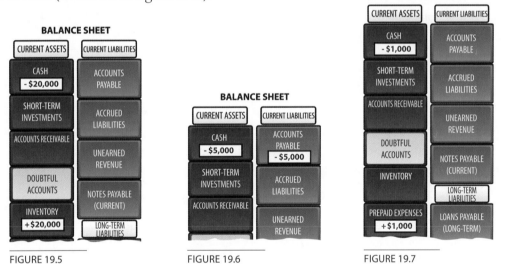

Now let us start preparing our cash flow from operations. Remember that cash flow from operations under the indirect method starts with net income and then adds or subtracts certain items from the income statement and changes on the balance sheet. In our current example, the company's net income for 2012 is $637,704.

Net income is added to (or net loss is deducted from) our opening cash account balance. Since we are focusing on cash flow instead of accruals, we need to only account for the money that actually changes hands during a period. Therefore, in the cash flow from operations section, we begin with net income and initially add or subtract for non-cash items from the income statement such as depreciation. Since depreciation is simply the decrease in the value of an asset, without any change to cash, depreciation deductions are taken out of any equations involving cash flow. Then, we add or subtract changes in items related to operations that do not flow through directly to the income statement (i.e. specifically, changes in current assets and current liabilities such as accounts receivable, inventory and accounts payable).

Therefore the next step in assembling the cash flow from operations section is to add back any depreciation that was originally deducted. As shown in the income statement, Soho's depreciation expense for 2012 is $43,262.

Here is how our opening cash balance changes: As you can see in figure 19.8, we take our opening cash balance, add the net income (or deduct the losses if any) and add back depreciation expense. This gives us an updated cash balance of $753,608.

This column is used to calculate the updated cash balance to help you understand the process.

You will not see this theoretical column illustrated in a regular cash flow statement.

Cash Flow Statement for 2012	Amount	Updated Cash Balance
Opening Cash Balance		$72,642
Cash Flow from Operations		
Add: Net income	$637,704	710,346
Add: Depreciation	43,262	753,608

FIGURE 19.8

Figure 19.8 is only the first part of our cash flow from operations. We start with cash, then add net income or deduct losses and then add depreciation. The second part involves referring back to our comparative balance sheet and going down the list of current assets and liabilities. Loans will be dealt with in the cash flow from financing section, below.

Cash Flow Statement for 2012	Amount	Updated Cash Balance
Opening Cash Balance		$72,642
Opening Cash Balance		
Add: Net income	$637,704	710,346
Add: Depreciation	43,262	753,608
Changes in Current Assets & Current Liabilities:		
Increase in accounts receivable	(220,326)	533,282
Increase in prepaid expenses	(5,987)	527,295
Increase in inventory	(843,469)	(316,174)
Increase in accounts payable	307,957	(8,217)
Change in Cash due to Operations	**(80,859)**	

FIGURE 19.9

Our first listed current asset in our comparative balance sheet (after cash) is accounts receivable. As indicated in the balance sheet, this account increased by $220,326 from 2011 to 2012. Remember that since accounts receivable increased, it will decrease cash because it is yet to be collected. We therefore deduct this amount from the cash balance of $753,608. As indicated above, the updated cash balance is $533,282.

Prepaid expenses increased by $5,987 resulting in a decrease in cash because the prepaid expenses must have been paid with cash, resulting in an updated cash balance of $527,295.

Inventory increased by $843,469, resulting once again in a decrease in cash because cash must be used to pay for the additional inventory resulting in a negative updated cash balance of $316,174.

Accounts payable increased by $307,957. This will result in more cash in the bank, causing the updated cash balance to increase and ending up with a decrease in cash from operations of $80,859, as indicated in bold in figure 19.9.

Under the indirect method of preparing cash flow statements, the following figure outlines the impact on the cash flow statement an increase or decrease to current assets or current liabilities will have.

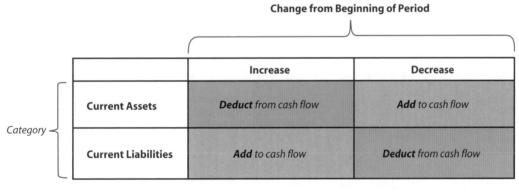

Impact on Cash Flow Statement:
Change in Current Assets and Current Liabilities

FIGURE 19.10

Cash Flow from Investments

Changes in the value of long-term assets (i.e. property, plant and equipment) affect cash flow. However, measuring the affect is not as straightforward as observing the change in the property, plant and equipment balance from one year to the next.

This section of the cash flow statement deals with the way cash flow changes through the investment in or sale of capital assets. In our current example with Soho Supplies, the information required to complete the cash flow from investments section is provided in the 'Additional Information' portion below Soho's balance sheet (figure 19.2).

The proceeds from the sale of the land in the amount of $50,000 is added to the updated cash balance since the transaction represents a cash inflow. The $202,518 in purchases of property, plant and equipment is deducted from the updated cash balance because it represents a cash outflow. In figure 19.11, the cash flow from investment section is the new addition to our illustrative cash flow statement.

Cash Flow Statement for 2012	Amount	Updated Cash Balance
Opening Cash Balance		$72,642
<u>**Cash Flow from Operations**</u>		
Add: Net income	$637,704	710,346
Add: Depreciation	43,262	753,608
Changes in Current Assets & Current Liabilities:		
Increase in accounts receivable	(220,326)	533,282
Increase in prepaid expenses	(5,987)	527,295
Increase in inventory	(843,469)	(316,174)
Increase in accounts payable	307,957	(8,217)
Change in Cash due to Operations	**(80,859)**	
<u>**Cash Flow from Investments**</u>		
Sale of land	50,000	41,783
Purchase of property, plant & equipment	(202,518)	(160,735)
Change in Cash due to Investments	**(152,518)**	

FIGURE 19.11

This is our change in cash due to investments, and essentially constitutes that entire section of the cash flow statement.

Cash Flow from Financing

Cash flow from financing is the last section of the cash flow statement that we need to prepare. As loans or contributed capital (i.e. in our example, common stock) increase or decrease, cash flow is correspondingly affected.

If loans or common stock increases, this means that cash has been received, resulting in an increase in cash. If, on the other hand, loans or common stock decreases, this would lead to a decrease in cash.

Remember that this section accounts for cash resulting from any financing activities during the year. It includes borrowing money or receiving cash as a result of a stock issue. In addition, this section also includes any payments involved with financing, such as dividend payments or loan repayments. While repayments of loan principal amounts are an outflow in this section, the interest expense related to this loan has already been accounted for in the operations section as part of net income.

The cash flow from financing section is somewhat different from the other cash flow sections in that it involves changes to more than one section of the statement. For example, in the operations section of the cash flow statement, accounts receivable is one account, inventory is another, and so on.

Cash flow from financing is divided into two areas in our balance sheet: long-term and current. In addition, payments in the form of dividends also affect the cash position directly from year to year. That is why it is especially important to keep track of money as it changes hands while the cash flow statement, particularly the financing section, is being assembled.

First, we need to take a look at our balance sheet again and check all aspects pertaining to financing. The three parts that are affected are notes payable, bank loans and dividends.

Let us look at notes payable in the current liabilities section of the balance sheet. This is relatively simple since there is only one account here. The decrease in notes payable of $30,000 implies that cash also decreased by $30,000 from 2011 to 2012. Notes payable could be classified as either long-term or short-term depending on its due date. In this chapter, we assume that it is due in less than one year; therefore it appears as part of the current liability section. Regardless of being a short-term or long-term, notes payable would be part of the financing of the cash flow statement.

Now look at bank loans. An extra step is involved because bank loans are divided into two areas on our balance sheet: current and long-term. We must extract from the balance sheet the changes from period to period that occurred for both combined.

As shown in figure 19.12 (the liabilities portion of the balance sheet), the current portion of the bank loan increased by $140,000 from 2011 to 2012. The long-term portion of the bank loan increased by $64,000. Therefore, the total increase in the bank loan balance is $204,000 ($140,000 + $64,000). This amount is an increase to cash since Soho is taking additional money out as a loan. Therefore, it represents a cash inflow.

	2012	2011	Changes
Liabilities			
Current Liabilities			
Accounts payable	$783,602	$475,645	$307,957
Current portion of bank loan	380,000	240,000	140,000
Notes payable	170,000	200,000	(30,000)
Total Current Liabilities	1,333,602	915,645	417,957
Long-term portion of bank loan	420,000	356,000	64,000
TOTAL LIABILITIES	1,753,602	1,271,645	481,957

❶ Sum = $204,000

FIGURE 19.12

Next, we need to look at dividends. In the 'Additional Information' section under Soho's balance sheet (figure 19.2), it is mentioned that Soho declared and paid $10,000 in dividends during 2012.

A CLOSER LOOK

In most problems that ask you to prepare a cash flow statement, total dividends paid is provided to you. However, there are a few cases where this number is not explicitly stated. An alternate way to determine total dividends paid is by referring to the calculation of retained earnings. Recall the following formula for calculating closing retained earnings for a given period:

Closing Retained Earnings = Beginning Retained Earnings + Net Income - Dividends

Rearranging for dividends, the formula is expressed as:

Dividends = Beginning Retained Earnings + Net Income - Closing Retained Earnings

Now, dividends can be calculated provided that beginning retained earnings, net income and closing retained earnings all are provided in the question.

This represents a decrease to cash because it is a cash outflow.

Lastly, the balance of common stock increased by $10,000 from 2011 to 2012. This means that new stock was issued for $10,000 in cash. Therefore, the cash balance is increased by $10,000.

As should now be clear, changes in cash due to financing account for an increase to our cash account of $174,000 (-$30,000 + $204,000 - $10,000 + $10,000). The cash flow from financing section is added on in figure 19.13 below.

Cash Flow Statement for 2012	Amount	Updated Cash Balance
Opening Cash Balance		$72,642
Cash Flow from Operations		
Add: Net income	$637,704	710,346
Add: Depreciation	43,262	753,608
Changes in Current Assets & Current Liabilities:		
Increase in accounts receivable	(220,326)	533,282
Increase in prepaid expenses	(5,987)	527,295
Increase in inventory	(843,469)	(316,174)
Increase in accounts payable	307,957	(8,217)
Change in Cash due to Operations	**(80,859)**	
Cash Flow from Investments		
Sale of land	50,000	41,783
Purchase of property, plant & equipment	(202,518)	(160,735)
Change in Cash due to Investments	**(152,518)**	
Cash Flow from Financing		
Payment towards notes payable	(30,000)	(190,735)
Proceeds from bank loan	204,000 ❶	13,265
Payment of cash dividend	(10,000)	3,265
Issuance of common stock	10,000	13,265
Change in Cash due to Financing	**174,000**	

*Note that the $204,000 proceeds from the bank loan is from the calculation in figure 19.12.

FIGURE 19.13

Summary of the Indirect Method

We have now completed the three sections of our cash flow statement: cash flow from operations, investments and financing. It is now just a matter of putting them all together to form one complete cash flow statement in proper format for 2012 as shown in figure 19.14 below.

Soho Supplies
Cash Flow Statement
For the Year Ended December 31, 2012

Cash Flow from Operations		
Net income	$637,704	
Add: Depreciation	43,262	
Changes in Current Assets & Current Liabilities:		
Increase in accounts receivable	(220,326)	
Increase in prepaid expenses	(5,987)	
Increase in inventory	(843,469)	
Increase in accounts payable	307,957	
Change in Cash due to Operations		($80,859)
Cash Flow from Investments		
Sale of land	50,000	
Purchase of property, plant & equipment	(202,518)	
Change in Cash due to Investments		(152,518)
Cash Flow from Financing		
Payment towards notes payable	(30,000)	
Proceeds from bank loan	204,000	
Payment of cash dividend	(10,000)	
Issuance of common stock	10,000	
Change in Cash due to Financing		174,000
Net increase (decrease) in cash		(59,377)
Cash at the beginning of the year		72,642
Cash at the end of the year		$13,265

FIGURE 19.14

Sale of Property, Plant and Equipment

In the sample balance sheet and income statement used to prepare the cash flow statement above, the land was sold for the book value. Remember that selling assets for the book value does not affect equity (since there is no gain on the sale) and therefore does not appear on the income statement. Determining the book value of assets other than land is a little more complicated, since accumulated depreciation must be taken into account. This topic is discussed in the appendix at the end of this chapter.

Suppose the land was sold for $60,000 instead of the $50,000 book value. This would mean that the company made a profit (or gain) of $10,000 on the sale. Anytime long-term assets are sold for more than their book value, a gain is recorded. If the sale price is less than the book value, a loss is recorded.

By selling the land for a gain of $10,000, the financial statements will have to change. On the balance sheet, the extra $10,000 will increase cash and also increase equity (specifically, retained earnings). Because equity increased, the $10,000 gain will also have to be reported on the income statement.

The updated balance sheet is shown in figure 19.15. The items that are different from the balance sheet in figure 19.2 are outlined in green.

Soho Supplies
Balance Sheet
As at December 31

	2012	2011	Changes
ASSETS			
Current Assets			
Cash	$23,265	$72,642	($49,377)
Accounts receivable	1,286,138	1,065,812	220,326
Inventory	1,683,560	840,091	843,469
Prepaid expenses	48,612	42,625	5,987
Total Current Assets	3,041,575	2,021,170	1,020,405
Property, plant & equipment[(1)]	322,518	170,000	152,518
Less: Accumulated depreciation	(79,262)	(36,000)	(43,262)
TOTAL ASSETS	$3,284,831	$2,155,170	$1,129,661
LIABILITIES AND EQUITY			
Liabilities			
Current Liabilities			
Accounts payable	$783,602	$475,645	$307,957
Current portion of bank loan	380,000	240,000	140,000
Notes payable	170,000	200,000	(30,000)
Total Current Liabilities	1,333,602	915,645	417,957
Long-term portion of bank loan	420,000	356,000	64,000
TOTAL LIABILITIES	1,753,602	1,271,645	481,957
Stockholders' Equity			
Common stock	15,000	5,000	10,000
Retained earnings[(2)]	1,516,229	878,525	637,704
TOTAL STOCKHOLDERS' EQUITY	1,531,229	883,525	647,704
TOTAL LIABILITIES AND EQUITY	$3,284,831	$2,155,170	$1,129,661

Additional Information:

(1) Property, Plant & Equipment:
   a) During 2012, land was sold for a gain of $10,000. The cash proceeds from the sale totaled $60,000.

   b) During 2012, Soho made purchases of property, plant & equipment for $202,518.

(2) Retained Earnings:
   Soho declared and paid $10,000 in dividends in 2012.

FIGURE 19.15

The income statement must now show a gain on the sale of the assets as a separate line item. The new income statement is shown on the next page. The items outlined in green represent the differences from the income statement shown in figure 19.3.

Soho Supplies
Income Statement
For the Year Ended December 31, 2012

Sales	$8,685,025
COGS	5,998,612
Gross Profit	2,686,413
Operating Expenses	
Administration charges	8,652
Advertising & marketing	42,645
Depreciation	43,262
Bonuses	65,000
Commission	420,250
Interest	51,875
Insurance	16,000
Sales and administration salaries	610,325
Management salaries	320,560
Occupancy	52,000
Consulting	22,500
Repairs and maintenance	36,860
Professional fees	11,560
Other operating expenses	61,200
Total Operating Expenses	1,762,689
Operating Income	923,724
Other Revenue	
Gain on Sale of Land	10,000
Net Income Before Tax	933,724
Income Tax	286,020
Net Income	$647,704

FIGURE 19.16

The gain or loss that occurs when property is sold for a value that is different from the book value is not part of day-to-day operations. Therefore, gains and losses must be reported separately from sales and operating expenses. They will appear in a section called "Other Revenue" or "Other Expenses".

On the cash flow statement, the gain of $10,000 from the sale of land is deducted from net income in the cash flow from operations section. The net income includes the gain; however the gain is not part of day-to-day operating activities and must be removed from this section. Although the gain will be removed from the operations section, it will be included in the proceeds that Soho received from this sale. The proceeds will be reported in the cash flow from investments section. *Therefore,* *the $10,000 gain is deducted from net income in the cash flow from operations section to avoid double counting.* If, instead, Soho incurred a *loss* from the sale of land, the amount would be added back to net income in the cash flow from operations section.

The cash proceeds of $60,000 from the sale of land are added in the cash flow from investments section since it represents a cash inflow. The new cash flow statement is shown below. The sections in green outline how the gain and the proceeds from the sales are reported on the cash flow statement.

Soho Supplies
Cash Flow Statement
For the Year Ended December 31, 2012

Cash Flow from Operations		
Add: Net income	$647,704	
Add: Depreciation	43,262	
Deduct: Gain on sale of land	(10,000)	
Changes in Current Assets & Current Liabilities:		
Increase in accounts receivable	(220,326)	
Increase in prepaid expenses	(5,987)	
Increase in inventory	(843,469)	
Increase in accounts payable	307,957	
Change in Cash due to Operations		($80,859)
Cash Flow from Investments		
Sale of land	60,000	
Purchase of property, plant & equipment	(202,518)	
Change in Cash due to Investments		(142,518)
Cash Flow from Financing		
Payment towards notes payable	(30,000)	
Proceeds from bank loan	204,000	
Payment of cash dividend	(10,000)	
Issuance of common stock	10,000	
Change in Cash due to Financing		174,000
Net increase (decrease) in cash		(49,377)
Cash at the beginning of the year		72,642
Cash at the end of the year		$23,265

FIGURE 19.17

Direct Method

We have assembled a cash flow statement using the *indirect method*. The term indirect refers to tracking the changes to cash without direct reference to cash receipts or payments. In other words, this method analyzes cash flow indirectly by starting with accrual-based net income and making related adjustments for changes on the balance sheet and income statement.

We will now turn our attention to the **direct method**, which is another way of tracing the changes to cash from one period to the next. Like the indirect method, the **direct method** breaks down the three ways of generating and using cash into: operating, investing and financing activities. In this section, we will illustrate how the direct method accomplishes this by looking at, specifically, *cash receipts* and *payments*. The direct method is not often used because it can be burdensome to execute.

Here is a simple example to illustrate the fundamental difference between the indirect method and the direct method presented in this chapter. Jane is a student who currently pays her tuition in cash and gets paid in cash for her part-time job. In an attempt to control her spending, she has opted to use her debit card for all purchases and never pays by credit card. Suppose that, at the end of the year, Jane wants to determine by how much her cash situation changed in the year. There are two ways she can go about doing this:

1. She can review her bank statements and calculate the difference between the December (end of year) bank balance and January (beginning of year) bank balance. Since all her transactions are made with cash, she can simply subtract the beginning of year balance from the end of year balance and determine how her cash situation changed during the year. Or,

2. Jane can calculate her cash flow for the year by adding together all the individual purchase receipts and pay stubs she received throughout the year.

Both methods will add to the same value, assuming all receipts and stubs are accounted for and there are no errors.

Method 1 is, essentially, the indirect method. This is because Jane indirectly determined her cash flow situation by reading off the balances on her bank statements. Method 2, on the other hand, demonstrates the direct cash flow method because Jane directly summed up all her collections and disbursements for the year using source documents. Notice that the direct method can be a lot more time-consuming and prone to error since Jane would have to search for all her documents (e.g. she may have accidentally thrown out some receipts). Similarly to Jane, most companies opt to use the indirect method for simplicity purposes.

In the following example, we will examine how to determine the cash flow of a company using the direct method.

Suppose ArmorVilla Corporation had the following transactions at year end July 31, 2011.

a)	Depreciation expense	$22,000
b)	Cash sales	284,000
c)	Loan to another company	75,000
d)	Credit sales	966,000
e)	Cash received from issuing current debt	26,000
f)	Dividends received in cash on investments in stock	9,000
g)	Payments of salaries	180,000
h)	Accrued salary expense	105,000
i)	Collection of interest on notes receivable	32,000
j)	Cash received from issuing common stock	81,000
k)	Purchase of inventory on credit	605,000
l)	Declaration and payment of cash dividends	144,000
m)	Collections from credit customers	638,000
n)	Payments to suppliers	313,000
o)	Payment of long-term debt	175,000
p)	Cash received from selling equipment (includes gain of $5,000)	30,000
q)	Interest expenses and payments	21,000
r)	Cash payments to acquire capital assets	204,000
s)	Cash balance: August 1, 2010	178,000
	Cash balance: July 31, 2011	$166,000

FIGURE 19.18

Since we are using the direct method, we are interested primarily in *cash receipts* and *payments*. Therefore, let us identify only those items that affect cash flow:

b)	Cash sales	$284,000
c)	Loan to another company	75,000
e)	Cash received from issuing current debt	26,000
f)	Dividends received in cash on investments in stock	9,000
g)	Payments of salaries	180,000
i)	Collection of interest on notes receivable	32,000
j)	Cash received from issuing common stock	81,000
l)	Declaration and payment of cash dividends	144,000
m)	Collections from credit customers	638,000
n)	Payments to suppliers	313,000
o)	Payment of long-term debt	175,000
p)	Cash received from selling equipment (includes gain of $5,000)	30,000
q)	Interest expenses and payments	21,000
r)	Cash payments to acquire capital assets	204,000

FIGURE 19.19

Now let us categorize each cash item into the appropriate category to create our statement of cash flow. First, we will consider cash receipts/disbursements that relate to regular business operations.

Cash Flow from Operations		
Cash Sales	$284,000	
Collections from Credit Customers	638,000	
Dividends Received on Investments in Stock	9,000	
Collection of Interest on Notes Receivable	32,000	
Total Cash Receipts		$963,000
Payment of Salaries	180,000	
Payments to Suppliers	313,000	
Interest Expenses and Payments	$21,000	
Total Cash Payments		514,000
Change in Cash due to Operations		449,000

FIGURE 19.20

Notice that to perform a cash flow calculation using the direct method, a company has to be able to track information regarding cash inflows and outflows. This makes it more difficult to use the direct method.

Note that the cash flow calculations for investing and financing activities using the direct method are very similar to the indirect method.

The gain that is realized on the sale of the equipment is already included in the sales price of $30,000. There is no need to list the gain anywhere when using the direct method.

Also, the current debt that is issued is considered part of financing activities. The reason for this is that the debt is incurred specifically to help finance the company. This makes it different from other current debt such as accounts payable, which is simply a supplier allowing the company some time to pay their bills.

Cash Flow from Investments		
Loan to Another Company	(75,000)	
Sale of Equipment	30,000	
Capital Asset Acquisition	(204,000)	
Change in Cash due to Investments		(249,000)
Cash Flow from Financing		
Issuance of Current Debt	26,000	
Issuance of Common Stock	81,000	
Declaration And Payment of Dividends (Cash)	(144,000)	
Payment of Long-Term Debt	(175,000)	
Change in Cash due to Financing		(212,000)

FIGURE 19.21

Summary of the direct method

In summary, the cash flow statement of ArmorVilla Corporation prepared by using the direct method is shown in figure 19.22.

Although the direct and indirect method use different approaches to determine the cash flow, both approaches still provide the same end result and allow for an assessment of a company's cash management effectiveness.

ArmorVilla Corporation
Cash Flow Statement
July 31, 2011

Cash Flow from Operations		
Cash Sales	$284,000	
Collections from Credit Customers	638,000	
Dividends Received on Investments in Stock	9,000	
Collection of Interest on Notes Receivable	32,000	
Total Cash Receipts		$963,000
Payment of Salaries	180,000	
Payments to Suppliers	313,000	
Interest Expenses and Payments	$21,000	
Total Cash Payments		514,000
Change in Cash due to Operations		449,000
Cash Flow from Investments		
Loan to Another Company	(75,000)	
Sale of Equipment	30,000	
Capital Asset Acquisition	(204,000)	
Change in Cash due to Investments		(249,000)
Cash Flow from Financing		
Issuance of Current Debt	$26,000	
Issuance of Common Stock	81,000	
Declaration And Payment of Dividends (Cash)	(144,000)	
Payment of Long-Term Debt	(175,000)	
Change in Cash due to Financing		(212,000)
Net increase (decrease) in cash		(12,000)
Opening Cash Balance, August 1, 2010		178,000
Ending Cash Balance, July 31, 2011		$166,000

FIGURE 19.22

Ethics and Controls

The accounting scandals that began in 2001 with Enron served as a warning to much of the financial community that income statements and balance sheets can be manipulated to present a false financial picture of a business. As a result, an increasing number of people started using the cash flow statement as a more revealing snapshot of a company's financial well-being.

Indeed, the motivation behind relying more on cash flow statements to analyze company performance is understandable. Cash flow statements are supposed to show where the money is coming from and where it is going. However, no financial statement is immune from flaws, and this is certainly also the case with cash flow statements.

The following three situations should be viewed with caution when analyzing the cash flow statement of a business:

- *Some companies may stretch out their payables.* One way of artificially enhancing a company's cash position from operations is to deliberately delay paying bills. In fact, some companies will even go so far as to institute such a policy and label it as a form of shrewd cash flow decision making. Of course, the company has not improved its underlying cash flow, but has simply manipulated it.

- *Some companies may finance their payables.* Some companies try to manipulate their cash flow statements by having a third party pay their payables for them – although regulators have tried to crack down on this practice. This means that the company itself shows no payments in its cash flow and, instead, pays a fee to the third party at a later date. Picking and choosing the periods in which this is done artificially manipulates the cash flow statement — almost at will.

- *Cash flow categories can be artificial.* Although businesses may handle their finances differently, including receiving and paying out cash, cash flow statements should exhibit the same categories listed under the same headings for every business. In essence, information can be lost in translation, and analysts can become too dependent on numbers that are made to fit into the cash flow statement.

In Summary

↪   Balance sheets and income statements are prepared on an accrual basis, which involves recording transactions that do not necessarily involve any exchange of money. Cash flow statements differ in that they reveal both the sources and uses of cash within a business.

↪   The three ways of generating cash flow, which form the basis of the way cash flow statements are structured, are operations, investments and financing.

↪   Two generally accepted methods of preparing a cash flow statement exist for a business: the direct method and the indirect method.

↪   The indirect method of preparing cash flow statements starts with net income and then tracks changes in balances (within the cash flow from operations section).

↪   The cash flow statement contains three sections: cash flow from operations, cash flow from investments and cash flow from financing.

↪   The cash flow from operations section tracks the movement of cash related to day-to-day activities of the business.

↪   The cash flow from investments section tracks the movement of cash on the basis of the purchases and sales of long-term assets.

↪   The cash flow from financing section tracks the movement of cash related to the way a company receives money for financing purposes and pays it back.

↪   The indirect method tends to be universally used in preparing cash flow statements, since the direct method takes a more burdensome approach to tracking cash receipts and payments.

↪   The direct method of preparing the cash flow statement breaks down cash flows based on actual receipts and payments associated with sales and expenses.

Review Exercise

Shown below is the balance sheet for MLF. Net income for 2010 was $207,144.

Required: Prepare the cash flow statement for 2010. Use the indirect method.

MLF Balance Sheet As at December 31, 2010	2010	2009
Assets		
Current Assets		
Cash	$28,222	$64,494
Other Current Assets	605,379	902,417
Total Current Assets	633,601	966,911
Long-Term Assets		
Property, Plant and Equipment	3,490,970	3,389,108
Less: Accumulated Depreciation	(1,126,727)	(1,080,293)
Total Long-Term Assets	2,364,243	2,308,815
Total Assets	$2,997,844	$3,275,726
Liabilities		
Current Liabilities	$591,199	$778,299
Long-Term Liabilities	1,245,218	1,502,985
Total Liabilities	1,836,417	2,281,284
Stockholders' Equity		
Contributed Capital	790,027	790,027
Opening Retained Earnings	204,415	231,907
Net Income for the Year	207,144	4,525
Dividends Paid	(40,159)	(32,017)
Closing Retained Earnings	371,400	204,415
Total Stockholders' Equity*	1,161,427	994,442
Total Liabilities and Stockholders' Equity	$2,997,844	$3,275,726

*Total Stockholders' Equity = Contributed Capital + Closing Retained Earnings

Assume current liabilities include only items from operations (e.g. accounts payable, tax payable). Long-term liabilities include items from financing (e.g. bonds and other long-term liabilities)

Note that there was no sale of property, plant & equipment throughout the year.

MLF Cash Flow Statement For the Year Ended December 31, 2010		
Cash Flows from Operations		
Net Income	$207,144	
Add: Depreciation	46,434	
Decrease in Other Current Assets	297,038	
Decrease in Current Liabilities	(187,100)	
Total Increase in Cash from Operations		$363,516
Cash Flows from Investments		
Purchase of Property, Plant and Equipment	(101,862)	
Total Decrease in Cash from Investing		(101,862)
Cash Flows from Financing		
Paid Long-Term Liabilities	(257,767)	
Dividends Paid	(40,159)	
Total Decrease in Cash from Financing		(297,926)
Net increase (decrease) in cash		(36,272)
Cash at the beginning of the year		64,494
Cash at the end of the year		$28,222

Appendix 19A: Selling Long-Term Assets

In the example presented in chapter 19, when a long-term asset is sold, it is presented in the investing section of the cash flow statement. The example showed land being sold, which does not depreciate, so the cost or purchase price of the land is equal to its book value. Therefore the decrease in the value of property, plant and equipment is equal to the book value of the land. This makes it easy to determine if a gain or loss was recorded. A gain is reported if the amount received is greater than the book value of the land, and a loss is reported if the amount is less than the book value of the land.

When selling equipment or any other long-term asset that depreciates in value, determining the book value of the item requires more investigation. Presented below is a sample balance and sheet and income statement for a company.

Soho Supplies
Balance Sheet
As at December 31

	2013	2012	Changes
ASSETS			
Current Assets			
Cash	$746,000	$54,000	$692,000
Accounts receivable	850,000	800,000	50,000
Inventory	950,000	600,000	350,000
Prepaid expenses	35,000	30,000	5,000
Total Current Assets	2,581,000	1,484,000	1,097,000
Long-term investments[1]	400,000	500,000	(100,000)
Property, plant & equipment[2]	1,150,000	900,000	250,000
Less: Accumulated depreciation	(290,000)	(213,000)	(77,000)
Total Long-Term Assets	1,260,000	1,187,000	73,000
TOTAL ASSETS	$3,841,000	$2,671,000	$1,170,000
LIABILITIES AND EQUITY			
Liabilities			
Current Liabilities			
Accounts payable	$750,000	$475,000	$275,000
Current portion of bank loan	380,000	240,000	140,000
Notes payable	170,000	200,000	(30,000)
Total Current Liabilities	1,300,000	915,000	385,000
Long-term portion of bank loan	420,000	356,000	64,000
TOTAL LIABILITIES	1,720,000	1,271,000	449,000
Stockholders' Equity			
Common stock	150,000	100,000	50,000
Retained earnings	1,971,000	1,300,000	671,000
TOTAL STOCKHOLDERS' EQUITY	2,121,000	1,400,000	721,000
TOTAL LIABILITIES AND EQUITY	$3,841,000	$2,671,000	$1,170,000

Additional Information:
(1) During 2013, Soho did not purchase any long-term investments.
(2) During 2013, Soho made purchases of property, plant & equipment for $375,000.

FIGURE 19A.1

Soho Supplies
Income Statement
For the Year Ended December 31, 2013

Sales	$7,000,000
COGS	4,500,000
Gross Profit	2,500,000
Operating Expenses	
Administration charges	9,000
Advertising & marketing	40,000
Depreciation	95,000
Bonuses	60,000
Commission	30,000
Interest	50,000
Insurance	16,000
Sales and administration salaries	600,000
Management salaries	300,000
Occupancy	55,000
Consulting	85,000
Repairs and maintenance	90,000
Professional fees	20,000
Other operating expenses	70,000
Total Operating Expenses	1,520,000
Operating Income	980,000
Other Revenue and Expenses	
Loss on Sale of Investments	(5,000)
Gain on Sale of Factory Equipment	16,000
Net Income Before Tax	991,000
Income Tax	280,000
Net Income	$711,000

FIGURE 19A.2

The creation of the cash flow from operations section will be identical to the way it was created in chapter 19.

For the cash flow from investments section, recall that changes in long-term assets are recorded here. In our example, the income statement indicates that some equipment has been sold for a gain. To determine how much cash was actually received, we must determine the book value of the asset. This is done by examining the changes in the balance sheet accounts. Figure 19A.3 helps illustrate this.

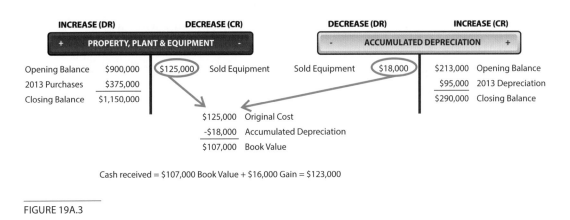

FIGURE 19A.3

From the balance sheet, we see that property, plant and equipment increased by $250,000, however the note indicates that $375,000 was purchased during the year. This means that equipment that originally cost $125,000 was sold. Also from the balance sheet, we see that accumulated depreciation increased by $77,000, however depreciation expense on the income statement was $95,000. This means that $18,000 was removed from accumulated depreciation when the equipment was sold.

The difference between the cost of the equipment and the associated accumulated depreciation indicates the equipment had a book value of $107,000 when it was sold. The income statement tells us that the equipment was sold at a gain of $16,000, which means the total amount of cash received must have been $123,000 ($107,000 + $16,000). This will represent an increase in cash flow in the investments section of the cash flow statement.

Long-term investments held at cost were also sold during the year, as is shown by the decrease in this item on the balance sheet. However, the $100,000 decrease represents the cost of the investment, not necessarily the amount of cash received. The income statement indicates there was a loss of $5,000 when the investment was sold. Thus, the amount of cash received was $95,000 ($100,000 – $5,000) and this will represent an increase in cash

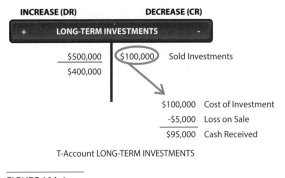

T-Account LONG-TERM INVESTMENTS

FIGURE 19A.4

flow in the investments section of the cash flow statement. Note that a gain on the sale would be added to the cost of the investment for calculating the amount of cash received on the sale.

In this example for long-term investments, we assumed that there was no additional purchases in the year. If there was any purchases of long-term investments during the year, we would add the amount to the debit side of the investment account and then calculate the amount (cost) of investment sold. The calculation is similar to the example shown in the property, plant and equipment account from figure 19A.3.

Lastly, we turn our attention to the financing section of the cash flow statement. There is no note regarding the amount of dividends paid, however figure 19A.5 will illustrate how we can calculate the amount of dividends.

From previous chapters, we know that the retained earnings account will increase if there is a net income for the year and decrease if there is a net loss for the year. Additionally, dividends are paid out of the retained earnings account, decreasing its value. The balance sheet shows that the retained earnings account increased by $671,000, however the income statement shows that net income was $711,000. Therefore, the difference of $40,000 must be the dividends paid. This will represent a decrease in cash flow in the financing section of the cash flow statement.

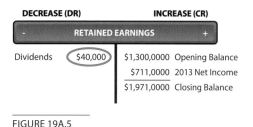

FIGURE 19A.5

The rest of the items on the cash flow statement have already been discussed in chapter 19. The complete cash flow statement is shown in figure 19A.6.

Soho Supplies
Statement of Cash Flows
For the Year Ended December 31, 2013

Cash Flow from Operations

Net Income	$711,000	
Add: Depreciation	95,000	
Deduct: Gain on sale of equipment	(16,000)	
Add: Loss on sale of investments	5,000	
Changes in Current Assets & Current Liabilities:		
Increase in accounts receivable	(50,000)	
Increase in prepaid expenses	(5,000)	
Increase in inventory	(350,000)	
Increase in accounts payable	275,000	
Change in Cash due to Operations		$665,000

Cash Flow from Investments

Sale of equipment	123,000	
Sale of investments	95,000	
Purchase of property, plant & equipment	(375,000)	
Change in Cash due to Investments		(157,000)

Cash Flow from Financing

Payment towards notes payable	(30,000)	
Proceeds from bank loan	204,000	
Payment of cash dividend	(40,000)	
Issuance of common stock	50,000	
Change in Cash due to Financing		184,000
Net increase (decrease) in cash		692,000
Cash at the beginning of the year		54,000
Cash at the end of the year		$746,000

FIGURE 19A.6

Additional Items for the Cash Flow Statement

We already discussed some of the non-cash items such as depreciation and a gain or loss on the sale of assets under the operations section of the cash flow statement. As for the investing and financing activities, there could also be some non-cash transactions which have no impact on cash. For instance, the company may issue some shares to pay off a note payable or they may buy assets in exchange for shares. Note that although these non-cash transactions are not shown on the cash flow statement, GAAP requires their disclosure in the notes to the financial statements.

Additionally, an income statement may report discontinued operations and extraordinary items in addition to regular operations. When it comes to the cash flow statement, the cash flows related to discontinued and extraordinary items should be presented separately based on the appropriate operating, investing or financing activities.

Review Exercise

Shown below is the balance sheet, income statement and notes for MLF Inc. Prepare the cash flow statement for 2013 using the indirect method.

MLF Inc. Balance Sheet As at December 31		
	2013	**2012**
ASSETS		
Current Assets		
Cash	$1,085,700	$27,000
Accounts receivable	370,000	400,000
Inventory	290,000	250,000
Prepaid expenses	29,000	21,000
Total Current Assets	1,774,700	698,000
Long-term investments(1)	560,000	600,000
Property, plant & equipment(2)	1,300,000	1,100,000
Less: Accumulated depreciation	(206,000)	(156,000)
Total Long-Term Assets	1,654,000	1,544,000
TOTAL ASSETS	$3,428,700	$2,242,000
Liabilities		
Current Liabilities		
Accounts payable	$461,000	$342,000
Current portion of bank loan	75,000	65,000
Notes payable	96,000	90,000
Total Current Liabilities	632,000	497,000
Long-term portion of bank loan	275,000	215,000
TOTAL LIABILITIES	907,000	712,000
Stockholders' Equity		
Common stock	400,000	320,000
Retained earnings	2,121,700	1,210,000
TOTAL STOCKHOLDERS' EQUITY	2,521,700	1,530,000
TOTAL LIABILITIES AND EQUITY	$3,428,700	$2,242,000

Additional Information:

(1) During 2013, MLF Inc. did not purchase any long-term investments.

(2) During 2013, MLF Inc. made purchases of property, plant & equipment for $400,000.

MLF Inc. Income Statement For the Year Ended December 31, 2013	
Sales	$5,600,000
COGS	2,968,000
Gross Profit	2,632,000
Operating Expenses	
Administration charges	6,200
Advertising & marketing	38,500
Depreciation	80,000
Bonuses	40,000
Commission	20,000
Interest	34,500
Insurance	8,000
Sales and administration salaries	521,000
Management salaries	245,000
Rent	34,000
Consulting	25,100
Repairs and maintenance	95,000
Professional fees	18,000
Other operating expenses	56,000
Total Operating Expenses	1,221,300
Operating Income	1,410,700
Other Revenue and Expenses	
Gain on Sale of Investments	8,000
Loss on Sale of Factory Equipment	(10,000)
Net Income Before Tax	1,408,700
Income Tax	422,000
Net Income	$986,700

Cost of equipment sold = $1,100,000 + $400,000 - $1,300,000 = $200,000

Depreciation of equipment sold = $156,000 + $80,000 - $206,000 = $30,000

Book value = $200,000 - $30,000 = $170,000 - $10,000 loss = $160,000 cash received on sale of equipment

Cost of investment = $600,000 - $560,000 = $40,000 + $8,000 = $48,000 cash received on sale of investments

Dividends paid = $1,210,000 + $986,700 - $2,121,700 = $75,000 cash paid for dividends

<table>
<tr><td colspan="3">MLF Inc.
Statement of Cash Flows
For the Year Ended December 31, 2013</td></tr>
</table>

Cash Flow from Operations		
Net Income	$986,700	
Add: Depreciation	80,000	
Add: Loss on sale of equipment	10,000	
Deduct: Gain on sale of investments	(8,000)	
Changes in Current Assets & Current Liabilities:		
Decrease in accounts receivable	30,000	
Increase in inventory	(40,000)	
Increase in prepaid expenses	(8,000)	
Increase in accounts payable	119,000	
Change in Cash due to Operations		$1,169,700
Cash Flow from Investments		
Sale of equipment	160,000	
Sale of investments	48,000	
Purchase of property, plant & equipment	(400,000)	
Change in Cash due to Investments		(192,000)
Cash Flow from Financing		
Payment towards notes payable	6,000	
Proceeds from bank loan	70,000	
Payment of cash dividend	(75,000)	
Issuance of common stock	80,000	
Change in Cash due to Financing		81,000
Net increase (decrease) in cash		1,058,700
Cash at the beginning of the year		27,000
Cash at the end of the year		$1,085,700

Chapter 20
FINANCIAL STATEMENT ANALYSIS

LEARNING OUTCOMES:

❶ Understand the importance of analyzing a combination of financial ratios to determine financial performance

❷ Calculate and comprehend ratios that pertain to profitability

❸ Use the DuPont framework to analyze the ROE of a company

❹ Calculate and comprehend ratios that pertain to cash flow

❺ Calculate and comprehend ratios that pertain to management performance

❻ Perform horizontal and vertical analysis of financial statements

The Importance of Financial Statement Analysis

It might be tempting to believe that once the financial statements are prepared and read, the job of the accountant, or anyone interested in analyzing the health of the business, is over. However (with perhaps the exception of some added notes), these financial statements do not provide all the answers needed to form conclusions on where the business is heading. These answers are, however, needed by the organization's accountants, its management team, potential lenders and investors, or others with an interest in the state of the business.

In order to start getting answers, and to draw conclusions on the financial state of the business, accountants and other interested parties perform what is known as a **financial analysis** of the financial statements. **Financial ratios** are used to perform this kind of analysis.

We have learned about different financial ratios in previous chapters, each providing a snapshot of a particular area of the business. Some financial ratios provide answers relative to profitability, while others address inventory, and so on. No financial ratio, on its own, can form the basis of the financial analysis of a business. Instead, a combination of ratios must be used to draw a complete picture of the state of an organization's finances. In a sense, financial analysis is much like peeling an orange. An orange with its peel on can give you a sense of how ripe it is. Peel away the skin, and you get a closer picture. Does it have bruises? Is it firm or soft? To truly know how good the orange is, it is then necessary to take a bite. Finally, more bites are taken and a conclusion is formed as to the taste and quality of the orange.

Our approach to financial analysis follows a similar logic. Here is the progression that we take:

Revenues are Vanity

Much like an orange with its peel on, glancing at business revenues does not necessarily give us an accurate picture. In other words, sales do not guarantee profits.

Profits are Sanity

Some serious weaknesses can exist within a business if profits are not quickly transformed into cash. In other words, a business should have a good degree of liquidity. Just as taking off the orange peel provides a better look at the fruit, but not necessarily an accurate judgment as to its quality, a company's profit figures may not provide all the information we need.

Cash Flow is Reality

Getting more information about the well-being of a business comes from looking at its cash flow. It gives us the most accurate picture of the true state of the financial affairs of a business. Accountants and analysts can only give a business a clean bill of health if they are satisfied that profits result in enough cash flow for the business.

Management Ensures Stability

You will not get a sense of what the orange tastes like unless you put it in your mouth and start savoring its flavour. Similarly, you will not get a sense of how the company's cash flow is managed unless you take a look at some management ratios.

The rest of this chapter is dedicated to performing a financial analysis based on this precise sequence. Soho Supplies is a manufacturer of office supplies and was introduced in the previous chapter. Soho's financial statements will be used for analysis in this chapter. Throughout this chapter, current year financial ratios will be calculated, and these ratios will be compared to Soho Supplies' previous year and to its related industry. This comparison can shed some light on the overall performance of Soho Supplies. By comparing the current year to the previous year, we can conclude how Soho is performing in relation to its previous year's performance. By comparing Soho's ratios to the industry average, we can conclude how Soho is performing in relation to its competitors in the office supplies industry. This type of analysis gives us a better understanding of where Soho Supplies stands financially compared to itself and its competitors. The income statement is presented below.

Soho Supplies Income Statement For the Year Ended December 31		
	2012	**2011**
Sales	$8,685,025	$6,482,000
Cost of goods sold	5,998,612	4,397,200
Gross Profit	2,686,413	2,084,800
Operating Expenses		
Administration charges	8,652	6,861
Advertising & marketing	42,645	32,975
Depreciation	43,262	15,862
Bonuses	65,000	62,432
Commission	420,250	325,210
Interest	51,875	31,253
Insurance	16,000	12,000
Sales and administration salaries	610,325	435,951
Management salaries	320,560	226,548
Occupancy	52,000	48,000
Consulting	22,500	21,356
Repairs and maintenance	36,860	26,845
Professional fees	11,560	8,642
Other operating expenses	61,200	48,672
Total Operating Expenses	1,762,689	1,302,607
Operating Income Before Tax	923,724	782,193
Income Tax	286,020	223,652
Net Income	$637,704	$558,541

FIGURE 20.1

Revenues are Vanity

The first part of our analysis is to consider changes in revenue. Presented below is a portion of Soho's income statement, illustrating the change in revenue.

Soho Supplies Income Statement For the Year Ended December 31			
	2012	**2011**	
Sales	$8,685,025	$6,482,000	$2,203,025 (or 34%)
Cost of goods sold	5,998,612	4,397,200	
Gross Profit	2,686,413	2,084,800	
Operating Expenses			
Administration charges	8,652	6,861	

FIGURE 20.2

As shown in figure 20.2, revenue jumped from $6,482,000 in 2011 to $8,685,025 in 2012. This constitutes an increase of $2,203,025 (or 34%).

Revenues only form the first superficial glance at the numbers for the business. In this case, growing revenues, numbering in the millions of dollars, might look great. However, we need more analysis and ratios to determine if they are in fact great figures, or merely superficial indicators of business health. For example, if revenues increased by $2.2 million but costs increased by $4 million then just looking at changes in revenues, alone, will not give us a true understanding of how the company has performed in the past year.

Profits are Sanity

The next step in our approach to financial analysis is to look at profits. Remember, profits are sanity. In other words, profits can serve as a deeper indicator of financial stability, beyond revenues. For Soho Supplies, gross profit (revenues minus cost of goods sold) has increased by $601,613 (from $2,084,800 in 2011 to $2,686,413 in 2012).

However, just as with revenues, gross profit figures can only tell us so much. In this case, they indicate the business is turning revenues into profit. But we need more information — which means that we need to introduce some ratios into the mix. We will start with the gross profit margin.

Gross Profit Margin

We use the gross profit margin to demonstrate the impact of cost of goods sold on the financial statements. In other words, the gross profit margin subtracts cost of goods sold from sales revenue, the result of which is divided by sales revenue. Here is the formula:

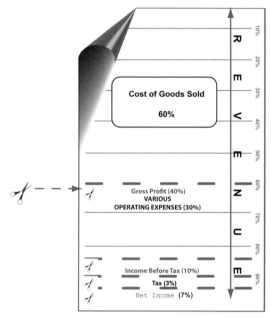

Our approach to analyzing the entire income statement is rather simple, and is depicted in this diagram of a piece of paper. The entire paper represents business revenues. As our analysis proceeds, a certain chunk - or percentage - is taken from revenues, which leaves something behind for us to analyze. By the end of the income statement, we are left with the smallest chunk, which is net income. By then it will be time to move on to the balance sheet.

FIGURE 20.3

$$\text{Gross Profit Margin} \quad = \quad \frac{\text{Gross Profit*}}{\text{Sales Revenue}}$$

* Gross Profit = Sales Revenue – Cost of Goods Sold

Gross profit margin tells us how much money is left to pay expenses, other than those directly involved in producing the goods or services of the business. That is, how much profitability remains after deducting the cost of goods sold.

The following chart calculates the gross profit margin using figures from the income statement:

	2012	2011
Sales	$8,685,025	$6,482,000
COGS	5,998,612	4,397,200
Gross Profit	2,686,413	2,084,800
Gross Profit Margin	30.93%	32.16%

FIGURE 20.4

As you can see, gross profit margin has decreased by more than one percentage point over the course of the period. Suppose the industry's average gross profit margin is 33.23% for 2012. Soho is doing worse compared to its competitors in the industry as its 2012 gross profit margin is lower than the industry average by more than 2%. There are many reasons why this might occur, ranging from increasing discounts to customers, a change in the product mix to lower margin products, increased waste, shrinkage or breakage of inventory or an error in counting or valuing the inventory.

EBIT

It might be tempting to believe that the next step in our analysis is to start peeling away all costs after gross profit has been calculated. As enticing as it might be to jump from gross profit to net income, there is a step in between that many accountants and analysts take to get an even clearer picture of business performance. Specifically, certain costs (that are considered largely under the control of management) are added back after net income is calculated. These costs generally include interest and tax. The calculated amount is referred to as EBIT or earnings before interest and tax.

Adding these costs back after net income is calculated essentially levels the playing field when analyzing the performance of one business compared to another. In other words, items such as taxes are not the result of day-to-day managerial decision-making. Instead, these types of costs can vary from jurisdiction to jurisdiction or from one business to another. Net income, therefore, does not reflect the direct performance that the business controls.

The expenses that are added back to net income to calculate EBIT are highlighted below. Thus, EBIT for 2012 is $975,599 and EBIT for 2011 is $813,446.

Soho Supplies
Income Statement
For the Year Ended December 31

	2012	2011	
Sales	$8,685,025	$6,482,000	
Cost of goods sold	5,998,612	4,397,200	
Gross Profit	2,686,413	2,084,800	
Operating Expenses			
Administration charges	8,652	6,861	
Advertising & marketing	42,645	32,975	
Depreciation	43,262	15,862	
Bonuses	65,000	62,432	
Commission	420,250	325,210	
Interest	51,875	31,253	Add back
Insurance	16,000	12,000	
Sales and administration salaries	610,325	435,951	
Management salaries	320,560	226,548	
Occupancy	52,000	48,000	
Consulting	22,500	21,356	
Repairs and maintenance	36,860	26,845	
Professional fees	11,560	8,642	
Other operating expenses	61,200	48,672	
Total Operating Expenses	1,762,689	1,302,607	
Operating Income Before Tax	923,724	782,193	
Income Tax	286,020	223,652	Add back
Net Income	$637,704	$558,541	Start with Net Income

FIGURE 20.5

EBIT Percentage to Sales

Given that we now have a better understanding of what EBIT is, and why associated expenses are added back to net income; it is time to start formulating some ratios as a result. You may have noticed a trend in the ratios we have used so far. Specifically, we have taken that part of the pie remaining after certain expenses are deducted — such as COGS, operating expenses, and so on — and divided it by revenues. In other words, we have been deducting slices of expenses from revenue and then dividing the remainder by revenue itself. This gives us a corresponding percentage relative to revenue, which, in essence, tells us how much money we are working with on a percentage basis. The exact same thing is done with EBIT.

In other words, we want to take our EBIT number and divide it by revenue, to obtain yet another percentage figure to work with in our analysis.

$$\text{EBIT Percentage to Sales} = \frac{\text{EBIT}}{\text{Sales Revenue}}$$

This ratio has been calculated for us in the following chart:

	2012	2011
Sales	$8,685,025	$6,482,000
EBIT:		
Net Income	637,704	558,541
Add back:		
Interest Expense	51,875	31,253
Income Tax	286,020	223,652
EBIT	$975,599	$813,446
EBIT Percentage to Sales	11.23%	12.55%

FIGURE 20.6

As you can see, although EBIT has increased in absolute dollars from 2011 to 2012, the percentage has, in fact, decreased. This probably means that the business has become less efficient during the period and further analysis needs to be done to find out which expenses are contributing to the decline. Suppose the industry's EBIT percentage to sales is 12.35% for 2012. In this case, Soho is doing worse compared to the competitors in the same industry as its 2012 EBIT percentage to sales is lower than the industry average.

In addition to EBIT, some corporations may use another measure called **EBITDA** or earnings before interest, tax and depreciation. EBITDA is calculated by adding back costs such as interest, taxes, and depreciation to the net income. EBITDA is mainly used internally by management to measure the profitability of the company and to compare the results to other companies in the same industry. This eliminates the items over which management has no or little control to make a fair comparison between companies. Note that although EBITDA can be a useful tool when analyzing financial statements, EBITDA is not allowed under GAAP. This means that businesses may exercise some flexibility when it comes to what is included in EBITDA calculations which could decrease the objectivity of this measurement. This should be kept in mind when reading published financial reports released by an organization.

Interest Coverage Ratio

You may have noticed that financial ratios are often nothing more than a comparison of numbers involving one figure divided by another. In fact, most of the ratios analyzed so far in this chapter involve dividing a number by revenue, which provides us with a percentage relative to revenues.

The second ratio we will look at with respect to EBIT is the **interest coverage ratio** which is very similar to the EBIT to sales ratio. The only difference is that instead of dividing EBIT by revenue, it is interest that serves as the denominator in the ratio. In other words, the interest coverage ratio measures the extent to which earnings before interest and taxes covers the interest payments that are to be made by the business. That is, to what extent does EBIT cover the ability to pay lenders cash in the form of regular interest payments that are due within the period?

For example, an interest coverage ratio of only 1 time would mean that the business has just enough earnings (before EBIT expenses are deducted) to cover the amount of interest paid during the year.

Here is how the interest coverage ratio is calculated:

$$\text{Interest Coverage Ratio} = \frac{\text{EBIT}}{\text{Interest Expense}}$$

The corresponding numbers related to interest coverage are provided in the following chart:

	2012	2011
EBIT	$975,599	$813,446
Interest Expense	$51,875	$31,253
Interest Coverage Ratio	**18.81 times**	**26.03 times**

FIGURE 20.7

As you can see, total interest has increased at a rate greater than that for EBIT. Although the interest coverage ratios for both periods are well above 2 times (which is desirable), if this downward trend continues, it may mean that the business will have an increasingly difficult time covering its interest payments with EBIT. In addition, Soho might find itself in a more concerning position if we assume that the industry average is 22.67 times in 2012. Therefore, Soho is doing worse than its competitors as its 2012 interest coverage ratio is lower than the industry.

Net Profit Margin

Now that we have taken EBIT into account, we can finally move on to net income. Specifically, we can use **net profit margin** to assess profitability after all expenses have been deducted.

$$\text{Net Profit Margin} \quad = \quad \frac{\text{Net Income}}{\text{Sales Revenue}}$$

Here are the net profit (i.e. net income) numbers from the income statement we have been using:

	2012	2011
Net Income	$637,704	$558,541
Sales	$8,685,025	$6,482,000
Net Profit Margin	**7.34%**	**8.62%**

FIGURE 20.8

Although the absolute revenue and net income dollar figures have risen over the course of the period, the net profit margin has decreased. In order to perform a complete analysis of net profit margins, comparisons should be made on a monthly and yearly basis to historical company performance, industry averages and direct competitors. Only then will these net income figures be placed in context so that assessments can be made and conclusions drawn. For instance, if the industry average is 8.87% in 2012, we can conclude that, on average, Soho is doing poorly compared to other competitors in the same industry due to its lower than industry net profit margin in 2012.

As was alluded to earlier in this chapter, you should notice another trend in the ratios we have been calculating so far, especially those done with respect to revenues — where revenues serve as the denominator in the corresponding ratio.

Specifically, these percentages, or margins, are getting smaller as we go along. That is because as expenses get deducted from revenues, the remaining figure gets increasingly smaller. Therefore, gross profit margin will be larger than EBIT percentage to sales, which will be larger than net profit margin. In other words, the more we break down the income statement, the less we have left to analyze.

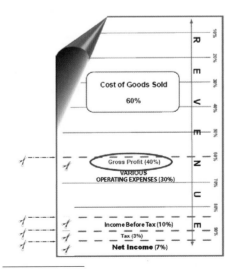

FIGURE 20.9

Linking the Income Statement to the Balance Sheet

The next part of our approach to analyzing financial statements takes us from the income statement to the balance sheet. We will analyze Soho Supplies' balance sheet.

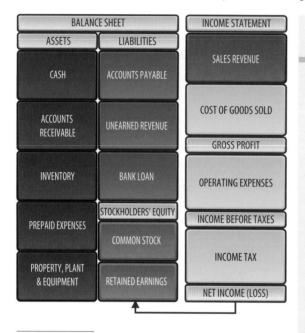

FIGURE 20.10

As the diagram shows, the next step in our analysis of Soho Supplies' financial statements is to essentially link the income statement to the balance sheet. We do this by moving from net income on the income statement to stockholders' equity on the balance sheet.

Soho Supplies Balance Sheet As at December 31		
	2012	**2011**
ASSETS		
Current Assets		
Cash	$13,265	$72,642
Accounts receivable	1,286,138	1,065,812
Inventory	1,683,560	840,091
Prepaid expenses	48,612	42,625
Total Current Assets	3,031,575	2,021,170
Property, plant & equipment	243,256	134,000
TOTAL ASSETS	$3,274,831	$2,155,170
LIABILITIES AND EQUITY		
Liabilities		
Current Liabilities		
Accounts payable	$783,602	$475,645
Current portion of bank loan	380,000	240,000
Notes payable	170,000	200,000
Total Current Liabilities	1,333,602	915,645
Long-term portion of bank loan	420,000	356,000
TOTAL LIABILITIES	1,753,602	1,271,645
Stockholders' Equity		
Common stock	15,000	5,000
Retained earnings	1,506,229	878,525
TOTAL STOCKHOLDERS' EQUITY	1,521,229	883,525
TOTAL LIABILITIES AND EQUITY	$3,274,831	$2,155,170

FIGURE 20.11

Return on Equity (ROE)

We went from gross profit margin, to EBIT, to net profit margin. Each step of the way told us something more about how well the company was using the revenues it earned in comparison to last year and this year's industry average. It is now time to move onto the balance sheet of the business, which essentially tells us how strong a position the organization is in with respect to what it owns versus what it owes. We proceed with our analysis of financial statements by assessing owners' equity, stockholders' equity, capital accounts, or other accounts that describe the net worth of the business.

IN THE REAL WORLD

One of the most important assessments that owners of a business can make is to know if they are getting a decent return on their investment. How is this done and how do they know if they are getting their money's worth out of the business?

Any determination of return on investment revolves around stockholders' equity. In other words, how much cash would the owners have left if they sold all the assets of the business and paid off all their debt? Given that this is a hypothetical question, and that the owners do not have to sell everything to assess the return on investment, there are other ways of assessing the value of the investment in the business.

For example, the owners could ask themselves another theoretical question: Should we keep our money in the business, or put it elsewhere? Safe investments such as fixed deposit accounts come with relatively lower returns on investment. Investing in a friend's new business comes with a potentially much larger return on investment — but also with greater risk.

In fact, a general rule of thumb can be applied to assessing return on investment associated with certain levels of risk. Generally speaking, investments in publicly traded companies come with the expectation of a return ranging from 15%- 25%. Alternatively, the rate of return associated with private companies is expected to be much higher. In fact, it is not unusual to expect a rate of return of 100% or more for an investment in a small private company.

As with most things in life, everything comes at a price. With return on investment, the price can be a matter of risk. If owners want a better return, they must have a greater tolerance for risk.

The first basic analysis to be performed on the balance sheet involves assessing **return on equity (ROE)**. ROE is a measure of what the owners are getting out of the business relative to the amount they invested.

Although there are various ways to calculate ROE, we will examine the most common method:

$$\text{Return on Equity} = \frac{\text{Net Income}}{\text{Average Stockholders' Equity}}$$

First, we calculate average stockholders' equity by adding opening stockholders' equity and closing stockholders' equity and then dividing the result by two. Second, net income is the numerator for the ratio, which means that the last figure on the income statement serves as the basis from which we start measuring balance sheet performance. That is, net income serves as our link to the balance sheet at this stage of our financial analysis.

A CLOSER LOOK

The return on equity formula assumes that there is no preferred stock equity included in stockholders' equity. If preferred equity exists, the formula would be as follows:

Return on Equity = (Net Income - Preferred Dividends) ÷ Average Common Stockholders' Equity

In this course, only common stock will be illustrated.

The following chart provides a breakdown of the ROE calculation for our ongoing example. Two assumptions are made. One, assume that the beginning stockholders' equity balance for 2011 is $716,475. Two, assume that the sample company has no outstanding preferred stock.

	2012	2011
Net Income	$637,704	$558,541
Average Stockholders' Equity[1]	$1,202,377	$800,000
Return on Equity	**53.04%**	**69.82%**

(1) Average Stockholders' Equity for 2011: (716,475 + 883,525) ÷ 2 = 800,000
Average Stockholders' Equity for 2012: (883,525 + 1,521,229) ÷ 2 = 1,202,377

FIGURE 20.12

Although net income and average stockholders' equity values have increased, the return on equity has decreased fairly significantly from 2011 to 2012. Suppose the industry's return on equity is 68.54% in 2012. In this case, on average, Soho is doing worse compared to the competitors in the same industry as its 2012 return on equity is lower than the industry average.

Return on Assets (ROA)

During the income statement portion of our financial analysis, we peeled away certain layers by starting with revenues and then working our way down to net income. We do much of the same thing during the balance sheet portion of our financial analysis. Specifically, we start with net income from the income statement, jump over to the stockholders' equity account on the balance sheet, and are now ready for the next step. That is, we are ready to take liabilities out of the equation and focus specifically on assets. We do this by using the **return on assets (ROA)** ratio, which is calculated as follows:

$$\text{Return on Assets} = \frac{\text{Net Income}}{\text{Average Total Assets}}$$

ROA essentially provides an assessment of what the company does with what it has; it measures every dollar earned against each dollar's worth of assets. A business invests in assets for the purpose of generating sales and making a profit. This is what ROA tries to measure. Although assessing ROA depends on the type of business being analyzed, a higher ROA number is generally considered better than a lower one. A higher ratio means that the business is earning more money on its investment in assets.

Let us now calculate ROA using our sample company. We have already used the net income numbers needed from the income statement. The total asset figures are to be found on the balance sheet. Assume that the balance of total assets as at December 31, 2010 was $1,844,830.

The following chart provides the necessary ROA calculations:

	2012	2011
Net Income	$637,704	$558,541
Average Total Assets[1]	$2,715,001	$2,000,000
Return on Assets	**23.49%**	**27.93%**

(1) Average Total Assets for 2011: (1,844,830 + 2,155,170) ÷ 2 = 2,000,000
Average Total Assets for 2012: (2,155,170 + 3,274,831) ÷ 2 = 2,715,001

FIGURE 20.13

As you can see, although both net income and asset values have increased, the rate of return has decreased. This discrepancy between absolute figures and percentages is precisely why we use the latter. It also reveals a trend in the business. Specifically, although revenue, income and asset values keep increasing, they can also go down in relative terms.

Regarding our ROA calculations, the ratio for 2012 is 23.49%. This essentially means that the business earned more than 23¢ for each dollar invested in assets. This is a decrease from 28¢ in the 2011. Also suppose the industry's return on assets for 2012 is 28.43%. In this case, on average, Soho is doing worse compared to the competitors in the same industry as its 2012 return on assets is lower than the industry average. Various factors might explain the decrease ranging from an increase in the cost of capital assets, to an increase in production costs that affect the cost of goods sold directly.

In fact, the list of factors contributing to a change in ROA can be almost endless. Some of the most important business decisions by managers pertain to how well resources are allocated. Efficient use of assets should increase ROA. A less productive use of assets can ultimately lead to a decrease in ROA. In essence, ROA measures how efficiently business assets are used relative to profits generated.

As a general rule, an ROA of below 5% is considered capital-intensive or asset-heavy. This means that the business is investing a considerable amount in assets relative to profits. Industries that tend to display low ROA figures include manufacturers and large transportation companies such as railroads. Alternatively, an ROA of over 20% is considered much less capital-intensive or asset-heavy. In other words, such businesses tend to get more 'bang for the buck' when it comes to investing in assets. Examples include professional practices, software companies and retailers.

Asset Turnover

Another way to assess how well business assets are being utilized is to test how much revenue is generated for every dollar of assets. This is calculated by dividing revenue by average total assets.

Asset turnover measures the ability of a company to generate sales revenue from asset investments—the higher the number the better.

$$\text{Asset Turnover} = \frac{\text{Sales Revenue}}{\text{Average Total Assets}}$$

Using our sample statements, let us compare the results for 2011 and 2012.

	2012	2011
Sales Revenue	$8,685,025	$6,482,000
Average Total Assets[1]	$2,715,001	$2,000,000
Asset Turnover	**3.20 times**	**3.24 times**

(1) See Figure 20.13 for calculation of average total assets.

FIGURE 20.14

In 2011, the business generated $3.24 of revenue for every dollar tied up in assets. In 2012, however, the return dropped to $3.20 in revenue for every dollar tied up in assets. What does this tell us? If the business invested less cash in assets but generated more revenue this would mean that the business is "selling more with less". Suppose the industry's asset turnover for 2012 is 3.48 times. In this case, on average, Soho is doing worse compared to the competitors in the same industry as its 2012 asset turnover is lower than the industry average. The higher the revenue per dollar tied up in assets the more efficiently the assets are being utilized.

The DuPont Framework

Return on equity is one of the most important profitability ratios frequently reviewed by investors. In this chapter, we have learnt that the ratio is calculated using the following equation:

$$\text{ROE} = \frac{\text{Net Income}}{\text{Average Stockholders' Equity}}$$

Return on equity measures the amount of return earned in comparison to the resources the owners provide. In general, the higher the ROE, the more efficient a company is in using its owners' resources.

Suppose that you are examining the return on equity ratio for a company in two consecutive years. If the ratio remains the same from the first to second year, it may be easy to conclude that the company performed equally well in both years. However, the manner in which the company generated the ROE can be drastically different and would be of interest to stockholders.

Looking back to the concepts taught in this course, stockholders' equity is equal to assets minus liabilities (denominator of ROE). Based on the ROE equation, this indicates that an increase in ROE can be caused by an increase in net income, a decrease in assets, or an increase in liabilities. If a company's ROE increases or decreases, examining ROE in its simplest form does not provide information on what caused ROE to change.

The **DuPont Framework** resolves this problem by breaking the ROE equation into three components to provide more information on where the changes in ROE are coming from. The ROE equation can be expanded and rearranged to formulate the DuPont formula as shown below:

$$ROE = \frac{\text{Net Income}}{\text{Revenue}} \times \frac{\text{Revenue}}{\text{Average Total Assets}} \times \frac{\text{Average Total Assets}}{\text{Average Stockholders' Equity}}$$

The formulation of this equation from ROE is mainly mathematical and easy to understand. It starts with the basic ROE equation:

$$ROE = \frac{\text{Net Income}}{\text{Average Stockholders' Equity}}$$

Then apply two common multipliers (revenue and average total assets) to both numerator and denominator.

Apply the first common multiplier:

$$ROE = \frac{\text{Net Income}}{\text{Average Stockholders' Equity}} \times \frac{\text{Revenue}}{\text{Revenue}}$$

$$= \frac{\text{Net Income}}{\text{Revenue}} \times \frac{\text{Revenue}}{\text{Average Stockholders' Equity}}$$

Apply the second common multiplier:

$$ROE = \frac{\text{Net Income}}{\text{Revenue}} \times \frac{\text{Revenue}}{\text{Average Stockholders' Equity}} \times \frac{\text{Average Total Assets}}{\text{Average Total Assets}}$$

Finally, the equation can be rearranged to formulate the DuPont framework:

$$ROE = \frac{\text{Net Income}}{\text{Revenue}} \times \frac{\text{Revenue}}{\text{Average Total Assets}} \times \frac{\text{Average Total Assets}}{\text{Average Stockholders' Equity}}$$

The DuPont framework provides important insight to ROE by connecting the following three measurements together:

1. Net Profit Margin (Net Income/Revenue): This measures operating efficiency
2. Asset Turnover Ratio (Revenue/Average Total Assets): This measures asset usage efficiency
3. Total assets as a percentage of stockholders equity (Average Total Assets/Average Stockholders' Equity): This measures how much a company relies on the use of equity vs. debt. In financial accounting, this ratio is called *an equity multiplier.*

Substituting the above three measurements, ROE can be represented as:

ROE = Net Profit Margin X Asset Turnover Ratio X Equity Multiplier

Based on this DuPont framework, an increase in ROE can be caused by an increase in one of the three components or a combination of all components. Recall from the previous sections that an increase in net profit margin and total assets turnover is generally a positive sign for a company. However, an increase in equity multiplier could mean that a company is using more debt (i.e. hence lower stockholders' equity) to finance its business. While this could represent an efficient usage of debt to generate returns, it also makes the business riskier.

Let us now return to our sample financial statements. Recall that ROE decreased from 69.82% in 2011 to 53.04% in 2012. Using the values calculated earlier in the chapter, we can calculate the components of ROE for the two years as follows:

	2012	2011
Net Profit Margin	7.34%	8.62%
Asset Turnover	3.20	3.24
Equity Multiplier	2.26	2.50

FIGURE 20.15

The net profit margins and asset turnover ratios were taken from figure 20.8 and figure 20.14 respectively. The equity multiplier was calculated using average total assets (from figure 20.14) divided by average stockholders' equity (from figure 20.12).

For our sample company, the net profit margin and the equity multiplier had significant decreases from 2011 to 2012. The asset turnover ratio was approximately the same in both years, which means asset usage efficiency was approximately constant for both periods. Therefore, the asset turnover ratio can be factored out of the analysis on the change in ROE. Therefore, the company's reduction in ROE can be explained by a combination of a decrease in net profit margin and a decrease in the equity multiplier. The decline in net profit margin suggests that the company's ability to control expenses decreased from 2011 to 2012. The decrease in the equity multiplier suggests that the company was relying on less debt and more equity (as a percentage) in 2012 than in 2011 to finance its assets. A combination of the discussed effects results in a decreased ROE from one year to the next.

The DuPont framework demonstrates that examining ROE as a single number is not enough to make sound business decisions. Even if a company's ROE stays the same from year to year, applying the DuPont framework can provide useful insights. If a company's net profit margin and total assets turnover have increased from year 1 to year 2 but the equity multiplier has decreased, this is generally a good indicator although the overall ROE may remain the same. On the other hand, if the company's net profit margin and totals assets turnover have decreased from year 1 to year 2 but equity multiplier has increased significantly, this most likely is not a favorable sign.

Cash Flow is Reality

Our analysis of the balance sheet so far has been related to net income. It is now time to leave the income statement altogether. We will focus on the balance sheet exclusively to look at cash flow and related financial ratios.

An analysis of business cash flow determines the extent to which profits are transformed into actual cash in the bank. In other words, cash flow analysis is an attempt to assess the liquidity of the business. Will the business have enough cash on hand when needed? Does it have the ability to get cash when necessary? Can this cash cover debts and more? We will provide the answers to these questions as we look at liquidity ratios. Liquidity ratios are used to evaluate a company's ability to meet debt obligations (primarily short-term debt).

Current Ratio

The **current ratio** assesses the ability of the business to pay its current debt. The formula for the ratio is:

$$\text{Current Ratio} = \frac{\text{Current Assets}}{\text{Current Liabilities}}$$

The "current" label on the balance sheet is almost always associated with a period of 12 months or less. Therefore, current assets and current liabilities both have terms of less than a year.

Soho Supplies
Balance Sheet
As at December 31

	2012	2011
ASSETS		
Current Assets		
Cash	$13,265	$72,642
Accounts receivable	1,286,138	1,065,812
Inventory	1,683,560	840,091
Prepaid expenses	48,612	42,625
Total Current Assets	3,031,575	2,021,170
Property, plant & equipment	243,256	134,000
TOTAL ASSETS	$3,274,831	$2,155,170
LIABILITIES AND EQUITY		
Liabilities		
Current Liabilities		
Accounts payable	$783,602	$475,645
Current portion of bank loan	380,000	240,000
Notes payable	170,000	200,000
Total Current Liabilities	1,333,602	915,645
Long-term portion of bank loan	420,000	356,000
TOTAL LIABILITIES	1,753,602	1,271,645

FIGURE 20.16

The current ratio assesses business liquidity by determining the extent to which current assets can cover current debts. No business wants to find itself in a position of having to sell capital assets to pay current bills. A current ratio of at least 1 indicates that the business has just enough current assets to pay for its current liabilities. If the current ratio is less than 1, the business will have to pay close attention to its cash balance to ensure it can pay the current liabilities as they come due.

Depending on the industry in question, the higher the current ratio, the more assurance that the business has enough of a cushion that it can afford to have some cash tied up in current assets, such as inventory and accounts receivable. Once these assets are cashed, so to speak, they can be used to pay for current liabilities such as current portions of bank loans or bills to suppliers.

It may seem counterintuitive to say that a business that is too liquid is using its capital inefficiently. For example, if the current ratio of a business is 5, it has $5.00 in current assets for every dollar that it owes in the next 12 months. This could indicate that the business has too much cash. Money in a bank account earning 1% is not an efficient use of assets, especially if the business is earning a return on investment of 20%. Cash should either be invested in new capital assets or perhaps invested in the short-term until a better use for the cash can be established.

The following chart calculates the current ratio using the numbers provided in Soho Supplies' financial statements:

	2012	2011
Current Assets	$3,031,575	$2,021,170
Current Liabilities	$1,333,602	$915,645
Current Ratio	**2.27**	**2.21**

FIGURE 20.17

In this case, our ratio indicates a healthy state of affairs. Not only is the ratio above 2 for both years, but it has increased from one year to the next. In addition, in comparison to industry's current ratio of 2.19 in 2012, Soho is doing better with a higher current ratio in relation to the competitors in the same industry.

Investing too much money in capital assets that are not liquid enough could compromise a healthy current ratio. Property, plant and equipment should be financed with long-term liabilities such as term loans. Current liabilities should not be used for this purpose.

Quick Ratio

The other liquidity ratio that is relevant to our current analysis of business cash flow is the **quick ratio** (also known as the acid test).

Here is the calculation for this ratio:

$$\text{Quick Ratio} = \frac{\text{Cash} + \text{Short Term Investments} + \text{Accounts Receivable}}{\text{Current Liabilities}}$$

The quick ratio is much like the current ratio; the only difference is that the quick ratio excludes some current assets which cannot be quickly converted to cash (such as inventory and prepaid expenses). Short term investments occur when a company has excess cash and wishes to invest it. This cash can be invested in stock of other companies.

In essence, the quick ratio assesses the ability of the business to meet its most immediate debt obligations without relying on the liquidation of inventory (which may take some time to sell). A quick ratio of at least 1 indicates that the business has just enough liquid assets to pay for its current liabilities. Anything below 1 might mean the business has too much of its money tied up in inventory and may be unable to pay its short-term bills.

Quick ratios have been calculated using the numbers in our sample financial statements. Note that Soho Supplies does not have any short-term investments.

	2012	2011
Cash + Accounts Receivable	$1,299,403	$1,138,454
Current Liabilities	$1,333,602	$915,645
Quick Ratio	**0.97**	**1.24**

FIGURE 20.18

With a quick glance, you will notice that the quick ratio has decreased from 2011 (1.24) to 2012 (0.97). This means that the business has gone from a sound short-term liquidity position to a potentially dangerous one. As for the industry comparison, assume that industry's quick ratio for 2012 is 1.57. Since Soho's quick ratio of 2012 is lower than the industry average, the company is doing poorly in relation to the competitors in the same industry.

To address any potential problems here, and since the balance sheet provides only a snapshot of business finances, further analyses should be performed over the course of the next few months on the specific assets and liabilities of the business. This is to ensure that bills can in fact be paid on time.

The situation could have developed due to too much money being invested in inventory or capital assets. A review should be performed to address the situation and rectify any problems found.

Debt-to-Equity Ratio

The **debt-to-equity ratio** is used to assess how much of a company is being financed by lenders, and how much is being financed by the owners or stockholders. In other words, this ratio assesses the extent to which a business is indebted to lenders and whether it can afford to borrow more cash if necessary.

Here is the how the debt-to-equity ratio is calculated:

$$\text{Debt-to-Equity Ratio} = \frac{\text{Total Liabilities}}{\text{Total Stockholders' Equity}}$$

It is simply not healthy for a business to borrow too much relative to what it is worth. The industry the business is in will usually have a bearing on how much will have to be borrowed. If a business has a debt-to-equity ratio of 0.50, this means that for every $0.50 of debt, it has $1.00 in stockholders' equity.

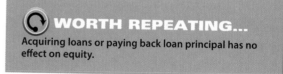

WORTH REPEATING...

Acquiring loans or paying back loan principal has no effect on equity.

Look at the debt-to-equity numbers from Soho's balance sheet:

Liabilities		
Current Liabilities		
Accounts payable	$783,602	$475,645
Current portion of bank loan	380,000	240,000
Notes payable	170,000	200,000
Total Current Liabilities	1,333,602	915,645
Long-term portion of bank loan	420,000	356,000
TOTAL LIABILITIES	1,753,602	1,271,645
Stockholders' Equity		
Common stock	15,000	5,000
Retained earnings	1,506,229	878,525
TOTAL STOCKHOLDERS' EQUITY	1,521,229	883,525
TOTAL LIABILITIES AND EQUITY	$3,274,831	$2,155,170

FIGURE 20.19

Entering these numbers into the debt-to-equity formula, we get the following:

	2012	2011
Total Liabilities	$1,753,602	$1,271,645
Stockholders' Equity	$1,521,229	$883,525
Debt-to-Equity	**1.15**	**1.44**

FIGURE 20.20

As you can see, although the debt-to-equity ratio has improved from 2011 to 2012, it is still above 1. Suppose that the industry's debt-to-equity ratio for 2012 is 0.98. Since Soho's debt-to-equity ratio of 2012 is higher than the industry average, the company is doing poorly in relation to the competitors in the same industry.

There are a few ways a business can improve the debt-to-equity ratio. First, making more profit might do the trick (although it is easier said than done), since it directly results in an increase to stockholders' equity. Second, the business might think about issuing equity (possibly in the form of stock), in exchange for cash.

The debt to equity ratio above is calculated as total liabilities divided by total stockholders' equity (as at a given date). This form of the calculation of the debt to equity ratio will be used throughout the book, unless otherwise stated. There exist slight variations of the debt to equity ratio such as long-term debt divided by stockholders' equity or average liabilities divided by average stockholders' equity. Any one of these forms of the calculation is acceptable as long as the company uses the same form from year to year and discloses how the ratio is calculated.

Management Ensures Stability

We have reached the last part of our approach to analyzing the financial statements of a business. We started with revenues on the income statement, worked our way down to net income, jumped over to stockholders' equity on the balance sheet, and looked at various relationships between assets and liabilities on that balance sheet. Now it is time to assess some of the decision-making aspects of running a business. We need to take a look at what management is doing.

Using financial ratios, we can assess managerial performance by looking at two components of the business: accounts receivable and inventory. Ratios related to each of these components provide us with some sense of what people are doing with the business. It is not just about the bottom line. The further we get into our analysis, the more we try to go beyond the bottom line. That is why we look at managerial performance indicators.

Accounts Receivable Ratios

One key to business success is the ability to collect on its bills. In other words, sales have to result in cash. If customers are buying a product or service on credit, they have to pay within a reasonable amount of time to ensure cash flow and financial health. That is what the **days-sales-outstanding** (DSO) and **accounts receivable turnover** are all about.

Days-Sales-Outstanding (DSO):

The formula for days-sales-outstanding is as follows:

$$\text{Days-Sales-Outstanding} = \left(\frac{\text{Average Accounts Receivable}}{\text{Net Credit Sales}} \right) \times 365$$

From here on in, we will assume that all sales revenues are credit sales for the DSO calculation. The DSO provides an indication of how many days it takes for customers to pay their bills. This number is important because late payments can cost a business lost interest from cash, or additional administration costs required to collect payments from customers.

We will take a look at DSO as they relate to our ongoing example for Soho Supplies. Assume that the accounts receivable balance for Soho as at December 31, 2010 was $934,188.

		2012		2011
Average Accounts Receivable[1]		$1,175,975		$1,000,000
Revenue (all credit sales)		$8,685,025		$6,482,000
	×	365	×	365
Days-Sales-Outstanding		**49.42 days**		**56.31 days**

(1) Average Accounts Receivable for 2011: (934,188 + 1,065,812) ÷ 2 = 1,000,000
    Average Accounts Receivable for 2012: (1,065,812 + 1,286,138) ÷ 2 = 1,175,975

FIGURE 20.21

As you can see, the business is improving its ability to collect from customers. The DSO decreased from over 56 days in 2011, to below 50 days in 2012. Suppose the industry's DSO for 2012 is 51.85 days. In this case, on average, Soho is doing better compared to the competitors in the same industry as its 2012 DSO is lower than the industry average. That is the kind of performance that owners, investors, and analysts want to see from an organization. If the DSO increased, it might be an indication of disputes with customers, a slowdown in sales resulting in slower payments to the company, or problems in the billing and credit function of the company. None of these items would be considered favorably by owners, investors or analysts.

However, there are some cautionary notes to keep in mind related to the DSO. First, the revenue figure used in the ratio should exclude all cash sales, since it is only sales on account (credit sales) that are of concern, relative to collecting customer payments. Second, sales to a major customer should be kept out of the total revenue figure used to calculate DSO, because they can skew the ratio.

Accounts Receivable Turnover

The accounts receivable turnover ratio (ART) is similar to DSO. It involves dividing a company's net credit sales by the average amount of accounts receivable.

$$\text{Accounts Receivable Turnover} = \frac{\text{Net Credit Sales}}{\text{Average Accounts Receivable}}$$

A higher ratio indicates a greater ability to convert accounts receivable into cash. If a business turns its receivables over 12 times per year, it would mean that it is collecting the average balance of receivables every month.

Inventory Ratios

The second component of a business that we look at to assess managerial performance is inventory. We can use two ratios to measure how successful a business is at moving inventory out the door: **inventory days on hand** (also known as day-sales-on-hand) and **inventory turnover**. Let us take a look at these ratios.

Inventory Days on Hand

There are various ways of calculating some of these ratios. For our purpose, we will calculate inventory days on hand this way:

$$\text{Inventory Days on Hand} = \left(\frac{\text{Average Inventory}}{\text{Cost of Goods Sold}} \right) \times 365$$

In other words, the inventory days on hand ratio calculates approximately how many days inventory stays on the company's premises before being moved out.

Inventory Turnover

The inventory turnover ratio is calculated as follows:

$$\text{Inventory Turnover} = \frac{\text{Cost of Goods Sold}}{\text{Average Inventory}}$$

In other words, inventory turnover takes the basic fraction used for the inventory days on hand calculation, flips it, and leaves out the factor of 365 days. The result essentially tells us how many times inventory is "turned over" within a year. If the value of the inventory on hand is equivalent to 100% of how much was used (cost of goods sold) for one year, then it was turned only once. If, however, the value of the inventory on hand is equivalent to 50% of how much was used then it was turned twice. Here is an example: If the cost of goods sold for the year is $120,000 and the value of inventory at the end of the year was $40,000 then the inventory was turned over three times ($120,000 ÷ 40,000).

Now, we will calculate these two inventory ratios for Soho Supplies.

Soho Supplies Balance Sheet As at December 31		
	2012	2011
ASSETS		
Current Assets		
Cash	$13,265	$72,642
Accounts receivable	1,286,138	1,065,812
Inventory	1,683,560	840,091
Prepaid expenses	48,612	42,625
Total Current Assets	3,031,575	2,021,170
Property, plant & equipment	243,256	134,000
TOTAL ASSETS	$3,274,831	$2,155,170

Soho Supplies Income Statement For the Year Ended December 31		
	2012	2011
Sales	$8,685,025	$6,482,000
Cost of goods sold	5,998,612	4,397,200
Gross Profit	2,686,413	2,084,800
Operating Expenses		
Administration charges	8,652	6,861
Advertising & marketing	42,645	32,975
Depreciation	43,262	15,862
Bonuses	65,000	62,432

FIGURE 20.22

Assume that Soho's inventory balance as at December 31, 2010 was $359,909. Applying our inventory days on hand formula to these numbers gives us the following:

	2012	2011
Average Inventory[1]	$1,261,826	$600,000
Cost of Goods Sold	$5,998,612	$4,397,200
	× 365	× 365
Inventory Days on Hand	**76.8 days**	**49.8 days**

(1) Average Inventory for 2011: (359,909 + 840,091) ÷ 2 = 600,000
    Average Inventory for 2012: (1,683,560 + 840,091) ÷ 2 = 1,261,826

FIGURE 20.23

As you can see, the average number of days that inventory was on the premises rose dramatically, from 50 to 77 days in one year. If we assume that industry's inventory days on hand is 47.28 days for 2012, then, on average, Soho is also doing worse compared to the competitors in the same industry as its 2012 inventory days on hand is more than the industry average. Unless something unusual occurred during the year that can account for such an increase, the business might be in jeopardy of having too much inventory on hand. This freezes capital that could be used in other parts of the organization.

Now let us apply the inventory turnover ratio to the same inventory and cost of goods sold figures:

	2012	2011
Cost of Goods Sold	$5,998,612	$4,397,200
Average Inventory[1]	$1,261,826	$600,000
Inventory Turnover	**4.75 times**	**7.33 times**

(1) See Figure 20.23 for calculation of average inventory.

FIGURE 20.24

In essence, inventory turnover tells us the same thing, but in a different way. It tells us that in 2012, inventory was turned over only slightly more than 4.7 times. This is a sharp decrease from 7.3 times in the previous year and indicates that inventory is staying too long in the organization's warehouse. The same conclusion is re-enforced when we also compare the turnover of 4.75 to industry's inventory turnover of 7.72 in 2012. This comparison emphasizes the fact that inventory is staying too long in Soho's warehouse in relation to other competitors in the same industry.

Like any other financial ratio analysis done so far in this chapter, inventory performance also should be assessed relative to the industry involved. For example, winter skis will be turned over less frequently (and on a seasonal basis), as compared to loaves of bread in a bakery. It might take months for a sporting goods store to sell a pair of skis it has stored in the back room, and probably much longer in the summer. Conversely, a loaf of bread normally stays on the shelf no longer than a couple of days — regardless of the time of year.

Investors Measure Performance

In addition to calculating financial ratios for internal measurements, some ratios are used by investors to determine whether a public corporation has desirable stock to purchase. The ratios that measure the stock performance of a public corporation were covered in a previous chapter, so this is a review of them.

Stock that is publically traded on the stock markets can have its price change daily, hourly, or even by the minute. The changes in market value will affect investors as they buy and sell stock, but the corporation does not record any of these changes in their books.

According to the balance sheet shown in figure 20.11, Soho Supplies does not have preferred stock, only common stock. Assume that the number of common shares outstanding at the end of 2011 was 1,250 and the number of common shares outstanding at the end of 2012 was 3,250. Dividends paid out during 2012 amounted to $10,000 and the market value on December 31, 2012 was $650 per share.

Book Value per Share

Book value represents the theoretical value of stock based on the net worth of the business. This assumes that all assets would be sold for their book value and all liabilities would be paid off. It will not necessarily match the market value of the stock.

The calculation of book value per share is relatively simple. Here is the formula that is often used:

$$\text{Book Value per Share} = \frac{\text{Stockholders' Equity} - \text{Preferred Equity}}{\text{Number of Common Shares Outstanding}}$$

Note that preferred equity should include preferred dividends if there are any outstanding. The formula calculates the amount of money that each common stockholder would receive if all the company's assets were immediately liquidated.

For Soho Supplies the book value per share at the end of 2012 can be calculated as:

$$\text{Book Value per Share} = \frac{\$1,521,229}{3,250}$$

$$= \$468.07$$

The company has a very high dollar amount for the book value per share. This would indicate that the company has a large amount of equity in comparison to the quantity of shares. For Soho Supplies, it appears that the company has been generating a large amount of income based on a relatively small equity investment.

Dividend Payout Ratio

Since dividends, or at least the potential for dividends, must form part of an analysis of company stock, the investing community has produced a ratio to assess just how much in dividends a corporation is paying out to stockholders. This is called the *dividend payout ratio* and calculates dividends paid as a percentage of net income. Here is the basic formula that is used:

$$\text{Dividend Payout Ratio} = \frac{\text{Dividends Paid in a Year}}{\text{Net Income after Tax}}$$

For Soho Supplies, they paid out $10,000 in dividends and had a net income of $637,704. Their dividend payout ratio is:

$$\text{Dividend Payout Ratio} = \frac{\$10,000}{\$637,704}$$
$$= 1.6\%$$

Soho is only paying out a small portion of their after tax income, deciding to keep most of the profits within the company.

Earnings per Share (EPS)

Another stock market term that one might see frequently used in the financial press is **earnings per share**. This measures how much profit is made for each share that is outstanding. Here is the basic formula for earnings per share:

$$\text{Earnings Per Share} = \frac{\text{Net Income} - \text{Preferred Dividends}}{\text{Average Number of Common Shares Outstanding}}$$

Since Soho Supplies does not have any preferred stock, there are no preferred dividends to subtract. Therefore, Soho's earnings per share ratio is:

$$\text{Earnings per Share} = \frac{\$637,704}{(1,250 + 3,250) \div 2}$$
$$= \$283.42$$

In other words, the company is making $283.24 for every outstanding share. The general interpretation is the larger the number, the more profitable the company.

As noted in a previous chapter, companies may use various methods to calculate the average number of shares outstanding, which is why reproducing the exact number provided in published financial statements might be difficult. For example, companies might use a monthly average number instead of a yearly number.

Price-Earnings Ratio

Another ratio commonly used by stockholders to evaluate their investment in a corporation is that of the **price-earnings ratio** (P/E ratio), which provides the investor with a measurement of stock price to actual earnings of the corporation. It is sometimes used as an indicator to buy/sell or hold stock. The formula is shown below:

$$\text{P/E Ratio} = \frac{\text{Market Price}}{\text{Earnings Per Share}}$$

Soho's EPS was $283.42 and the market price on December 31, 2012 was $650 per share. Therefore, the P/E ratio is:

$$\text{P/E Ratio} = \frac{\$650}{\$283.42}$$
$$= 2.29$$

The ratios indicate the stock is selling for 2.29 times the earnings in 2012. The P/E ratio can be used when comparing stocks between companies, although the comparison should be done with companies in the same industry. This will allow for a more even and fair comparison.

Horizontal and Vertical Financial Statement Analysis

Now that we have a better understanding of the various ratios at our disposal, we need to look at a few methods of comparing the results from the above calculations.

Management and other readers of financial statements use **horizontal analysis** to quickly compare the changes, both in dollars and percentages, in a given financial statement from one period to the next. Using the balance sheet accounts from the above examples, we can now calculate the dollar and percentage changes.

Balance Sheet	2012	2011	$ Change	% Change
Assets				
Current Assets				
Cash	$13,265	$72,642	($59,377)	-81.74%
Accounts Receivable	1,286,138	1,065,812	220,326	20.67%
Prepaid Expenses	48,612	42,625	5,987	14.05%
Inventory	1,683,560	840,091	843,469	100.40%
Total Current Assets	3,031,575	2,021,170	1,010,405	49.99%
Long-Term Assets				
Plant & Equipment	322,518	170,000	152,518	89.72%
Less: Accumulated Depreciation	-89,262	-46,000	(43,262)	94.05%
Total Long-Term Assets	233,256	124,000	109,256	88.11%
Total Assets	$3,264,831	$2,145,170	1,119,661	52.19%
Liabilities				
Current Liabilities				
Accounts Payable & Accrued Liabilities	$783,602	$475,645	$307,957	64.75%
Current Portion of Bank Loan	380,000	240,000	140,000	58.33%
Notes Payable	170,000	200,000	(30,000)	-15.00%
Total Current Liabilities	1,333,602	915,645	417,957	45.65%
Long-Term Debt	420,000	356,000	64,000	17.98%
Total Liabilities	1,753,602	1,271,645	481,957	37.90%
Stockholders' Equity	1,511,229	873,525	637,704	73.00%
Liabilities & Equity	$3,264,831	$2,145,170	1,119,661	52.19%

FIGURE 20.25

To calculate the dollar increase (or decrease), we simply take the current year amount for one line and deduct the amount reported for the previous year. For example, we see that cash decreased by $59,377, a decrease of 81.74%, calculated as follows:

$$(\$59,377) \div \$72,642 = (81.74\%)$$

This appears to be a significant decrease and may prompt readers to inquire about the reason for such a large decrease in cash.

Horizontal analysis is most effective when comparing a number of years, say, three to five. Comparative statements for these years are presented and, using horizontal analysis techniques, we can determine possible trends in the results.

Let us look at some key elements of a published income statement for American Eagle Outfitters, a U.S. retail chain.

American Eagle Outfitters In Millions of USD				
	2011	**2008**	**2007**	**2006**
Revenue	$2,988.87	$3,055.42	$2,794.41	$2,321.96
Operating Income	279.25	598.75	586.79	458.69
Net income	179.06	400.02	387.36	294.15

FIGURE 20.26

We must first select a base year. In this case we will pick 2006 as the year against which we will compare all other years.

Here are the results:

	2011	**2008**	**2007**	**2006**
Revenue	$2,988.87 ÷ $2,321.96	$3,055.42 ÷ $2321.96	$2,794.41 ÷ $2,321.96	$2,321.96 ÷ $2,321.96
% of Base Year	128.72%	131.59%	120.35%	100.00%

FIGURE 20.27

The horizontal analysis reveals that sales in all three years were higher than in the base year, and 2008 was the highest of the four years.

However, when we do a horizontal analysis of net income, we get a different picture of the company. Using the data from the above table, we calculate the following:

	2011	**2008**	**2007**	**2006**
Net Income	$179.06 ÷ $294.15	$400.02 ÷ $294.15	$387.36 ÷ $294.15	$294.15 ÷ $294.15
% of Base Year	60.87%	135.99%	131.69%	100%

FIGURE 20.28

What happened during 2011 to cause net income to be so much less than in the other years, even the base year? The answer to this question will require further financial analysis, perhaps using some of the ratios discussed above.

Vertical analysis is another common type of financial statement analysis. This method expresses individual accounts in the same period as a percentage of another account. For example, vertical analysis of the balance sheet indicates each account as a percentage of total assets. Vertical analysis of the income statement indicates each account as a percentage of net sales. Once again, we will use the financial statement data provided earlier in the chapter. Using the income statement data, the following table reports each line of this statement as a percentage of net sales:

Income Statement	2012	% of Net Sales	2011	% of Net Sales
Revenue (Net Sales)	$8,685,025	100.00%	$6,482,000	100.00%
Cost of Goods Sold	5,998,612	69.07%	4,397,200	67.84%
Gross Profit	2,686,413	30.93%	2,084,800	32.16%
Operating Expenses				
Administration Charges	8,652	0.10%	6,861	0.11%
Advertising & Marketing	42,645	0.49%	32,975	0.51%
Depreciation	43,262	0.50%	15,862	0.24%
Bonuses	65,000	0.75%	62,432	0.96%
Commission	420,250	4.84%	325,210	5.02%
Interest	51,875	0.60%	31,253	0.48%
Insurance	16,000	0.18%	12,000	0.19%
Sales and Admin Salaries and Benefits	610,325	7.03%	435,951	6.73%
Management Salaries	320,560	3.69%	226,548	3.50%
Occupancy (Rent, Cleaning, etc.)	52,000	0.60%	48,000	0.74%
Other Operating Expenses	61,200	0.70%	48,672	0.75%
Consulting	22,500	0.26%	21,356	0.33%
Repairs and Maintenance	36,860	0.42%	26,845	0.41%
Professional Fees	11,560	0.13%	8,642	0.13%
Total Expenses	1,762,689	20.30%	1,302,607	20.10%
Operating Income Before Tax	923,724	10.64%	782,193	12.07%
Tax	286,020	3.29%	223,652	3.45%
Net Income (Loss) Added to Retained Earnings	$637,704	7.34%	$558,541	8.62%

FIGURE 20.29

For example, COGS is calculated as 69.07% by dividing $5,998,612 by net sales of $8,685,025. Finding out each item's percentage of net sales, using the vertical analysis, helps management and other company stakeholders to compare the financial results of the current and other years presented. For example, the income statement above clearly shows that gross profit as a percentage of net sales has decreased by more than 1% from 2011 to 2012. This could indicate a serious problem such as theft of inventory or errors in recording transactions, and should be investigated.

Other methods of analyzing the financial statements exist, such as preparing **common-size statements** and benchmarking. Preparing common-size statements simply involves stating all dollar amounts on the statements as percentages. All items on the balance sheet are reported as a percentage of total assets and all items on the income statement are reported as a percentage of net sales. The above data have been used to prepare the common-size income statement below.

Common-size Income Statement	2012	2011
Revenue (Net Sales)	100.00%	100.00%
Cost of Goods Sold	69.07%	67.84%
Gross Profit	30.93%	32.16%
Operating Expenses		
Administration Charges	0.10%	0.11%
Advertising & Marketing	0.49%	0.51%
Depreciation	0.50%	0.24%
Bonuses	0.75%	0.96%
Commission	4.84%	5.02%
Interest	0.60%	0.48%
Insurance	0.18%	0.19%
Sales and Admin Salaries and Benefits	7.03%	6.73%
Management Salaries	3.69%	3.50%
Occupancy (Rent, Cleaning, etc.)	0.60%	0.74%
Other Operating Expenses	0.70%	0.75%
Consulting	0.26%	0.33%
Repairs and Maintenance	0.42%	0.41%
Professional Fees	0.13%	0.13%
Total Expenses	20.30%	20.10%
Operating Income Before Tax	10.64%	12.07%
Tax	3.29%	3.45%
Net Income (Loss) Added to Retained Earnings	7.34%	8.62%

FIGURE 20.30

The purpose of preparing common-size statements is to make the statements as easy to read as possible without overwhelming the reader with details and large numbers. Because dollar amounts are not used, these statements are quite often used to compare and analyze the results of different companies within the same industry. For example, suppose Company A had a net income of $100,000 and Company B had a net income of $200,000. If the statements were only reported in dollars, we might conclude that Company B had a more profitable year than Company A; however, after converting the dollar amounts into percentages, we see that Company A's net income represented 20% of net sales whereas Company B's represented only 5%. A common-size statement would have revealed this difference immediately.

Another term often used in conjunction with common-size statements is **benchmarking**, whereby the financial statements are compared against averages in the relevant industry, not just with the financial statements of another company. Using the data for the above company, we will now benchmark the company's performance against the following industry averages:

Common-Size Income Statement for Comparison with Industry Average		
2012	Company	Industry
Revenue (Net sales)	100.00%	100.00%
Cost of Goods Sold	69.07%	68.50%
Gross Profit	30.93%	31.00%
Operating Expenses	20.30%	25.00%
Income Taxes	3.29%	3.00%
Net Income	7.34%	3.00%

FIGURE 20.31

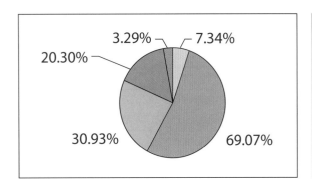 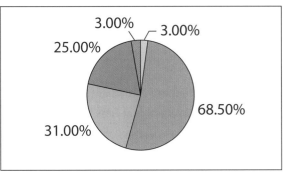

FIGURE 20.32

Pie charts and other graphics are often used to report differences between the company and others in the industry when benchmarking tools are applied. The above reveals that our company is more effective at generating net income from its sales (7.34% vs. 3.0%) than players in the same industry.

Ethics and Controls

When a company borrows a loan from a bank, the bank often imposes debt covenants in the contractual agreement. A **debt covenant** is a limitation on the behaviors or financial performance measures of a company. If a company violates a debt covenant while the bank loan is outstanding, the loan is said to be in default. Thereafter, the bank may penalize the debtholder by reducing the term of the loan or by negotiating a more unfavorable loan agreement (from the perspective of the debtholder).

Some of the covenants that banks impose are in the form of ratios. For instance, the bank may require the debtholder to stay below a specific debt to equity ratio throughout the term of the loan. Assuming that the company is close to the maximum debt to equity ratio, management may unethically take measures to manipulate the numerator or denominator in order to satisfy the bank covenant. For instance, overstating net income will reduce the debt to equity ratio (since equity increases). Understating liabilities will also reduce the ratio. It is up to the bank to decide which covenants will be used and define exactly how they will be calculated. The bank should always request audited financial statements to be reasonably assured of the debtholder's reported financial information and covenant calculations.

In Summary

↪ Performing a comprehensive financial analysis on a business is important because it gleans important information from the financial statements.

↪ The financial ratio is the primary tool used to analyze financial statements. The well-being of a business can be assessed by using a combination of these financial ratios.

↪ Our approach to analyzing financial statements can be summarized in four phrases: "revenues are vanity", "profits are sanity", "cash flow is reality", and "management ensures stability".

↪ The income statement is broken down by expense category. This produces a percentage relative to revenue along the way. We start with gross profit, and then consider EBIT (earnings before interest and taxes). Finally, we move on to net income.

↪ The jump over to the balance sheet portion of our analysis is made through net income and stops first at stockholders' equity. The analysis then breaks down the balance sheet just as it did the income statement.

↪ Cash flow analysis tends to focus almost exclusively on the balance sheet and assesses the extent to which the company has satisfactory liquidity.

↪ The performance of management can be assessed by using financial ratios that measure accounts receivable and inventory. It is these components of a business that are a result of decisions made by real people in the business.

↪ Other methods and tools used in financial statement analysis include horizontal and vertical analysis of the balance sheet and income statements as well as preparation of common-sized statements used in benchmarking.

Review Exercise

Use the financial statements for Basil's Bakery to calculate the following for 2010:

- gross profit margin
- net profit margin
- EBIT
- EBIT percentage to sales
- interest coverage ratio
- return on equity
- current ratio
- quick ratio
- debt-to-equity ratio
- days-sales-outstanding
- inventory days on hand

Prepare a common-size income statement for Basil's Bakery for 2010.

Basil's Bakery Balance Sheet As at December 31		
	2012	2011
ASSETS		
Current Assets		
Cash	$1,605	$987
Accounts receivable	1,175	573
Inventory	396	256
Other current assets	301	103
Total Current Assets	3,477	1,919
Property, plant & equipment	2,034	1,170
TOTAL ASSETS	$5,511	$3,089
LIABILITIES AND EQUITY		
Liabilities		
Current liabilities	$1,474	$547
Long-Term liabilities	104	58
TOTAL LIABILITIES	1,578	605
Stockholders' Equity	3,933	2,484
TOTAL LIABILITIES AND EQUITY	$5,511	$3,089

Basil's Bakery
Income Statement
For the Year Ended December 31, 2010

Sales Revenue	$6,009
Cost of goods sold	2,928
Gross Profit	3,081
Operating Expenses	
Depreciation	108
Interest	518
Other operating expenses	723
Total Operating Expenses	1,349
Income from Operations	1,732
Investment income	79
Operating Income Before Tax	1,811
Income tax	516
Net Income	$1,295

Review Exercise – Answer

Name	Calculation	Result
Gross Profit Margin	$\dfrac{3{,}081}{6{,}009}$	51.3%
Net Profit Margin	$\dfrac{1{,}295}{6{,}009}$	21.6%
EBIT	$1{,}295 + 518 + 516$	$2,329
EBIT Percentage to Sales	$\dfrac{2{,}329}{6{,}009}$	38.76%
Interest Coverage Ratio	$\dfrac{2{,}329}{518}$	4.5 times
Return on Equity	$1{,}295 \div \left(\dfrac{(3{,}933 + 2{,}484)}{2} \right)$	38.76%
Current Ratio	$\dfrac{3{,}477}{1{,}474}$	2.36
Quick Ratio	$\dfrac{(1{,}605 + 1{,}175)}{1{,}474}$	1.89
Debt-to-Equity Ratio	$\dfrac{1{,}578}{3{,}933}$	0.4
Days Sales Outstanding	$\dfrac{(1{,}175 + 573) \div 2}{6{,}009} \times 365$	53.09 days
Inventory Days on Hand	$\dfrac{(396 + 256) \div 2}{2{,}928} \times 365$	40.64 days

**Basil's Bakery
Common-Size Income Statement
For the Year Ended December 31, 2010**

Sales Revenue	$6,009	100.00%
Cost of goods sold	2,928	48.73%
Gross Profit	3,081	51.27%
Operating Expenses		
Depreciation	108	1.80%
Interest	518	8.62%
Other operating expenses	723	12.03%
Total Operating Expenses	1,349	22.45%
Income from Operations	1,732	28.82%
Investment income	79	1.31%
Operating Income Before Tax	1,811	30.14%
Income tax	516	8.59%
Net Income	$1,295	21.55%

Appendix I
SUMMARY OF FINANCIAL RATIOS

The following is a guide to some common ratios used to measure the financial performance of a business. Different industries have different benchmarks for each ratio. It is important to understand the trends in a company's performance from period-to-period and the relative performance of a company within its industry for each ratio.

Revenue Growth

$$\frac{\text{Year 2 Sales} - \text{Year 1 Sales}}{\text{Year 1 Sales}} \times 100$$

Measures the percentage growth of revenues from one year to the next.

Gross Profit Margin

$$\frac{\text{Gross Profit}}{\text{Revenue}} \times 100$$

Measures the percentage of revenue remaining to contribute towards operating expenses, after deducting product costs per dollar of revenue. The higher the percentage, the higher the contribution per dollar of revenue.

Overhead Margin

$$\frac{\text{Overhead Expenses}}{\text{Revenue}} \times 100$$

Measures the relative cost of operating the business. Can be measured for each individual expense (e.g. rent, wages, etc.) as a percentage of revenue. The lower the percentage, the lower the expenses relative to revenue.

EBIT Percentage of Sales

$$\frac{\text{EBIT}}{\text{Revenue}} \times 100$$

EBIT measures the **E**arnings **B**efore **I**nterest, and **T**ax.
EBIT margin measures the operating costs of a business relative to sales.

Net Profit Margin

$$\frac{\text{Net Profit}}{\text{Revenue}} \times 100$$

Represents the profitability and efficiency of the business. Generally, the higher the percentage, the better because it indicates efficient management and expense control.

Interest Coverage Ratio

$$\frac{\text{EBIT}}{\text{Interest Expense}}$$

Measures an organization's ability to pay interest owing. Generally, the higher the number the better – 2 times interest coverage is a common benchmark in many industries.

Return on Equity (ROE)

$$\frac{\text{Net Income}}{\text{Average Owner's Equity}} \times 100$$

Tests the financial return the owners of a business are earning, relative to their investment. Generally, the higher the percentage, the better. Use this ratio to assess risk and reward.

DuPont Framework

$$\text{ROE} = \frac{\text{Net Income}}{\text{Revenue}} \times \frac{\text{Revenue}}{\text{Average Total Assets}} \times \frac{\text{Average Total Assets}}{\text{Average Stockholder's Equity}}$$

Breaks the ROE equation into 3 components to provide more information on where the changes in ROE are coming from. An increase in ROE can be as a result of an increase in one of the 3 components or a combination of all components.

Current Ratio

$$\frac{\text{Current Assets}}{\text{Current Liabilities}}$$

Measures the ability of the company to pay current debt over the next 12 months (specifically, the number of times current assets can cover current debts). Generally, the higher the number the better (2:1 is a common benchmark in many industries). If the ratio is too high (e.g. 4:1), it indicates inefficient use of capital as current assets generally have the lowest returns.

Quick Ratio (or Acid Test)

$$\frac{\text{Cash} + \text{Short-Term Investments} + \text{Net Accounts Receivable}}{\text{Current Liabilities}}$$

The number of times the most liquid assets (e.g. cash, short-term investments, and accounts receivable) can cover immediate debts (usually 90 days). Generally, the higher the number the better (1:1 is a common benchmark in many industries). If the ratio is too high, it indicates inefficient use of capital (see current ratio).

Debt to Equity Ratio

$$\frac{\text{Total Liabilities (Debt)}}{\text{Total Owners' Equity}}$$

Used by lenders to examine their risk relative to the owners' risk. Some debt is good, but too much can cause financial distress. $1 of debt for every $2 of equity is a common benchmark in many industries (1:2).

Debt to Total Assets

$$\frac{\text{Total Liabilities (Debt)}}{\text{Total Assets}}$$

Measures how much a company's assets are financed through debt. The higher the ratio, the greater the difficulty a company will have in repaying its creditors.

Days Sales Outstanding (DSO)

$$\frac{\text{Average Accounts Receivable}}{\text{Credit Sales}} \times 365$$

Calculates the average number of days the A/R is outstanding, and indicates how well it is being managed. Generally, the less days outstanding, the less risk. This ratio is crucial in the service industry. DSO should be compared to similar periods in a cyclical business.

Inventory Days on Hand

$$\frac{\text{Average Inventory}}{\text{Cost of Goods Sold}} \times 365$$

Calculates the average number of days the current inventory will last, and how well the inventory is being managed. Generally, the lower the inventory days on hand, the less the holding costs (e.g. shrinkage, interest, etc.). Inventory days on hand should be compared to similar periods in a cyclical business.

Inventory Turnover

$$\frac{\text{Cost of Goods Sold}}{\text{Average Inventory}}$$

Calculates the number of times inventory is replenished within one year. Generally, the lower the inventory turnover, the less times per year inventory is being replenished which results in elevated holding costs. Inventory turnover should be compared to similar periods in a cyclical business.

Return on Assets (ROA)

$$\frac{\text{Net Income}}{\text{Average Total Assets}} \times 100$$

Compares the net income earned in a period to the amount of assets used to generate that income. Generally, the higher the percentage, the better.

Assets Turnover

$$\frac{\text{Revenue}}{\text{Average Total Assets}}$$

Tests how efficiently a business utilizes its assets to generate sales.

Accounts Receivable Turnover (ART)

$$\frac{\text{Net Credit Sales}}{\text{Average Net Accounts Receivable}}$$

Calculates how many times a business collects its accounts receivable throughout the year. The higher the ratio, the more times per year accounts receivable is being collected.

Earnings per Share (EPS)

$$\frac{(\text{Net Income} - \text{Preferred Dividends})}{\text{Average Number of Common Shares Outstanding}}$$

Tests the amount of dollar return a company is making for every outstanding common share. This ratio assesses the profitability of a company.

Book Value per Common Share

$$\frac{(\text{Stockholders' Equity} - \text{Preferred Equity})}{\text{Number of Common Shares Outstanding}}$$

Determines the value associated with each common share after all debts are paid.

Dividend Payout Ratio

$$\frac{\text{Dividends Paid in a Year}}{\text{Net Income after Tax}}$$

Calculates dividends paid as a percentage of net income.

Price to Earnings Ratio

$$\frac{\text{Market Price per Share}}{\text{Earnings per Share}}$$

Provides the investor with a measurement of the stock price to actual earnings of the corporation. It is sometimes used as an indicator to buy or sell stocks.

Note:

The purpose of ratio analysis is to help the reader of financial statements ask the appropriate questions and understand which issues need to be addressed. Keep in mind that no single ratio will be able to provide the complete story. Much like a puzzle, you need all the pieces to see the whole picture.

Appendix II

HOME DEPOT'S FINANCIAL STATEMENTS

THE HOME DEPOT, INC. AND SUBSIDIARIES
CONSOLIDATED STATEMENTS OF EARNINGS

amounts in millions, except per share data	Fiscal Year Ended[1]		
	January 29, 2012	January 30, 2011	January 31, 2010
NET SALES	$ 70,395	$ 67,997	$ 66,176
Cost of Sales	46,133	44,693	43,764
GROSS PROFIT	24,262	23,304	22,412
Operating Expenses:			
Selling, General and Administrative	16,028	15,849	15,902
Depreciation and Amortization	1,573	1,616	1,707
Total Operating Expenses	17,601	17,465	17,609
OPERATING INCOME	6,661	5,839	4,803
Interest and Other (Income) Expense:			
Interest and Investment Income	(13)	(15)	(18)
Interest Expense	606	530	676
Other	—	51	163
Interest and Other, net	593	566	821
EARNINGS FROM CONTINUING OPERATIONS BEFORE PROVISION FOR INCOME TAXES	6,068	5,273	3,982
Provision for Income Taxes	2,185	1,935	1,362
EARNINGS FROM CONTINUING OPERATIONS	3,883	3,338	2,620
EARNINGS FROM DISCONTINUED OPERATIONS, NET OF TAX	—	—	41
NET EARNINGS	$ 3,883	$ 3,338	$ 2,661
Weighted Average Common Shares	1,562	1,648	1,683
BASIC EARNINGS PER SHARE FROM CONTINUING OPERATIONS	$ 2.49	$ 2.03	$ 1.56
BASIC EARNINGS PER SHARE FROM DISCONTINUED OPERATIONS	$ —	$ —	$ 0.02
BASIC EARNINGS PER SHARE	$ 2.49	$ 2.03	$ 1.58
Diluted Weighted Average Common Shares	1,570	1,658	1,692
DILUTED EARNINGS PER SHARE FROM CONTINUING OPERATIONS	$ 2.47	$ 2.01	$ 1.55
DILUTED EARNINGS PER SHARE FROM DISCONTINUED OPERATIONS	$ —	$ —	$ 0.02
DILUTED EARNINGS PER SHARE	$ 2.47	$ 2.01	$ 1.57

(1) *Fiscal years ended January 29, 2012, January 30, 2011 and January 31, 2010 include 52 weeks.*

THE HOME DEPOT, INC. AND SUBSIDIARIES
CONSOLIDATED BALANCE SHEETS

amounts in millions, except share and per share data	January 29, 2012	January 30, 2011
ASSETS		
Current Assets:		
Cash and Cash Equivalents	$ 1,987	$ 545
Receivables, net	1,245	1,085
Merchandise Inventories	10,325	10,625
Other Current Assets	963	1,224
Total Current Assets	14,520	13,479
Property and Equipment, at cost:		
Land	8,480	8,497
Buildings	17,737	17,606
Furniture, Fixtures and Equipment	10,040	9,687
Leasehold Improvements	1,372	1,373
Construction in Progress	758	654
Capital Leases	588	568
	38,975	38,385
Less Accumulated Depreciation and Amortization	14,527	13,325
Net Property and Equipment	24,448	25,060
Notes Receivable	135	139
Goodwill	1,120	1,187
Other Assets	295	260
Total Assets	$ 40,518	$ 40,125
LIABILITIES AND STOCKHOLDERS' EQUITY		
Current Liabilities:		
Accounts Payable	$ 4,856	$ 4,717
Accrued Salaries and Related Expenses	1,372	1,290
Sales Taxes Payable	391	368
Deferred Revenue	1,147	1,177
Income Taxes Payable	23	13
Current Installments of Long-Term Debt	30	1,042
Other Accrued Expenses	1,557	1,515
Total Current Liabilities	9,376	10,122
Long-Term Debt, excluding current installments	10,758	8,707
Other Long-Term Liabilities	2,146	2,135
Deferred Income Taxes	340	272
Total Liabilities	22,620	21,236
STOCKHOLDERS' EQUITY		
Common Stock, par value $0.05; authorized: 10 billion shares; issued: 1.733 billion shares at January 29, 2012 and 1.722 billion shares at January 30, 2011; outstanding: 1.537 billion shares at January 29, 2012 and 1.623 billion shares at January 30, 2011	87	86
Paid-In Capital	6,966	6,556
Retained Earnings	17,246	14,995
Accumulated Other Comprehensive Income	293	445
Treasury Stock, at cost, 196 million shares at January 29, 2012 and 99 million shares at January 30, 2011	(6,694)	(3,193)
Total Stockholders' Equity	17,898	18,889
Total Liabilities and Stockholders' Equity	$ 40,518	$ 40,125

THE HOME DEPOT, INC. AND SUBSIDIARIES
CONSOLIDATED STATEMENTS OF STOCKHOLDERS' EQUITY AND COMPREHENSIVE INCOME

amounts in millions, except per share data	Common Stock Shares	Amount	Paid-In Capital	Retained Earnings	Accumulated Other Comprehensive Income (Loss)	Treasury Stock Shares	Amount	Stockholders' Equity	Total Comprehensive Income
Balance, February 1, 2009	**1,707**	**$ 85**	**$ 6,048**	**$ 12,093**	**$ (77)**	**(11)**	**$ (372)**	**$ 17,777**	
Net Earnings	—	—	—	2,661	—	—	—	2,661	$ 2,661
Shares Issued Under Employee Stock Plans	9	1	57	—	—	—	—	58	
Tax Effect of Stock-Based Compensation	—	—	(2)	—	—	—	—	(2)	
Translation Adjustments	—	—	—	—	426	—	—	426	426
Cash Flow Hedges, net of tax	—	—	—	—	11	—	—	11	11
Stock Options, Awards and Amortization of Restricted Stock	—	—	201	—	—	—	—	201	
Repurchases of Common Stock	—	—	—	—	—	(7)	(213)	(213)	
Cash Dividends ($0.90 per share)	—	—	—	(1,525)	—	—	—	(1,525)	
Other	—	—	—	(3)	2	—	—	(1)	2
Comprehensive Income									$ 3,100
Balance, January 31, 2010	**1,716**	**$ 86**	**$ 6,304**	**$ 13,226**	**$ 362**	**(18)**	**$ (585)**	**$ 19,393**	
Net Earnings	—	—	—	3,338	—	—	—	3,338	$ 3,338
Shares Issued Under Employee Stock Plans	6	—	42	—	—	—	—	42	
Tax Effect of Stock-Based Compensation	—	—	2	—	—	—	—	2	
Translation Adjustments	—	—	—	—	206	—	—	206	206
Cash Flow Hedges, net of tax	—	—	—	—	(116)	—	—	(116)	(116)
Stock Options, Awards and Amortization of Restricted Stock	—	—	214	—	—	—	—	214	
Repurchases of Common Stock	—	—	—	—	—	(81)	(2,608)	(2,608)	
Cash Dividends ($0.945 per share)	—	—	—	(1,569)	—	—	—	(1,569)	
Other	—	—	(6)	—	(7)	—	—	(13)	(7)
Comprehensive Income									$ 3,421
Balance, January 30, 2011	**1,722**	**$ 86**	**$ 6,556**	**$ 14,995**	**$ 445**	**(99)**	**$(3,193)**	**$ 18,889**	
Net Earnings	—	—	—	3,883	—	—	—	3,883	$ 3,883
Shares Issued Under Employee Stock Plans	11	1	196	—	—	—	—	197	
Tax Effect of Stock-Based Compensation	—	—	(2)	—	—	—	—	(2)	
Translation Adjustments	—	—	—	—	(143)	—	—	(143)	(143)
Cash Flow Hedges, net of tax	—	—	—	—	5	—	—	5	5
Stock Options, Awards and Amortization of Restricted Stock	—	—	215	—	—	—	—	215	
Repurchases of Common Stock	—	—	—	—	—	(97)	(3,501)	(3,501)	
Cash Dividends ($1.04 per share)	—	—	—	(1,632)	—	—	—	(1,632)	
Other	—	—	1	—	(14)	—	—	(13)	(14)
Comprehensive Income									$ 3,731
Balance, January 29, 2012	**1,733**	**$ 87**	**$ 6,966**	**$ 17,246**	**$ 293**	**(196)**	**$(6,694)**	**$ 17,898**	

THE HOME DEPOT, INC. AND SUBSIDIARIES
CONSOLIDATED STATEMENTS OF CASH FLOWS

amounts in millions	Fiscal Year Ended[1]		
	January 29, 2012	January 30, 2011	January 31, 2010
CASH FLOWS FROM OPERATING ACTIVITIES:			
Net Earnings	$ 3,883	$ 3,338	$ 2,661
Reconciliation of Net Earnings to Net Cash Provided by Operating Activities:			
Depreciation and Amortization	1,682	1,718	1,806
Impairment of Investment	—	—	163
Stock-Based Compensation Expense	215	214	201
Changes in Assets and Liabilities, net of the effects of acquisition and disposition:			
Receivables, net	(170)	(102)	(23)
Merchandise Inventories	256	(355)	625
Other Current Assets	159	12	4
Accounts Payable and Accrued Expenses	422	(133)	59
Deferred Revenue	(29)	10	(21)
Income Taxes Payable	14	(85)	(174)
Deferred Income Taxes	170	104	(227)
Other Long-Term Liabilities	(2)	(61)	(19)
Other	51	(75)	70
Net Cash Provided by Operating Activities	6,651	4,585	5,125
CASH FLOWS FROM INVESTING ACTIVITIES:			
Capital Expenditures, net of $25, $62 and $10 of non-cash capital expenditures in fiscal 2011, 2010 and 2009, respectively	(1,221)	(1,096)	(966)
Proceeds from Sale of Business, net	101	—	—
Payments for Business Acquired, net	(65)	—	—
Proceeds from Sales of Property and Equipment	56	84	178
Proceeds from Sales and Maturities of Investments	—	—	33
Net Cash Used in Investing Activities	(1,129)	(1,012)	(755)
CASH FLOWS FROM FINANCING ACTIVITIES:			
Proceeds from Long-Term Borrowings, net of discount	1,994	998	—
Repayments of Long-Term Debt	(1,028)	(1,029)	(1,774)
Repurchases of Common Stock	(3,470)	(2,608)	(213)
Proceeds from Sales of Common Stock	306	104	73
Cash Dividends Paid to Stockholders	(1,632)	(1,569)	(1,525)
Other Financing Activities	(218)	(347)	(64)
Net Cash Used in Financing Activities	(4,048)	(4,451)	(3,503)
Change in Cash and Cash Equivalents	1,474	(878)	867
Effect of Exchange Rate Changes on Cash and Cash Equivalents	(32)	2	35
Cash and Cash Equivalents at Beginning of Year	545	1,421	519
Cash and Cash Equivalents at End of Year	$ 1,987	$ 545	$ 1,421
SUPPLEMENTAL DISCLOSURE OF CASH PAYMENTS MADE FOR:			
Interest, net of interest capitalized	$ 580	$ 579	$ 664
Income Taxes	$ 1,865	$ 2,067	$ 2,082

(1) Fiscal years ended January 29, 2012, January 30, 2011 and January 31, 2010 include 52 weeks.

GLOSSARY

A

Accountant — A professional, who develops and maintains the accounting system, interprets the data, prepares various management reports and supervises the clerksto ensure that the information is correct.

Accounting — Accounting accurately measures all the financial activities of an individual or a business. Personal accounting tracks how much an individual is worth.

Accounting Cycle — The steps repeated each reporting period for the purpose ofpreparing financial statements for users.

Accounting Equation — The equation is: Assets = Liabilities + Net Worth

Accounting Ethics — The standards of reporting, practice, professionalism and behavior an accountant must meet in discharging this responsibility.

Accounting Income — Accounting income represents the amount of profit a company makes during a specific period of time (as reported on the income statement).

Accounts Payable — This account tracks the amount a business owes a supplier. Accounts payable is a liability.

Accounts Payable Subsidiary Ledger — A subsidiary ledger listing individual credit supplier accounts.

Accounting Period — The length of time covered by financial statements and other reports; also called reporting periods.

Accounts Receivable — This account often represents a significant percentage of a company's assets.

Accounts Receivable Subsidiary Ledger — A subsidiary ledger listing individual credit customer accounts.

Accounts Receivable Turnover Ratio — This ratio involves dividing a company's net credit sales by the average amount of net accounts receivable.

Accrual Accounting — This approach recognizes revenue (increases net worth) and expenses (decreases net worth) in the time period in which they occur, regardless of when the payment is received or made.

Accrued Expense — This is an expense incurred in one accounting period but not paid until a later accounting period. An adjusting entry is required for recording the accrued expense.

Accrued Revenue — Revenues earned in a period that are unrecorded and/or not yet received in cash (or other assets); adjusting entries for recording accrued revenues involve increasing (debiting) assets and increasing (crediting) revenues.

Acid-Test Ratio — A ratio used to assess a company's ability to cover its current debts with existing assets calculated as quick assets (cash, short-term investments and receivables) divided by current liabilities; also called quick ratio.

Adjustments — They ensure that all account values are properly reported. Adjustments are done at the end of an accounting period.

Adjusting Entry — A journal entry at the end of an accounting period to bring an asset or liability account balance to its proper amount while also updating the related expense or revenue account.

Adjusted Trial Balance — A trial balance that is prepared once adjusting entries have been made and posted to the general ledger.

Allowance for Doubtful Accounts (AFDA) — A contra account used to record debts that may not be collected.

Allowance Method — The method uses the bad debt expense account and the allowance for doubtful accounts (AFDA) account to record bad debts in the same period as when the revenue is actually generated, which adheres to the matching principle.

Amortization — The decline of an intangible asset such as a patent or a copyright.

Assets — All the items that are owned such as cash, inventory, land, machinery, accounts receivable, etc.

Asset Turnover — A general measure of a firm's ability to generate sales in relation to total assets.

Auditing — An examination and verification of the records and systems of a company, and an assessment of the fairness of a company's financial statements.

B

Bad Debts — Money owed to the company (accounts receivable) that has been proven as non-collectable. This non-collectable money is regarded as an expense.

Balance Sheet — A permanent document that is used to record what you own (assets) and what you owe (liabilities) on a specific date.

Bank Reconciliation — An internal control that involves comparing and reconciling the items in the company's cash records with the items shown on the bank statement.

Bookkeepers — (also known as accounting clerks) People who enter all the daily accounting transactions, accounts payable and receivable, payroll and employer-filed taxes; or they may work with an accounts receivable clerk, an accounts payable clerk and a payroll clerk.

Bank Statement — The document provided by the bank, which summarizes deposits, checks, withdrawals, interest received, and other debits and credits to a bank account.

Bonds — An "IOU" issued by a company. The corporation pays interest on the bond and pays the entire amount (called principal) when due. Corporate bonds are usually traded publicly and they will rise and fall in value on the bond market. These are included in long term debt on the Balance Sheet.

Book Value — The cost of the asset less its accumulated depreciation.

C

Capital (Owner's Capital) — The difference between total assets and total liabilities (same as net worth, owner's equity).

Capital Assets — Tangible long-term assets that often constitute a significant proportion of the value of a company's assets.

Cash — Either cash in the bank, petty cash, or cash equivalents.

Cash-Based Accounting — Revenues are recognized when cash is received and expenses are recorded when cash is paid.

Cash Disbursement — Cash spent during the reporting (or accounting) period.

Cash Discount — A reduction in the price of merchandise that is granted by a seller to a purchaser in exchange for the purchaser paying within a specified period of time.

Cash Flow — Cash flowing into and out of the bank account, which is not necessarily directly connected to net worth.

Cash Flow from Financing — The movement of cash related to the way a company receives money for financing purposes and pays it back.

Cash Flow from Investments — The movement of cash on the basis of the purchases and sales of long-term assets.

Cash Flow from Operations — The movement of cash related to day-to-day activities of the business.

Cash Flow Statement — A financial report that shows the inflows and outflows of actual cash during a specific period of time; where the company's cash came from and where it was spent.

Cash Payments Journal — This is a journal used to record all cash payments made by the business (e.g. rent and wages expense) including payments made to suppliers.

Cash Receipts Journal — Used to record all cash deposits (e.g. cash sales) and collections from outstanding accounts receivable.

Cash Short and Over — The difference between cash receipts and cash disbursed from petty cash.

Certified Public Accountants(CPA) — An accountant in the United States who is licensed by a state to practice public accounting in a professionally competent manner.

Certified Management Accountants(CMA) — A specialists in managerial accounting topics; she or he assists internal users in making business decisions.

Chart of Accounts — The listing of all the accounts being used by a business.

Classified Balance Sheet — The type of balance sheet where assets and liabilities are subdivided into current and long-term categories to further define a company's financial position.

Closing Entries — Journal entries recorded at the end of each accounting period that transfer the end-of-period balances in revenues, expenses, and withdrawals accounts to the permanent owner's capital account in order to prepare for the upcoming period and update the owner's capital account for the events of the period just finished.

Common Stock — The name for a class of stock in a company that has a claim on the assets of the company after preferred stockholders.

Controls — Procedures and methods used to protect assets, monitor cash payments, and ensure transactions are authorized and the accounting records are accurate.

Contra Account — An account linked with another account and having an opposite normal debit or credit balance; reported as a subtraction from the other account's balance so that more complete information than simply the net amount is provided.

Consulting — Some professionals use their knowledge and expertise to advise the actions of other businesses. Their services could include providing advice on information technology (IT), financial matters and investments.

Conservatism — A principle that states that whenever an accountant needs to exercise their own interpretation or judgment in applying an accounting standard and has several options, the least optimistic or least favorable option should be selected.

Consistency Principle — The accounting requirement that prevents people from changing accounting methods for the sole purpose of manipulating figures on the financial statements.

Contingent Liabilities — A financial obligation that will happen only if a certain event occurs. Companies establish a contingent liability account to try and cover the costs involved with the possible occurrence of an event; also known as an estimated liability account.

Comparable — The financial statements of a company must be prepared in a similar way year after year.

Cooperative — An enterprise or organization that is organized, owned and democratically controlled by the people who use its products and services, and whose earnings are distributed on the basis of use rather than investment.

Copyright — An intangible asset that is similar to a patent in that it gives exclusive rights of ownership to a person or group that has created something.

Corporation — A business that is registered with the State government or Securities and Exchange Commission (SEC); it is considered as a separate legal entity from its owners, the stockholders.

Cost of Goods Sold — The cost to directly produce the product or deliver the service. In the case of retail the "cost of goods" is the cost that the store paid for the goods. In manufacturing the "cost of goods" is the material cost, labor overheads, supervision or any other cost attributing to produce the product.

Cost Principle — This principle states that the accounting for purchases must be at their cost price.

Credit Note — The form issued by a vendor to reverse charges made on a regular sales invoice.

Credit Period — The time period that can pass before a customer's payment is due.

Credit Terms — The description of the amounts and timing of payments that a buyer agrees to make in the future.

Current Assets — Assets that will be converted into cash within the next 12 months.

Current Liabilities — Liabilities that are due to be paid within the next 12 months.

Current Ratio — This ratio is calculated by dividing current assets by current liabilities. It shows the company's ability to pay off its short-term debt.

D

Database — An electronic information storage space that allows information to be inputted and reports to be inputted in a variety of ways, depending upon the information required.

Days of Inventory on Hand — An estimate of how many days it will take to convert the inventory on hand at the end of the period into accounts receivable or cash; calculated by dividing the ending inventory by the cost of goods sold and multiplying the result by 365.

Days Sales Outstanding — A management ratio that tracks how long take customers to pay their bills. It is one way of organizing accounts receivable information.

Debit — An entry that increases asset, expense and owner's withdrawals accounts or decreases liability, owner's capital and revenue accounts; recorded on the left side of a T-account.

Debt-to-Equity Ratio — This ratio is another tool that investors and analysts have at their disposal to assess a corporation's financial statements.

Debt-to-Total-Assets Ratio — Measures how much of a company's assets are financed through debt. Debt-to-equity ratio is used to assess how much of a company is being financed by lenders, and how much is being financed by the owners or stockholders.

Deferred Income Tax — The difference between income tax expense and income tax payable.

Deficit — A business loss; an owner's capital account with a debit balance.

Depletion — The decline in value of natural resources due to its use over time.

Depreciation — The process by which accountants reflect changes in the book value of a capital asset.

Discount Period — The time period in which a cash discount is available and a reduced payment can be made by the buyer.

Determinable Liabilities — Debts taken on by the company for which the terms are readily known.

Discontinued Operation — A segment of a business that is no longer part of regular operating activities.

Dividends — The amount paid to the shareholders from the profits of the company.

Dividends in Arrears — Dividends on current stock that are not paid currently but will be paid to the holder at a future date.

Dividend Payout Ratio — Assess how much in dividends a corporation is paying out to stockholders.

Double Entry Accounting — An accounting system where every transaction affects and is recorded in at least two accounts; the sum of the debits for all entries must equal the sum of the credits for all entries.

E

Earnings per Share — Net income divided by the total number of shares of the company owned by the shareholders. This gives a good indication of the earning ability of the company relative to the number of people who may at some point share in the benefit of those earnings.

EBIT — Earnings before interest and tax.

EBITDA — Calculates earnings before interest, tax, depreciation and amortization because generally these expenses cannot be controlled by most business operators.

EBIT Percentage to Sales — Calculated by taking our EBIT number and dividing it by revenue, to obtain yet another percentage figure to work with in our analysis.

Economic Entity — This principle states that accounting for a business must be kept separate from the personal affairs of its owner or any other business.

Electronic Data Interchange (EDI) — A computerized system that allows companies to transfer electronic information to one another.

Electronic Fund Transfers (EFTs) — Automatic cash payments to other accounts or automatic cash receipts from others.

Equity — It takes the form of stock in a company. Income is earned from the shares, either through an increase in its value or through dividend payments.

Estimated Liabilities — A financial obligation that will happen only if a certain event occurs. Companies establish an estimated liability account to try and cover the costs involved with the possible occurrence.

Expense — A decrease in net worth from the costs of day-to-day activities.

External Stakeholders — People or organizations that are outside the business, such as suppliers, banks and external accountants.

F

Financial Accounting — Concerned with the recordkeeping or bookkeeping of the business and preparing the financial statements, similar to what you have learned so far.

Financial Statements — Written records of the financial status of an individual, association or business organization. It usually includes balance sheet, income statement, statement of owner's equity and cash flow statement.

Financial Ratio — The primary tool used to analyze financial statements. The well-being of a business can be assessed by using a combination of these financial ratios.

First-in-First-Out (FIFO) — This method is used when a business assumes that the first items received in inventory are also the first items moved out of inventory.

Fiscal year — Defined as a period consisting of 12 consecutive months. A fiscal year does not necessarily start and end in a calendar year.

Fixed Assets — Long-term assets used in producing goods or services.

FOB Destination — Means that the seller pays the shipping costs and the ownership of the goods transfers to the buyer at the buyer's place of business.

FOB Shipping Point — Means that the buyer pays the shipping costs and accepts ownership of the goods at the seller's place of business.

Freight — The cost of shipping goods.

Full Disclosure Principle — Requires financial statements (including footnotes) to report all relevant information about the operations and financial position of the entity.

G

Generally Accepted Accounting Principles (GAAP) — A set of standards and acceptable ways of reporting accounting activities.

General and Administrative Expenses — Costs that support the overall operations of a business and include the expenses of such activities as providing accounting services, human resource management and financial management.

General Ledger — A book or file used to record all the accounts of the business (other than those in the subsidiary ledgers); these accounts represent the complete financial position of the business.

General Partnership — A type of business in which the owners are jointly liable for business operations and as such share the unlimited liability.

Going Concern — This principle assumes that a business will continue to operate into the foreseeable future.

Goodwill — An intangible asset of a business that has value in excess of the sum of its net assets.

Gross Pay — The total amount earned by an employee before any deductions.

Gross Profit — The difference between service revenue and cost of sales in a service based business. It is the amount of profit remaining after selling inventory that is used to cover operating expenses in a manufacturing business.

Gross Profit Margin — The gross profit as a percentage of sales.

Gross Profit (Inventory) Method — A method for estimating ending inventory using a company's historical gross profit figure.

I

IFRS — International Financial Reporting Standards; the uniform international accounting standard that many countries have adopted; a transition from GAAP that is the accounting profession's response and contribution to globalization.

Income Statement — Primarily used as a temporary document to record transactions relating to revenue and expenses.

Income Summary — A temporary account used only in the closing process to which the balances of revenue and expense accounts are transferred; its balance equals net income or net loss and is transferred to the owner's capital account.

Income Tax — The amount of money the government charges the company for making money. The more the profit, the more the tax.

Income Taxes Payable — Money owed to various tax agencies but not yet paid. This is a liability to the company.

Indirect Method — Analyzes cash flow from operations indirectly by starting with accrual-based net income and adding or subtracting certain items from the income statement and changes on the balance sheet.

Intangible Assets — Long-lived (capital) assets that have no physical substance but convey a right to use a product or process, e.g. patents, copyrights and goodwill.

Interest — A charge related to money borrowed; imposed on the borrower by the lender.

Interest Coverage Ratio — A ratio which indicates the ability of a company to cover net interest expenses with EBIT.

Internal Controls — Procedures set up to protect assets, ensure reliable accounting reports, promote efficiency and encourage adherence to company policies.

Internal Stakeholders — People who own the business and/or work in the business.

Inventory — Composed of three classes of material: raw material used in making goods; work in progress, which is goods in the process of being manufactured; and finished goods ready to be shipped to customers. In a retail store or distribution business the value of the inventory would generally be what the company was charged for it plus the shipping costs.

Inventory Days on Hand — Tells us how many days inventory is held before being sold.

Inventory Turnover Ratio — Estimates how many times a year a company replenishes the full value of inventory.

Invoice — An itemized statement of goods prepared by the vendor that lists the customer's name, the items sold, the sales prices and the terms of sale.

J

Journal — A record in which transactions are recorded before they are posted. Journals are known as *books of original entry*. Amounts are posted from the journals to the general ledger.

Journalizing — A process in which all business activities are recorded initially in a journal. It contains all the initial entries used to record every transaction (each of which includes at least one debit and one credit) and the purpose of the transactions.

L

Last-in-First-Out (LIFO) — This method is used when a business assumes that the last items received in inventory are also the first items moved out.

Leasehold — Involves a lessor lending an asset (usually land or property) to a lessee.

Ledger — A record containing all accounts used by a business.

Liabilities — All the debts and legal obligations that the business owes and must pay.

Limited Liability Partnership (LLP) — Allows partners to have limited liability regarding the misconduct or negligence of the other partners.

Limited Partnership — Includes at least one general partner who accepts unlimited liability and one or more limited partners with liability limited to the amount they invested.

Liquid Assets — Can be easily converted to cash or used to pay for services or obligations; cash is the most liquid asset, (e.g. accounts receivable and inventory).

Liquidity — The ability to pay day-to-day obligations (current liabilities) with existingliquid assets.

Liquidation — The sale of the assets of the company. This is done when the business goes broke. The assets are sold and the proceeds are used to pay the creditors.

Long-term Assets — These assets are used to operate a business and are not expected to turn into cash or be used up within the next 12 months unless they are sold for reasons other than the day-to-day operations of the business.

Long-Term Liabilities — Amounts due to be paid after 12 months. Examples of long-term liabilities would include bank loans and mortgages.

Long-Term Investment — Along-term asset and it is an investment that the company intends to keep for longer than one year.

Lower of Cost or Market (LCM) — The required method of reporting merchandise inventory on the balance sheet, where market value is reported, when market is lower than cost; the market value may be defined as net realizable value or current replacement cost on the date of the balance sheet.

M

Managerial Accounting — Serves the internal users of the business by providing special analysis of financial statements and assisting with decision making.

Market Value — The value of an asset that buyers are willing to pay for in the market; market value is not tied to the book value of an asset.

Matching Principle — Requires expenses to be reported in the same period as the revenues to which they are related.

Materiality Principle — Requires accountants to use Generally Accepted Accounting Principles except when doing so would be more expensive or complicated relative to the value of the transaction.

Merchandising Business — Buys and resells products for a profit.

Merchandise — Products, also called goods, which a company acquires for the purpose of reselling them to customers.

Miscellaneous Assets — Most of the asset accounts on the balance sheet represent well-defined types of assets. However, many companies own an asset that does not fit into any of these clearly defined categories.

Monetary Unit Principle — Requires that the accounting records are expressed in terms of money.

Multistep Income Statement — An income statement divides revenue and expenses further to show subtotals such as COGS, gross profit, operating expenses and operating income. This format highlights significant relationships because gross profit and operating income are two different but important measures for a merchandising business.

N

Net Accounts Receivable — Total accounts receivable less allowance for doubtful accounts.

Net Income — The excess that is left after all expenses have been paid; also called net profit.

Net Pay — This is gross pay; less all deductions (i.e. take home pay).

Net Profit Margin — A profitability ratio, which measures how much profit, a company generates relative to their revenue.

Net Realizable Value — The expected sales price of an item minus the cost of making the sale.

Net Sales — The value of sales after taking into account sales returns and allowances and sales discounts.

Net Worth — If you were to sell all your assets and pay all your debts, the remaining cash represents how much you are worth.

Not-for-Profit Organizations — Profits made by not-for-profit organizations may be paid out (redistributed) to the community by providing services. Not-for-profit organizations include religious organizations, community care centers, charitable organizations, hospitals and the Red Cross.

No-Par Value — Means that the stock has no "stated value" so that when they are sold, the stock account is credited for the entire proceeds.

Notes Payable — Represents a more formalized contract between a company and a supplier for an amount owed, as opposed to a standard bill or invoice.

Note Receivable — An unconditional written promise to pay a definite sum of money on demand or on a defined future date(s); also called a promissory note.

NSF Check — Nonsufficient funds check, returned due to a lack of funds.

O

Objectivity — This principle states that transactions will be recorded on the basis of objective and verifiable evidence.

Operating Expenses — The various costs of running a business.

Operating Income — Calculated by subtracting operating expenses from gross profit. This figure shows what a company is making or losing when it produces and sells the product or service.

Other Assets — See miscellaneous assets definition.

Other Income/Expenses — Money earned or expenses incurred not directly involved in making and selling the product or service. For example, interest earned on bank deposits or paid for bank loans.

Outstanding Checks — An outstanding check is one that has been recorded in the general ledger, but has not been recorded on the bank statement. This is so because after the company records the check, it is mailed to the supplier. The supplier then records it in the books, prepares the deposit and takes it to the bank.

Outstanding Deposits — An outstanding deposit is one that has been recorded in the company's general ledger but not shown on the bank statement. This can occur when the company makes a deposit in the bank (perhaps using the night deposit box) on the last day of the month, but the bank does not record the deposit until the following business day.

Overhead Margin — A management ratio which measures the relative cost of operating the business as a percentage of sales; the lower the percentage the better.

Owner's Contributions — The amount of cash or assets invested into the business by the owner.

Owner's Equity — Everything that the company owns, less what it owes.

Owner's Withdrawals — The amount of cash or assets taken by the owner of the business for personal use.

P

Partnership — A business owned by two or more people called partners.

Par Value — For stocks , when a stock is issued with a stated value on each share; for bonds, when a bond is issued at the value printed on the bond, also known as face value.

Patent — Gives inventor exclusive rights to use a product.

Periodic Inventory System — Updates inventory when a physical count of the inventory is taken, usually at the end of a period.

Perpetual Inventory System — Constantly updates inventory whenever a purchase or sale is made.

Petty Cash — Small amounts of cash to pay for petty (small) expenses.

Petty Cash Custodian — Deals with specific transactions involving the petty cash fund.

Post-Closing Trial Balance — Once the income statement is cleared, it is necessary to ensure that the balance sheet still balances. This is done by completing another trial balance called the post-closing trial balance

Posting Reference (PR) Column — A column in journals where individual account numbers are entered when entries are posted to the ledger; a column in ledgers where journal page numbers are entered when entries are posted.

Prepaid Expenses — Arise when a business pays for expenses before they are incurred.

Preferred Stock — Shares of a company that have preference with respect to dividends and distribution of assets in case of liquidation.

Present Value — Determines the amount invested today to produce a certain amount in the future.

Price-Earnings Ratio — A ratio commonly used by stockholders to evaluate their investment in a corporation is that of the price-earnings ratio (P/E ratio) which divides the market price per share of common stock by earnings per share.

Principal — The amount of a loan or note payable on which interest is calculated.

Proprietorship — A business owned by one person also known as a sole proprietorship. The financial affairs of the business must be separate from the owner. However, from a legal perspective, a sole proprietor is personally liable for the business.

Promissory Note — An unconditional written promise to pay a definite sum of money on demand or on a defined future date(s); also called a note receivable.

Purchase Allowances — Occur when the buyer agrees to keep the undesirable goods at a reduced cost.

Purchase Discount — A term used by a purchaser to describe a cash discount granted to them for paying within the discount period.

Purchases Journal — A journal that is used to record all purchases on credit.

Purchase Returns — Goods often need to be returned for reasons such as incorrect product, over-shipments, or inferior quality product.

Q

Quick Ratio — The total of cash, short-term investments and accounts receivable divided by the total of current liabilities. In other words, those items that can be rapidly converted into cash with which the current liabilities can be paid. Another way of calculating the quick ratio is simply to add cash plus accounts receivable divided by current liabilities; also known as the Acid Test.

R

Return on Assets (ROA) — Shows the after tax earnings of assets. Return on assets is an indicator of how profitable a company is.

Retained earnings — All the profits kept by the business (i.e. not distributed).

Return on Equity — Net income divided by average shareholders' equity. This is an indicator of how well the company is making use of its equity to bring a return to its investors.

Return on Investment — Annual revenue less annual costs, both associated with a specific project, divided by the total investment required for that project.

Relevant — Means that all information useful for decision making is present in the financial statements.

Reliability — Means that information is free from material error and bias.

Revenue — An increase in net worth caused by providing goods or services.

Revenue Recognition — This principle states that revenue can only be recorded (recognized) when goods are sold or when services performed.

Residual Value — The amount remaining after all depreciation has been deducted from the original cost of a depreciable asset, also known as Salvage Value

S

Sales Discount — A term used by a seller to describe a cash discount granted to the purchaser for paying within the discount period.

Sales Journal — A journal that is used to record all sales made on account.

Sales Returns — A business may have to deal with numerous returns from customers, and these returns must be tracked over a period of time. High return levels may indicate serious problems. Therefore, instead of reversing the revenue account with a debit when recording returns, a contra-revenue account called sales returns and allowances is used to track the amount of returns.

Sales Revenue — The earnings generated from selling products.

Sales Tax — A tax that is applied by the state government to goods or services that are sold.

Salvage Value — The amount remaining after all depreciation has been deducted from the original cost of a depreciable asset, also known as a residual value.

Short-Term Investment — Instead of investing surplus cash in a bank account (with minimal returns), forward-looking business managers invest in short-term opportunities which mature within one year and provide a higher rate of return.

Service Revenue — The earnings generated from providing services.

Shrinkage — The cost of goods "not sold", which is typically caused by theft, goods signed for and not received, spoilage, reject production, etc.

Single-Step Income Statement — An income statement format that includes cost of goods sold as an operating expense and shows only one subtotal for total expenses.

Special Journals — Individual journals that are used to record similar repetitive activities on a regular basis – for example, sales and purchases journals.

Specific Identification — A method that is used when a business wants to value specific items individually.

Sole Proprietorship — A business owned and generally operated by one owner.

Source Documents — Provide evidence that a business transaction has occurred, come in many different forms.

Statutory Deductions — Are mandatory deductions, or those required by law.

Statement of Cash Flow — A financial report that shows the inflows and outflows of actual cash during a specific period of time; where the company's cash came from and where it was spent.

Stockholder — An owner of the business through ownership of shares.

Stock Dividends — Companies can choose to give a dividend payment in the form of additional shares rather than cash.

Stock Split — A corporate action that increases the number of a corporation's outstanding shares which in turn diminishes the individual price of each share of stock.

Stockholders' Equity — The owner's equity category in a corporation. It shows how much of the business is owned by the owners, or stockholders.

Straight-line Depreciation Method — Allocates equal amounts of an asset's cost to depreciation expenses during its useful life.

Subsidiary Ledgers (also called *subledgers*) — Are used to provide details that are not kept in the general ledger because there is so much information that will clutter up the general ledger accounts.

Sundry Assets — See miscellaneous assets definition.

T

Taxable income — The portion of income subject to taxation by law.

T-Account — A simple characterization of an account form used as a helpful tool in showing the effects of transactions and events on specific accounts.

Temporary Accounts — The type of accounts that are used to describe revenues,expenses, and owner's withdrawals for one accounting period; they are closed at the end of the reporting period; also called nominal accounts.

Time Period — This principle requires that accounting takes place over specific time periods known as fiscal periods.

Trademark — A formally registered symbol identifying the manufacturer or distributor of a product.

Trial Balance — A list of accounts and their balances at a point in time; the total debit balances should equal the total credit balances.

U

Understandable — Means that the financial information can be reasonably understood by its users if the users have a reasonable knowledge of the business and a basic knowledge of accounting.

Unearned Revenue — Arises when customers pay before the service is delivered. The income statement is not initially affected. Unearned revenue is a liability.

Units of Production (Method) — Amortization Method of amortizing an asset based on its usage.

V

Voluntary Deductions — The type of deductions agreed upon between employer and employee.

W

Wage — An hourly rate that an employer pays an employee based on the actual number of hours worked.

Weighted Average Cost Method — When a business simply applies an average cost to its entire inventory.

Wholesaler — A middleman that buys products from manufacturers or other wholesalers and sells them to retailers or other wholesalers.

Workers' Compensation — An insurance program paid for by the employer that represents a statutory deduction to be tracked by accountants and/or the payroll department.

Working Capital — Current assets less current liabilities; called "working capital" or "operating capital" because it is capital that has been put to work in the business and has taken the form of inventory, accounts receivable, cash etc.

Notes

INDEX

A

accounting, defined, 11–12

accounting cycle
adjusted trial balance, 130–131
adjusting entries, 125–127
balance sheet
formalized format, 135–136
worksheet, 131–132
bookkeeping, 101
debits and credits, 101–105
chart of accounts, 104–105
defining accounts, 105
journal entries, 103–104
ethics and controls, 116–117, 150
evolution from manual to computerized
accounting, 148–150
income statement
formalized format, 133–135
statement of owner's equity, 134–135
worksheet, 131–132
post-closing trial balance, 136–147
close directly to capital
account, 137–142
close using income summary, 142–147
formalized format, 147
steps in, 106–116
general ledger, 110–113
journals, 106–109
trial balance, 114–116
worksheets, 127–132

accounting designations, 62

accounting equation, 16–20
net worth calculation, 19
process, 20
T-accounts, 19–20

accounting ethics, 72
. *See also* ethical issues

accounting income, 475

accounting information systems
controls and ethics, 199
integrated approach to learning
accounting, 181
modern accounting information systems,
197–198
paper trail, 182–186
special journals, 186–196
cash payments journal, 183, 192–196
cash receipts journal, 183, 188–190
purchase journal, 183, 191–192
sales journal, 183, 186–188
types of, 183–184
subsidiary ledgers, 186–196
. *See also* software for accounting

accounting periods, 16

accounting policies, changes in, 481–482

accounting principles and practices
controls in business, 69–72
definition of, 69–70
implementing, 70–72
ethics and insights, 72–75
attributes of good accounting
system, 75
4-way test, 74
fields of accounting
accounting designations, 62
financial accounting, 61
managerial accounting, 61–62
GAAP. *See* Generally Accepted
Accounting Principles (GAAP)
International Financial Reporting
Standards, 68–69

accounting system, attributes of, 75

accounts, defining, 105

accounts and notes receivable
bad debt accounting, 237–242
allowance method, 239–242
direct method, 237–239

bad debt estimating approaches, 242–246
 balance sheet, 244–246, 257
 income statement, 243–244, 257
 controls for, 96–97, 199, 250–253
 definition and description of, 5–6, 83, 98
 ethical approach to managing, 256–257
 managing information using
  reports, 246–247
 measuring effectiveness of collections
  using ratios, 249–250
 outsourcing, 236
 overview, 235–237
 promissory note and notes receivable,
  253–255
 strategies for managing and controlling,
  247
 subledger, 247–249
accounts payable, 87, 98
accounts payable subsidiary ledger, 185
accounts receivable turnover ratio
 (ART), 250, 579, 600
accrual accounting, 21–25
 cash flow vs. accruals, 22, 38
 cash-based vs. accrual-based, 22–23
 defined, 21, 38
 matching principle, 23–25
accrued interest expense
 adjustments, 94–95, 150
 defined, 98
 short-term notes payable and, 377–378
accumulated depreciation, 30, 125, 341–342
accumulated surplus (deficit), 42–44
acid test, 399
additional paid-in capital, 459
adjusted trial balance, 130–131
adjusting entries, 125–127
adjustments, 91–95, 98, 480–481
AFDA (allowance for doubtful accounts),
 239–242, 257
AICPA (American Institute of Certified
 Public Accountants), 62
allowances

for doubtful accounts, 239–242, 257
 purchases, 266, 310
 sales, 270, 271–272, 313
American Institute of Certified Public
 Accountants (AICPA), 62
amortization, 355, 420
annuity, 411
ART (accounts receivable turnover ratio),
 250, 579, 600
Arthur Andersen (accounting firm), 368
asset register, 342
asset turnover ratio, 364, 569–570
assets
 buying, 29, 334
 capital, 333, 335–338
 defined, 12
 insuring, 367
 long-term. See long-term assets
 selling, 29, 334, 503–504, 549–552
 sequence of, 42
 stock in exchange for, 456
assets turnover ratio, 600
auction-rate securities, 498
authorized shares, 455
available for sale investments, 497–498,
 511–513

B

Bacanovic, Peter, 467
bad checks, 213
bad debt
 accounting methods, 237–242
  allowance method, 239–242
  direct method, 237–239
 defined, 237
 estimating approaches, 242–246
  balance sheet, 244–246, 257
  income statement, 243–244, 257
balance sheet
 classified, 168–172
 comparative financial statements, 174
 description of, 13–14

distinction between short-term and long-term assets, 498

estimating bad debt, 244–246, 257

formalized format, 135–136

limitations of, 523

stockholders' equity section of, 480

worksheet, 131–132

bank errors, 216–217

bank loans, accounting effect of, 54, 150, 576

bank overdraft, 13

bank reconciliations

    bank errors, 216–217

    outstanding checks, 215–216

    outstanding deposits, 213–214

    recording errors, 217–219

    unrecorded charges, 210–213

    unrecorded deposits, 208–210

bank reconciliations summary, 219–222

banking industry, mortgage defaults in (2009), 37

benchmarking, 589

blue chip stocks, 496

bonds

    debenture, 408

    description of, 8

    issued at discount, 415–419

    issued at par, 412–415

    issued at premium, 420–422

    purchasing between interest dates, 507–511

    retiring, 423–424

    types of characteristics, 407–408

bonds payable, 411–412

book value, 47, 488

book value differing from market value differing, 441–443

book value per common share, 600

book value per share, 483–485, 583

bookkeeping, 101

borrowing money, 26–28

bounced checks, 213

business accounts, 41–44

    overview, 41

owner's equity vs. net worth, 42–44

sequence of assets and liabilities, 42

business structures, 44–47, 431–432

buying assets, 29

C

callable bonds, 408, 423

capital, 36

capital account, 43, 137–142

capital assets

    changes in, 336–338

    defined, 333

    lump sum purchases of, 335–336

    . *See also* long-term assets

cash

    controls for, 228–230

    converting accounts receivable into, 252, 253

    petty cash, 222–227

    sources and uses of, 36

    stocks in exchange for, 455–456

cash account, 5

cash controls

    ethics and controls, 228–230

    overview, 207

cash discounts, 266

cash dividends, 460–462

cash equivalents, 207

cash flow, description of, 8

cash flow statements

    balance sheet and income statement, examination of, 526–528

    balance sheet and income statements vs., 523–524

    direct method, 526, 541–544

    discontinued operations, 477–478, 479, 553

    ethics and controls, 545

    extraordinary items, 477, 479, 553

    generating cash flow, 524–525

    indirect method, 528–536

        cash flow from financing, 532–535

cash flow from investments, 531–532

cash flow from operations, 529–531

defined, 526

overview, 524–525

preparing, 526–536

sale of property, plant and equipment, 537–540

selling long-term assets, 549–552

cash flow vs. accruals, 22, 38

cash flow vs. balance sheet and income statement, 523–524

cash out, 12

cash payments journal, 183, 192–196

cash receipts journal, 183, 188–190

cash registers, 228

cash-based vs. accrual-based, 22–23

Certified Management Accountants (CMAs), 62

Certified Public Accountants (CPAs), 62

charges, unrecorded in bank statement, 210–213

charitable donations, employee deductions, 389, 393

chart of accounts, 104–105

checks, outstanding, 215–216

classified balance sheet, 168–172

client lists, 199

closing entries or closing the books

to capital account, 137–142

for corporations, 475

description of, 136–137, 299

inventory, 274–276, 317–319

post-closing trial balance, 147

using income summary, 142–147, 437

closing retained earnings, 534

CMAs (Certified Management Accountants), 62

COGS. *See* cost of goods sold

collaborative self-insurance groups, 367

common stock, 175, 457–459

common-size statements, 588

company stock, 455

comparability, defined, 64

comparative financial statements, 174

compound interest, 410

comprehensive income, 479

computerized accounting, 148–150, 219

. *See also* software for accounting

conservatism principle, 66

consistency, defined, 64

contingent liabilities, 394–397

contra accounts, 125–127, 239

contra-revenue account, 270

contributed capital (paid-in capital), 161, 452–453, 480

control accounts, 184

controls in business

account entries, 116–117

accounting cycle, 116–117, 150

accounts payable, 199

accounts receivable, 96–97, 199, 250–253

cash, 228–230

cash flow statements, 545

current liabilities, 400

debt covenants, 590–591

definition of controls, 69–70

implementing controls, 70–72

inventory, 294–296, 299

investment assets, 516–518

long-term assets, 365–367

long-term liabilities, 425

petty cash, 226–227

convertible bonds, 408

converting accounts receivable into cash, 252, 253

cooperative, 46

copyright, 362–363

corporate charter, 455

corporations

cash dividend accounting, 460–462

definition or description of, 46–47, 431

ethical issues, 466–467

financial statements, 452–455

overview, 449–450

public vs. private, 450

separating management from ownership, 451–452

stockholders' equity, 452–455

stocks

common, 175, 457–459

company, 455

dividends, 463–464

issuing, 455–457

preferred, 175, 457–459

splits, 463

treasury, 464–466

corporations, financial statements

closing entries for, 476

earnings of, 473

equity, measuring changes in, 479–482

accounting policies, changes in, 481–482

prior period adjustments, 480–481

financial position, measuring, 482–483

financial ratios, calculation of, 483–489

income, measuring, 477–479

income tax expense, 474–475

cost of goods sold (COGS)

defined, 164, 175, 299

impact of on gross profit, 284–285

sales reporting, 313–314

cost of inventory, determining, 277

cost principle, 66

coupon bonds, 408

CPAs (Certified Public Accountants), 62

credit approval, 96, 251

credit controls, 251

credit information, 251

credit policy, 252, 253

credits

chart of accounts, 104–105

defining accounts, 105

journal entries, 103–104

current assets, description of, 6, 168, 175

current assets vs. long-term assets, 168–169

current liabilities

controls related to, 174, 400

defined, 175

estimated and contingent liabilities, 394–397

ethical approach to, 400–401

financial ratios, 398–399

current ratio, 171–172, 175, 398–399, 598

quick ratio, 399, 572–576, 598

long-term liabilities verses, 169–172

overview, 375–376

payroll accounting, 381–386

employee deductions, 383–385

employer contributions, 385, 390–391

example of, 386–394

gross pay to net pay, 382

paying deduction liability, 386

sales tax, 379–381

short-term notes payable, 376–379

accrued interest expense, 377–378

current portion of long-term liabilities, 378–379

current ratio, 171–172, 175, 398–399, 573–575, 598

customer billing, 97

customer lists, 199

customer payments, 97

D

date of declaration, dividend payments, 460–461

date of payment, dividend payments, 461–462

date of record, dividend payments, 461

days sales outstanding (DOS), 249–250, 578–579, 599

debenture bonds, 408

debits, 101–105

chart of accounts, 104–105

defining accounts, 105

journal entries, 103–104

debt

defined, 499

doubtful debts, 5–6

repaying, 26–28, 500–501

subprime, 37

debt account, description of, 7

debt covenant, 590–591

debt investments, 496

debt to equity ratio, 424, 599

debt to total assets, 599

debt-to-equity ratio, 485–486, 576–578

debt-to-total assets ratio, 424

declining-balance depreciation method, 343

deferred income taxes, 475

depletion, 355–357

deposits

    outstanding, 213–214

    in transit, 213

    unrecorded in bank statement, 210–213

depreciation, 30–32

    accumulated, 30, 125, 341–342

    adjustments, 95

    concept of, 338–339

        actual salvage value, 339

        residual value, 338–339

    description of, 7

    disposal of, 349–354

    methods of, 339–346

        declining-balance, 343

        determine method to use, 346

        double declining-balance, 344–345

        straight-line, 340–342

        units-of-production, 345–346, 355

    for partial years, 347–348

    revising, 354–355

    trading-in, 353–354

determinable liabilities, 375, 394

direct method of recording bad debt, 237–239

discontinued operations, 477–478, 479, 553

discount, bonds issued at, 415–419

discount on capital stock, 459

discounts

    purchases, 266, 310–311

    sales, 272, 313

Disney Studios, 445

disposal of capital assets, 349–354

dividend earned, 512

dividend payout ratio, 486, 583–584, 600

dividends

    in arrears, 462

    cash, 460–462

    defined, 162, 175

    payments, 460, 534

    recording of, 502–503

    significant influence on, 515

    stock, 463–464

division of income or loss in partnership, 436–439

    earnings according to agreed-upon ratio, 437

    earnings according to agreed-upon salary allocation, plus share of remainder, 438–439

    earnings according to capital contribution, 438

    earnings equally divided, 437

DSO (days sales outstanding), 249–250, 578–579, 599

double declining-balance depreciation method, 344–345

double entry, 102, 106

doubtful debts, 5–6, 239–242

DuPont framework, 570–573, 598

E

earnings per share (EPS), 487–488, 584, 600

EBIT, 561–562

EBIT percentage to sales, 562–563

EBITDA, 563

economic entity principle, 65

Effective Interest Method of Amortization, 420

electronic communication of financial entities, 149, 198

employee payroll deductions, 383–385, 387–389

employer payroll contributions, 385, 390–391

Enron, 72, 95, 545

EPS (earnings per share), 487–488, 584, 600

equipment

description of, 7

sale of, 537–540

equity

definition or description of, 8, 499

measuring changes in, 479–482

stockholders' equity, 42–44, 162

equity investments, 496, 501

errors

bank errors, 216–217

in inventory, 284–286

recording errors, 217–219

in trial balance, 115–116

estimated and contingent liabilities, 394–397

estimating

bad debt, 242–246, 257

inventory, 288–291

gross profit method, 289–290

retail method, 290–291

ethical issues

account entries, 116–117

accounting cycle, 116–117, 150

cash flow statements, 545

client or customer lists, 199

corporations, 466–467

current liabilities, 400–401

debt covenants, 590–591

4-way test, 74

inventory estimation and evaluation, 297–298

long-term assets, 367–368

long-term liabilities, 425–426

overview, 72–74

revenue and expenses, 95–97

evolution from manual to computerized accounting, 148–150

expense recognition, 86–88

expenses

defined, 13

income tax of corporations, 474–475

interest, 94–95, 98, 150, 377–378

operating, 86, 98, 164

prepaid. *See* prepaid expenses

recognition of, 86–88

. *See also* revenue and expense recognition

Extensible Business Reporting Language (XBRL), 149, 198

external stakeholders, 48

extraordinary items, 477, 479, 533, 553

F

factoring, 253

Fannie Mae, 501

federal income tax, 387–388

Federal Insurance Contributions Act (FICA), 388–389, 390

Federal Tax Administration, 380

Federal Unemployment Act (FUTA), 390–391

feedback value of information, 63

FICA (Federal Insurance Contributions Act), 388–389, 390

fields of accounting

accounting designations, 62

financial accounting, 61

managerial accounting, 61–62

FIFO (first-in-first-out) inventory method, 277, 279–280, 299, 321

financial accounting, 61

Financial Accounting Standards Board, 91

financial analysis, description of, 8, 557

financial ratios

accounts receivable turnover ratio, 250, 579, 600

asset turnover, 364, 569–570

book value per share, 483–485, 583

current ratio, 171–172, 175, 398–399, 573–575, 598

days sales outstanding, 249–250, 578–579, 599

debt to equity ratio, 424, 599

debt to total assets, 599

debt-to-equity ratio, 485–486, 576–578
debt-to-total assets ratio, 424
dividend payout ratio, 486, 583–584
earnings per share, 487–488, 584, 600
interest coverage ratio, 564, 598
inventory days on hand, 293–294, 580, 599
inventory turnover ratio, 292, 580–582, 599
net profit margin, 565–566, 598
price-earnings ratio, 198, 489, 585, 600
profitability ratio, 167–168
quick ratio, 399, 572–576, 598
return on assets, 364, 568–569, 599
return on equity, 566–568, 598
financial statement analysis
    accounts receivable ratios
        accounts receivable turnover ratio, 250, 579, 600
        days sales outstanding, 249–250, 578–579, 599
    assets turnover ratio, 600
    cash flow, 573–578
        current ratio, 171–172, 175, 398–399, 573–575, 598
        debt-to-equity ratio, 576–578
        quick ratio, 399, 575–576, 598
    DuPont framework, 570–573, 598
    ethics and controls, 590–591
    horizontal analysis, 585–587
    importance of, 557–559
    inventory ratios
        inventory days on hand, 293–294, 580, 599
        inventory turnover ratio, 292, 580–582, 599
    investors, 582–585
        book value per share, 583
        dividend payout ratio, 583–584, 600
        earnings per share, 487–488, 584, 600
        price-earnings ratio, 198, 489, 585, 600
    management, 578–582
        accounts receivable ratios, 578–582
        inventory ratios, 580–582

profits, 560–570
    asset turnover, 569–570
    EBIT, 561–562
    EBIT percentage to sales, 562–563
    gross profit margin, 167–168, 175, 560–561, 597
    interest coverage ratio, 564, 598
    net profit margin, 565–566, 598
    return on assets, 364, 568–569, 599
    return on equity, 566–568, 598
revenues, 559–560
vertical analysis, 587–590
financial statements
    accounting, meaning of, 11–12
    accounting equation, 16–20
        net worth calculation, 19
        process, 20
        T-accounts, 19–20
    accounting periods, 16
    accrual accounting, 21–25
        cash flow vs. accruals, 22
        cash-based vs. accrual-based, 22–23
        matching principle, 23–25
    balance sheet, 13–14
    borrowing money, 26–28
    buying and selling assets, 29
    capital, 36
    cash, sources and uses of, 36
    depreciation, 30–32
    income statement, 15
    inventory impact on, 297
    market value vs. book value, 37
    materiality, 35
    net worth principle, 12–13
    prepaid expenses, 32–35
    repaying debt, 26–28, 500–501
financial statements of different types of businesses, 48–50
    manufacturing business, 50
    merchandising business, 49–50
    service business, 49
financing, cash flow from, 525
FOB destination, 269, 315

FOB shipping point, 268, 314
4-way test (ethics), 74
fraud, 297–298, 299, 368, 401
Freddie Mac, 501
freight cost, 268
freight-in, 311
full disclosure principle, 66
FUTA (Federal Unemployment Act), 390–391
future value, 410

G

general journal, 148, 183
general ledger, 110–113, 148
general partnerships, 46, 434
Generally Accepted Accounting Principles (GAAP), 62–67
    accounts receivable, 246, 256
    AFDA and, 240
    bad debt estimates, 242
    basic concepts and principles, 65–67
    characteristics of, 63–64
    classification of investments, 497–498
    different jurisdictions, 67
    discontinued operations, 479
    earnings of corporations, 473
    equity changes, 479
    extraordinary items, 479
    IFRS and, 68
    non-cash transactions, 553
    physical inventory count, 283
    pro forma financial statements and, 289
    stockholders' significant influence factors, 514
    trade-off of reliability and relevance, 64–65
Global Crossing, 368
going concern principle, 65
Goldman Sachs, 498
goodwill, 358–361
gross pay, 381
gross profit
    cost of goods sold and, 284–285
    defined, 49, 164, 175
    method of estimating inventory, 289–290
gross profit margin, 167–168, 175, 560–561, 597

H

health plans
    employee deductions, 389, 393–394
    employer deductions, 391, 393–394
held to maturity investments, 497, 505–511
Hewlett, Bill, 445
Home Depot's financial statements, 601–604
horizontal analysis, 585–587
hybrid business types, 50

I

IFRS (International Financial Reporting Standards), 68–69
ImClone, 467
imprest system, 222
income of corporations, measuring, 477–479
income statement
    comparative financial statements, 174
    description of, 8, 15
    estimating bad debt, 243–244, 257
    formalized format, 133–135
    limitations of, 523
    multistep, 172–174, 273
    statement of owner's equity, 134–135
    worksheet, 131–132
income summary, closing books using, 142–147
insider trading, 466–467
insuring assets, 367
intangible assets, 357–363
    copyright, 362–363
    description of, 7
    goodwill, 358–361
    leasing long-term assets, 363
    patents, 361–362
    trademark and trade name, 363

integrated approach to learning accounting, 181

interest
    on bonds, 420, 507–511
    compound, 410
    recording of, 501

interest coverage ratio, 564, 598

interest earned, 499–500, 506–507

interest expense
    accrued, 94–95, 150, 377–378
    defined, 98

internal controls, 70

Internal Revenue Code (IRC), 474–475

internal stakeholders, 48

International Financial Reporting Standards (IFRS), 68–69

inventory
    actual quantity of inventory, 283
    closing entries, 274–276, 317–319
    controls related to, 294–296
        compliance and regulations issues, 295–296
        defined, 299
        economical and efficient use of resources, 296
        objectives, 296
        safeguarding, 296
    description of, 6, 164, 175
    effect of errors in, 284–286
        cost of goods sold and gross profit, 284–285
        overstating, 285–286
    estimating, 288–291
        gross profit method, 289–290
        retail method, 290–291
    ethical issues, 297–298
    FOB and inventory count, 314–317
    Just In Time, 298
    measuring using financial ratios, 291–294
        inventory days on hand, 293–294, 580, 599
        inventory turnover ratio, 292

overview, 263–264
perpetual inventory system, 265–273
    income statement, 273
    purchases, 166–167, 265–269
    sales, 166–167, 270–272
perpetual vs. periodic, 165–167, 264
physical count, 283
purchase of, 166–167, 265–269, 309–311
sales of, 166–167, 270–272, 312–314
valuation methods, 277–282, 319–324
    applying valuation methods, 277–278
    determine cost, 277
    effect of different methods, 282, 322–324
    FIFO method, 277, 279–280, 299, 321
    LIFO method, 277, 281–282, 299, 322–323
    lower of cost or market, 287–288
    specific identification method, 277, 278–279, 299, 320
    weighted average cost method, 277, 280–281, 322

inventory days on hand, 293–294, 580, 599

inventory turnover ratio, 292, 580–582, 599

investments
    available for sale investments, 497–498, 511–513
    cash flow from, 525
    controls related to, 516–518
    description of, 5
    held to maturity investments, 497, 505–511
    overview, 494–498
        classification of, 497–498
        terms of, 496–597
        types of, 496
    short-term investments, 207, 497
    significant influence on, 514–518
    trading investments, 497, 499–504

investors measure of performance, 582–585

invoices, 83, 400

IRC (Internal Revenue Code), 474–475

J

journal entries
  format for, 103–104
  general journal, 148, 183
  special journals. *See* special journals
  steps in, 106–109
journalizing, 106, 136
Just In Time (JIT) inventory, 298

K

Kroc, Ray, 445

L

last-in-last-out (LIFO) inventory method,
  277, 281–282, 299, 322–323
laws, compliance with, 295–296
LCM (lower of cost or market) inventory
  method, 287–288
lease agreement, 363
leasing long-term assets, 363
Lehman Brothers, 498
lessor, defined, 363
liabilities
  contingent, 394–397
  current. *See* current liabilities
  defined, 12
  estimated, 394–397
  long-term. *See* long-term liabilities
  payroll liabilities, 391–394
  sequence of, 42
liability, unlimited, 44
LIFO (last-in-last-out) inventory method,
  277, 281–282, 299, 322–323
limited liability partnership (LLP), 46, 434
limited partnerships, 46, 434
liquidating, defined, 13
liquidation of partnership, 443–445
liquidity, 42
LLP (limited liability partnership), 46, 434
loans
  bank, 54, 150, 576

investment, 499–501
local income tax, employee deduction, 388
long-term assets
  acquisition of, 334–336
  capital assets
    changes in, 336–338
    defined, 333
    lump sum purchases of, 335–336
  controls related to, 365–367
  current assets vs., 168–169
  defining, 333–334
  depreciation, concept of, 338–339
    actual salvage value, 339
    residual value, 338–339
  depreciation, revising, 354–355
  depreciation and disposal, 349–354
  depreciation for partial years, 347–348
  depreciation methods, 339–346
    declining-balance, 343
    determine method to use, 346
    double declining-balance, 344–345
    straight-line, 340–342
    units-of-production, 345–346, 355
  ethical approach to, 367–368
  intangible assets, 357–363
    copyright, 362–363
    goodwill, 358–361
    leasing long-term assets, 363
    patents, 361–362
    trademark and trade name, 363
  natural resources, 355–357
  overview, 331–332
  selling, 549–552
  total assets and financial ratios, 364–365
  trading-in, 353–354
long-term debt, 8
long-term investments, 497
long-term liabilities
  controls related to, 174, 425
  current liabilities vs., 169–172
  current portion of, 378–379
  ethical issues, 425–426
  financial ratios, 424

overview, 407

present value, 409–412

    bonds payable, 411–412

    time value of money, 411–412

lower of cost or market (LCM) inventory method, 287–288

lump sum purchases of capital assets, 335–336

M

managerial accounting, 61–62

manual accounting to computerized accounting, 148–150

manufacturing business, financial statements for, 50

market value, defined, 47

market value differing from book value, 441–443

market value vs. book value, 37

Martha Stewart Living Omnimedia Inc., 467

matching principle, 23–25, 56, 66, 87

materiality, 35, 91, 333

materiality principle, 66

McDonald brothers, Richard and Maurice, 445

Medicare payroll deductions, 388–389

merchandising business or corporation

    classified balance sheet, 168–172

    defined, 161, 175

    ethics and controls, 174

    financial statements for, 49–50

    financing a business, 161–163

    gross profit margin, 167–168

    multistep income statement, 172–174

    perpetual vs. periodic inventory, 165–167, 265–269

    sales of, 164–165

Merrill Lynch, 498

modern accounting systems

    computerized accounting, 148–150

    electronic data, 149, 198

    information systems, 197–198

software for accounting, 106, 116–117

    source documents, 148–149

monetary unit principle, 65

money, time value of, 411–412

money market securities, 499

mortgage bonds, 408

mortgage defaults in banking industry (2009), 37

mortgages, subprime, 425

multinational corporations, 68

multistep income statement, 172–174

mutual agency, 45

N

natural resources, 355–357

net pay, 381

net profit margin, 565–566, 598

net purchases calculation, 311

net sales, 273

net worth calculation, 19

net worth principle, 12–13

neutrality of information, 64

night deposit boxes, 229

no par value, shares or stock, 458–459

non-cash transactions, 553

non-determinable liabilities, 375, 394

non-sufficient funds (NSF), 212, 213

notes payable, 376–379

notes receivable. *See* accounts and notes receivable

O

objectivity principle, 66

off-balance-sheet financing, 425

operating expenses, 86, 98, 164

operations, cash flow from, 525

organizational types for businesses, 431–432

other comprehensive income, 479

other revenue and expenses, 173

outstanding shares, 455

overhead margin, 597

overstating inventory, 285–286

owner's drawings, 43

owner's equity

    defined, 42–44

    net worth verses, 42–44

    statement of, 134–135

    transferring assets, 224

P

Packard, David, 445

paid-in capital

    additional, 459

    contributed capital, 161, 452–453, 480

par, bonds issued at, 412–415

par value, shares or stock, 455, 458–459

partial years depreciation, 347–348

partner addition and withdrawal, 440–441

partner drawings, 439

partners, defined, 45

partnerships

    addition and withdrawal of partner, 440–441

    advantages of, 432

    description of, 45–46

    disadvantages of, 433

    division of income or loss, 436–439

        earnings according to agreed-upon ratio, 437

        earnings according to agreed-upon salary allocation, plus share of remainder, 438–439

        earnings according to capital contribution, 438

        earnings equally divided, 437

    formation of, 435–436

    liquidation of, 443–445

    market value differing from book value, 441–443

    notable companies that started as partnerships, 445

    partner drawings, 439

    structuring ownership, 431–432

types of, 434

patents, 361–362

payroll accounting, 381–386

    employee deductions, 383–385

        statutory deductions, 383

        voluntary deductions, 383–385, 389

    employer contributions, 385, 390–391

    ethical issues, 401

    example of, 386–394

    gross pay to net pay, 382

    paying deduction liability, 386

pension fund assets and liabilities, 425

periodic inventory system, 165–167, 175, 264, 299, 308–317

perpetual inventory system, 265–273

    defined, 175, 299

    income statement, 273

    perpetual vs. periodic, 165–167, 264

    purchases, 166–167, 265–269

    sales, 166–167, 270–272, 312–314

personal accounting, linking to business accounting

    business accounts, 41–44

        overview, 41

        owner's equity vs. net worth, 42–44

        sequence of assets and liabilities, 42

    business transactions, 50–56

    financial statements of different types of businesses, 48–50

        manufacturing business, 50

        merchandising business, 49–50

        service business, 49

    organizational types for businesses, 44–47

        corporation, 46–47

        not-for-profit organizations, 47

        partnership, 45–46

        sole proprietorship, 44–45

    stakeholders, 48

petty cash, 222–227

    controls, 226–227

    posting to general ledger, 224–226

    setting up fund, 223–224

petty cash custodian, 223

physical inventory count, 283

plant & equipment
description of, 7
sale of, 537–540

point-of-sale (POS) cash registers, 228

policies, procedures, and plans, compliance with, 295–296

post-closing trial balance, 136–147
close directly to capital account, 137–142
close using income summary, 142–147
formalized format, 147

posting reference (PR) column of journals, 109

predictive value of information, 64

preferred equity, 567

preferred stock, 175, 457–459

premium, bonds issued at, 420–422

prepaid expenses
adjustments, 93–94
definition and description of, 6, 98
financial statement and, 32–35, 88–91

prepaid insurance, 89

present value, concept of, 409–412

price-earnings ratio, 198, 489, 585, 600

principles-based accounting, 66

prior period adjustments, 480–481

private corporations, 47, 450

pro forma financial statements, 289

product warranties, 394–397

profit
analysis of, 560–570
asset turnover, 569–570
EBIT, 561–562
EBIT percentage to sales, 562–563
interest coverage ratio, 564, 598
net profit margin, 565–566, 598
return on assets, 364, 568–569, 599
return on equity, 566–568, 598
gross profit margin, 167–168, 175, 560–561, 597
. See also gross profit

profitability ratio, 167–168

promissory notes, 253–255

. See also accounts and notes receivable

property
description of, 7
sale of, 537–540

proprietorship, 431

prudence, defined, 68

public accounts, 61

public vs. private corporations, 450

purchase, of inventory, 166–167, 265–269, 309–311

purchase journal, 183, 191–192

purchases, inventory and, 166–167, 265–269

Q

quick ratio, 399, 572–576, 598

QuickBooks, 106

Qwest, 368

R

ratios. See financial ratios

recognizing, defined, 81

recording errors, 217–219

registered bonds, 408

regulations, compliance with, 295–296

relevance
defined, 63
trade-off of reliability and, 64–65

reliability
defined, 63–64
trade-off of relevance and, 63–64

repaying debt, 26–28, 500–501

representational faithfulness, 64

residual value, 338–339

resources, economical and efficient use of, 296

retail method of estimating inventory, 290–291

retained earnings, 162, 175, 452–455, 480, 534

retirement plans
employee deductions, 389, 393–394
employer deductions, 391, 393–394

retiring bonds, 423–424

return on assets (ROA), 364, 568–569, 599

return on equity (ROE), 566–568, 598

returns

    purchases, 265, 309

    sales, 270–271, 312

revenue

    analysis of, 559–560

    defined, 13, 81

revenue and expense recognition

    adjustments, 91–95

    ethics and controls, 95–97

    expense recognition, 86–88

    prepaid expenses, 88–91

    revenue recognition, 81–84

    unearned revenue, 84–86

revenue growth, 597

revenue recognition principle, 66, 82

ROA (return on assets), 364, 568–569, 599

ROE (return on equity), 566–568, 598

Rotary, 74

rules-based accounting, 66

S

safe storage of cash, 229

safeguarding

    inventory, 296

    investments, 517

salaries payable (net pay), 389–390, 392

sale of inventory, 166–167, 270–272, 312–314

sales journal, 183, 186–188

sales returns and allowances contra-revenue

    account, 270

sales revenue, 81

sales tax, 379–381

salvage value, 338–339

Sarbanes-Oxley Act of 2002 (SOX), 72

secured bonds, 408

security guards, 229

self-insurance, 367

selling assets, 29, 334, 503–504, 549–552

separation of duties, 97

service business, financial statements for, 49

service revenue, 81

services, stock in exchange for, 456–457

setting credit terms, 252–253

shareholders' equity, 42–44

shares of stock, 46–47, 161

short-term investments, 207, 497

short-term notes payable, 376–379

    accrued interest expense, 377–378

    current portion of long-term liabilities,
        378–379

Simply Accounting (software), 106

Social Security payroll deductions, 388–389

software for accounting, 106, 116–117

sole proprietorship, 44–45

source documents, 149, 182

SOX (Sarbanes-Oxley Act of 2002), 72

special journals

    cash payments journal, 183, 192–196

    cash receipts journal, 183, 188–190

    defined, 148, 183

    purchase journal, 183, 191–192

    sales journal, 183, 186–188

specific identification, inventory method, 277,
    278–279, 299, 320

stakeholders, 48

state income tax, employee deduction, 388,
    392–393

State Unemployment Taxes (SUTA), 390–
    391

stated value (stock or shares), 459

statement of cash flow. *See* cash flow
    statements

statement of owner's equity, 134–135

statutory deductions, 383

Stewart, Martha, 467

stock dividends, 463–464

stock exchanges, 47

stock splits, 463

stockholders, 46, 431, 514

stockholders' equity, 42–44, 162, 175, 452–
    455, 480

stocks
    buying for short term, 504
    common, 457–459
    defined, 161
    dividends, 463–464
    issuing, 455–457
        in exchange for assets, 456
        in exchange for cash, 455–456
        in exchange for services, 456–457
    preferred, 457–459
    selling, 503–504
    treasury, 464–466
straight-line method of amortization, 420
straight-line depreciation method, 340–342
subprime debt, 37, 425
subsidiary ledgers (subledgers)
    accounts receivable, 247–249
    description of, 184–186
    special journals and, 186–196
SUTA (State Unemployment Taxes), 390–391
swaps (in telecom industry), 368

T

T-accounts, 19–20
taxable income, 475
taxes
    federal income tax, employee deduction, 387–388
    FICA, 388, 390
    FUTA, 390–391
    income tax expense of corporations, 474–475
    local income tax, employee deduction, 388
    sales tax, 379–381
    state income tax, employee deduction, 388
    SUTA, 390–391
Taylor, Herbert J., 74
Telus Corporation, 174
term bonds, 408
terms of sale, 251, 252–253
tickler files, 400

time period principle, 66
time value of money, 411–412
timeliness of information, 64
total assets and financial ratios, 364–365
Total Quality Management (TQM), 298
trade discounts, 266
trademark and trade name, 363
trade-off of reliability and relevance, 64–65
trading investments, 497, 499–504
trading-in long-term assets, 349–354
transposition errors, 115–116
treasury bills (T-bills), 499
treasury stocks, 464–466
trial balance
    adjusting, 130–131
    creating, 114–116
    errors in, 115–116

U

understandability, 64
unearned revenue
    adjustments, 92–93
    defined, 98
    recognition of, 84–86
    relationship between prepaid expenses and, 91
unemployment taxes, employer contribution, 390–391
union dues, employee deductions, 389, 393
units-of-production depreciation method, 345–346, 355
unlimited liability, 44
unrecorded charges from bank statement, 210–213
unrecorded deposits from bank statement, 208–210
unsecured bonds, 408

V

valuing inventory
    effect of different methods, 282

methods, 277–282
  applying valuation methods, 277–278
  determine cost, 277
  FIFO method, 277, 279–280, 299, 321
  LIFO method, 277, 281–282, 299, 322–323
  lower of cost or market, 287–288
  specific identification method, 277, 278–279, 299, 320
  weighted average cost method, 277, 280–281, 322
verifiability of information, 64
vertical analysis, 587–590
voluntary deductions, 383–385, 389

W

Waksel, Samuel, 467
weighted average cost method, inventory valuation, 277, 280–281, 322
worksheets, 127–132
WorldCom, 72, 95, 368
Wright brothers, Wilbur and Orville, 445

X

XBRL (Extensible Business Reporting Language), 149, 198

Notes